All the World at War

All the World at War

People and Places 1914–1918

James Charles Roy

'Nowhere do events correspond less
to men's expectations than in war.'

Livy, *History of Rome*

Pen & Sword
MILITARY

First published in Great Britain in 2023 by
Pen & Sword Military
An imprint of
Pen & Sword Books Ltd
Yorkshire – Philadelphia

Copyright © James Charles Roy 2023

ISBN 978 1 39906 032 5

Typeset by Mac Style
Printed in the UK by CPI Group (UK) Ltd, Croydon, CR0 4YY.

Pen & Sword Books Limited incorporates the imprints of Atlas, Archaeology,
Aviation, Discovery, Family History, Fiction, History, Maritime, Military,
Military Classics, Politics, Select, Transport, True Crime, Air World, Frontline
Publishing, Leo Cooper, Remember When, Seaforth Publishing, The Praetorian
Press, Wharncliffe Local History, Wharncliffe Transport, Wharncliffe True
Crime, White Owl and After the Battle.

For a complete list of Pen & Sword titles please contact

PEN & SWORD BOOKS LIMITED
47 Church Street, Barnsley, South Yorkshire, S70 2AS, England
E-mail: enquiries@pen-and-sword.co.uk
Website: www.pen-and-sword.co.uk

Or

PEN AND SWORD BOOKS
1950 Lawrence Rd, Havertown, PA 19083, USA
E-mail: Uspen-and-sword@casematepublishers.com
Website: www.penandswordbooks.com

Endpapers: The Belgian city of Ypres after four years of war. The Canadian nurse Mabel
Clint visited the ruins after the Armistice. She wondered if anything there could ever be put
right again.

For Jan Victoria
There for every mile

Contents

Preface

The centenary of the First World War has passed. Before, during and immediately after 2014–18 came what can only be described as a deluge of printed matter: standard academic surveys, revisionist commentaries, detailed narratives of specific personalities, political happenings and individual (usually epic) battles. Readers may wonder why we need yet another book on what appears to many a fairly straightforward matter of historical record. Subtlety is not an adjective usually applied to anything regarding World War I.

The enormity of events between 1914 and 1918 – the largest and most destructive industrial-scale war ever launched and fought until then – tends to obscure smaller matter under its enormous tent. With something like seventy million people under arms, and civilian populations of millions more dragged into the daily torment of conflict or privation, few corners of the earth could escape its consequences. Individual behaviour and individual personality somehow appear to shrink when movements of such magnitude involving numberless men, economies, nation states and powerful aspirational impulses, rule the stage. The background colours are usually grey, brown or muted. As T. E Lawrence wrote in 1915, after receiving news of his brother's death in France, 'The hugeness of this war has made one change one's perspective, I think, and I for one can hardly see details at all'. A figure like Lawrence, in fact, is striking, in so far as he was unusual and stood out from the mass.[1]

Having said that, no one can deny that individual people, with their collective mix of virtue and vice, certainly initiated, directed, coordinated and, in many cases, bungled the terrible events that both began the conflict and prolonged the agony of its progression. It takes only the act of turning an ignition key to start a car, whereupon a complicated, ingenious and powerful machine powers into life. A car, of course, has an accelerator and a brake (even an emergency brake), so oftentimes the skill of a driver, or his incompetence, determines which way to go and at what speed.

This book is an attempt to personalize the landscape with what I hope are interesting, often neglected items that will bring many of the better-known episodes of the war more vividly to life. Each chapter is a series of vignettes, mostly dealing, in chronological order, with the major highlights of the conflict. Yes, another treatment of Sarajevo, likewise Verdun and Passchendaele; Winston Churchill turns up all over the place. But I have attempted to give each of these subjects something of a twist; not necessarily revisionist, but guided by contemporary observation in the form of diaries, letters, personal reminiscences and, of course, memoirs. Many of these I have culled from relative obscurity; in the process they added light to many a dark corner.

Judgments of 'People and Places' are my own. If they fail to convince the reader, I take full responsibility.

Chapter 1

The European Landscape: Victoria's Web

'No queen was ever loved so well.'

Lord Esher, on the unveiling of
Victoria's statue on The Mall, 1911

Among the many innovations witnessed in the latter half of the nineteenth century was the development of photography. In an age that saw incredible growth in manufacturing, architecture, medicine, the press, military advances (at least in killing power) and even the notion that men could fly in the air, photography might not seem particularly earth-shattering. But in fact it was. Photography was one of many tools that democratized society, particularly in Europe, a landmass governed for centuries by a very narrow oligarchy of individuals, the crowned heads of dynasties both large and small that cluttered the landscape. A few of these individuals were blessed with intelligence and imagination, others less so. In some cases, monarchs ordered affairs as they saw fit; where crowned heads did not have sufficient intelligence to manage their nation's business, they were usually ruled themselves by ministers or favourites. The numbers of people who 'counted', however, were generally very few.

Some countries had evolved into governments of volatile republicanism, or were forever under assault by its baleful influences (France, for example), but these societies often found themselves susceptible to *coups d'état* where popular, right-wing strongmen, supported by the mob, might seize power (Napoleon III comes to mind). These experiments, which generally allowed full rein to the eccentric predilections of often unstable individuals, ended badly more often than not. General Georges Boulanger, for example, ended his brief flirtation with fame by shooting himself at the grave of his mistress, thereby climaxing a career in embarrassingly operatic fashion. In a few nations, constitutional monarchs were the rule. Britain is the prominent example, where power gradually did devolve to parliament, however restricted the right of the masses to vote for their representatives actually was. On the other end of the spectrum lay Russia, a country mired in not just feudalism, but outright tyranny.

Monarchical authority was consciously reinforced by spectacle. Marx had said that religion was the opiate of the masses; in terms of sovereigns, pomp and circumstance did the same thing. Sacred majesties by the dozens organized military parades, histrionic displays of wealth and display, court festivities that were cemented in a maze of procedure, etiquette and obsequious manifestations of hierarchy and loyalty. One might have thought (as many did) that they were in the presence of gods.

Portraiture was one method of mass indoctrination. Court painters had always been valued in princely circles. What king did not enjoy being depicted in gorgeous robes, sceptre in hand, with angels blowing trumpets in the background; or, after a battle, riding a noble steed and trampling the standards of a defeated foe. No one looking at a formal portrait of Kaiser Wilhelm II would ever have known he was born with a deformed left arm or that, in his heart of hearts, he was a weak and faint-hearted man. One look at his fierce scowl was meant to shrivel the soul of any would-be dissident. So too with formal sculpture, portraying kings, at double the size of normal men, on highly strung horses just panting for combat. Photography changed all that.

Queen Victoria of England reigned for sixty-four years, from 1837 to 1901. After the death of her admittedly devoted husband, Prince Albert of Saxe-Coburg-Gotha, she habitually dressed in black for an unnatural span of forty years. As she aged, her mourning became almost a caricature. Progressive photographs of the queen, as time passed, ruthlessly catalogued the ravages of age: diminished stature, graying hair, burgeoning stomach, shrivelled posture – all signs of advancing decrepitude. Looking over these 'snapshots' one can almost smell the approaching grave. This was the woman who stood at the head of the greatest empire in the world?

The answer to that, of course, was yes. Here she was, in all her glory, a somewhat grotesque comedown from the artificiality that formal art had accorded her. Great Britain genuinely mourned the queen's passing in 1901 (though characters in James Joyce's *Ulysses* referred to her as 'the old hag with the yellow teeth ... the flatulent old bitch that's dead'), but an appreciation of her regal authority lay suspended for several years. The unveiling of a monumental statue of Victoria in front of Buckingham Palace in 1911 did much to make people forget the stunted images that ruthless photography had generated for more than two decades.

Socialists, republicans, labourites, anarchists, revolutionaries – along with a large segment of thinking people everywhere – despised monarchical power during the first decade of the twentieth century. They resented the unbridled authority and seemingly unlimited riches that preceded, and followed, the imperial train. The entire network struck many as inbred, and any examination of the late queen's dynastic tree could do nothing but reinforce that perception.

Victoria herself was a daughter of King George III's younger brother (he of the American Revolution, to say nothing of a nine-years enforced confinement due to mental illness that marked the finale of his reign).[1] George was a Hanoverian (as were his two predecessors) brought to the English throne from Germany as Protestant bulwarks against Catholic pretenders. King George I, in fact, spoke not a word of English. Victoria, an only child, was a wilful, opinionated and very stubborn girl, traits that would never desert her. Her private secretary once wrote that 'When she insists that 2 and 2 make 5, I say I cannot help thinking they may make 4. She replies there may be some truth in what I say, but she knows they make 5. Thereupon I drop the discussion.' She came to the throne without experience, true close friends, any semblance of a rounded education or realistic notions as to the character of her subjects. The man in the street was as foreign to her as a Chinaman. She suspended this imperiousness, to some degree, during her marriage to Albert, a somewhat penniless 'adventurer' (in the eyes of the radical press), who had been proposed as a suitable match by the arch schemer of Europe, Leopold I of Belgium, a man with a superb genealogical memory. Albert of Saxe-Colburg-Gotha was Leopold's nephew; Victoria's mother was also Saxe-Coburg. Victoria, in fact, had married her first cousin, a not uncommon occurrence between the royal houses of Europe. Her offspring would continue, and complicate, this very pattern.

The story of Victoria and Albert's progeny is comparable to a spider's web of royal incestuousness that ran through just about every royal house of consequence in Europe. The couple had nine children in twenty-one years of marriage, of whom eight were wedded to either German or Russian aristocrats. The most consequential of these unions was that of the eldest daughter, engaged and then married to the Hohenzollern crown prince, who later became emperor of Germany; their son was Kaiser Wilhelm II. The interpersonal relationships among all these individuals were complex and highly personal. It seemed that everyone knew everyone else by their first name. The infamous correspondence between Kaiser Wilhelm II and Tsar Nicholas II was marked by 'Dear Willy' and 'Dear Nicky' salutations. Wilhelm, in particular, felt diplomacy was little more than an exchange of informal notes between members of the same family, and in a way he was correct – he and the tsar were first cousins. Not only that: Wilhelm was the first cousin of George V, Great Britain's king since 1910. Overseeing this entire mélange for over six decades, which eventually consisted of thirty-four grandchildren, was Queen Victoria, the great matriarchal figure.

Over her long life, Victoria could alternate between friendship and disdain for the various prime ministers who passed before her. Some she respected, and followed their advice (Disraeli for instance); others she detested and sought to frustrate (Gladstone, 'a humbug', was mostly unwelcome).[2] Her influence in the political affairs of the country could wax and wane; but in private family matters the queen was an unyielding despot, whose sense of diplomacy escaped her. She approved or utterly rejected various marriage proposals without regard for any opinion other than her own, lectured those of her extended family who displeased her, and admonished anyone who veered beyond the boundaries of accepted decorum. A whiff of scandal could launch a royal tirade. Nine years before her death, the queen expressed her fatigue with running this royal menagerie much longer: 'I really cannot go about keeping everyone in order'.

This remark was directed at Wilhelm in Berlin, whose treatment of his own mother (she was Victoria's beloved eldest child) was indeed deplorable. He called his aged grandmother, more than once, 'an old hag'. Yet in this hothouse environment, the affairs of Europe were often decided. Wilhelm, for example, had an elevated sense of regard for his own abilities, whether on the battlefield (he saw himself as the current embodiment of Frederick the Great, an illustrious ancestor) or negotiating table (Bismarck was a drug-addled 'pigmy' who rarely knew what he was doing; Wilhelm would correct that). The best-known diplomatic coup of the kaiser involved what later became known as the Treaty of Björkö (1905) with 'Nicky'. This agreement was hammered out by the two men, alone: no professional diplomats, no advisers, no observers were present. The result was a fascinating display of royal ineptitude, Nicholas agreeing to an arrangement whereby, in the event of war between Germany and France, Russia would be contractually obliged to assist both. It took his own foreign office several days to enlighten their master to the incongruity of the terms to which he had agreed. Wilhelm was additionally discomforted when his own circle of sycophantic confidants blanched, and his reaction was predictably excited. Diplomats in their little cubbyholes on the Wilhelmstrasse in Berlin, or pestering him in the corridors of his palaces, had 'filled their pants' and 'stank of shit'; you could smell it all over the city. Wilhelm would not be deterred from running things as he saw fit.

The turmoil of European politics (and particularly those involving the Balkans) would put an end to such pretensions. When a situation called for common sense or compromise, the powers-that-be often chose a 'right-wing' solution, usually selecting one of their own to 'become a king'. A Danish prince had been foisted on Greece, and another royal of Austrian heritage became 'Tsar' of Bulgaria, turning that country into a 'Balkan Prussia'. But private agreements within monarchical circles would prove incapable of thwarting the many complicated impulses in which long-suppressed peoples were indulging. Royal bloods continued their exhaustive excursions through genealogical tomes to find the best 'mixes and matches' for specific applications, but the tides of history were running against them. Anarchists, ultra-nationalists, assorted madmen – they were only the most obvious stumbling blocks. Their spectacular outrages galvanized readers who scrutinized the trashy front pages of the growing popular press: Tsar Alexander II, attacked on three separate occasions, did not survive the fourth in 1881; Emperor Franz Joseph's wife, the Empress Elisabeth, was murdered with a crude ice pick in 1898; Premier Stefan Stambolov known as the 'Bismarck of the Balkans', was riddled with some twenty bullets on a street in Sofia, 1895; King Umberto I of Italy was shot four times and killed on 29 July 1900;[3] the king and queen of Serbia were both stabbed repeatedly in their bedroom, 1903, the corpses thrown out of a palace window onto the garden dung heap (it is said that the king, still alive, clung to the windowsill, whereupon his fingers were cut off with a knife, and he fell to his death); the king of Portugal and his son, killed by republicans in 1908; a deranged workman had even thrown a piece of iron at the kaiser, hitting him on the cheek, while he was visiting Bremen. These were but symptomatic of bottled-up contempt.

In May 1910, the largest assembly of royals in world history gathered in London for the funeral of King Edward VII, Victoria's son, after a mere eight years on the throne. Nine European kings attended, along with five crown princes or heirs apparent, seven queens and untold numbers of aristocratic notables. This was a royal reunion on the grandest scale, and a deeply reactionary event. Stéphen Pichon, the foreign minister from Republican France, was furious when he saw his positioning in the formal procession: relatives from the French royal house of Orleans, who had last held the throne in 1848 before being ousted in the succession of revolutions that year, were actually ahead of him in line, an insult to France![4] But by 1918, the final year of the Great War, five of these kings were either dead or had been swept from their thrones. The twentieth century would be nothing like that of its predecessor. World War I made certain of that, as Friedrich Engels had predicted hyperbolically thirty years before: 'Crowns roll in the gutter by the dozens', he wrote, 'and there will be nobody to pick them up'.[5]

During Victoria's interminable reign, however, few such rumblings could be heard over the horizon. Her rule, despite the Crimean War, had been generally one of peace and prosperity. The British empire was the largest in the world, her maritime reach extended to everywhere a ship might dock. The historian Paul Kennedy called the English 'virtually satiated' when it came to imperial power (as a German general put it, in envy, 'England is now at three o'clock, when the sun shines the brightest'). Occasionally there were international embarrassments. No one was amused when General Gordon died at Khartoum, and the Boer War was an ugly smudge on Britain's reputation for invincibility; only disharmonious reverberations from the direction of Germany spoiled the tableau. Her leaders had been used to a divided European landscape, where no power held undisputed sway over the others. This allowed Britain to follow a policy of 'splendid isolation'. The Franco-Prussian War changed that scenario, as Prime Minister Disraeli acknowledged in an address to parliament in February 1871. 'We used to have discussions in this House about the balance of power ... but what has really come to pass in Europe? The balance of power has been entirely destroyed, and the country that suffers most, and feels the effects of this great change most, is England'. In the forty years since he made those remarks, the rapid industrialization of imperial Germany had become the talk, and concern, of all Europe. Touring the Ruhr Valley in 1909, the newspaper baron Lord Northcliffe ominously viewed the landscape. 'Every one of those factory chimneys', he said to a companion, 'is a gun pointed at England'.

Chapter 2

The Kaiser

'Wilhelm the Great'

> Sarcastic Remark of Edward,
> Prince of Wales, 1888

There had never been in modern times a united Germany. German-speaking peoples, it is true, were dominant from the Baltic Sea to the Italian Alps – they could disrupt the politics of Europe with seeming ease from Hamburg on the river Elbe to Königsberg on the Russian border; what generals and statesmen decided in Berlin and Vienna had major implications anywhere on the continent. But a united Germany remained an illusion until the career of Prince Otto von Bismarck.

Bismarck remains the most intelligent, calculating, profound, and Machiavellian figure in German history. As the distinguished historian John Röhl has noted, Bismarck was only one of three statesmen in modern European history, other than royalty, to hold the reins of indisputable power for at least three decades (only Metternich and Stalin were his equals in that respect). He was appointed to office by Wilhelm I of Prussia in 1862 at a time when what we call Germany today was a motley collection of petty states (Hanover, Hess, Saxony and so forth), interspersed with other independent kingdoms of more considerable prowess and ambition (Prussia and Bavaria being the most important). Coequal in pride and arrogance with these was Austria, a power Bismarck would put in its place during the war of 1866. In that conflict, several of the 'German' principalities had sided with the Habsburgs, much to their regret.

With Austria's defeat, this once-great power was shunted to the side when it came to central European affairs, forced to relinquish its primacy in the German-language world to Berlin. Unfortunately for Vienna, this resulted in forcibly having to reorient her concentration to eastern issues, issues involving a polyglot collection of peoples – Magyars, Slavs and the heterogeneous populations of the Balkans for the most part – whose multicomplicated racial, religious and national aspirations would, in just a quarter of a century, break Austria into pieces. It has been often observed that if the Habsburg diplomatic corps had displayed a more judicious and accommodating gaze on these varied questions (and a more realistic geo-political assessment of its relationship with Russia), perhaps its empire might have survived the turbulence of 1914 and after; but the fact remains that centuries of prominence in grand European designs had given Austrian statesmen the idea that their skills remained peerless, despite recent indignities suffered at the hands of Bismarck. Their refusal to adapt – from sheer arrogance and ill temper – would prove their ruin.

In the new, unified Germany of Bismarck's creation, Prussia, as intended, was by far the dominant partner, even though most member states (there were twenty-seven in all) retained their monarchs, foreign embassies, armed forces and all the seeming paraphernalia of independent rule.[1] But Prussia, in practical terms, was top dog. It occupied well over half the geography, her army represented eighty percent of the entire force (its officer corps dominated by Prussian Junkers) and its king was crowned 'Emperor' of the entire conglomeration. In times of war, his authority was deemed supreme. Complicating the organizational chart, however, were concessions to popular, democratic forms of government. Several tiers of parliamentary houses, one elected by universal suffrage, enjoyed far-reaching authority, particularly in budgetary matters, necessitating considerable dexterity on the part of Bismarck to control.[2] These formed a counter-reactionary voice representing the viewpoints of centrists, Catholics (predominantly from southern Germany) and, with the growth of densely populated industrial centres, many little better than slums, socialists. By 1914, in a contradiction little appreciated by some historians, the most important political party in the Reichstag would be Social Democrats, the 'people's' party, the choice of over a third of Germany's population. These representatives were consistently opposed to excessive militarism, colonial ambitions and the type of sabre-rattling that was synonymous with the word 'Prussia'. As Bismarck's tenure progressed through the 1880s, the overall indigenous feeling about the stature of Germany was one of dissatisfaction, a large machine whose several parts did not seem to mesh. No one was particularly happy with the status quo. When particularity exasperated, Bismarck would often dream of *coups d'état* whereby all his opponents could be suppressed.

Nevertheless, Bismarck consolidated his central authority, and that of his kaiser, in impressive and generally amoral fashion. The independence of more powerful components in the federation were quietly whittled away. Bavaria, for example, was undermined by simple bribery. Its king, Ludwig II, the patron of Wagner, was in constant financial difficulty. His lavish spending, perhaps a reflection of mental instability, underwrote the construction of grandiose castles and spectacular operatic spectacles, but these were largely funded with 'loans' arranged by Bismarck. When Ludwig died, 1886, in mysterious circumstance, the royal house of Wittelsbach was virtually bankrupt, and its independence of Prussia surrendered.[3]

What Bismarck could not totally manipulate, however, were the powers of appointment, and this proved a matter where any kaiser of the moment exercised great authority. He could dismiss anyone he wished, he could appoint anyone he wished. Bismarck felt confident that his advice in such matters would always be respected. He also assumed that his son, Herbert, would eventually succeed him. All would go well so long as his imperial master was 'not totally eccentric' (his words). Unfortunately for him, Kaiser Wilhelm II was exactly that, a man who had a messianic belief in the divine right of kings, a feudal notion that one would have thought the French Revolution might have thematically buried for good during the eighteenth century.

Caesar or Caligula?

> *'A monarch must always speak the final word, but His Majesty always wants to have the first word, and that is a cardinal failure.'*
>
> Baron Marschall von Bieberstein, state secretary, 1895

No man strutted the world stage at the turn of the twentieth century with more attendant commotion than the emperor of Imperial Germany, Wilhelm II. He was a man of considerable spirit who, to the despair of most of the diplomatic community from the city of London to the city of St. Petersburg, had few notions of verbal restraint. What came to his mind of a moment was generally what came out of his mouth less than a second later. He was the epitome of spontaneous combustion, given to eruptions occasioned by the most trivial of incidents. If these had been confined to his domestic apartments, the repercussions would have been non-existent, but Wilhelm, unfortunately, often unleashed his usually impromptu broadsides in the midst of public occasions or ceremonies where the widest audiences possible would be there to hear and wonder (to say nothing of dinner parties and diplomatic receptions, where his commentary could be equally indiscreet). The majority of such pronouncements, to the consternation of all, were generally bombastic and war-like. Wilhelm was a medievalist in many ways, and his rhetorical allusions often involved sabres and swords, usually in the process of being unsheathed and waved menacingly in the air.

He was a man much given to threats and, when feeling put upon or slighted, much given to unleashing promises for revenge. Reversals in political affairs, whether international or domestic, were taken as personal affronts and darkly remembered, however irrationally. For years Wilhelm regarded his uncle, King Edward VII of Britain, as 'satan'. To the end of his life he blamed Edward, who died in 1910, as responsible for World War I, which did not begin for another four years.

Wilhelm's verbosity (not restrained to just speech; his marginalia on official dispatches and communiques, described by one of his circle as 'expectorations', could make a person's blood curdle) was thematically consistent with the regime he consciously styled during his thirty years on the throne. His building projects were loud and ostentatious, his taste in the arts, garish; curiously, he disliked Wagner, whom he dismissed as 'noisy', when in fact the music he enjoyed most were brassy and repetitive military marches with their drums and horns.[4] He personally designed military uniforms, which during his reign became noted for their theatrical flourish; likewise, the excessively ornate medals and decorations that flowed from his sketchbooks. The eagle, that noble bird, became as ubiquitous in symbol and design as the common pigeon eating crumbs on the Unter den Linden. Wilhelm was determined to transform Berlin into a capital city that would rival a London or a St. Petersburg (though not a Paris, which he visited but once in his long life, the morals and loose atmosphere of which he intensely disapproved). The result was a Berlin that embarrassed more refined Germans. The wealthy industrialist Walther Rathenau called it 'Parvunopolis'.

By 1900, the kaiser's uneven forays into national affairs had brought him notoriety, a generally negative press and unfavourable reputation abroad. An open topic of discussion around dinner and conference tables was the degree to which Wilhelm might be deemed out of his mind. Tsar Nicholas called him 'raving mad' at one point. Whenever the kaiser made one of his spectacular blunders, the Marquess of Salisbury, a three-times British prime minister, would generally point his index finger towards his head and lightly strike it. Everyone knew what he meant.

Irrational or merely shrewd? It didn't really matter. The kaiser's mood swings were a fact of life, according to Edward Grey, another important English diplomat, who wondered if Wilhelm was 'not quite sane', feeling that the kaiser's unpredictability made him particularly dangerous. One could never anticipate properly or plan an initiative knowing with confidence what Germany's response might be. Wilhelm enjoyed the collective uncertainty shared by all his international opponents. It made them wary of him, which suited the image he had of himself as a character to be reckoned with. You

English 'have all gone mad', he quipped to Edward Goschen, the new ambassador to Berlin during the 1900 New Year's reception. 'You seem to think that I am always standing with my battle-axe behind me waiting for an opportunity to strike.' The issue was, however, that the kaiser's battle-axe was not some imaginary prop that could be hauled out during one of the several masquerade balls that he so enjoyed giving. Germany had what most observers felt was the most professional army in Europe; its navy was embarking on a course of expansion that threatened the sovereignty of Britain; its foreign policy seemed determined to establish a colonial empire that would rival those of the other great powers. The axe, in other words, had an edge to it.

On the eve of the Great War, and in the two decades following it, a flood of literature – both serious memoirs and cheap, psychological pieces of journalism – attempted to fathom the kaiser's true personality; to seek some sort of rational explanation for his fascinating, albeit erratic character. None was ever wholly successful; none ever presented a balanced portrait (if one was even possible). 'Tell-all' exposés were common, usually written by intimates of the inner circle such as Count Robert Zedlitz-Trützschler, a court functionary for twelve years (partisans of the kaiser dismissed his generally negative portrait as a 'spittoon' where Zedlitz-Trützschler vented his spleen). Others were so partisan and biased in favour of the kaiser that they strained belief (Wilhelm's second wife wrote a remembrance that was embarrassingly florid). The results were mixed, to say the least. By the time Wilhelm died on 4 June 1941, the European landscape was engulfed in a second, even more cataclysmic world war. Hitler sent his overweight and heavily bemedalled Luftwaffe chief, Herman Göring, to attend the kaiser's funeral in Holland. The führer had neither the time nor the inclination to go himself, and besides, no one by that point cared about the kaiser at all.

This strange, bewildering man was born eighty-two years before, and one thing that can be said without dispute is that Wilhelm's upbringing was no easy business. That might seem a strange thing to say about someone delivered into the lap of luxury: grandson to the aged Kaiser Wilhelm I; son of Crown Prince Frederick, next in line to the throne; and himself destined, if all went well, to wear the crown himself one day. But even the titled and wealthy among us can have a difficult time of it, and Wilhelm was no exception to that rule.

There were several issues. His mother, familiarly known as Vicky, was English, the eldest daughter of Queen Victoria and Prince Albert of Saxe-Coburg-Gotha. She was but a young girl of seventeen when she removed to Prussia after her marriage, where she ran into a wall of intense Anglophobia.

Given her own free and determined spirit (doubtless inherited from her mother) she returned the enmity with a vengeance. Vicky was no wallflower, she had no intention of denying her roots, background or opinions which, unfortunately for her, ran contrary to those most dearly held in the reactionary Prussian court, whose current king, Wilhelm I, was a man of no education and behaved accordingly. Vicky was a constitutional monarchist by nature, with a full appreciation for the necessity of parliamentary cooperation, a reflection of her father's political persuasions. She held Bismarck, militarism and any sort of jingoism in utter contempt, and made no mistake about hiding these views from anyone who might care to listen. Although her husband, the crown prince, was a war hero, she persuaded him to her unwavering points of view, in essence herding him into 'the opposition'. Since he was the kaiser-in-waiting, this alienated just about everyone who mattered in Berlin; court opinion saw her as an English spy, a sinister, witch-like figure who had turned the head of her husband in treasonable directions. Bismarck did everything in his power to frustrate her designs; Vicky, in her turn, became more doctrinaire and wilful than ever – she was good for not one occasional misstep now and again, 'but two big ones every day' – generating a predisposition to stridency that translated itself into her domestic life as well. One observer labelled her 'a little tyrant'.

Whether it mattered or not, Vicky decreed that an English doctor should deliver her first child, and the results were calamitous. Her baby boy emerged into life, after a lengthy and frightening delivery, with a dislocated left arm that at first no one noticed. This had apparently occurred when the physician, in fear over the boy's life, had applied excessive force in extricating the baby from his mother's uterine canal, in the process of which several ligaments around the shoulder socket were torn as well. Modern surgical techniques today could have remedied this situation, but a century ago doctors were largely in the dark when it came to internal injuries. The left arm, despite several remedial (and painful) attempts to increase 'circulation' and movement, never responded. The arm essentially withered into a useless appendage that, for his entire life, Wilhelm attempted to conceal, especially during ceremonies or in any public venue. It is to his great personal credit that he never appeared self-conscious or defensive among intimates, playmates, fellow soldiers or family members. It was a fact of personal misfortune that he accepted. Wilhelm became a proficient rider with but one arm to control his mount (many falls notwithstanding), was athletic throughout his youth and never minded when people cut his food for him. Amateur psychiatrists have often blamed this impediment for Wilhelm's strident behaviour, seeing in his aggressiveness a mechanism to overcompensate for an obvious and embarrassing weakness.

Sigmund Freud felt otherwise. The problem with Wilhelm, he wrote after the war, was his mother.

Vicky was not happy at all to have given birth to a boy with such a deformity; as he grew older, and as his character seemed to develop into a catalogue of stereotypical Germanic traits that she so disliked – the boy was headstrong, boisterous, uncontemplative – she emotionally turned her back on him, becoming something of a harridan of a mother. Her letters home to Victoria make unpleasant reading even today; her son could not do anything right. He was a dull student (the tutor she employed, given almost dictatorial powers, played a part in this, a deadening pedant and taskmaster), a poor sport in athletics and, while dutiful, showed no genuine affection for anyone. Wilhelm was entirely self-centred and susceptible to any kind of praise. Early on he found the advantages of surrounding himself with sycophants who understood their role only too well: to swell the royal vanity. His father's family relations continually undermined Vicky's authority by feeding into the young boy's childish delight in military paraphernalia. At one point he was dressed from top to toe in the uniform of a famous Guards division. Vicky wrote to her mother that Wilhelm reminded her 'of some unfortunate little monkey dressed up standing on the top of an organ'. This was not exactly a manifestation of maternal love. In point of fact, Vicky gradually withdrew her affection from Wilhelm, showering her attentions on the several children she had thereafter. The crown prince, who reigned over the German empire for only ninety-nine days (he died of throat cancer, an affliction that was dreadfully misdiagnosed by another English physician, a specialist brought over from London), had also grown estranged from Wilhelm, a disdain that proved mutual. Wilhelm unfeelingly mentioned to his mother that if Frederick was to die, it should be on the battlefield, not at the hands of an English doctor. Their communications thereafter were generally painful.

When Wilhelm came to the throne in 1888, he had already made up his mind as to the sort of king he planned to be. Despite his inexperience in military affairs – he never seemed to mature from his days as a Potsdam lieutenant, where he spent much of his time in fraternal horseplay and regimental frivolities – he had no doubts that he had inherited the military genes of the greatest of all the Hohenzollerns, Frederick the Great. As for diplomacy, the wily Bismarck might think he controlled the imperial government, but Wilhelm knew better. When the time was right, he would 'drop the pilot' over the side and take control of things himself. It was, after all, his destiny: he was to be the new Caesar of his age. The politician Ludwig Quidde disagreed. In 1894 he published his essay *Caligula*, drawing a none-too-subtle comparison between the kaiser and a Roman counterpart who allegedly appointed his horse as consul. As crude as the comparison seemed, the follies initiated under Wilhelm's now personal rule collectively reminded one German diplomat of an 'operetta'. Caligula and Wilhelm might have had more in common than was at first apparent.

'This man wants to live as if every day were his birthday.'

Otto von Bismarck

One thing the new king seldom lacked was self-confidence. His childhood heroes – Caesar, Charlemagne, the warriors of the Trojan War – were hardly shy or bashful role models of any subtlety. Wilhelm was sure of himself – 'He has no doubts', as Bismarck put it – and absolutely determined that the Almighty sanctioned his every step. The kaiser's relationship with God was deeply personal and conventional. God was on the side of monarchs: that was the simple part of the political equation (God was also, as a Belgian diplomat said, a German); on the other end was democracy, represented by the Reichstag, 'that pigsty', whose leaders he publicly snubbed and, behind their backs, viciously slandered. They were a 'band of apes' occupying a 'chatter chamber'. Within Wilhelm's mind-set, he had the right to send any ordinary lieutenant with ten grenadiers inside the parliament building with orders to either shoot the whole lot of them or else clear the chambers at bayonet point. Occasional blood letting was a good thing, he often told his entourage, a way to keep insolent members of the population under control. 'Five hundred people being shot down' on a city street – dead socialists – would not disturb his conscience or keep him up at night. He had never read the German constitution (written by Bismarck) and boasted that he never would.

Wilhelm, in keeping with most monarchs of the time, was both contemptuous and fearful of the red menace. One of his first initiatives as kaiser was, in fact, an intelligent effort to provide workers in fast-industrializing Germany with a series of social benefits that horrified conservative elements in Prussian society (many of these were rural landowners in the east, wedded to the ethos of the Teutonic Order of Knights). Even Bismarck, who had earlier in his career tried much the same thing, felt that Wilhelm was going too far, and openly sabotaged the program. This was probably the first and last attempt by the kaiser to reach out to this vital segment of Germany's people, among whom he rarely mingled and knew less about. It was a learning moment, in retrospect. Wilhelm had tried to provide an alternative to Marxist radicalism, only to be rebuffed. That being the case, he would respond to any further ingratitude with grapeshot.

As any observer of parliamentary procedure would know, political rebuffs are a daily occurrence in democratic societies, but to Wilhelm they represented intolerable insults to his authority and each was keenly felt, resented and remembered. This tendency to personalize every setback was seized upon by his small and influential coterie of advisers and hangers-on, who reinforced the notion that the kaiser was under siege, disrespected and vulnerable. This deeply militaristic group, almost a cabal, was always ready to recommend drastic countersteps, usually violent and extreme, that tended to strengthen Wilhelm's authoritarian impulses. The fact that most of these men were dolts tended to reinforce Wilhelm's sense of intellectual superiority (one contemporary observer called them 'clowns at a village fair'). When the kaiser made one of his many sweeping generalizations – 'How stupid the rest of the world is' – there was always someone at his elbow demurely agreeing. They were also the butt of his many violent outbursts, reminding Zedlitz-Trützschler of 'Newfoundland dogs, which let themselves be kicked and cuffed, and still wag their tails'.

Certainly the women in Wilhelm's daily life proved either unable or unwilling to soften his edges. Wilhelm was never truly happy in female company. He could be *galant* on social occasions, and certainly admired pretty and accomplished women, though largely from afar. Too much intelligence in either sex discomforted him. He had married Princess Augusta Victoria of Schleswig-Holstein in 1881, a woman of little education but of fine breeding stock. She delivered seven children to the kaiser in quick succession (Bismarck referred to her as the 'Holstein cow'). Her own suite of ladies in waiting were pretty much like her: conservative, pious, dowdy and boring. Wilhelm soon tired of their collective company. He was happiest, according to his closest friend in the 1890s, the charming (and homosexual) Count Philipp zu Eulenburg, when he was off riding to a hunt or a bachelor excursion, leaving the 'chicken coop' behind. On his annual summer cruises, he could not bring himself to waste time sending letters to the kaiserin, ordering Eulenburg to write her instead. It didn't help that his wife was taller than he was. He generally sat on a pillow at dinner so that he could dominate the room, which he did both physically and rhetorically. Wilhelm had a great capacity for talk, which often degenerated into loud and lengthy monologues which no one, and certainly not Dona (Wilhelm's nickname for her), dared to interrupt. When there was a pause in these orations, which were generally kaiser-centric and full of self-congratulation, the responses were usually adulatory.

Zedlitz-Trützschler could hardly stand it. The air, he said, was always 'thick with incense'. Dona was given to outbursts of her own, usually ignited by lapses in what most considered the stifling etiquette of the royal court, or operas and plays that offended her sense of morality. On political matters she seldom ventured, as the kaiser brushed her off. 'The emperor always says in these cases', she once said, "Go away. You don't understand these things"'. Wilhem thought the glory of German women had but three outlets: 'Küche, Kirche, Kinder' ('Kitchen, Church, Children').

Despite initial impressions, which generally left the uninitiated with the notion that Wilhelm was 'energetic [and] clever', it did not take long for anyone in his company for a reasonable period of time to realize that the kaiser was essentially a quick study, a 'flash in the pan' as it were. He had an amazing ability to read and absorb information on a superficial level. Zedlitz-Trützschler noted 'his rapid grasp'. He could read twenty or so pages full of technical matter 'and have an astonishing command of its contents for purposes of discussion'. He was, in fairness, better suited to be a royal personage from the year 2000 as opposed to 1900, a man who could be given a quick briefing before being handed a pair of scissors to open a new bridge – he would know the names of the committee, the architect, the purpose of the project and who the bridge was being named for. The problem for the real kaiser at the turn of the twentieth century, however, was more consequential. He often would veer from programmed remarks and extemporize, frequently with unfortunate results; and he had the knack of immediately losing interest in any subject of the moment, in a matter of minutes forgetting all the information he had just seen. This was satisfactory for innocuous civic occasions, but far more serious when it came to vital issues affecting war and peace.

Wilhelm soon tired of Otto von Bismarck. The aging chancellor was a firm believer in restricting the powers of dynastic kings; the notion of a Louis XIV – 'L'état, c'est moi' – was obsolete in his opinion (the radical press was more blunt – Wilhelm's notion of divine right was 'junk from a dead past'). Wilhelm could not have disagreed more, and chaffed at Bismarck's imperious nature. The common nickname for Bismarck's suite of offices was 'Olympus': the kaiser took offence at that; there was room for only one Greek god in his universe. From childhood, Wilhelm had detested people who either hectored him or assumed professorial or superior airs. Although Bismarck was careful in his dealings with the young kaiser, Wilhelm resented the notion, quite correct as it turned out, that his chancellor knew more about diplomacy and running Germany than he did. He said after the war, 'I saw that Bismarck would be the uncrowned emperor. *I could not tolerate that.*' In 1890 he forced the retirement of Europe's most influential statesman, a process he completed with uncharacteristic aplomb and tact. Bismarck, an egomaniac, was sullen and spiteful by contrast, which to a small degree became apparent to the general public and made the transition somewhat palatable. Wilhelm took about a decade to squander that good feeling.[5]

For the next several years the kaiser ruled virtually unfettered – approximately to the *Daily Telegraph* affair of 1908. His independent predilections were not given a sudden full reign – the process was more gradual than that – but by 1897, Wilhelm was consistently 'on his own'. His worst tendencies were abetted by weak chancellors chosen specifically for their pliability: Leo von Caprivi, a general whose shared belief in the divine right of his master to rule without restraint undermined his personal misgivings when faced with the grotesque reality of Wilhelm's wilfulness; Prince Chlodwig Hohenlohe, a septuagenarian whose energy had evaporated years before; Count Bernhard von Bülow, a fawning creature whose unctuousness even the emperor sometimes found excessive (courtiers called him 'the eel'). These men, while privately horrified by many decisions capriciously made, were nonetheless generally steadfast in supporting the emperor's prerogatives.[6] They were not Bismarckian characters and learned, with varying degrees of success, how to get things done obliquely, which always began with mastering the technique 'of presenting [their] ideas as if [the emperor] had inspired them' (an art form, as a Belgian diplomat observed). Even they, however, eventually reached their limits. Wilhelm's gratuitous decision to send German troops halfway round the world to help suppress the Boxer Rebellion in 1900 stunned Hohenlohe. He had never been consulted, knew nothing specific about the expedition (timetable, size, commanders chosen, political objective, duration of mission, potential allies and so on), and had no control over the kaiser's public statements, which were inflammatory to say the least (among others: 'No Chinaman, no matter whether his eyes be slit or not, will dare to look a German in the face'; and, the Chinese are 'by nature, cowardly like a dog'; and, 'Peking must be razed to the ground'; and, 'Take no prisoners' and so forth). Yet Wilhelm expected his chancellor to explain and justify the entire matter before a hostile Reichstag. Impossible! said Hohenlohe. I 'must answer in the Reichstag for policies about which I know nothing?' He finally, after six years in office, resigned (and promptly passed away).[7] One diplomat on the Wilhelmstrasse said that the kaiser acquired, and discarded, chancellors as a man would his mistresses. Others referred to them as 'eunuchs'.

Wilhelm oversaw (but certainly would not recognize them as such) a string of dispiriting reverses in German affairs. His desire to placate socialist tendencies among German workers failed; his public utterances thereafter fuelled the growth of the opposition Social Democrats in succeeding Reichstag elections. Bismarck's emphasis on maintaining close relations with Russia was cavalierly jettisoned; in any future European conflict, the likelihood of Germany having to fight a two-front war both east and west was exponentially increased, a fateful, to say the least, development. An expensive and thoroughly gratuitous 'naval race' with Britain was initiated, ostensibly on the notion that German world trade required a formidable and protective maritime presence in order to thrive (the example of unarmed Holland and Norway, which possessed two of the larger merchant fleets in the world, was apparently deemed an unworthy comparison). Several diplomatic crises were carelessly initiated, pursued and bungled, some in regions of the world that had little international significance (Morocco, for one). Wilhelm's colonial ambitions added little to German prestige, despite his grandiose pronouncements ('We must now go out in search of new spots where we can drive in nails on which to hang our armour'); some, like the acquisition of portions of the French Congo, added nothing but hundreds of square miles of barren countryside, devoid of minerals or any other kind of wealth. All these episodes and trends, following one another or occurring simultaneously, created an atmospheric of ratcheting tension that put everyone's nerves continuously on edge, not least Wilhelm's own. Eulenburg often complained that being around the kaiser necessitated walking on eggshells; the slightest annoyance could result in a volcanic explosion of temper. He likened it to sitting on a keg of gunpowder, and to what purpose? Wilhelm often depicted himself as a martyr for Germany; but in fact, his often frantic scrambles, whether in domestic or international politics, usually achieved nothing. As one of his chancellors put it, 'Challenge everybody, get in everyone's way, and actually, in the course of all this, weaken nobody.'

The volatility of Wilhelm's rhetoric made for wonderful newspaper copy. 'He approached every problem with an open mouth', as one historian put it. Above all (other than socialists, parliamentarians, gossipy women and civilians of most stripes), the kaiser detested the press, a loathing that was often reciprocated. His loquaciousness exacerbated the environment; most every tactless phrase, expression or indiscreet remark made its way into print, along with reams of his more innocuous (or vacuous, depending on one's point of view) pronouncements on just about every topic under the Germanic sun. In 1895, a cartoonist for the journal *Simplicissimus* depicted Wilhelm as King Philip of Macedonia consoling his son, Alexander the Great, who was sketched weeping into a Grecian vase (Wilhelm adored Greek lore and history; the buffoonish Achilles was, aptly enough, one of his boyhood heroes). Alexander (in this case Wilhelm's son, the crown prince) responds to his father's query as to why he is crying: 'I fear that if you go on ruling for much longer', he says, 'you will leave nothing for me to say.' Wilhelm's infamous *Daily Telegraph* interview, however, showed the crown prince mistaken; the kaiser still had plenty to say.

The *Daily Telegraph* Affair

'You English are mad, mad, mad as March hares.'

With these words, Kaiser Wilhelm II began what can only be described as the most maladroit address ever given by a reigning German emperor. It was not, in reality, a straightforward interview undertaken by a newspaper reporter or editor, but rather a compilation of remarks taken down by a British admirer of the kaiser during a state visit to England, and published in London's *Daily Telegraph*. When his crazed and megalomaniacal rants were published in Germany, they caused an immediate uproar. 'Great debate on *D.T.* interview', Ambassador Goschen wrote in his diary from Berlin. 'People are rabid here as they say he had made them ridiculous before the whole world.... The line the debate [in the Reichstag] took was that everyone has had enough of the "Personal" regime of the Emperor.'

By this point in his career, Wilhelm had managed the impossible; he had offended just about every segment of German popular opinion. The '*D.T.* Affair' just brought accumulating dissatisfactions to a boil. Socialists felt he was beyond repair, a menace to world and domestic peace. Warmongers from the extreme right thought he was 'soft and weak'. Militarists had tired of his superficiality.[8] When artillerymen in the German army recommended gun shields to provide protection from enemy shrapnel, Wilhelm vehemently objected (it would foster cowardice); likewise the abandonment of gaudy uniforms in favour of field grey (it would lessen regimental pride). Prussian conservatives recoiled from the emperor's perceived encouragement for industrialization, tending as it did to undermine traditional rural values. They also scorned his garish monumentalism ('Of a machine, one had [only] to tell him that it is the biggest in the world.') Monarchists supported the crown, but excoriated Wilhelm's erratic personal behaviour, which only undermined popular support for the institution. His public persona, 'fierce and forbidding', seemed after a while a mere caricature of imperial power.[9]

There was no one Wilhelm could please. A foreign correspondent noted the near-universal opinion that 'Germany is a new, crude, ambitious, radically unsound power'. The kaiser was no more than 'a flashy schoolboy', all 'cant, talk, appearances'. This was a damning portrait that too many knowledgeable people shared, to Germany's later regret. When World War I started, most would point the finger of blame directly at the kaiser. For the life of him, Wilhelm could never figure out why.

Wilhelm's response to the outpouring of scorn after the *Daily Telegraph* interview was near hysteria. He suffered what can only be described as a nervous breakdown, took to his bed and refused to see any of his advisers. Even the drastic step of abdication was discussed, as his own chancellor deserted him on the Reichstag's floor and the press went after him with a vengeance. 'The business of the Reich demands a political temperament, not a dramatic one', the radical *Die Zukunft* editorialized. 'We don't want a Jupiter who sends lightning from the clouds'. General Karl von Einem, a monarchist of the first order, later complained that 'we have not had a functioning head of state for twenty-five years.'[10]

After almost a month in seclusion, the kaiser began to reappear in public, though much chastened. He even made promises to mend his ways, to practise more restraint and generally to behave with more constitutional respect. In some regards he kept his word, paying a little more attention to the counsels of his new chancellor, Theobald von Bethmann Hollweg; but Morocco was soon replaced by the Balkans as a *casus belli*, presenting situations of enormous complexity that required a discrimination the kaiser simply did not possess to comprehend fully. His rhetoric soon reached its normal levels of stridency, though with some circumspection. Admiral von Tirpitz noted in his memoirs that 'when the emperor did not consider the peace to be threatened, he liked to give full play to his reminiscences of famous ancestors'. This was usually manifested with blood-soaked imagery of the usual sort, but 'in moments which he realized to be critical he proceeded with extra caution'. This, at least, was a slight improvement, but his sense of personal humiliation remained keen. Something had been stripped from him; his feelings of omnipotence had been battered. He became less inclined to give matters of state the kind of study they deserved. Never a workaholic, he drifted into a state of spasmodic attention, and became more distracted than ever. Wilhelm now seldom read entire position papers; his staff pared them down to extracts or summaries, as they did with newspapers, cutting out selected articles on any given subject but excising many more. It became commonplace for the restless kaiser to rush off on the spur of the moment for cruises, 'vacations', archaeological expeditions or week-long excursions visiting the estates of often startled, bewildered and not exactly appreciative members of the nobility or nouveau riche. When Wilhelm travelled, he did so in style, accompanied by at least one hundred retainers (Dona was usually left behind), all of whom required accommodation, meals and incessant entertainment. Hunting became a serious obsession. His entourage, at one venue, shot 4,200 pheasants. At another, Wilhelm alone brought down 550. As he aged, he grew lazier; the game was brought to him; he no longer stalked deer or elk, they were driven to his shooting blind by an army of woodsmen. All the kaiser had to do was shoot them down. One meeting with his counsellors was interrupted by news that a stag was nearby. He rushed out of the chamber, was handed a gun and off he went for the kill. Evenings were full of dinner parties, largely dominated by monologues delivered by the kaiser on any number of subjects, the object of which, according to one observer, was his 'intent' on showing his audience 'that he was little short of omniscient'. Although Wilhelm was generally abstemious when it came to alcohol, his companions (usually male) were not. Their duties mostly entailed dreaming up risqué theatricals which the kaiser so loved. In one, an aged and overweight general danced a ballet for the kaiser dressed in a tutu. When finished, he staggered offstage and died of a heart attack. Wilhelm insisted the musicians play on as though nothing of consequence had happened. The conversation on these occasions, according to many commentators, was often coarse, though rarely lewd (the kaiser was a prude). He was rough with his compatriots. Wilhelm slapped people on the back or rump, he hit them (playfully, he thought) with his baton or staff, he pushed guests around in crude pranks. In public his salutations could often be grotesque, loud and impolite. At one reception, greeting a respected and distinguished old soldier, he cried out, 'What, you old pig. Are you invited too?' An evening in Wilhelm's company could be excruciating. 'When I left the palace', wrote one guest, 'I felt like an escaped prisoner.'

The kaiser's hectic schedule, which proved the despair of his personal staff, was seen by one historian as a subconscious defence mechanism, a 'conspiracy against self-understanding.'

The decade before the Great War was a stressful one, full of crises, ill-founded decisions and several opportunities for collective mayhem. The kaiser was in the middle of many of these – 'this drilling, trampling foolery in the heart of Europe', as H. G. Wells termed it – where his nerves were often tested. Eulenburg, no longer in favour, had predicted the confusion that would follow his monarch's directives.[11] Wilhelm retained his conviction that he, and he alone, would direct Germany's military affairs. In fact, professional soldiers did all the planning and implementing, often behind the kaiser's back. He didn't want to know the details anyway, nor did he feel that his officials at the foreign office needed any insight either. When the time came, Wilhelm would leap from saddle to saddle. In other words, from the saddle in his office (which he used instead of a chair) to the one on his charger, whence he would lead his troops into battle, a superb eighteenth-century scenario. The final dilemma, however, created by the assassination of the heir to the Austro-Hungarian throne in June 1914, found Wilhelm at the very centre of a storm where he did not wish to be; his remarks and actions proved a major contributor to the initiation of hostilities, even as he lost his courage at the very last moment. What else would one expect from a man who had said to his advisers, on more than one occasion, that 'All of you know nothing; I alone know something. I alone decide.' Anyone seeing in remarks like these a macabre similarity to those of Adolf Hitler in his bunker, as the Red Army closed in on Berlin during those bleak days of May 1945, would not be far wrong.

Chapter 3

Alfred von Schlieffen

'To make war is always to attack.'

Frederick the Great

O tto von Bismarck was the towering figure of German political life almost from the moment he was appointed minister president of Prussia in 1862. His long tenure of office lasted until 1890 when he was finally ousted by the young, headstrong and self-confident new kaiser, Wilhelm II. Bismarck, an autocratic and arrogant personality, had experienced difficulties with the two previous kaisers under whom he served, but they were reasonable men who could be convinced as to the soundness of the policies he proposed, if indeed he deigned to share his views with them. Wilhelm II was a different personality altogether, a man who often could not be reached on any serious level.

Bismarck, though a militarist of the first order, often had no use for army officers, whom he usually lampooned as 'demi-gods'. They were an instrument to be used as he, Bismarck, saw fit. He recognized the tendency of the institution to veer into extreme behaviour, understanding that the excitement of wars and the allure of fame and promotion were often too much for mere mortals in uniform to resist. When Bismarck unleashed his armies, as he did on three occasions between 1864 and 1870, he did so with the utmost resolve that once his goals were attained, he would reattach the leash and bring his dogs of war back under control. After German armies defeated Austria in 1866, the then kaiser wanted a triumphal entry into Vienna to further humiliate his foes. Bismarck cracked the whip and forbade it. Austria, though beaten, was to be a useful ally for Germany in the future.[1] Bismarck had a subtle game in play, the details of which neither the kaiser nor his generals ever seemed to fathom, and he meant to keep it that way. Writing later to his counterpart in Vienna, he put the matter succinctly: 'We must both take care that the privilege of giving political advice to our monarchs does not in fact slip out of our hands and pass over to the general staffs.'

Carl von Clausewitz, the famous Prussian military theorist of the early nineteenth century, is often portrayed as a kind of evil genius whose works helped spawn the entire ethos of German aggressiveness that so marred the history of Europe from Bismarck's time to 1945. Von Clausewitz's seminal work, *Vom Kriege* ('On War'), for example, represents the gospel; the great German general staff, the acolytes; sitting out in the congregation, the entire mass of Germany's population, all geared up, trained and indoctrinated to the theorems of total war. These views are often spread about by people who have never read *Vom Kriege*, which, as it turns out, was often the case as regards large numbers of German officers who never opened a book in their lives.[2]

Perhaps the most oft-quoted proposition from the pen of von Clausewitz, ironically, was a pivotal distinction he made regarding the proper role of the army: it did not exist for the gratification of blood lust or as the primitive outlet for those seeking glory or booty or the women from a neighbouring village. It was simply an extension of the political process, the tool by which diplomats and civilians attained their goals when the negotiating table could no longer produce the desired result. Politicians controlled generals, not vice versa. This was a Clausewitzian given, one that Bismarck (who also never read *Vom Kriege*) believed implicitly. Professional soldiers, on the other hand, despised these constraints. General Erich Ludendorff, for instance, advised his readers to 'throw Clausewitz overboard'.[3]

In order to curb the seemingly genetic impulse of German generals to act independently of civilian (and sometimes monarchical) control,[4] Bismarck and the various kaisers devised a series of bureaucratic roadblocks that in many respects provided unintended results and, perversely, actually increased the influence of militarists on the general staff. Broadly speaking, the military hierarchy evolved into three separate entities that, over time, grew competitive and secretive as regards one another, thereby sapping efficiencies and disrupting the smooth course of military affairs. The minister of war, originally an office of great authority (especially under Albrecht von Roon before the Franco-Prussian War), was over time relegated to a largely political role, dealing with the ever-contentious Reichstag over budgetary matters, an issue of great importance when the army and navy exponentially grew as the nineteenth century rolled over into the twentieth. The war cabinet, the second entity, became a social registry of sorts, dedicated to the preservation and advancement within the officer corps of aristocratic bloodlines, to the exclusion of middle classes or, heaven forbid, the proletariat. Promotion lists were its specialty. The third component was the great general staff, a body of some importance, of course, but mostly a bureaucratic office within the army's infrastructure, dedicated to war planning, troop training, mobilization guidelines, compiling wish lists for new equipment and, most importantly, troop levels. Helmuth von Moltke the Elder, however, changed the dynamic of these arrangements through his spectacular battlefield successes during the Franco-Prussian War, and the resultant idolization of his abilities through the pages of an ever-burgeoning popular press. In 1883, von Moltke's status was elevated. No longer was he (or his successors) subservient to the minister of war. He now enjoyed the independent status of his own department, with the right to demand a direct audience with the kaiser. This, not unnaturally, would eventually provoke the jealousy of both the war minister and those in the military cabinet. It also ensured that the kaiser – any kaiser – would now be receiving advice, admonition, threats of resignation, unbridled praise or any combination thereof, from a variety of bemedalled, beribboned and highly opinionated officers. Some imperial warlords could sift through the resultant barrage of conflicting verbiage and come to coherent decisions but others, such as Wilhelm II, often could not.

A lack of oversight thus developed with regard to the general staff. They were beholden to no one, however much Kaiser Wilhelm II, for instance, believed to the contrary. This was especially true during the tenure of Alfred von Schlieffen, who held the post of chief of the general staff from 1891 to 1906. His run of fifteen years has often been described in monastic terms, Schlieffen the abbot (or hermit), running his 'church' as he saw fit, developing war plans about which no one knew anything, except for the inconvenient fact that they in essence committed the nation, in case of hostilities, to a course of action about which no deviation was possible. For seven of those years, Schlieffen worked on his 'plan' to attack France, and France alone, without the knowledge or oversight of anyone else in the imperial government other than officers serving under him on the staff itself. For better or worse, he was operating 'in a vacuum'. Wilhelm II considered himself a warlord. The army was 'his', the generals were 'his', everyone did as he commanded. He enjoyed telling members of the general staff that when war came, he would dispense with most of their services, especially senior officers, those 'old asses' as he called them. He would be the chief of the general staff, he would be the next Frederick the Great. Wilhelm would learn, to his chagrin, that this was just another in a long list of fantasies with which he continuously deluded himself.

Unlike many of his contemporaries from the social caste of rural Prussian nobility, Alfred von Schlieffen was not born into abject poverty, nor was his mother forced to take in laundry in order to pay off the indebtedness of some dirt-scrabble family estate, held for innumerable years by reedy descendants of the Teutonic knights. Indeed, his parents enjoyed both a modestly noble pedigree and the rewards of several large and remunerative properties, enough for them to maintain a Berlin residence (where von Schlieffen was born in 1833) and to finance a reasonable education, not the sort of spartan, intellectually impoverished curriculum provided by cadet academies where most boys destined for army life were invariably sent, there to be brutalized and turned into martinets or worse. Von Schlieffen's boyhood living rooms were saturated with Hutterite and pietist proselytizing, which emphasized the rigid Prussian virtues of duty, self-effacement, industry, with heartfelt attachment to king, country and protestantism thrown in.[5] Schlieffen was a religious man to his dying day, which predestined him to look forward all his life to the 'cold, cold grave' that figured to be the destiny of every cold, cold man.[6]

That von Schlieffen had a frigid disposition is the universal observation of the few contemporaries who put pen to paper in order to record their impressions of this aloof and distant personality. Hermann von Kuhl, for example, a great admirer, stated quite bluntly that von Schlieffen was not a well-rounded or normal man. He had no sense of humour, no inner life to speak of and no social acuity. Some ascribe this detachment to several personal tragedies that beset his family life within a very short span of time: the death of a brother in the Franco-Prussian war, that of a beloved sister and, finally, the passing of his wife after just three years of marriage. Von Schlieffen internalized distress by channelling all his energy into careerism; not so much for advancement through the ranks, but in order to master his profession, the success in which few men would ever match. 'He lived exclusively for his work and his great tasks', von Kuhl wrote.

Slowly winding his way through army life, Schlieffen gained a reputation for meticulous attention to detail, and myopic absorption in the strategic and tactical issues that rapid industrialization was forcing the armed forces to acknowledge and adapt accordingly. He was a glutton for work. Whereas von Moltke the Elder was a man of some refinement (he read Goethe and Shakespeare, and had once begun to translate into German Gibbon's *The Decline and Fall of the Roman Empire*), whose horizons had been considerably broadened by extensive travel, Schlieffen had no time for culture or the arts. He absorbed technical papers and studies on gun calibres instead. Apocryphal stories circulated that after long and difficult days he would return home after midnight, awake his two daughters, and read to them until 2 a.m. He disdained fables or *Grimms' Fairy Tales*, however, confining his bedside reading matter to history books relating battles and Napoleonic strategy.

Because (at least according to von Schlieffen) he was a man largely devoid of ambition – or, more precisely, proved temperamentally unsuited for the kind of ingratiating, obsequious and grovelling submission that angling for preferment usually required – his advancement to the chief of general staff was essentially a succession of fortuitous happenstance. When von Moltke the

Elder first laid eyes on Schlieffen, he dismissed the notion immediately that the officer before him could be candidate for high command. This middle-aged gentleman was overly quiet, reserved, dull, and held back too often, both physically and intellectually. He was part of the woodwork. Watching him perform on a staff ride in 1875 changed the field marshal's mind, however, and he made a mental note that this was a man to keep his eye on. Appointed head of a Uhlan regiment to see what he could make of it, von Schlieffen rarely left a minute wasted, beginning each day at 4 a.m. in the stables where one of the pressing issues he spent a good deal of time and research resolving was what to do with excess manure. Some considered him a drudge, but in another piece of unexpected good fortune he was promoted to the staff of von Moltke's successor, the politically ambitious Alfred von Waldersee, a close and intimate friend of the kaiser (one of the few Wilhelm had). This should have guaranteed for Waldersee a long career as chief of the general staff, but he presumed too much on his familiarity with the kaiser. Hoping to commingle his top position in the military with its equivalence in political affairs, the general overstepped himself by his involvement in several squalid intrigues that, tangentially at least, were intended in his own mind to lead to the chancellorship, a miscalculation of the first order. The kaiser sensed this ambition; other hangers-on not only sensed it, but warned the kaiser more bluntly that he was being manipulated. Waldersee capped his downfall by having the temerity to criticize Wilhelm's performance during an annual summer war game – the kaiser, it appears, attacked some of his own forces by mistake – and he was summarily banished to an obscure army command. In 1891, 'without my effort or desire', von Schlieffen found himself suddenly promoted to Waldersee's position.

This was not a move that made headlines. Alfred von Schlieffen was a figure almost unknown outside of Germany, however old his family and however well connected he was to important figures of the Prussian aristocracy.[7] He was just a name, as it were. His fame, or notoriety, was really a postwar concoction, as we shall see later in this narrative. During the remaining years of his formal military career, Schlieffen's motto remained steady, 'Do much, but stand out little'. This desire for relative anonymity was fully achieved; so too, and closely associated, became the growing myth of the German general staff which, after the events of 1914, was seen as an entity without any individual personality other than that of a ruthless, impersonal, technocratic war machine peopled by automatons, not individuals. The monolithic nature of this image, most assiduously crafted by von Schlieffen himself, did much to ensure that after two world wars the very institution of the general staff would be stigmatized as a collective 'war criminal' and banned. This did not prove successful after the First World War, but was accomplished after the Second. There is today no great general staff in the *Bundeswehr*.

Within Germany, von Schlieffen's ascension to chief of the general staff reflected a genuine turning point in the direction (and methodology) of long-term planning within the imperial army. Helmuth von Moltke the Elder, on the occasion of his official retirement, had set the bar very high. The victor of the Franco-Prussian War, among others – the man who had won the battles of Königgrätz and Sedan – in his old age almost regreted that Germany was now the powerhouse of central Europe, for with the prestige and glory came both danger and temptation. Germany was paying the price for its success; it was also paying the price, and would continue to do so, for its new kaiser, a man whose insistence on personalizing a direct rule over the empire, and trusting his instincts to do so, would within two decades essentially isolate Germany from the rest of the continent. Relations with the several European powers that mattered – France, Russia, Great Britain, Italy and Austria-Hungary – while hardly warm and comfy, were certainly within reasonable degrees of diplomatic civility in 1888, the year of Bismarck's ouster. That would not last long. By the eve of war, Germany's sole ally was the weakest reed of them all, Austria-Hungary, the others (especially France and Russia) irretrievably alienated. Von Moltke the Elder realized the deteriorating situation very keenly, and had thought long and hard about the developing isolation. If the trend continued, any future war would see the fatherland engaged on both its eastern and western frontiers, outnumbered, encircled, attacked from all directions save its common border with Vienna. Von Moltke had war-gamed the situation many times. He saw no path to easy victory, at least by the force of arms. His final address to the Reichstag is memorable for two important points. In the first, he predicted that the next round of hostilities would raise havoc equivalent to that of the Thirty Years' War from the seventeenth century. That was an image to give any German nightmares. In the second, which may have been a thinly disguised warning to the new kaiser, he said 'Woe to him that sets Europe on fire', which he referred to as a 'powderkeg'.

Von Moltke's solution, generally shared by his immediate successor, Waldersee, was that Germany would adopt a defensive posture on the western front against France. The French, since the Franco-Prussian War, had built a solid wall of concrete facing the lost provinces of Alsace-Lorraine. The entire north-east corner of France was, in von Moltke's opinion, now 'hermetically sealed'. There was no way to run around the fortress system, nor were frontal attacks to be even considered, given the appalling casualties that would certainly result. The better idea was to let France, allegedly full of resentment and desires for revenge, attack Germany's two great fortress systems, centred in Metz and Strasbourg or, failing that, to have German armies fall back to the Rhine, a physical barrier that would present a formidable challenge to any would-be invader. The bulk of the Fatherland's forces would deal with Russia first, on the eastern front, where the ability to manoeuvre was somewhat less constricted, and the chances of inflicting a stunning defeat on an inferior foe more pronounced. If Russia was blooded first, the opportunity of a negotiated settlement was good, since Germany – even its most hidebound imperialists – wanted little that Russia possessed. After all, wrote Moltke, the country 'had no gold, and we don't need land'. By the time of von Moltke's death in 1891, this was the basic operational plan. By the time von Schlieffen replaced Waldersee, he inherited the same viewpoint. But not for long.

The Von Schlieffen Concerto

'Gigantic, strategic Cannae!'

General Wilhelm Gröner

During his first years on the general staff, Schlieffen contributed little originality to the prevailing drift of von Moltke's strategic ideas. When promoted to the top position, in fact, his first significant deviation was to suggest that perhaps a defensive posture in the west was incorrect, and that frontal attacks on the French defensive line was not such a far-fetched idea after all. The idea was to outflank French forces on the country's northern borders, but it was predicated on attacking and capturing Nancy, the capital of Lorraine, first. Alfred von Waldersee, now languishing in Hamburg, was horrified. 'We are doing exactly what the French have hoped and prepared for', he wrote in his diary. The very idea curdled his blood.

But Schlieffen was a patient, thorough man. Before most officers had even shown up for work at army headquarters, Schlieffen could be seen in the chart room, poring over the newest topographical maps. Few dared engage the general in idle conversation; he was 'insensible' to everyday conventions of bonhomie, preferring to be left alone with his thoughts, twisting an ever-present monocle in his eye socket. (An Austrian officer noted that Schlieffen was 'the most taciturn [person] one could ever meet'.) During these long inner monologues, a new version to his operational ruminations began to take form. He developed these notions at first by himself; then shared them with selected colleagues whom he could trust (Schlieffen never hesitated to cull officers who disagreed with him); and finally put them to the test in simulated war games and staff rides, the latter of which he led on thirty-one separate occasions. He never came to any of his decisions lightly.

Schlieffen was the epitome of the apolitical officer, unlike Waldersee whose dabbling in foreign and domestic affairs had led to his premature exile. This is not to say that Schlieffen was an innocent in political matters; just that he kept his opinions to himself. The resident intellectual of the foreign service for some three decades, Friedrich von Holstein, mentioned in his memoirs that during times of crises, many fostered by the loose-lipped kaiser, the general would visit his office for updates. 'While I sit here', Holstein noted in 1897, 'Count Schlieffen sits beside me reading documents, which is usually the case once a week in troubled times.' Political calculations definitely influenced Schlieffen's thinking on strategy. Who were Germany's potential opponents, whose forces should be deemed more dangerous than others, which enemies could inject their forces into the field first? The answers to these questions put into Schlieffen's mind variations on logical responses, conditioned by his understanding of Germany's strengths and weaknesses, particularly in the evolving field of technology. As the kaiser's erratic policy decisions increased, rather than decreased, the probable coalition of opponents, Schlieffen's task became more complicated. By 1905, the year of his own retirement, he based his final plan on a very bleak scenario: Germany would, to all intents and purposes, be fighting every nation in Europe save one, Austria-Hungary. How could it hope to win? And if he could figure that out, with whom would he share the secret?

Much has been written (and argued) over the alleged morbidity of men like Schlieffen, who tended to view the world in apocalyptic terms that, it is alleged, put gears into motion towards a doomsday scenario that any sensible person would have avoided. Many historians have rejected the hysteria that greeted the outbreak of the Great War – jubilant crowds, bouquets of flowers, a delight in the glory of battles to come – as proof that European societies ingenuously welcomed the conflict as they would a bank holiday. The average man in the street clearly did not, but the average man mostly reacted to events, he did not initiate them. When mobilizations began, and volunteers marched through the streets, he cheered. In thinking it over, he would have probably preferred doing something else.

The First World War was clearly a turning point in European history, a moment when the decisions of just a handful of men – many of them dim-witted hereditary kings – could launch a war almost at whim. It can be argued that monarchs like Wilhelm, Tsar Nicholas, and George V were merely figures of straw, manipulated by a cadre of diplomats and soldiers who, in fact, directed the flow of events and pulled the various switches to initiate hostilities. But the fact remains that, up until the very eve of war, an individual crowned head could say no and be obeyed. By the end of 1918, such monarchical authority had been destroyed. But the lesson remains clear as regards 1914. Just a few individuals controlled the arena.

As the baker baked his bread, as the farmer ploughed behind his horse, as the worker poured molten steel into forms, men like Alfred von Schlieffen toiled in relative obscurity at their particular specialties. In his case, it was exclusively preparing for war. Within his own narrow world, with few associates, a brush now and then with men like von Holstein, an avalanche of technical advisers focused on single subjects surrounding him, it was the only topic that mattered. Without a doubt, the atmosphere in which he worked was cloistered. As such, everyday events might take on more significance than they should have; portents of seeming innocuity might be misinterpreted by individuals more obsessed with searching out negativities and dwelling on them; people engorged on constricted visions could prove unable to open their minds to other, less ominous interpretations. All the signs that Alfred von Schlieffen saw was a world preparing for battle: an arms race underway, alliances disintegrating and then renewed elsewhere, seething ethnic difficulties on the edges of Europe, seemingly insignificant but interpretable as mortal threats. Added into the mix were fashionable Darwinian principles that could be twisted into motivations for aggressive actions; millenarianism, or the notion of unfathomable destiny beyond human ability to avoid; public rhetoric and imprecise monarchical talk that focused like a heady drumbeat on drawing swords, drawing blood, fulfilling one's destiny as a Teutonic knight. Von Schlieffen and his ilk could feel it coming on; the notion preyed on their minds.

As a generalization, one might say that von Schlieffen's conclusions from his strategic ruminations evolved into three fundamental strands. The first was his choice of a target, and political considerations determined this decision. Would it be France? Or Russia? Simultaneously, or one at a time? Would he divide his armies more or less equally, or concentrate more powerfully on one, while hoping to keep the other at bay? At what point, if any, would Britain and Austria-Hungary play a role, and what would the significant contribution, or debit, be from either? After mulling over his options, Schlieffen made up his mind and selected his victim of choice, one from which he never deviated. It would be France. 'The *whole* of Germany must throw itself on *one* enemy', he concluded, 'the strongest, most powerful, most dangerous enemy.'

The second strand, obviously, was how to do it. Schlieffen, though not a cultured man, was well read within the confines of his particular interests, and he was a student of history. Hans Delbrück, a pre-eminent (and controversial) military writer and historian who published widely from his university chair in Berlin, began releasing his several-volume *History of the Art of War* in the first decade of the new century. Schlieffen was fascinated, most particularly by a battle that had been fought some twenty-one centuries ago in 216 BC in south-eastern Italy, near a village called Cannae. Hannibal of Carthage, with an army of about 45,000 men, crushed a far larger Roman force under the command of consuls Gaius Varro and Lucius Paullus. Varro and Paullus, amassing their foot soldiers in a solid and unwieldy block or phalanx, attacked Hannibal's centre, which bent (but did not break) under the impact of the Roman advance. Eventually, Hannibal's line assumed a concave form, drawing the Romans into his centre. The Carthaginian cavalry had meanwhile scattered its Roman counterparts on both wings, and proceeded to attack the Roman rear. At just this moment, Hannibal ordered both his infantry wings to advance on an 'end around', meeting up with his cavalry in the rear in a dual pincer movement. The Romans were now completely surrounded, compressed into a small area, and physically reduced to immobility. Many legionnaires had no room to swing their swords or wield their heavy spears. Hannibal's men then slaughtered some 70,000 of the enemy, ceasing only when the sun went down. It is said by some ancient scribes that only 3,000 Romans escaped what turned out to be, in effect, a battle of almost complete extermination.

An 'annihilating embrace' were words that warmed Schlieffen's heart, which in general was impervious to any emotion.

Schliffen wondered what lessons could be learned from Cannae. It might even be suggested that he became obsessed with this battle; certainly some of his fellow officers thought so. As war games and theoretical problems were thrashed about, all seemed aimed in one direction, and with a single query that begged for an answer: in the modern age, with battlefields enveloping hundreds of square miles, and with weaponry at a degree of complexity where 'the conceivable [in terms of mass destruction] has been achieved', was it possible to think in terms of a Cannae-type victory, a double envelopment so complete that it could bludgeon the enemy into insensibility? And if so, by what means? Schlieffen began to think that such a feat could be done, and he had his disciples surrounding him who thought so too. Critics called this 'church' and its members 'encirclement' fanatics.

Von Moltke the Elder had stated that 'no strategic plan goes with any certainty beyond the first encounter with the enemy's main forces. Only the layman believes he can see in the course of a campaign the carrying through of the initial idea, thought out in advance, considered in every detail, and adhered to right to the end.' Schlieffen disagreed, and von Moltke, after all, was dead and no longer in charge.

The Schlieffen 'plan' was predicated on several dogmas, the first involving concentration of force. 'We must be stronger at the point of impact', he wrote. 'Our only hope of this lies in making our own choice of operations, not waiting passively for whatever the enemy chooses for us.' This was in clear lock step with what Napoleon had once said: 'Do not do what the enemy wants, for the sole reason that he wants it.' Out the window with these declarations was any sense of opting for a defensive posture. Schlieffen was not prepared to keep his men and artillery cooped up in fortress cities or underground bunkers. 'Annihilation', as one of his staff put it, 'can only be achieved by movement, not immobility.'

A second dogma flowed from the first. Whatever Schlieffen devised would be predicated on speed. The killing power of modern weaponry made brisk and bold operations necessary, and would require hitting the enemy where he least expected it. Frontal attacks might have their place in certain types of operation, but on the whole should be avoided. Infantry trooping across open fields in packed formations against prepared positions bristling with machine guns and cannon firing shrapnel, was simply a form of suicide. In this regard, again referring to Napoleon, Schlieffen contrasted how differently that great warrior had fought at the height, and then at the end, of his career. At Austerlitz, Napoleon had simply overwhelmed his Austrian opponents, throwing all he had into the battle and attacking from every conceivable angle. '*Activité, activité, vitesse*', he allegedly cried. But ten years later, at Waterloo, he had lost that spark of inventive inspiration, throwing his infantry and then cavalry again and again at Wellington's front line in dull, plodding attacks. 'One ages rapidly on the battlefields', the emperor had remarked, and he proved it at the worst possible moment of his life.[8] As far as Schlieffen was concerned, 'The attack must never come to a standstill.' Even more importantly, it must never be wasted against the main strength of the enemy.

This led inevitably to the principal lesson from Cannae. As Hannibal had done, so would Schlieffen. He would not attack the French frontier fortifications that faced the German border, but would outflank them. This was easily said, but the placement of the various enemy systems did not allow for manoeuvres of such scope within French territory. French planners had designed their forts and entrenched guns to funnel German attackers into killing grounds of their own choosing, which would certainly not do for Schlieffen. The alternative, therefore, was to bypass frontal obstructions and circle to the right or left to attack the flank and rear of the enemy. In strictly military terms, which were the only criterion about which Schlieffen cared, the application was simple – ignore the French frontier, and push forward through either Switzerland or Luxembourg/Belgium to achieve the desired envelopment. The political ramifications of such a move, all three of these countries being neutral, and Belgium's status 'guaranteed' since 1839 by both Britain and France, did not enter Schlieffen's thinking. As a matter of fact, he threw his net even wider, deciding that if the northern route was the one selected, he might additionally violate Holland's borders as well.

In looking over these routes, Schlieffen selected what was, militarily, the obvious choice: Luxembourg, Belgium and Holland. He needed relatively open space because, in what several military historians have called his 'gambler's throw', he intended to use 85 per cent of his force level on just one flank, his right. Not 85 per cent of the forces allocated to the western theatre (von Moltke had projected dividing German strength equally between those fighting Russia and those fighting France), but the entire strength of the whole German army. The key to this allocation was the intent not to fight a two-front war simultaneously (one in the east, one in the west), but to fight two one-front wars in succession. This is one reason why Schlieffen chose to face off with France first. Russia, still reeling from its disastrous defeat by Japan and the revolution in St. Petersburg that had followed, was not prepared, or conditioned, to another even more difficult struggle; nor was its infrastructure sufficiently upgraded to allow the type of efficient mobilization of which France, Germany and Britain were all capable. In other words, Schlieffen had time to achieve his speedy victory in the west before turning to face the slower giant to his east. Thrashing the French, along with the few men that Britain might throw into the fray, would all be over in 42 days. Or so the theory went.

Schlieffen's goal was not just victory but the obliteration of his enemies. To achieve this, he did not want a static front, but a fluid one marked by Napoleonic *vitesse*, endurance and overwhelming force. His strong right wing, 'never [coming] to a standstill', would sweep through the Low Countries before France even knew what had happened, crossing the border between roughly Bastogne and Hasselt (north of Maastricht); it would be like a swinging door, the hinges resting at Metz, the arc of the door's outer edge brushing the English Channel. It would inflict a series of hammer blows, winning battle after battle with no rest between encounters. The trick was to 'relentlessly pursue the enemy, and bring him to defeat again and again', a process that would eventually find French forces crushed against their own fortress system overlooking the river Meuse and Alsace-Lorraine. In such a scenario, the French forest of heavy guns in their concrete pens would be useless, all pointing in the wrong direction.

Speed was essential. Schlieffen had an appreciation for the sensibilities of modern society and the limits of its patience. A long drawn-out affair, or anything that threatened to bog down in stalemate, would threaten disaster. Wars of the future would require subservience from the entire state; farm workers, factory labourers, shopkeepers, all would be required to don a uniform and shoulder a rifle. But commerce and business were the order of the day in the modern, 'soft', mercenary world; the disruption of civil society and the ability of people to make money would never brook an endless breach in normal life. Schlieffen had no fear of a Thirty Years' War, society would never tolerate such a thing. Without a quick victory that destroyed the enemy, countries would find themselves drowning in the 'red ghost' (as he put it) of socialist revolution. Kaiser Wilhelm had, notoriously, lectured a graduating class of cadets at Potsdam that, upon his command, they must be ready to shoot or bayonet their own kin should they find them rioting in the streets or attacking the royal prerogative. Schlieffen knew those triggers would never be pulled; few men would skewer their brother with a bayonet. Rioting in the streets of St. Petersburg had convinced him that the same peril was possible for Berlin.

In order to achieve total superiority, German forces would have to rely on inbred (and racial) superiority: their discipline, bravery, indifference to fatigue, rigorous attention to detail and technological savoir-faire. They also required a bigger army, and the steel nerves of the men who would direct it. This was no place for weaklings; it was also no place for men who did not know what they were supposed to do. Schlieffen was adamant that every layer of command should coordinate perfectly with the soldiers above and the soldiers below, and be in synchronism with how the plan was to unfold. His subordinates were to play the game just as Schlieffen intended they play it. He would not be on the battlefield himself, but they were to know implicitly, within the set of orders they had received, how he wanted them to act. At points where individual initiative was required, they were to be so ingrained with the philosophy of the entire operation that they would respond with a set of 'Schlieffen principles'. This is why Schlieffen took such pains in his war gaming; why he rotated so many like-minded officers in and out of the general staff, familiarizing them with his ideas; why he favoured those whom he felt had learned the lessons best, in effect establishing a 'school' devoted to his points of view. With timetables planned to the very minute, he expected absolute compliance. Von Clausewitz had warned about 'the fog of war', the probability of things going wrong at the most awkward or crucial moments.

Schlieffen seemed to believe that he could overcome that obstacle through vigorous indoctrination. Of the many criticisms levelled at his reputation when the Great War ended, this unrealistic assumption was perhaps the gravest flung in his direction.

In the end, in order for the 'plan' to achieve its highest potential, Schlieffen yearned for the advantages to be gained from exploiting the right opportunity. Earlier in this chapter, three strands were mentioned that coalesced into the broad complexion of the Schlieffen scheme. The third strand slides quite comfortably within the overall texture of everything discussed to date, whether it be Schlieffen's personal mindset, the atmosphere of strategic thought within the upper circles of Wilhelmine society, or the popular notions of the day concerning Germany's 'precarious' and threatened international and geographic position – the notion of 'preventive war'.

The German tradition of battle had traditionally been that of the advance. The career of Frederick the Great, Germany's most revered warrior, was an exemplar of aggressive action. Frederick was famous for attacking everything in sight, even when seriously outnumbered, and the results were sometimes calamitous, though often obscured by his many spectacular victories. Men like von Schlieffen were never entirely comfortable with 'defensive' strategies; they much preferred to walk in Frederick's bootsteps.

With this predilection for the attack, it was but a small step, in addressing tactical situations, to search for the upper hand, the opening, the sliver of opportunity that might tip the balance in one's favour. Combined with the generally unfavourable portents that men like von Schlieffen saw as endangering Germany's security, the notion of attacking first became ingrained as operational thinking. The hostility of its neighbours and the antipathy they all felt for Germany seemed reflected in growing armies and military expenditures, infrastructural improvements aimed at facilitating mobilizations, warmongering in the hostile demagogic press – all seeming to predict the inevitability of conflagration. As Schlieffen's successor put it, 'there may be war for the simple reason that everyone has prepared for it so long', a validation of the American industrialist Henry Ford's dictum that 'I am against preparedness, because preparedness means war.' To the average citizen, all this may have been background noise, but to the German high command it represented a clear and insistent bugle call, the reverberations to which they were peculiarly attuned. The conclusions they drew became clearly understood: why let the enemies of the Fatherland get stronger while we get weaker? Why allow Russia the time it needs to recover from the Japanese defeat and the social unrest that came in its wake? Why let France take the lead in building bigger and better armies? Britain is increasing its dominance in naval strength, why let her advantage become simply overwhelming? Doctrinaire thinkers in the German armed forces tended to view these trends from the point of view of an aggrieved party – 'The whole world has conspired against us', wrote one. It is a testament to their blinkered points of view that they rarely understood their own country's contribution to the atmosphere of growing tension. Von Moltke the Younger, for example, consistently wrote to his wife that war was being pushed on Germany by its enemies. Germany's response, the invasion of France, was without a doubt 'a righteous war'.

Of course, 1914 was the year Germany took the plunge. The chancellor at the time, Bethmann Hollweg, described it as 'a leap in the dark', but it was hardly an unexpected moment that caught everyone by surprise. The entire first decade of the twentieth century had been one crisis after another, with sparks from the arid wastes of western Africa to the tangled affairs of the Balkans ever threatening to lead to something bigger. The drift towards imminent conflict had been a constant on the front pages of every European newspaper. Von Schlieffen was correct in calling this period one of 'cold war' (he coined the phrase). In several of these crises, the German high command had argued ferociously that the moment was ripe and that Germany must strike, and strike first, to maintain the upper hand in what would be an engagement involving many combatants. The cliff was there, and they were willing to go over its edge. This predilection to go to war was thus, in and of itself, a form of wish fulfilment when the opportune moment arrived. The unsettling brake on several of these occasions, however, came from the most surprising individual of all. For all his sabre-rattling rhetoric, Wilhelm II was, in fact, a man of little nerve, afraid to give the signal to go. As the younger von Moltke said on several occasions, the biggest problem he faced was neither the French nor the Russians, but the kaiser.

When von Schlieffen urged that war be sprung in 1905, it had nothing really to do with Morocco, the contretemps of the moment. It had to do with Germany's preponderances versus those of other countries. The moment, according to the now field marshal, was 'tailor-made'. 'Russia is tied up in the east, England still weakened by the Boer War, France still behind with its armaments. Before long the German Reich has to prove its worth through war. Now is the most convenient time. Therefore my solution: war with France.' When von Moltke the Younger next pushed for the attack seven years later – once more, the dispute involved Morocco – it again had nothing to do with that insignificant backwater of a country, but rather involved the question of timing. All Britain's policies were intended to 'squash' German commercial interests worldwide. Though statistics could be deceiving when looked at from a predisposed outlook, there was no question that Russia had recovered to some degree from her losses in the Japanese war. Her manpower was frightening, however impoverished its new troops were in terms of training, equipment and desire. Its armament industries were on the move, and the rapid expansion of railways heading west could not be overlooked. By 1916/17, a Schlieffen plan that relied on a slow Russian mobilization would be obsolete. Russians would be in Berlin as fast as Germany was in Paris. As for France, the assumption that bitter memories of Alsace-Lorraine continued to inflame that nation's alleged desire for revenge remained as solidly embedded in the German consciousness as the millions of tons of cement that were being poured all along their common border.[9] 'I regard war as inevitable', von Moltke declared, 'the sooner the better'. When the kaiser backed away yet again, von Moltke tried hard to conceal his contempt and frustration. Writing to his wife, he complained that Germany was 'creeping out of this affair with our tail between our legs'. We might as well 'abolish the army and place ourselves under the protection of Japan. Then we will be able to make money without interference and to become imbeciles.' In 1914, the mood in the kaiser's entourage was 'joyous' when it appeared that Britain might intervene with France for peace. Von Moltke stood 'shattered'; he had 'reached a state of despair'. What had to be done to get Germany's war machine in gear? What had to be done to begin the von Schlieffen Concerto?

Railways

One of the generalized stories about the beginning of World War I was the near heart attack that Wilhelm gave von Moltke the Younger when the kaiser insisted on a last-minute change to the entire war plan. Convinced that Britain, faced with the appalling notion of being dragged into a general European-wide war, was seeking some sort of option to remain on the sidelines (respect Belgian neutrality and do not attack France and we shall stay out of it, seemed to be the notion), the kaiser appeared to have the reed of hope that he, at the very last minute, so desperately wanted. Forget France, he now said – there was no need to attack her at this very moment; we now gather up 'my' entire collection of armies and attack Russia instead. When he heard this volte-face, Von Moltke nearly collapsed. Indeed, after the ensuing tumultuous interview with Wilhelm, where he managed, with tremendous difficulty, to maintain the agreed-upon course of action, he went back to his office and reportedly burst into tears. It was a strain he could hardly endure, and one that his famous uncle had never experienced on the eve of the Franco-Prussian War ('The first day of mobilization in 1870', that gentleman had written, 'was the quietest day of my life, as everything had been arranged'). Some say that von Moltke the Younger was never the same man again after this psychologically devastating collision, wherein one single individual's neurotic outburst had threatened to derail a decade's worth of work and planning ... and it all had to do with railways.

Beginning largely in von Moltke the Elder's tenure, railways had become the dominant factor in German war planning, as indeed they had to be. For over fifteen years the general staff had envisioned a two-front war. It was the *de rigueur*, preconceived 'given'. Germany possessed neither the manpower nor the resources to fight with equal strength simultaneously on both its eastern and western fronts. The idea was to mobilize quickly, mass on one frontier and fight a *Titane Kampf*, or 'Battle of the Titans', there, then shift the bulk of one's remaining forces in the opposite direction to deal with the next opponent. Being in the 'middle of the European house' had given Germany the unique opportunity of focusing its attentions on an integrated transportation system that both served the nation during peacetime as a commercial stimulant, and doubled during wartime as a powerful tactical weapon. With typical Teutonic efficiency, Germany tackled the issue with focused organizational zeal. By 1904, the year before Schlieffen's retirement, the German grid stood at 35,000 miles, serviced by some 20,000 locomotives. France, by contrast, could muster only 12,000 engines, and Russia a mere 10,000. A decade later, Germany's locomotive fleet had increased thirty percent, and they were hauling close to 700,000 freight cars, capable of carrying ten million tons of equipment. This does not even include 65,000 passenger cars. Technological innovations in rail and engine design increased productivity, load capacities and, most of all, getting from Point A to B in good order. As one historian has noted, several speed records at the turn of the century in both Europe and the United States were not surpassed until the 1960s. Innovation in signals design, telegraph and telephone communications and 'convoy' planning reached mathematical levels of extraordinary complexity. The army's railway section, largely the preserve of non-aristocratic officers with presumably more proficiency in the mundane details of industrial life than their more cavalry-obsessed aristocratic comrades, worked closely with civilian counterparts to create one of the largest bureaucratic entities within the German government. No detail proved too small for intense analysis: which types of coal did which engines use, and how were efficiencies affected; what was the continuous speed required that might keep multiple train convoys in more or less perpetual motion along a single line of track (20 km an hour, as it happens);[10] how could arrivals and departures from intertwining trunk lines be both added and diverted to a variety of destinations; wouldn't it be helpful if Germany could convert from its five separate time zones into one, in order to simplify scheduling? Of course it would, but the Reichstag initially refused until it was instructed as to its benefits from a wartime perspective.

Railways were a decisive factor in helping von Schlieffen's determination to deal with France first, given his dual concerns involving speed and time. Belgium had an impressive rail network that could assist Schlieffen where it most counted, speed. Troops would be where they were meant to be in good order, as scheduled, and ready for jump-off. Russia, according to officers the field marshal had sent to that country with the express purpose of reconnoitering its iron landscape, reported back that it would take that country a decade to equal Germany's system. A much slower mobilization process in Russia would give Schlieffen what he needed most for a second front: time, time in which to destroy the French army, with a sufficient margin to turn again eastwards to deal with a slower-mobilizing Russia. All this enormously complicated schedule, planned to the most minute dimension, could be destroyed if something hiccuped along the line; let us say, for example, that the All Highest Warlord changed his mind at the last second. In keeping with Wilhelm's mercurial personality, and his inability to grasp anything other than the superficial overview of any topic, his conception of the logistical efforts required for moving hundreds of thousands of men hither and yon to their appointed task by rail was marginal at best. The kaiser was an autocrat; what he ordered, he expected could be done without undue difficulty. If mountains had to be moved, then move them. In a way, he was a throwback to King Canute, ordering the tides to cease their inevitable rise. That might have worked in the ninth century … but, in fact, it hadn't.

A Conundrum

It should never be assumed that Count Alfred von Schlieffen ran a ship that could not be sunk or that he was immune to the criticisms of others. The gist of his plans for attack were certainly well known within military circles, even if German diplomats and chancellors were deliberately kept in the dark. Indeed, the kaiser himself, the alleged supreme warlord, had only the vaguest idea of what the earliest days of the coming war were intended to look like. He understood that France was the preferred target. 'In order to march on Moscow, Paris has to be taken first', he said in 1909 to people he shouldn't have been talking to; but as for details, 'around the left' and 'around the right' seemed to be the sum of it. Within the powerful and select circle of corps commanders and top military officials, however – what we might call true professionals within the army – von Schlieffen's ideas were analyzed, discussed and often disparaged. The notions of swift and almost easy envelopments, followed by a single overwhelming victory, some deemed naive. One general told von Schlieffen to his face that modern war would not allow such an outcome; you can't just take the French 'like a cat in the sack'. He had better get used to the notion of battle becoming a slog, a 'tedious and bloody crawling forward step by step here and there by way of an ordinary attack in siege style', which turned out, sadly enough, to be the coming reality of World War I and its trench warfare. Schlieffen did not like hearing that. Others were off put by the rigidity of the war plan, which seemed to diminish the relevance of individual officers, who could not improvise on the battlefield. War no longer assumed the status of an art form, 'it becomes a trade', one colleague wrote, 'and the commander is, as it were, a mechanic'. The notion of a single decisive battle also drew criticism. Hannibal, it was pointed out, might have won at Cannae with his outnumbered Carthaginians, but who won the war? Rome.

Divisions within the army ran deep. Traditionalists grew wary of von Schlieffen. His strategy, in order to succeed, would require vast infusions of men and equipment into the military, and even then victory was not assured. In the staff ride of 1904, for example, following the 'plan' in significant detail, the French had won; in a ride the following year, von Schlieffen himself devised the exact riposte that Gallieni and Joffre were to employ on the Marne in 1914, which in effect derailed the German invasion. Von Schlieffen's acolytes, after the war, kept referring to the 'plan' in symphonic terms. Von Schlieffen was the composer, a genius like other German greats, Beethoven, Brahms and all the rest. The conductor would be the commander of the great general staff; he would read the score and follow it exactly – it would not do to alter a single note. The orchestra would be the army, charged with following the director's commands. Staff rides and war games, unfortunately, could not duplicate the exact experience of actually going into battle, and no symphony orchestra can ever execute a score correctly without numerous rehearsals. Some of the intelligentsia within the German army believed in the beautiful music that Schlieffen intended for his grandest opus, but others simply would not, however varied their reasons.

An officer like Erich Ludendorff symbolized the significant philosophical split that seriously aggravated the jealousies and competition between the three military enclaves that ran the army. Ludendorff, as will become apparent as this narrative continues, was a 'new' man, largely self-made, without pedigree, a nonentity when it came to anything to do with ceremonial court appearances or the aristocratic pecking order. He was not an individual who would have ordinarily gained the attention of either the kaiser or his retinue. Certainly his boorish manners and brusque disregard for decorum made him persona non grata with the kaiserin and her prudish ladies in waiting.

In 1911 Ludendorff was a colonel on the general staff in charge of deployment and mobilization policies, in the course of which he became a master of statistics involving the relative birthrates of various European countries, the figures of which appalled him. Despite Germany's booming population, far outreaching that of France, for instance, the harvest for military trainers was drastically inferior. France managed to cadge 82 per cent of its eligible, arms-bearing men into some sort of training programme, Germany, a mere 52 per cent. To Ludendorff, these figures did not lie. He would not, as many officers managed over their cups at regimental dinners, harp on the glories of 1870 and 1871. The Franco-Prussian War, in his unsentimental view, was as irrelevant as Thermopylae (though not Cannae; he was a von Schlieffen devotee).[11] The Prussian armies that had crushed Napoleon III had numbered only 335,700 men; by 1892, that figure had reached 1.2 million, by 1905, another 700,000 had been added to the rolls. Still, these were not enough. Ludendorff saw the coming great conflagration for what it had to be, a total war that would drag every element of society into its maw. Nothing could be held back from the military effort, even if it meant destroying the traditional Prussian army. He pressed for universal conscription, emphasizing the word 'universal': ever more men, ever more army corps, ever more training. In doing so, his career was nearly destroyed.

If the great general staff had a realistic view of the future, the other entities of the army – the minister of war, the military cabinet and the kaiser – often did not. A 'universal' army entailed several negatives, in the opinion of important segments within the military establishment. For the minister of war, it meant unrealistic financial demands, demands the democratically elected Reichstag would never approve. It was already an institution full of 'Red apes', according to the kaiser, a nest of subversives and traitors. The war ministry, which was to massage as much funding out of the Reichstag as possible, did not have the appetite for grandiose proposals that had no chance of implementation. It poured as much cold water on Ludendorff's insatiable appetite as possible, just as it had von Schlieffen only a few years before. The minster of war wrote him without mincing words that his troop demands were in the 'realm of fantasy ... the chief of the general staff must remain content with what the army provides him'. The military cabinet did not want a larger army either, which seems illogical to most people's ideas of warmongering generals. However, a larger army, or a 'people's army' as Ludendorff correctly viewed the coming ensemble, meant the inclusion of social elements that would dilute the purity of Prussia's most prized and valued institution. The officer corps, for instance, had always been the preserve of the aristocracy, the 'vons' of East Prussia and the genealogical offspring of countless petty princes, counts and nobles, no matter their relative impoverishment. In 1865, over half the army's 8,000 or so officers were members of the aristocracy; by the eve of the Great War, officer numbers had exploded to nearly 30,000, with a dramatic diminution in aristocratic bloodlines. An even larger army of the sort envisioned by pragmatists would require more officers, more sergeants and more corporals. The agricultural population, especially in East Prussia, could no longer supply the necessary numbers.[12] For every peasant tilling the sandy soils of Pomerania, there were ten in the burgeoning slums of the Ruhr industrial basin, infected as they were with notions of strikes, better working conditions and anti-monarchical sentiment, who would be required to fill the gaping manpower void that a von Schlieffen plan required. Such dilution would democratize the military and turn it into socialist slosh, as was happening all too plainly in France. The war cabinet, whose purview was the ever-important promotion list, felt people like Ludendorff were anathema. Already the general staff itself was full of men like him, having grown from 88 in von Moltke's tenure to 650 under his nephew. When Schlieffen retired in 1905, 70 per cent were commoners.

Then there was the kaiser himself. Early in his reign he had further complicated the chain of command – or, to put it more precisely, muddied the path by which he could be approached on military matters – by creating yet another layer of military officialdom, an entire 'court' of military adjutants, aides-de-camp, attachés ... call them what you will ... who formed an almost independent *maison militaire* around the impressionable warlord within the walls of his various palaces and hunting lodges. These men were sometimes old cronies from his Potsdam years, often selected for their manliness or the cut of their figures in uniforms overloaded with braids, medals, shoulder epaulettes and other baubles. They were generally uneducated boors, but their bloodlines had been carefully vetted, and the political views espoused within their company were unvarnished anachronisms, generously larded with militaristic bombast that Wilhelm could seldom resist. Philipp Eulenburg, one of Wilhelm's few close friends, deplored the exaggerations that flew back and forth between the kaiser and these men. After the war he wrote, 'I read our *doom* in the spirit and influence of the Kaiser's military entourage, which found their *echo* in his exclamation points'. In this circle, the army was viewed as a select, restricted, almost religious brotherhood, a throwback to the Teutonic knights in whose medieval garb the kaiser enjoyed dressing up on re-enactment days. The idea of commoners flooding the ranks was unappealing to this group, to put it mildly, and their insinuations often dominated the conversation buzzing around the kaiser's ears.

Ludendorff, who rarely hesitated when speaking his mind, antagonized all these multifarious entities within the army. His aggressive, strident and argumentative positions on the inadequacy of army troop levels led to his demotion from the great general staff in 1913 by the then war minister who, one day, in the inevitable turn of fate, would be licking Ludendorff's boots. Ludendorff was dispatched to an army post in Dusseldorf, where he presumably would be silenced and retired. The coming war saved him from the obscurity his enemies had hoped Dusseldorf would provide.

Von Moltke's Nephew

'The hussar let his single eye-glass fall, and showed an astonished face.

"Manoeuvres, my dear fellow? Why, all's plain sailing in them!"

"How do you mean, plain sailing?"

"The rendezvous all fixed up beforehand, with friends on the enemy's side; simultaneous lunches arranged for when possible. Every detail settled in advance."

The little hussar suddenly burst out laughing. "Reimers! My dear fellow!" he cried, "don't pull a face like a funeral march! Do you mean to say you didn't know it? You didn't?"'

from the novel Jena' or' Sedan'?
Franz Adam Beyerlein, 1904

During the summer of 1905, Count von Schlieffen suffered a serious accident while riding his horse. Most observers, including the kaiser, felt he was no longer physically capable of staying on, and Schlieffen largely agreed. 'I am almost seventy-three years old', he said, 'nearly blind and have now a broken leg. It is high time to resign.' At the annual New Year's reception at the Neues Palais in Potsdam, Wilhelm announced the coming change. As his 'will and testament', Schlieffen left the 'plan' behind him. Would his successor remain true to it? Would he 'conduct' it in a manner that the composer would approve? Would it remain relevant?

It is interesting to analyze the pool of candidates from whom the kaiser would eventually select the new chief of staff. Two men rejected from consideration were Schlieffen disciples, which is a hint of sorts that the 'plan' was never wholeheartedly accepted as a gospel; two others were men with reputations for independence of thought, never a selling point where Wilhelm was concerned. The final choice, Helmuth von Moltke the Younger, had been part of the kaiser's entourage as an aide-de-camp since 1891. He was an agreeable man, had seen combat during the Franco-Prussian War (something that had eluded von Schlieffen), and had experience on the general staff where he served as an adjutant to his uncle, von Moltke the Elder. Unlike many professional officers, he was a relatively well-rounded man who read widely, played the cello, was a pleasant conversationalist and even painted recreationally. Wilhelm certainly saw in him an amenable individual who would not cause undue stress or inconvenience. After all, as he told von Moltke, 'The little work that is to be done in peacetime you can do, but in war I will be my own chief of staff', yet another instance of the kaiser's inability to fathom reality. With little fanfare he was appointed von Schlieffen's successor. One newspaper editorialized that 'the great name alone won't do the trick', but few were listening.

Von Moltke has often been portrayed as a genial nonentity. Churchill called the man 'ordinary', and other critics described him as a mere 'courtier' who had no genuine grasp of either strategy or technology. These are mostly postwar judgments. Von Moltke was a capable officer with just the right blend of expertise and interpersonal skills; he managed what von Schlieffen had never even attempted, to ward off the kaiser from his infernal meddling. A case in point were the annual summer manoeuvres.

As Wilhelm grew into middle age, his restlessness increased. Family life, the paragons of which he constantly trumpeted as a national pride, in fact bored him to death. His wife and her retinue of overly pious attendants were the epitome of everything he wished his own court not to be, a collection of dowdy and unimaginative 'donkeys'. The kaiserin was so unglamorous that Wilhelm equated her with a 'parson's wife', and set out to redesign her clothes and jewellery so as to remind people that Berlin was no second to Paris or London. According to one of Wilhelm's court officials, the kaiser did not hesitate to inform his wife that life in her company was 'incredibly dull'. He was never happier than when he set off from Berlin, without Dona, to attend a ceremonial parade or a hunting party, or to start a progress to one or another of his castles (he owned seventy-six) or lodges. He could be accompanied on such outings by an entourage of some one hundred assorted colleagues, mostly men. But the highlight of his annual schedule was certainly the summer manoeuvres.

By the time of Schlieffen's tenure, the size of this operation had grown exponentially. It now involved some 100,000 men, 18,000 horses, innumerable logistical details, considerable inconvenience to the local population and untold deutschmarks to pay for the kaiser's unceasing entertainments. This was the grand occasion to show off in spectacular fashion, a platform Wilhelm embraced with his customary fervour, the opportunity for all the world to see the All Highest Supreme War Lord in action. The kaiser never failed to shine which, of course, was the entire problem.

As far as von Schlieffen was concerned, manoeuvres had lost their allure; they were no longer teaching opportunities or particularly effective vehicles for trying new tactics or new weaponry. The kaiser insisted on personally leading one of the two opposing forces fighting in the mock engagement, issuing orders right and left (many contradicting each other), and generally behaving in the manner of a Potsdam lieutenant, full of swagger and braggadocio. 'The emperor upset everything to such an extent that no operations could develop normally according to the rules of the game', one observer recalled. 'Everything was confusion and mad haste. His Majesty himself frequently rode into the line of fire in order to hustle everyone still more.' The crescendo, reserved for the final day, was a grandiose tableau straight out of the Battle of Waterloo, a grand cavalry charge led by the kaiser himself which would determine the battle. In 1903, Wilhelm charged across 6,000 yards of open ground, overrunning some eighteen artillery batteries and two infantry brigades. In another spectacle, twenty-four cannon and twenty-four machine guns were stormed in a 2,000-yard rampage, uphill, covering open ground. Three years later, in what Winston Churchill, an observer, called the 'Grand Finale', Wilhelm led thirty cavalry squadrons into the teeth of a prepared defensive position full of 'venomous-looking little cannon', a spectacle as ostentatious as it was absurd. Churchill, who 'galloped along with the greatest glee', witnessed the happy outcome as umpires declared the kaiser victor of the field, guided in their verdicts, no doubt, by the comic opera of 1890, when the kaiser was injudiciously deemed 'decreased' after an equally impulsive mock melee with his horse guard (the referees in that instance were demoted). Count Robert von Zedlitz-Trützschler could not help but notice 'the depression' of various officers as they looked on in disbelief at these 'perfect lessons on how not to do it'. Von Schlieffen, however, never flinched. 'Silently, seriously, and without moving a muscle of his face, he carries out the commands given him by the All Highest, and his stereotyped answer [always] is: "As Your Majesty commands." ' In one instance of frivolity, the kaiser found himself outnumbered and threatened with defeat. He immediately ordered his opposite number to detach several squadrons of cavalry from his own force and transfer them to the kaiser's. Wilhelm then regrouped and charged again, carrying the day. Von Schlieffen complimented the kaiser on his 'novel solution'. He knew not to rock the boat; allowing Wilhelm's vivid imagination full play during manoeuvres gave him a free hand in just about every other facet of his work, an exchange he evidently deemed worth the annoyance. It did not bother him that *Operationstag* ('Exercise Day') had degenerated into *Ovationstag* ('Ovation Day').

As one of the kaiser's adjutants, Helmuth von Moltke the Younger had been a witness to all this. He generally 'took refuge in eloquent silence' when things became too outrageous, discretion being the better part of valour in such instances, but, like many officers, he was disturbed by the unprofessionalism that such displays occasioned. When approached about possibly replacing von Schlieffen, he insisted on a private interview with Wilhelm. It became his painful duty to inform the All Highest that the annual manoeuvres were rigged, that his 'victories' were predetermined; 'Count Schlieffen says that when the kaiser plays he must win', von Moltke told him. Wilhelm, who generally took tidings such as these in very ill humour, was shocked but, at the same time, gracious for once. As a precondition to accepting the chief of staff position, von Moltke insisted that the kaiser refrain from personally participating in any future manoeuvres. Wilhelm was unhappy about that and momentarily abashed. He shook hands with von Moltke not once, but twice, determined to amend his ways. While the kaiser's rhetoric remained largely unfettered – he 'repeatedly talked about the general staff in the most degrading way', wrote one officer – he did restrain himself at future manoeuvres. Wild cavalry charges became largely a thing of the past. In 1911, for instance, aeroplanes made their first appearance during the summer war games. Traditionalists, especially those obsessed with horses, could not help but complain, however, that a certain panache had been lost. Wilhelm recognized von Moltke for his candour in 1909 when, after that summer's martial festivities, he awarded him the nation's highest honour, The Order of the Black Eagle. The irony was not lost on Von Moltke. 'We *épigones* [13] achieved it in three days of [bloodless] manoeuvres.'

Although an accomplished individual, von Moltke the Younger did come to his new office with psychological baggage, the first being a sense of premonition that he would be labouring in the shadows of two such accomplished predecessors, one of whom (his uncle) occupying the niche of genuine national hero. Could he equal their achievements?

He was also, to some degree, emotionally vulnerable and subject to raging internal dichotomies. He loved the arts, indulged in intellectual debate, but had dark forebodings about the consequences that any European-wide war might have on 'culture', an appreciation for the destructiveness of war to which many of his fellow officers never gave a thought. He could sit for hours at his desk in serious depression over the implications of what his orders and plans might unleash, what a diplomat described as the potential 'overturn of everything that exists'. There was, he wrote his wife, 'enough flammable matter around' to start something that no one could stop, and the prospect frightened him. He was too sensitive for his own good.

On the other hand, von Moltke was a staunch monarchist, with the usual contempt for constitutional democracies, and was further burdened by anti-Semitic inclinations that often accompanied such views. He was xenophobic to an alarming degree, willing to throw caution to the wind when opportunities presented themselves for preventive war. On such occasions he turned into a fire-eater, and seemed to forget his several ruminations that no war should be started for 'frivolous' reasons. Yet the most damaging aspect of his personality revolved about something more insidious, a predilection to spiritualism.

Von Moltke's wife, Eliza, was a strong-willed and opinionated individual who dominated her husband in several critical respects. Many of the general's comrades disdained her influence. In the first days of the war, when von Moltke finally moved army headquarters closer to the front, the kaiser, the general staff and a host of attachés and adjutants were discombobulated to find, on the official train, Frau von Moltke accompanying her husband as a sort of muse or nurse. This was not considered a good omen.

Eliza von Moltke, among her assorted enthusiasms, was a committed disciple of a Goethe scholar by the name of Rudolph Steiner, one of several 'prophets' committed to the abstruse, otherworldly and occult principles of theosophy, which had several near fanatic cells all over Europe, but primarily in England and Germany. Steiner was a legitimate academic figure; whether he was also something of a charlatan is open to debate, but his charisma was undoubted as he peddled what he called 'spiritual science' to a gallery of well-placed, intelligent and often influential members of Wilhelmine society. While the general theorems of Steiner's teachings were often murky, the overall tenet was Darwinian in nature: the belief in cycles, the spirit world, and continuous 'rebirth'. Life did not end in the grave, which he proved in seances where he often connected those attending with loved ones who had moved over 'to the other side'. After von Moltke's death in June 1916, for example, Steiner conveyed messages to Eliza from her deceased husband with constant regularity. Some of these were more garbled than others, but Eliza believed in their authenticity. Her dead husband was equally enraptured.

There was, additionally, another element to throw in the pot: a dark, brooding, Wagnerian notion of an impending doomsday, an inevitable clash of the gods where civilization would be at stake. Von Moltke and many of his friends were conscious of a messianic mission just over the horizon which they must not shirk. Instead of meeting this challenge with the boldness of a Nietzsche, they instead viewed the impending conflict with morbid resignation; some called it fear.

Certainly von Moltke was no dilettante when it came to his official duties. He did not share von Schlieffen's work ethic, to be sure, but he chaffed when the kaiser distracted his attention either by formulating the usual string of diplomatic crises, or inundating his desk with a blizzard of outlandish ideas. He had enough on his mind without having to worry about Wilhelm, and he usually went to incredible lengths to avoid or get away from the emperor's presence, a tactic that often annoyed his imperial master. Zedlitz-Trützschler noted Wilhelm's irritation every time von Moltke said that urgent business required him to return to headquarters in Berlin. 'The emperor can never admit that anyone can have anything important to do anywhere away from himself, even if he is chief of the general staff.'

At the back of his mind, von Moltke obsessed over von Schlieffen's operational plans, always against the backdrop of a millenarian day of reckoning that Germany would have to confront. He often tinkered with details, some important, others not, but he left its bold core essentially intact. As for Count von Schlieffen himself, he also obsessed – in isolation, now that he was retired – with the culmination of his life's work. In 1909, the journal *Deutsche Revue* asked the old field marshal to write an article on the rather amorphous topic of 'preserving the peace'. Schlieffen obliged, though the *Revue*'s editors may not have been prepared for the bellicose and entirely pessimistic result, entitled 'War Today'. In it, von Schlieffen repeated the encirclement theory, painted a dire description of modern battle and weaponry that he felt too few people truly understood, and generally depicted a rather bleak landscape full of foreboding war clouds on the proverbial horizon, mostly fomented by France. At the end of pages of gloom, he offered one ray of hope: 'The horrible cost, the possible high casualties, as well as the phantom of danger threatening from anarchism [in case of a lengthy war], have [all] emerged', he wrote. Were there any other factors that might discourage the initiation of hostilities, that might 'preserve the peace'?

Universal conscription, which uses high and low, rich and poor alike as cannon fodder, has dampened the lust for battle. The supposedly impregnable fortresses, behind which one feels warm and safe, appear to have reduced the incentive to storm out and bare one's breast to combat. The arms factories, the cannon foundries, the steam hammers that harden the steel used in fortresses have produced more friendly faces and more amiable obligingness than all the peace conferences could. Everyone carries just as many doubts about attacking a numerous and well-armed enemy for fear of using their own destructive instrument, which has been laboriously created but which they do not know if they understand how to handle. And even when all these doubts and all the difficulties have been overcome and when the decision is ripe to set out on the powerful advance against the centre from all sides,[14] questions [by the French authorities] must still be anxiously asked: Will the 'others' come? Will the far-away allies intervene at the rightful time? Will we be abandoned and left to face the hammer blow of a superior power [i.e. Germany's] alone? These doubts force a pause, a delay, the revenge to be postponed, the drawn sword to be put back in its scabbard.

The article was signed anonymously, but everyone in Berlin knew pretty quickly who the author was. The questions Schlieffen raised were pivotal, provocative, timely, to the point and depressing. Armageddon was staring Europe in the face, pretty much as the Book of Revelation predicted. Schlieffen's conclusion that restraints were at hand to prevent the contagion of war was, at best, tepid. He certainly had little faith in their efficacy. His deathbed utterance, while possibly apocryphal, would become one of the most famous in German military history. 'Whatever you do, keep the right wing strong.'

Chapter 4

Sarajevo: Where It All Began (And Why)

'Violence was, indeed, all I knew of the Balkans.'

Rebecca West, 1941

In 1936 Rebecca West, a woman forty-four years old and well established in London literary circles, travelled to the Balkans on a lecture tour. Accompanied by her husband and assisted by various guides and locals recommended to her, she followed in the hallowed footsteps of any number of British eccentrics who, in their inimitable fashion, tramped the byways of faraway and impossibly exotic locales with an air of both wonderment and condescending hauteur. It was in many ways a difficult journey, broken up by sicknesses and marred (in her view) by the condescending and sexist attitudes of the men she encountered who wanted nothing to do with intelligent or independent females. No matter, her heart was taken by the places she visited, and broken by the tales of woe and human misery that she dutifully recorded. Published in 1941 as German troops overran the lands she had grown to love, *Black Lamb and Grey Falcon* was hailed from the start as its author's 'magnum opus', and received a second huge bump of recognition during the savage civil wars of the 1990s, when the world again stood witness to the maelstrom of what might possibly be the most convoluted region on earth. Interpreting and understanding the Balkans has never been an easy task; 'an unendurably horrible book to have to write', as she put it about her own work. After 1,100 pages, even she seemed to give up.

Sarajevo was still a place of oriental appeal when West visited it. The old quarter had the genuine allure of the fabled spice routes, with the town's population marked vividly by its diversity in religion, culture, language and costume – 'like a fancy dress ball', as she remarked. It seemed a perfect place to visit in 1936. By contrast, the city today is barren, unhappy and still marked by deserted buildings and a damaged infrastructure. Many of the Stalinist apartment complexes that line the main avenue from Sarajevo's airport to the centre of town are pockmarked by artillery shells fired twenty years ago. Riding the antiquated trams is an exercise in sullen theatrics: people are dour, repressed, sullen and make no effort to disguise it. If the bugle call sounded today, one has the impression that fighting could resume in about ten minutes, or however long it might take to find a gun. Situated in the centre of an amphitheatre of surrounding hills, Sarajevo generally takes half a day for the sun (if there is any) to burn off coagulating blankets of mist and pollution. The tourist areas have little glamour and the markets are a hodgepodge of cheap souvenirs and plastic flotsam from China. Even the food is pretty poor.

This town is famous for what happened here on a sunny day in June 1914, when the heir to the Austro-Hungarian throne, Archduke Franz Ferdinand, was murdered along with his wife, an event that proved the catalyst for World War I. The actual site of the assassination is an anticlimax: pedestrian, ordinary, matter of fact. On the sidewalk there used to be a set of footprints embedded in concrete, which marked the exact spot where Gavrilo Princip pulled twice on the trigger of his pistol, but for some reason this is now gone. The building in front of which he stood, which used to be an upscale food shop, is now a one-room museum containing mannequins of Ferdinand and his wife, along with several interesting artefacts skilfully presented. Princip's pistol hangs on the wall in a display case, an insignificant handgun that looks about as lethal as a plastic toy, a reminder that even smallish packages can deliver heavy goods. To see what just one tiny projectile can do, one must travel nearly 500 miles to Vienna. Franz Ferdinand's body went the long way, from Sarajevo to the port of Metković, then by sea to Trieste, and train the rest of the way in a journey that took four days. This observer went by plane. At the impressive military museum in Austria's capital city called the *Heeresgeschichtliches*, an entire room is devoted to Sarajevo. The fated automobile in which he died is there, an open touring car manufactured by Gräf & Stift, as well as interpretative exhibits full of compelling material. In the centre of the room, lying flat under glass, is Franz Ferdinand's attire from that gruesome day, laid out in full funereal repose. The breast of his coat is torn and covered in blood, mostly the result of attendants who cut its fabric apart in order to find the wound. The actual entry point of Princip's bullet, however, is so minuscule that it requires a small pointer, or arrow, to show its passage through the uniform. It is remarkably circular and precise, and no stains surround it.

Of all the countries involved in the First World War, Austria-Hungary is perhaps the least understood, and for good reason. It was certainly the most complicated, its multiplicity of racial components, religions, languages, borders and social currents a maze of contradiction and cross-purposes. It comprised almost 52 million people, incorporating eight distinct kingdoms and an equal number of duchies, many of which wanted nothing to do with Vienna, the Habsburgs or any association with Roman Catholicism. Northern Italy seethed with discontent, Hungary yearned for its independence, Bohemia had no idea what it really wanted, and Slavs, comprising half the empire's population (both orthodox and Muslim) and splintered into various factions, united mostly in but a single though intense desire to free themselves from what they considered alien rule. To further twist the picture, Vienna itself, a thoroughly Germanic entity, was divided in what its goals should be, distracted by the vision that its true destiny really lay to the north, as a leader of a united or federated Germany, and that everything to the east was a distracting rabble of inchoate aspirations wherein only danger lay.

In some ways such diversity helped Habsburg rule, if only to continue its time-honoured appreciation of 'divide and conquer'. Ancient racial animosities allowed an emperor of the moment to summon troops from one corner of the kingdom to crush dissidents in another, between whom little love had ever been lost. Particularly contentious issues involving a certain subset of the empire could often be meaningless somewhere else along the Danube, allowing minor episodes of repression to occur without undue or universal objection. 'My people are strange to each other', as one emperor put it, 'and that is all right. They do not get the same sickness at the same time.' That was not to be the case in 1848.

Eighteen forty-eight, the year of revolution, was a difficult one for hereditary monarchs trying to stem the tides of constitutionalism, socialism, communism or, what was even worse, out and out anarchy. Up to the eve of that fateful year, the fortunes of Austria-Hungary had largely been determined by the wiles and stratagems of Prince Klemens von Metternich, who often described himself as 'the Rock of Order'. He was now, unfortunately, a man of seventy-five years and well past his prime, inured by habit to ignoring the will of the people, however confused its manifestations might appear, and oblivious of rioting in the streets or noisy demonstrations (he was immune to both, both by inclination and by the fact that he was now deaf). No one was more surprised than he was in March of that year when the emperor's brother demanded his resignation, largely to appease the mob. In order to save himself and his family, Prince Metternich escaped the city, fleeing his mansion by a back door from the garden, and from there in a common hackney until well outside the city gates. He would settle for a while in London, where he was regularly visited by that other famous septuagenarian, the Duke of Wellington, and then he moved to Brussels. In 1851 he was allowed to return to Vienna at the invitation of the new emperor, Franz Joseph, but his days of influence were over.

Also over, as Franz Joseph himself was heard to mutter, was 'my youth'. The emperor was barely eighteen in 1848, pushed onto the throne by his overwhelming mother, Archduchess Sophie. Too many years of interbreeding with first cousins had produced Emperor Ferdinand I, charitably called by one historian 'a half-wit' barely able to sign royal documents.[1] His younger brother (Sophie's husband) wasn't much better, though their son Franz Joseph was. Handsome, already battle-tested, a man of spartan tastes and military bearing, he seemed the perfect person to assume the throne, at least in his mother's opinion. The royal entourage had been forced to flee the capital in May of that year (they would flee again five months later), the streets of the capital overrun with rioting students from the university (inside the city walls) and by desperate, impoverished workers (who lived mostly outside the city walls). This seemed a wise decision in light of what happened to their minister for war, Count Latour, whose offices were swamped by Viennese rioters in October. Displaying his disdain a bit too boldly, Latour walked down a marble staircase to confront the rabble; forty-three stab wounds later, his body was stripped, further mutilated and hung from a lamppost. Like the French revolutionaries half a century before at the site of the guillotine, his murderers soaked their handkerchiefs and scarves in Latour's blood as souvenirs.

Karl Marx was originally encouraged by what he heard and saw, rushing to Vienna to take advantage of the revolution-in-progress. He was soon disillusioned. The students actually wanted the emperor to return to Vienna, not a recipe for proletariat liberation! By the turn of the next year, Marx was a political refugee on the run, Vienna had been dragooned by royal troops, Ferdinand had abdicated and Franz Joseph installed as the new emperor. The archduchess Sophie would remain a potent force behind the scenes until her death in 1872; some have claimed that her overbearing ways doomed Franz Joseph's marriage to the beautiful, high-spirited, independent, but ultimately unstable Princess Elisabeth of Bavaria. That may or may not be true. The emperor's personal happiness was something he sacrificed out of duty, not so much for the sake of Austria as for his dynasty.[2]

Franz Joseph ruled for an astounding sixty-eight years, a long enough period to see him well settled in his ways. He was a conscientious creature of habit, his work days an often tedious progression of sifting through reports, making imperial decisions, dismissing ministers if and when he saw fit, and attending to details surrounding royal weddings and court etiquette, the last mentioned of which was the most hidebound and stifling in Europe. He enjoyed everything to do with his army, though presumed too much that he was competent to lead it. Like his fellow monarch, the upstart Napoleon III, he took personal command of his forces in the disastrous Italian campaign of 1859, the battles of which were clumsy affairs that were horrifyingly bloody. One, at the village of Magenta, even gave its name to a particularly florid dye of red discovered there. Franz Joseph learned enough from those experiences to relinquish command seven years later when Austria fought Prussia for control of the emerging German empire, but the results were largely the same. The emperor endured substantial reverses throughout his long career, both personal and political, and though he suffered acutely through all of them, he managed to project a relatively unruffled image to his subjects, which encouraged calm when news was bad. This required considerable self-control, a byproduct no doubt of his military training. It also made of him a somewhat roboticized figure, devoid of genuine intellect or insight, and unable (or unwilling) to recognize such traits in those who served him, who were therefore largely mediocre. As he aged, his appearance became 'fatherly' and totally familiar; portraits and photographs of the kindly old gent were, after all, everywhere. He was impossible not to like.[3]

'*When the Turk gets up from the Sick Man's bed,*
Austria will take its place.'

Albert Sorel, French historian

Probably more nonsense has been written about the *belle époque* ambiance of prewar Vienna, a city with a population of two million people (seventh biggest in the world at that time) than any comparable descriptions of, let us say, Paris, Berlin or St. Petersburg during the same period. Vienna, the abode of Beethoven, Schubert, Brahms, Klimt, Mahler, the Strauss family – and, of course, Sigmund Freud – is often depicted as a waltz-crazed mecca of frivolity, famous for its idle aristocracy, absorption with sex and the 'fluff' of everything else (pastries, opera, funerals, sartorial extravagance). Freud, who loved and despaired of Vienna with equal fervour, once said that listening to his Viennese patients often reminded him of cheap novellas, a critique of what many observers noted as the Austrian obsession with 'surface delight', and what the *Times* correspondent called a 'merry-go-round existence'. These kinds of generalizations distort a true picture of Austria's capital, 'an old and tough organism' as complex as the empire it ruled.

Freud, whose office and apartment at 19 Berggasse is now a museum, received his patients in a study full of curios, statuettes and odd *objects d'art* that he had collected, mostly from Greece, a country that had always generated his interest, and where he toyed as an amateur archaeologist over many visits. Digging into the past with a tool in one's hand, sifting through the dirt of centuries to uncover some small knickknack from Homer's time, was the same thing as delving through a patient's memory bank, trying to understand present behaviour from what happened years ago. The same obsession haunted Vienna. The past had generated great prestige, glory and vast territorial dominions, personified by the Habsburgs and the splendour of central Vienna that its wealth created. No dynasty in Europe had a longer history, no family a richer list of distinguished statesmen, warriors and emperors, no individual ruler a more splendidly diverse collection of subjects. Pretensions centuries old, however, presented problems as societies all over the continent sped up: communications, industry, transport systems, arms races, the incredible stride of varied technologies, all could mock a system of government that refused to change, that was all too wedded to old ways of doing things. The gigantic statuary that decorated the imperial palaces and government buildings of old Vienna – Hercules wrestling with mythic monsters, and always in triumph – seemed a brittle boast when Emperor Franz Joseph refused to use a telephone, avoided railway or automobile travel whenever he could and agreed to indoor plumbing only when his wife insisted on it.

'Decadence' is a word often heard when describing Viennese society at the turn of the century. The symphonies of Gustav Mahler did not astound his audiences the way Stravinsky's *Rite of Spring*, with its shocking dissonance, would to Parisians in 1913; instead, they oozed a rich sensuality that seemed slightly sick and cloying, an excess of emotion. Klimt's canvases, veering towards pornography in the opinion of some, also leeched a sense of excess that seemed slightly repulsive and, therefore, alluring, an unhealthy obsession with the dark underbelly of psychotic obsession. Freud was the serious embodiment of these lurid themes, his 'Jewish' specialty of analysis closely related to sexual matters. Is it any wonder that the sensational Mayerling episode of 1889, wherein Franz Joseph's son, Crown Prince Rudolph, the heir apparent to the throne, murdered his mistress of the moment and then himself in a supposedly mutual suicide pact, was embellished by the ugly rumour that Rudolph had made love to the corpse of his beloved before shooting himself. This admixture of the grotesque with the romantic ensured that this episode would live forever in novels, operas and cheap, sensational exposés. His funeral ended with the traditional burial in the ghoulish mausoleum of the Capuchin Kaisergruft, but not before his entrails and heart were removed for separate entombments in two other nearby churches. The cult of death, embellished by the morbidity of certain Roman Catholic practices (to say nothing of Mozart's *Requiem*), seemed a Viennese specialty.[4]

In point of fact, Vienna was no more obsessed with cheap entertainments or criminal sensationalism than any other cosmopolitan city of the times. What did differentiate it from other European capitals, however, was the extreme rigidity of its social caste system, strongly reinforced by the emperor and those of the aristocracy whom he favoured (largely on the basis of birth and pedigree). At the beginning of Franz Joseph's reign, Vienna was a walled city whose layout resembled the medieval town that had resisted the Turkish siege of 1683. Palaces, mansions, offices of the immense bureaucracy and banking houses competed for space with purveyors to the crown, small artisans, the two thousand or so students who attended the university and, originally unique to Vienna, its plethora of coffee emporia. A long and sloping glacis, or green swath, stretched downwards from the city's fortifications to sprawling slums below, packed with an underclass (many of them peasants from the countryside) without hope, employment or any cash to speak of. Vienna's gates were there for a reason: to keep these people beyond reach.[5]

Within the court, intrigues, social climbing and political nuance were closely studied. This was a complicated process, given the empire's diversity. Factions existed everywhere, allegiances could be surprising. Competing political cauldrons contributed to the confusion, each of which was represented in Vienna by wealthy noblemen, landowners, petitioners, emissaries, official delegations and assorted hangers-on. Prague, for example, ancient capital of Bohemia, perhaps best exemplified the issues most corrosive to harmony in the Austro-Hungarian empire. Three 'peoples' strove within its boundaries, none of whom wished to live in harmony with the other. Germans comprised the most prosperous and intellectual of the population, their language and culture at the top of the social order. Obsessed with worries over their personal security, they feared the majority Czechs, a seething underclass, who naturally despised all aspects of a people who lorded it over them in every conceivable phase of daily life. In between were Jews; everyone was contemptuous of them. In the ghetto, orthodox Jewry followed their centuries-old customs and spoke Yiddish; those educated and with pretensions to the intelligentsia escaped the ghetto and spoke both Hebrew and German. The strange, twisted, inbred writings of Franz Kafka, though devoid of specific references to Prague itself, do reveal the pressures of the place and, ultimately, its desolation.

In Hungary, the situation was more straightforward. The Magyars, intensely nationalistic, sought a variety of solutions to disassociate themselves from direct (and thus, to their eyes, oppressive) Habsburgian rule. Hungary enjoyed a long, tumultuous history, much of it as an independent state. Its people had a reputation for wild behaviour, and a romanticized image of themselves as irrepressible, a gypsy-like flare that appealed to rebellious spirits like Elisabeth, the emperor's wife. As Byron and Shelley had idolized Greece, so too in that self-deceiving light did the empress regard Hungary, though in her mind the association of high-spirited horseflesh – she loved riding – with a nation's unbridled desire for liberty, seems just as confused as those of the noble poets for the 'perfect civilization' of Greek culture. Hungarians genuinely chaffed at their subordinate status, so much so that Vienna appealed to the tsar for help in crushing revolution in Budapest during the 1848 troubles, which restored order if not affection. An elaborately orchestrated arrangement two decades later whereby Franz Joseph was crowned King of Hungary, in effect a formalization of federalism within the empire and called the 'Dual Monarchy', applied a patch, though not a remedy, to the Magyar desire for independence.[6]

Northern Italy presented yet another instance of nationalistic impulses that boded poorly for the empire's future. Austrian armies marched back and forth over Piedmont, Lombardy and Venetia for years, fighting everyone from patriots, anarchists, Garibaldian red shirts, the self-styled king of Sardinia, a French emperor and all manner of vicious guerrillas. They responded with bayonets and the noose (as Metternich commented, he loved the sound of cannon). Italy was important; fully a third of all the empire's revenue came from taxes generated south of the Alps. Austria would not willingly let the place go, though its fortunes fluctuated in this arena for all the years of Franz Joseph's reign. In 1866, the emperor managed to lose control of Venetia, which prompted his predecessor, in perhaps the only lucid remark he ever made, to say 'Is this what they made me abdicate for? I could have lost those provinces myself.'

On top of all this, there were the Balkans.

Habsburgs had a tradition of not identifying themselves too exclusively with one race or another; they were cosmopolitan in outlook which, given their history of domination in countries all over the European map (seven centuries' worth), is not surprising. The justly famous Charles V, the man who divided the Habsburg holdings into two geospheric entities in 1555 (one centred in Madrid, the other in Vienna) just gave up working at only fifty-five years of age, when the effort of conceptualizing all the various interests in his empire grew too much for one man to manage. He retired to a monastery for the remaining years of his adventure-filled life. Franz Joseph's court reflected the same dilemma. Like ancient Rome, a model to which it compared itself, Vienna was full of partisans; instead of Gauls, Greeks, Franks, Spaniards, Egyptians and Jews, all clamouring for favour and rewards, Vienna's corridors prowled with Magyars, Germans, Slavs, Venetians, Czechs, Poles and the occasional Jew (the Rothschild bankers, for example, were always welcome). But again like Rome, Austria-Hungary was an empire, not a nation, all-encompassing of nationalities and thus open to divisions, ethnic strife and stifled expectations. A major difference is that it had no Edward Gibbon to record its decline and fall.

'I remember old Bismarck telling me the year before he died that one day the great European war would come out of some damned foolish thing in the Balkans.'

Albert Ballin, German shipping magnate,
to Winston Churchill, over dinner, 24 July 1914

As if friction within the empire was not enough, the progressively accelerating collapse of the Ottoman Empire presented even graver problems for Vienna, although initial warnings of potential instability in that region were often dismissed with an insouciance that even by today's standards seem uncritically casual. By 1913, the Ottomans had lost effective control over most of the Balkan peninsula. Greeks, Bulgarians, Serbians, Albanians, Montenegrins et al. – ancient peoples with long memories and entrenched resentments – competed for both political coherence (involving ever-changing borders), and any advantage they could generate at the expense of both friends and foes alike (meaning fellow Slavs and the hated Turk). In a geopolitical sense, the most volatile of the emerging antagonists was also, ironically, the least significant in most people's eyes, the landlocked, minimalist state of Serbia, described by the Austrian foreign minister in 1907 as 'a negligible quantity'. Within its capital city of Belgrade, however, visions as grandiose as any that a Julius Caesar might have considered circulated freely, the urge to forge a mega-Slavic entity along the lines of Marshal Tito's Yugoslavia, a creation of 1946 – anti-Muslim, anti-Habsburg, anti-Turk, anti-Greek, anti-Italian and anti any other ethnic or imperial entity. The sweeping nature of this ambition was often derided, given Serbia's minuscule population (four million), inadequate army (250,000) and chaotic internal politics that could witness the barbaric slayings of its king and queen in 1903 by disgruntled army officers. The reality of the ambition might be dismissed, but its allure should not have been, especially given the more potent demographic statistic that thousands of people of Slavic origin lived outside Serbia's boundaries but within the Balkans as a whole, a tremendous pool of aggrieved and yearning peoples. Political and nationalistic daydreams are perhaps only slightly less dangerous than religious fantasias; they should, as a rule of thumb, be carefully and prudently analyzed. The problem with Serbia was the combination of all three elements packed together in one explosive and often inarticulate muddle. Added to the complexity was Mother Russia, the bastion of Christian and Slav orthodoxy, which saw itself as something of a guardian when it came to its co-religionists in the Balkans. It kept one watchful eye focused on the doings of its proxy clients there, with the other on Constantinople and the Dardanelles.

In a diplomatic stroke of dubious long-term advantage, Vienna decided in 1908 to annex the provinces of Bosnia and Herzegovina. This was a provocation of the first order to Slavs everywhere, but especially to Belgrade, as well as being an entirely unnecessary procedure; the Habsburgs had administered these territories since 1878 (at the expense of Turkey), and there had been little urgency to formalize their possession other than to teach other, less powerful people a humiliating lesson. Serbia rose to the bait, as did Russia (though weakened by its recently concluded struggle with Japan), but Austria, with German support and the kaiser's threat of war, cowed both into submission. As one historian has noted, 'It was an accepted convention of the time that great powers bullied small ones. The new factor was the resolve of Germany's rulers to bully great powers also.' This was a devastating loss of face to Slavs, no matter the country in which they lived, and an unfortunate template for Austrian behaviour five years later in 1914, when the outcome would be entirely different. Berlin's pledge to support Vienna in its dealings with Serbia was merely a continuation of the kaiser's habitual bellicosity, easily aroused and indiscriminate. The Serbs were 'Orientals, therefore liars', and he never lost the opportunity to bolster his Austrian counterparts. (Count Leopold von Berchtold recalled a later episode involving Serbia when the kaiser yelled, 'I am behind you, and am ready to draw the sword whenever your action requires', invigorating his pledge by grabbing the pommel of his sabre. These 'swelling words ... ran like a scarlet thread' through all their mutual conversations.) The coup of 1908 was followed by two Balkan wars which proved ruinous for the Ottoman Empire; commingling with these were 'internecine' conflicts which saw Serbia, Bulgaria, Romania and Greece all fighting with one another over what was left in struggles that were vicious, marked by numerous atrocities and often fought on the level of clan feuds, or one valley against another. To summarize the Balkan landscape in just these few sentences does little justice to the complexity of what happened, but its labyrinthine nature does not reward patient dissection, nor does it generate a dose of respect for human nature. On the ground, however, this was the reality.

The foreign secretariat in Vienna, largely running on its own fumes and unsupervised, to all intents and purposes, by an aged Franz Joseph, played the diplomatic game in the same fashion as its counterparts in Paris, Berlin, St. Petersburg and London. It was, it should be repeated, a game, the best analogy perhaps being chess, with its full panoply of kings, queens, knights, castles and pawns. Even bishops played their role (though to call Rasputin a 'bishop' is perhaps pushing it too far). The rules of campaign called both for strategy and tactics. Pawns – indeed, even major players – could be sacrificed, wasted, led into death traps, maliciously sacrificed, all to achieve the final victory. Foreseeing defeat, one side of the game might 'resign', seeing no hope in continuing play; but oftentimes, if the game is played to conclusion, only a few pieces are left standing … chess as life.

In their anterooms, chambers and offices located on the famous Ballhausplatz near the imperial palace, Austrian diplomats pored over maps, contemplated treaties, tried to figure out how their moves might be interpreted in any number of other capitals, and parsed the official and unofficial communiques of both friends and rivals for hidden meanings and the divination of intent. Bluffs were a constant, as were bullying threats; so too were brave words hiding desperation. In Austria's case, there was a sense of both lineage and melancholy. The Habsburgs were an ancient family, a mainstay in European politics, though, as Talleyrand had once put it, they had developed 'the annoying habit of always losing battles'. Their pre-eminence in the German-speaking world had been supplanted by Berlin, which was regrettable; their prospects to the east, in Hungary, were problematic, which was worrisome; but their issues in the Balkans, while often inscrutable to them, were generally just embarrassing. For an empire in decline – and almost every contemporary observer saw Vienna in just this light – there seemed an added insult that such fleas should disturb the lion, however decrepit he may be. A determination in Vienna solidified as the years after 1908 strode forward: Serbia was looking for trouble, would find it, and the price she would pay would be an object lesson for all the rest of the Balkans to heed.

For diplomatic historians, the two decades that preceded the outbreak of war in 1914 have been a treasure trove of rich and diverting material, much of it mesmerizing, much of it trivial, a full panoply of human motives gone awry. Never has there been a period in history so entangled in a myriad of treaties, alliances and misplaced confidences; never a period of more swagger and intrigue; never a more fundamental misunderstanding of societal pressures that, when ignored or inadvertently sparked, had the potential to destroy everything in its path. The very few individuals who sought to manipulate events back and forth in the summer of 1914 can be viewed in the photographs of their times in ways that exalt their character more misleadingly than they should. We see statesmen in their frock coats and top hats, carrying canes or perhaps wearing ceremonial sashes to liven up their mostly dark attire; we see proud and fearless generals, their sturdy shoulders festooned with epaulettes and decorations; we see monarchs and their spouses adorned in unimaginable splendour. All these surface embellishments provoke the uniform illusion that these well-bred, and sometimes well-educated, people knew what they were doing, had prepared themselves for all eventualities, understood most of the ramifications that their policies could engender. This is entirely the wrong conclusion. When the heir to the Austro-Hungarian empire, Archduke Ferdinand, lay bleeding to death in the utterly insignificant market town of Sarajevo on 28 June 1914, done in by a tubercular nineteen-year-old nobody with a crude automatic pistol, his death unleashed a sequence of moves and countermeasures that bewildered those who pulled the levers as the consequences played themselves out. Vienna, for example, thought there might be a small brush fire, which it was prepared for (but bungled nonetheless). Berlin had blown the bugle call more vigorously than any other power, but when the moment came, its kaiser fell apart and nearly collapsed in terror, unable to harness or restrain the impulses he had encouraged in twenty-five years of careless rule. St. Petersburg mostly reacted, out of vanity for the most part, eager only to show the European world that a decade of military reversals and insults to its dignity would not go unanswered for ever, even though aware that the only real weapon it possessed was manpower. Paris saw itself as a victim of aggression; though anxious to reacquire its lost provinces of Alsace and Lorraine, these were never so important that it wished for war. But once Germany mobilized, France matched the effort, placing undue regard for élan above a more commonsensical defensive posture. She would lose 300,000 men in just four months. London could have stood apart from the entire conflagration, but antique notions of honour and responsibility overthrew the hesitant, and Britain stumbled onto the continent where its small, professional army was largely exterminated. None of these capital cities foresaw what was to come except Brussels. It had nowhere to hide, its rulers fully aware that many of the combatants would march back and forth across its territory more or less at will. The only decision was whether to resist or not. The fervent hope for Belgium was that the war might be a short one, a notion disabused very shortly. None of these entities cared too much about Archduke Ferdinand, an insignificant and unpopular figure, yet his death started the whole 'game'. The checkmate, when it finally came in 1918, saw an allied victory over warmongering Germany, but most of the principal actors in the drama of four years before would find themselves swept from the landscape, something none of them had ever expected.

'I am not a criminal.'

Gavrilo Princip, assassin

Franz Ferdinand offers little to the history of World War I other than the obvious fact that he was murdered in Sarajevo on 28 June 1914. He was effectively unknown outside the German-speaking world, and inside it he was a man that few others either respected or admired. The emperor himself could hardly stand him. He was, however, heir to the Habsburg throne. As such, his death mattered.

His route to the projected crown had been a complicated one. The suicide of Franz Joseph's son at Mayerling had cleared the way for the emperor's younger brother (Franz Ferdinand's father) to succeed him in case of an untimely royal death. But in an excess of religious zeal, this unfortunate gentleman had taken a sip of water from the Jordan River, no doubt against the advice of whomever happened to be his guide. Whatever ghastly malady he caught from doing that killed him, putting his son next in line. So far the procedure was not entirely out of order, but Ferdinand next did a very foolish thing: he married what one historian called the equivalent of a chambermaid. This earned him the emperor's near total contempt.

Autocrats are more conscious of their bloodlines than any other class of human beings, and the Habsburgs more than most. Habsburg diplomacy, seven hundred year's worth, revolved around political and dynastic marriages, which in the olden days of greatness generally involved property. The British historian A. J. P. Taylor, in fact, once snubbed the Habsburg emperors by calling them landlords, not rulers, emphasizing the value they placed on well-arranged and profitable marriages where a dowry often meant a duchy or two. By 1900, of course, the year of Franz Ferdinand's marital transgression, such considerations no longer truly applied, but habits honed by generations usually die hard, and the emperor was genuinely appalled and furious at the projected union.

The object of his disdain was not exactly a nobody. Sophie Chotek had been born into a high-ranking family of the Czech nobility, counts and countesses since the fourteenth century; but her bloodlines were insufficiently regal for an heir apparent to the Habsburg throne, and the emperor made his nephew pay for it. In a series of embarrassing concessions, Franz Ferdinand was forced to surrender the rights of succession to any of his future children should he ascend the throne, and though eventually granted a decent title his wife was purposefully humiliated in any number of cutting ways by the royal chamberlain, the ultra-reactionary Albert, Prince of Montenuovo (no doubt with the connivance of the emperor) who controlled every facet of the protocol that suffocated court life in Vienna. Sophie Chotek, for instance, could not participate in a procession on the arm of her husband; given her diminished stature, she usually walked by herself, and well down the line behind Franz Ferdinand, following any number of other titled dignitaries, many of them youngsters. When she entered public chambers, alone, for a reception or ball, only one portal of a double door would be opened for her. Attending the opera or theatre, she could not sit in the imperial box with her husband, some less visible seating being provided. These snubs were noted by everyone who mattered, and tended to isolate Franz Ferdinand in more ways than one. Deeply devoted to wife and family (his one endearing quality, it appears) he created in effect an 'opposition' court at his private residence, entertaining advisers, diplomats and other notables who were generally not in good odor at the imperial palace. This placed him out of touch with people who surrounded the emperor and controlled his policies, especially as Franz Joseph aged, became 'very tottery' in the words of a German officer, and drifted towards an inclination to decrepitude. Perhaps in response to this exclusion, the archduke became something of a patron to unpopular political views: he favoured some inclination to constitutionalism, realizing that change was inevitable, and held unfashionable ideas regarding concessions to Slavs, which were anathema to just about everyone (even Slavs). He seemed deliberately self-cast as an outsider, however reactionary his views regarding military, religious and societal matters really were. Looking at photographs of his hard, unyielding face, what he appears to have been was a man looking for prey, a chance to avenge the slights that conventional society had thrown in his face.[7]

His trip to Sarajevo, for instance, was a display of defiance aimed at Uncle Franz. His wife, under Viennese stipulations, would never have been allowed to accompany him on such a visitation, but the archduke flagrantly took her along by the clever use of a technicality.[8] This would have fatal consequences for them both. Indeed, just about every aspect of his decision to 'show the flag' in this volatile little city would prove foolhardy; but then again, this was the kind of man Franz Ferdinand was. Austrian intelligence was aware that plots were in place to disrupt the royal progress. The archduke himself had contributed to the unsettled atmosphere by supervising military manoeuvres along the Serbian border, a provocative display that was meant to unnerve various groups of extremist hotheads but instead, to no one's surprise, only angered them more. The date of the excursion into Sarajevo was also purposely insulting, 28 June being the anniversary of a devastating military defeat of Serb armies at the hands of the Turks some five centuries before … as stated earlier in this narrative, memories in the Balkans ran far away into the distant past (28 June was, in effect, a day of mourning throughout the region). One would have thought, given such background, that security measures along the streets of Sarajevo might have been formidable, but in fact they were scanty. The archduke's motorcade, rumbling down the narrow streets at slow speeds, were barely distanced from people lined up on either side (some period photographs show crowds at some points, but sparse numbers at others). The first would-be assassin, one of six young men dedicated to the task, had no difficulty tossing a bomb towards one of the vehicles at 10:30 a.m.; the fact that he missed was due more to incompetence than to the lack of opportunity. Two officers in the entourage were wounded. Everyone stopped, everyone alighted from their vehicles, everyone milled around. If four out of the five remaining terrorists had followed orders, high-level carnage could have ensued, but they had all run for it in panic. The sixth, Gavrilo Princip, arrived on the scene too late, the five cars now all speeding along the Miljacka river to Sarajevo's town hall. Discouraged, he went and had a cup of coffee.

There are a multiplicity of photographs showing the archduke's progress that day: alighting from the train, being met by dignitaries, sitting in the automobile with his wife, going into and out of the town hall. He was a heavily built man, bulging here and there with unwanted middle-aged weight. His uniform, a pale blue jacket with red-stripped black trousers, topped with a helmet covered in plumes, seemed ill-fitting and too tight (Freud thought Austrian officers looked like parakeets). His demeanour occasionally revealed a smile, but that disappeared when Sarajevo's mayor began a speech of welcome in the assembly room after the first assassination attempt. 'That's all a lot of rot', he is said to have shouted. 'I come here to pay you a visit, and you throw bombs at me. It's an outrage.' His wife said something in his ear, and the archduke restrained himself. When it was his turn to make a reply, his written remarks, when handed to him, were covered with the blood of his adjutant, occasioning another few moments of rank fury as the archduke goose-stepped about the room. It was decided that the state occasion was now over, and that the royal party should leave the town with all necessary speed. Princess Sophie's suggestion that they visit the local hospital first to check on the wounded, would finish their day in Sarajevo. No one bothered to give this information to the driver of the first motorcar in the cavalcade.

Had not the princess made her suggestion, proffered with the best of intentions, Franz Ferdinand would not have been murdered that day, and the beginning of World War I might never have happened, or not have started exactly how or when it did. This is one of the many cruel turnings of fate that so affect human history. The chauffeur, having been given no fresh instructions, assumed the schedule for the rest of the day remained unchanged. At the intersection where the famous Latin Bridge crossed the Miljacka, leading into the old town, the driver took a right in that direction, followed by the second car carrying the royal couple. Realizing the mistake, an officer yelled, 'Stop you fool, not this way.' Doing as he was told, the poor minion applied the brakes and put his gears into reverse. Standing right there but ten feet away, no doubt dumbstruck in disbelief, stood Gavrilo Princip. With no hesitation he pulled out his pistol and fired two shots. One struck the archduke just below the collarbone and severed his jugular vein, the other pierced his wife's abdomen. Both bled to death within fifteen minutes. The archduke's last words were, 'It is nothing', but again, he was wrong. This was the excuse that foolish men in Vienna were looking for.

There is a vivid photograph showing policemen or soldiers (it is difficult to tell which) arresting Princip. Actually they are beating him. He suffered a broken rib and his arm was so mangled and shattered that it later had to be amputated. He made no effort to deny his guilt. At his trial he said the killing was a political action. 'I am no murderer', he told the court. This diminutive, inconsequential young man died of tuberculosis in prison a little over three years later. He is regarded as a hero in Serbian circles, and there can be no question as to his bravery. When he saw his chance, he never wavered for a second.

'The Austrians are quite the stupidest people in Europe.'
British Prime Minister Asquith, 26 July 1914

The archduke would probably have been mortified (but not surprised) had he able been to observe the reaction to his death back in Vienna. Concerts throughout the city were cancelled for one night only, but thereafter went on as usual; no great outrage immediately burst through the pages of Viennese newspapers, and few threats of war circulated about the neighbourhoods, usually hotbeds of rumour and emotion. The spiteful lord chamberlain, Prince Montenuovo, initially forbade the next in line for the throne, Archduke Karl, aged twenty-seven, from greeting the funeral train carrying the bodies back from Sarajevo. Montenuovo had arranged for them to arrive late in the evening, well after dark, and it would be inconvenient, surely, for the prince to attend. To his credit, Karl refused. In the privacy of his apartments, the emperor, now eighty-four, apparently had a tearful fit over the news. God had passed judgment, he is said to have whispered, on the marriage that Franz Ferdinand had entered into without his uncle's approval. At least he had the generosity to overrule Montenuovo on the more egregious aspects of the proposed funeral arrangements. The prince had suggested that Sophie's coffin should not lie in the royal mortuary chapel next to her husband's, nor should she be buried with him there. The emperor said no to that, but Montenuovo managed to slight the poor woman anyway, arranging that her casket be eighteen inches lower in height than the archduke's, and minimally adorned with rank and insignia. Franz Ferdinand, in a posthumous snub to his uncle, wrote in his will that he was not be buried in Vienna among his royal relations, but at Artstetten, a family castle some distance from Vienna where he had slaughtered so many animals. Montenuovo managed to make this journey as logistically inconvenient as possible (Rebecca West outlines this fiasco in lurid detail).[9] To Viennese citizens old enough to remember, the contrast between Franz Ferdinand's funeral and that of the Empress Elisabeth sixteen years before (both horrific murders) was astonishing. No expense had been spared for the empress, the entire city had been draped in black, the ceremonies and obsequies so lavish as to verge on the grotesque. Franz Ferdinand, when his remains left the capital, did so in the same fashion they arrived, in the middle of the night. Many courtiers and army officers, offended at Montenuovo's insensitivity, assembled an informal cortege to accompany the bodies, but, aside from his immediate family, the archduke had inspired little affection in anybody and he was quickly forgotten.

The circumstances surrounding his death, however, were thoroughly aired. Princip and his accomplices were all tried, their guilt a foregone conclusion, and Vienna went through the motions of assembling a learned commission to conduct an investigation. All leads pointed to Serbia in general and Belgrade in particular, and with good reason, for they were certainly the guilty party no matter their flood of protestations to the contrary (details, in a way, hardly mattered). Members of the Serbian government, and certainly members of the Serbian armed forces, had all encouraged, bankrolled and facilitated any number of disillusioned Slavic nationalists, recruited from among the several secret societies that were, and are still today, a hallmark of the Balkan political scene. The most sinister of these, variously labelled the Black Hand, was run by a colonel in the Serbian army well versed in conspiratorial intrigues, Dragutin Dimitrijević, more generally known by his nickname Apis, or 'the holy bull'. This sinister figure had been among those soldiers who murdered the Serbian king and queen in 1903 (their bodies were hit by nearly fifty bullets, after which the assassins hacked their corpses with swords), so his hands were already well stained with royal blood. Princip and the others received rudimentary training in Serbia, were provided with the tools of their trade, and assisted in crossing the border into Bosnia. The only thing Apis and his colleagues did not do was pull the trigger, but they might as well have. This was common knowledge in Vienna, and played into the hands of two exceedingly reckless individuals, General Franz Conrad von Hötzendorf and the Austrian foreign minister, Count Leopold von Berchtold.

Conrad was a fiery, irresponsible, headstrong personality. He seemed to believe that if Austria-Hungary did not immediately take control of its destiny in the most aggressive fashion possible, only 'catastrophe' and 'collapse' would follow. He was, by inclination, a ham-fisted descendant of imperial generals such as Prince Alfred of Windisch-Grätz, who in 1848 had had no compunction turning Vienna into dust if it meant saving the dynasty. By controlling the empire's destiny, Conrad meant dealing with the centrifugal forces that he rightfully saw as disintegrating the nation, most particularly to the south and east. In 1911, with Italian forces tied up in Libya, he had advocated a pre-emptive strike to regain Austro-Hungarian dominance in the northern third of that country, one of several adventurous ideas that constantly roiled his imagination. Franz Joseph and his foreign minister at the time were appalled and vetoed the scheme; in the disrespectful shouting match that followed at Schönbrunn Palace, Conrad was sacked. Between that episode and 1917, in fact, Conrad would be dismissed three times. Luckily for him, he had the engaging personality of a gamecock, and always bounded back. Again in office during the Sarajevo incident, he saw another chance to wipe the slate clean. He intended to settle the Balkan question once and for all, a notion fully shared by Berchtold. For Conrad, the time for war was a constant. He feared the interference of timid politicians or outside powers, and despaired that some peaceful resolution would complicate his plans as they had in the past. 'If you pull up twice at the fence', he said, 'the third time your horse will not jump.' More worrisome was Russia. Conrad seemed to have a death wish at times, because he realized all too well that the odds were long on Austria-Hungary being able to counter a Russian military intervention (he called the projected war 'a hopeless struggle'); but harking back to the crisis of 1908, he saw a possible counterweight to that threat in Kaiser Wilhelm II.

The narrative of events that occurred in July 1914 have been recounted almost to the minute by dozens of capable historians. It is a story that begins slowly, rounds into form in almost plodding fashion, gains tempo seemingly from nowhere, then reaches a climax of blaring trumpets, clashing cymbals and thundering cacophony. Conrad should be seen as the flickering flame that, once lit to its fuse, snaked along for thirty or so days until it reached the stick of dynamite. Although Archduke Ferdinand had once been his patron, the assassination in Sarajevo did not personally sadden Conrad (they had had a falling out; Franz Ferdinand, it seemed, was passionately opposed to any sort of preventive war).[10] Fortified to stand firm and take a hard line, Conrad did everything he could to encourage an aggressive response – war if possible – to humble Slavic pretensions. The fact that his army was in a poor position to win any sort of conflict, whether big or small, is another matter.[11]

Elsewhere in Europe, there was no sign of panic. In London, politicians were obsessed with the possibility of civil war in Ireland, and the murder of a foreign archduke did not particularly resonate at 10 Downing Street, even though one observer questioned what the local reaction might be if the Prince of Wales were to be assassinated riding through Dublin. In Paris, the President of the Republic, Raymond Poincaré, went as usual to the races at Longchamps. The tsar was nervous, though not unduly so. His internal problems were such, to say nothing of private issues regarding his family, that he spent more emotional energy on them than on what was happening in Sarajevo. In Berlin, the kaiser was furious, but then again he always was, and Von Moltke saw no reason to delay his annual visit to the chic spa of Karlsbad in Bohemia. 'A lot of water will flow down the Danube before [this] comes to anything', he wrote. Such was not to be the case. On 30 June, the German minister in Vienna, Heinrich von Tschirschky, advised Count Berchtold not to be 'too hasty' when formulating a response to the murder. In Berlin, the kaiser exploded. His ambassador was 'stupid', talking 'nonsense', and had better straighten the record immediately. 'The Serbs must be disposed of', he wrote in the margins of von Tschirschky's report. Von Tschirschky, no fool when it came to prolonging his career, reversed himself immediately, and even gave an interview to a German newspaper saying that the kaiser would support Austria-Hungary 'through thick and thin'. On 5 July, in

Potsdam, Wilhelm more or less said the same thing to a special emissary sent expressly by Franz Joseph, urging Vienna to act immediately. This was the famous 'blank cheque', and yet another instance of the kaiser's penchant for spontaneity, which usually landed him in trouble. The second the Austrian diplomat left the room, Germany was more or less chained to whatever Conrad and Berchtold chose to do.

Prince Karl Max Lichnowsky, the kaiser's minister to the Court of St. James, could not believe this chain of events, and warned Berlin repeatedly that linking its own grandiloquent fortunes so closely to those of a declining state, obsessed as it was with a matter of only local significance, would bring ruin. 'Even had ten archdukes been murdered' in Sarajevo, he wrote a year later, 'that was no concern of ours. It was for Austrians to settle their affairs with their neighbours as they saw fit.' Nowhere was the contrast between a Bismarck and a Wilhelm more apparent. The kaiser 'practised the politics of sentiment, not *Realpolitik*', Prince Max noted in some dejection. Bismarck would have shrugged the whole matter aside, and 'declared the subject of the dispute to lie outside the alliance', meaning Vienna could not look to Berlin for any material support. (For these and other unpopular views, Lichnowsky became something of a social outcast within Germany, expelled from the Prussian House of Lords in 1917.)

The Emperor, Franz Joseph:	*'How will you carry on a war if they all then fall upon us, especially Russia?'*
His chief of staff, Conrad von Hötzendorf:	*'Surely Germany will protect our rear!'*
The Emperor, looking at Conrad questioningly:	*'Are you sure of Germany?'*

5 July 1914
Schönbrunn Palace, Vienna

It took three weeks for Berchtold to present Serbia with an ultimatum; up to that point, the summer of 1914 seemed no different from any other. But this brusque and ominous document, to which Serbia was given a ludicrously short forty-eight hours in which to respond, was the warning signal that things were heating up both quickly and dangerously. The terms of Austria-Hungary's conditions were, according to Churchill, 'the most insolent document of its kind ever devised' and were a direct affront to Serbia's sovereignty, the kind of thing, as another British diplomat put it, that 'no independent power could swallow'. Amazingly enough, however, Serbia initially did swallow, with only a single exception. But Belgrade realized that even that would not be sufficient; they understood that Vienna meant to attack. The Serbian general staff ordered mobilization several hours before their note of acquiescence was even delivered. Once started, mobilizations were viewed as a process fraught with the notion of grim inevitability, or so the argument went, war seen more or less as unavoidable.

When the kaiser was eighty-two years of age and exiled in Holland, one of his last interviews was with a British writer, John Wheeler-Bennett. World War II would erupt in just a few days, and Wilhelm had a lesson for Adolf Hitler. If the führer wasn't careful, he warned, 'the machine will run away with *him* as it ran away with *me*'. These were prophetic words.

The kaiser returned from his summer cruise on 27 July, unaware that the turn of events, which he had stimulated more than any single individual, had more or less left the station without him, approaching a denouement he had never considered possible. Inordinately pleased with the Serbian show of abject submission, he was astonished to learn that it had had no effect on Vienna; that Berchtold had rejected the reply from Belgrade without even bothering to consult him. Chaos, in other words, lay just over the horizon. Seeking to reassert his authority, he found instead that Berlin stood gripped in confusion, with no steadying hand at the helm. His reputation for feckless behaviour, and the personal disdain that many within his government felt for him, proved a fatal chasm in the hours and days that followed. Leaderless, generals and diplomats proceeded as though the kaiser did not exist, and followed their own interests as they thought best. General Helmuth von Moltke, for example, who had been wanting war for over two years, urged his counterpart, Conrad von Hötzendorf, to mobilize immediately and initiate hostilities while the opportunity remained alive. Chancellor Bethmann Hollweg, at just the same time, was trying to suppress his eager colleague in Vienna, Foreign Minister Berchtold, with the same energy that he had previously used to urge him on to drastic action, belatedly realizing that the situation was careening to an end that he had not anticipated just a week or two before. In Vienna, the appearance of German paralysis was perfect. 'Who runs the government?' Berchtold asked, delighted that he still had the free hand. With his minions acting at cross-purposes, the kaiser found himself with no one to turn to for a realistic picture of what was going on or which course he should follow, earning the scorn of Winston Churchill, who later wrote that the entire conflagration had been needlessly caused by 'stupid kings'. Max Weber put it even more succinctly when he asked whether the German-speaking world was being led by a herd of lunatics.

Within three days, Wilhelm's minister for war, Erich von Falkenhayn, bluntly told his kaiser the truth: 'I remind him that he is no longer in control of these matters.'

The linchpin to the evolving crisis was, in the end, Austria-Hungary. Von Schlieffen had predicted the problem many years before. As far as he was concerned, Vienna was a liability. 'She demands support from her ally' [meaning Berlin] 'but cannot offer any in return.' Leaning too confidently on this shaky entity was a risk which the kaiser had ignored out of simple *Nibelungentreue*[12] three weeks before when he issued his 'blank cheque'. With no restraining hand placed on Count Berchtold's shoulder, as there should have been, Germany was looking at a generalized European inferno where, at the very least, she would be fighting France and Russia in a two-front war, with Britain looming over the horizon. Berchtold himself seemed immune to the greater risk. He assumed, naively, that Russia would refrain from involving itself to defend Slavic interests in the Balkans (what was he thinking, Lichnowsky later wrote, 'that Russia would give her blessing to the annihilation of Serbia?'). Instead, Berchtold relied on the purportedly shared 'conservative, monarchical and dynastic interests' where kings would band together to combat forces of social and anarchist unrest which threatened it, trumping any pan-Slavic concerns the tsar might have. This proved to be fanciful thinking. Upon reading Vienna's note to Belgrade, Russia's foreign minister warned Berchtold directly that 'You are setting Europe alight. You have burned your bridges.' Berchtold ignored him. While Austria-Hungary was dealing with the Serbs, Germany would 'have our backs covered' by fending off the Russians if they chose to fight. This was news to Berlin. In the end, as George Bernard Shaw lamented, the note to Serbia represented 'the escapade of a dotard'.

During von Schlieffen's tenure as chief of the general staff, relations with his counterparts in Vienna had been chilly. Von Schlieffen, in the words of one Austrian officer, was generally 'taciturn' and not at all 'forthcoming' when it came to discussing Germany's intentions. But Schileffen's successor, the more affable von Moltke, was the reverse. Conrad and von Moltke engaged in frequent discussions with regard to war plans; at times the exchange of information had been perfunctory and minimalist, but at others considerable amounts of technical details were passed back and forth. Conrad had a good picture about the Schlieffen Plan, but von Moltke had fudged one important detail that would prove critical in the summer of 1914. While encouraging Austria to deal immediately and authoritatively with Serbia, he in effect had his eye elsewhere, towards the west. Von Moltke wanted Conrad to open an immediate offensive out of Poland into Russia. In order to secure the promise of cooperation from his allies, he promised that German forces in East Prussia would attack at the same time, sharing the burden, as it were. He was not at all forthcoming over his truest intentions; he never revealed that almost eighty per cent of his entire troop strength would be deployed in Belgium and France, leaving the eastern theatre effectively unattended. Austria-Hungary, in other words, was expected to go it alone.

The German attitude all along had been that the fate of Franz Joseph's empire would be settled on the Seine, not some nondescript river in Galicia (modern-day southern Poland), which immediately consigned Austria-Hungary, in the minds of Berlin, to the status of a satellite or client state, not the great world power it aspired to be again. If diplomats in Vienna had been privy to that rather telling fact, its bellicosity would have shrivelled to that of a pet mouse. Such fundamental miscalculations between two allegedly allied countries beggars the imagination, but such was the case as beleaguered officialdoms tried to make sense out of the deteriorating political morass. The finale ended, somewhat farcically, in the kaiser's bedroom. Wilhelm, in a frantic and utterly hysterical effort, had attempted to cobble together a last-second reprieve to the initiation of hostilities, which had led to the partial breakdown, both mental and physical, of his commanding general, Helmuth von Moltke the Younger. Von Moltke, trying in his way to undermine the kaiser without appearing to do so, finally had to report to the All Highest that the war was on, like it or not. Wilhelm, in his pyjamas, exhausted from the strain of it all, told him to go away, to do what he wanted, to leave him alone. 'I don't care', he said. Thus began the most destructive war in the history of the world.

Ruin

'Well, I don't think I'll be seeing them again.'

Franz Joseph, reviewing troops
about to leave for the front, 1915

In just five months of war, Austria-Hungary would lose close to a million men in combat: killed, wounded, missing in action or captured. Their professional army, and in particular junior and non-commissioned officers, largely disappeared, replaced by conscripts drawn from its multitude of nationalities. By 1918, as General Foch remarked, they had degenerated into a pack of 'slovenly fighters' and deserved no respect. By that time, the Austro-Hungarian empire had ceased to exist, with neither Conrad nor Berchtold in any position of authority. Prince Max predicted the whole thing in 1915. 'What the outcome of the war will be: Austria's disintegration. We shall stand with Austria and Turkey, two states which we can expect by then to be in ruins, quite alone in Europe.'

The war was an unmitigated disaster for the empire. Conrad's skill as a strategist was above ordinary; the imposing campaigns that swept back and forth over Galicia on into Russia were ambitious and well designed, a reflection perhaps of his Napoleonic personality, but unrealistic given the quality and quantity of men, equipment and supplies that he had at his disposal, to say nothing of the enormous theatre itself, some 500 miles of front. German support, right from the start, proved indispensable to prevent a more or less general collapse, much to the annoyance of Berlin, which soon realized they were 'chained to a corpse'. As one German officer put it, 'Those characters will only desert or run away to the enemy', which is pretty much what von Schlieffen had predicted.

The Italian campaign, begun in 1915, was another colossal waste, a landscape of broken armies (both Italian and Austro-Hungarians, depending on the occasion) fleeing pell-mell and in panic along country roads crammed with men, guns and ambulances (one driven by Ernest Hemingway); or, alternately, fighting existentially in the frozen Alps amid the splendour of ice packs and glaciers. Far and away the largest misperception of Conrad's career, however, was tiny Serbia.

Distinctive components of Austria-Hungary had different notions of how they saw the post Franz Joseph era (surely soon to commence, given his age) with what might be called a new and revamped empire. The Magyars in Buda and Pest were uninterested in occupying Serbia. That would merely enlarge the empire to include more Slavs, corrrespondingly threatening their status. Franz Ferdinand, before his untimely death, detested Hungarians (he called them 'rabble'); anything that dropped them down a peg (more Slavs would be fine) was acceptable to him. Conrad, who despised anyone other than Germanophiles, believed in the constant rule of martial law. The revolting and random execution of civilians in Galicia during the first months of war, for example (some 36,000 it is alleged), did not disturb his conscience.[13] Slavs had to be firmly ruled, after all, to keep them in place. But, in the end, what did he truly know about the Slavic personality? Before 1914 he had had little experience of war. When he visited outposts of the empire, he no doubt did so in contempt. He did not see in the vagabond countryside riffraff of the Balkans – goat herders and hard scrabble farmers who lived off 'our pigs and our plums' – anything but a motley collection of Asiatic trash. He did not recognize, in other words, what a tough lot they were.

Conrad had a plan in place for Serbia called 'War Case B', where overwhelming numbers of his units would simply brush aside the enemy and occupy Belgrade. The sudden realization that Russian forces were mobilizing and taking to the field, and that German expectations were focused on the west, not the east, gave him pause and fatally muddied his first moves. His goal all along had been to pulverize a weak and cringing Serbia; he realized he had been duped only when he received a cable from von Moltke saying, 'We have only one goal, Russia!' This switch, which entailed a fatal revision of transport and logistical plans, spelled disaster for both Austrian campaigns. Troops diverted from Serbia to the Russian front arrived too late to be effective. The moment von Moltke threw in the sponge on the Marne, Conrad did the same thing in Galicia. And when his men belatedly marched into Belgrade, behind schedule, they stayed there a mere two weeks before being thrown out. What had been meant to be little more than a heavy-handed police action suddenly turned grim, and would remain so throughout the war.

As a portent for what was to come on the other, larger fronts of war in the east, the Serbian campaign was a back-and-forth affair. Conrad had discounted the geography of the Balkans, which any traveller through its various countries today can appreciate for its wild and undeveloped character. Mountainous, largely unpopulated, with few roads, amenities or infrastructure of any sort, it was inhabited by a clannish people used to hardship and privation, and additionally infused with a fierce and primal sense of who they were – Slavs. They were used to fighting, both with each other, with Turks and now with Conrad's armies. In just one month, Serbian forces had repulsed the Austrians and plunged into Bosnia, so close to Sarajevo that Archduke Ferdinand's assassins were hastily transferred to a more secure prison in Bohemia (it would never do for these scum to be rescued, and then worshiped as heroes). But as autumn turned to early winter, the combined resources of Germany and Austria-Hungary reversed the tide, and the *shvaba* (or 'cockroaches', as Serbians referred to their German-speaking enemies) again occupied Belgrade. The Serbian king, Peter I, addressing his troops as 'heroes', released them from their their bonds of allegiance. His resolute character, however, reflected that of his people. Picking up a discarded rifle, he returned to the front and took his place in the line, and most of his troops followed him. By the end of this incredible year, Conrad faced the humiliating face of defeat in Serbia, a campaign he had waged for almost entirely personal reasons, because it had no immediate impact on the larger struggle of the war. He had managed, however, to lose well over 40,000 men. There would be revenge in the future – Serbia would be all but destroyed in the next year's campaign. There are poignant photographs of Peter I taking part in the retreat through the treacherous mountain passes of Albania during winter, seated on a donkey cart. The later-to-be-famous reporter John Reed asked a Serbian in 1915 why there were no men in his village. They were all in the army, he replied, 'or dead'. But the empire of Austria-Hungary would be long gone as well just two years later, and a 'Yugoslavia' created from some of its remnants that would be, as usual, wracked by internal fissures (King Peter's son was assassinated in 1934). Today's conglomeration of Balkan states, with its uneasy mixture of catholic, orthodox and Muslim populations, is probably no more certain of its future and its borders than it was when the Turks ruled here. That sort of continuity will never change.

As for Conrad, his opinion of his German allies evolved more or less as diminished circumstances ordained. He resented being treated with condescension; he resented being ignored. Unfortunately, reversals on the battlefield more or less warranted the coming disdain. The Germans, he said, 'were cold, compromising calculators. It is part of their method to portray us as weaklings and inferiors and to belittle our accomplishments so as to be able to step forward arrogantly and deprive us of our rights.' By the end of the war, he called the great general staff in Berlin 'our secret enemies'.

The Aftermath

The town of Sarajevo reacted to the assassination of Franz Ferdinand by indulging in ethnic riots. Serb properties were attacked and looted, and known pan-Slav agitators went underground as best they could, fleeing both the police and vengeful mobs. Assassinations of royal personages were a common enough event in European life. In most such instances, the heat of the moment would pass; if international relations were involved, a period of some instability, leading to crisis, might evolve, but a European-wide conflict had not broken out for several decades. 'Maybe the tensions of 1914 seem greater only because they ended in war', wrote A. J. P. Taylor.

Of the six youthful assassins, three died in prison before the end of the hostilities they had done so much to foment. The others survived well into the century; one even became minister for forests under Marshal Tito. Dragutin Dimitrijević, or Apis, was arrested by his own government thirty-one months after the assassination; he knew too much, or was intriguing to pull down the prime minister, probably both. After a show trial in which he presented little in the way of a defence, he was sentenced to death. It is said that Dimitrijević was either told or assumed that his removal from the scene was a necessity for the furtherance of 'Serbian interests', and in that light he was willing to sacrifice himself. 'It is fate', he said on the day of his execution at dawn on 13 June 1917; he and two others kissed the hands of a priest, stepped into their graves, and were shot. It took twenty bullets to kill Apis. In 1953, he was retried (in absentia, naturally) and acquitted of all the charges for which he had been condemned. Unlike Princip, however, no monuments or commemorative plaques have been erected in his honour, nor any public buildings named after him, patriot though he was. His methodology was too sanguinary, and his appetites too coarse, not the appropriate example to encourage a future generation of would-be Serbian nationalists. A large monument to Franz Ferdinand and his wife was, however, erected in Sarajevo, overlooking the site of their murder – 'the last folly of these idiots', as Rebecca West's guide put it – but it disappeared after 1918. Also disappearing during the following war were Archduke Ferdinand's two sons and daughter. They were arrested after the *Anschluss* with Germany in 1938 and sent to the notorious Dachau concentration camp. While imprisoned there for seven years, two of the daughter's four sons died on the eastern front fighting in yet another of greater Germany's wars.

Chapter 5

Fort de Loncin

'Not one of us will surrender!'

Victor Naessens
Commandant, Fort de Loncin, Liège, Belgium

Not without some justification, German general staff officers had not expected stiff resistance from the armed forces of Belgium. This was not a slur on Belgian manhood, just a realization that geography, demographic data and German superiority in equipment and *matériel* would overwhelmingly tip the scales in their favour. The population of Belgium was a mere seven million, its field and garrison forces a relatively insignificant 340,000. It had almost no field artillery and very few machine guns. There are pictures of Belgian infantrymen, in quaint headgear that resembled formal top hats, leading dog trains pulling boxes of ammunition belts, a kind of lampoon on the notion of military efficiency. Most of the country was wide and flat, which was its attraction to von Schlieffen and the generals who came after him. Once able to cross the Meuse river anywhere between Namur and Maastricht, there was room to manoeuvre, room to push into France. Belgium realized that as well as anyone, which is why they invested heavily in three major fortification systems to protect their most strategic railway hubs and industrial cities: the aforementioned Namur, along with Liège and Antwerp. Some romantics on the Belgian high command espoused offensive tactics in the case of a German invasion, but the commander in chief, the king himself, threw cold water on such fantasies. Belgian troops would defend their positions; they would not fritter themselves away on reckless frontal attacks or suicidal charges. The Germans would have to come to them. King Albert had no doubt they would.

Belgium was a rich and prosperous country, just as it is now. Its foundation was largely made after the Congress of Vienna in 1814/15, when today's Belgium and Holland were artificially thrown together as a single nation, an impossible amalgam of differing religions and tongues that was bound to fail, as it did in 1830 when Belgium rebelled and gained independence. Because of its politically sensitive location (in everyone's way, salt water harbours, industrial potential, a long history of commercial prosperity), its lowlands became important as a crossroads, both physically and economically. It was also a nation that could not protect itself, having no genuinely defensible borders, and a reputation for the pursuit of comfort that undermined many people's confidence in its resolve. A great deal of this had to do with King Albert's father, the notorious Leopold II.

Several monarchs were easy targets for political cartoonists, who were now flooding the popular press with malicious and defamatory caricatures. Any Russian tsar of the moment could count on being portrayed with a knout in his hand, flailing serfs into submission. The minute Kaiser Wilhelm invaded 'plucky' Belgium, he was depicted as a bloodcurdling Attila, and after reports of German atrocities there, the imagery became even more florid. But Leopold II belonged in a separate category. The rape of the Congo (and such it was), undertaken with an avarice and a cruelty not often matched by a civilized country, shocked the world, and deservedly so. Leopold grew rich (and by extension, so did his country), reinforcing the notion that only profit motivated his people. There was something comfortably bourgeois and cosy about mercantile peoples like the Dutch and the Norwegians, but something decidedly less flattering when it came to Belgians.

Kaiser Wilhelm was well aware of Leopold's failings, both public and private. He had nothing but contempt for the Belgian king, calling him 'satan', and his long and sordid sexual peccadillos made his a truly odious figure as far as the kaiser's wife was concerned. Nevertheless, Wilhelm presumed on Leopold's greed during a state visit in 1904. It was certainly common knowledge that any war between France and Germany would probably involve Belgium, the temptation to violate its neutrality having to do with the aforementioned geographical character of a basically featureless and easily traversed landscape. In one of his diplomatic, or 'genius' moods, the kaiser decided that a personal agreement between the two kings would be a good thing. Wilhelm proposed that any movement of German troops through Belgium be recompensed by the creation, at Wilhelm's hand, of a new and rich Burgundian kingdom, the likes of which had not really existed for five centuries, which Leopold would rule in splendour. Leopold replied that, however appealing in the medieval sense, such a vision was impossible; in this age of parliamentary government, he could not imagine his ministers even thinking of such a thing. Wilhelm then exploded. Leopold was betraying monarchical principles; no king ever submitted to the will of politicians; only God could rule a royal's conscience – in all, a tirade on the divine right of kings to do as they wished. Then he threatened his now cowed guest. In case of war, the kaiser 'could not be played with'. He was the direct descendant of Frederick the Great – he had inherited that man's military genius – and he would not be obstructed by an imposter who had not the courage to be a true king. 'Whoever in the case of a European war was not with me, was against me'. If Belgium was not 'on my side, [the emperor] would be actuated by strategical considerations only'. Leopold was many things, but stupid he was not. The rattling sabre deeply disturbed him, given the implications of Wilhelm's threats. It is said that on leaving this interview for the railway trip home, he put his helmet on backwards and was unaware of the rather ludicrous figure he cut until he reached the train.

In 1888, Belgium undertook the expense of a major programme of military modernization, mostly an investment in concrete. Old fortresses designed two centuries previously by Vauban, the French military engineer, and largely sited within city walls, were replaced by a ring of gun sites that were generally emplaced far outside urban centres. These were usually designed as either triangles or trapezoids and were buried in the ground. Huge excavation pits, dug at mostly elevated sites that overlooked (in particular) Namur and Liège, were then filled with wooden forms into which concrete was poured to create firing platforms, observation towers, barracks, corridors and everything else required for a troglodyte existence (bakeries, kitchens, cisterns, latrines and so forth). The roofing was in some places over thirteen feet thick. When finished, the entire complex was then reburied with the previously extracted earth, giving each of these forts an essentially non-existent profile. The gun turrets, the largest of which encased 21-cm howitzers, were ingeniously encased in steel cylinders or cupolas that could 'pop up' out of the ground in their amoured casings when called upon to fire. Some of these were capable of discharging twenty rounds per minute. At night, a powerful and technologically advanced electric searchlight could illuminate the approaches for a distance of three kilometres. At Liège, twelve of these fortresses were built around the city on a perimeter that stretched for thirty-four miles; at Namur, a somewhat smaller city, seven were built. In between the forts, earthworks and infantry positions were designed to provide flank protection with enfilading fire. By the time of their completion in just three years, these were the most modern expressions of 'active defence' anywhere in the world. They were also, in the relative blink of an eye, largely obsolete.

Mankind's ingenuity when it comes to weapons of war is just about unlimited. Perhaps the allure of firepower, the attraction of the male persona to violence, power and just plain noise, or the fascination with deadly gadgetry in and of itself, explains this preoccupation; but the fact of the matter is that once any protective mechanism is put into place, it becomes an obsession for others to undermine it. In an engineering sense, the problem at the turn of the nineteenth century was a simple one. Given the strength of concrete, given the buffering qualities of protective layers of dirt thrown on top, what type of shell from what type of artillery pierce could render or destroy its most important properties? It did not take long to figure that out: bigger shells, bigger cannon to propel them, more effective (meaning delayed) fuses ... that's about all it would take. This sort of solution appealed to a man like Kaiser Wilhelm, who gloried in 'the massive, the colossal, the overloaded', according to the Belgian ambassador to his court. The details would be left to the engineers of Krupp AG.

War had barely been declared before German troops were on the march. Luxembourg rolled over immediately: resistance was pointless. It was to be hoped, by the Germans anyway, that Belgium would follow its example and put up a mostly token effort to repel invasion. This proved a nasty first surprise. King Albert, who had succeeded his father in 1909, had the usual aristocratic notions of honour. It did not behoove any king to surrender without a fight, no matter what the destruction wrought to his kingdom or subjects, whose opinions did not matter when it came to such topics. 'Oh, the poor fools!' one German diplomat said in exasperation at such niceties. 'Why don't they get out of the way!' In Liège, one diarist noted that 'it is not decided yet if we will go to Brussels considering what is rather sure to happen here'. Some residents outside the city had buried containers full of petrol in their backyards, just to be ready in case. On 5 August 1914, when the first shots began to fly, many packed their wives and children into the family car and fled. The roads west towards Brussels and the coast were soon clogged with civilian traffic. The last train out of the city left the central station at 7 a.m. with thousands of refugees on 7 August, passing beneath the guns of Fort Loncin which were busy firing.

Seven German army corps, approximately 300,000 men, were headed for Liège. A vanguard under the command of a veteran officer, General Otto von Emmich, recklessly attacked several of the forts on the eastern bank of the Meuse, thought to be lightly defended. They were not. King Albert had directed that over 35,000 men defend the city, some inside the fortresses, others in the field works located in between. These initial forays were repulsed with considerable casualties. When rain began falling the next day, spirits sagged in both armies. Glenna Bigelow, an American house guest of a Belgian count whose château lay in the suburbs, watched the estate grounds fill up 'with Belgian troops, bedraggled with mud, trying to regain order. And there they halted for hours and hours in the rain – an absolute picture of dejection'. Their enemies were not much happier. The first shock of war had proved discomforting to German troops. Many who had lost their officers milled about in confusion, upset by their first sight of dead comrades. Even

Erich Ludendorff, who arrived on the scene, confessed to queasy feelings. 'I shall never forget', he later wrote, 'hearing the thud of bullets striking human bodies'. After the first day of fighting, the Germans regrouped. With precious time slipping away (they had von Schlieffen's schedule to keep, after all) the last thing they wanted was a prolonged siege. The roads leading west over their border into Belgium were already jammed with elements of both the First and Second German armies, which were meant to burst into the open on either side of Liège. Too much of a delay would bog the entire delicate mechanism into a form of gridlock. Wilhelm, behind the lines at army headquarters in Berlin, turned viciously on von Moltke, saying, in effect, 'I knew this would happen'. Von Moltke did not quite comprehend what to make of this tirade, but it clearly had something to do with not having an instant victory to report to the All Highest. As was usual with Wilhelm, the highs and lows of any particular situation were extremely taxing on all who had to bear the emotional results. With the onslaught of these difficulties, the German response was predictably heavy-handed: more artillery.

Tempers were being frayed, generals were shouting, results demanded. Belgian troops in exposed positions began feeling the effects of heavier shelling, and German forces were turning their flanks from both the north and south of the city itself. There was danger that the entire contingent might be encircled and trapped inside Liège. With considerable reluctance, Gérard Leman, the general in charge of the defence, authorized a retreat on the 6th, leaving the twelve fortresses to carry on alone. On the 7th, Ludendorff himself, who had peremptorily taken charge of a leaderless brigade, boldly entered the city and approached the ancient citadel, demanding its surrender. Since this ancient structure had no real military value, it did so. Ludendorff considered himself the master of Liège – 'the favourite recollection of my life', he later wrote – but he was not, as yet. The fortresses still held.

Despite the undoubted ability of the Belgian engineer General Henri Brialmont, who had designed the system two decades before, these concrete strong points had a variety of Achilles heels which all the forts universally shared. Communications between the forts were primitive. So much of the system had an 'underground' quality, except for those elements that allowed commanders to stay in touch with one another. Telephone lines, for example, were strung along poles from fort to fort. These were destroyed right from the start. Target coordination for the various artillery pieces required spotters on the ground, either in exposed observation points or in vulnerable spots such as church steeples. For much of the fighting, as a result, many fortress guns fired blind or generalized rounds. The innovative searchlights that were meant to protect the forts at night proved vulnerable to enemy fire. Once darkness fell, many of the forts were isolated from everything except danger. As the Germans brought up heavier and heavier artillery pieces, however, the true weaknesses of the system were ruthlessly exposed.

Krupp AG had been a busy company for the preceding two decades (to say nothing of the previous three centuries). One of the great industrial and military conglomerations in the history of Europe, it specialized in 'heavy lifting' when it came to weapons of war. Huge dreadnought battleships, naval guns, humongous artillery of any sort, these were the types of outsize weaponry that few futurists could even dream about. The Krupp dynasty, however, was not unimaginative. From a bay window at their former headquarters in Berlin, which somehow survived World War II, and decorated with Krupp AG's famous logo, three intertwined circles, it is said that Gustav Krupp doodled a sketch of a revolutionary 420-mm calibre howitzer that later would be famously nicknamed 'Big Bertha'. During the siege of Liège, this behemoth made all the difference.[1]

Technically speaking, the German *Dicke Bertha* translates as 'Fat Bertha', but given the namesake after whom this enormous piece of ironmongery was named, Bertha Krupp von Bohlen und Halbach, the principal heir of Friedrich Alfred Krupp, some modicum of discretion was evidently called for (Bertha was not an ugly woman by any means, though she was solid). Many writers have misapplied the moniker 'Big Bertha' to any number of outsized artillery pieces manufactured by Krupp AG – in particular, the enormous 'Paris Gun', a piece with a range of seventy-five miles that shelled Paris in 1918 – but Big Bertha is factually attributable to one gun only, a multi-ton howitzer that the historian William Manchester once referred to as a slug, given its ponderous nature. *Dicke Bertha*'s predecessor, a prototype known as Gamma-Gerät, was a fixed-position instrument of death that weighed 300,000 lbs. It required ten railway cars to transport, six allocated to the gun itself, broken down into pieces, the other four to its concrete foundation. When offloaded on site, which had to be accessible by rail, the firing platform was emplaced into the ground, and the gun reassembled. The logistical requirements were so formidable that the gun's practicality proved excessively limited. Just two years before the war, the German high command commissioned Krupp AG to come up with something more mobile, and Big Bertha was the result. Weighing less than a third of Gamma-Gerät, Big Bertha could be dragged by horse teams or, where possible, by a specially designed tractor. It too came in pieces but, once assembled, it had the advantage of mobility. It could be pushed around here and there, on specially designed treads that, it was hoped, would prevent it from sinking into the earth. It had a 420-mm specification, more than double that of the heaviest howitzers then in army use, and it packed a powerful punch, specifically designed to pierce the outer shells of concrete structures. By 12 August, two Big Berthas began concentrating on the fortresses, their range, generally speaking, being ten miles. No gun anywhere in Liège could fire farther than six. It now became a matter of human endurance. How much could the Belgians take?

These grotesque howitzers, preceded during the fighting by other heavy guns with 28-mm barrels, exposed Brialmont's blithe disregard for the capacity of men to absorb punishment. With the beginning of the siege, the forts had buttoned themselves up for action: all embrasures were closed and bolted, basically entombing everyone inside. Ventilation had barely been thought of, a few primitive fresh air pipes scattered about, with no circulation system provided.[2] Electrical systems were primitive, the few lights inside the buildings barely able to illuminate anything. Soldiers had been provided with miners' lamps, fuelled by petrol, but in the chaos of continuous shelling, these proved next to useless. Men often found themselves trapped in complete darkness, yet were still expected to operate the many complicated pieces of equipment that would keep the guns firing. Latrine systems broke down right from the start. After just a few hours, with no fresh air, every fort stood smothered in vile odours, which were compounded by a variety of gaseous fumes caused by gun smoke and explosive shells now pounding, and sometimes penetrating, the forts themselves. Hits on the metal gun turrets reverberated throughout the fort like a carillon of bells ringing at once. These were truly hells on earth, and one by one the forts began to crack.

The first surrendered on 8 August; by the 14th, all the forts on the eastern side of the Meuse were finished. Some had absorbed shelling at the rate of 400 hits per hour. German artillerymen now hauled Big Berthas even closer to the western ridge overlooking the far side of the city, on the most commanding of which was Fort de Loncin, which controlled both the road and the railway line to Brussels. It was here that General Leman had moved his command post. An elderly gentleman, he had told his staff that he would not surrender. He also refused to remove his sword. If he was to die, it would be in the correct manner.

Célestin Demblon, a university professor, described the arrival of a Big Bertha from his vantage-point on Rue Saint-Pierre near the city centre on the 15th. It was dragged, in pieces, by horse teams through the streets, accompanied by the 300 or so men that its assembly and operation required. Winches, levers and human sweat put the whole contraption together with scientific precision, the citizens of Liège looking on in mute amazement. 'Hannibal's elephants could not have astonished the Romans more', as Demblon put it. When the first shot was fired – the 3-foot projectile flew a mile in the sky before its descent, a process that took an entire minute – the earth shook under Demblon's feet, and every downtown window shattered.

Fort Loncin suffered barrages almost unknown in the history of warfare to that point. Some survivors later claimed to have counted fifteen direct hits that struck the place simultaneously. How they were able to figure that out is a mystery. In a tale that might be apocryphal, the fort's commandant supposedly asked a group of troopers if they were afraid. They replied that they were only afraid that he might *think* they were afraid, and thus unworthy of his trust. By the next day, in darkness, the air befouled, some men died for lack of oxygen. At a single moment on 15 August, at 5:20 in the afternoon, about 300 of their comrades followed suit in one terrible explosion. A single 42cm shell, weighing some 1,600 lbs, penetrated the powder magazine, blowing up 24,000 pounds of gunpowder. The entire roof of the chamber blew up. The encased 21-cm howitzers in their turrets flew through the air 'like champagne corks'. When the dust settled, two-thirds of the garrison lay buried in what Leman called 'a chaos of rubbish', either dead or soon to be. Fort Loncin was now *hors de combat*.

The Germans were delighted. Only two forts were left. Under flags of truce, they invited the two remaining Belgian commandants safe passage to take a look at Loncin. If that's the way they wished to die, it was fine with them. They surrendered the next day, Liège finally taken. The Big Berthas were then dismantled, trundled up with Teutonic efficiency and transported to Namur, which held out for just three days. The much-heralded Belgian forts had, according to a British general, fallen 'like scraps of paper'.

Enemy troops made perfunctory efforts to dig out survivors at Loncin. 'We were no Huns', said Ludendorff. The carnage was too great, however, and exhuming all the bodies would have taken too much time. The Belgians were left buried in the rubble, as they are to this day. General Leman miraculously survived, however. He was found unconscious and partially buried. After regaining his senses, he demanded that his captors write a statement that he had fallen into their hands involuntarily (his honour demanded it). In captivity for three years, he finally returned home to Belgium a national hero. Ludendorff received Germany's highest war-time decoration, the *Pour le Mérite*. He deserved it. Von Moltke suddenly found the kaiser fawning all over him in delight, kissing his cheeks. Wilhelm was irrepressible. Glenna Bigelow, working during the day as a volunteer at a field hospital, returned to her host's château in the evening to find herself required for a formal dinner party; the count, it seems, had about twenty German officers billeted in his spacious mansion, all of whom had to be wined and fed. The gathering was an 'odd affair', she remembered, with one or two tactless statements from their guests, such as 'Paris in a fortnight'. Bigelow found herself seated next to an older officer. 'I asked him as stupidly as possible (perhaps I did not need to simulate that) if he liked "War". He hesitated just a second and I was prepared for the usual self-respecting denial when he horrified me by answering a simple "Yes". *Voilà le sentiment prusse!'*

Edith Cavell

'Patriotism is not enough.'

The road now lay open. Two German armies began their great sweep south into France as the extreme elements of von Schlieffen's right wing. They had been delayed by the courageous defence of Liège, and to some degree by Namur, but analysis after the war suggests that von Moltke lost only two days or so from his original schedule, not a critical span given the always uncertain nature of war. More damaging in some ways was the behaviour of German forces who were split off from the main attack force, their intention to capture Brussels (easily done), then to take Antwerp to its north, an objective completed in workmanlike fashion by 9 October.[3] King Albert, who had intended to remain in the city no matter what, was persuaded to withdraw, and rode out while he still could with his staff in a decidedly pessimistic frame of mind. This mood was not helped by French and British efforts to tell him what to do. Albert, thirty-nine years old, was a stubborn, opinionated man. As a king, naturally, he had an autocratic state of mind. Winston Churchill had come over to assess the situation at Antwerp. As was to prove standard behaviour for him, he urged no retreat or surrender. From the French side, Ferdinand Foch appeared in his usual whirlwind fashion, crying for the Belgians to 'Attack! Attack!' Albert deeply distrusted both men; they had no interest in Belgium, especially when his alleged allies asked him to relinquish command of what Belgian forces were left, and sublimate them to the wishes of London and Paris. At one point, the king turned on his French liaison officer and called him 'an untrustworthy dog'. His bitterness that much of the following four years of bloody, destructive war would take place on Belgian territory led him on several occasions to contemplate a separate peace with the kaiser. London and Paris generally viewed him with suspicion, Margot Asquith noting in her diary that Albert hates 'the French quite as much as the Germans'. Early in 1915, in fact, her husband sent one of his many indiscreet notes to Venetia Stanley, his would-be lover, stating that the Belgians 'are in a very bad way, and there is a serious risk, if we do not back them up by every means in our power, of their going over lock, stock and barrel to the Germans. A pretty end to our "scrap of paper"– wouldn't it be? They are certainly the most disenchanting of protégés.' On 25 October, in resignation, the king decided that the only way to stop the enemy's juggernaut was to turn to mother nature. He approved orders that sluices at the mouth of the river Yser at Nieuwpoort be opened which, after three days, created a moat of seawater almost two miles wide by twenty long. Behind this wall of water, four feet deep, which turned farm fields into mud, the Belgian army recovered its breath. The king then had time to absorb, and to disseminate, the news of what had occurred in their wake, not least of which was the fate of Louvain.

Louvain, an ancient university city between Liège and Brussels, had been made famous by two factors from its ancient history: the cloth industry and the busy work of long-since-disappeared Irish monks. During the dark ages of European history, Louvain had been a monastic centre traditionally attractive to wandering Celtic scholars, missionaries drawn by barbarian kings and their licentious courts, always in need of corrective advice, reformation and, over time, education. The Irish were both spirited scolders and enthusiastic teachers, Louvain soon becoming what historians like to call a 'seat of learning'. The Catholic university here, formally established in 1425, was if not the oldest, certainly one of the oldest in Flanders, its library an irreplaceable repository of illuminated manuscripts, ancient printed material, and books that represented, more than just about anywhere else, the essence of civilization. On 25 August 1914, German troops burned the entire building to the ground in a wanton display of heathenism.

Belgian atrocity stories were quickly the staple of newspapers all over the continent. Wildly inflated by the yellow press, and quickly drenched in exaggeration, such press coverage was devastating to Germany's image abroad, and sealed for it the enmity of millions of people. It did not take long for most casual readers to care not a fig who actually started the war or who invaded whom. The villain was Germany and its kaiser. He was depicted as an ogre, and his generals as enthusiastic grim reapers, skewering Belgian babies with their bayonets and swords. Negative publicity of this sort hardened people's hearts. When 1918 rolled around, there were few onlookers anywhere who had much pity for the German people.

In any war, outrages occur. If ever there was a fact of life regarding invasions, battles and poor people defending their homesteads, this was it. Modern European conflicts were no strangers to guerrilla fighters taking part as irregular combatants without uniforms, flags or identifying insignias. Napoleon's invasion of Spain had seen particularly nasty incidents of local people ambushing and murdering French soldiers, thereby inviting ugly reprisals by enraged troops, depicted in horrifying fashion by the great artist Francisco Goya. Urban disturbances during the famous uprisings in 1848 had seen ordinary citizens, in emulation of the French Revolution, tearing up cobblestones to create barricades, and fighting uniformed soldiers in vicious street battles. Their fate, if captured, was often summary execution. After the collapse of Napoleon III's regular armies during the Franco-Prussian War, the revolutionary commune issued calls for a people's army to procure and bear arms. Not only in Paris, but out in the countryside over 100,000 men (and boys) answered the call. These individuals, known as *franc-tireurs* or 'irregulars', as far as German army commanders were concerned lay outside the rules of engagement. If they surrendered (a foolish choice) or were captured on the battlefield, they could expect only the harshest consequence. Nineteen-fourteen was to be no different.

In the early days of the Liège campaign, there was considerable confusion in and around the city. German authorities were caught off guard by the occasional appearance among Belgian forces of seemingly civilian elements, most likely members of what was, in practical terms, a civil defence force. These few men, some armed, were intended to be local police auxiliaries, their purpose to guard facilities or provide basic law and order duties in place of uniformed personnel needed elsewhere. The Germans looked upon these people as guerrilla fighters. It is impossible today to state how many actual incidents of firing on German soldiers by these 'irregulars' actually occurred, but it is certainly true that rumours within the invading army exaggerated both their numbers and their activities. The response was draconian, heartless and clumsy, a collective case of what one historian called 'mass self-suggestion', the results of which were militarily ineffective and politically ruinous.

At first, lower grade officers reacted on their own. Hostages were routinely taken, often the local priest, burgomaster or resident landowner. Human shields were also employed, which could include women and children. If a captain or major found himself truly nonplussed, five to ten civilians could find themselves indiscriminately shot. General Karl von Einem, as reports of *franc-tireurs* reached his ears (whether true or false), made matters worse by issuing a blanket authorization that houses could be burned and innocent people executed in reprisal. This considerably intensified the situation. In the town of Dinant, over 600 civilians were more or less butchered ('Up against the wall', a German Major Schlick would yell). It did not take long for incidents such as these to be embellished: roadside murders had stories of rape thrown in for good measure, then even more lurid descriptions of babies being stabbed with bayonets and pitchforked into ditches. The kaiser's reaction did not help matters. He had it on good authority that Belgian children were mutilating wounded German soldiers, cutting off their privates and poking out their eyes with specially crafted spoons. Belgian irregulars were 'blood-thirsty' villains, he said, and deserved the punishments they received. Sensationalist rhetoric of this sort contributed to the three-day rampage through Louvain, which destroyed the ancient library with its collection of some 230,000 books, and almost twenty percent of the ancient city centre. German officers set up dinner tables in the main square and drank looted wines and liqueurs, watching the flames do their work. In all, during an eleven-day period, it has been estimated that some 6,000 innocent Belgian civilians were killed, and 20,000 buildings knocked to pieces. For the great German theorist von Clausewitz, this sort of excess was a perfectly natural occurrence. 'To introduce into the philosophy of war a principle of moderation would be an absurdity', he wrote. 'War is an application of violence which in its application knows no bounds.' That looked fine and good on the printed page, but in the minds of educated people the question inevitability arose: was this the *Kultur* that the rest of Europe could look forward to?

An even worse public relations disaster, and one that easily could have been avoided, was the 'martyrdom' of a hitherto utterly obscure English nurse by the name of Edith Cavell. Her statue, a monolithic and not especially appealing rendition, stands boldly at the foot of Charing Cross Road in London, looking down towards that considerably more famous hero, Lord Horatio Nelson, whose figure on top of a very tall column dominates Trafalgar Square. Most people today have heard of Nelson (or so one would hope), but most pedestrians hurrying by Cavell's memorial have not the slightest idea who she was. In 1915, however, everyone knew.[4]

Edith Cavell represents an almost archetypal English cliché: the homely spinster, excessively pious, who was preordained from day one by her severe father (a minister, of course) to be farmed out into service. Reserved, chilly in disposition, virginal and formal, she was first employed in a variety of nanny and governess positions. As her father lay dying, she returned from her position in Belgium to care for him by his bedside; thereafter she determined to become a nurse. At one point in her career, she was the night matron in a hospital ward, which was certainly not conducive to either finding a husband (if indeed she ever wanted one) or making any money. She had no close friends to speak of, only a Jack Russell terrier who, after her death, was somehow returned to England. When his day of reckoning came, he was for some reason stuffed and placed on exhibit at the Imperial War Museum, yet another manifestation of English idiosyncrasy.

Cavell returned to Belgium in 1907. As part of a local doctor's attempts at reforming Belgian nursing standards (nurses, in his opinion, had been dominated too long by religious orders, whose practices had little changed since medieval times), she was named director of his new clinic. Whatever work she had embarked upon, however, was interrupted by the German invasion. Wounded prisoners came and went from her facility, but not always into POW camps where they were supposed to be placed after their recoveries, as German authorities soon noticed. Cavell, it seems, was organizing escapes for English captives: providing false papers, arranging itineraries and facilitating their return behind allied lines. On 5 August 1915, she and nine co-workers were arrested and later put on trial by a military court, which did not last more than one day before all were found guilty. Edith, as it turned out, was disinterested in a defence of her behaviour. It was against her principles to lie, so she blithely admitted everything; having little concept of the real world, she also implicated several of her associates, apparently not realizing the danger in which she was placing them, Cavell seeming to think that no real harm would result from the verdicts. After all, she did what any decent-minded person would do in her place; how could she be punished for doing her duty? Whether or not she was shocked into silence when condemned to death we shall never know. Edith Cavell epitomized the stiff-upper-lip syndrome that heroines are routinely expected to display.

No one could really believe that Cavell would be executed, but, as the appointed date approached and no reprieve seemed forthcoming, the world began paying attention. Were the Germans really serious about this? Many members of the diplomatic corps on the Wilhelmstrasse in Berlin tripped over themselves trying to figure out how the military ruling could be overturned, but legally they could not find a solution on short notice. The American and Spanish ambassadors to Belgium tried their hardest, but the generals ignored them. Appeals were discreetly made to the kaiser and his wife but Wilhelm, for whatever reason, was in an angry mood and had no idea that world opinion really cared one way or the other. He was obtuse enough not to realize that Cavell was a woman, and that there was something rather unsightly about pumping sixteen bullets into a slight, shy, defenceless creature of the weaker sex. His wife, the empress, was entirely unmoved. If Edith Cavell wanted to play a man's game, she must be willing to pay a man's price. On 12 October 1915, Cavell was shot by a firing squad, an act that Admiral Georg von Müller, Wilhelm's naval attaché, called an act of 'incredible stupidity'. He was not far wrong in that judgment.

Cavell's death became the stuff of English legend: her fortitude, courage and indifference to anything but what was right. During the final visit of a chaplain, she apparently said the words inscribed on the pedestal of her statue, 'Patriotism is not enough'. Sentiments like these would not survive four long years of dreadful war, but it was a tonic for harried recruiters early on in 1915. Between the 'rape of Belgium' and the example of Edith Cavell, men shirking their duty on the home front might find themselves looking over their shoulder to find people pointing them out. She was a copywriter's dream.

In 1919, Cavell's body was disinterred and brought home to England. She had a magnificent funeral service at Westminster Abbey, from where she was taken to the ancient town of Norwich and buried in the shadow of that fine city's beautiful cathedral. The grave site is a modest one; remnants of floral bouquets are usually always visible. Innumerable streets, hospital wings, nursing homes, schools, parks, a bridge in New Zealand, a new rose variety and Edith Piaf have all been named after her.

George Bellows

Bellows, an American artist remembered today for his depictions of the urban grit of New York City, including energetic paintings of boxing matches in places like Sharkey's Club, where the combatants seem to tear the life out of one another, was a forceful contributor to the anti-German sentiment caused by bloody events in Belgium during 1914. His raw, vigorously depicted scenes of brutality, full of bold flesh tones and caricatured violence, took the breath away from many Americans who, before the days of colour cinema, could only imagine what blood and gore might look like. The depiction of a naked woman nailed to the wall of a house, her left breast severed by a bayonet, while the perpetrator sits idly by smoking a cigarette, was shocking beyond description, though typical of the near hysteria that rumours of such behaviour had incited. Bellows worked an entire summer on a series of lithographs, and then five very large paintings, that the conflict in Belgium inspired. Some of the canvases were tableau of Calvary-type catharsis, the *Massacre at Dinant* being a prime example. A group of over twenty civilians, including nuns, priests, women and children, react at the moment that shots are about to be fired; likewise, *The Germans Arrive*, where Bellows painted a boy having his hands cut off as a salutary example to other villagers that they had better behave. The most effective is *The Barricade*, showing eleven naked Belgians, their hands in the air, being used as a human shield behind whom the hideous invaders advance, rifles aimed and at the ready. There is no emotional middle ground. Bellows also helped immortalize Edith Cavell. Unusually for him, the image of Cavell calmly descending a stairwell to the execution yard is saccharine, an angel going to her death without a second's hesitation, ignoring some reports that she had fainted from fright at the last minute. Pedestrians strolling along Fifth Avenue, being urged to buy bonds or support the war effort, could not pass by any of these without a response of some sort. One art critic wrote that the canvases were 'reeking with truth'.

This was all a classic example of rumour run rampant. The first 'official' report on atrocities in Belgium was commissioned by the British government in 1915 and headed by a respected historian, Lord James Bryce. Prime Minister Asquith made sure 40,000 copies were shipped to the United States upon its release, to stir up American feelings. Whether Bellows read it or not is unknown, but he certainly scanned papers and magazines and no doubt found his subject matter there, as presented by journalists whose prejudices and/or competence were rarely questioned. As many observers have noted, the first casualties in any war are reliable facts.

Bellow's artistic vehemence was questioned after the armistice, and particularly as rumours about the Versailles Treaty negotiations began circulating in the United States, which seemed to show the various bickering powers as having learnt nothing from four years of war. This was a period of growing anti-European sentiment, the notion perhaps that the United States had been hoodwinked once again by corrupt politicians from the Old World, who had involved the world's greatest democracy in just another of its squalid wars. As was the case in every combatant country, many questioned the value of unfettered patriotic feelings, and disparaged the raw appeal to emotion that 'propaganda' sought to encourage. Bellows was a 'fine arts' artist, but the astonishing brutality of his renditions no longer seemed morally appropriate, especially since postwar commentary suggested that the Belgian atrocity tales might have been exaggerated. Some wondered if he was appealing to some grotesque strain of voyeurism, the kind that bystanders often exhibit when they pass a gruesome accident. Others said that Bellows did not know what he was talking about, never having seen the battlefields himself or had any personal experience of such bloodshed. His response was to ask whether Leonardo da Vinci had been invited to The Last Supper.

Much to his disappointment, the Belgian paintings were soon forgotten. He did not exhibit them again in his lifetime (he died at the early age of forty-three in 1925), nor did he ever sell one. People seemed to prefer the violence of the boxing ring to the real (or imagined) violence of war.

Liège Today

This interesting Belgian city retains much of an old-world character, though its location in the bowels of the Meuse River valley, surrounded by heights on either bank, generally guarantees gloomy mornings before the sun can burn off pervasive mists. Suburban development has climbed up the valley walls, topped the ridges, and sprawled over to the other side, which was not the case a century ago when it was all farmland and woodlots. Railway lines are still everywhere. The front gate of Fort de Loncin, enveloped in a nondescript residential quarter, comes as a surprise. This is clearly not a tourist attraction of any significance. I had to ask directions several times as I made my way there. Many people I stopped had no idea who or what the place was. World War I seems a long time ago in comfy Belgium.

There is a fine museum inside the fort, run by volunteers. The tour is self-guided. The place is gloomy beyond belief; knowing that you are walking over the graves of several hundred men will do that. Many of the corridors have pictures of soldiers who died here, all in blue uniforms, some with family expressions of grief inscribed below. To walk along the former roof of the fort reminds me of a jungle gym twisted into grotesque distortions: gun barrels upside down, masonry tossed around like chips, the cacophony of war. A sculpture of sorts rises out of the ruins, a silver hand holding a torch, to memorialize the mass grave. I don't know how effective this symbolism really is. There should be more.

In 2007, the Belgium army began wondering if the site was really safe enough for visitors. During the Second World War, a Halifax bomber had crashed nearby, almost hitting the fort; apparently some people had wondered even then what might have happened if that aircraft, with its own load of bombs, had acted as a detonator to what might be still buried in the earth. A thorough survey was undertaken, and 147 tons of explosives removed from the fortress site. The remains of twenty-five additional bodies from Fort Loncin's garrison were also recovered.

Chapter 6

Tannenberg: 'The Siamese Twins'

*'World history knows three great battles of annihilation:
Cannae, Sedan, and Tannenberg.'*

Adolf Hitler

No one could be blamed today if the word 'East Prussia' means nothing to them – what it was, where it was, the connotation of the very words that might, given the listener, roil their blood in either anger or nostalgia. Older Germans of the generation just born at the end of 1945 would certainly know the details, particularly if their families had had their origins there, tediously detailed over wintertime's long cold nights as fathers and mothers recalled the old days, with scrapbooks and odd photographs that might have survived wartime disaster. Nearly four million German refugees fled East Prussia as the Red Army launched its last drive from the east towards Berlin in the final days of the Second World War, an advance that was as ruthless and vengeful as it was overwhelming. Many thousands of that number never made it anywhere alive, marking it as one of the largest, and least known, humanitarian disasters of World War II. Once the Russians had finished, *Ostpreussen*, or East Prussia, ceased to exist. Its population or, more aptly, those who had survived, fled as far west as they could go. By 1947, there wasn't a German left in the entire province.

The long decades of the Cold War put the geography of *Ostpreussen* even further adrift from western eyes. Idle tourists were not allowed to roam about what was now Polish territory; Prussia became a word in the dictionary more associated with the generic definition of 'militarism' than with specific terrain, not helped by the fact that every German town and village was linguistically wiped off the map, to be replaced by Polish nomenclature. Did the place ever exist?

My first visit to the region, along with most other people, coincided with the Berlin Wall coming down, and what a revelation it was, a countryside still ploughed by the horse. Vestiges of Germany remained, but often in a humbled state. Guided by the directions of German émigrés then living near Frankfurt, I sought out the site of Field Marshal Paul von Hindenburg's first grave, a vast mausoleum that marked his greatest victory, the Battle of Tannenberg. This edifice – a huge, mock-Teutonic fortress in red brick – was long gone, blown up by retreating Germans in 1945, then trashed by oncoming Russians, and finally 'desecrated' by Poles returning to what they considered sovereign territory of their own. The place was levelled, like Carthage, to the very ground, but I wondered if a trace or two might still survive. I knew the task would be a difficult one when I was advised to ask for directions at the equivalent of a diner on a lonely country road. That did not bode well that my objective was considered by anyone there as a major tourist attraction.

East Prussia was the very heart of the Prussian military mystique, or 'monster' if you happened to be Polish, Lithuanian, Estonian, Latvian or Russian. Originally, the territory running east of present-day Gdansk, and shouldering the Baltic Sea, stood as a no-man's land of sorts, a fluctuating frontier between the Germanic and Slavic races that has been fought over for centuries. With no genuine physical barriers save several great rivers running from the interior, the fluidity of territorial boundaries has been a constant puzzle for historians to keep up with or figure out, as they track the tensions and continual invasions that have crisscrossed these amorphous plains. Poland, for instance, always in the middle (and often, in speaking of 'sovereignty', non-existent), has paid the price over and over again for having no fortifiable frontiers. It has made up for this lack by an often defiant and belligerent posture that has frequently cost it dearly.

From the German perspective, the heart and soul of East Prussia, the entity that in fact created it, was the monastic Teutonic Order of Knights, who eventually settled themselves most ostentatiously in the great fortress of Marienburg (now Malbork in Poland). From this citadel, and many others, the knights advanced Germanic arms (and, as they would add, Christianity and Culture) ever towards the east. Without simplifying things too drastically, the knights created the genetic gene pool that evolved, ever so slowly, into what we might call the German General Staff of the nineteenth century. The Hohenzollern dynasty, with Berlin (or, more properly, Potsdam) as its emotive capital, recruited the core of its officer pool from the sons of *Junkers* in East Prussia – country gentlemen, often dirt poor, with estates as large as they were unproductive, and generally ill-equipped to provide income or support for those foolish enough to sire large numbers of boys. This did not, of course, diminish the intense affection that such people held for their lands. When something is won with the sword, it is usually very hard indeed to give it up.

Younger sons were generally shunted off to military schools or academies, there to bulk up, both physically and morally, imbibing the traditions and teachings of military men famous to them, if not particularly to others: Scharnhorst, Gneisenau, von Clausewitz, Blücher. Upon graduation, they had no homes to return to, their addresses usually a barracks or military station somewhere in the country, or perhaps elsewhere as a mercenary in some foreign army. There they were known for their arrogance, stiff-necked pride and boorish manners. Marriage to a family with money was always welcome, providing the wherewithal to purchase land in *Ostpreussen* for their eventual retirement; lacking that, it was always hoped that a war might arise, and with it the chance for glory and advancement. The Prussian conflict of 1870 with the hated French was a God-sent opportunity of which many took advantage. As the century closed, with its crises and arms races, many engineered by the volatile new kaiser, Wilhelm II, there seemed a good chance that more opportunity lay ahead. By this time, East Prussia had become a settled and Germanic creation, an agricultural and somewhat feudal landscape devoid of heavy industry. Small market towns, often with a restored Teutonic castle in their midst, radiated bourgeoisie comfort with ubiquitous brick townhouses and market squares, their railway stations anchoring a spider's web of steel tracks that connected them to the university city of Königsberg, made famous by Kant, and the great port of Danzig, an ancient seat of the Hanseatic League. Kaiser Wilhelm loved this countryside. His favourite summer palace was a stud farm at Cadinen, with its acres of horse trails and endless vistas of the Baltic. When he prayed in his private chapel there, he no doubt did so in the utter satisfaction of knowing that all was right with the world. It was his to rule and dominate.

German strategy in August 1914 was bold, aggressive and, most of all, dangerous. To achieve the numerical superiority required by Schlieffen's formula meant denuding its eastern front, leaving East Prussia open to invasion by Russia, should it intend to honour its treaty commitments to France, as expected. This would present the 'two-front-war' scenario that the German general staff had been thinking about for forty years, and the key to its resolution was quick victory in France. Russia, derided by the kaiser as a lumbering, antiquated and primitive opponent, would certainly mobilize, but could she become what Churchill called 'that mighty steamroller' quickly enough to make a critical difference on the western front? That was the dilemma, and every German general realized it. Victory delayed in France meant a fearful day of reckoning on the banks of the Niemen or, even worse, the Vistula and Oder, but no other strategy seemed to make sense. The German army could not simultaneously fight its two major enemies with enough manpower to beat either. But in 1914, as the first month of the war began, such was the catastrophe facing the High Command.

German troops entered Belgium on 4 August, seven of its eight armies systematically commencing the application of von Schlieffen's so far theoretical plan. Delays at Liège were irritating but not unduly disruptive to the all-important timetable, and the German wing crossed into France more or less as envisioned. Casualties on both sides were unexpectedly high, particularly for the French, who, as yet, had misunderstood the enemy's intentions and frittered away their strength through the misguided élan of *offensive à outrance*, or 'offence at any price'. The horrific five days of 20 to 24 August, when the north-east frontier of France found itself engulfed in battle and pierced everywhere by German troops, were among the darkest in French military annals.

At German headquarters, the chief of staff, Helmuth von Moltke, found his nervous system equally tormented. The great envelopment was proceeding just as planned. The question was: could the German army sustain its momentum, maintain its strength and essentially continue to dictate the character of battle as a gun-and-chase affair – the very mobility von Schlieffen's ghost demanded? But with all eyes riveted on France, von Moltke heard news that shrivelled his spirits. Contrary to all expectations, Russia had launched not one but two field armies toward the core of East Prussia, forces that totalled well over half a million men and something like 600 pieces of artillery. The sacred soil of the Fatherland, the emotional heart of its martial spirit, was being trampled by barbarians just as Paris stood within reach. What good was a triumphal march down the Champs-Élysées if Cossacks put Berlin to the torch? Such was the inevitable result should the sole German army in the east, the Eighth, numbering only 210,000 men, be brushed aside, and that seemed unavoidable.

Von Moltke could hardly stand the strain. A man of ability but incapable, as he had warned the kaiser, of generating the sang-froid that every great commander must sustain during a crisis, he saw himself staring down the abyss of utter ruin. His knees may have shaken even more when he spoke by telephone on 20 August with Max von Prittwitz, commander of the Eighth and a favourite of the kaiser. Von Prittwitz, known as 'Fatty' to his fellow officers, reported that his forces had been sufficiently bloodied by one of the Russian pincers, and threatened in the rear by the other, that a withdrawal beyond the Vistula was now necessary. East Prussia was to be abandoned.

The newness of war – many generals had last heard the sound of serious gunfire some forty-four years before in 1870 – may partially explain the timidity and upset that officers such as von Prittwitz displayed when adverse tidings reached their headquarters. Von Prittwitz, sixty-six years of age, had certainly panicked on that 20 August when he heard that General Pavel Rennenkampf's First Army had advanced to the Insterburg Gap, a 43-mile stretch of level country between the fortresses of Königsberg and the obstructive maze of Masuria's forests and lakes, dealing two serious blows to German forces in the process. Simultaneously the staff of XX Corps, acting as a screen on the southern side of Masuria, reported the approach of Russian General Alexander Samsonov's Second Army from Warsaw, advance units of which were now pouring over the border and threatening the town of Neidenburg. Von Prittwitz should have known better but he signalled his intention to retreat, thus marking the end of his career.

German officers had been trained to withstand adversity. It was their duty when confronted with a deteriorating front to consider options and countermeasures that would stem the decline and reverse the fortunes of battle. The aid to this process had supposedly been decades' worth of war games and simulations, along with the annual staff rides, whereby every detail of landscape could be considered and filed away. Von Prittwitz momentarily forgot himself, whereas members of his staff did not.

Colonel Max von Hoffmann, a cynical man, whose diary is one of the few eyewitness accounts of the great battle that has any verve or nuanced assessment, saw opportunity in the tactical situation, not ruin. Appalled at the notion of retreat, he pulled calipers from his pocket and demonstrated that Samsonov was actually closer to the Vistula than the Eighth Army and could beat them to the river if it came to a race. The key was to turn once again to the von Schlieffen gospel. Draw off strength from before one of the Russian armies and attack the other with all your might, then turn and strike down the survivor. The essential requirement for such a scheme was in place: the Prussian railway grid. Since 1862, annual war games had relied heavily on the transport and manoeuvre of troops by rail, and indeed Hoffmann was an expert in their deployment. He proposed denuding forces ranged against Rennenkampf and shifting them south-west to attack Samsonov, relying on the commonly held conviction that the Russians were incapable of exploiting their earlier successes with any speed or vigour. This, in keeping with von Schlieffen's maxims, constituted a gamble, but Hoffmann felt sure of success. After Samsonov was defeated, the Prussians could concentrate another blow against Rennenkampf. 'Enough of war on two fronts', von Schlieffen had said in 1899; 'one front is ample'. Von Prittwitz was brought around to

Hoffmann's view and issued the necessary instructions. Von Moltke then relieved him of his command.

The saviour of East Prussia arrived in a special train from the western front on 23 August. Headquarters staff at Marienburg gave him a chilly reception, their honour doubly offended when they realized that new commands intended to rectify the position were in fact no different from Hoffmann's . The newcomer was indifferent to their notions of self-esteem, however. Erich Ludendorff was not a sentimentalist. He had come to take charge, to issue orders, to win a crucial victory. In his train came the nominal commander in chief, Paul von Hindenburg, a man neither Hoffmann nor anyone else 'had ever seen before'.

The partnership between von Hindenburg and Ludendorff is undoubtedly the most revered in the tradition of Prussian arms, on a certain par with its illustrious predecessor from the Napoleonic era, that of Marshal Blücher and Scharnhorst. Whereas the latter arrangement was more or less between equals, however, that of Ludendorff and von Hindenburg was very much weighted in the younger man's favour.

Ludendorff was forty-nine at the time, a general staff officer of Prussian, though minor-aristocratic background, whose abrasive personality and dogged adherence to principle had, as related earlier, actually earned him demotion before the war. A fervent disciple of von Schlieffen and his plan, many of whose intricacies he had himself put into the detailed minutes of battle orders, Ludendorff was the lucky recipient of gratuitous opportunity before the gates of Liège in the first days of August. Encountering a leaderless brigade mired in confusion, Ludendorff immediately took command and fulfilled its orders to force an entry into the ring of Belgian forts surrounding the city, orders he knew by heart. This achievement won him instant fame.

Von Moltke, in urgent need of merciless housecleaning for the Eighth Army, detached Ludendorff from what everyone thought was the brink of a glorious victory on the western front, with renown for all, and ordered him to 'prevent the worst from happening' in Prussia. Within fifteen minutes of receiving this message from von Moltke, Ludendorff was packed and on his way, first to an audience with the kaiser and from there by train to the east.

What went through Ludendorff's mind as he sat in his private coach is unknown. His memoirs are spare in colour, being, like their author, direct, plain and to the point. He was not a complicated or a reflective man. His entire attitude towards life was aptly summarized in his remark that 'all I stand for is authority and order'. His path, as he also frequently observed, was nothing if not 'straight'. A pathological worker, Ludendorff proved the master of detail, the epitome of drive, the cliché of a merciless, single-minded Prussian officer to whom the pursuit of personal reward was a mere afterthought in comparison to the greater glory of kaiser and Germany. No comparable figure in any army, any war or any epoch so wholeheartedly sank himself with such unrelenting concentration into his work as did Ludendorff. In the end he emerged from the four years of war in a kind of shell shock, utterly devoured, a wreck of nerves, the victim of what von Hindenburg himself called his 'ruthless energy'. It is probably with some confidence, then, that we can assume what Ludendorff was thinking on that train. He was thinking, in a clinical sort of way, just how to annihilate as many Russians as possible.

One necessity of army protocol remained before Ludendorff assumed his new duties. At 4 a.m. on the morning of 23 August, his command express consisting of three cars stopped at the Hanover station. Standing on the platform, dressed in the outmoded blues of a Prussian general and unable to tightly clasp his formal collar on account of a bulging neckline, was von Hindenburg with his wife. Eleven hours before he had been just another retired officer, a man whose climb through the ranks had been steady if unspectacular, whose decorations, in the none-too-charitable assessment of a contemporary observer, had been the 'minimum consistent with his rank'. When war began, he had written letters to old friends still in the army, obsequious pleas not to be forgotten, but he had abandoned hopes of any further employment. His routine seldom varied, his meals never so: ten hours of sleep every night; mornings in his apartment; a short daily walk; afternoons at the Linden café drinking beer 'with the gravity of a hippopotamus'. No one was more shocked by his recall than he, but his reply to the summons was resolute – 'I am ready'.

How von Hindenburg received command of the Eighth Army was chance and little else, a decision that caused no one at headquarters undue amounts of thought. Ludendorff was the key element, the man entrusted with responsibility and worry, the 'robot Napoleon' (in Liddell Hart's phrase) who was to seize control of the Prussian situation and redeem it. What the brash and impolitic Ludendorff required was a figurehead of some respectability to give authority to whatever orders Ludendorff deemed necessary. Von Hindenburg was merely a name on the list, a figure of age, lineage and the required deportment. As the train left Hanover, Ludendorff briefed von Hindenburg on the general situation, outlined the remedy and went to bed. Von Hindenburg's value was not at first sufficiently appreciated.

Proceeding east, the train stopped in Berlin to pick up another passenger, Ludendorff's wife, who accompanied her husband for several hours before being dropped off at a later stop before the battlefield. She found Hindenburg a sweet old gentleman, 'calm and almost cheerful', in contrast to her husband, who was immersed in his own thoughts, not a very personable companion in the private dining car. 'There was a time when he could be cheerful', she wrote in her memoirs later. 'His features did not always wear that look of unbending obstinacy, the expression of a man whose feelings had turned to ice.' Looking out the window, she noted endless lines of military troop trains and motorized convoys, heading to the front, all 'decked with flowers'.

Arriving in Marienburg on 23 August, the two generals found that Colonel Hoffmann's dispositions were already set in motion, with neatly scheduled trains hauling all the scattered elements of the Eighth Army, save two corps, southwards to face Samsonov and his Russian forces heading up from Warsaw. In just forty hours, for example, General Hermann von François's I Corps, later to play a key role in the coming battle, would be dropped quite precisely on the right wing of Ludendorff's force. Some troops marched only three miles from their depots to the front lines.

In contrast, Russian soldiers of the Second Army were shambling forward with only the vaguest notion of where they were or where they were going. What they did know was hunger and fatigue. The Russian mobilization had been haphazard and chaotic, Tsar Nicholas and his uncle, the commander in chief, Grand Duke Nicholas Nikolaevich, being anxious to fulfil their pledge to France and Britain that Russia would take the field immediately to create a second front. As a result, Samsonov's forces, in particular, were in disarray on their march to the Prussian border. The weather was hot, the Polish roads sandy, rutted and difficult to traverse, the bread ovens far behind, and their orders contradictory and often inappropriate to immediate circumstances. Once on or near the battlefield, units were sometimes marched all day in one direction and, come evening, commanded to turn around and tramp back the way they had come. Officers were irresolute or unaware of the general tactical plan, other than a vague notion that they should advance. It was their universal expectation that they would soon encounter and mop up the desiccated remnants of the Prussian field army that Rennenkampf had so proudly announced he had routed some days before. They were to a man ignorant of the German forces being arrayed against them.

The allied equivalent to Hoffmann's diary is that of Major Alfred Knox, the British military attaché assigned to the Russian high command. Knox was a breezy fellow, a typical British officer of the period: addicted to the hunt, full of admiration for 'good chaps' hither and yon, a lover of wine and port, an eager photographer who snapped away at peasants and princes alike, a rumpled figure, his pockets bulging with scraps of paper and notes to himself. He also had an eye for terrain. In 1911 he had bicycled from Warsaw all the way to Königsberg, a 'staff ride' of sorts, and understood that, although Prussia was not strategically important in and of itself, the province certainly represented a 'delicate spot' in the German psychological armour. He was delighted with the Russian plan to take it.

Knox was a professional traveller and managed, in his usual insouciant fashion, to secure a berth on the last pre-war train from Berlin to Moscow. Russians on board reserved comment until they had crossed the border between the two countries, whereupon the conversations became animated about 'those pigs of Germans'. Knox eventually made his way to the grand duke's railway command car somewhere in Poland, commenting in approval on its cuisine ('We lunch at 12:30 – three courses – and dine at 7:30: soup, joint, and sweet, a glass of vodka, claret or Madeira, and a glass of cognac with our coffee'). Nicholas granted Knox's request to join General Samsonov at the front, more than delighted, perhaps, to rid himself of this determinedly cheerful Englishman. Knox noted the ragged villages through which he passed, 'dirty and dusty, the streets swarming with Jews', and jotted down the prophetic remark of a despondent Russian recruit – 'They say it is a wide road that leads to war and only a narrow path that leads home again.'

The attaché reached General Samsonov on 24 August, his headquarters still being in Russian Poland. The general struck Knox as a fine fellow, 'of a simple, kindly nature', yet possibly over his head in this command. Knox nonchalantly observed that neither Samsonov or Rennenkampf had ever commanded forces larger than a division, the implication being that their understanding was necessarily no broader than what they saw in front of them.

The vision at Marienburg was decidedly more expansive, though it is now impossible to say in whose mind the idea of manoeuvring a full-scale envelopment of the enemy had originated. Quite possibly it was a collective notion, a process in keeping with the general staff tradition of orchestral management, wherein disparate elements or talents blend towards the same solution, although occasional soloists might take the lead. Uniting them all, as students of von Schlieffen, was the notion of Cannae, transferring its lessons to a modern battlefield hundreds of miles large and encompassing numbers of combatants that Hannibal, for one, could never have imagined: give way in the centre but do not break, send stronger forces around the flank of your enemy and, in effect, overwhelm him with superior might at a point of weakness. A double envelopment, if possible, would bring even greater profit; that is, send out two flanking forces that could meet at the enemy's rear, thereby surrounding your opponent. Ludendorff, Hoffmann, François and Hindenburg all saw that exact possibility in southern Prussia, though, as

Solzhenitsyn remarked years later, 'the task of convincing history that *he* had thought it first still lay ahead'.

The disquieting element to their plan, however, was Rennenkampf. If the Russian First Army sensed that the enemy had decamped from its front, the road into East Prussia lay clear and open. A resolute commander could burst through to support Samsonov by taking the Germans from the rear. With superior manpower, it lay well within the Russians' ability to crush the Eighth Army, and nothing would then lie between a ransacking horde of Slavs and the capital city of Berlin. On the evening of the twenty-fourth, during dinner, Ludendorff quailed at this possibility and questioned the disposition of his battle plan, some of which was already in motion. Hoffmann, a heavy drinker who never had qualms about anything, was aghast at these remarks. Was yet another general officer about to lose his nerve? It was here that von Hindenburg won the Battle of Tannenberg.

No one witnessed the conversation between Ludendorff and Hindenburg which took place outside the officers' mess that evening, neither man giving details in his respective memoir, but its broadest tenor is clear. Von Hindenburg, the old bear, in a few minutes of honest, quiet, deliberative counsel, calmed the excitable Ludendorff with a show of stoicism and fortitude, a 'trust in yourself and the Almighty' kind of performance: Ludendorff had done his best, the execution of his orders was under way, so let the matter take its course. Hindenburg would accept responsibility in case of failure. The next day, intercepted wireless messages sent in the clear between the Russian commands ('quite incomprehensible thoughtlessness', according to Hoffmann) showed that the gamble could work, as Rennenkampf was advancing too slowly to influence the outcome of battle in the south. Ludendorff immediately ordered the second enveloping wing, hitherto in a holding pattern in front of Rennenkampf, to head by forced march to the new battlefield. Samsonov's doom was seriously in motion.

In broadest terms, the German plan was to entice Samsonov forward into what Solzhenitsyn would later term 'the wolf pit'. At the very moment that the Russian general was trading toasts with Major Knox, the centre of his army was already engaged with the German centre, XX Corps, near the village of Orlau on a front of about ten miles long. It is interesting to note that XX Corps contained units of the *Landwehr*, or reservists, older men not previously considered to be first-line troops. But XX Corps was an East Prussian regiment. These soldiers were truly fighting to save home and hearth, and thus they unwaveringly accepted the sacrificial nature of their task, for XX Corps was to be the 'anvil' the Russian army would repeatedly be lured into striking. It might bend, but it must not break. In a series of sharp contests, the XX Corps absorbed a rain of blows and frequently came close to collapse, yet it managed, over the course of the battle, to realign its formations in such a way that Samsonov, still far to the rear, remained assured that the Germans were fleeing in some disorder.

In fact, with each localized victory and marginal advance, the Russians' centre was sliding farther toward destruction. On 25 August, Ludendorff's noose began to tighten, aided immeasurably by the steady stream of intercepted Russian messages that indicated little change in the enemy's intent. Hindenburg was sufficiently confident that he retired to bed at an early hour. 'We can sleep soundly tonight', he said to Ludendorff, a man to whom rest was anathema.

Over the next three days, a Cannae, the likes of which the deceased von Schlieffen had designed for the western front, played itself out in the east. Though Ludendorff faltered on one or two occasions, the resourcefulness (and often insubordination) of his generals, in particular the aggressive von François, put all the finishing touches on what became a rout. Although the Russian centre performed heroically, its right and left wings were summarily shattered and reduced to ineffectiveness, separated corps acting independently of one another in the absence of both communications equipment and any knowledgeable direction from Samsonov, who initially had no idea as to the seriousness of his position. Knox recorded in his diary that 'things have developed rapidly', but it was not until the 27th that he observed the onset of 'nerves'. By then the Russian right had already dissolved, with the left about to, their commanders disgraced and fleeing helter-skelter for the border. Samsonov, out of touch, had only just entered Germany. Already he was receiving messages from headquarters that his lack of forward progress had been deemed 'cowardly', but on the very next day he suddenly realized that the battle was as good as over.

Knox caught up with Samsonov in fields north of Neidenburg. He found him 'sitting on the ground poring over maps and surrounded with his staff. I stood aside. Suddenly he stood up and ordered eight of the Cossacks who were with us to dismount and give up their animals. I prepared to go off too, but he beckoned to me and took me aside. He said that he considered it his duty to tell me that the position was very critical. His place and duty was with the army, but he advised me to return while there was still time'. Samsonov then broke off all contact with his superiors and rode northwards into the hopeless battle and oblivion.

Tonight I am driving the lonely road from Neidenburg to Willenberg, enjoying a panorama little changed from those days in 1914. The usual avenue of ancient trees lined up on either side of the road heads due east. Farm fields spread in parallel strips 200–300 yards off to either side, boxed in by stands of pine through which dirt tracks criss-cross. In this morass of wood, fragments of the Russian Second Army thrashed about seeking escape. Units that still had officers generally followed compass readings south, while stragglers or bands of common soldiers fled wherever the sounds of gunfire seemed least appalling. The general retreat was therefore aimed for this road.

The two corps detached from Rennenkampf's front had done their work, wrecking the Russian right flank and closing in from the north-east. Von François, after dispensing with the Russian left and in direct disobedience of Ludendorff, who had ordered him to stop, plunged eastwards towards Willenberg to close off the cordon. Ludendorff realized his mistake and later sanctioned this move. Von François emphasized speed to his men, many of whom travelled on bicycles. At intervals along the narrow road, detachments peeled off to take up firing positions towards the forest. On 29 August, the Russians began to emerge.

This was the glorious finale for German arms but little more than slaughter for the dispirited Russians, who found themselves cut down in the killing zone between forest and road. From my vantage-point near Muschaken, where I camp for the evening, my sight line is unrestricted. Groups attempting a breakout fell back on fresh stragglers trying themselves to push forward, resulting in a dreadful mayhem throughout the tangled undergrowth. The final, semi-organized attempt to escape encirclement occurred exactly here. German soldiers saw an Orthodox priest come out of the woods holding a crucifix. Behind him several hundred starving Russians, many of whom had not eaten so much as a crust of bread in the last five days, charged with fixed bayonets. Not a single one made it through the German line. Von Hindenburg referred to this final episode as 'the harvest'.

Knox heard about Samsonov's fate several days later. The befuddled general had gone to the centre to take personal command, but there was little he could do. Despair and fatherly concern for his poor recruits, the men of the army, racked his soul. 'How can I face the tsar?' he was overheard saying. When Knox reached Russian Poland on 1 September, he asked an officer to direct him to Samsonov. 'He shook his head, and as I pressed for a reply, he drew his hand significantly across his throat.' Samsonov, on foot with his staff, lost in the great wilderness of forest, had shot himself in the head. 'This is a disaster', Knox wrote in his diary. 'The Russians are just great big-hearted children who had thought out nothing and had stumbled half-asleep into a wasp's nest'. The Germans, by contrast, had thought of everything. As night fell, searchlights were brought up and splayed across the landscape. They did not want anyone to escape.

No more authoritative military victory could have been achieved, and even von Hindenburg and Ludendorff were overwhelmed at its immensity. To have accomplished the utter ruination of such enormous forces on a fluid battlefield in modern times may have been theoretically feasible, but it was a hardly anticipated outcome. Yet the Germans had prisoners and spoils to prove it: over 125,000 captives and untold thousands dead and rotting in fields and woods. It took weeks for the methodical victors to scour the forests for all the booty left behind, and the final tally amounted to some 500 artillery pieces.

In Allenstein, von Hindenburg and Ludendorff went to church. When the Russians had entered this small town just a few days earlier, they had in their naiveté thought they had captured Berlin. Most of those men were now dead. Von Hindenburg found himself overwhelmed with emotion. In the shadow of the red brick castle built by his revered Teutonic Knights, he piously gave thanks for the victory. Ludendorff knelt beside him and went through the motions of prayer, but his thoughts were elsewhere. Already formulating in his mind were plans of action against Rennenkampf.

One could reasonably expect in driving about the countryside to find some indication that a battle so famous in the annals of war had taken place here, but such is not the case. The great Hindenburg mausoleum is gone, as one would expect, and so too is nearly every trace of battle. Unlike a Ypres or a Verdun, the landscape is devoid of memorials or remembrance. Taking a chance in the village of Willenberg, I approach a group of Polish officers standing by the roadside, in charge of a convoy with twelve enormous tanks that are being trucked to who knows where. They strike extremely noble poses in their handsome uniforms and distinctive caps, known in Polish as *rogatywka*. Two of these gentlemen speak some French, and I ask if the grave of General Samsonov has ever been formally located in the wilderness or marked by any memorial or commemorative stone. They have no idea who Samsonov was and in fact are ignorant of the battle itself. 'There were so many fightings here, so many campaigns', one said, 'but they have nothing to say to us.' As I go back to my car, each of the officers gives me a very smart salute.

Despite the enormity of its success, the Battle of Tannenberg, as it came to be called (in revenge for the famous drubbing German knights had received 500 years before by Poles on these very grounds), resulted in no lasting influence over the course of the war, and in one respect may have negatively affected German fortunes. Von Moltke, impressed by the kaiser's fury that Prussian soil had been violated and responding to reports of terrified civilians fleeing en masse from the province, diverted two entire corps and a cavalry division from the von Schlieffen right flank then wheeling into France and entrained them to reinforce Ludendorff in Prussia. These troops failed to reach the battlefield in time and thus assisted neither front. Military historians have long debated whether the French recovery at the Marne (5–12 September), which in effect destroyed the German effort for a short, knockout war, could ever have succeeded had these troops remained in line. A French officer called this error 'our salvation'.

Tannenberg did, however, save Prussia, and Ludendorff's immediate follow-up against the enemy's First Army proved another humiliation for Russian arms, its commander, Rennenkampf, so unnerved that he jumped into a staff car and fled from the field of battle. Foreign attachés at Nicholas Nikolaevich's railway command car behind the lines commiserated on these dreadful losses. He famously replied, in French, 'We are happy to have made these sacrifices for our allies', wherein lie the seeds of the bolshevik revolution.

Ludendorff and von Hindenburg continued to inflict enormous suffering on the various Russian armies that would oppose them over the next two years. Gigantic battles raged through East Prussia and then farther afield in Galicia and Poland, campaigns about which most Western readers know very little, their attention more focused on the Somme, Ypres, Passchendaele and Verdun. But to Germans, the dual focus was a genetic trait, warfare in the east a logical extension of so much bitter history and too much racial animosity. 'Will any German now, as then, suffer the Latvian, and more especially the Pole, to take advantage and do us violence?' wrote Ludendorff. 'Are centuries of German culture to be lost?'

And yet German victories could not eliminate Russia from the war, no more so than the single Battle of Tannenberg, though a dreadful battering, could prevent the tsar from fielding another assemblage of ill-equipped and ill-trained peasant armies, and another and another after that when necessary. Ludendorff's great sweeps, envelopments and pincers shamed them, but no defeat or even series of defeats brought cries for surrender. A partial explanation lay with Austria's performance as Germany's ally, Ludendorff himself ruing the day that ever made him dependent on such 'a corpse'. And, of course, Germany's resources were wearing thin, the eastern front at one time stretching from the Baltic city of Riga in Courland all the way south to the Black Sea, though still secondary in terms of men and material to the cauldrons of trench warfare that raged from the North Sea to Switzerland.

In August 1916, with stalemate everywhere, the eastern commanders were brought west, thereby initiating Ludendorff's reign as virtual dictator of Germany. It had been the hope of the general staff that this by now legendary team could somehow transfuse their penchant for mobility into the stagnant morass of stationary warfare in which the western front was mired. This 'ironmongery', as one German officer put it, was an affront to what many men considered to be the 'art' of war. Mobility, however, required a breakthrough, and by that time the front was a churned-up sea of mud and fortified lines, a ground fought over so many times that it lacked any features. None of Ludendorff's subsequent offences achieved the desired Tannenbergian result. No armies were enveloped from the rear, no blow, however strong, brought enemy proposals for an armistice. Ludendorff, dulled by relentless strain, grew to rely on strength in numbers. Whereas at Tannenberg he had 500 artillery pieces at his disposal, his last great push, Operation Michael, had 6,000 guns on the firing line. Whatever subtlety he had once possessed was gone for ever. When asked about the strategic logic that lay behind Operation Michael, he brusquely replied, 'I forbid myself to use the word "strategy". We chop a hole. The rest follows.'

Chapter 7

Gallipoli: The Sideshow

'The most damnable folly that ever amateurs were enticed into.'
Lieutenant-General Sir George Macmunn, 1930

The approach as one flies into Istanbul's Atatürk Airport is an eye-opener. So many famous deep-water ports in the world are disappointing today, empty of the great passenger ships and steamers young and old that so glamourized the notion of going to sea. A modern Joseph Conrad might find the romance decidedly lacking if he were to sail into a New York or Halifax or England's Portsmouth Harbour. The life, in a maritime sense at any rate, seems to have leeched away entirely. But Constantinople is different. The roadstead leading from the Sea of Marmara to the Bosphorus is a logjam of shipping, dozens upon dozens of ships lined up at anchor waiting for their turn to head in, an enormous panorama as viewed from a descending plane. The skyline is a forest of silhouettes, from cruise ships to ungainly freighters piled high with cargo containers, many from the Far East, interspersed with an amazing collection of tramps, generally covered with rust, flying flags from places I hardly recognize and crews from all corners of the earth. You can call the Bosphorus many things – pipeline, conduit, highway, gateway – but the adjective that seems most pertinent is busy. This stretch of water connects the Black Sea in the north to the Aegean Sea in the south, flowing in a fast surface current through the Bosphorus into the Sea of Marmara and, after that, thirty-eight miles through another choke point known as the Dardanelles straits. On one shoreline lies Europe, on the other Asia, the great divide of cultures, religions, peoples and languages so complex as to defy easy comprehension. To cross from one to the other, as heroes have done for centuries, is often to leave one world behind and step into the gauze of the unknown, enshrouded in myth, rumour and, oftentimes, danger. Alexander the Great never came back, and he is only one of many.

Churchill

Most mottoes – high-sounding expressions of fidelity, allegiance and virtue – are often thoroughly distorted by many deviations from the straight and narrow that the histories of allegedly noble families on whose arms they are emblazoned reveal. Winston Leonard Spencer Churchill, born on 30 November 1874 in the ducal mansion of Blenheim Palace, which he visited innumerable times during the many years of his gilded youth, was surrounded by the blurriness of grandeur that, on closer examination, often displayed corrosive blemishes of greed, ambition, duplicity and behaviour regarded by many as treacherous and more worthy of the executioner's axe than public gratitude and financial reward (Blenheim, largely built at public expense between 1705 and 1724, cost more than £300,000). How many times did the young boy assemble his sizable collection of lead soldiers to replicate the tactics of the great Duke of Marlborough, his illustrious ancestor, who had outmanoeuvred the French at the Battle of Blenheim in 1704? How many times did he spend contemplating the spectacular (and garish) tomb of that great general who, along with his celebrated wife Sarah, are buried in the mansion's chapel? How often did he pore over history books which detailed the many diverse twists in fortune that bedevilled the duke's enormously complicated career, and debated not when, but how often, Marlborough contemplated treason against his king or queen of the moment? (Enough times, need it be said, that Winston put his oar into the stream himself beginning in 1933, writing a magisterial four-volume work, *Marlborough: His Life and Times. Faithful but Unfortunate* could just as easily have read, *Unfaithful and, luckily, Very Fortunate*.[1]

It is certainly too much a strain to hold people's conduct over lengthy careers strictly to the letter of high-minded slogans. The Duke of Marlborough was a man of his times, as slippery as the shifting winds of political allegiances allowed during an era of mind-numbing turmoil, much of it generated by religious strife that contributed directly to dynastic and geographical confusion. The political arena in and of itself demands attention to one's own ambitions; very rarely in public life can behaviour be separated from personal motivations. The desire to do good deeds for peoples, nations or sovereigns is generally a byproduct of doing good deeds for oneself. As such, Winston Churchill was probably no different from anyone else inhabiting his genealogical tree (certainly true in the case of his father, an equally celebrated, and often scorned, political figure). Winston too saw himself as a faithful servant to crown and country, even though his enemies, and there were many, accused him of faithlessness throughout his lengthy career in British politics. He also saw himself as deeply 'unfortunate' during several depressions in his career, when in fact he was probably the recipient of more abundant luck than most of his contemporaries. Few had been placed with more good precedents for success than he; few had more influential patrons and easy access to important people, especially in the beginnings of his career, than he; and few of his contemporaries had the talent, drive and intense desire to succeed as did he. Not just to achieve a position, a sinecure or wealth, but to achieve greatness (to which he aspired above all else). Churchill, along with Stalin, Hitler and Roosevelt, would prove to be the towering personalities of the twentieth century, despite their collective disappearance from the scene by the 1950s. Can there be any doubt that Churchill was the most attractive personality of the Big Four?

Churchill's enshrinement as an indisputably great man of history was certainly late in coming. He was sixty-five when World War II commenced, a man with a chequered past and dubious reputation that five years at the helm of an embattled Britain from 1940 to 1945 has largely obscured. Few casual observers realize that Churchill's career was considered largely finished in 1938. Too old, too dated and altogether too bloodthirsty. His entry to 10 Downing Street on 10 May 1940, the fulfilment of all his political desires, came far later than he ever expected. He had, in fact, given up hope many years before, though his thirst for the position never slackened.

Churchill's father, Randolph, a political figure of great ability and promise, was a template he both idolized and copied and, in many ways, their careers (and what people said about them both) were at first eerily similar. Randolph was criticized on more than one occasion for being 'wayward and headstrong' (as would his son), and Lord Salisbury, prime minster on three occasions, complained that the elder Churchill, a member of his cabinet, seemed always to be fiddling away at one tune or another while Salisbury and everyone else wished to play something different. The same was said about Winston throughout his early years in parliament and governmental office. Both Churchills were noted for irreverence to party ideology, a lack of loyalty to political superiors and/or mentors and their obsessive propensity for keeping a sharp eye out for the main chance.

Churchill's education was spotty. Sent to Harrow, a famous public school, he performed poorly in academics, was scolded for boisterous behaviour and presented a generally sloppy figure in dress and deportment. Team sports were never for him; he preferred solo pursuits such as fencing and riding where the spotlight would never wander to anyone else. Unlike his father, who went to Oxford, Winston was shunted off to Sandhurst, a military academy, which he struggled to enter because of difficulties with entrance exams. His father despaired, as did the son, who always regretted the lack of an Oxford education. An army career at this point in the late nineteenth century was not considered to be a particularly attractive destination for people with a brain in their head. The opportunity for military glory as an avenue for advancement remained alluring, however, though there had not been a major war for the army to fight since the Crimean adventure of 1854. Luckily for Winston, a series of spats presented themselves, of which he took full advantage: the Sudanese campaign of 1898, where he participated in the last great formal cavalry charge in British history at the battle of Omdurman (this attack, as it turned out, had no major impact on the outcome of the fray, though Churchill drew his first blood, killing three tribesmen with his pistol; and the Boer War, where he was captured and then escaped, a feat that made him famous back home). Although Churchill loved military life with all its paraphernalia, pomp and spectacle – he always had 'a genius for war', as one observer put it – he was mature enough to realize that true power lay in the hands of those who ordered generals when and where to fight, in other words, the political arena. While seduced and distracted on many occasions by the sudden excitement of action, he said on more than one occasion that the House of Commons would be his true testing ground and battlefield.

By the start of the Great War, Churchill had over a full decade of parliamentary experience behind him, and the award of several departments over which he had presided with customary vigour. In 1911, he held the most important of his career to date, placed in charge of the Admiralty. In his hands lay real authority, responsibility for the fleet, upon which Britain's true strength historically resided. The country was not a land power per se; its far-reaching empire depended on superiority at sea. In 1914, Britain's army numbered but 100,000 men, while its navy encompassed nearly five hundred capital vessels and more sailors than it could employ at sea.[2] 'The British Navy is to us a necessity', he said in a speech in Glasgow, whereas 'the German Navy is to them more in the nature of a luxury.... It is the British Navy which makes Great Britain a great power. But Germany was a great power, respected and honoured all over the world, before she had a single ship.' With the war, and all the alarums that came with it, his days became, as Churchill wrote his brother, 'an unbroken succession of events & decisions'. And later, 'This is what I live for'. Margot Asquith, seated next to him at a dinner party in January 1915, recorded the following exclamations: 'My God! This is living history. Everything we are doing and saying is thrilling. It will be read by 1000 generations – think of <u>that</u>!! Why, I would not be out of this glorious, delicious war for anything the world could give me (Eyes glowing, but with slight anxiety lest the word "delicious" should jar on me). 'I say, don't repeat that I said the word "<u>delicious</u>" – you know what I mean'. Winston was only thirty-nine years of age, the youngest and most vital member of Herbert Asquith's cabinet, or so his wife Clementine thought. He was also, according to Asquith, by 'far the most disliked'.

The dichotomy of Churchill's character was a trademark of the hot-and-cold attitude with which many of his contemporaries regarded him. No one denied his talent, drive or fertile imagination, but many deprecated the seeming haste and arrogance of his many opinions, most of which were launched with the intensity of biblical certitude on often unwilling recipients. Many disparaged the notion of ever having a conversation with Winston; they were 'monologues' wherein divergent views were utterly disregarded. Churchill never hesitated to lecture his associates, none of whom he considered to be his equal. He had 'what someone said of genius – "a zigzag streak of lightning in his brain," ' as Asquith put it, which could produce spectacular effects intended to dazzle and convince. But was it ever 'wisdom'? Some thought he had only 'a noisy mind', and had become as erratic a figure as his father, whose career had fizzled out in pathetic fashion after an abrupt and ill-timed resignation from government position in 1886.[3]

Rhetoric

'Although we hope the navy will have a chance of settling the question of the German fleet, if they do not come out and fight in time of war, they will be dug out like rats in a hole.'

Churchill, to great applause, at a rally, 21 September 1914

While always deeply reverential to the British royal family, many of whom he individually disparaged, and as firmly ensconced as he was into the fabric of the landed gentry (with all its virtues and vices), Churchill was always his own man.[4] His speeches at rallies and political gatherings often excoriated the principles his own extended family felt dearest to heart, and many of his statements and proposals could prove deeply antagonistic to people he certainly did not wish to offend. Some slights and insults were unintended; he should have known better. In 1911 he recommended to Edward VII that a new battleship be christened the *Cromwell*, a man best known for cutting off the head of Charles I, an indiscretion to sovereign sensibilities if there ever was one. But other offences were largely the result of his own enthusiasms, which often got the better of him. Naval officers (indeed, the king himself) were infuriated at Winston's 'rats in a hole' allusion. Aside from being bombastic and not the language suitable for a king's minister, it inappropriately raised the expectation around the country that if the first lord's underlings did not enter the hornet's nest at once to ferret out the German Imperial fleet (an action clearly suicidal), the British navy would somehow have failed in its duty out of simple cowardice. The fact remains, however, that the 15,000 people who attended the speech in question howled with pleasure. Churchill knew how to get people's blood up, and he usually relished the opportunity to deliver speeches of 'tremendous voltage'.

Churchill's oratorical mannerisms, often dubbed 'high Victorian', were standard fare in late nineteenth- and early twentieth-century parliamentary debate. Many intelligent men, such as Disraeli and Gladstone, mastered the form, others debased it as they wallowed in portentous or imperial sentimentality more Gothic than circumstances usually demanded. All could agree, however, that Winston Churchill was a master of its form and delivery, perfected in the House of Commons where he made over 2,300 speeches, a record that will never be broken. On moments of high occasion, he could rally men to his standard who, in other instances, would never rise to the bait; in the maelstrom of his long parliamentary life, few ever could question the ferocity of his interests. As a generalization, it can be said that he seldom trimmed sails to accommodate the coming or going of fashion in idiom or expression. This rigidity proved costly at times. Churchill was a serious student of formal delivery, and generally spent days and weeks preparing his speeches. Like that other great speaker of the twentieth century, Adolf Hitler, he often practised for hours, in front of a mirror, perfecting the craft. This led to a certain inflexibility on his part, a refusal to alter content in the face of spontaneous reactions or evolving circumstances regarding whatever issue he was addressing. This often blunted his effectiveness, and led critics to think of him as doctrinaire, unyielding and stubborn. His greatest weapon, though recognized as formidable, could be dismissed by a contemporary as 'powerful but not very mobile artillery'.

At the height of his early career, in 1914 and 1915, his style was often the subject of considerable critique. It embodied, as the historian David Cannadine suggested, the Victorian characteristics of 'abundance, confidence and ostentation'. But as his fortunes later waned, his star in decline, whatever brilliance of speech that he could produce had more of a melancholy impact upon his listeners, such obvious talent falling helplessly on deaf ears. As he himself so often lamented, his abode in the wilderness of the 1930s produced comparisons with biblical outcasts wailing in the desert (compelling but, in effect, background noise, his stridency seeming old-fashioned and obsolete). The Second World War re-established the primacy of his tone and vigorous rhetoric; just the thing for reviving tired souls. But the minute the guns went silent, so too did receptivity for his evangelical style of 'sham-Augustan' grandeur. Britain became ordinary, as did the spoken word. It had no need for a man of the last century and his flourishes, which took on the *faux* characteristics of (in the words of one critic), 'St. Patrick's Cathedral on Fifth Avenue'. [5]

During the first months of the Great War, Churchill was called upon on several occasions to justify his conduct at the Admiralty. Although the Royal Navy was prepared for this war, in many ways due to Churchill's vigilance, several embarrassing lapses and losses had at times stunned the general public and demoralized his departmental officials. Churchill's own exuberance had also, on more occasions than was considered permissible, led him far beyond the stated duties of his office. 'No one department, hardly one war, was enough for him', as a friend was to say. In October 1914, with Belgium teetering, the defence of Antwerp was suddenly deemed critical, and Churchill set off on mostly his own initiative to survey the situation and report back to London. Once there, he impetuously took command of British forces in the city, and offered his resignation so as to remain in Antwerp to supervise its defence to, presumably, the very last man. This was yet another in a long line of injudicious conduct influenced more by the emotions of the moment than by common sense (both military and political). When Asquith presented Churchill's request to the assembled cabinet, he did so as a joke. Everyone laughed, but the unease was palpable.

As far as Churchill was concerned, his enthusiasm was justified. He saw confusion and incompetence all around him; men ill-suited to command, yet in command, men too old doing work that younger men were far more suited to attend. He sensed right from the beginning that things were going wrong, not just in the navy, but everywhere, and he applied every fibre of his being to initiate action, almost for its own sake if necessary. 'Winston is like a torpedo', Lloyd George said of his on-again, off-again-friend. 'The first you hear of his doings is when you hear the swish of the torpedo dashing through the water'. Memoranda flowed from his pen and often submerged the cabinet in deliberations for which their competence was questionable. Asquith was no generalissimo, nor was anyone else in the room, Kitchener included. Yet Churchill hammered away on pet projects: incursions to the

Baltic Sea, invasions and occupation of 'crucial' German islands, landings hither and yon to isolate and capture Berlin. Captain Herbert Richardson, attached to the Admiralty staff, would become a bitter critic of the first lord (at least in his diary). In September 1914 he noted that Churchill 'wanted to send battleships – old ones – up the Elbe; but for what purpose other than to be sunk I did not understand'. Later he would remark that, 'I really believe Churchill is not sane.' Nevertheless, after only three months of war, Churchill accurately sketched the future to anyone who would listen. The western front was now defined and ossified, one long line from the North Sea to the Swiss border, busily being fortified, entrenched and battered to pieces, a killing ground where the collective resources of all the combatants would be ground up in useless slaughter. Churchill's notion of romance and chivalry stood appalled at the prospect ahead, which he correctly defined as 'chewing barbed wire', and his restless mind sought some alternative that might both relieve pressure on the primary front and, at the same time, deal a crushing blow to the enemy. Much debate among historians has swirled about as to whose idea it actually was to focus on the Dardanelles, the long strait that connects the Mediterranean with the Sea of Marmara, and from there to that glittering prize of Constantinople and the Bosphorus, entry point to the Black Sea, and it seems the finger cannot be pointed exclusively at Churchill. But from his lifetime of reading the classics, with his continuous study of atlases and maps, and his imagination stirred by the Trojan War, Winston grabbed onto the idea as almost his own. That his career survived the debacle that followed represents one of the true miracles of his extraordinary life.[6]

The Turk

The notion of attacking on the eastern/Asian perimeter was attractive on many counts, some realistic, others fanciful. Certainly the condition of Russia was causing grave concern to the allied cause, the alleged colossus suffering one disaster after another. Perhaps the most consistent imperial desire from the corridors of St. Petersburg was widely known throughout the various European capitals: Constantinople. Russia and the Ottoman Empire had been traditional antagonists for centuries, their differences encompassing everything from religion (Orthodox versus Muslim) to commerce. Russia had no all-weather access to reach European and world markets. This was particularly important in peacetime with regard to her wheat exports, but became more urgent as war commenced.[7] While Churchill considered Russia 'unconquerable', its response to the demands of a truly modern European war had exposed grave deficiencies in every level of support. Not enough guns, not enough shells, not enough heavy artillery, not enough of anything but men. Britain alone supplied Russian forces with emergency supplies on industrial levels: over eight million hand grenades, 27,000 machine guns, one million rifles and, among other things, the extraordinary figure of three trillion rounds of ammunition. With the allegiances of the Turkish government at first unknown – which side would it support? – the strategic importance of the Black Sea passage to the Mediterranean and beyond grew ever more obvious. If Turkey closed the straits, Russian wheat would never reach its markets, and its balance of payments would collapse. Someone had to pay for that ammunition.

A manoeuvre guaranteeing the unrestricted passage of the Dardanelles would, in very important ways, bolster the Russian war effort, secure that nation's goodwill in return for their sacrifices already made and produce the first positive news for Russians to enjoy in some time. A sense of reciprocity existed in both Paris and London when it came to Russia, the sense that it was time to offer their ally a substantial boost. Russia not in the war was a notion no one wanted to even consider.

This conspicuously sensible thrust for a Dardanelles expedition was offset by chaotic thinking when it came to the Balkans, a sphere of action in which Churchill for one (and joined by Lloyd George) should have been wary. Churchill, in particular, easily glossed over the enormous complications this region presented, seemingly oblivious of the long history of Vienna's difficulties in this impossibly complicated political and geographical theatre. He seemed to think that a coalition of Christian Balkan states which would enter the war on the allied side presented a realistic possibility of success, especially when these obstreperous countries (particularly Greece, Romania and Bulgaria) saw the collapse of the Ottoman Turks right on their doorstep, which the Dardanelles venture would precipitate. While Churchill was certainly correct in assessing the greed that all these countries collectively possessed, he underestimated the racial and religious complexity of the region; nor did he correctly understand the venality of Balkan diplomacy. The idea of a wartime 'union' was a daydream. It might look agreeable on paper, or from a quick glance at a map, but the reality on the ground was torturous to a degree that he did not fully comprehend until later, when he lumped the entire Balkan quagmire, 'that devil's kitchen' in Asquith's phrase, as baggage to be avoided at all costs.

While many of these factors were debated at 10 Downing Street, one aspect of the equation was largely glossed over, namely that of the projected enemy. The Ottoman Empire, it was quickly agreed, was finished. All it needed was a nudge. T. E. Lawrence complained, after the fact naturally, that planners in London thought smashing Turkey would be 'a promenade'.

The great bugaboo of European liberals, aside from the tsar and his knout, was the sultan, usually portrayed as a fat lout surrounded by eunuchs and harem girls traipsing about the corridors of the Topkapi Palace, a den of iniquity in Constantinople overlooking the Bosphorus, and oblivious of everything except his pleasures and persecuting Christians. This was hardly an acceptable picture of the current caliph, Mehmed V, whose troubles were legion. He and his immediate forebears were witnessing the steady diminution of the once formidable Ottoman Empire; in fact, the appropriate metaphor was that of a dying beast, mortally wounded, surrounded by jackals feasting on extremities but focused, nonetheless, on the animal's entrails. At one time in history the Turks had threatened Vienna, and their kingdom's border had touched the Atlantic rim at Tangier, covering the entire northern coast of Africa. By 1914, they had been largely expelled from Europe, having lost nearly all their holdings in the Balkans, and Italy's invasion and consequent acquisition of Tripolitania (present-day Libya) was but the latest huge chunk of territory lost to their south (the most serious of which was Egypt which, after decades of instability, was placed under a British protectorate in the early days of the war). The Turks were surrounded by enemies: all the Balkan states were hostile, Russian avarice for control of the Dardanelles had never wavered, and faraway European powers such as France and Britain had envious eyes for the Middle East. One of Churchill's endeavours as first lord had been the conversion of the Royal Navy's propulsion fuel from coal to oil; this made sense only if easy access to oil fields was a secure option. Even the country's financial purse strings were tainted; Turkey's debts to western banks had forced the sultan to cede important tax-gathering powers to the Ottoman Bank, largely controlled by capital from London and Paris, a blow to Turkey's prestige that reminded many of an occupation by the medieval crusaders. Whenever a caliph of the moment felt particularly aggrieved, he could turn his urge for revenge on the Christian minorities in his kingdom (largely Armenians) on whom dreadful pogroms were unleashed which, with regard to world opinion, did the country little good.[8] As if all this was not bad enough news for anyone to digest, the sultan had closer problems to consider, such as his own life and safety.

Mehmed V was no longer the ruler of his own house. In a convoluted and constantly changing political environment, unfolding in what Churchill called the 'labyrinth of Turkish duplicity and intrigue', a cabal of younger army officers since known as the Young Turks, had wrested important strands of power from the sultanate's hands in 1908, leaving him in the ambiguous position of being a chief of state with no clear or delineated authority. When Mehmed clapped his hands, he might receive his dinner, but the amorphous nature of his army commanders (who was in charge, who controlled what, who had been replaced by whom in innumerable struggles for advantage) left him in a vacuum. He did not truly know with whom he had to deal; nor did, at many junctures, the revolving leadership cadre of the Young Turks themselves. General Liman von Sanders, the head of the German military legation, claimed that the ruling committee 'ever remained a mystery. I have never learned how many members it consisted of, or ... who the members were.'[9]

The vital question of what to do as the Great War began was typical of the confusion then rampant in Constantinople. Most officers seemed to favour strict neutrality; the weakness of Turkish forces, who had been mauled in the Balkans, marched to and fro through Africa, and, consequently riven by discontent in the ranks, seemed to favour a passive stance. But important individuals, whose motives were often unbeknownst to their colleagues, found themselves negotiating on their own with the representatives of warring powers, often committing their country to important concessions without consultation. The most powerful and conspiratorial Young Turk, Enver Pasha, signed a formal treaty with the German ambassador that came inches short of committing Turkey to the war; he did so without notifying anybody. Germany found itself invited to send additional military and naval advisers, which it did with alacrity, just as the British attaché, negotiating with others, felt he had a deal in place to deliver two modern, British-built battleships (built on the River Tyne by Armstrong Whitworth) to Constantinople. The left hand, in other words, had no idea what the right hand was doing.

Amidst no real insight as to what was going on in Constantinople (other than the fact that German military officers seemed to be everywhere), Asquith's cabinet, whenever its members deemed the subject worth discussing, spent most of their time analyzing potential spoils, resembling, in the prime minister's words, 'a gang of buccaneers': which favoured country would end up with this desired piece of territory, which would have that, and so on. It was predetermined that Turkey, in Asquith's words, was a 'carcass' there to be divided, hardly an unprecedented conversation within the foreign offices of various European capitals. Old decayed empires, whether Spanish, Portuguese, Chinese or Turkish, no longer served any function other than that of a desirable trophy. 'General euphoria' was the usual mood in such discussions; obstacles, difficulties, inconvenient details or a realistic appraisal of possible Turkish resilience were barely considered. The 'sick man of Europe' was there for the taking. 'The Dardanelles seems too good to be true', wrote one enthusiast.

> *'He will write his name big in our future,*
> *let us take care he does not write it in blood'.*
>
> A.G. Gardiner, *Pillars of Society* (1913), on Churchill

In 1916, desperate to clear his name, Churchill lobbied aggressively for an official inquiry into the Dardanelles operation, thinking it would vindicate the initiatives he had proposed and overseen. The final verdict, based on some but not all the appropriate documentation, generally offered a bland appraisal of what went wrong. One of its more damning judgments was that the entire enterprise was characterized by an 'atmosphere of vagueness and want of precision'. Churchill and all the others involved were certainly guilty of that.

With the western front already in stalemate, enthusiasm for a diversionary operation gained momentum among strategists already complaining that a 'fresh start' to the war was required. The issue in question was how to force passage through the Dardanelles straits, a key to the major goal of seizing Constantinople. Could the navy, guns blazing, run the straits unsupported by land forces? Could it neutralize the Turkish artillery emplacements located on both the European and Asian shores for a stretch of forty miles? Could it effectively sweep the channel of mines beforehand? Once in the Sea of Marmara, could it destroy two modern German cruisers that would certainly challenge it? If the fleet made it to Constantinople, could the threat of its 12"- and 15"-guns be enough to force a Turkish capitulation? All these were interrelated, run-on questions, and all depended on the very first: could the straits be rushed? Lord Salisbury was of the opinion that everyone thought the navy could do it, but added the slightly worrisome caveat, 'except the Admiralty'. George Joachim Goschen, a well-travelled British politician, scoffed at the notion. People who thought the Dardanelles was a simple cavalry charge 'know nothing of the defences'. The military attaché in the Turkish capital cabled that the navy might go it alone successfully, 'but to command situation properly at Dardanelles requires also the use of military force and point arises whether substantial enterprise should be attempted in quite a subsidiary theatre of war'. This warning was a reflection of controversies already brewing among army officers who considered any diversion of resources from the western front as tantamount to undermining the war effort. Killing Germans, they said, was more important than killing any other nationality. On 14 November, whether to kill Turks or not turned out to be a moot point. The sultan in Constantinople formally declared a *jihad*, or holy war, entering the conflict on Germany's side. Turkey, in the words of a British admiral who had been trying to argue the Young Turks into maintaining neutrality, sadly concluded that they had 'finally committed suicide'.

Turkey's unfortunate action opened the floodgates in London. Schemes for the Dardanelles were discussed, argued over and dismissed on a weekly basis. Military men were especially in a quandary; it seemed to many of them that amateur politicians were forcing an issue over which they themselves remained lukewarm. Lord Esher, courtier and confidant of many important figures both in and out of government, was particularly scornful of the cabinet. 'Every member has a different plan; it is like a game of ninepins; one plan is knocked over, and, in falling, knocks over the next one, and so on until the board is clear; the result is a total want of initiative of any kind.' Churchill played an active role in all these deliberations, convinced that a second front would make all the difference, particularly if he had a hand in its planning. At first he proposed a purely naval operation, but when souls more timid than he felt a back-up entity was required, meaning a major contribution by the already overextended army, he supported that as well. The important thing, in his opinion, was to launch the operation before German leadership, training and supplies had the chance to stiffen the resolve of Turkish forces, already the recipients of two disastrous military reversals (one involving an excursion into Russia, the other at the Suez Canal). He ran roughshod over all who disagreed with him, particularly the controversial, volatile and elderly John Fisher, whom Churchill had resurrected as first lord of the Admiralty in October 1914. Fisher's support of the mission was, alternately, encouraging, enthusiastic, wavering, 'a little uneasy', negative and volcanically pessimistic. At one point he was all in – whole hog, as he wrote, *totus porcus*; at another, he in effect abandoned his post as first lord and disappeared, all in protest to the criminal 'foolishness' he saw around him. Asquith ordered him to 'return to duty' but Fisher was essentially done in. The old admiral scolded Churchill, 'You are just eaten up with the Dardanelles and can't think of anything else! Damn the Dardanelles! They'll be our grave.'

Aside from men, munitions and all the energy wasted over this expedition, the most glaring loss was that of time. Time was wasted in prodigious quantities; nothing seemed synchronized or at all in gear. The navy finally arrived in the Aegean Sea during February 1915. In his breezy, self-assured way, Churchill had stressed the fact that the operation carried little threat of weakening the grand fleet itself, assembled at Scapa Flow in the Orkney Islands, ready to meet any sally by German battleships seeking to break out into open water. Only obsolete battleships were to be employed, vessels that the launching of the technologically advanced *Dreadnought* in 1906 had condemned to uselessness in the event of a real battle in the North Sea or the Atlantic. Churchill saw nothing wayward in that; if a few ships went to the bottom in Turkish waters, what was the harm? They were expendable, so long as the objective was achieved. 'Unavoidable losses must be accepted', he wrote to the admiral in charge, Sackville Carden. The only ship of real significance was the *Queen Elizabeth*, a super-dreadnought of 36,500 tons, launched in 1913, thrown in almost as an afterthought. This mighty firing platform – eight 15-inch guns – guaranteed in the minds of many that Turkish forts guarding the straits were doomed. The lessons of the early days of war, after all, had seen impregnable forts surrender almost from the moment they were first bombarded. What was there about Turkish masonry that would prove more durable?

The first significant salvos, fired on 19 February, were directed at gun emplacements protecting the entrance to the straits. These were launched from open water. Turkish defences had been placed under the command of General von Sanders, but he was uncertain where, when or even if the British would invade after this initial bombardment. On the Asiatic side of the straits were large, flat, farming plains, surrounding the fabled site of Troy. The alleged grave of Achilles looked straight out to sea at Carden's guns as they cruised by, firing broadsides. The European side was entirely different, a long peninsula forty miles long from its head (Bulair), to its Aegean tip (Cape Helles), its greatest width only fourteen miles (between Suvla Bay and Gallipoli, a small town overlooking the straits). It narrowed like a thumb as it stretched southwards, now also facing the British fleet. This was an entirely different landscape from its Asian counterpart: scrub and waste, for the most part, with few if any roads and barren of many habitations, villages or agricultural activity. A spine of hills, many steep and running off in various directions, intersected by ravines and gullies, overlooked the shorelines and beaches on either side of the finger. Tactically speaking, these dominated difficult terrain. Then Lieutenant-Colonel George Patton, who wrote a staff paper on the Gallipoli campaign in 1936, was impressed by the 'tremendously jumbled nature of the country, which seems to follow no geological formula in its construction, but has valleys and spurs running in all directions'. It

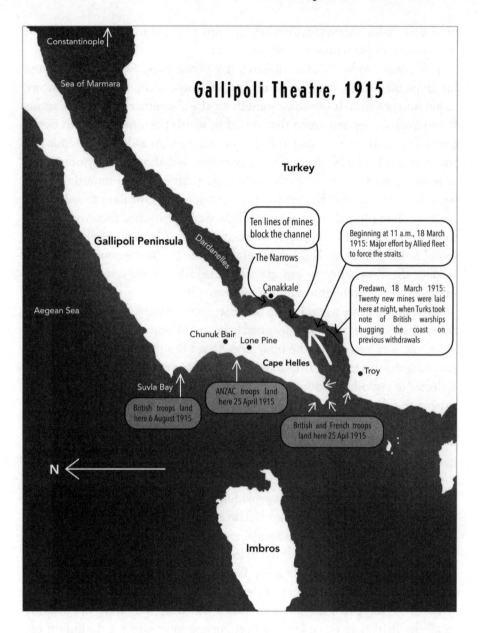

Gallipoli Theatre, 1915

Constantinople

Sea of Marmara

Turkey

Gallipoli Peninsula

Dardanelles

Ten lines of mines block the channel

The Narrows

Çanakkale

Beginning at 11 a.m., 18 March 1915: Major effort by Allied fleet to force the straits.

Predawn, 18 March 1915: Twenty new mines were laid here at night, when Turks took note of British warships hugging the coast on previous withdrawals

Aegean Sea

Chunuk Bair   Lone Pine

Cape Helles

Troy

Suvla Bay

ANZAC troops land here 25 April 1915

British troops land here 6 August 1915

British and French troops land here 25 April 1915

N

Imbros

seemed to him a place to avoid, a thought von Sanders shared. He was fairly certain that a projected allied invasion would land in Asia Minor, near Troy, and he distributed his land forces accordingly.

Carden's fleet of twenty-two major warships so enveloped the gun batteries on both sides of the mouth in smoke, flame and general destruction that Turkish gunners quickly abandoned their fixed positions. When small parties of scouts and marines landed on Cape Helles, for example, they found the place deserted. Carden, greatly relieved, wrote to London that he hoped to be in Constantinople within two weeks.

This proved to be wishful thinking. It was one thing for Carden to stand his ships offshore, out of range of Turkish guns, and pound every known target into oblivion. It would be something else altogether to enter the straits themselves, a confined arena that varied in width from four miles to barely over one, the latter at a spot called 'The Narrows', which Lord Byron had swum in 1811. The Narrows were heavily fortified, though many of its guns were antiquated or not of sufficiently large calibre, and ammunition levels were dangerously low (Krupp, the great patriot, was unwilling to ship more shells without immediate payment). These were established facts well known to the Admiralty, which excited the impatience of officers there when Carden found himself stymied. Neither he, nor anyone else, had seriously taken into account the less glamorous aspects of the Turkish defence system, namely its minefields, its searchlights and its mobile artillery.

Trouble first arose when British minesweepers attempted to enter and clear the straits, where nearly 400 mines had been set. Minesweeping was dangerous work; the idea was to cut the buoy lines to set the mines adrift. Flowing to sea along the surface on a five-knot current, these would be spotted and either collected or exploded. Working at night, the minesweeper crews, mostly civilian fishermen culled from trawlers all along the British coast, panicked when they found themselves lit up by searchlights from the shore, and then exposed to withering shrapnel and small arms fire. They hadn't signed up for this kind of mayhem. Support from the battlewagons was generally ineffective because the Turks moved their mobile field howitzers from place to place, never firing from the same spot, and thus not providing a fixed target. Carden could batter the forts at will, but he could not isolate and destroy roving Turkish artillery pieces. Churchill might have assured Carden that some losses were acceptable, but no British admiral ever wanted to lose a battleship, especially at the hands of something as mundane as a mine. Careers had been scuttled over less, and the admiral's resolution began to fade.[10]

Carden represented the dilemma that a widening war effort was creating in all the British services. He had been, over a long career, a dutiful officer, but approaching sixty years of age, he saw his final assignment, overseeing the repair dockyard on Malta, for what it was, the last step before hauling down his flag and drifting off into retirement. Being handed the command of the Dardanelles operation was probably the shock of his life; it certainly exceeded his abilities as a front-line commander. General William Birdwood, who did in fact distinguish himself during the coming campaign, dismissed him as 'very second-rate'.

With the mine-sweeping operations seemingly foiled, Carden had to deal with firebrands on his staff, particularly a young commodore, Roger Keyes, who would prove a problem for many elderly officers to come. Keyes was impatient, imperious, opinionated, rash and undeniably brave (foolishly so, in the opinion of some). A British general labelled him 'that desperado'. Calling for volunteers to replace the recalcitrant fishermen, he led the sweeping crews himself into repeated fierce hailstorms of lead, more or less futilely. His resolution, however, made Carden look like an old woman. With pressure mounting fiercely from London, this unfortunate admiral was faced with no options at all. He was to attack the Narrows no matter what, and a date was selected, 18 March. On 16 March, with two days to go, Carden essentially threw in the towel and collapsed, but not before managing to get a Harley Street physician to certify that he was unfit for service. Carden's retirement thereafter unfolded more or less on schedule.

John de Robeck, another undistinguished senior officer, now took command (David Beatty, one of the more flamboyant admirals in the Royal Navy, admitted that though de Robeck was 'a born leader of men', he 'was no genius'). At the very least, however, de Robeck maintained his nerve, and the attack commenced on schedule at 10:30 in the morning of the 18th, the objective being to reduce the established forts at the Narrows. These were punished, just as their predecessors had been at the mouth; since the British battleships remained out of their range, there was little they could do but absorb salvo after salvo. Mobile batteries along the straits unleashed a great deal of fire on the more or less stationary ships, but nothing powerful enough to do serious damage was inflicted. Later in the afternoon, however, when de Robeck ordered a flotilla of minesweepers to proceed ahead of the firing line to further clear the fleet's path, these secondary Turkish guns wreaked dreadful havoc on the defenceless small craft, which broke and ran for it. This was not a glorious sight for de Robeck, Keyes or anyone else with a knowledgeable eye to witness; in fact, the lapse was critical. The mines, more than anything else, were crippling the initiative, as the afternoon would prove.

To the uninitiated, the day seemed on the surface a brilliant success. The din of bombardment, unlike anything ever seen or heard in Mediterranean history, was an undeniable expression of British sea strength: irresistible, implacable, dominant and awe-inspiring. Sir Ian Hamilton, the commander of the British land units being slowly assembled on nearby Greek islands in case landings were deemed necessary, viewed the bombardment from a cruiser (unfortunately for Hamilton, he would find himself spending far too much time watching events unfold from the deck of ships, instead of seeing things for himself on the ground at first hand). He noted with satisfaction that that the Turks were 'very half-hearted' in their return fire ('frightfully keen to see the fun', he wrote in his diary). By nightfall his tune was a bit different.

Unbeknownst to anyone, a Turkish minelayer had set a string of twenty new mines parallel with the Asian shoreline, nine miles downstream from the Narrows. Supplies being as slim as they were, these may have been Russian mines indiscriminately released at the head of the Bosphorus several weeks before, aimed to float by Constantinople to disrupt Turkish shipping or – better – strike the two German warships anchored there. Many of these were netted by the Turkish navy and redeployed at the Dardanelles. A Turkish officer had noted how the British manoeuvred their ships as they entered, and left, the Straits, and under night's cover he had, with considerable ingenuity and foresight, laid this new line. Three of the twenty were subsequently discovered and detonated, but the mine sweeping capability of the British fleet had become so inchoate and demoralized, the concept of a whole new field was apparently not considered possible. Incredibly, four of the remaining seventeen mines would find a target, a stunning success rate that essentially scuppered the entire expedition.

At 1:54 in the afternoon, the French battleship *Bouvet* hit one of these mines and immediately exploded. In the space of about 130 seconds, it disappeared from sight. Almost 700 sailors went down to the bottom. This shocking sight was replicated in about two hours when the *Inflexible* hit another mine and immediately began listing. Three to five minutes later, the *Irresistible* was put out of action, and would later sink. The *Ocean*, rushing to aid *Irresistible*, would then meet the same fate. It was a gruesome thing to watch British sailors line up as ordered on the decks of their crippled ships, waiting helplessly for them to go under. Amazingly enough, less than a hundred of these men drowned. Hamilton's diary ended on a more sombre note than it had begun, 'a very bad day for us'. De Robeck viewed the situation in more personal terms: 'I suppose I am done for' he remarked to his staff. Even though he retained his command – was there anyone better available? – he did not retain any lingering affection for rushing the Dardanelles. A far better idea was to turn the whole thing over to the army ... or was it? Kitchener couldn't believe it. The navy had 'chucked up the sponge'.

'I am counting much in Hamilton.'

Churchill, 15 March 1915

Even before the disaster of 18 March, Churchill had been pressing the war minister, Lord Kitchener, to prepare for a land assault in support of the naval operation. As bad news filtered in from the battlefront, most of his cabinet colleagues supported such action. Kitchener, though generally agreeable, was hard-pressed (both organizationally and mentally) to undertake speedy action. He had a manpower issue on his hands, trying to assemble million-soldier armies for the western front, and he was never in the mood to be ordered about by civilians. Early spring saw few battle-tested regiments available. To be sure, raw recruits from Australia and New Zealand were being trained in Egypt and they could be released for duty in Turkey. After all, as Kitchener said disdainfully, they were good enough to cruise about the Sea of Marmara as though on holiday, a dreadful thing to say about men who were soon to be regarded as the cream of the British army. He had one serviceable, reliable infantry group ready, the 29th Division in England, but he was loath to waste it on the Dardanelles. Furious cabinet-level arguments went on for weeks trying to dislodge these men from Kitchener's very 'sticky' grasp for service in the east. After all the wrangling was done, and the men secured, far too much time had been squandered.

Experts on the Balkans and Turkey had explicitly warned about delay. The idea had originally been to pounce on the Turks, overwhelm them with superior firepower and demoralize them to the point of a sullen acceptance of defeat. A friend of Churchill, Sir Mark Sykes, had been attached to the diplomatic corps of Constantinople in 1905. He was an old 'Balkan hand' who knew the region and its politics well. He warned that any military action, whether by land or sea or in combination, 'should be hard, decisive, and without preamble'.

Turks always grow formidable if given time to think; they may be lulled into passivity, and rushed, owing to their natural idleness and proneness to panic, but they are dangerous if gradually put on their guard. During the Balkan war, they were at one moment ready to abandon Constantinople but in 18 days they had recovered and were ready to fight until the last man.

Unbeknownst to Sykes, or anyone else in the Asquith cabinet, the powers that be in Constantinople were even then contemplating their very own flight from the capital. The sultan had two trains, fully coaled, waiting for himself and his entourage on the Asian shore, their goal some refuge in the Anatolian wilderness. Several of the railway carriages were full of treasure and luxury goods to sustain his accustomed lifestyle. Talaat Pasha, one of the more important Young Turks, commandeered a Mercedes sedan from the Belgian embassy, petrol cans full of fuel strapped to its running boards, ready to flee at a moment's notice. Preparations were made to destroy any supplies that might prove useful to the invader; included on the list was the Hagia Sophia, the irreplaceable church-turned-mosque allegedly first built by the Emperor Constantine the Great (certainly not true). The American ambassador was so chilled by this news that he motored over to government headquarters to plead for its exception. We do 'not care for anything that is old', he was told.

Turkish troops and their German advisers along the Straits were of divided opinion as to what was in store for them. On the one hand, they were to some degree numb from the events of 18 March. They had absorbed a gruelling barrage of firepower, a test of both their nerves and their eardrums. It seemed inevitable that the British fleet would come again, and hammer them once more. With ammunition running low, could they prevent a breakthrough? On the other hand, they could hardly believe their eyes at the sight of crippled and sinking battleships, or of the great fleet calling it quits when their minesweepers were scattered. Had Allah answered their prayers for a great victory, or had they simply won a respite? The next few days would answer that question.

Commander Keyes was blind with fury. He had recklessly exposed himself to enemy fire continuously, trying to organize a salvage operation for the doomed *Irresistible*. He had seen, heard and experienced the tremendous cacophony of battle, and could not help but sense that the Turk was a beaten foe. 'I am spoiling to have at it again', he said in a letter to his wife, who was no doubt worried sick over such blind impetuosity.

Keyes's opinion, however, stood alone. De Robeck was understandably in deep despair. The French had lost a ship; he had lost three. The main Turkish forts were no longer of real concern, but the roving artillery pieces were. Until these were suppressed, the minesweepers could not function, and the fleet would not be placed in hazard's way again until the minefields were clear. De Robeck turned to Ian Hamilton. Could what forces he had be landed; could they occupy the Straits and neutralize the enemy? Hamilton dithered. Although advised by some on his staff to seize the moment while the dazed Turks were pulling themselves together again, he feared to disobey Kitchener, who had advised from the start that the army was to play 'string number two', a supporting role to the navy. The vaunted 29th Division was three weeks from arriving on the scene, just the first in any number of excuses for delaying action. Hamilton advised London to pause, reorganize and then overwhelm the Gallipoli peninsula with several coordinated landings that would trap the Turkish land forces, disable their forts and open the way to Constantinople for the navy. That attack would not commence for another five weeks, a delay that guaranteed that the sultan's trains would never be called upon to flee eastwards.

Ian Hamilton was not unskilled in his craft; at one time (36 years old) the youngest colonel in the British army, a man twice considered for the Victoria Cross.[11] He was probably the most qualified field officer in the British army not already employed in France or Belgium. He was great friends with Churchill. They had experience together, mostly during the Boer War; an expedition there led by Hamilton had been the subject of one of Churchill's books. He had spent twenty-five years or so in India, was a great exponent of thorough training and expertise with modern weaponry, and carried on in the face of whizzing bullets with the kind of insouciant cheerfulness that seemed to typify so many British officers. If there was a battle to be had – or, in keeping with his actual level of experience, more accurately a fray – he wanted nothing better than to be in the middle of it. 'Gallant, chivalrous Sir Ian!' as one of his fellow officers said of him. As was so typical of the officer corps, Hamilton was an excellent rider and devotee of the hunt. In India, he seldom lost an opportunity to join parties for a solid afternoon searching for big and dangerous game. His ardent, breezy spirit could be infectious; no one would ever best him in dash, courage or elegance in the face of fire, the last a trait that distinguished him from one's average boyhood hero running amuck in a haze of blood lust. John Singer Sargent caught this elusive feature of Hamilton's 'thin eager form' in his 1898 portrait.

By 1914, he was sixty-two years old, and still looking for a front-line command. On 10 March 1915 he got it. An intimate of Kitchener, Hamilton was selected to lead the land component at the Dardanelles, since 18 March now the primary focus of attention and responsibility – the baton, as it were, passed from sea to land. It cannot be said that he did anything but throw his heart and soul into it; 'worked all day in the office like a nigger', as he put it. This was to be the pinnacle of a long and so far successful career, the commander in chief of a major, possibly war-changing, expedition. It was a shame, as everyone was to say afterwards, that his obvious abilities lacked one major characteristic that all the great captains of war must possess: cold-blooded heartlessness.

Churchill was delighted with Hamilton's appointment, revealing his own deficiencies as a judge of character. He was deceived by Hamilton's 'nobility', equating it with competence. He would be sorely let down on that count. Asquith was more cautious in his assessment. 'He is a sanguine enthusiastic person, with a good deal of *superficial* charm', he wrote Venetia Stanley, 'but there is too much feather in his brain.' The literary gadfly Compton Mackenzie, who had somehow wangled a spot on Hamilton's staff as affairs there began disintegrating (Hamilton had admired one of Mackenzie's novels, *Sinister Street*, which seemingly reassured him that he would be a capable officer), was himself unimpressed when they first met on board the command ship.

Sir Ian Hamilton came striding around the deck and I was presented to him. He must have said something which allowed me without impertinence to ask him why Lord Kitchener did not grasp the difficulties of the enterprise and the full implications of its success, for his next words are cut like a chisel on my heart. 'Lord Kitchener is a great genius, but like every great genius he has blind spots'. As he spoke his eyes turned eastward to the long line of cliffs beyond that dancing deep blue sea, and in one illuminated instant I divined with absolute certainty that we should never take Constantinople.

To Mackenzie, it seemed perfectly clear that 'Sir Ian's own brave hope had been shaken'.

Hamilton planned an elaborate scheme for putting about 70,000 men onto the Gallipoli peninsula. During staff exercises in Malta, he had managed two such trial operations from the sea against entrenched forces, both of them deemed successes. The Gallipoli theatre, however, presented additional challenges. There were no decent maps,[12] no accurate notion of terrain or local currents and little intelligence as to what the Turks were doing: where they were, the state of fortifications at the various obvious choices for landings, how accurate reports now were regarding their ammunition woes, morale, leadership and so forth. These vacuums were worrisome, and to recompense for what he did not know, Hamilton placed his reliance on 'no half measures, no tentatives …. Prudence here is entirely out of place.' His spirit was the same as the navy's had been: irresistible numbers, irresistible firepower and irresistible resolve would simply push the Turks aside. This did not work for the navy on 18 March, and it would not work for the army on 25 April.

The plan was to envelop the southern tip of the peninsular, Cape Helles, at five separate landing sites. These would scatter the Turkish defenders, the rationale being that if one or two or even three of these were contested, others would succeed, push inland and encircle the Turks from the rear. Simultaneously, New Zealanders and Australians, now identified by the acronym ANZAC, would disembark at a spit of land jutting out from the western coastline at Gaba Tepe, about thirteen miles north of Cape Helles, and head cross country for the eastern shore, taking the important heights of Sari Bair in the process, a range of hills, 'the high backbone of the peninsula', as Hamilton called them, three of which were about 1,000 feet, that ran slightly north, then east. This successful manoeuvre would both cut off the supposed bulk of the Turkish force (or split them in two), and also secure domination of the Narrows, which the Sari Bair overlooked, clearing the way for de Robeck and the fleet. Many of the logistics were minutely prepared, from landing craft to shuttling artillery ashore to ammunition dumps, though some categories were given shorter shrift (medical stores and field hospitals, for one, were poorly organized, as though Hamilton did not expect any casualties). At Zone V, for example, the most critical objective at the mouth of the Straits, a clever landing technique involved an old tramp steamer, the *River Clyde*, which was to beach itself on the shore; two barges would then be towed forward, connected and formed as a ramp or bridgehead over which the landing troops would disembark ... on the run if opposed, in good marching order if not. All these plans looked fine on paper, and the actual schemes for assembling the troops (largely on the Greek island of Lemnos), embarking them on over 200 miscellaneous transports, and managing to get everyone at their landing stations by 4 a.m. on the morning of 25 April, worked marvellously. Hamilton doubtless had an imaginative mind, men were eager to go. As ships left Lemnos for the beachheads, they were sent off with resounding cheers.

On a clear bright morning, the attacks were launched, and very early on the major flaw in Ian Hamilton's style of command revealed itself. Stationing himself on the ponderous *Queen Elizabeth*, he remained on the periphery of the action. Hamilton 'had a deckchair on the bridge below the rails', a naval officer recalled. 'He couldn't see anything. He didn't want to see anything. He wouldn't look at anything.' The *Queen Elizabeth* slowly cruised the coast, lobbing barrages on supposed Turkish positions ashore. The noise and reverberation of these fusillades, to say nothing of smoke, must have been thrilling, but in terms of enabling Hamilton to get a clear view and idea as to what was going on at the beachheads, it proved an injudicious choice. Hamilton could have boarded a frigate or some other fast conveyance that might hug the shore, enabling him to intervene where necessary, because as the landings progressed, communications broke down more or less immediately.

His divisional commanders, emulating their chief, also remained afloat, and very quickly they too had little notion of conditions on the ground.

The *River Clyde*, as intended, ploughed full steam ahead towards the beach, grinding to a stop many yards short of land at 6:22 a.m. The great surge of water ploughing out of the Dardanelles into the Aegean made for currents far stronger than anticipated, however, and connecting the land bridge from ship to shore proved exceedingly difficult. Some men in the water actually held the barges together by hand, but all to little avail. Hamilton had expected the preliminary barrage from the fleet to make the zone 'as healthy as Brighton', but, as he later recalled, the immense shelling 'might as well be confetti for all the effect they have upon Turkish trenches'. Enemy defenders unleashed a gruesome field of fire, not only on the 2,000 or so men on the *River Clyde*, but on hundreds more who approached in open boats. The slaughter was horrific, a veritable sea of blood, as witnessed by a shocked observation pilot circling above. After three hours of futility, with a mere 200 men on shore, the *River Clyde* contingent essentially gave up. While all this was going on, officers were breakfasting on board ship. Major John Gillam, a supply officer, wrote in his diary, 'The steward calmly hands the menu round, just as he might on a peaceful voyage. What a contrast! Two boiled eggs, coffee, toast and marmalade. Here we are sitting down to a good meal and men are fighting up cliffs a few hundred yards away.' Like Gillam (but with less excuse) the divisional commander of the 29th, General Aylmer Hunter-Weston, had no idea of any difficulties. His second wave was ready to go, just waiting for the small landing craft to return from the initial landing, but only six came back from the original flotilla. The brigadier in charge could not believe it, and went ahead for a quick look. As he approached the *River Clyde*, he didn't see any men on board (they were all taking shelter inside the ship). Several shouted out, warning him to find cover; he refused and, as though taking a Sunday stroll, was shot dead on one of the barges. He was but one of dozens of senior officers who did not survive the day. It was not until the cover of night, when the exhausted Turks withdrew, that the holds of the *River Clyde* were emptied of its men.

The other beachheads, though originally deemed secondary to Zone V, encountered few initial difficulties. There was plenty of barbed wire to navigate, but Turkish resistance was initially slight. At Zone Y, for instance, there was no opposition at all, not a Turk in sight. But here the initial success was irretrievably botched. For all his technical abilities, Hamilton had allowed one glaring deficiency to fester: his officers down the command chain had no real idea as to their objectives. This incredulous omission at first seems largely impossible to fathom. Hamilton, Hunter-Weston and Birdwood (in charge of the ANZAC landing) certainly knew what was intended. They had masterminded the whole thing in Alexandria and Lemnos, but for some inexplicable reason junior officers on shore were never fully apprised as to what they were to do once on Turkish soil. One problem was the lack of maps, the other that Hamilton just assumed that British troops would show their customary initiative and move forward. Moving forward meant moving inland; moving inland meant pushing out the Turks; pushing the Turks out meant that the entire peninsula would be occupied. In his memoirs, Hamilton put a gloss on all this in very breezy fashion. The men, out of their boats, would go 'on the war path'. What else was there for them to do?

The fact remains, however, that, once on shore, the troops at zones S, X and Y did almost nothing. Beach W faced resistance, engaged in heavy firefights, and began entrenching positions as an exercise in self-preservation; other beachheads saw troops boiling water and having tea. On Y the situation was complicated by the fact that two colonels were apparently confused as to which one of them was in command. Their 2,000 men, who landed unopposed and saw barely a trace of the enemy, should have marched east towards the centre of the peninsula. They were ideally positioned to attack the Turks who were shooting up the *River Clyde* with impunity. Instead, they remained where they were, waiting for additional orders that never came. Ian Hamilton had forgotten an essential point of command: never assume anything.

As the afternoon progressed, the commander in chief finally sensed that things were not running smoothly. At one point that nettlesome character, Commodore Keyes, approached with the impertinent notion that perhaps the c-in-c should do something. Instead of contacting Hunter-Weston or Birdwood directly, however, to either receive an update or to 'apply the spur' for more progress, Hamilton deferred to his sense of gentlemanly behaviour. It would not do, he reasoned, to interfere in the affairs of his subordinates. They had a job to do, and he would let them do it, even though at times, as when the *Queen Elizabeth* moved in close to turn the village overlooking the *River Clyde* into a 'lyddite ruin', he could plainly see for himself that his men were not moving as they should. (Churchill's brother Jack was on board as well, and wrote that when Hamilton came on deck after tea, he 'asked if there was anything new' going on.) His troops had an overwhelming advantage in numbers; only 2,000 Turks had been deployed on the cape. As the long, sunlit day stretched on, the splendid opportunities to wrap up the entire Turkish position evaporated.

The ANZAC landing was also becoming problematic. Instead of debouching on a mile-long accessible beach just on the coastline of Gaba Tepe, the small craft full of Australians and New Zealanders, rowed by sailors some of whom were barely fifteen or sixteen years old, were carried well north of their intended drop-off. Initial reports blamed local and unknown currents, but it seems that, given the pitch-black darkness, they simply lost their way. Whatever the cause, troops found themselves disembarked in the water fifty feet from the shore of a small cove, but facing an entirely unexpected environment. Instead of a fairly flat locale, they were barricaded by the very foot of the Sari Bair range, a tangle of trackless ravines, gullies and dead-end canyons. On the beachhead itself, they looked up at a forbidding ridge that poked up higher than the rest, dominating their position. This would come to be known as The Sphinx. They brushed aside a few Turkish soldiers roaming about, and proceeded piecemeal, and largely without direction, up the various heights that presented themselves. The force, eventually to number 8,000 men by eight in the morning, and 16,000 by evening, inevitably broke into splinters. Some groupings actually made it to the heights themselves, and looked down at the Dardanelles and the Narrows itself, without seeing a single Turk; others became disoriented, lost or utterly bewildered as they climbed hither and yon through the wilderness, often caught in crossfire from Turkish soldiers firing on them from all directions. As the day progressed, some of these skirmishes turned into vicious firefights, but a success achieved in one locale could be offset by a reversal a few hundred yards in another direction. There never was an actual battle line established, nor were communications between any of the diverse spheres of action ever achieved – on board ship, where Birdwood's headquarters were positioned, the beach site, where men and supplies were peremptorily dumped ashore, or the hinterlands, where small detachments found themselves fighting for their lives – all these epicentres operated more or less independently of one another. Birdwood, when he did go to shore for an inspection, was shocked at what he saw. The entire landing force, with its waves of supplies, were being funnelled onto a small beach only ninety feet deep, and perhaps 3,000 feet long, much of it rapidly being taken up by wounded men lying in rows, many of whom were hit a second time as shrapnel fire burst overhead. The site was vulnerable to Turkish fire on all three sides which, if it fully developed, would find every inch of the cove littered with targets. If the ANZACs could not broaden their attack zone into the interior, the entire operation would choke itself into formless gridlock. The only option was to climb, and keep climbing, a distinct tactical advantage for the defenders, and, as the afternoon progressed, the tide began turning against the ANZACs. This was largely the result of the determination of one man, a Turkish officer by the name of Mustafa Kemal, and his ability to encourage his troops to throw away their lives.

'I order you to die.'

Mustafa Kemal
Order of the day to the 57th Infantry Regiment

General von Sanders played a cautious hand at first. The French contingent of the allied force had staged a diversionary attack on the Asiatic side of the Dardanelles, at Troy. He had always worried over this possibility, so early reports of activity there gave him pause. During the five-week-lull after the naval action of 18 March, he had given full vent to another preoccupation that preyed on his mind. He knew a landing was coming; security was about as lax for this operation as any in the entire war. The press in Egypt, for example, gave daily reports on British preparations in Alexandria where, as one officer put it, 'the fearful hugger-mugger of ship funnels … was apparently infinite'. Any fool could see that something was on, and German agents, not being fools, dutifully passed their observations along to Berlin. Von Sanders was also concerned that Hamilton would land considerably farther north on the peninsula, in the hope of cutting off the entire Turkish army. As such, he positioned a sizable contingent of his forces in reserve around the Bay of Bulair, thirty-five miles away from the tip of Cape Helles, and maintained his headquarters there. He would wait and see how things developed before committing the bulk of his men. Of six Turkish divisions, only two were anywhere near Cape Helles (one to defend the cape itself, the other held in reserve about 15 miles away). A previously inconspicuous Turkish officer, Lieutenant-Colonel Mustafa Kemal, was placed in charge of the reserve division; he was not to move them unless ordered to by von Sanders.

How much confidence General von Sanders had in his men can be inferentially understood only from the reminiscences he left behind. He was discreet enough not to openly criticize the Turkish army and its officers, but small details are telling. When he arrived in Constantinople to assume his command, the guards of honour who met him at the railway station were largely barefoot. On inspection trips to various barracks, he was initially delighted at the quality of dress, until he noticed, after several parades, that the uniforms were exactly the same as the ones he had seen the day before (they were constantly shipped ahead in anticipation of his visits).[13] German advisers and officers numbered about 500; many of them, like von Sanders, spoke not a word of the indigenous language, so interpreters were always in demand; they witnessed several temper tantrums on the part of the frustrated and often arrogant foreigners. An inevitable frigidity developed between the two officer corps. The Turks, used to what von Sanders called a 'musing existence', disliked being told what to do and the often incessant criticisms. Once the fighting started, and the stresses accumulated, rumours were rampant that Sanders had been murdered by angry Turks; that did not happen, but his sheets and pillowcases were stolen from his Gallipoli headquarters within days of his arrival.

As with most German officers, von Sanders could be brusque, impolitic and lacking in finesse. He did not have the common touch; indeed, it was with some reluctance that he was persuaded to wear a Turkish fez instead of his regimental cap. An acquaintance in Berlin suggested that only a psychiatrist could really fathom his motives, but he had a good technical eye and appreciated character when he saw it. Lieutenant-Colonel Mustafa Kemal came to his attention. Kemal was opinionated, stubborn and arrogant, qualities shared with Sanders. The general noted that the young officer 'delighted in responsibility', not a trait he recognized in too many other Turks. He would soon 'have full confidence in his energy'.

Wondrous indeed is the nature of fate. The word most often used to describe Mustafa Kemal at this point in his career is 'obscure'. Details of his background have always been confused and often contradictory, a state of affairs Kemal himself did little to clarify. Perhaps rumours of Jewish blood in his make-up contributed to this reticence; perhaps he just didn't care enough, as fame engulfed him, to satisfy everyone's curiosity about his origins or family genealogy. His great feats, he seems to have suggested, was all anyone needed to know. He was certainty in the right spot on the morning of 25 April. He had experience in battle, was a veteran of the Balkan Wars and other inglorious actions that had generally resulted in failure, but was deemed sufficiently competent to have been sent as an official observer of the French military manoeuvres of 1910. From these he learned no lessons in subtlety, to be sure, for his tactics on the Dardanelles were generally unimaginative and wasteful of life. To be fair, he saw no alternative, and his determination never failed him. Turks, in the opinion of many condescending European officers, were good for only one thing, running away. If this canard was indeed true, the one exception would be Mustafa Kemal.

Early on 25 April, the first garbled reports of various landings came into his headquarters. While it is easy to judge from hindsight what his true reactions were, Kemal's behaviour suggests he did come to one immediate and resolute conclusion: this was no sideshow, this was the real thing. Not only did he decide to go out himself to reconnoitre around the Sari Bair range, but he took his reserve division with him in direct contravention of von Sanders' instructions. He had the conviction, he later said, that they would be needed. This, in fact, saved the day.

Setting out, Kemal let himself be generally guided by the sound of gunfire from ANZAC Cove since his maps were not much better than Hamilton's, and local guides seemed as confused as everyone else. This was truly a wilderness marked by scrub and goat trails. Relying on compass bearings and considerable common sense, he manoeuvred himself and the vanguard of his division, the 57th infantry regiment, into the path of the oncoming foreigners, some of whom were nearing the tops of various ridges and hillocks. It did not take Kemal long to realize that these were the key to the entire strategic situation. He had two tasks: the first, to repel the Australians and New Zealanders from getting a foothold on these heights; the second, to convince von Sanders that this was the eye of the storm.

In these initial contacts between the opposing troops, the bayonet often ruled the day. Many Turks had little or no ammunition to start with, but Kemal ordered them to charge anyway. Some ANZACS, despite the occasionally horrifying aspects of this, their first exposure to combat, were delirious with excitement: 'A brief pause to fix bayonets', one recalled later, having just landed on the beach, 'and swearing and cheering we charged up a hill so steep in places we could only just scramble up. No firing, all bayonet work. Clean over a machine gun we went, men dropped all around me, it was mad, wild, thrilling … not until I was near the top did I realize that in the excitement I hadn't even drawn my revolver.' Unfortunately for him and his men, the day proved to be a long one. Turkish resistance stiffened. A first wave of counterattack was driven back, but it was followed by a second wave, then a third, and a fourth. By early afternoon, the wear and tear of the fighting began to tell on the ANZACs. Kemal fed his division into the fight all day long with little or no respite, often leading charges himself. His objective was a simple one: the ANZACs were not to establish any sort of control on the heights. Messages he managed to send Sanders stressed the crucial nature of the struggle and, to his credit, the German general, putting aside any prejudices he may have harboured for the men under his charge, required no second opinion from one of his own countrymen to conclude that Lieutenant-Colonel Kemal was correct. He began ordering up his troops from Troy, and directing the two divisions in Bulair to proceed south. The main battle, he agreed, would be joined on the heights.

Kemal never let up. In one order of the day to his men, he wrote the most famous lines in modern Turkish history: 'I do not order you to attack, I order you to die. In the time it takes us to die, other troops and commanders can come and take our places.' And the *Mehmetçik* under his command mostly did as they were commanded, though Kemal added an afterthought by telling his officers not to hesitate shooting anyone they saw retreating from the battlefield.[14] By the end of the Gallipoli defence, the 57th Regiment no longer existed; it had been fully wiped clean from the slate. As a tribute, no other infantry division in the Turkish army has ever been reconstituted as the 57th.

These brutal assaults on the rapidly tiring ANZACS led to piecemeal retreats from the ground they had occupied, unopposed, in the morning. By nightfall the 'front', if it could be called that, was a series of strong points scattered here and there on the hillsides over what is known today as ANZAC Cove; nowhere did the allies hold a commanding ridge or high spot. And it was clear to the two most senior officers on the ground that Turkish forces were likely to be reinforced. The element of surprise had been squandered. Meanwhile the beachhead was a scene of indescribable confusion, supplies offloaded helter-skelter, men and animals milling about in confusion, troops from the front wandering down to the water in a state of utter exhaustion. On Birdwood's first inspection of the scene, he found many of the troops despondent. 'Small groups would tell me that they were all that was left of their respective battalions – "all others cut up!" On such occasions I would promptly tell them not to be damned fools ….This always had an encouraging effect.' When the general returned to his headquarters on board ship, he felt not unduly pessimistic, but after nightfall 'Birdie' was asked to come ashore for a second inspection. He was told, in no uncertain terms, that the only thing to do was evacuate the cove. After assessing these reports, he was forced to agree. Hamilton, who had gone to bed on the *Queen Elizabeth*, was jolted awake before midnight and given a message from Birdwood saying that the operation had the potential of degenerating into a 'fiasco', and to authorize retreat. Sitting in his pyjamas, Hamilton did not know how to respond.

The dilemma was acute. The landings on Cape Helles, while not the success he had envisioned, seemed capable of achieving some sense of cohesion the next day. He expected the five landing forces to unite and push inland, their objective a height of 700 feet called Achi Baba. He wanted the ANZACs to force their way inland too, and for the life of him refused to grasp why they couldn't, having little comprehension, other than the fact that the terrain was 'difficult', about the physical nature of the battleground. The consequences of a retreat would be an immediate career-breaker, the inevitability of which surely shrivelled his spirits. On top of that, the navy insisted that a debarkation would take days to accomplish, and if it was to undertake the task at all, an order had to be instantly given before Turkish reinforcements arrived and turned the entire landing zone into a bloodbath. This in itself was a powerful argument to stay put, and that is the decision Hamilton made. 'Your news is indeed serious', he wrote Birdwood, 'but there is nothing for it but to dig yourselves right in and stick it out.' In a postscript, he added, 'You have got through the difficult business, now you have only to dig, dig, dig, until you are safe.' This was an incorrect assessment on two points: the first is that 'the difficult business' was only just beginning; and the second was that the admonition to 'dig' ignored facts on the ground. The steep inclines of hills and gullies made creating sustainable trenches near the beachhead a near impossible task, the shaley rock sliding down the embankments when pick and shovel were applied. This was not the flat goo of Flanders. Over the next eight months 'shanty towns' and improvised dugouts held in place by scrub pine poles, millions of sandbags, wooden crates, and the assorted flotsam of the battlefield would sprout all over the landscape of ANZAC Cove, with coils of barbed wire strung out everywhere. Some Australians compared the scene to that of a mining camp in the outback, both transitory and yet permanent at the same time; the poet John Masefield called it a vision from prehistory, 'a city of cliff dwellers'. It would certainly give the lie to any notion of a fluid, evolving front. The whole point of the Dardanelles operation had been to bypass the inertia of trench warfare in Belgium and France, but Hamilton's decision pretty much guaranteed that ANZAC Cove would become a twin to the stagnation of Western Europe.

The story of ANZAC Cove would be written in blood, bayonets, flies, faeces and rot. Those are clichés of the first order, but true nevertheless. Week after week, desperate schemes were put forward to scale the heights of the Sari Bair range and achieve the breakthrough that everyone wanted; these would generally be repulsed by Kemal's forces, who would then return the favour with ill-advised counter-attacks that wasted thousands of Turkish lives. Some soldiers compared these onslaughts with turkey shoots, as they thinned down with ease waves of the enemy. 'You can't help hitting the brutes', wrote one officer; 'they simply walk into our bullets'. According to Birdwood, the ANZACs poured nearly a million rounds into the Turks on 16 May alone. Hamilton condescendingly called the enemy 'stupid but exceedingly brave', which, with some irony, was the identical judgment of many allied soldiers for their own commanders. A New Zealand doctor could not get over the absurdity of landing reinforcements at ANZAC Cove in full daylight; 'damnable indifference to human life, absolutely German in its callousness ... I call it murder and nothing else'. ANZAC losses were dreadful in killed and wounded, all more or less for nothing gained. At Cape Helles, minimal results as well; the heights of Achi Baba, 'that accursed hill', remained tantalizingly close but were never taken, despite over six attacks engineered and carried out between 28 April and 12 July by General Hunter-Weston, who was soon tagged with the unenviable nickname 'The Butcher'. Some 23,000 men either killed or wounded in wasteful frontal attacks inevitably will generate such resentment, as did his widely reported remark, 'Casualties? What do I care for casualties?'[15]

By June, Hamilton conceded that the ANZAC operation had stalled, and both sides settled into what can only be called siege conditions. The physical environment decayed accordingly. No proper drainage, hygiene non-existent, water scarce, food (on the allied side) effectively uneatable, especially as warmer weather settled in, bringing its own species of hardship, a Biblical plague of flies. By the time a trooper had put his fork to canned bully beef, or spread his hardtack with jam, and then put it in his mouth, it could be covered with insects, whose previous meal may well have been a corpse rotting twenty yards away.[16] On one sector of the Helles front, Compton Mackenzie saw approximately 4,000 Turkish bodies rotting in the sun. They had been there for an entire month. 'You've got your foot in an awkward place', he was told by a soldier. 'Looking down I saw squelching up from the ground on either side of my boot like a rotten mangold the deliquescent green and black flesh of a Turk's head.' Dysentery and other intestinal disorders ravaged the troops, necessitating periodic truces to clean up the battlefield of disease-spreading decay. On such occasions, the allies met their enemies for the first time (other than when they were trying to kill them). One New Zealander came away impressed. 'The Turkish officers were charming', he wrote to his wife, particularly when compared with the Germans, who were 'rude, dictatorial swine'. Another ANZAC, walking among the bodies, recorded this comment from his Turkish counterpart: pointing to the newly dug graves, he said, 'That's politics', and to the dead still lying on the ground, 'That's diplomacy'.

The entire theatre quickly degenerated into a parody of military 'science', wherein the buoyant independence of ANZAC soldiers, in particular, became an exasperation to their British superiors. Australians seemed inherently disrespectful. As the weather and conditions degraded their uniforms and equipment, so too their soldierly demeanour. This place was a mess, and who was to blame for it? The officers with their red tabs, who no longer headquartered on a ship near to shore, but had returned to the relative comfort of Imbros, fifteen miles offshore (where Hamilton dined on fresh crayfish to celebrate the centenary of the Battle of Waterloo). Many refused to salute and became openly contemptuous, especially when staff officers relied on formerly tried-and-true methods to instil pride, obedience and the stiff upper lip. One of Hamilton's officers commiserated with a group of Australians over the loss of a particularly popular commander. 'They've given [him] a posthumous K.C.M.G.' 'Really?' said one of the Aussies, 'that won't do him much good where he is now, will it, mate?' In all, the ANZAC 'were rather difficult', but, as Mackenzie put it, 'so was Achilles'. When called upon to go over the top, they always did.

In a pattern reminiscent of the western front, Hamilton finally asked, with considerable trepidation, for more men and more ammunition. 'The only sound procedure is to hammer away', he told a reporter, terminology that would be worked to death by Douglas Haig in Flanders for three long years. The navy too, having passively lost three additional ships to submarines, began getting edgy. Kitchener was losing patience with them. 'The navy was afraid to wet its feet', he grumbled. Junior officers, such as Keyes, agreed among themselves that perhaps another try at the Narrows was worth undertaking, but there was little support for that in the cabinet, excepting, of course, from Churchill, whose position was eroding daily. 'My reputation is at stake', he declared to Lloyd George, 'I am wounded.' His career standing in jeopardy, he was desperate that some sort of action be undertaken to redeem the situation. Ian Hamilton provided one in August, but by then it was too late for Winston.[17]

'Our third Sunday in Gallipoli – sounds like a quotation from the prayer book.'

Dr. Percival Fenwick
ANZAC Cove, 9 May

Lieutenant-Colonel Percival Fenwick of the New Zealand medical corps was one of the first to set foot on ANZAC Cove, where he worked and lived for the next two months before being invalided out with fever and dysentery. His reports home were well written, informative and full of interesting detail. He wanted to do his job, and do it well, and was generally supportive of the mission, but, as conditions moved from barely adequate to deplorable, a certain wariness set in to his narrative. 'What good we are doing here I can't say", he noted almost from the start. 'We are like a rat in a trap. The rat cannot get out and the owner of the trap does not like putting his hand in, and can only annoy the rat by pushing things through the bar. Unquestionably we are held up.' Several days later he added, 'We are here; we don't like it; but we mean to stick till we are blown out of our funk holes.' This is the very definition of futility. Fenwick was sickened and depressed by the human losses, but equally saddened by the sight of dead mules towed a mile off shore and dumped. 'No one seems inclined to go fishing.'

'Naturally I shall tell you *everything.*'

Prime Minister Asquith to
Venetia Stanley, 9 February 1915

It is astonishing to see how desire, romance and sex can never be separated or compartmentalized away from the everyday course of daily life, with its many alterations between mundane routine and moments of crisis or high political drama. The salons and gatherings of the social elites, whether it be London, Paris or St. Petersburg, with their intermingling of important guests and mere hangers-on looking for gossip, rarely equalled the astonishing exchange of letters between lovers or would-be lovers which put the notion of mere rumour to shame. Churchill told his wife just about everything that mattered in a ceaseless barrage of letters (she called them 'tidbits'). Lloyd George held nothing back from his mistress, Frances Stevenson, who promptly recorded everything in her diary. Prime Minister Henry Herbert Asquith showed no discretion at all when he wrote long summaries of cabinet meetings over which he presided, where secrets of all sorts were discussed, to the love of his life, Venetia Stanley, often just minutes after they had occurred. She saved all of it, over 500 letters of 300,000 words. Examples abound of indiscretions. Early in 1915, Lloyd George and Churchill both wrote long memoranda outlining 'new objectives & theatres' for military action. 'I will bring them to you on Monday', Asquith wrote Stanley '& we can talk it all over'. As the Dardanelles situation fell into crisis mode later that year, forcing Asquith to consider a coalition government with the (to him) hated Tories, her revelation that she meant to marry another man incapacitated the prime minister to such a degree that he effectively disappeared from the scene for several days. Without your 'counsel & consent', he wrote her in despair, how could he make the 'astounding and world-shaking decisions' that his office required? These words to a twenty-eight-year-old dilettante. The slovenly and casual spread of confidential material disseminated to people who had no right to share in it is, in retrospect, astonishing, and a further black mark on the notion that human beings are, in the main, intelligent.[18]

Asquith had been something of a patron to Churchill, promoting him to important cabinet positions on three occasions. Although he often despaired of Winston's vanity and ambition, he admired the younger man's persistence, abilities, eloquence and vigour. As he said, 'I can't help being very fond of him', all well-meant but with one caveat: he knew where Churchill's primary interest always lay. Asquith summarized for his wife what meant the most to him when it came to his political colleagues: 'Character is better than brains, and loyalty more valuable than either'. But the ministerial crisis of late

May 1915 found him in a damaged mental state, Venetia Stanley's marital decision coming right out of the blue when he least expected it. Stanley had dropped hints to Asquith that his obsession with her had become oppressive, but the prime minster never dreamed that she would sever all contact. When Admiral Fisher's abrupt resignation from the Admiralty on 15 May became common knowledge, the Tory opposition saw its chance to cripple Asquith, largely over his conduct of the war (the Dardanelles in particular), by forcing him to form a government that would include members of the opposition, most of whom, on a political level, he loathed. Ordinarily, Asquith would have employed his usual arsenal of political manoeuvrability to thwart this challenge, but he was emotionally played out. One price the Tories extracted was the removal of Churchill from the Admiralty. To Winston's amazement, Asquith did so with barely a step of hesitation.

This most depressing moment of Churchill's career was hardly softened when Asquith offered him a chance to remain in the cabinet; the largely irrelevant post of Chancellor of the Duchy of Lancaster was tossed his way, a sinecure of no consequence, duties, staff to speak of or influence. He took it as to a lifeline. This presented him, as his cousin the Duke of Marlborough put it, with 'a bone on which there is little meat'. At least Winston retained a seat at the table, and the opportunity to present his views and opinions, but Tories like Carson and Bonar Law were smug in their disdain. Churchill could talk his head off, it made no difference to them. 'Poor Winston!' wrote Margot Asquith. 'His political situation is nil – no tenor off the stage was more helpless than he is'.[19]

Suvla Bay

'Men swift in the work of war?'

Simonides, Greek poet, c. 500 BC

Ian Hamilton's psychological state was by now fairly standard given the circumstances. The venture he was commanding had been from the start full of both promise and peril; the promise had been frittered away, the peril growing more ominous as each day passed by in futility. So much had been committed, however, and so many men had died, that the thought of walking away seemed almost beyond consideration. Hence the decision to remain at ANZAC Cove, which merely worsened Hamilton's overall tactical situation, given that no progress was ever realistically possible. He would rationalize that decision with his customary bravado. 'Better to die like heroes on the enemy's ground than be butchered like the runaway Persians at Marathon.' Thrashing for a way out, any way out, he concocted a scheme to relieve pressure on the ANZAC front by proposing yet another amphibious operation farther north along the coast, at a spot called Suvla Bay. A landing there, he reasoned, would draw Turkish defenders away from the cove, giving the Australian and New Zealanders yet another chance to break out and capture Sari Bari. As with most of Hamilton's ideas, this looked promising on paper, a chance to salvage what had so far been little more than a disaster. The landing site was sandy beach, behind which a considerable salt lake (now dry) approached yet another ridge of low hills, all lightly defended. Kitchener, Asquith, Churchill … indeed, the entire cabinet … grasped this straw of hope and approved. As had become symptomatic of the entire campaign, this operation only made matters worse.

The fault, as usual, lay in the by now familiar lack of communication and inept leadership. Kitchener did send out more men, five divisions, many the result of his initial recruiting surge and hastily trained; they have come to be known since as 'Kitchener's New Army', and, once landed, many professional officers regarded them as 'a very weedy lot'. He gave Hamilton a choice of the commanders still available. The Darwinian principle of survival of the fittest did not apply to the men he proposed; these generals were old in the tooth, far removed from the rigours of modern war and selected more or less on the basis of seniority. Sir Frederick Stopford, for instance, who would lead the landing at Suvla Bay, was sixty-one at the time, his last posting being a largely honorific one, lieutenant in charge of the Tower of London. He was the epitome of what Churchill called 'dug-out trash … mediocrities who have led a sheltered life mouldering in military routine'. Stopford was certainly one of these, and would prove a disastrous choice.

On 6 and 7 August Hamilton's three-pronged operation began. 'It was to be a triple battle', as John Masefield later explained to a British public begging for details, 'fought by three armies not in direct communication with each other.' While Masefield did not intentionally wish to criticize Hamilton's direction (or non-direction) of the coming battle, he certainly planted the seeds of doubt by admitting that 'here was no place from which the battle as a whole could be controlled'. Sir Ian sat in his headquarters tent on the island of Imbros, some sixteen miles away.

Troops first attacked from their foothold on Cape Helles. This was a diversionary exercise meant to deceive von Sanders, that nonetheless ground up a great many bodies. Later on, ANZAC forces launched one of their own at the ever-problematical heights of Sari Bair, where the fighting was predictably savage and costly. The third and most crucial surge was to be Stopford's men, who achieved more or less total surprise. Turkish commanders were certainly not stupid – they had considered the possibility of a landing at Suvla – but had dismissed the notion that the enemy could successfully link up with the ANZACs from there, the country in between being the usual labyrinth of gnarly hills. 'Only bandits can walk in these gullies', said one. Twenty thousand men landed at Suvla Bay in almost complete darkness on 7 August, an impressive logistical feat. Only 1,500 Turkish troops were anywhere near them, mostly dispersed and hardly a serious obstacle. It should have been clear sailing to the day's first objective, the occupation by dawn of an adjacent series of hills. Capturing these heights would enable Stopford both to link up with the ANZACs, and catch Mustafa Kemal in the middle, attacked front and rear by allied troops. That, at least, was the point Hamilton envisioned; whether he shared it with anyone else is open to question.

The minute Stopford's men landed, they stopped: no advance, no surge inland, no sense of urgency. A German officer scanning the beachhead with binoculars the next morning said it reminded him of a Sunday school picnic: men bathed in the sea, had tea, lined up for their daily rum ration, harassed only by occcasional sniper fire. The blame for this incredible lapse must surely rest with Hamilton. His obsession with secrecy apparently extended to the men under his immediate command; the fullest details were only known to the 'tiny circle' (as he called it) of his own staff. Stopford was fully briefed, knew and accepted what was expected of him (or so Hamilton assumed, who claimed that the general 'fell in love with our plans'), but others on Stopford's team were either unclear or unenthusiastic about what they heard, especially his chief of staff, H. L. Reed, and a divisional general, Frederick Hammersley, both of whom brought the prejudices of the western front with them to the Dardanelles. Although Hamilton assured Stopford that Suvla Bay itself was a puff cake, Hammersley apparently convinced his superior that the exact opposite must surely be the case, and until the Turkish trench systems were pulverized by heavy artillery (Hamilton had reviewed the shoreline himself from a destroyer, and knew there were no trenches) an advance was impossible. Compton Mackenzie nicknamed Hammersley 'General Dash', and felt Stopford should have 'squashed' him, but the old general was too 'deprecating, courteous, and fatherly' to do it.[20] Stopford's love affair with Hamilton's schemes withered away, and grew into something close to terror. Fear of a debacle was the last thing he wished added to his résumé.

Stopford, in retrospect, was over his head. He did not himself land until almost forty-eight hours had passed, grew obsessed with petty details, deferred in everything to his staff and began feeling frail and sickly (which he was). For all intents and purposes, the operation was without a commanding general. It did not help that the great majority of his men were untested. They were poorly trained, poorly led by junior officers and not in any particular rush to experience the terrors of war. It also did not help that many had been cooped up on board ships for over three weeks, or that some of their lieutenants, majors and colonels had not received any orders as to what was expected of them. As snipers (always a serious and dangerous menace) began dropping their mates with increasing regularity, the word went around to dig in and wait for the artillery. Meanwhile it was hot and water was scarce.

Hamilton's first word from Stopford did not arrive at HQ until noon on the 7th, wherein Sir Ian learned that his twenty-two battalions were indeed onshore, or about to be, but not far inland off the beach. This was disturbing, but Hamilton, again assuming more than he should have, felt sure Stopford would advance. It was still early in the timetable, and with a bit of effort his men could still take those pesky hills before the Turks arrived in force. All that day Hamilton waited for more reports, but none arrived. He was now nervous. This was not the 'fog of war', about which so many great generals have complained, wherein the din and utter confusion of battle almost obliterate thoughts and comprehension about what might be happening. This was the silence of war, a commander far removed from the front, desperate for news. 'I'd sooner storm a hundred bloody trenches than dangle at the end of this wire', he wrote.

Hamilton did not hear from Stopford again for fourteen hours. No doubt feeling sick to his stomach, he finally dispatched a trusted officer of his staff, Lieutenant-Colonel Cecil Aspinall, to find out what was happening. Maurice Hankey, an 'insider' from both the war department and 10 Downing Street (in Gallipoli as a spy, or so the soldiers felt) went with him. They did not arrive at Suvla Bay until 1 p.m., and what they saw was shocking. Landing on the beach, they walked several yards inland, and asked where the front was. You're standing on it, was more or less the reply. An officer, noting the red tabs on Aspinall's collar, none too respectfully approached and suggested that he 'get a move on … nothing is being done!' Needing no further advice of this sort, Aspinall and Hankey cadged a ride to Stopford's headquarters off shore, where they found the general satisfied and impervious to any talk about rushing things, Sunday being, as one officer noted, 'the day of rest'. Aspinall immediately sent off a cable to Hamilton. 'Just been ashore where I found all quiet. No rifle fire, no artillery fire, and apparently no Turks. IX corps resting. Feel confident that golden opportunities are being lost and look upon the situation as serious.' His chief never received it.

In keeping with the tragi-comic aspects of Hamilton's day, he finally decided to inspect Suvla Bay himself, but when he rushed down to the dock where his destroyer lay berthed – what Roger Keyes, with a note of racial condescension, called – an 'Italian-made Portuguese destroyer' – imagine the shock when he heard that the boilers had been doused (engine trouble of some sort). Although the waters 'were alive and bustling with ships and small craft', there was nothing available to convey the commander in chief to his front. As he himself admitted, he was essentially 'marooned'.

Hamilton finally managed to arrive at Suvla Bay in the early evening. He found Aspinall quickly enough; he 'was in a fever, said our chances were being thrown away with both hands'; and Hankey with all his bad news; and the combustible Keyes as well, in a racing boat of some sort. All of them immediately sped off to Stopford's ship. If there was ever a time for resolute command, this was it. Hamilton was as aware as the others that time was running out, and but a sliver remained to achieve their goals.

His interview with Stopford lasted a mere five minutes; until he had his artillery ashore, the old man said, what could he do? The men were exhausted, drained like 'sucked oranges'. Everything would have to wait until the next day. Keyes, 'in a fever of resentment', was appalled at these 'leisurely proceedings', writing afterwards that he stood momentarily 'deprived of the power of speech', a rarity for him. This was hopeless, and Hamilton decided quickly to tackle Hammersley instead. When he returned to shore to hash things out with him, however, he ran into another hailstorm of excuses, and here his fundamental misunderstanding of the nature of command was exposed. He was, according to Compton Mackenzie, 'in the position of a man who has to coax jibbing mules along by holding carrots in front of them'. Instead of ruthlessly firing every slacker in sight, and turning authority over to junior officers with more nerve – or, more drastically, taking command himself – Hamilton maintained the correct decorum expected of a British general, and barely raised his voice. On more than one occasion during his fly through of the sector, he voiced thoughts such as 'this is what I felt [but] I did not say it' or 'I kept these views to myself'. When Stopford, Hammersley and the rest refused to advance until the next day, Hamilton seethed. Pleading and cajoling, he managed to extract a pledge from Hammersley to mount a night attack, then rushed off almost by himself to wander aimlessly among the troops, never following through to see if the attack would indeed be pulled off (the answer to that was no). Tomorrow would just have to do.

'Tomorrow', of course, would not do. Liman von Sanders, who never hesitated to throw incompetents out of his office, consolidated the overall command of both Suvla and the Sari Bair ridge line to Kemal. Ordinarily, the accepted procedure on such occasions called for a German officer to be placed in charge, but Sanders knew a fighter when he saw one, and Kemal did not disappoint. When allied troops finally crossed the great salt lake and began advancing up the hill line, Kemal was there and ready. Hamilton, viewing the debacle from a ship close to shore, nearly cried in despair at the chaos that unfolded before his binoculars, men streaming down the hillsides and running for it. Broadsides from the fleet blew deadly sheets of shrapnel over the Turks, but they also set the dry brush afire. Many wounded men were burned to death. 'My heart had grown tough amidst the struggles of the peninsula but the misery of this scene well nigh broke it', Hamilton later wrote in his memoirs. 'Words are no use.' After just a week of further dithering, Hankey cabled back to London that 'the surprise attack has definitely failed'.[21]

'I think they are finished.'

Kemal's battlefield assessment,
Chunuk Bair, 10 August

Above ANZAC Cove the struggle was more even and desperate. Australian troops, attacking from their soon-to-be famous redoubt called Lone Pine, suffered gruesome casualties in their advance. New Zealanders finally captured the critical height, Chunuk Bair, and held on to it, by inches, for thirty-six hours. This was a Pyrrhic victory, as one of them noted. 'The position was untenable and had no future', he wrote. 'It was found almost impossible to supply even this handful of men', a generalized admission of the obvious, given the torturous terrain. Ian Hamilton would note on many occasions the geographical difficulties that the Gallipoli campaign presented, but it seems certain that he never fully realized them. Ammunition, grenades, water, food, artillery ....none of these would ever reach Chunuk Bair in sufficient quantities to enable its retention. This simple logistical detail seemed to have eluded not only the commander in chief, but also his generals on the ground, one of whom called the operation 'a hopeless mess'. Birdwood certainly should have understood by now the potential dilemma that would arise if the ANZACs had taken and, more importantly, retained Chunuk Bair and/or the adjoining two hills. What he could have done about it, given the geography, dreadful heat and exhausted men is another question. He seemed to be of the mindset, as one historian put it, of Mr. Micawber: 'something will turn up'.

Mustafa Kemal rode cross-country from the Suvla Bay battlefield back to Sari Bair in late afternoon sun. He and his men were thirsty, hungry, weary and just about all in. Kemal himself had not slept for four days, and it is left to our imagination as to how he managed to inspire, goad or frighten what remaining troops he had to charge the New Zealand position at 4:30 the next morning. Perhaps the power of rhetoric had spent itself, because Kemal himself led the attack. He was the first man out of the trench. He walked a few yards ahead, then gave the signal, raising his whip and pointing it to the enemy line. Inspired by this signal act of bravado, two regiments launched themselves forward and regained the summit. To all intents and purposes, the Dardanelles enterprise was now finished. It would drag on for another four months; the summer heat and its decay would be transformed into the chill of winter, where men would suffer freezing rain followed by chilling wind storms. The infamous blizzard of 27–29 November, 'the like of which I had never seen', according to Birdwood, resulted in 5,000 cases of frostbite, 300 deaths from exposure and the loss of one or both feet to fifty Gurkhas. One general likened its effects to the winter of 1812, when Russian snowstorms obliterated the Grand Armée of Napoleon.

Raids, forays and serious attacks continued, but the essential character of the respective field positions would not change – 'a great army hanging on by its eyelids to a rocky beach', as Churchill put it. Hamilton, in a moment of utter delusion, crowed that the 'spirit of the Turks had been broken'. It was his own men, on the contrary, who were finished, even the swaggering ANZACs. 'Their heart and guts [were] torn out ... even they could cheer no more.'

One journalist on the scene no longer believed his eyes, as frontal attacks continued without an end (or victory) in sight. 'The muddles and mismanagement [here] beat anything that has ever occurred in our military history.'[22] On 16 October, Hamilton was sacked. When the question of a possible evacuation had been broached in London, he called the idea 'the bloodiest tragedy in the world!' His prediction that half his entire force would be wiped out by enemy fire shrivelled the souls of even his most ardent supporters, and encouraged the defeatists. He followed that by requesting another 90,000 men to continue the campaign which, for some, made an even worse impression. His star declined over the horizon with incredible speed; Hamilton never held a command of importance thereafter. A replacement was sent to the Dardanelles, a member of the 'western cathedral',[23] who took one look at the situation and advised London to pull out. Churchill wrote of him that 'he came, he saw, he capitulated'. A marvellously executed withdrawal of ANZAC forces took place over eleven nights in December from Suvla

Bay with the loss of barely a man, and Helles was similarly emptied between 8 and 9 January.[24] Generals, admirals and politicians who had so botched the entire operation for twelve months took singular satisfaction in this feat, comparing it favourably with the sort of military triumph that had eluded them up to that point. Men in the trenches fooled themselves as well with numberless rationalizations. 'We were not driven off by the Turks', one said in defiance, a sentiment echoed by many. Others of more serious bent, though still defiant, showed more reflection. 'We have a lot of fellows sleeping in those valleys', one ANZAC said to Jack Churchill, Winston's brother, 'and we should never have been told to leave them.' John Masefield, the future poet laureate, admitted the obvious, equating the retreat as 'creeping off in the dark, like thieves in the night', one of the few negative observations in his book, which was mainly an apologia.[25]

Liman von Sanders claimed that it took over two years to pack up all the booty left behind, but this was little solace to Mustafa Kemal who, enfeebled by exhaustion and sickness, had been granted leave. 'Had I been there', he later said, 'and had the British got away without loss as they did, I would have blown out my brains.'

The Aftermath, and How to Explain It

'I will not attempt to even summarize the story of the Dardanelles Campaign with its incomprehensible blunders and its tragic failure.'

David Lloyd George, *Memoirs*

Kitchener's death in June 1916 enabled him to escape much of the blame for the Dardanelles. Many of the generals were cashiered on a haphazard basis, which would prove especially damaging to Ian Hamilton. Hemmersley and Stopford, for example, were among the many sent home rather quickly, where the former suffered another breakdown and never served again. Stopford, having now received 'the order of the Bowler Hat', immediately proceeded to criticize Hamilton for interfering in his operations during that disastrous span of 6 to 10 August. Incredible as it seems, the commission formed to investigate the affair agreed with Stopford. Hamilton's reputation was shot by the time he arrived back in London.[26] The new man at the Admiralty, Arthur Balfour, wrote Admiral de Robeck as follows: 'I am sorry but not surprised to hear from Commodore Keyes that you are badly in need of a holiday. Please consider yourself at liberty to take one'. Winston Churchill, more than any other individual, paid the heaviest price. He badgered Asquith repeatedly to publish the full appropriate documentation, which he felt would exonerate him of primary guilt, but Asquith had his political survival, among many other things, on his mind, and the general public by that point was ready for scapegoats, not protracted, legalistic defences. For years and years thereafter, Churchill would be greeted at rallies and speeches with the cry, 'What about the Dardanelles?' In a stew, he resigned from the cabinet on 11 November. The Dardanelles, he wrote Admiral John Jellicoe, were 'like a Greek tragedy', its principal victim not so much the thousands of men who perished, but his own career. He requested a military assignment on the western front, which he received, the command of a battalion raised in Scotland. When he arrived to take up his quarters, he brought along far more than the customary allotment of personal goods (35 pounds), including a bathtub and boiler to heat his water. He asked his wife to send him a book of poetry by the Scottish bard, Robert Burns. 'I will soothe & cheer their spirits by quotations from it'. His mother continued giving dinner parties, inviting as many powerful men as she could to keep Winston's name in circulation, but even she admitted these were like going to see *Hamlet*, but Hamlet wasn't there.

Churchill had been raised from an early age on the great martial feats of legend and romance; Marlborough's blood, after all, ran through his blue veins. In the early days of the war, his office at Whitehall could seem tame and dreary. Asquith wrote that Churchill's mouth appeared to water when they discussed the army's first battles, and that he seemed like a chained tiger wanting more blood. He 'declared that a political career was nothing to him in comparison with military glory'. He reminded the prime minister of a schoolboy. The reality of trench warfare two years into the struggle, however, presented a different picture. He was not going over as a field marshal, or a general, or even as a brigadier. He would not be directing anything, but just following orders, and orders of the day were usually brutal attacks against entrenched machine gun positions. There was no need for a sword here, nor for bugles, flags or bearskin hats. Writing 'daily at the lack of power to make things move', the gloss of a military life soon grew stale. His troops had suffered horrific casualties in the Loos fiasco of September 1915. Attending a lecture given for officers to go over lessons learned, Churchill had to bite his tongue when asked what he had learned. 'Don't do it again' was what he wished to say, but what was the point? 'They will [do it again]', he wrote his wife, 'I have no doubt', a reflection of his growing discontent with the contemporary military mindset. This was, he concluded, no place for a man of his talents, and he soon agitated to return home, which he did three months later. 'I have left the army', he told Lord Riddell, 'I was in the trenches for eighty days. I did not see why I should remain at the mercy of some ill-directed shot.' Thereafter, the glory he dreamed about would always be political.

After the war, publishing houses vied with one another to bring out memoirs and histories that, unsurprisingly, varied in both literary quality and reliability. In their wake (usually by many years) came the more or less 'official' histories: broad and dense narratives, often under the auspices of royal commissions; also regimental histories where, in the words of one commentator, 'chaotic retreat becomes an orderly withdrawal. Everything seems to have gone exactly to plan' and so on; and, inevitably, individual reminiscences both by generals, privates and every rank in between. Those written by the former group of gentlemen could be counted upon for their dry and frequently bloodless recapitulations of operational detail, their desire to 'straighten the record' (usually at the expense of someone else's reputation), and their obliviousness of day-to-day reality. Memoirs by men in the trenches, by contrast, usually fell into two categories. The first, though full of gruesome detail, generally revelled in the adventure of it all. A Captain Lynch relayed in some satisfaction his encounter with a German officer leading Turkish troops, whom he bayoneted not once or twice, but six or seven times, just for the hell of it ('I gave him a fine death'). The second, also detailed, would emphasize futility. Some slathered their stories with glory, others with dirt and blood; there seemed to be little middle ground.

The Dardanelles campaign presents anyone interested in it with more than the usual tidal wave of material. Much of this had to do with the inordinate pride that the Australian and New Zealand peoples developed for this enterprise. It was presented to them in ways that Darwin himself might have authored: two far-flung, extraneous colonial outposts (one first settled by convicts) entering the grand stage of nationhood by their free expenditure of blood and treasure on this immense imperial enterprise – a rite of passage, as it were, and one that would exact a heavy sacrifice willingly accepted by all. In the earliest explosion of war fever, the leader of the Australian opposition had said it point blank, Australia would support the empire 'to our last man and our last shilling'. Fifty-two thousand signed up almost immediately, and were at Gallipoli within two months, fighting and dying. Twenty percent of these recruits had been born in England, but the remainder represented the cream of Australian towns, cities and the outback. Three-quarters were of prime military age, between 18 and 29, and eighty percent of these young men were single. Proportionate to the population, the losses by 1918 were actuarily staggering, which considerably dampened the initial rush of enthusiasm for war.[27] After the Gallipoli evacuation, the Australians and New Zealanders were generally lost in the vast manpower pools of allied units in Flanders and France, and, given the larger theatre, their casualty figures climbed exponentially. Their reputation for gallantry, along with the Canadians, remained high, but they were now part of a bigger narrative, whereas at the Dardanelles they had stood out front and centre, both for what they won and for what they lost, becoming in many ways the major story. As such, their feats in Gallipoli have received special prominence 'down under', and provided a deep wellspring of both national pride and regret, depending on people's points of view.

Commentators at the time had welcomed this test. Darwin was fashionable. Until you had killed someone in battle, how could you call yourself 'a people' or 'a nation'. Some ANZAC diaries repeated this mantra over and over again. Gaining the respect of London was supremely important. Perversely, however, the highly embellished 'rugged individuality' for which the ANZACs became known, also manifested itself in an ugly undertone of contempt for aspects of the mother country, especially its politicians and officers. If it hadn't been for the ANZACs, could Britain have possibly won the war? The answer to that depended on whom you talked to. Many staff officers at Whitehall saw the ANZACs as numbers, men to throw into the breech; ANZACs resented that. They saw themselves as saviours, steel ramrods who put some energy into the faltering and exhausted British ranks. The truth lies somewhere in between. Many recollections of old veterans refused to enter into the argument, or avoided the blandishments of pride or macho heroics. 'My uncle's most vivid … memory of this period was that he spent most of his time at ANZAC sitting on the latrine', said one family historian. Certainly by 1918, neither of the ANZAC nations was prepared to be considered a mere appendage of Britain, what one called 'a joint in the tail of a great empire'. Their prime ministers, along with their counterpart in Canada, would no longer be taken for granted. Woodrow Wilson caused a major contretemps at the Versailles peace conference when he initially vetoed the notion of granting any of the 'little three' a seat at the conference table. In former times, the British prime minster of the moment might well have agreed, but in political terms that sort of imperial arrogance was no longer possible.

'Sing the epic.'

Lieutenant-General Sir George MacMunn

Augmenting and embellishing the mock-heroic dimensions of the ANZAC experience – making it unique, in fact – were the imagistic fetishes that so enthralled those Britons who took pen to paper after the war, men who had been educated at public schools or who had studied the classics at Oxford and Cambridge. These men could not get Homer out of their minds.

Veneration of all things Hellenistic has a long history in British tradition. Athens, the alleged birthplace of democracy, with Sparta as its 'Prussian' counterpart, figured in the fantasies of countless generations: Shelley translated Plato and Aristotle from their original Greek, Byron died as he prepared to lead a brigade in the Greek revolution of 1824, Herodotus proved the inspiration for Gibbon's magisterial *The History of the Decline and Fall of the Roman Empire*, Elgin could steal panels from the Acropolis without a thought, Rupert Brooke was seen as a latter-day Apollo and everyone was enthralled with the Aegean, 'that calm and crystalline sea'. The greatest classic of them all was Homer, the greatest epic of them all the *Iliad* – the perfect emotive backdrop to the Gallipoli campaign.

Standing on or near the fabled plain of Troy, witnessing the arena of the mighty but feckless Xerxes, disparaging the oriental decadence of the Turks, commingled into an almost homo-erotic worship of virility on the part of countless British observers. The Australians and New Zealanders were 'physical specimens' of incredible grace and power, their 'superb physiques' perfectly suited to hurling the discus, bathing naked at ANZAC Cove as shrapnel swirled overhead or killing Turks. Compton Mackenzie outdid himself in one of his descriptive odes, published in *Gallipoli Memories*:

> There was not one of those glorious young men I saw that day who might not himself have been Ajax or Diomedes, Hector or Achilles. Their almost complete nudity, their tallness and majestic simplicity of line, their rose-brown flesh burnt by the sun and purged of all grossness by the ordeal through which they were passing. These united to create something as near to absolute beauty as I shall hope ever to see in this world.

'They should be celebrated in hexameters', he wrote, 'not headlines.'

Sir Ian Hamilton agreed. He saw in these buckaroos some idealized vision of the perfect killer. 'The spirit of war has breathed fires into their hearts', he wrote with his usual exaggeration, 'They are spoiling for a scrap!' If only they could wear armour, carry shields and skewer their enemies with sword or spear, the picture would be perfect.

Hamilton's memoir is possibly the most interesting of all that were published on the Gallipoli experience, if only because he was at the centre: the 'show' was all his, the 'stunts' of landing at Cape Helles and ANZAC Cove, then at Suvla Bay, were his creations; the responsibility for what happened there uniquely his. This was certainly not the way he had intended it to be. In all fairness, his instructions from London had been incredibly vague. When he read them out to de Robeck and his officers upon his arrival in the theatre, he was finished in just a couple of minutes. Roger Keyes, after an awkward silence, asked, 'Is that all?' When told it was, 'everyone looked a little blank'.

This was due to the fact that Kitchener had envisioned the navy doing all the hard work and earning the laurels; Hamilton was there in case everything at sea went wrong. When everything did go wrong, Hamilton and his staff were placed in the position of planning the invasion, for such it was, of this 'barren trackless extremity of an Empire', all on their own. He did so with complete confidence; he did not start going sour on the enterprise until the operation itself went sour. Then he looked for someone to blame.

Memoirs are usually, by their very nature, slippery threads. Details can be forgotten or omitted (consciously or not sometimes does not matter), and people with an axe to grind can often be utterly untrustworthy. Setting the record straight usually entails stabbing someone else in the back, for rarely – especially in military reminiscences – is it ever the intention of their authors to blame themselves. Even accepting these bare truths, however, Hamilton's rendition stands more slyly dishonest than most. It is possibly the most disingenuous rendition of any coming out of this war, and, in its bravado and cheap sentimentality, perhaps the most dislikable. Beneath the frantic, slightly hysterical, tone of presentation and style, there is one deep undercurrent of some subtlety. While not an unabashed character assassination, its main object is to crucify Kitchener.

Lord Kitchener will be dealt with more fully later in this narrative. Suffice to say here that during the Gallipoli campaign his inefficiencies, egotism and anachronistic ways all came under heavy though indirect fire from his colleagues in the Asquith government (most generally whispers, not to his face). Originally deemed an infallible presence, he was gradually embarked on a long slide towards irrelevancy, several schemes now afoot to shunt him off to India or some other faraway place. There can be little doubt that his amorphous goals for Gallipoli (reflecting, in all honesty, the inchoate thinking of others in the cabinet) did not help Hamilton in his task.

Capturing Constantinople was the agreed upon goal, but how to achieve it was left fairly open. The miscoordination between the army and navy's roles is only the most obvious manifestation of this confusion.

While Kitchener and the rest had high hopes for the expedition, they sought to do it, according to Hamilton, 'on the cheap', a charge that was accurately put to some degree. On the one hand, the projected harvest from beating the Turk was considered immense – the war would be won! – but on the other, the western front consumed the lion's share of men, artillery, ammunition and, most importantly, attention, a fact of life that would not change. Having said that, Hamilton never quailed at the prospects ahead of him; never initially questioned the resources to be made available; and assumed that the Turk was ready to fold. Everyone knew the enemy foot soldier was an impoverished and illiterate peasant, brutalized by his officers, seldom paid, poorly equipped and the recipient of several military humiliations over the previous five years. He was not considered a worthy or difficult opponent. Hamilton does not say so explicitly, but this assumption is obvious on every page. His surprise and chagrin at the string of rebuffs he suffered, beginning on 25 April, are at first impossible for him to accept. Though none of his objectives were met, it is clear to him that he is winning: losses are severe, but the Turks suffer more; allied morale is cresting higher every day, the Turk's is low; the racial qualities of the Anglo-Saxon are obvious to see, his opposite number thirty yards away in the enemy trench line is just waiting for a chance to surrender or desert; the *Queen Elizabeth* turns the countryside into rubble, the Turk can't take much more.

As days stretch into weeks and then months, however, all Hamilton can do is stew. His effective strength declines, whether due to enemy shells or dysentery does not matter. It becomes obvious to him what is now needed: more men, more shells, more help. Kitchener, however, was loath to receive such pleas (and had warned Hamilton against sending them, as Sir Ian specifically noted: when given Fortune's purse, don't ask 'for an extra half-crown'). But without them, this golden opportunity might be lost.

What golden opportunity? The element of surprise had been lost months before. General von Sanders might not know exactly where the allies would land (Kemal, however, did in his heart), but he had a plan and the reserves to meet them. As the allies incrementally poured more men and equipment into the struggle, so did the Turks. The Gallipoli operation had stalemate written all over it, but a deadlock was not something Hamilton was prepared to accept.

Hamilton styled his memoirs as a diary, a grossly misleading characterization. He published the book in 1920, five years after the campaign. While he did employ notes, memos and correspondence between his headquarters and London, and published many of these in allegedly verbatim form, he did so selectively and, apparently, with an editor's eye (i.e. scissors). Though claiming absolute fidelity to Lord Kitchener, a man who had done much for his career and whom he generally admired, the objective was to portray the now-deceased field marshal as more niggardly than he should have been with the expedition's growing needs, therein the cumulative cause of defeat. The two-volume 'diary' is almost a daily recitation of wants and needs. With more of just about everything, Hamilton suggested, he would most certainly have won the day, but Lord Kitchener was either recalcitrant or too late in supplying the necessities. The barrage of Sir Ian's always cheerfully written requests succeeds as it was intended to, in a wearying sort of way. Kitchener bungled it, Hamilton did the best he could against overwhelming odds (yes, the Turk had suddenly became 'well clothed, well nourished' and 'well commanded', their reinforcements of 'better character and resolve'. Hamilton even threw in the allusion of David [being the allies] and Goliath [the Turk], against whom he had only 'pebbles' to throw, an allusion to his want of artillery shells).

The problem with Hamilton's recollections is the usual one for individuals caught in a bind trying to justify their every decision and action. Attempting to have it both ways, the general slips into contradictions and lapses in ordered thinking. The western front is the 'cudgel', it demands and absorbs everything; the Dardanelles is the 'rapier', it doesn't need all that much to be a success, but it gets nothing. This is contradicted by Hamilton's 'cudgel' approach to his own problems: he wants supplies on 'a western scale', more artillery to crush the enemy's defences and more men to rush forward in daylight frontal attacks, their aim to capture a line of earthworks behind which are three or four more. He is, in fact, applying western front tactics to what was supposed to be a nimble and quick approach to outflanking the enemy. Hamilton prefigured Douglas Haig with each passing day; his appetite became omnivorous. Casualties were to be regretted, but there was never a hesitation to suffer more.

In personal terms, Sir Ian comes across pretty much as the man he was. A 'cheerio' type full of enthusiasm, positive thoughts and endless optimism; no obstacle too high, no mountain that could not be climbed. His thinking processes, at least as exemplified on the printed page, were not measured or consistent, however. What he thought one day could be entirely reversed the next, a curious juxtaposition that more thorough editing might have corrected. As problems and reverses piled up, his frustrations kept pace. Furious that press censorship had not been applied in Egypt, where reports on the initial preparations for the campaign had been daily reported, he was frustrated five months later when the still-applied press blackout prevented him from writing 'one or two articles' declaiming the 'truth' about his supply problems. 'I could kill' the censor, he notes in the spirit of full disclosure.[28] He continues to batter and belittle the Turk: they 'are afraid of us', 'the enemy has been brought to a standstill', 'they have had a belly full', he was 'singeing his beard', 'It was worth ten years of tennis to watch the Australians and New Zealanders go in'. No doubt all this was true, but what had Hamilton to show for it? A static line, failure on every front, gridlock. The whole thing was unfair. Why couldn't the two combatants just meet in an open field and go at it, man to man, bayonet to bayonet, the field of Agincourt transplanted to Turkey? Instead some 'dirty Turk' with a machine gun can cut down fifty fine men in a minute, 'each of whom is worth several dozen' of the wretched enemy. If Kitchener comes off, as intended, rather poorly in this narrative, at the end of over 700 pages so too does Hamilton.

ANZAC Day

'And the scrub held other secrets. As you peered among the shadows you might find the grizzly remains of men, lying stiller than the leaves in a hot noon. They had become horrid black and swollen figures, causing you to turn and push for more open spaces. At times a sickly wind would drift over, warning of more spots to be left alone. It was not that we were careless with our dead and left them where they died. But some men fell in lonely places and some lay under enemy fire where the search parties could not go in. In the strangest, most difficult, mostly wayward places little graves were dug, each with simple marks of a man's name, which winter winds would wash away.'

Australian trooper

The high-water mark of the New Zealand advance to the summit of Chunuk Bair is marked by a modest though impressive memorial of white bleached stone. It is overpowered, however, by a nearby Nelsonian pillar, crowned with a statue of Mustafa Kemal. Even taller than that is a huge flagpole flying the Turkish standard, white crescent on a red background. It is not often that visitors from any number of countries that made up the British Empire come to a battleground like this to commemorate a defeat. The Dardanelles was not, as Lloyd George put it, 'Victory as Usual'. What one does read are the usual praises sung for the triumph of human spirit in the face of adversity, but at times one must even question that. Courage, grit, endurance? All these were amply demonstrated here, but the overall impression is that of waste. People were slaughtered, but to what end? After the Turks retook this position, all that was left were bodies, sometimes two and three deep in the various trenches, many of whom had been dead for days. In the euphemistic jargon of official histories, they had been 'swept away' by human tidal waves yelling 'Allah' at the top of their lungs. 'Bloated and blackened by decay and crawling with maggots.... This is war and this is glory', wrote one ANZAC veteran later. The Turks buried some 850 New Zealanders in mass graves.

Wandering about the scrub, one comes across small plots here and there with eight or nine headstones recording names of soldiers who had come across oceans and seas 'from the uttermost ends of the earth' (meaning New Zealand and Australia), followed by the words 'believed buried here'. But does anyone know for sure? Of the 60,000 Australian soldiers killed in World War I, 25,000 have no known grave, a testament to the obliterating character of modern war. For the Turkish dead, who greatly outnumbered those killed on the allied side, those who were not conflagrated in ghastly funeral pyres lie mostly in communal pits, largely undecorated, unnamed, anonymous. Commanders on both sides were certainly profligate with their troops, sending them out on missions that were closer to suicide than reasoned military operations. The consequences often cost them the respect of their troopers, their careers and their sanity. 'You are not fit to command pigs, let alone men', one New Zealander said to a superior British officer. Another trooper wrote in his diary about a new batch of colonels and brigadiers assigned to his unit. 'I give them about a fortnight in this place and then home with shattered nerves.' Looking out from the summit of Chunuk Bair at miles of desolate territory – truly the middle of nowhere – I can understand why.[29]

Most of the battlefield is noteworthy only for this, the geography, and in nearly all of it the scars of battle have disappeared. There is very little left to remind a person that some one million combatants struggled here. ANZAC Cove might as well be the setting for a beach resort, so perfect is the vista of shimmering sea and mountain backdrop. The only things missing are cabanas, palm trees and people. As is typical of the peninsula as a whole, it seems largely devoid of tourists.

On ANZAC Day, however, 25 April, the place exudes a decidedly surreal atmosphere, as tourists from Australia and New Zealand arrive here in the spirit of both sober commemoration and noisy cheer (in 2001, over 15,000 of them), perhaps a reflection of conflicted feelings. Many would prefer that ANZAC Day be formal and solemn; in Australia, for instance, there have been bitter squabbles over whether liquor stores and bars should be open. Prohibitionists won some early battles, but the day has come to be largely a wet one, where many wave flags and live a little, as though to cement in everyone's eyes the general cliché about these cheerful and boisterous peoples. It goes to show that life is not neat; no one is ever fully satisfied.

On ANZAC Day the small and tidy cemeteries on Gallipoli are overrun. People eat picnics sitting among the rows of gravestones. Most of the more famous outposts, particularly Lone Pine, double as cemetery plots, so for a couple of days of the year there's enough commotion here almost to resemble the din of battle. A single pine still stands on the site, planted with a seed from its famous ancestor, a nice touch. The British know how to make a place of death look serene and comfortable. The Turks, on the other hand, have more tangible artefacts to exhibit. The forts at both the head of the Dardanelles and at the Narrows are still there, many with their guns still intact. Aside from memorials to Mustafa Kemal, which are everywhere, the most common representation is that of the Turkish artilleryman, Corporal Seyit Ali Çabuk who, when a winch broke during battle, carried three shells on his back weighing six hundred pounds to and fro from an ammunition storehouse to the Krupp-built 14-incher that he was serving. Bronze statues of this fellow are ubiquitous. Ferries ply back and forth at the Narrows, weaving in and out of the ship traffic that steams by without interruption. These evasive manoeuvres remind me of the British and French attempts to dodge the minefields. It seems incredible that the Royal Navy could not force its passage on through to Constantinople, but the channel is only a mile or so wide at this point and, being here, one can imagine in such a confined space how menacing the mine situation must have been.

As for the *River Clyde*, which Asquith had light-heartedly compared to the Trojan Horse (until he learned the actual bloody details of the botched landing), it lay for some time beached at Zone V. When the allies occupied Constantinople immediately after the war, 'they took [her] away and sold her to tramp the Mediterranean with coal', according to Compton Mackenzie.

For the sake of a few hundred pounds they were not willing that her plates should slowly rust away in memory of that April morning, rust away in red flakes and like the blood of the men she carried be mingled at last with the sea. And maybe those white and purple caper flowers will again have nodded to her in the June breeze when she has steamed past

Sedd-el-Bahr, carrying coals for her Greek owner up the Dardanelles to Constantinople, she who once anchored off here with a cargo of heroes, they too bound for Constantinople.

The ship remained in service until 1966, last seen plying the Spanish coast as the *Maruya y Aurora*, selling her dirty cargo at various ports of call. She ended on the scrap heap, but no one can remember where.

Chapter 8

Verdun

The city of Verdun sits mostly on the left bank of the river Meuse. Along with other long-established frontier posts along the north-eastern edge of France – Thionville, Metz, Nancy, Belfort, Toul and so on – its lineage is largely linked to war. Verdun and its compatriots have all served a single purpose, to stem the flow of barbarism that inevitably had its origins on the other side of the rivers Saar and Rhine, the former only ninety miles away. The Romans first identified the site, *Virodunum Castrum*, meaning strong fortified 'camp', and its geographic characteristics certainly justified the name. At a bend in the river, the old town sits on a rocky elevation 130 feet high, dominating the approaches of small ravines and gullies which pierce a small circular buckler of higher hills, part of the *Côtes de Meuse* that rise up from the other bank. Before the days of artillery, this was a commanding situation, enhanced by hundreds of years spent erecting walls, moats and heavy gates, enough tảo discourage the primitive armies that periodically laid siege to it. Verdun rarely cracked.

In the late seventeenth century, gunpowder changed all that. The great Vauban, chief engineer to Louis XIV, designed one of his most formidable works here, an enormous and largely 'subterranean' fortification carved into the stony escarpment that was designed to absorb the shock of cannonballs and various other explosive devices. His sprawling citadel monopolized much of the town's physical space, which was largely clustered about its eastern edge in typically congested proximity. Even today the upper town retains a claustrophobic air, its battered cathedral and episcopal palace cramped together amid twisting alleyways and narrow streets. In 1914 about 15,000 people lived here, in what had become the quintessential garrison town, somnambulant in times of peace but packed with men, vehicles and commotion in times of war. Its obsolescence was perfectly described by an American journalist in 1916. 'Verdun is like a lump of sugar in a finger bowl', he wrote, and from his perch on one of the surrounding hills, 'I was standing on the rim'.

The conflicted thinking in French military circles after the Franco-Prussian War had a dramatic effect on Verdun and its surroundings. That conflagration, known in France as *la Débâcle*, had proved a humiliating experience not only for Napoleon III but for French arms in general. The result saw the emergence of a great divide in the field of strategic theory, almost a 'fault line' dividing two schools of thought. At issue, as always, was how to protect French interests from their perennial (and encroaching) foe. Germany had seized Alsace-Lorraine from the defeated French in 1871. Instead of being 250 miles from Paris, German armies were now only 150 or so miles away. In the spirit of *revanche* (or revenge), no French officer doubted that another day of reckoning lay ahead at some indeterminate but inevitable moment in time, and the question became: how were French armies to be deployed in the next round? The just-concluded war with Bismarck had witnessed stupendous and unimaginable fiascos. Two French marshals, Bazaine and MacMahon, had found themselves boxed and trapped in the fortress cities of Metz and Sedan. Their collective defeats had seen nearly 300,000 French soldiers marched away into captivity. The inelegant phraseology of a French general trapped in Sedan pretty well summarized the dilemma: 'We're in a chamber pot and we're going to get covered in shit.'

Contemplating the future, strategists asked themselves why anyone would ever contemplate repeating such an experience. French martial spirit existed in open fields and fluid encounters, situations where the spirit of attack could flourish. France should determine its fortunes in movement. Such views coalesced in the operational Plan XVII, which coloured the first phase of the war in 1914, and is best expressed in the phrase *l'offensive brutale et à outrance*, or 'attack to the bitter end'. The results were just as disastrous as anything Napoleon III oversaw at Metz and Sedan. In just fourteen days, over 300,000 Frenchmen were killed or wounded, and the officer corps trimmed by ten percent of its total complement, many of whom had died leading charges wearing white gloves and waving canes. The chief architect of this doctrine, Colonel Louis de Grandmaison, exemplified both the approach and its inevitable result when carried forth under modern conditions of war. In one day, 20 August, his 153rd Infantry regiment was effectively obliterated. He himself was wounded six times during the Battle of the Frontiers, and was killed the next year when a shell fragment hit him in the head.

The other side of the coin was best exemplified by what the Third French Republic actually did between 1873 and the turn of the century. The secular Third Republic, born amid the rubble, both intellectual and physical, of Napoleon III's feckless military adventurism – as well as by the experience of seeing Paris under siege in 1870 – was riddled with both suspicion and disgust for the officer corps of the standing army. Too many of these soldiers, especially those connected to the general staff and Saint-Cyr, the military academy, were Catholic, clerical, monarchical in sympathy, vainglorious and opinionated, the very embodiment of 'gold-braided infallibility'.[1] They were not to be trusted, nor their theories left unquestioned. Purges within the officer corps were frequent: going to church each Sunday was often a justification for banishment to some remote garrison in the south or, worse, perhaps to South-East Asia. Republican ministers of war could come and go with depressing regularity, but they held the administrative power. At one point they even banned the playing of drums and bugles in barrack squares, and efforts to replace traditionally gaudy uniforms with camouflage green were strenuously opposed. When French soldiers advanced in 1914, many of them looked to be straight from the pages of Waterloo.

Whereas cavalry officers, still the social elite within establishment circles, envisioned charges of cuirassiers and dragoons up to the crests of undulating hillocks, politicians, bureaucrats and engineers in Paris put their faith, and budgets, behind something considerably less glamorous: concrete. By losing Alsace and Lorraine, France had not only stood embarrassed, but also undressed. The great fortress cities of Metz and Strasbourg were now gone. All Germany had to do was spent a handful of marks to reorient artillery mounts to face west, not east. France, on the other hand, had to start from the very beginning. An entire system based on forts was soon proposed by General Séré de Rivières, an engineering genius, and lavishly funded. His idea was to erect a concrete barrier; it was between Verdun and Toul, a line that would so discourage the Germans that they would be forced to direct their attacks either to the north or to the south of it. Mobile French units could bring the enemy to battle there on ground of their choosing. He ridiculed the notion of building 'a Wall of China' along the entire frontier; his idea was to funnel the Germans into geographical situations that would favour the French. Twenty-five percent of France's postwar budget went towards military spending, and large proportions of that sum were allocated to construction costs. Some of this money went into the pockets of a legion of Italians who were imported into the country as construction workers. Little villages like Douaumont and Vaux were flooded by them.[2]

There was nothing fundamentally radical in the fortress designs; they were, in simple terms, a modernization of Vauban. Indeed, a diagram of any French fort subsequently built during these three decades is nothing if not a reiteration of Vaubanesque principles: bastions, angles, supporting fire fields, simple polygon design. Instead of one fortification, however, the evolution of Vauban's mathematically driven schemes was an entire interlocking system of multiple strong points, in Verdun's case twenty major forts supported by three dozen smaller ancillary posts, each intended to cover a neighbour's flank here or a vulnerable approach there. The most important of these, such as the famous Fort Douaumont, were strung along the eastern heights across the river Meuse from Verdun. Aside from covering each other, they overlooked the expansive plain of Woëvre stretching east. This would prove, it was believed, a defensive wall of strength against which the attacking enemy could batter himself senseless if he so chose.[3]

The breath and complexity of the Verdun fortress system is not as readily apparent to the visitor today as it was a century ago, unless one first approaches the complex from the plain of Woëvre and the east (as would the Germans, theoretically). The Côtes de Meuse were so pulverized during the Great War that in many places they were simply abandoned to human use when hostilities finally ceased. Nine villages, *Mort pour La France*, were not reinhabited after 1918 by order of the government. The ground was so saturated with heavy ordnance, much of it unexploded, that authorities expected there to be a whole new round of casualties should farmers be allowed to till the soil again. Instead, large swaths of forest were planted, obscuring the landscape (and views), concealing the symmetry and design rationale of de Rivières' overall plan, and making most of the forts visually inaccessible to the general public. Wandering through the woods, as I did in some trepidation, maps in hand, often did not reveal the chill gray stone of blockhouses and enormous gates until you had more or less stumbled upon them. In 1914 many of these forts, though built into the ground, were open to view; standing on top of Fort Douaumont, for example, provided a fine panorama, easily encapsulating the implications of the defensive design. Every gun position had been mathematically plotted. There was not a single target that a gunner could not hit, given proper observation. And far below, stretching into the distance, was the Woëvre plain, so typical of the Lorraine countryside: flat, featureless, with nowhere to hide. Driving today west from Briey towards Verdun, for example, the Côtes de Meuse seem more formidable than they really are, looming over the entire approach. Its strategic value was pretty obvious in 1914, when fields of fire were unobstructed by vegetation; they still give a chill now, even though the forts are largely invisible from a distance.

This was a view that might have dampened the Germans (it did not); and it might have reassured the officers of the Grand Quartier Général, or *GQG*, (but did not). At the turn of the twentieth century, the French army was not looking for *sécurité*, nor was it interested in the boredom of sitting in drafty, dripping, cavernous bunkers waiting for the enemy. Four decades of time to think things over, four decades of having no wars to fight, had rekindled the collective imagination of officers who had grown weary of garrison duty. Too much time on one's hands usually results in trouble, and such was the case up and down the halls of France's leading military academies.

The French, until the recent past, have generally considered themselves to be the elite of military nations. The career and example of Napoleon has generally had that effect. The exaggerated paintings of Jacques-Louis David, Antoine-Jean Gros and others, showing the emperor in some histrionic pose or another – who can ever forget Gros's *Napoleon at the Bridge of Arcole* – embody the nation's concept of itself: heroic beyond imagination, colourful and daring, a style second to none.[4] The Franco-Prussian War had disturbed this image, but that conflict had had its moments, the heroic cavalry charges at the Battle of Sedan in 1870 being one (even Wilhelm's grandfather, Kaiser Wilhelm I and present at the moment, was heard to utter words of astonishment – 'Oh, such brave gentlemen!' which he said in French). With no recent war to study, theorists turned instead to the glorious past and, in the process, lost touch with reality. Louis de Grandmaison proved an example of that. It did not take long before many officers, trained in the ethos of *l'attaque à outrance*, had learned their lesson. Men like Grandmaison 'performed the function of corporals, not commanders', in the opinion of some contemporaries. Others refused to be discouraged.

Louis de Grandmaison is not a name that most people will recognize today. Joffre, Robert Nivelle, Pétain and Ferdinand Foch are a different matter. Foch, for instance, remains one of the heroes of the Great War, the man all the allied leaders turned to when the western front nearly collapsed in 1918. His resolution and grit – 'Everyone to the battle!' he said at a moment of great peril – stiffened people's nerves and staunched the mood of growing panic. It was he who oversaw the great counterattacks that finally overwhelmed the enemy's armies; it was he who presented the terms to German delegates in the woods of Compiègne to end the war 100 days later. Few people recall, however, that just twenty-nine months into the war, he was a figure in eclipse.

The Generals

Ferdinand Foch was born in Tarbes, a village at the foot of the Pyrenees. His father was a functionary in the civil service, intensely religious and patriotic – his first name, Napoleon, manifests the usual idolatry, reinforced by the exploits of two long-deceased relatives, one of whom had fought with the emperor at Austerlitz, and the other who had attained the rank of general. On solemn occasions, his father's old uniform was brought out for reverenced attention. On the religious front, Tarbes stood witness to the amazing miracles of Lourdes, only ten or so miles away to the south-west, which solidified in devout souls the importance of Catholicism in everyday life. Ferdinand, like his parents and siblings, was a religious man; his younger brother would become a Jesuit.

Foch attended several schools, some far away, a number run by religious orders. He was studying mathematics at Metz when that city found itself deluged with retreating troops in 1870. In his memoirs, Foch remembers seeing Napoleon III riding by in his carriage. Napoleon was a sick man at the time, suffering gallstones, and he looked like death. His face was covered with rouge to deceive the public, but Foch was not fooled. He also heard, with contempt, that Marshal Bazaine, soon to be disgraced, had set up headquarters in the Grand Hotel, where he spent his time playing billiards. Catching one of the last trains out of Metz before its fall, Foch shared a railway compartment with refugees. One peasant woman had fled with but a single possession, a potted geranium. These sorts of things impressed his mind.

Foch's technical abilities marked him as an artilleryman when he decided to join up at nineteen years of age. He studied at various military schools, some passed through with moderate distinction, and served the usual stints in garrison towns around the country. Promotion was slow, but Foch was earmarked as someone to pay attention to. He was seen as 'the future', a designation made quite apparent when he was appointed as an instructor at the École Supérieure de Guerre in Paris, a post held for six years. In 1908 he returned, as the school's superintendent. He was clearly acknowledged as one of the foremost thinkers and theorists of the new French army. By this time he was also fifty-seven years old, and younger men, with more vigour, viewed him as only young men can do: Foch was 'old school', *démodé*, and lacking dash. His opinions needed updating and an infusion of energy.

Foch, while not a true academic, was well read, at least by the standards of his fellow officers, many of whom never dared open a book.[5] He was as familiar with von Clausewitz as he was with Napoleon, and certain conclusions from their careers and writings deeply influenced his thinking.[6] He was aware that the mechanics of warfare were changing. He recognized new weapons for what they were: machine guns could not be dismissed as inconsequential gimmicks; railways did more than just carry freight and passengers along scenic routes during holidays – they could also move entire armies from Point A to Point B in mere hours; heavy artillery, when used properly, could grab an enemy by its throat.[7]

Modern technology had to be met in modern ways, a fact Foch understood, but he was determined not to leave the past behind. He was patriotic enough, a student of history enough, and a complete enough devotee of French spirit and *élan* to point out where victory, in such mechanistic confrontations, could ultimately be found. The difference maker was 'will'. Nietzsche must have turned over in his grave to think that a Frenchman, of all people, was among those who fully appreciated his creed.

Foch, as a man of spirit, believed that human qualities could both win and lose battles, that one side could 'impose its will' on the other even if numerical factors on the battlefield were stacked the opposite way. Armies with fewer men, fewer resources and fewer capable officers could still defeat their enemy if – and this was the significant 'if' – they decided they would not accept defeat. Psychological factors mattered even in modern warfare, and Foch was clever and sufficiently agile that he could encapsulate his motivational messages in short, catchy phrases that grabbed the attention of students: 'No victory without fighting'; 'War can only be learnt by war'; 'I desire nothing so much as a big battle' (quoting Napoleon), so on and so forth, rolled off his lips and were dutifully entered into notebooks. His acolytes, with less discernment than his, would put these largely undigested theorems into action beginning in 1914. The military historian Liddell Hart called Foch 'a preacher more than a teacher', and Georges Clemenceau, with whom he would have bitter disputes, dismissed his printed lectures as 'metaphysics', not military science.

Ferdinand Foch appeared to be an up-to-date, current officer. Theories of superheroes and men of destiny were popular at the turn of the century. It seemed a humanist response to a world rapidly industrializing, a world where numbers took on exaggerated importance and buried individuality. But, in fact, Foch had his feet in two worlds, both the past and the present (though not the future). He recognized defensive warfare as a regrettable fact of life; he did not believe the boring Belgian forts would prove ineffective, he could not envision that the ring of concrete protecting Verdun would, on the eve of battle, be deemed obsolete and stripped of its weaponry. These were facts of life.

The logic of modernity depressed him, however, and he often fell back into Napoleonic daydreams, always a comforting support for any French soldier. Any way you looked at it, war was by definition 'offensive' in nature. Victory rarely lay in 'defending' something, it more often turned on plunging ahead into the unknown, attacking almost for the sake of it. In modern war, a general had to be careful when and where he unleashed the offensive spirit – Foch believed in artillery – but 'Forward! Forward!' remained his primary weapon, the most important arrow in his quiver. There was no renown, and no gain, to be found sitting in one's dugout or always confined in an undergound bunker. At some point, one had to advance. Foch's ideology was in many ways the same old thing wrapped in the veneer of new and trendy terminology, even if the terminology was a stale rehash of Napoleon's. At end of peace in 1914, Foch remained stuck in the arid desert of confusion. The Russo-Japanese war, for instance, had no lessons for him. Other generals, more alert, knew better than that.

One thing Foch had was complete confidence in himself. In keeping with a determinist (and Napoleonic) concept of leadership, he felt that armies, even modern ones with millions of men, could be inspired and manipulated by the personality of the man who led them. This despite the fact that generals no longer rode to critical points on a battlefield at critical moments, leapt from their horses, grabbed the standard and led their men in a desperate, high-stakes charge. Frederick the Great had done that at Zorndorf, and had won the day; Napoleon had refused to do it at Waterloo – had he lost the great battle on that account? Modern generals rarely saw the front, and Foch was no exception. Still, he believed in destiny: 'As Napoleon said, it was Caesar, not the Roman legions, who conquered the Gauls'. Georges Clemenceau thought Foch was a little crazy, like a man who 'heard voices'. That may have been so, but one thing Ferdinand Foch did have that an entire array of incompetent generals on both sides of the war did not: he was adaptable.

As World War I broke out, Foch was actually in command of troops, his stint as a superintendent of the staff college over. His XX corps, attached to the First Army, was stationed in Nancy on the eastern frontier. German troops were only ten miles away. Initially advancing, as all the French armies would, he was engaged in stiff fighting right from the beginning, and forced back on the city. He conducted what would be called today a 'fighting retreat', and did reasonably well for himself. In just two weeks he was reassigned by the commander in chief, General Joffre, to oversee the left wing of the far larger Fourth Army, which would be called upon to perform important duties during the 'Miracle' of the Marne in early September. Foch was one of the few generals in whom Joffre would place his faith; after just four weeks of war, Joffre would need all the help and support he could muster.

The pinnacle in the career of Joseph Césaire Joffre had apparently arrived in 1911, though at the time his appointment as chief of the general staff was almost a by-product of what was, in fact, a far more profound change in the structure and attitude of the French army. Since the Franco-Prussian War, what passed for organizational thinking within the officer corps remained transfixed with Germany. Peacetime manoeuvres and staff college exercises could sometimes be oriented towards the crisis of the moment – at one time, Britain was the focus of attention – but most operational blueprints that were meant to be the basis of future action focused on Germany. Many of these, through Plan XVI (adopted in 1909) were primarily defensive in nature. As they were churned out every few years, restive souls became increasingly roiled by their passive nature. Defence, in their minds, 'implied avowal of inferiority' which was inimical to the French spirit. In 1911 the architect of Plan XVI was purged, replaced by a figurehead, in the opinion of some, Joseph Joffre, the seventeenth commander in chief of the French army since 1874 (in the same time frame, Germany had had only four). But the architect of what was almost a *coup d'état* was, in fact, Louis de Grandmaison.

Grandmaison's credentials were, in certain circles, impeccable. He was an ardent nationalist, deeply patriotic and totally committed to the army. He was not the ideal republican, however. His brother Léonce would become an oft-published theologian of considerable repute, called by the future Cardinal Baudrillart 'the perfect Jesuit'. Grandmaison, a graduate of Saint-Cyr, was marked for early promotion, and selected to attend the war college. He studied there during Foch's tenure as superintendent and, we may presume, took to heart his superior's penchant for the attack. A continuing argument today between historians is the degree to which Foch influenced Grandmaison and those of his 'school'. Some claim that the younger officer took Foch's teachings to an extreme that Foch himself would never have tolerated; that Foch had no intention of having his generalized theories adopted as a gospel of sorts, and that 'Young Turks' were alone responsible for the distorting effect that *l'attaque à outrance* produced on official army doctrine. A slightly demuring school of thought asserts that Foch, like so many long-winded Frenchmen, became so carried away by the rhetoric of Napoleonic jingoism that he had little idea of the effect it might have on impressionable pupils (he had, after all, only once heard a shot fired in anger or seen a dead corpse on the field of battle before 1914); and that, once sensing the drift of his principles being taken up with such fervor by his pupils, did little to tamper their ill-advised enthusiasms.

No matter. Grandmaison soon found himself on the general staff, where he and fellow zealots conspired to remove General Victor Michel, the author of Plan XVI, from his position. Several choices of an offensively minded replacement were bandied about, but in the end a compromise candidate was accepted, General Joffre. With his ensconcement, Grandmaison oversaw the creation of Plan XVII, whose first sentence set the tone for all that followed: 'The French Army, returning to its traditions, no longer knows any other law than the offensive'. This was followed by several other *bons mots*, most of which encouraged the notion of cold steel: not the impersonal variety of artillery shells or machine gun bullets, but the bayonet, which would eviscerate one's enemy in face-to-face combat. As a Russian general had observed, bombs and projectiles of any sort were mechanical, they had no 'thought processes' to speak of: 'bullets are blind, only the bayonet is intelligent' (as one observer later commented, generals had accepted the notion of a rifle only 'in order to stick a bayonet on the end of it'). Grandmaison even wrote, implausibly it seems, that 'in an offensive, rashness is the safest policy', the bayonet charge being the apogee of nobility. He gave little thought to casualties. 'Bloody sacrifice' was 'the very nature of war'. Anyone afraid to face that stark fact of life would do well to find another profession. Grandmaison's enthusiasm was infectious, and produced often surrealistic responses, although some critics were unimpressed. 'Are we to attack?' said one general. 'Then let us attack the moon!'[8] Civilian observers, who took the time to notice such things, were appalled at the intellectual vacuity of bayonet enthusiasts. A Polish banker who spent much of his business career in Russia, Jan Bloch, wrote a prescient analysis in 1899, *Is War Now Impossible?*, which was loaded with statistics that essentially forecast most of what happened between 1914 and 1918. He wondered, in some puzzlement, at the closed military mind that could never learn lessons from the past. In the Franco-Prussian War, for instance, intensely studied at French military academies, it was a known fact that only one percent of German casualties could be attributed to 'cold steel'. The days of the bayonet were undeniably over, yet men like Grandmaison acted as though the Franco-Prussian War had never happened.

Joffre might seem, at first glance, to be a strange figure indeed for the man who ultimately authorized the headstrong and flamboyant war policy that Plan XVII embodied, for he was, if anything, hardly a dramatic personality. A man who delighted in the domestic pleasures of home life and the dinner table, he was rarely given to histrionic displays of emotion. His career had been a relatively quiet ascent up the promotional ladder, interspersed with occasional war experiences with small regimental groupings. He saw action as a young man during the siege of Paris, 1870/71, and in 1894 he led one of a two-pronged expedition up the Niger River to secure Timbuktu for French control. This latter expedition required diligent leadership. He commanded a column of mostly Senegalese troops on a 500-mile forced march that was constantly harassed and badgered by fierce local tribesmen. When he finally reached Timbuktu, he had the unfortunate experience of seeing the other French column, which had arrived before him, all dead and rotting in the sun. He separated the French officers from the grisly pile and buried them separately; the native troops were interred in a mass grave. He then had the presence of mind to occupy the city, raise the flag, scatter the enemy and consolidate his position.

In times of relative peace, Joffre was stationed all over the French colonial empire: Formosa, Hanoi, Senegal and Madagascar. A specialist in engineering, Joffre laid out and built fortresses, harbours and almost every kind of infrastructure. He made few friends but, more importantly, few enemies. It was a conscious point of personal discretion that he kept most of his opinions to himself. In none of his several stations, however, did Joffre command substantial numbers of men or units; he was generally part of someone else's staff, as opposed to being in charge of one himself. As such, it is something of a surprise to note his appointment in 1905 to the Supreme Council of War in Paris, a sort of 'high command' made of up a dozen or so generals and chaired by the minister of war, a position in constant flux. In memoirs and diaries of those times, Joffre was mostly noted for his comparative silence during meetings; during the war years, this translated into a somewhat less complimentary descriptive ... Joffre 'chewing the cud'. Six years later, he succeeded the ousted General Michel and sat atop the pyramidal structure that produced Plan XVII. Liddell Hart called him the 'fountainhead' of the plan 'who knew nothing of strategy'. Grandmaison was the 'oracle', and the fiercely Napoleonic (and cleric-ridden) General Castelnau, the 'high priest'. All these men would be stunned in the summer of 1914 as Plan XVII imploded. Grandmaison, as we have seen, died for it; Castelnau absorbed the shock, but remained determined that its ethos should work; and Joffre simply sat in stunned turpitude as everything collapsed around him. Stoicism is a fine quality to have as preconceptions disintegrate, but, unfortunately for Joffre, his sense of calm was often betrayed by a non-military and unpresupposing demeanour. Edward Spears, a British liaison officer assigned to French headquarters, was unimpressed by the general's martial appearance. Joffre was not a horse enthusiast; he preferred walking to riding as a form of relaxation. Spears noted his propensity for wandering slowly about, hands behind him. 'He wore the red and gold cap of a French general, and a black tunic that from about a third down sloped gently outward. His red breeches were baggy and ill-fitting.' Joffre's voice was 'toneless, coming through the sieve of his big whitish moustache, all giv[ing] the impression of an albino'. Spears, who was an elegant figure himself, despaired of the general's lack of sartorial deportment. 'A bulky, slow-moving, loosely built man, in clothes that would have been the despair of Savile Row.' He didn't seem long destined for the rigours of high command.

The Marne

Joffre's imperturbability had been put to the test in the first two weeks of the war, when Plan XVII's utter bankruptcy became apparent to most, if not all, observers. What came to be known as the Battle of the Frontiers had proved a disaster for French arms. It can be said that the enormity of casualties was not at first fully appreciated in the cozy confines of army headquarters but in fact, within that limited circle, individual losses served to symbolize and encapsulate the deteriorating situation. French privates and corporals were not the only men being killed; generals' sons were being mowed down as well, the news of which spread rapidly throughout the upper echelons of the tightly knit officer corps. General Noël de Castelnau lost a son in the first few days, with two more to follow; Ferdinand Foch's only son, along with the husband of his daughter, were both killed on the same day – and the list went on. Maps at *GQG* were also diviners of bad news: a substantial portion of French territory and population, a significant percentage of her industrial base and much of her mineral wealth now lay under German control. Far from recovering the 'lost' provinces of Alsace and Lorraine, the nation now saw the possibility that many of her cities – Lille, Amiens, Verdun, Laon, Soissons, Rheims, even Paris – might fall. For this (and other reasons perhaps) Joffre refused to have maps on the walls of his office, not that that mattered according to Douglas Haig, who said Joffre couldn't read one anyway. Details distracted him, as his staff well knew; only the big picture mattered. Joffre's inner sanctum became known as the 'secret Temple', and only acolytes were generally allowed to enter. He avoided his telephone like the plague, because the news conveyed over it was generally sour.

Most of the postwar memoirs and histories of 1914, and there are hundreds, usually part company over an assessment of Joffre's role in the first six weeks of the war. One school posits that Joffre's great inner wealth of calm is what saved the day, and saved France, during the utter peril of August and September. Joffre did not cave in; he did not succumb to nerves; he refused to panic when others were losing their heads all around him. This is true, as most witnesses attest. Joffre ate three full meals a day, religiously. He took an hour's walk each afternoon, that usually ended up with the general sitting down on a bench, lost in thought (or a nap). He went to bed each night at 10 p.m, and woe to the staff officer who even thought of waking him up (Joffre always locked the door as a discouragement). But disagreement lies in the discussion of what lay behind this reservoir of sang-froid. An empty vessel, some say; Joffre was incompetent, lazy, jealous, a bureaucratic infighter more concerned with maintaining his position and, later, his posterity, than with a serious engagement to the principles of strategy and military fact. He was, after all, an engineer, not a cavalryman. Others dispute this denigration, and assert that Joffre had a sound appreciation of military operations, that he delegated tremendous authority to his staff, who immersed themselves in day-to-day planning and whom he trusted implicitly, but always reserving final judgment to himself after carefully assessing all the possibilities. As is usual in such matters, the truth seems to be in the middle.

Joffre's imprimatur is all over Plan XVII. It was the rage of the prewar French officer corps, and he was not a man who enjoyed upsetting other people's presuppositions. Aside from its overriding concern, however, to launch offensive operations against the German armies no matter what, the real character of the plan – its formlessness – directly reflected the void in Joffre's strategic purview and, perhaps, his mind. Plan XVII had no real goal, other than that of immediate combat. French armies would attack, mostly north and east in the direction of the Rhine, but their primary duties would be to await developments, see how situations developed, and take advantage of presumably fluid battlefields to strike the enemy when he made a mistake or left an opening. By 3 August 1914, Joffre's generals were asking for some sort of direction from their commander as he assembled them for a last emergency conference. All they got from him, said one, were 'banalities'. One general, Auguste Dubail, head of the First Army, attempted to provide details as to what he intended to do when hostilities began. 'That may be your plan', said Joffre in reply, 'it is not mine', but he would commit himself to nothing more, offering only 'the broad lines of the manoeuvre I would probably execute'. This did not generate an overflow of confidence or enthusiasm. General Charles Lanrezac had these contemporaneous comments to make on Joffre's style of leadership:

> It is certain that General Joffre will never be willing to listen to advice or to demands for explanation from his lieutenants, that he will limit himself to prescribe movements for them without saying anything to them of the end that he has in view. The system is Napoleonic. In war of a hundred years ago, it was acceptable, in the name of discipline, for a Napoleon, but not for a general of lesser genius.

While a vocal minority of French military thinkers made strong cases that the primary German threat would be through Luxembourg and Belgium, by far the majority considered the old battlefields of the Franco-Prussian War to be the arena of coming battles. Joffre, despite indications to the contrary, went along with this last assumption. When the dimensions of the Schlieffen Plan started to become apparent – let us say, seven days into the invasion, or about 12 August – Joffre did not believe it. When the indicators became blatant, he still misunderstood the depth of the German commitment to turn the French left flank, and the consequent danger of envelopment that this portended for the entire army. He disregarded the warnings and concerns of many of his top generals in the field: they were incompetent or defeatist, and he sacked dozens in the first two weeks. They were told to give up their commands and to report for duty in Limoges, a backwater in the middle of the country and hundreds of kilometres from the front, hence the slang expression to '*allez à Limoges*', meaning one's career was over. Joffre had a healthy respect for self-preservation in his make-up. Like many high-ranking officers, he had his share of resentments towards men he had served with (mostly under) whom he disliked or envied. Many of these ended up in Limoges. But some were too powerful or well-respected to dismiss, men like de Castelnau and Joseph Galliéni, the soon to be appointed military governor of Paris. Politicians, of course, could always be ignored. When Paris was threatened, Joffre encouraged the ministers to flee to Bordeaux (as did Galliéni). The Germans were distracting enough, who needed these dross around who wasted time in endless, acrimonious meetings? People like Castelnau and Galliéni, however, were different. They couldn't be bossed around.[9]

By 23 August, the situation was everywhere grave. French offences had been fiascos, all five armies were retreating or attempting just to stand fast. The eastern front around Nancy and Verdun was the site of fierce battles. The intentions of von Schlieffen's plan were now obvious, even to Joffre. Paris, in his mind, was to be written off. The city was a 'conception'; it had no military value. There were not enough men on his left flank to stop the Germans, yet if he transferred troops from Nancy and Verdun, those vital strong points would stand equally endangered. Joffre was no coward; he was looking for a place to make his stand, a launch point for counterattacks, and initially he decided that it would be the river Seine. His armies were utterly exhausted, at the end of their rope. He would withdraw.

Three days later, Galliéni accepted command of the city of Paris. In keeping with the Republican notion of dividing responsibility – specifically, to avoid the 'man on horseback' syndrome that had so often bedevilled French politics – his position vis-à-vis Joffre was complicated. Joffre assumed Galliéni was under his control, while Galliéni demurred. There was some history behind this jockeying for position.

Galliéni, like Joffre, had served many years overseas: Madagascar (where Joffre was one of his subordinates), French Sudan, Indo-China. He was

The Schlieffen Plan, Projected & Actual: Originally, von Schlieffen intended an especially powerful right wing to sweep in a wide arc west of Paris. Four other armies would invade directly south, and another two west, from Lorraine and Alsace, towards Verdun and Toul. General von Kluck, sensing opportunity, altered this concept by having his 1st Army curve inwards, east of Paris, alongside the other armies. However, a gap developed between his force and von Bülow's, which the allies exploited along the river Marne (signified by narrow black arrows).

a rigorous, upright, tough man, and no stranger to the irregularities and harshness of colonial wars. He did not enjoy being disputed or argued with, hence his contempt for politicians who, in his opinion, should all be shot. Paris could not be defended, given the troops at his disposal; nor could it be abandoned. Galliéni, a sick man (he would soon die from internal bleeding after two operations on his prostate) decided he would perish in Paris ... but not without a fight.

Joffre had given in to Galliéni's badgering that a new army just formed should be positioned to defend the northern approaches to Paris. It was to be known as the Sixth. In reality, this would be a grab bag collection of whatever Joffre might cobble together. It included Moroccans, Zouaves just arrived from Algiers and broken remnants of regiments that had been minced from non-stop fighting. Joffre promised two divisions as well from the eastern front. In order to buy time for their assembly into something that might be regarded as a cohesive force, he turned to one of his irascible generals, Charles Lanrezac, for one final and seemingly hopeless gesture. Lanrezac's Fifth Army, on the extreme left wing of the French force, was ordered to undertake a difficult manoeuvre to shift its front from due north to the west, in order to delay the onrushing right wing of his opposite number, General Alexander von Kluck. Such a move exposed both his flanks, and was unorthodox, to say the least. Lanrezac grew apoplectic when given this order. He damned the instructions, damned *GQG* and damned Joffre in the bargain. He did this in full earshot of his staff.

The Fifth Army had suffered grievously in almost continuous action from the beginning of the war. It had been pummelled by von Kluck, had absorbed numbing casualties, was in a damaged psychological state given its constant retreating, and had been betrayed (in Lanrezac's opinion) by the British Expeditionary Force led by Sir John French, which had been expected to support his left flank. As far as Lanrezac was concerned, the British had deserted the battlefield, an opinion that was not far from the truth. Sir John now had his eye myopically on the coast, on how to extricate his forces from what he considered to be an onrushing catastrophe. He was not in the mood to be judged by history as the general who had lost Britain's entire army in just three weeks.[10]

Joffre, while an opaque man in many respects, now rose to the occasion. He understood Lanrezac's contempt, he knew that many people thought of him as a fat old man more familiar with roast chicken than a battlefield. But Lanrezac must be made to obey. Joffre wedged himself into a staff car and sped to Lanrezac's headquarters, where the atmospherics grew heated, and quickly. Lanrezac was at breaking point, his army in tatters, France on the brink of ruin. Tempers flared, a rarity in Joffre's case, who seldom expressed himself with vehemence. The two generals withdrew to a room and began yelling at each other, in a scene rarely duplicated in the next four years. Staff officers, overhearing the abuse, cringed. There are variations in what was reportedly said, some versions more explicit and colourful than others. One had Joffre shouting, 'Do as you're told, and don't argue. If you refuse to carry out my orders, I'll have you shot!' In the end, Lanrezac accepted the instructions, though demanding that Joffre put them in writing. From then on, the Fifth Army did as Joffre commanded. The results were not exactly what he expected, but they bought the necessary breathing space. For his reward, Lanrezac was *Limogé*. Joffre's next problem would be Galliéni.

❧

Taxis

One of the many enduring legends from World War I is the story of Parisian taxicabs assembled by Galliéni, which would drive reinforcements out of the city to beef up the Sixth Army during its moment of both crisis and victory, known collectively as the Miracle on the Marne. There is certainly a semblance of truth to the tale. Galliéni did exclaim, as he saw the taxis all lined up and ready to move out, five soldiers with full gear in each, on the unusual sight – 'My goodness, here at least is something out of the ordinary', but as is standard for historical exaggeration, the reality was far more ordinary. Galliéni needed transports and he commandeered what he required. When he ran out of trucks and vans, he resorted to cabs. If he had run out of cabs, he would have turned to horses and carriages. There wasn't much fuss to that; he was not a man who stood on ceremony. And if Paris was to fall, he would make it as inconvenient for the Germans as possible. He was already in the process of laying explosives under several dozen Parisian bridges, the exquisite Pont Neuf included. Even the Eiffel Tower was slated for demolition, given its usefulness as a radio transmitting station. But he knew in his heart that defending the city was impossible. His only hope lay in a German mistake, and on 3 September, based on reports from aviators, he thought he saw one in the making.

General von Kluck, commander of the German First Army, was a typical hard-bitten Prussian soldier. A man of little refinement, he often walked around with a rifle on his shoulder, or clutching his pistol, as though to intimate that he might prefer shooting a person as opposed to talking to him. He pushed himself when he had to, and expected no less from those under his command. Extremely aggressive, he had been given command of the far right wing of the German invaders; as such, he had more ground to cover, and the need for more speed, than any of the other six armies. His initial goal, in keeping with von Schlieffen's plan, had been to pass around Paris from the west, but the seeming collapse of French forces caused an alteration. Von Kluck was convinced that he had the enemy on the run. Instead of encircling Paris, wasting time and resources, he saw the chance to obliterate any hope that the French could collect themselves for a final stand. Finish them off now was his mantra. He proposed to wheel inside of Paris, not outside; to envelop the French army more quickly, not to give them a second of repose. By doing so, he would expose his own right flank to whatever forces were north of Paris, but von Kluck, in his greed, professed not to care. These particular French troops were vagabonds, there were not enough of them, he was supremely confident of victory. Von Moltke, far from the front, could only trust that von

Kluck was right. Everyone at headquarters in Luxembourg were luxuriating in all the positive developments. General Gröner, the railway expert, wrote to his wife that the enemy's government no longer seemed functioning; there was no one around who could even surrender! The French seemed entirely beaten, all signs but one confirmed it. Von Moltke was insecure enough to keep harping on this solitary negative: where were the French prisoners? If all his generals were sending accurate communiques from the front, there should have been hundreds of thousands of defeated Frenchmen marching to the rear under guard. There was nothing like that number in any report that he had seen. Von Moltke was getting anxious.

Von Kluck not only underestimated the extent of French resolve, he overestimated the durability of his own men. As the English general Sir Henry Wilson observed in his diary, 'the German corps of today [are] very different indeed to their corps of a month ago, and they [are] no longer an avalanche'. The German First Army was numb with fatigue; it had suffered not inconsequential casualties itself, and was also starving. Von Kluck was almost 100 miles removed from his railway depots. Supplies were now scant. Everything had to be brought up by horse power, some two million pounds of hay were required to sustain each German army, and the French countryside was fast being nibbled to the ground. On top of everything else, the summer heat was proving unbearable. In the last month, von Kluck's troops had not had a single rest day, had been continuously in battle, and had marched, with full packs, some 312 miles. On 3 September, his First Army had covered over 25 miles alone. Nonetheless, von Kluck crossed the river Marne and ordered the advance to continue, a decision that held (in his own mind) both promise and peril. He could crush the French opposing him, but the same manoeuvre meant increasing the gap between the First Army and that of its lagging neighbour, von Bülow's Second. Von Kluck chose to run the risk, and go for glory. His men could sleep in Paris when the whole business was over.

It was Galliéni who manoeuvreed Joffre into accepting battle on 6 September. Everything about the operation disturbed the rotund commander in chief. He had to be convinced that von Kluck was indeed exposing his flank. He had to be certain that shifting divisions from the eastern front and inserting them against von Kluck could be accomplished in time. He had to know in confidence that his generals were willing to fight. And he had to be reassured that the British would stop retreating; their presence between the French Sixth and Fifth Armies was crucial to the plan's success. On top of everything else, he delayed the operation by a full day. Even that Galliéni would not grant. He informed Joffre that the Sixth Army would attack on 6 September. This was pretty much what it appeared to be: an ultimatum.

Joffre, as was his wont, took precious time to make his decision. In the unrelenting heat of 4 September, he went outside his headquarters and sat alone in the shade of a tree. He had no maps, no memoranda, no intelligence reports, no written material. He just sat there and thought. Most everything he had done in the first month of war had been a disaster. Few fighting generals had any faith in his resolve. They considered him a bureaucrat without energy or resolution. He was 'fat and heavy', according to Galliéni, an indolent drag on *élan*. He was, however, the man at the top, an indisputable fact of which Joffre was fully aware. What he finally decided would determine the fate of France. He knew *that* in his heart; however fearful he might have been in reaching his decision, he was never unaware of the implications it held, both for him and the nation, two considerations that he considered equal in weight. At about 5 o'clock in the afternoon he made up his mind. The attack would proceed as Galliéni had conceived it. *GQG* suddenly launched into action. Orders were written, arrangements made, dispositions put in motion. Then the bombshell dropped. The British would not cooperate.

Sir John French had had enough of this war. It had become too complicated for him to understand and nothing had gone as intended; according to Churchill, French's heart had been 'chilled' by the experience. As far as this particular field marshal was concerned, France was finished. Galliéni had personally visited British headquarters, where French proved unavailable. Galliéni exhorted the field marshal's staff, explained the coming manoeuvre in detail, asked where in heaven's name could Sir John French be? He left discouraged and dismayed. The British Expeditionary Force was absolutely critical to the plan of operation. The only officer of any standing who was convinced it could work was Sir Henry Wilson, who also happened to be one of the few British officers who could speak fluent French. That alone earned him the distrust of many colleagues. When Joffre heard all this, he reacted immediately, ordering his car and setting off on a hundred mile or so journey to French's headquarters. He arrived at 2 p.m. on the 5th and, luckily, found everyone of any importance assembled in conference. Wasting no time, he launched into a violent tirade, little of which Sir John French understood. These intra-service get-togethers, in fact, were often called 'Towers of Babel'. But Wilson understood, and roughly translated when he could get a word in. Joffre was passionate, infuriated, pleading and wholly convincing. He pounded the map table with his fists, waved hands in the air and, with the conviction that no actor could replicate, told French that 'the honour of England was at stake. It is France that begs you for help!' Some claimed that tears rolled down Joffre's cheeks. French was speechless. He attempted to construct an appropriate reply in French, but emotion ruled the day in his heart as well. He simply told Wilson to tell Joffre 'Yes'.

The 'Miracle' of the Marne went off more or less as planned, though as regards actual combat and casualties it proved a relatively modest affair. As Liddell Hart put it in 1931, when most of the paper trail could be examined in some leisure, 'In proportion to its scale and its historical effect, no decisive battle has seen less fighting than that of the Marne'. Some military writers have claimed that German failures in the eastern theatre to invest Verdun and Nancy, being fought simultaneously and at far higher expense in terms of lives and resources, more spelled the doom of an early German victory than the Marne. But there can be no doubt that, psychologically speaking, the Marne was a tonic and propaganda 'victory' that France desperately needed, but for that perhaps the credit (or blame) must rest more with the German foe than with taxi cabs struggling to reach the battlefield at a crucial juncture in the action. Helmuth von Moltke, when given the opportunity to go for the French jugular, refused to take the chance. Like his troops in the field, his nerves were also frayed to breaking point. He was so exhausted, he hardly knew where to turn. Guilt overwhelmed him; the colossus he had helped put in motion, engines of vast destructive power that were already, even before trench warfare had begun, turning western Europe into a charnel house, oppressed his spirits that were already in a downward spiral. 'Terror often overcomes me when I think of this', he wrote his wife, 'and the feeling I have that I must answer for this horror.' A few days later he suffered an emotional collapse.

Even before the French counter-attack began, he had ordered von Kluck (through his surrogate, one Lieutenant Colonel Hentsch, sent expressly to the front with plenipotentiary powers) to withdraw and, simultaneously, reorient his front towards Paris. The great enveloping manoeuvre was to stop short of its goal, because von Moltke, unlike von Kluck, was worried about the First Army's exposed flank; was worried that French and British forces were stronger than von Kluck believed; and was worried that a thrust to the underbelly of von Kluck's army (graphically described by Winston Churchill as 'the German liver') would lead to an even greater haemorrhage in von Bülow's adjoining Second Army. Von Kluck was, understandably, absolutely stunned. Victory was there for the taking; he believed that as firmly as he believed anything, but 100 miles behind the front, von Moltke had lost his courage. As von Moltke's soon-to-be-successor, Erich von Falkenhayn, observed, 'Schlieffen's notes [had] come to an end, and with this, Moltke's nerves.' Another officer wrote in his diary, 'Moltke and his followers were completely sterile. All they could do was turn the handle and roll Schlieffen's film, and they were clueless and beside themselves when the roll got stuck.'[11]

The scene at von Kluck's headquarters on 10 September when Lieutenant Colonel Hentsch arrived was full of portent. Before Hentsch, an intelligence officer, had even opened his mouth, everyone present (aside from von Kluck, who was absent) knew the truth: that the deciding moment in the German thrust for total victory was about to be decided. Although Hentsch was junior in rank to many of the men in attendance, he had the power from von Moltke to use his own judgment about what to do next. His directives were to be 'absolute' and obeyed; there was to be no dispute as to his authority. Hentsch began by sketching the entire battlefront. Von Kluck's staff were amazed to hear of the difficulties around Verdun, were shocked to hear that von Bülow's Second Army was falling back, and were aghast at the tactical situation that Hentsch described as 'not favourable'. The assembled officers, led by von Kluck's chief of staff, General Hermann von Kuhl, tried arguing. Attacks by the French Sixth Army were negligible; Sir John French's British forces were slow moving up and could be repulsed; they were beaten men – one of their own officers had just reported seeing the Eiffel Tower with his binoculars from a church spire, just thirty miles away, with not a single French soldier in the vicinity. Yes, there was a gap between von Kluck and von Bülow, but recent manoeuvring had taken this into account. To reposition themselves along the lines of Hentsch's suggestions – 'drawn on my map with a piece of coal', said von Kuhl – meant, as Liddell Hart would describe it, 'performing a sort of backwards somersault'. Von Kluck, in his memoirs, called it a 'difficult backwards wheel' which no army was well trained to execute, and certainly not one as exhausted as von Kluck's. Hentsch remained adamant. In von Kuhl's opinion, the younger officer had been infected by the 'depressed atmosphere' of von Bülow's Second Army headquarters, the site of his previous visit, and their assessment of the situation, which had been presented in 'very dark colours'. No matter. He issued his orders, and then 'hastily departed' before von Kluck could meet him. Many officers after the war were bitter regarding Hentsch's performance, some blaming him exclusively for the German failure to win the war in one swoop. It was unfortunate, wrote one, that the colonel had not 'crashed into a tree somewhere' or 'been shot by a French straggler' before ever arriving at von Kluck's headquarters. If misfortune felled him, 'we would have had a ceasefire in two weeks … and received a peace in which we could have demanded everything'. The withdrawal began, however, assisted by French and British pressure, and by General Ferdinand Foch's success in holding the French centre to the east. The German First and Second Armies fell back forty miles in five days, and established themselves in favourable

Queen Victoria and her eldest daughter, familiarly called Vicky, empress dowager of Prussia, the mother of Kaiser Wilhelm II. Both are in mourning clothes in memory of their husbands.

Kaiser Wilhelm II in warlord mode.

Bejewelled, bemedalled and bearing swords, nine monarchs attended the funeral of Edward VII, Windsor Castle, 20 May 1910. By the end of the war, only four remained on their thrones.

German Strategists

Alfred von Schlieffen, 1890, before assuming his duties as chief of the Imperial German General Staff.

The kaiser, in command vehicle, with von Moltke the Younger to his left, at annual manoeuvres, 1913.

The Spark that Started It All

Archduke Ferdinand, the hunter, with his wife and children.

His assassins, and other conspirators, on trial in Sarajevo, October 1914. This image sits in the front window of the former food shop that overlooks the sidewalk where Gavrilo Princip fired the fatal shots, currently a small museum. 'I am not a criminal', he said in his defence.

Fort de Loncin

Big Bertha, one of which
pummelled Fort de Loncin,
Liège.

Memorial to the
fallen.

Aerial photograph
showing the effects
of the explosion that
destroyed the fort.

Generals

Generals Ludendorff, centre in trench coat with walking cane, and von Hindenburg, to his left, tour the Tannenberg battlefield after 'the harvest'.

Allied Commanders in 1918: Front row, l. to r., Joffre, Foch, Haig and Pershing.

Gallipoli

Statue of Turkish artilleryman, Corporal Seyit Ali Çabuk, carrying a 600-pound shell on his back, at his gun position overlooking The Narrows.

Lone Pine.

Present-day billboard of Mustafa Kemal (Atatürk), Çanakkale, Turkey.

Verdun

Fort de Vaux.

General Erich von Falkenhayn, architect of the 10-month Verdun campaign of attrition, 1916.

Philippe Pétain awards battle ribbons to two regiments that defended Côte 304 in 1916. Note that both flags have been shredded by shrapnel and bullets in several places.

Verdun

La Voie Sacrée.

The hill known as
Le Mort Homme
('The Dead Man').

The Tavannes Tunnel.

Verdun

'Max' firing.

After the war, French tourists frolic on, about, and in the abandoned 'Max'.

NT, VA DIRE
RES PEUPLES
/ILLAGE EST
UR SAUVER
ET POUR QUE
SAUVAT LE

E 10 AOUT 1924
R. POINCARÉ.

Site of the village of Vaux. 'Passerby, go tell other peoples that this village died to save Verdun, and with it, Verdun saved the world.' Raymond Poincaré, president of the Third Republic.

Aerial photograph of Passchendaele in the early stages of the Allied attack.

Passchendaele one week before its capture. The only recognizable structure is the village church, in ruins.

Despair, Disillusionment and Death

German war veteran and artist Otto Dix, in this famous etching, *Shock Troops Advance Under Gas*, best captured the nihilistic character of trench warfare.

Canadian Major-General Sir Arthur Currie and Field Marshal Haig, 1918. By this point in the war, the two did not see eye to eye.

'Potter's Field', Pentonville Prison, London, where Roger Casement was first buried.

Vice-Admiral David Beatty, centre right, hands in pockets and his hat at a characteristically rakish angle, with officers on deck of the battlecruiser HMS *Lion*.

Naval Ordnance, a caricature of then-Captain John Jellicoe, drawn by the cartoonist SPY (Leslie Ward) for a 1906 edition of *Vanity Fair*.

After Jutland, the heavily damaged German battlecruiser SMS *Seydlitz* struggles home, its bow nearly submerged, having been flooded by over 5,300 tons of sea water. Approaching Wilhelmshaven, and fearing the ship might sink, her captain was forced to approach port stern first.

A battered *Seydlitz* undergoing repairs. She suffered twenty-three direct hits and a torpedo strike.

Halifax, after the explosion. The *Imo*, beached on the far side of the ship channel, is at the extreme left of the photograph. The Richmond neighbourhood, pictured here, was largely destroyed. Everything below ground level on the ship in dry dock survived without damage; almost everything above was swept away.

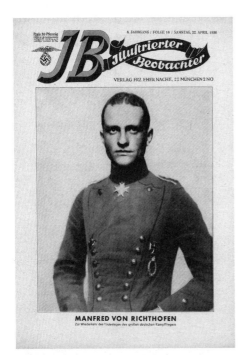

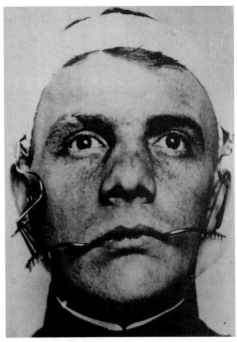

Manfred von Richthofen, in a photograph from 1916. It appears here on the front page of a 1933 edition of 'Illustrierter Beobachter' (*Illustrated Observer*), a Nazi propaganda magazine published from 1926 to 1945.

Manfred's brother, Lothar, who crashed in March 1918. This photograph shows some of the damage, his jaw wired shut.

An unusual photo of a German observation plane taken from above by another observation plane, a Belgian. If the Belgian had been a fighter pilot, this would have been an easy 'kill'. Observation crews generally had very short careers. That of T.E. Lawrence's brother lasted only a week.

British aviators examine the twin machine guns recovered from von Richthofen's Fokker fighter plane, the wreckage of which lies in the background.

Rasputin

The Siberian village of Pokrovskoye, on the river Tura, where Gregory Rasputin was born. It lies well over 1,000 miles from St. Petersburg.

Gregory Rasputin, respectably dressed, by Karl Bulla, a German-born photographer frequently patronized by the Romanovs.

Rasputin's assassin, Prince Felix Yusupov, dressed for a costume ball, 1910.

defensive positions on the river Aisne. An expatriate, Mildred Aldrich, who owned a cottage overlooking the small town of Meaux on the Marne River, sensed that the tide had turned. She was no strategist, but her eyes and ears were enough. 'There could be no doubt of it, the battle was receding', she wrote. 'The cannonading was as violent, as incessant, as it had been the day before, but it was surely farther off.' There were so many bodies to collect in Meaux that the Parisian Fire Department was sent to assist. Many German corpses were bloating under the hot sun, gorged on looted champagne, the liquor fermenting in their stomachs. British troops, to the tune of *Pop Goes the Weasel*, sang verses that included lines such as 'We don't give a fuck for old von Kluck/And all his bleeding army'. But in the next four years, it would be the British who bled more than most.[12]

The Marne certainly saved Joffre's career; or, to put it more succinctly, delayed the day of his sacking. French spirits revived to some degree; they remained physically and spiritually capable of maintaining an 'offensive' attitude. Again, this would change. It is ironic that three of Joffre's most important decisions … stopping the blind, near suicidal attacks that characterized Plan XVII, the insertion (like the Germans) of reservists into the front lines and drawing forces away from the east to the Marne … were all heresy to the Grandmaison school of thought. But without so doing, Joffre would have lost the battle for France then and there.

For the moment, Joffre basked in glory. When time allowed for it, his staff allegedly excised various communiques, orders and memoranda that might heap too much attention on Galliéni's contribution to the victory. Joffre was an expert plotter. Indeed, one of his admirers called him a natural politician, a species for whom Joffre, unlike most generals, held a modicum of respect. Several officers remained critical of his performance, but Joffre knew how to handle them. 'He was always on the lookout for squalls', wrote Jean de Pierrefeu, a journalist who was assigned to *GQG* to write the equivalent of today's press releases for the general public (the usual combination of misinformation and cliché). Joffre 'worked alone, seeking to break up the cabals against him by a series of incomprehensible silences, of stubborn denials, made without heat or ulterior motive. He rolled himself into a ball, so to speak. The cleverest intriguer retired in defeat from this stone wall.' To all outward appearances, he was the perfect general, at least in the eyes of the governmental establishment, who were always on the lookout for flaws in the high command. He disdained undue pomp and circumstance, telling Pierrefeu on one occasion not to describe the soldiers guarding his headquarters as a 'personal guard'. Too 'praetorian', in his opinion. Joffre refused to wear spurs on his boots, to the annoyance of his more aristocratic staff. He discouraged negative remarks about particular politicians, which greatly decreased the conversation level around his dinner table which, after all, was to be reserved for matters of more importance, the menu (*gigot agrave la bretonne* was his favourite dish). During Holy Week in 1915, his chef proposed a week of fish. Joffre exploded. 'I am a republican general', he is said to have yelled, ordering that roast beef, chicken and pork make their usual appearance. Meals were enhanced by the veritable flood of gifts that were showered on Joffre after the Marne: 'Sweets, cases of champagne, every kind of fruit', according to Pierrefeu, along with 'games, clothes, smoking requisites, inkstands and paperweights. Every part of the world sent its own specialty … the commander in chief, although no sign of it appeared on his impassive face, sniffed appreciatively at this incense.' Joffre's Buddha-like reserve, however, was soon to be tested yet again.

The man on the other side of the rapidly expanding trench system was no longer Helmuth von Moltke. German headquarters after the Marne reminded one officer of 'a mortuary'. Clearly a change was necessary; von Moltke's health, recently precarious, deteriorated as his nerves disintegrated. The kaiser, still more or less in command of the German armed forces, removed him as commander in chief on 9 September, and replaced him with the Prussian Minister for War, Erich von Falkenhayn. Moltke, as befits a man of honour, initially refused to step down. 'My place is here', he told the kaiser, 'I stand and fall with this army'. But go he did. Von Falkenhayn convinced the kaiser to combine the two offices under his sole authority, and Wilhelm agreed. Von Moltke summoned enough strength to argue against Falkenhayn's appointment, but his days of influence were over. He was assigned a meaningless desk in Berlin.

Erich von Falkenhayn, a stereotypical Prussian, seemingly enters the annals of this war straight from central casting. Born in East Prussia to a Junker family that could trace its ancestors back several centuries to the Teutonic Knights, von Falkenhayn followed the well-trodden path of a young, patriotic and myopically single-minded German boy. The army was to be his career, his life, the only thing that really mattered. He would learn to obey orders, then he would learn to give them, and in both cases compliance would be automatic. In keeping with every other German officer, he would serve in a variety of garrisons and, due to merit, be exposed to administrative details on the general staff and the overbearing persona of General Fieldmarshal

Count Alfred von Schlieffen. He would inherit the traditional contempt for politicians, the Reichstag and anything to do with democratic principles. When sabre-rattling became endemic, he, like his contemporaries, would all be in favour of war, the sooner the better. On the first day of hostilities, in fact, he was heard to say, 'Even if we perish, it will have been exquisite.' Appreciating the virtue of etiquette and flattery (when appropriate) he eventually became known to the kaiser, and in time was singled out as a 'favourite', his career enabled at several opportune junctures by a nod from Wilhelm. Max Hoffmann went so far as to say that Falkenhayyn 'has his Majesty in a bag'. This was beneficial and deleterious at the same time, as events would prove. By August 1914, Falkenhayn was the Prussian Minister of War, an office that by custom was held by a senior officer, usually appointed for the maturity of judgment that only a long career in the military could be expected to develop. Falkenhayn, by contrast, was only fifty-three years of age, with over thirty more experienced officers above him on the promotion list. By appointing Falkenhayn as his primary minister, in fact, Wilhelm had proven himself incompetent to lead the army, in the opinion of many disgruntled generals, a sentiment that would grow and ultimately undermine the kaiser as the war progressed.

The German officer corps, like those of every other warring power, was riven by the usual discords that bedevil most organizations: greed for advancement, envy, jealousy, paranoia, suspicion. Two of Germany's current military heroes, Von Hindenburg and Ludendorff, were vastly unpopular in many segments of the army, Hindenburg due to dotage, Ludendorff because of the unenviable suspicion that in order to get his way, anyone – friend or foe – was expendable. Wilhelm, as befits a man of extreme disposition who disliked sharing the limelight with anyone, disdained both men, no matter what their successes; Hindenburg because he was a simpleton, Ludendorff because of his 'dubious character, eaten away by personal ambition'. The antipathy to von Falkenhayn, however, was of a different sort. The kaiser believed in him, but no one else did. Few in the military hierarchy had much insight into his character or motivations. He had arrived at the top as an unannounced, unexpected and relatively unknown personality. He was the quintessential outsider, a man without a pedigree within the known avenues of advancement, and he intended to keep it that way.

The problem with Falkenhayn was his position within the cosmos of current military thinking or, to be more precise, his distance from its centre. The formative years of his young career were not spent in the general staff milieu of classrooms and staff rides, listening to the at times overbearing obsessions of Count von Schlieffen. In 1896 he was sent to China, where he spent a good deal of time improvising and reacting to the general chaos of the Boxer Rebellion. He learned one important lesson there, however, which he would apply to the western front eighteen years later: when something was in the way, remove it (in this instance, a large portion of Peking centre's Ming-era 'sacred' wall, flattened in the name of military exigency). Falkenhayn was therefore not a protégé of the von Schlieffen school of thought. Unlike Ludendorff, for example, who considered the master as something of a god, von Falkenhayn had never been susceptible to the gospel of Cannae; when Schlieffen had taught his class on that battle, as a fellow general quipped, Falkenhayn was off in China sightseeing. Schlieffen, to Falkenhayn, was a theorist; a genius, no doubt, but a man whose rigid conception of how the coming battle with France must be fought was too inelastic given modern conditions of warfare. Hannibal's army in 216 BC had probably numbered 50,000 warriors, and his envelopment of the enemy was conducted on a battlefield of just a few square miles; but in 1914 millions of men were in the field, so many that the kind of grand enveloping manoeuvres that von Schlieffen planned for the borderlands of France and Belgium seemed almost preposterous. It was a tribute to von Schlieffen, and the mechanical ability of German engineers and railway systems that delivered these astounding numbers of troops where they were supposed to be and when they were supposed to be there, that the entire scheme almost worked. But that was the point, according to Falkenhayn. It hadn't worked.

Then again, some things were working, though not particularly for Falkenhayn and the general staff over which he now presided, with its obsessive concentration on the western theatre. One continuing factor that hampered Falkenhayn's freedom of movement (and freedom of thought) was persistent rivalry with OberOst, the army headquarters of the eastern theatre run by von Hindenburg and Ludendorff, the latter of whom was no shrinking violet. He offered Falkenhayn a certain degree of respect by agreeing that ultimate victory lay in Germany's ability to knock at least one of its important opponents out of the war. For Falkenhayn that meant France, for Ludendorff it meant Russia, and a tally card showed disproportionate results between the two camps by the end of 1915. Falkenhayn had not 'won' the race to the sea. He had not 'won' the first battle of Ypres. He had not, in fact, 'won' anything. That was hardly the case with Ludendorff. His armies had crushed the Russians at Tannenberg, and his follow-up operations, Napoleonic in scope, had been devastating to the tsar's forces, inflicting over one and half million casualties.[13] Poland lay under German control. The Serbian army had been destroyed. If Austro-Hungarian forces could perform, at the very least, to merely competent levels, Italy, when and if it entered the conflict, would be stalemated. These were spectacular results – Ludendorff certainly thought so – but Falkenhayn did not return the compliment. When Ludendorff suggested more of the same, Falkenhayn refused to allocate the necessary troops. When Ludendorff promised decisive returns, Falkenhayn demurred, suggesting that victories in the east were mostly tactical, and could never deliver the penultimate blow that would destroy Russia's ability to wage war. When Ludendorff declared that wide-ranging offensive tactics, so successful against Russia, would work in the western theatre as well, Falkenhayn grew dismissive. 'The force of the defensive is unbelievable', he wrote a friend; the idea of breaking through the French or British lines and achieving a decisive victory was delusional.[14] Thus began a vicious stream of gossip and innuendo, mostly directed to the kaiser's ears and interspersed by several threats from Hindenburg to resign, which sought to undermine Falkenhayn, and very nearly did. The kaiser, by nature combustible, at first defended Falkenhayn. Hindenburg, in his opinion, was no better than that rascal from centuries ago, the freebooter Wallenstein; no field marshal, in times of war, should ever threaten the emperor with resignation! Even his wife was badgering him to dismiss Falkenhayn. 'Now the ladies room becomes involved', he complained. With no natural allies within the officer corps as a whole, Falkenhayn struggled to retain Wilhelm's support, but it became painfully obvious that what he needed most was a success, and in keeping with the stakes involved, it had to be a big success. In the wings, waiting to replace him, stood Hindenburg and Ludendorff.

Literature on von Falkenhayn in the century since the Great War's beginning is uniformly negative. He has been portrayed as weak-willed, prone to nervous anxiety, insufficiently bold and too obsessed with 'limited objectives'. But of all the Great War commanders, he alone had intellectual character. Vain, certainly arrogant and opinionated, he had an unpleasant and cold personality. He did not suffer fools gladly. When Austria-Hungary's aged Emperor Franz Joseph finally died in 1916, his successor to the throne, Archduke Karl, dared to dispute a certain point of military strategy. Von Falkenhayn would have none of that. 'What is your Imperial Highness thinking of?' he shouted. 'Whom do you think you have in front of you?' Nonetheless, he had a clearer vision of how the war was progressing as 1915 turned into 1916 than any of his contemporaries. He saw the issues more precisely, recognized realistically the parameters within which Germany might win the war, and devised a strategy to pounce on the one slender reed that, if realized, might satisfactorily conclude the struggle. At the decisive moment, he did indeed lose his concentration, and frittered away what was certainly his country's last chance for a favourable peace; had he not done so, the course of the war might well have been different.

As early as November 1914, von Falkenhayn had advised the imperial chancellor, Bethmann Hollweg, that Germany could not win the war by 'conventional' means. By that, he meant by military conquest. Falkenhayn could do the arithmetic. Added together, the allied (or Entente) nations simply outpopulated Germany. Germany in 1914 might have had a twenty-seven million more people edge over France, but the vast resources of the British Empire had barely come into play. Russia could be militarily diminished, but never completely defeated. 'An advance on Moscow', he wrote, 'takes us nowhere', this being the one and certain Napoleonic example that made Ludendorff's contentions to the contrary nothing short of absurd. The best hope for defeating Russia lay, perversely, in internal revolution, a premise that would come to be in 1917, to Germany's ultimate regret. Italy, which had entered the war with 'brigand's ambitions', could be discounted; nevertheless, the Italian front wasted resources, and Austria-Hungary was an ally in constant need of assistance. Serbia had been militarily neutralized, but Romania might join the Entente. The United States, in von Falkenhayn's opinion, was unlikely to enter a continental land war, but if it did, the eventual imbalance in material resources and troops would be devastating. A dictated peace, based on overwhelming military successes, was not to be. 'If Russia, France, and England hold together, we cannot defeat them in such a way as to achieve acceptable peace terms. We are more likely to be slowly exhausted.' A negotiated peace, however, was still possible, and von Falkenhayn recommended that Bethmann Hollweg pursue one. Germany had several chips to use in any prospective bargaining: large swaths of foreign territory and resources under its control, an undefeated military machine in the field and functioning superbly, a united people on the home front. The nation might be compelled to forfeit some assets in any future peace conference, but several prewar objectives had been achieved and could be retained if diplomacy was put to work right away. But time was running out for Germany, and von Falkenhayn was one of the few men who recognized that stark fact.

Perhaps the most famous strategic memorandum ever produced between 1914 and 1918 is also the most mysterious, in that several historians have questioned its validity and if, in fact, it was ever written in the first place. We have only von Falkenhayn's word that it is genuine. In December 1915 he claims to have delivered for the kaiser's review a blueprint for victory. It was probably not the sort of report that Wilhelm wanted to read, because it promised very little that was grandiloquent or heroic. It was a confession, in fact, that the opportunity for the kind of strutting, taunting and histrionic triumph that the megalomaniac warlord so longed for, had slipped from Germany's grasp with the failure of von Schlieffen's plan. In its place stood cold reality. All Germany's enemies remained still standing and still fighting, though in varying degrees of effectiveness, and the one most to be feared ('our arch enemy') had not nearly reached its fullest strength. This was Britain.

Germany could, at the very least, revert to a defensive posture that would ensure that the country suffered no catastrophic loss on the battlefield. On the western front especially, German positions were well chosen and favoured defenders as opposed to attackers. The French in particular could be counted on to continue their aggressive tactics; it was part of their military character to do so. Fine and good, concluded von Falkenhayn; French offensives had been so disastrous that 'any imitation of their battle methods' would be folly. As he would write elsewhere, the rationale of the defence 'in itself [is] quite worthy of consideration'. After all, 'If we do not lose the war, we will have won it.' However, 'our enemies, thanks to their superiority in men and material, are increasing their resources much more than we are. If that process continues, a moment will come when the balance of numbers will deprive Germany of all remaining hope.' A decisive blow must be struck, but unconventionally, and not initially directed towards Britain. The weak straw in the west was France, exhausted 'almost to the limits of its endurance'. Knock France out of the war, and Britain would follow. She had no territorial stake on the continent; in fact, her entry into the war had been idealistic – the protection of Belgium, a country now almost completely occupied by German troops. She was not fighting, in other words, to protect British soil; she was fighting in France, but for what reason? If France stood battered and defeated, Britain would simply retreat to its island sanctuary, bloodied but certainly unbowed. The contest for European supremacy might continue after a pause, but for the moment Germany would have achieved a breathing space. Settling with Britain could wait. France was 'England's best sword'. Make her drop it and all the rest would follow.

How to achieve this result? Not through the decisive battle of annihilation so favoured by German theorists like Clausewitz and von Schlieffen. Such a drama was no longer possible. Instead, a more wearying and analytic solution presented itself. The French would be 'bled white' in a battle resembling more of a siege than a sudden duel. 'Within our reach behind the French sector of the western front there are objectives for the retention of which the French General Staff would be compelled to throw in every man they have. If they do so the forces of France will bleed to death – as there can be no question of a voluntary withdrawal – *whether we reach our goal or not.*'[15]

The ingenuity of von Falkenhayn's approach (and disregarding its morally repugnant character) was that the plan would work either way. If the French 'threw everything they had' into the cauldron, that would achieve a German victory; if they did not, then they would inevitably lose whatever objective Germany had set out to attack, thereby achieving a different sort of victory, but victory nonetheless. 'The moral effect on France will be enormous' no matter what, Falkenhayn concluded. The trick was to pick the right target. For von Falkenhayn, it was Verdun.

Falkenhayn reproduced this memo in his memoirs, written three years after the war. No original copy has ever been uncovered, and neither the kaiser nor his son, Crown Prince William (who commanded the German Fifth Army that would spearhead the attack), mentioned it in their own written recollections. Indeed, the behaviour of the crown prince especially seems to indicate an ignorance of von Falkenhayn's truest intentions in the Verdun matter (he seemed to feel all along that the objective of the campaign was to capture the city). This has led several revisionist historians to speculate whether von Falkenhayn invented the memo after the fact, as though to justify (and incriminate) others in the decision to drain France of its lifeblood at Verdun, when in fact the operation turned out to be an equal disaster for Imperial Germany. This beggars belief. None of the participants in this campaign ever reacted in horror to von Falkenhayn's memoir, or even suggested that the former commander in chief was a fabulist. Von Falkenhayn has been accused of many things, but being a liar has never been suggested. As a great supporter of duelling among officers, he was seen by most as a paragon of honour. Other statements, moreover, recorded by a variety of observers, certainly corroborate the general gist of von Falkenhayn's intention. One of his trusted officers reflected his chief's contention that the French were 'morally mediocre' and ready to collapse. Walther Rathenau, a respected German industrialist, noted in his diary von Falkenhayn's opinion that beneath their crumbling façade there still lurked 'a remnant of noble quality' in the French: they would not stand by and let Verdun fall, and thus would sink unthinkingly into the German trap. Even the kaiser conceded in a conversation after the war 'that Falkenhayn's thinking was "Our goal was to hold the line, [a line] that would be solid enough to repel French counterattacks while causing the most damage".' This was absolutely the crux of his thinking. The French would recoil, then surge forward to recover lost territory, as they had throughout the first year of the war. As they did so, salients would develop that German artillery could enfilade from three angles. The hoped-for result would be a killing ground, 'a mere slaughter-house' that would sap the very marrow of France and scatter it into the ground. By the time they were finished, as one general said, not a mouse would be left alive in Verdun.

There is nothing particularly attractive about von Falkenhayn's train of thought. He intended to amass the greatest concentration of heavy artillery yet seen in the history of warfare, and to pulverize a very narrow front on the east bank of the Meuse, then move in. It was the sort of thing, he felt, that Britain would do if it had the chance. The British, after all, 'judged others by herself'; they had a 'will to war' that France no longer possessed. They were, in fact, the real target. With France stripped of its ability or sense of purpose to fight on, Russia neutralized and the United States not yet in the war, what would be the point of Britain's continuing the fight? German preparations to stake everything on Verdun sped forward. Von Falkenhayn named the operation *Gericht*, which translates loosely as 'place of judgment'; more literally, however, it means 'place of execution'.

German railheads lay just a dozen miles from the city. German preponderance of heavy artillery – everything from massive 15-inch naval guns to a plethora of hard-hitting mortars – were dragged into position, many by specially designed tractors, in order to take some of the strain from draught horses, thirty per cent of whom would die from overwork at Verdun. Elaborate underground bunkers, reinforced with concrete, were quickly built behind German lines, often at night to conceal evidence of their construction. The usual approach trenches into the front-line works were dispensed with, the idea being to give no clue as to the upcoming operation. Almost two and a half million shells would be transported to German gun emplacements for the first week of action, hauled by over thirty-three ammunition trains a day. Most significantly, von Falkenhayn specified the requirement that German planes rule the sky, which they mostly did through sheer numbers. French reconnaissance sorties were brushed from the scene. This was a very early recognition as to the value of air power. Although French intelligence gradually divined that some sort of attack was in the works, they had no idea as to the size of the hammer blow that would follow.

Given command of *Gericht* was Crown Prince Friedrich Wilhelm, the kaiser's eldest son. Like his father, Prince Wilhelm had received an odd education and upbringing, designed, if that is the proper word, to guarantee that not a sprig of affection might develop between father and son. Childhood was relatively harsh, in spartan quarters and ruled for the most part by military tutors, the idea being that, at least as a postcard image, the royal heir was to be trained, seen and appreciated as a Prussian soldier. In fact, he was barely that. He could look the part, as his father did, and be counted on to open his mouth at inopportune moments with the usual frothy mix of militaristic gibberish. He was little more than a dilettante: a lover of fast cars (with 'springs of first-rate German steel'), horses, beautiful women, music, tennis and fine French wine. Indeed, he was not much different from Edward, the Prince of Wales, his English counterpart, though in one important respect he stood apart. Prince William would never have forfeited his crown 'for the woman I love'.

William was, of course, a commander in name only, a figurehead. The real director of the Fifth Army was General Schmidt von Knobelsdorf, the chief of staff. The kaiser had put it plainly to his son, in a lesson that he too was gradually learning: act like a soldier, look the part, but do what von Knobelsdorf tells you to do. This was deflating to the ego of the crown prince, but nothing when compared to the indignities that the kaiser was beginning to feel at the hands of his generals. By the end of the war, both men would be relegated to doing what they did best, handing out Iron Crosses on ceremonial occasions.[16]

Be that as it may, on 21 February 1916 Prince William gave the order for the very first artillery salvo of the battle, the discharge of a 15-inch naval artillery piece which launched a projectile weighing over 2,000 pounds towards the general vicinity of Verdun. It landed on the cathedral. It was followed by a barrage over the eastern bank that lasted for ten hours; cannon fire seeming to obliterate everything in its path. German stormtroopers, 'coloured grasshopper grey', then emerged from their dugouts and advanced. They expected little or no opposition.

'The point is not only to strike the French army but to destroy it.'
Von Falkenhayn to the crown prince, February 1916

One of the major criticisms of von Falkenhayn's plan was his decision to focus on the eastern bank of the Meuse alone, where the major forts of Douaumont, Vaux and Souville were situated. Knobelsdorf had vigorously disputed this disposition, saying that a wider front should be employed that attacked on both sides of the river. Von Knobeldorf, in fact, had the traditional, von Schlieffen-esque goal in mind: a devastating attack that would lead to a more or less instant victory. He did not envision a long-drawn-out struggle. This would have required, however, a dilution of the artillery attack and more troops than Falkenhayn thought he could spare, but von Knobelsdorf's reservations gave him pause. He recognized the merits of the argument, and agonized just before the attack was to commence. Should he, or should he not, expand the scope of *Gericht*? By deciding not to, he essentially lost the war for Germany.

This critique proved valid. He had conceived a major offensive aimed at crippling the enemy, but an inherent sense of caution (unfortunately rare, to be true, in many World War I generals) caused him to hold back. Perhaps, in his own mind, he was confused as to his goal. Was it to take Verdun in one quick stroke, or was it to destroy the French army? It must be said that humanitarian concerns were not at the root of Falkenhayn's hesitation. Like Haig, like Foch, like Joffre, casualty figures were abstractions, numbers on a sheet of paper that hardly troubled his conscience. The implications of those figures, however, deeply unsettled him. Reserves took on critical importance. With no reserves, vulnerability on other fronts, where a crisis could emerge at any moment, might prove catastrophic. This reluctance to commit fully would cost him a battle he sorely needed to win. He sought victory 'on the cheap'. Only eight divisions attacked on 21 February. On the Somme, five months later, Douglas Haig and Joffre threw twenty-four into the battle.[17]

Joffre Makes a Miscalculation

Deep inside the citadel at Verdun, General Frédéric-Georges Herr sat mired in a strengthening depression. The state of Verdun – its readiness, or lack of same – had been a hotly debated topic within French military circles ever since the more-or-less static trench line stretching from the North Sea to Switzerland had been established after the Marne. France, though temporarily relieved by what the allied propaganda was already calling a miracle, stood in a state of some shock. Casualty lists had been deeply disturbing, the performance of the French army something of a mortification. Where would the rapacious Germans attack next, and would the country's forces be up to stopping it? To Herr and many others like him, everything pointed to Verdun, and when he reviewed the state of his defences, all he could say was 'Every day I tremble'.

The theories of Grandmaison and his 'Young Turks' had devalued the importance of concrete fortresses. Their rationale was buttressed by extensive testing that had been underway for some two decades, new generations of high explosives having a devastating effect on some of de Rivières's precious strong points. Indeed, some of his work proved obsolete in the span of just three years, requiring extensive and expensive alterations. The contempt also seem merited by the Belgian debacle: Liège humbled, Namur taken in just six days. General Joffre concurred. Just as von Falkenhayn was preparing his sledge for the eastern banks of the Meuse above Verdun, Joffre ordered the forts to be dismantled and abandoned. Nearly all the heavy artillery pieces were removed for other fronts, so desperate was the need for guns that could match the heavy German pieces, and garrison troops were dispersed for trench duty elsewhere. Fort Douaumont, perhaps the most advanced fortification in the world and called by Pétain 'the masterpiece of the system', was on 21 February manned by about 56 territorials and reservists, most of whom remained huddled in the nethermost subterranean quarters of the fort. Their commander was a tired-out sergeant-major nearing sixty years of age. These were not the *crème de la crème* of the French army. '*Les reserves,*' as one officer put it, '*c'est zero*'.

Rumours of Verdun's vulnerability were rampant in Paris, where Galliéni was now the minister of war. Indiscreet and unauthorized complaints had reached his desk, and he sent an insulting letter of inquiry to Joffre, seeking assurances that Verdun would be adequately defended if the Germans attacked there. Ever the bureaucrat, Joffre was furious that leaks could undermine his authority and, with intense *hauteur*, wrote a vigorous denial (marked by 'offended grandeur and ponderous rage') that anything was amiss. Despite the laurel of victory that had been deposited on his head after the Marne, 'Papa Joffre' (as he was now popularly called) had cause for concern. He trusted only a few generals now, having sacked over fifty in just the first month of war. Ferdinand Foch was among his favourites. He admired the man's refusal to panic. During the so-called Race to the Sea, Joffre had made Foch his 'point man', sending him hither and yon along the stretching front to succour, cajole, stiffen, encourage and invigorate an entire roll call of generals, field marshals, kings and admirals. In one span of 57 hours, he motored 530 miles, rushing into various headquarters 'like a gust of wind'. Foch was infectious; a few enthusiastic words from him, usually encouraging people to attack and keep on attacking, seemed just the tonic for exhausted commanders. He had done that at the Marne, after all, inciting his subordinates with spirited harangues. 'I won't hear anything! You understand! I won't hear anything! I'm deaf!' he said in one impromptu pep talk. 'I only know three ways of fighting – Attack – Hold On – Clear out. I forbid the last. Choose between the first two'. Few seemed to notice that Foch spent most of that battle in retreat, albeit fighting all the way.[18] Some who disparaged his rhetorical excesses called him 'The Tower of Babel'. De

Castelnau was another one, the 'fighting monk'. These men had spirit, the kind Joffre did not possess. That made them valuable to him. They were also not unduly doctrinaire, like the Young Turks. That made them invaluable. To check out the situation at Verdun, Joffre dispatched de Castelnau to take a look. A few days later, he went himself.

What they saw was not encouraging. General Herr had to be replaced, that much was certain; he lacked initiative and enthusiasm, and was bound to crack under any serious strain. Now that the forts were no longer considered essential, more earthworks and trench systems were required, and work started on them. More importantly, additional troops were ordered up. Indications certainly pointed to an attack, many of a small and seemingly insignificant character, but telling nonetheless when considered as a whole. Intelligence officers took note that church spires in German-held territory were disappearing, which could only mean that the enemy were removing easily identifiable markers that could be used by artillery spotters. German fighter planes were more numerous than usual. Deserters had disconcerting tales to tell, but could they be trusted? As was his wont, Joffre remained unperturbed. As he stated himself, if he believed every rumour, every intelligence report and every nervous general, the Germans would be attacking not just Verdun, but at every single point on the line, an impossibility. Joffre left the town no more or less convinced that von Falkenhayn would attack here. His inner calm would change, and quickly, on 21 February.

No one, up to that point, had ever witnessed or endured an artillery barrage of the intensity experienced on the 21st. German superiority in cannons and howitzers was in the four-to-one range, and nearly every piece was concentrating on a very small front of only eight miles. It seemed impossible that anything could live through it. Although natural features of the landscape were rearranged by the massive shelling – trees uprooted, splintered, thrown in all directions – the fact is that men did survive. Crawling out from half-buried dugouts, crazed or deafened by gunfire, stupefied by the sheer chaos of the destruction around them, which included flying body parts, debris and the scythe of shrapnel, they nevertheless resisted (for the most part) the impulse to flee. The great martial spirit of the common French soldier overwhelmed the more natural instinct to run for it. Pockets of resistance formed on the platoon level, perhaps ten to twelve men, often without officers, taking it upon themselves to fight on, no matter the hopeless odds. In the days of nineteenth-century warfare, such resistance would have been cast aside or overrun, given the number of Germans involved in the attack, but modern war had balanced the odds in such instances if defenders had at their disposal a machine gun or two. This weapon, in tactical circumstances, was the trump card: a few men with enough ammunition, hidden in the rubble of concrete shelters or cellar holes, were capable of stopping hundreds, especially if they caught them out in the open or from flanks ... and especially if they held their own lives for naught. Individual instances of superhuman bravery, most unrecorded or obliterated when these nameless men inevitably fell, in effect saved Verdun by delaying the numerical onslaught of Brandenburgers, Hessians, Saxons and Westphalians. In several instances, French divisions simply disappeared from the army rolls. The 72nd's complement, for example, 200 officers and some 10,000 men, all died in just four days. It was a grisly portent of what was to come.

The most famous to fall was Émile Driant, a lieutenant-colonel of the 'old school'. A fifty-seven-year-old army veteran, his career had been chequered by an unwillingness to bridle his tongue. Initially his prospects had been bright, especially when he married a daughter of Georges Boulanger who, in the midst of one of France's innumerable crises (this one in January 1889) had mesmerized the nation with a combustible mix of nationalistic pride, monarchist tendencies and an appeal to the Napoleonic past (Napoleon I, let it be said, not Napoleon III). Had Boulanger not wavered at the last moment, he probably could have engineered a successful coup and taken power but, like many men of dubious moral fibre, he lost his nerve to cross the line, to take the decisive step, to fulfil what he had previously characterized as destiny. Boulanger's fall from popular favour was lent a saccharine twist when he shot himself to death at the grave of his mistress who had died two months before. As a contemporary noted, he began as a Caesar but ended as a Romeo, not the progression that he or his followers had wished for.

Émile Driant dabbled in politics and wrote profusely. Some of his literary efforts were in the vein of Jules Verne, futuristic works that professional officers derided. Blimps? Submarines? What nonsense. In his seminal book, *The War of Tomorrow*, however, he took issue with the ethos of 'offence at any price'. That was not the way modern campaigns should be conducted, he wrote, appreciating the lethality of new weapons and their gruesome application. He attended the German army manoeuvres of 1906. Such events usually climaxed with a ritualistic cavalry charge, generally led by the kaiser, but Driant overlooked these comical manifestations of Wilhelm's medievalism to analyze everything he had seen beforehand, and his conclusions were anathema to the French general staff: France would lose any coming war with Germany, just as it had in 1870, he wrote in a French weekly, only this time the pounding would be even worse. No wonder he was stationed on the front lines of Verdun's defensive positions. He was expendable.

During the early hours of 21 February, Driant's command absorbed the initial onslaught that he had sensed was coming. He also sensed that he would not survive it. A fervent Catholic, he had received absolution the day before, and given his personal effects to an adjutant to return to Madame Driant. 'I feel very calm', he had written her. As his lines collapsed, he was seen as the pillar of strength, directing his men in what was a suicidal defence. Eighty thousand high explosive shells had been dropped on his sector alone, and nearly half his men were dead or wounded after the opening barrage. Driant himself grabbed a rifle. Witnesses heard him yell, 'We are here, this is our place, they shall not move us out of it'. Unfortunately, the Germans introduced a new and hideous weapon to their arsenal of inhumanity – flamethrowers – first deployed against Driant's *chasseurs*.[19] As with any innovation, this caused considerable terror among the French, and understandably so. While rallying his men, Driant finally fell, a bullet through the head. Even the Germans respected his courage. He was given a military funeral some days later, and a letter of condolence was written to his widow. His grave can be found fairly near to where he died, surrounded by the tombs of his *chasseurs*, mostly so mangled they could not be identified.

The next several days were trying ones for the French. Communications had almost collapsed. Telephone wires, many carelessly unburied, had been shredded during the bombardments, and runners sent back to headquarters in the rear invariably never made it. Generals sitting deep in the catacombs of Vauban's citadel or in towns behind the city had no idea what was going on, and issued orders which, by the time they were delivered, usually had no correlation to reality. Officers on the front lines often asked plaintively for direction. What shall I do? The reply, if they ever received one, was usually along the lines of: fend for yourself. Cold winter weather was an added detriment, especially for French colonial troops. Moroccans and Algerians had the ferocity, for which they were so well known, sapped right out of them. Many wounded lay where they had been hit, which was frequently less of an ordeal than being roughly carted to an emergency aid station, there to await attention that never came. Verdun's sole railway line was severed, its road system to the west gravely damaged. The question of supplies became more serious by the hour. On the morning of 24 February, Verdun's commander had, in effect, no reserves. The next day he heard even more grim news: Fort Douaumont had fallen, in circumstances that verged on the burlesque. A German sergeant of pioneers stumbled into the dry moat surrounding Douaumont.[20] Enterprisingly, he found a shell hole in the masonry and crawled inside the fort where, through bravado and bluff, he secured the surrender of probably half the Frenchmen inside. Not a shot

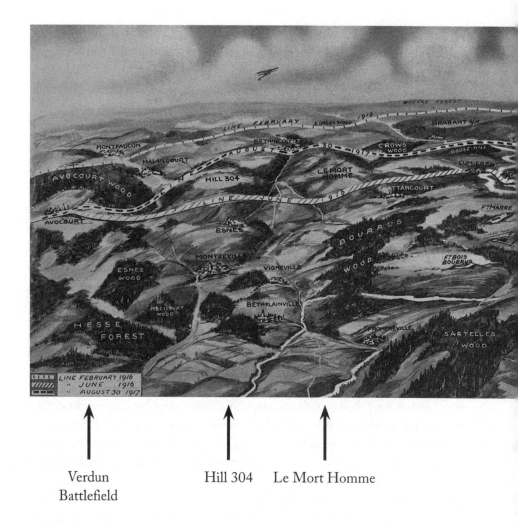

Verdun   Hill 304   Le Mort Homme
Battlefield

was fired. After locking up his prisoners in a bunker, he even sat down and
ate lunch, washed down by a glass or two of *vin ordinaire*. He was joined
later in the afternoon by other small parties of German infantry. The fort
was officially taken. 'Douaumont is like those distant and disdainful women',
wrote a disgusted Frenchman in his diary, 'who seem impregnable but yield
in an instant'. After General Herr reported this improbable information to
the man sent to replace him, he was told to pack up and report to Limoges.

Presumably, Verdun now lay there for the taking. Douaumont stood just
a few kilometres from the city centre. From its vantage-point overlooking
the entire battlefield, artillery spotters could direct fire not only into town,
but presumably at the bridges crossing the Meuse. If these were destroyed,
the entire east bank would be isolated and cut off from supplies, and, if that

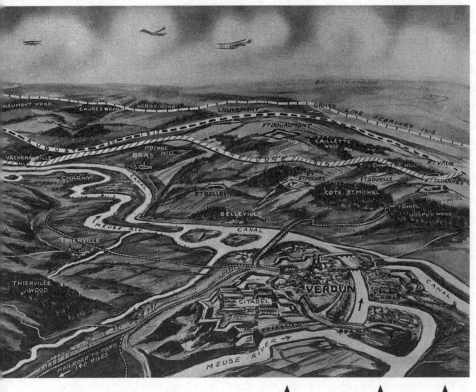

Ft. Douaumont   Tavannes   Ft. Vaux
Tunnel

happened, the end had surely come. Certainly the kaiser thought so. He reported for duty, watching the smoke from afar through a telescope and listening to the thunder of guns. He was ready to enter Verdun in triumph on his charger. That's what warlords were for, after all, to ride over the corpses of their enemies. Attila the Hun had wanted to do the same thing in Verdun fifteen centuries before, but he found only frustration, as indeed would Wilhelm II.

What was it that saved France in this darkest of hours? The answer is many-headed, but initially it was the fortitude displayed by common soldiers. They did not cave in; they fought back, they bought time. This elemental doggedness can never be marginalized in any discussion of Verdun. General de Castelnau, back again to assess the situation, and General Philippe Pétain, appointed by him to replace Herr, are mentioned again and again in histories of this battle. Their task was simple, however: they issued commands, they told people to stand fast, they allegedly inspired subordinates by their steadfast determination. Little of that translated to the front lines. Neither Castelnau nor Pétain ever fired a rifle at Verdun, shuddered as artillery shells churned up their trenches into mush or pulled on a gas mask when canisters flooded the now ghastly landscape with green poison. The common *poilu* did all this and more. Often of peasant background, inured to the harsh life of pre-mechanized agricultural work and generally obedient (if sullen) to the orders of superiors, whether they be military or clerical, the *poilu* endured. Told to hold a position, he would generally do so. Told not to give in, he would generally do so. Told to die … well, he would give it some thought. Enough were willing, in the end, that France had a chance.[21]

Erich von Falkenhayn could not have been happier with the way the situation was progressing just five days into the offensive. If he had known about the characters of his French counterparts, de Castelnau and Pétain, he would have grown (for him) positively merry. His devil's pact had succeeded extraordinarily well. Instead of defeatists like Herr, he now had two men more than willing to take up the challenge. France, just as he intended, would be bled white.

De Castelnau, Joffre's chief of staff, was the perfect man for the commander in chief to send to Verdun. He was prepared to defend the city to its very last inch. Casualties, costs, material losses mattered nothing. Verdun might be reduced to a pile of rubble (as it largely was), but it would not fall. He had a Napoleonic sense of mission, and a Napoleonic disregard for looking at the final bill. It was the fate of soldiers to die, and they would die by the thousands all over the hills and ravines of the Meuse valley. If he consoled himself at all, it was by the notion that such deaths would be *glorieux*, a sensation he hoped his men would appreciate. If they did not, it was their fault, not his.

As he assessed the darkening situation, and directed the initial measures of defence, de Castelnau sensed immediately that a fresh cadre of officers was required. Headquarters, in the words of one newly arrived observer, resembled 'a lunatic asylum'. It required a steady hand to lead it now, and he did not hesitate to appoint Philippe Pétain as the new commander. The situation was so dire, de Castelnau didn't bother consulting Joffre, who apparently shrugged off the impertinence. 'Let him do as he wants', he said of Castelnau. Joffre was comfortable taking advice from the few people he trusted.

One aspect of Pétain-esque lore is that no one on his staff could find the general once news of his promotion arrived by telegram at the town of Noailles, where his current unit was quartered. An officer intimate with

Pétain's nocturnal meanderings figured it out, however, and took a train to Paris, arriving at 3:00 a.m. He then made his way to an old haunt of the general's, the Hotel Terminus. Wandering about the corridors, he spotted Pétain's boots in the hall, alongside a pair of woman's shoes. Knocking on the door, he conveyed the portentous news. Pétain expressed no emotion one way or the other. He arranged for the officer to secure a room of his own, and went back to bed, but apparently not to sleep. Legend maintains that he spent the rest of the early morning making love.

Pétain

Philippe Pétain was born to peasant stock in the village of Cauchy, population in the 1850s approximately 400 souls, located in the north-west of France in the Department Pas-de-Calais. Some have assumed that Pétain's well-known taciturnity was the simple result of geography, that being an oft-recognized character trait of farmers and workers from this area. A sense of foredoom was perhaps warranted by the local populace: the area around Calais, full of harbours and ports, has been a battlefield for centuries, given that region's unenviable distinction of being the major entry point for English armies about to set off on military adventures throughout France. From Richard the Lion Heart to Edward III to Henry V to the dukes of Marlborough and Wellington, the long list encompasses nearly every British warrior of note. Aside from William the Conqueror (who actually embarked from St. Valéry-sur-Somme, somewhat farther south in Picardy), the favour has seldom been returned in the opposite direction. The region was also undergoing an industrial revolution of sorts, vividly depicted in Zola's important novel *Germinal*. Pétain grew up in trying personal circumstances as well, which helps explain several strands in his day-to-day behaviour and outlook: he disliked the English and most of what they stood for; idealized a peasant life that was fast disappearing around him; and grew to distrust intimate affection, no matter what his belief in the centrality of the family unit to French society. Completing his diffidence, he turned his back on the Catholic faith, despite his affection for several important clerics in his life, and the educational opportunities that the Church showered upon him in his youth. He was, however, no republican. Far from it. He distrusted socialism, politicians and any cant from the left, attempting instead, as many disinterested officers did, to remain above the fray. Pétain recognized the fact that the Third Republic, born in 1870, had destroyed the Communist Commune in Paris, killing some 30,000 Frenchmen in the process. It was worthy of his allegiance, if not his fullest trust.

Pétain, after 'cramming' at a Dominican college in suburban Paris, managed to gain admittance to the French military academy of Saint-Cyr in 1876. Four hundred and twelve young men were admitted that year; Pétain's academic credentials put him 403 on the list. Some biographers have suggested that he chose the military only because other forms of employment (the priesthood, for example) did not offer the relative security of an army career, security being (as the cliché has it) an extraordinarily important component of the peasant psyche. This is somewhat hard to believe. Pétain, like everyone else his age in school, was sensitive to the humiliations of the just-concluded Franco-Prussian War, and equally suspicious of the populist governments that succeeded Napoleon III. The mantra of his Dominican principal, after all, could not have stated the situation more succinctly: 'For the generation we are raising, the future is revenge – revenge against the foreigner … revenge also against the revolutionary spirit which surprised us'.[22] Pétain's admittedly slow climb up the promotional ladder should not obscure the fact that he worked diligently, mastered many aspects of his profession, was admired by several of his superiors and steadfastly adhered to tactical theories, increasingly out of vogue, which he considered to be inviolable.

Whereas Pétain was politically aloof, he was less than circumspect when it came to issues being discussed within army circles. He had no hesitation, especially when he received appointments to various technical schools and then the war college as a professor, to bucking the various popular notions of his day. The expositions of Colonel de Grandmaison, for instance, were greeted with some scepticism by the now middle-aged Pétain. This is not to say that he was controversial, only that he had a mind of his own and was not above expressing his opinions, no matter the negativity with which these might be received. Janet Flanner, an astute observer of France, summed him up in one brief sentence: 'He had arrived at middle life with a mental baggage of his own ideas, solid but not very numerous, which he lacked the warmth to put across but which it was part of his character to defend.' In many ways, Pétain's nature was similar to that of one of his pupils, a young *sous-lieutenant* by the name of Charles de Gaulle; both had considerable faith in their own good judgement, let others say what they may. De Gaulle and Pétain had other things in common. It is said, though hardly established in fact, that both often pursued the same women, to a degree of success that would be the envy of most men. De Gaulle, however, married in 1921 and gave up the hunt, whereas Pétain became a legend, 'a serial fornicator' who never stopped chasing women. As he said, 'I love two things above all, sex and the infantry.'

Every French officer loved the infantry. Cavalrymen were assuredly glamorous, but it was the foot soldier who could charge a position and then, more importantly, hold it. The stiffer the fight, the better, and the queen of weaponry was the bayonet. Nothing worked more effectively than cold steel, face to face with the enemy. There would even be instances in the coming world war when officers made their men empty their guns and haversacks of bullets, and ordered them to charge with bayonets only. French generals and colonels enjoyed repeating the Prince de Condé's quip that 'a French soldier can do anything with a bayonet except sit on it'. Pétain was not so sure.

Going against the grain, Pétain believed in firepower; not inaccurate field volleys, where men and artillery just fired blindly into the distance towards the enemy, but coordinated, aimed and concentrated discharges to achieve maximum killing effect. Infantry should never advance unsupported by artillery, especially against positions favourable to the defence. Throwing lives away was a sin. In his lectures, Pétain put the point succinctly. 'An offensive is gunfire leading an advance. A defensive is gunfire stopping an advance. The gun wins ground, the infantry occupies it.' If that was too subtle, he put it even more bluntly: *Le feu tue*, or 'Firepower Kills'. This was entirely opposite the dogma represented by Plan XVII, which stated that 'artillery does not prepare attacks; it supports them'. In de Gaulle's opinion, whatever faults might be placed at Pétain's feet, 'he, at least, did not prepare for the last war'.

As an aside, what all these men said was theory, nothing else. Few had been tested in war, few could predict the future. General Charles Mangin, known to his men as 'the butcher', simply stated the obvious. 'Whatever you do, you lose a lot of men.'

Up until 1914, real experiences of war being far and few between, officers had little opportunity to distinguish themselves or merit swift promotion. Daily life was often the dull routine of the barracks. Pétain's résumé was shorter than most, however, which had something to do with the unpopularity of his views. They were stodgy, unfashionable and lacking *élan*. In twenty-seven years he received only five advancements in rank. In his personnel file, researchers later found a handwritten notation that under no circumstances was Pétain ever to attain a rank over brigadier-general, and that distinction only on his leaving the army, a condition Pétain was making plans for. He purchased an old property fairly near to where he was born; he also bought a pair of garden clippers, in anticipation of all the flowers and shrubs that he intended to nurture. His remarks, to both subordinates and superiors, grew ever more acerbic. At the army manoeuvres of 1913, with forced retirement staring him in the face, he was asked to comment on the tactics of one particular general who had ordered a climactic infantry charge across open fields, uphill and against fixed defences. The regimental band, preceded by regimental standards, had led the manoeuvre. Pétain said, to a large group of observers, that the officer in question had authorized this theatrical display 'only to impress upon your minds a catalogue of all the mistakes that a modern army should not make'. His mordant sense of humour never left him either. 'I was old as a lieutenant, as a captain, as a colonel', he said, 'I have been old in all my ranks'. He expected his command of the 4th Infantry Brigade to be the last of his professional career. Luckily for him, war broke out in 1914. He would rise to that occasion.

'I have taken over command. Tell your troops. Hold fast.'

Pétain
26 February 1916

During the first frantic weeks of war, Pétain had distinguished himself as a disciplined and organized officer who knew what he was doing (or gave the impression that he did). Although his units participated in the early and disastrous offensives that had been planned on paper for the past decade, this is not where his star began to shine or be noticed. Rather, his rise was more due to the obvious incompetence of others above him in rank. As Joffre began purging the officer corps, this thrust those below into positions of authority they could only have dreamed about just a month before. In quick succession, Pétain was given command of a division; then an army corps; and in June of the next year, the Second Army. The promotions were startling by any standard. That being said, 1915 was a horrific year for the French army. The zeal for offensives remained strong; at least Pétain's were marked by as much artillery preparation as he could provide, but still the casualty figures were appalling: over one million men. Pétain saw what war was now. No more 'decisive battle as there used to be. Success in the end will belong to the side which will have the last man.' This was not an attitude that made him friends. Pétain's dour forebodings and his generally icy air of pessimism were not conducive to overall morale. It was universally believed at *GQG*, as Pierrefeu reported, that negativity of any sort meant that a man 'had lost his nerve'. But Pétain demonstrated mettle and resolve, two qualities the worsening Verdun situation required. He reported to Joffre's headquarters on 25 February, where the general assured him, in his usual clouded way, that the situation was manageable (Pétain would instantly see for himself that it was not). At least Joffre's orders were simple. Pétain was to hold Verdun, no matter what. He was not to even think of retreat, but to protect every inch of territory. '*Eh bien, mon ami, maintenant vous êtes tranquille*', he said to Pétain as he left for the front – 'Well, my friend, now you are easy in your mind'. Pierrefeu interpreted this cryptic remark, so characteristic of Joffre, to mean but one thing: 'Now you know what you have to do'.

Pétain's first order upon arrival to Verdun was to remove his headquarters farther to the rear. He chose the *mairie*, or town hall, of Souilly for this purpose, a simple and rather unadorned building still standing. Two years later, General John Pershing would use the same spot for his headquarters. As Pétain said to an aide, he needed a quiet place where he could think.

Pétain's contribution to the defence of Verdun was three-fold. The first was his stubbornness. Like de Castelnau, he had no plans to fail. Just because he doubted the theories of Grandmaison, just because he believed in defence, did not mean he was afraid to suffer casualties. Far from it. Clausewitz had said it best: anyone who led troops had to be indifferent to slaughter. Under his command, and that of his successor, Robert Nivelle, French forces would lose over 200,000 men. That is what it took to fulfil their collective mission. Where he differed from the 'Young Turks' was his determination not to waste lives unduly. His men would be killed in vast numbers, but they would be put in positions where they could extract a fearsome price for their sacrifice. They would slaughter as many Germans as the Germans were slaughtering Frenchmen. This may not represent innovative tactical thinking, but the defence of Verdun seemed to offer no alternative. Through all this mayhem, Pétain supplied the steady hand. 'He was a man on the bridge of a huge ocean liner', a visiting journalist noted; 'he was not "the man on horseback".'

His second contribution flows from the first. Pétain believed in firepower. He immediately reorganized the entire blueprint for what he saw as the coming duel between heavy guns. He badgered for new and better equipment, insisted on plentiful ammunition and realized the significance of defending the west bank of the Meuse to the last man. French batteries located behind a curtain of hills there were crucial to defending Verdun. German troops advancing southwards along the eastern bank were now opening their flanks to fire incoming from places like the Bois Bourrus and its five forts. As the days and weeks slogged on, thousands of German infantrymen, many fully exposed, would be shredded by Pétain's gunfire, so much so that von Falkenhayn would be forced, on 6 March, to attack these positions, thereby expanding his front by an extra eight miles, a stark admission that his decision to limit the initial attack had been mistaken. Fellow generals saw this as desperation. 'It should have been done at once', said one, 'now the moment of surprise is lost'. Vicious fighting for the possession of two vital hillocks, one the aptly named Le Mort Homme ('The Dead Man'), the other Côte 304 (signifying its height, 304 metres), raged back and forth for over two ghastly months. Côte 304, by the time it was all over, was so pulverized by heavy shelling that its summit was reduced by 20 metres.

In order to sustain these lengthy battles, Pétain had to devise a supply methodology to cope with what was fast to become a devouring maw of material. His solution was the famous *Voie Sacrée*, or Sacred Road, a stupendous organizational effort that he recognized as the key to sustaining Verdun.[23] Railway connections to the rear had been practically destroyed by constant shelling or were under the direct view of enemy guns. Resupply by barge was impossible. The only passage that enemy fire could not interdict was a dirt road from Bar le Duc, via Souilly, which is today's Route RD1916, a distance of 45 miles. In the first days of the battle, this track was a mass of disorder. In the description of Jules Romains, 'The details of the scene were far from cheering. The road was filled higgledy-piggledy by those engaged in carrying on the war and those intent on fleeing it.' It may sound prosaic, but to Pétain this represented the key to the defence of Verdun. It was his third great contribution to this battle that he ruthlessly put every consideration aside in order to make *La Voie Sacrée* operational, for he early understood the special character of the test that von Falkenhayn had presented him.

Much has been made of Pétain's sympathy with the common soldier. Some of this is misplaced mythology. Pétain was a traditionalist. He believed in discipline, and was a stern taskmaster whose taciturn character was widely viewed as cold-hearted – 'he froze people at a distance', said one acquaintance.[24] His memoirs, with one exception, are terse, without emotion and dull. When a florid declaration to the troops was required, he could often lapse into conventional orations full of the usual clichés. He was not inspirational by nature. Unlike many of his contemporaries, however, Pétain had a better understanding of how the *poilu*'s mind worked, and how to squeeze the very best effort out of him. Verdun, aptly christened 'a furnace' by the German writer Arnold Zweig, was to become what later historians would call 'a meat grinder'. The intensity of combat, the horrific conditions under which it had to be fought, the extenuating circumstances that made this battle unique – so sorely destructive of the human capacity to carry on – was something Pétain took into special consideration. No one, he felt, could stand this sort of strain for long. He understood Falkenhayn's attritional intentions, and countered them in unusual fashion. No troops would stay in line longer than eighteen days at a time. After units had done their tour, replacements would be cycled in to replace them; troops would then be transferred to the rear for rest, clean-ups and decent provisions; moral recuperation, if you will. This may appear to be a mundane scheme, but in fact it was novel. German front-line troops at Verdun often stayed in service months at a time without a respite. Driven into battle again and again, their spirits drooped as the campaign dragged on, with no resolution in sight. Some German generals, and some French as well, seemed indifferent to the morale or condition of their men. Orders to attack, and attack again, no matter what the cost, gave troops the impression that they were expendable, mere automatons being shovelled into hell. Pétain, reflecting his background as a peasant, 'was thriftily inclined to regard live French soldiers as valuable domestic animals', wrote Janet Flanner of *The New Yorker* in 1944, 'too useful to be slaughtered recklessly'. Arnold Zweig's novel, *Education Before Verdun*, dwells inordinately on individual German soldiers trying anything to get leave, often restricted to only six days per year served. Pétain sensed that no soldier, however well trained, could sustain such an effort and remain trustworthy. He had seen it himself at Souilly, which lay directly on the *Voie Sacrée*. He would come out from headquarters to take a walk or collect his thoughts, and mingle with men going forward. From his memoirs comes one of his few poignant comments:

> My heart bled when I saw our young twenty-year-old men going under fire at Verdun … I loved the confident gaze with which they saluted me. But the discouragement with which they returned! – either singly, maimed or wounded, or in the ranks thinned by their losses. Their eyes stared into space as if transfixed by a vision of terror. In their gait and their attitudes they betrayed utter exhaustion. Horrible memories made them quail. When I questioned them they barely answered, and the jeering tones of the old *poilus* awakened no spark of response in them.

An incredible statistic involving Verdun is that out of 330 battalions making up the French army, 259 moved in and out of the line defending the city at one time or another. Ninety thousand French troops could go up or down the road per week, in all some 1.2 million fought in this theatre of the war alone. This put an enormous strain on French manpower, and the capacity of Joffre to manage his reserves for other fronts. The casualty lists, if continued unabated, would prove disastrous. Lord Kitchener, Britain's secretary of state for war, promised Foch that a million Tommies would soon be in the fire. Foch, reflecting reality, replied that 'he would prefer fewer sooner'. The strain between Pétain and Joffre grew palpably. Joffre was of the opinion that Pétain, if left to his devices, would see every soldier in France killed at Verdun; Pétain returned the favour, saying that if Joffre intended for him to hold Verdun, he must provide the resources to do so. The logistical effort alone to feed, supply and sustain such numbers of troops was enormous, in food some 45,000 tons per month. Pétain immediately ordered the construction of a narrow gauge railway line to run along side *La Route*, but initially it was the road itself that had to carry the load.[25] Engineers first widened the track to two lanes, about 23 feet wide. After a few snowfalls, and recurring episodes of freezing and thawing, the entire length became a mess of mud and foundering trucks. Quarries were excavated along the track, and crushed stone laid along its entire length, eventually over 700,000 tons. This was shovelled, graded, compacted and maintained by a virtual army of 8,000 labourers who worked all hours of the day and night. The stone soon began shredding truck tires, so shops and repair facilities were spread about to manufacture wheels of solid rubber that could better withstand the wear and tear, even though, without treads, they were treacherous in icy conditions. More than one loaded *camion* went over the edge, rolling and tumbling into ditches or meadows below. Anything stuck or broken down was hauled to the side; if it was repairable, shops were set up at intervals along the way, fully equipped to deal with any eventuality, which were myriad, given the rudimentary nature of these early internal combustion engines. Anything too far gone to save was simply hauled to the side and dumped. Some 4,000 army trucks, going on average 15 miles an hour, traversed *La Route* bumper to bumper in one continuous line, at night, with headlights on, reminding some observers of an ethereal serpent crawling through the landscape. These were supplemented by thousands of assorted vehicles requisitioned from all parts of the country. The American novelist Edith Wharton, who had moved to Paris in 1910, remarked that commercial vans and buses had 'vanished' from the city; they were all at the front lugging men, food and, most importantly, artillery shells here and there. Between February and October 1916, the French fired 23 million rounds. These all arrived at the killing fields via *La Voie Sacrée*.

For most French soldiers, *La Voie Sacrée* was beyond anything they had ever seen before. The very immensity of scale, the sheer collective chaos of the effort, the numbers of men, trucks, artillery pieces and assorted equipment all in motion, was a kind of foretaste of doom, a predictive of what lay ahead. *La Voie Sacrée* became, in their minds, a sort of *Via Dolorosa*, the road to Calvary and, thus, to death. After the war, *poilus* who survived had only to say *J'ai fait Verdun*' ('I did Verdun') for everyone in the café or local *magasin* to know exactly what they meant.

As for refugees trying to escape the ghastly situation, they were brushed off to the side of the road. They marched by foot to the rear; anything they could not carry by hand, on their backs or on a packhorse was abandoned. The city of Verdun was soon largely empty of its civilian population, aside that is from a few entrepreneurs who set up shop from deserted store fronts or cellars to sell wine and a few luxuries to officers or those men lucky enough to be stationed behind the actual front. The city was not so much 'dead' as it was dying, 'vanishing by blocks and squares', according to an American journalist.

Growing antagonism between Pétain and Joffre at *GQG* partially explains Pétain's next promotion (he earned a general's star in each year of the war), which was actually something of a demotion. Joffre had grown tired of Pétain's refusal to launch offensive attacks, and especially tired of hearing snippets from some of Pétain's remarks, to the effect that he would abandon the right bank of the Meuse if he had to. His subordinate seemed content to absorb German attacks, to lose some ground, then to regain the same yardage at great cost. Never did Pétain seem to initiate offensive action, nor did he cease to clamour for more of everything. He spent most of his time, according to Joffre, 'scaring everyone' with his dire pronouncements. Pétain retained overall authority over the Verdun sector by being given command of the Central Army Group, four armies in all, but operational responsibility now fell to an entirely different personality, General Robert Nivelle. Under his command, several costly attacks were undertaken, especially to recapture Fort Douaumont, none of which did anything more than consume bodies. Pétain spent immense energy trying to keep apprised of Nivelle's plans, and devising various means to foil them.

'No longer war, but rather butchery.'

A German lieutenant

Indecision now reigned among the German generals. Unless he was to be given sufficient reserves, the crown prince was wary of more combat. Falkenhayn told him to soldier on, but his own inner confidence was also wavering. Falkenhayn, said a friend, was too often 'not sure of himself'. The prince's chief-of-staff, von Knobelsdorf, was never lacking in self-confidence, however. He was a typically stern Prussian, a hard-liner. He urged more costly attacks, reflecting the sentiment from general headquarters that 'France must be tapped of much more blood'. But on the west bank, especially, progress was glacial. When German troops finally took the summit Le Mort Homme (or so they thought), they were immeasurably depressed to see a second height in front of them, a hundred metres taller. Morale began to falter. 'We shall be in Verdun at the earliest by 1920', wrote one officer.

On the east bank, another symbol of French resolve fell to the enemy, Fort Vaux, just two miles south of Douaumont. The value of these strong points had always been recognized by Pétain, and he had energetically reinforced the more important with troops and munitions. Unlike the Belgian forts, mostly constructed with heavy blocks of cut masonry that blew apart and fragmented when hit by shells, Douaumont and Vaux were of poured concrete with reinforced steel girders. Some of the foundations were eighteen feet below surface level, with tons of alternating levels of sand to absorb and cushion heavy artillery shells. After the war, engineers proudly pointed out how well, in fact, some of these structures held up to the almost continuous pounding (at Douaumont, some 120,000 'hits'). Far from 'cracking like empty nuts', as a German general had predicted, they had remained as vital operational strong points.[26] During the Verdun battle, Vaux, Souville, Tavannes and Belleville housed hundreds of soldiers and shielded them from artillery barrages. Their garrisons were invariably reinforced by other troops who sought them out as refuges when their own outside trenches were obliterated. The village of Vaux, for example, just outside the fort of that name, was captured and recaptured thirteen times during the siege. French defenders, when they lost the edge, simply retreated to the fort, regrouped and were available to attack again. Vaux and the others had become veritable bastions in the defence scheme; but on 7 June, Vaux surrendered.

The capitulation of Vaux bore no similarity to the pusillanimous defence of Douaumont. It was fully garrisoned with experienced troops under a determined commander, Major Sylvain-Eugène Raynal, a veteran so badly shot up and wounded that, upon his recovery, he should never have been sent anywhere near the front lines. He reported for duty on 24 May, and found Vaux crammed not only with men who should have been there, but with men who should not: stragglers, battlefield vagabonds, masses of wounded, assorted ambulance personnel. The place was so packed (over 600 men) that Raynal could hardly move about to inspect the heavily damaged fort now under his command. What he did come to understand was that Vaux had no operational artillery. The fort would be protected by machine guns, and machine guns only. He also found four messenger pigeons. By 1 June, the Germans had reduced two positions that had protected the fort with flanking fire. They then sent in their pioneers and infantry.

Vaux was of similar design to Douaumont, but considerably smaller. An outer defensive work surrounded the central block of the fort. Its machine guns were intended to provide enfilading fire on an inner dry moat. This initial line of defence was connected to Vaux itself by a series of underground passageways, which could circulate men back and forth to a central barracks, ammunition depot, latrines and kitchen. But the main tactical defence of the fort was always meant to be its artillery pieces, now long stripped away. The only way to keep the Germans out would be a small-arms infantry war of the crudest and most vicious sort.

Raynal held out for a week. Vaux was pounded by German artillery, at one point by an estimated 1,500 shells per hour. Then German troops swarmed all over the outside of the fort. They eventually were able to silence the outer machine guns, mostly by dangling several grenades by line to the gun slits, then swinging them back and forth hoping they would explode in the gunners' faces. This was a hit-or-miss process but, over time, it worked. Taking possession of the trench, then clambering over the fort's superstructure like ants, gave them a chance to spy out crevices in the fort or sections of interior wall that had been blown away. These were defended by sandbag emplacements and determined machine gunners. The choice then became stark for the Germans. They either had to worm their way into the labyrinthine interior of Vaux, or be blown away like chaff by French artillery, which now began its own fusillades all over the fort. In order to defend Vaux, the French were shelling it themselves.

Inside, Raynal and his men suffered incredible torments. The din, the stench of rotting corpses in the summer heat and, most importantly, a cistern that was fast approaching empty, made life underground almost unsupportable. The Germans' new tactic of using flame-throwers, propelled through any opening the enemy could find, added another frightful element to what was fast becoming a torment far beyond anything that Dante's inferno might offer. Men fought in total darkness, yard by yard, machine gun bullets shattering and fragmenting in the narrow corridors, filling them with a whirlwind of deadly shrapnel. When the Germans finally knocked out one barrier, they found another one just a few feet farther on. Raynal attempted to rid the fort of unwanted soldiery. On the evening of 4 June, almost 300 stragglers were sent off to try their luck and escape. Approximately nine made it. Raynal, down to his last pigeon, sent off a desperate appeal for help. At first the poor bird, numbed by the cacophony of battle, refused to leave the fort. Raynal had him forcibly thrown through a crack in the wall. It made it to headquarters, and then died, its reward being immortal fame. A plaque commemorating the bird was placed on the outer wall of the fort; its body was stuffed and sent to Paris, where it presumably sits somewhere in the vast military museum located in Hôtel des Invalides.

Days without drinking water, the fort filled with nauseous smoke and gas, and many men beginning to go stark mad, convinced Raynal that honour had been satisfied and that it was permissible to surrender the fort. In a ceremony that, by 1916 standards, was hopelessly antique, he managed to conduct a negotiation under a white flag, replete with exchanges of written proposals, whereby his men marched out of Vaux with the full honours of war. He then turned over the largely ceremonial key to the front gate, long since splintered to pieces, and would have preferred his sword if he had had one. No matter; the crown prince, in a noble gesture, gave Raynal a sword in return when he met him, to signify the nobility of his behaviour.

Visiting the fort today is a nightmarish experience that makes any reference to medieval chivalry a veritable charade. From the outside, its walls are blistered, cratered and disfigured almost beyond recognition. Inside, the dank subterranean halls are soaked in dripping moisture; they reek of mould and dusky odour. People with claustrophobia should avoid the place. Imagining the smells is almost intolerable. For a truly authentic experience, the corridor lights should be extinguished every hour, and loudspeakers (at full volume) should flood the place with a solid cascade of noise. Trickles of water seeping down the walls could then be licked dry, as *poilus* did trying to assuage their maddening thirst. As a tourist, I considered myself lucky to leave the place alive. Three thousand German soldiers were not so fortunate.

From Vaux, von Knobelsdorf then directed his attention to other nearby forts, especially Souville. It now became 'the key' to the situation, but in fact every turn in the road presented a key of some sort: a ridge here, a dominating hillock there, some articulation of ground cover that suddenly became crucial. The landscape of Verdun, after all, was nothing but a melange of 'confused and tangled hills'. Men fell by the thousands on both sides. Pétain's system of rotating troops into and out of line began falling apart; morale lagged; officers who gave up ground of any sort found themselves condemned to death without a court martial, and executed by their own men. Von Falkenhayn had thought only one army would bleed to death, but in fact both were haemorrhaging blood. An admirer of his wrote in midsummer, 'Falkenhayn is very upset emotionally, and yesterday gave up completely'. Just a few days after that, the battle for Verdun, from the German perspective at least, was called off. German troops assumed a defensive posture, and let the French carry on with the initiative which, under Nivelle and the thoroughly merciless General Charles Mangin, became a burden almost cheerfully accepted. Mangin, an old colonial hand, was a fearsome, headstrong personality. Dead bodies did not bother him. Of unquestioned bravery, he was also impulsive, unreflective and oblivious of any sort of obstacle. 'There is no man more capable of getting you into a mess', one general said of him. Casualty figures continued to soar, but on 1 July, when Douglas Haig and the British army launched the disastrous Somme campaign, von Falkenhayn was forced to divert precious troops westward to the Flanders battlefield. After he accomplished that feat, he was sacked. When Hindenburg and Ludendorff, his replacements, toured the western front to get a feel for things, they immediately turned their backs on Verdun as a lost cause.

The crown prince, Friedrich Wilhelm felt somewhat vindicated as the battle wound down. He was a man thoroughly unfit to lead an army in the field. A dabbling amateur, he had little strategic or tactical skill, and was obtuse when it came to interpersonal relationships with men under his command. He is said to have taken time off from his tennis games (he loved the sport) to wave to troops heading off for the front lines with his racket, dressed in spotless whites from head to toe. Arnold Zweig, in a devastating scene from *Education Before Verdun*, has the prince tossing cigarettes from his elegant staff car to troops standing to attention along the sides of the road. He did, however, demonstrate some facility for political intrigue. His relations with his imperial father, never close, had become positively chilly as Verdun ground along. If he wished to speak with the emperor, he required an appointment to do so, and the interviews (in his view) were seldom anything more than a long lecture or rant from the throne which the prince was never allowed to interrupt. When father was finished speaking, the meeting was over. But the crown prince saw the Verdun battle for what it was, a growingly colossal failure. He counselled that it be stopped, but his chief-of-staff, von Knobelsdorf, simply ignored him. On 23 August, however, through devious backdoor negotiations with court officials who had access to the ever fickle kaiser, he finally secured von Knobelsdorf's dismissal. In his self-serving memoirs, he took pains to wash his hands of the battle when it became clear that its objectives had become unattainable.

In any event, the enormous Somme campaign necessarily diverted everyone's attention from the river Meuse (the virtual collapse of Austro-Hungarian troops in the face of a huge Russian offensive in the east was also a consideration). Most of the gruesome statistics from Verdun were quickly outstripped by Haig: numbers of artillery pieces, throw weight tossed back and forth, the gruesome casualties on the initial day of battle (the highest ever seen). Joffre and Foch involved French forces in the British offensive, which soon turned into yet another debacle for the allied cause. De Castelnau, when viewing the wreckage of so many grandiose plans, said in despair, 'Ah, Napoleon, Napoleon. If he were here now, he'd have thought of something else.' At GQG, the atmosphere was grim as staff officers reversed their earlier high opinions of Foch. 'The day of this great warrior was over', according to Pierrefeu. 'His original ways, his eccentricities which were once regarded as marks of genius, now seemed only to reveal the approach of senility.' Joffre felt compelled to sacrifice him to the wolves, which produced a gigantic explosion between the two men, a yelling match that went on for some time. Joffre reportedly pounded his fist on the table to terminate the discussion, stating that 'You are Stellenbosched, I shall be Stellenbosched, we shall all be Stellenbosched.' The next day, Joffre himself was told, in effect, to '*allez* à *Limoges*'.[27]

The circumstances of his dismissal were at first misunderstood, because Papa was promoted to Marshal of France. Sycophants lined up to gain positions on what everyone assumed would be an enlarged staff, but in fact Joffre was being shunted to the side. He was given a large office (again, with few maps to be seen), a telephone and a contingent of three aides. When word passed around on these considerably diminished prospects, only one officer volunteered to join Joffre in his exile. Joffre pulled on his moustache and uttered his usual lament, *Pauvre Joffre*, but a colleague advised him that personal annoyance was unwarranted. 'You must not blame those who have their career to make.'

Joffre, at least, had outlasted most his counterparts in high command. Sir John French was gone, Helmuth von Moltke was gone and Grand Prince Nicholas of Russia was gone too. Even so, he would never again assume any relevance in the management of important affairs. Foch, however, would restore himself to the pantheon of glory in spectacular fashion. By 1918, he had eclipsed everyone, even Pétain.

Dozens of other men who fought at or near Verdun would later become famous, but they would have to wait another twenty-two years, or until the second course was served, World War II. Charles de Gaulle, statistically speaking, was one of the few to suffer a bayonet wound, his left leg run through during a struggle for Douaumont village. This probably hurt his feelings as much as it did his leg; most soldiers in the trenches now devalued the bayonet as little better than a pocketknife. They wanted the killing power of grenades and machine guns. De Gaulle was captured and spent thirty months as a prisoner of war, attempting to escape five times, but never successfully. Future Admiral François Darlan commanded a naval siege gun, firing salvos against German troops on the east bank of the Meuse. Erwin Rommel, the Desert Fox, saw action in the crown prince's Fifth Army in 1914. Friedrich Paulus, the unfortunate field marshal who was told by Hitler to commit suicide rather than surrender Stalingrad (he ended up surrendering), saw action as a lieutenant in the trenches. Von Brauchitsch, Keitel, von Kluge, Guderian and Göring also served in the siege of Verdun. Perhaps the finest tactician of the twentieth century, Erich von Manstein, operated on the western bank of the Meuse as a staff officer. What he saw at Verdun convinced him that genius in war required mobility. Future General Karl-Heinrich von Stülpnagel was a battalion commander in the imperial army during the battle. Von Stülpnagel was one of the few senior officers in the assassination plot to kill Hitler who was prepared to follow through on his commitments that 20 July 1944, when Colonel Claus von Stauffenberg planted the bomb near the führer at Wolfsschanze, or the Wolf's Lair, in East Prussia. The minute von Stülpnagel heard the news, he rounded up all the senior S.S. officers he could find in Paris, where he was the military governor, and was prepared to shoot the lot of them when given the word. Hitler, however, miraculously survived, and von Stülpnagel was ordered to return to Germany, his fate all but certain. On the road travelling east, he had his car detour to Verdun, where he walked the old battlefield from twenty-eight years before, including the ravaged hillsides of Le Mort Homme, what one French soldier called 'a rubbish dump' by the time the whole thing was finished. Then he shot himself on the banks of the Meuse.[28]

On 24 October 1916, Fort Douaumont was retaken by French forces. Strategically, it hardly mattered, but psychologically the victory had considerable meaning. In Jean Renoir's 1937 film, *La Grande Illusion*, news of Douaumont's capture enervates French prisoners of war. Putting on a masquerade full of drag queens of questionable sexual orientation, someone cries out the news. Every 'man' there stands to attention and sings the *Marseillaise*, a curious juxtaposition at best, but emotionally effective.

Pétain never ceased to consider Verdun as the very zenith of the war; it was there that France stood alone, unaided by anyone, fighting the enemy to a standstill.[29] Paul Valéry said it best in his speech welcoming Pétain into L'Académie Française in 1931. 'Verdun is a complete war in itself, inserted in the Great War, rather than a battle in the ordinary sense of the word.' Pétain's ingrained contempt for Britain, shared by many French officers, solidified here on these blood-soaked grounds. Nothing he would see anywhere else in this or any war would match the sacrifice, effort and waste of a Verdun. No other nation could have done it but France; everything Britain did was a sideshow. Even as late as 1940, Pétain insisted that Britain had played only 'a secondary role'. When Ludendorff launched his final offensive, Operation Michael in March 1918, Pétain was ready to cut and run, leaving Douglas Haig and his British forces in the lurch. Pétain had experienced too much to maintain an optimistic frame of mind; he had none of Foch's panache. Clemenceau, after hearing Pétain give a characteristically negative assessment of the situation in 1918, wondered aloud if a general should express himself in such a way. He did not care for men who flinched.

Le Champ de Bataille

Verdun Today

The city of Verdun is now the very definition of 'sleepy'. During my several visits to the area, I stayed in a large and antiquated hotel in the centre of town, right on the Meuse. I have seldom seen more than ten or so guests at any single time. From my window I generally have a decent view of the imposing Victory monument that was unveiled in 1929. It is a stolid, heavy plinth or column, reached only after a long series of steps, atop of which is an imposing and grim representation of some ancient warrior from long ago, leaning on his sword, staring across the river to the east. Where else, after all, was the mortal threat to come from? After the fall of France in 1939, German generals enjoyed staging Victory parades of their own on ground where they had been humiliated in the past. Frenchmen cried when Germans marched down the Champs-Élysées. Here in Verdun, there are photographs of stormtroopers stomping past Verdun's old warrior, the monument draped with flags and bunting full of swastikas and iron crosses. At dinnertime there are a few people sitting in cafés and restaurants on the now standard pedestrian mall on the banks of the unprepossessing Meuse, but everything else shutters down pretty quickly.

Touring the battlefield by car is very simple. On the western bank, Le Mort Homme and Côte 304 are the usual destinations, but both are so covered in thick, unthinned forestry that their alleged importance to the course of the struggle is not easily understood. Maps help explain the situation more than actually being there. French commemorative statuary can often be, to put it bluntly, weird, and the statue on Le Mort Homme is an apt example. It depicts a skeleton (presumably death itself), holding a furled standard in one hand and a torch in the other. The pose is histrionic, but the message unclear. This figure is either screeching defiance or warning all who approach that they are entering an inferno from which there is no escape. Perhaps one should congratulate the sculptor, one Jacques Froment-Meurice, on establishing such ambiguities so dramatically. Inscribed on the base are the stirring words, *Ils n'ont sont passe* – 'They did not pass', a riposte to a famous order of the day issued (most people still believe) by Pétain, in which he allegedly said, 'They shall not pass'. This is incorrect on two points: Nivelle issued the order, and what he said exactly is, 'Comrades, you will not let them pass'. The statue, of poured concrete, could use some help. It is frayed, chipped and disintegrating; the iron rods holding it all together bleed their rust and discolour the coarse off-white cement. Fairly near is an interpretive plaque that quotes Maurice

Genevoix, a well-known French writer and veteran of the war. 'We have experienced something that is not communicable.'

On the other side of the Meuse, the right bank, are the most famous of the forts. Douaumont and Vaux are open for tourists, and suitably grim. There are expansive views of the Woëvre plain stretching away to the east, but the dominance of the heights is more apparent when viewed from the other direction. One notable place to visit are the woods of Warphemont, near Duzey, the site of a German 15-inch naval gun emplacement, one of the biggest calibre artillery pieces on earth at the time, and nicknamed 'Max'. The formidable concrete foundation on which this behemoth sat is still in place, along with underground ammunition depots. Pictures of the beast firing salvos into Verdun are awe-inspiring, if you happen to enjoy metallurgy; the bursts of flame with each salvo were 15 metres long. These are counterbalanced by period photos of day trippers having picnics on the site after the war, several of whom climb into the gun barrel with only their heads sticking out, as though 'Max' was a circus gun instead of an engine of death that could propel its payload twenty-five miles away. In autumn, the ground covered in leaves, I stumbled over what I thought was a small, rectangular boulder. It turned out to be a bag of German concrete, a century old, that has over time turned into solid rock. This is a souvenir I won't be bringing home on an airplane.

The most interesting things to see, in my opinion, crop up on walks through the grim forests. Thirty-nine thousand acres of wood lots around Verdun were destroyed during the war. Foresters have noted that many of the replacement trees are pale reflections of what was lost; diseased, slow-growing, fed by the poisons churned into the earth, it has been estimated that it might take well over a century for nature to truly recover. Turn a corner in a walk through these pallid stands of greenery, however, and a blockhouse, machine gun emplacement, troop shelter, observation post or piles of old rusted barbed wire can be seen. When I was twenty visiting here, I picked up an artillery shell from a French 75 that was just lying on a path. That was a pretty stupid thing to have done. Most of the forts survive. Signs forbid entry, but fences are easily climbed or circumvented. Still, they are so uninviting that I never went inside one.

Certainly the most bizarre sight is the great ossuary located near Douaumont. One of the truly disquieting photographs from the battle shows piles of bones, in many cases dozens upon dozens of intact ribcages, that peasants returning to the region began recovering from their fields. Absolutely sickening. Casualty figures are not precise for Verdun, but estimates are that about 470,000 men were killed here; double that figure for those wounded, gassed or otherwise incapacitated, which means that French and German soldiers managed to seriously harm 1.2 million of each other. In terms of inflicting damage, one would suppose that Pétain, Nivelle, von Falkenhayn and von Knobelsdorf were fairly proficient at their trade. But as Churchill asked on many occasions, where was the 'art of war' in all this mayhem?

The bishop of Verdun was understandably upset at the piles of human debris that were being collected along the sides of roads, and he spent the last twenty-eight years of his life travelling the world soliciting funds for a suitable repository in which to inter these remains [ossuary comes from the Latin *ossis*, meaning 'a bone']. The resulting edifice, which dominates the surrounding environs, is again a rather strange manifestation of French architectural taste. A huge clunky spire, with representations of either a sword or a cross on each side, is supported by two long, low vaults that stretch from the tower. Beneath the spire is a garish chapel; the two 'arms' cover the ossuary itself. When I first visited Verdun over forty years ago, there were several glass windows through which the bones could be seen. Today, these have been replaced by coloured stained-glass, much of it red, which gives the impression that crematorium fires are blazing on the other side. When farmers find human bones today, which is an almost routine occurrence, they bring them here, adding to the 26,000 or so pounds of human remains already collected. The place was packed with teenagers on school excursions during my most recent trip. Overhearing some of their conversations, it is clear they have little or no idea what all this means. Perhaps that is just the way it is with kids.

One of the stranger effects of this structure used to be a red beacon at the top of the tower that was turned on at night, spreading a strange glow over the countryside. I have never been able to understand the significance or intent of this feature, only that its effect on me was that of a science fiction movie; it reminded me of a line from the memoirs of Frances Partridge, one of the Bloomsbury group, who toured Verdun in 1932 and came away more than ever impressed by 'the French passion for the macabre'. I do not know if this bizarre mechanism is still in use.

Spreading below the ossuary are rows of crosses, the burial places of 15,000 men. To the side is a recent edition, a mosque-like structure that commemorates all the colonial soldiers, mostly Muslim, who fought and died here.[30] Those men must truly have been bewildered. What on earth had condemned them to this European mess?

In 1984, French president François Mitterrand and German chancellor Helmut Kohl performed a ceremonial reconciliation (Mitterrand had fought and been captured here in World War II; Kohl's father was a Verdun veteran). Both men held hands on a rainy September afternoon to solemnify the new rapprochement between these two inveterate enemies. The effect was spoiled a few years later when Kohl's successor, Gerhard Schröder, refused to participate in a similar exhibition of amity.[31]

My final research ramble took me where, I believe, few other tourists would bother to venture. On the morning of my departure, a Sunday, I drove across the Meuse trying to find the railway line that runs due east into Lorraine. At the foot of the hills, on top of which sits the entire bead of fortresses, with 'old Douaumont in the middle of it like the shell of a gigantic tortoise', begins a long tunnel that runs beneath them, exiting onto the plain of Woëvre. Clearly this presented a dangerous situation in 1916; had the Germans forced their way through here, they could have attacked French forces from the rear to devastating effect. General Herr, in fact, wanted to blow the tunnel up but was prevented from doing so, for what reason I do not know. During the long and gruesome battle, what was called the Tavannes Tunnel become almost a secondary fortress; jammed with troops, command centres, communication gear and hospital services, it also established itself as a refuge. During periodic bombardments, the place could be packed with several thousand men. Lighting was sparse, run from gasoline-powered generators. Candles and lanterns were everywhere. Munitions, flares, crates of hand grenades, jerry-built bunks and kitchens, hay for pack mules – the scene was one of utter confusion. Both ends of the tunnel could find themselves under artillery attack. Hygiene was non-existent, men urinated and defecated where they could find a space. The resulting stench can only be imagined. On 4 September 1916, after dark, something sparked an explosion, which in turn set off a chain reaction that ignited everything else in the tunnel. Billows of smoke emerged from both entrances, along with tongues of flame which incinerated everything in their path. One survivor recorded being hit by multiple body parts, as well as liquified flesh that 'poured over me'. The agonies suffered by several hundred men as they died was surely indescribable. The resulting shambles lasted three days. Fires could not be controlled, munitions continued to explode. When would-be rescuers finally entered the scene of this holocaust, all they found were charred remains.

The tunnel still exists and, in a way, is still in use. It took about forty minutes to reach, after I left the car at the end of a dirt road and climbed up to the rail bed to start walking. The line is single-tracked, and when I eventually reached the western opening, it became obvious that the original tunnel, out of respect I assume, had been 'retired'. A companion tunnel was built side by side to the other, which the current trains use. A coat-of-arms has been inserted between the two, but no other commemorative display has been erected here. I am not tempted to enter the tunnel.

Chapter 9

Field Marshal Sir Douglas Haig

'Nobody likes to see his father labelled as a butcher.'
Lord Haig, son of Field Marshal Sir Douglas Haig

Clifton College, one of the great public schools of England, was founded in 1862 and is located directly outside Bristol. A statue of one of its more famous graduates, the Lowland Scots soldier Douglas Haig, stands in front of School House, an original building on its campus. This rendition is not as imposing as the equestrian statue that adorns Whitehall in London (criticized by his widow, angry that the sculptor did not represent the field marshal on his favourite horse), but it sets an appropriate tone as to Haig's character: resolute, disciplined, stubborn and brave – the perfect soldier.

Haig was commander in chief of the British army in France for three years, a tenure marked by controversy not just then, but in the hundred years that have elapsed since the beginning of that great war. He was the epitome of British military pride, a student of the 'art', advanced to some degree in new technologies that emerged on the battlefield, and undeniably without fear. He did not quail from slaughter, that being the price, as he saw it, to the goal of defeating Imperial Germany, called by one of his contemporaries 'the road hog of Europe'. If it required two million British casualties, then so be it.

Lloyd George, Haig's civilian counterpart from 1915 to 1918, saw him differently. The prime minister's son related Lloyd George's remark that Haig was a soldier to the very top of his boots, but in private conversation he was far harsher. Haig, in his opinion, was a monster, and Lloyd George did everything he could to curb his authority, undermine his credibility and eviscerate his grand military schemes. For his part, Haig considered the prime minister 'a thorough imposter' and 'a cur'. Their power struggle is the fascinating story of two polar-opposite personalities, each convinced of his moral superiority, who fought for control of the nation's war policy. Neither achieved supremacy, but it must be said in the final analysis that Haig bested the prime minister when it counted. The war was fought on Haig's terms, and he was not afraid of accepting that responsibility. He proved to be the victor, both in London and on the field of battle. The fact that his career effectively ended on the day the troops marched home, however, is some reflection on the currency of contemporary British opinion that the bill had come in too high.

Before discussing Haig's role during the war years in greater detail, it is important to outline both the political circumstances with which he had to contend, and the personalities of the major players who either abetted his schemes or sought to derail them. Haig basically had to deal with three British governments, two led by the Liberal Herbert Henry Asquith from the beginning of the war until 1916, the third by the Welshman David Lloyd George.

No one ever doubted the political skills and general all-round intelligence of Asquith. He was a man much admired for his parliamentary adroitness and humanitarian impulses. In normal circumstances he was more than an adequate leader: even-keeled, contemplative, a man not to be rushed ('no tide of hot compassion engulfs him', as one observer put it). None of these qualities would do for wartime, however. As Max Aitken, the Canadian newspaper baron, wrote, he was a man 'hard to describe, because within his own limited sphere – the management of Parliament in quiet times – he was perfection, and he was a failure because outside those limitations, and yet within his own sphere of time, lay a world of battle, murder, and sudden death – and that time called for men of a different range of genius.' In a nutshell, Asquith was overwhelmed by the onslaught of decisions that had to be made, and quickly. His response was to temporize, delay, see how things turned out and, often enough, to take to his bed to avoid confrontation. Admiral Jacky Fisher's nickname for the prime minister was 'Wait and See'. His wife agreed; 'the Asquiths', she wrote, 'have not one drop of wild blood in their veins'. He was bright enough, however, to understand that his expertise did not encompass military matters in the least, and one of his first acts after realizing this limitation was to appoint Horatio Kitchener, Earl of Khartoum, to a new cabinet position, secretary for war. This was both a wise and a disastrous decision.[1]

Kitchener 'pays no attention to anyone.'

Lord Esher

Kitchener was a name everyone recognized, though few people really knew the man. His exploits in many colonial theatres, most especially in Egypt and the Sudan, had earned him the kind of adulation and respect that the British public traditionally bestowed on its more exotic heroes. The deeper the jungle, the more enthusiastic the accolades. But Kitchener's wide travels through eastern lands had made him a stranger in England where, as he admitted to a friend, he hadn't spent a Christmas in forty years; nor was he particularly current with twentieth-century military affairs or the complexity of organization required to make a modern army function. Long tours of duty with native armies had cemented his autocratic tendencies. 'He kept everything in his own hands', as he himself admitted, a trait that bogged him down in minutiae from the very start of his tenure at Whitehall.

In the first days of war, though, Kitchener stood supreme. A man of imposing physical presence, he dominated the initial cabinet meetings. When he entered a chamber, it was 'like the Day of Judgment', according to a reporter. 'A pillar of ice could not lower the temperature more quickly.' Although most professional officers in high command deprecated Kitchener's understanding of strategic matters, he is to be given credit for one supreme and sobering observation. This war would not be over soon. Any talk of being in Berlin by Christmas was absurd. The German enemy had been preparing for this conflict for thirty years; conscription, mandatory annual training, a thoroughly professional general staff, unparalleled technical and industrial skills, all precluded any sort of cheap and thrilling victory for Britain. As he had said before, the enemy would 'walk through [the French] like partridges', so that Britain, in the end, would have to win this war itself. It could do so only by committing its economy to a full wartime footing, by tapping its population of forty million to put an enormous armed force in the field and to be prepared to keep it in place for years. This was such a dismaying prospect that the cabinet, described by one observer as a pack of chatterboxes 'discussing strategy like idiots', greeted Kitchener's remarks in stunned silence.

Impervious to anyone else's opinion (including the public's, about which, said Churchill, he knew nothing), Kitchener immediately took steps to enlarge Britain's manpower reserves and, for the allies, it was a good thing he did.[2] From the beginning of the war through the disastrous Loos campaign of September and October 1915, Britain's professional standing army, ludicrously small, had stood crushed, with especially critical losses among the ranks of junior and non-commissioned officers.[3] France, thanks to its misguided ethos of 'advance at any cost', had suffered the extraordinary and pointless loss over this same time frame of over a million men. Churchill noted the irony when he wrote, 'Though the Germans invaded, it was more often the French who attacked. Long swaths of red and blue corpses littered the stubble fields.' These were the kind of 'wastages' (a euphemistic expression common with generals on both sides of the conflict) that could not be casually dismissed. Kitchener realized the enormous needs ahead and pushed forward to raise levies for what came to be known as 'Kitchener's New Army'. Our force, he said at the time, 'should reach its full strength at the beginning of the third year of the war, just when France is getting into rather low water and Germany is beginning to feel the pinch'. These predictions proved quite on the mark. This soon-to-be-enormous pool of manpower was propelled in some measure by images of the famed field marshal himself which were pasted on walls all over the United Kingdom showing this fierce and determined moustached figure glaring at passersby – pointing a finger at them in many instances – and saying 'Your Country Needs You!' Such recruiting posters in their many variations (a total of 12 million, with 140 different designs) represent some of the most effective and successful propaganda tools ever created, and the results were electric. Some two and a half million men, afterwards referred to as the cream of Britain's young manhood, rushed to the colours, though sceptics abounded. Sir Henry Wilson, a career officer born in Ireland, said the 'New' armies were just a 'mob' of untrained men without 'morale or tradition ... the laughingstock of every soldier in Europe'. As Wilson and other experts in the 'science' of war proceeded to order hundreds of thousands of such men to their graves, they would soon be grateful for any sort of replacements, trained or not, to fill in the gaps. This would prove to be an industrial-scale war the likes of which no general had ever experienced, nor was even remotely competent to wage.

Certainly the task would prove more than Kitchener could handle. As one society doyen would put it, he was 'not a great man, but a great poster', and Lord Haldane described him as 'a man of great authority and considerable ignorance'. Incapable of delegating responsibility, indifferent to the opinions of politicians, and unskilled in the ways of reaching consensus within parliamentary or cabinet circles, he retreated into a great cavern of silence and, when questioned, was often inarticulate in his responses. One contemporary heard the Duke of Teck ask Kitchener, '"I suppose there is no harm in asking you when our Brigade leaves for the Front". "None", said Lord Kitchener, and left it like that'.[4] Because he trusted no one, he rarely put his thoughts on paper or in reports. His antipathy to the democratic process of exchanging information with people he deemed unsuited to hear it proved extreme and discomforting to his colleagues. On one occasion Churchill, then a member of the cabinet, asked Kitchener to explain an aspect of his munitions policies. The field marshal, who considered the future prime minister in some ill odour as the progenitor of any number of 'wild cat schemes', turned to Asquith with contempt in his eyes and asked, 'Must I answer?' To his amazement, the prime minister said 'Yes'.

Kitchener was only the first in a long line of military men who found it difficult to translate their thoughts into coherent speech. Lloyd George felt him obscure and hard to understand, and especially unhelpful when his figures and statistics proved incorrect. Lloyd George sometimes asked himself whether 'the tropical sun had scorched and parched some of his intelligence, leaving merely oases of verdure and fertility'. Kitchener, he told Max Aitken, 'was like a great revolving lighthouse. Sometime the beam of his mind used to shoot out, showing one Europe and the assembled armies in a vast and illimitable perspective, til one felt one was looking along it into the heart of reality – and then the shutter would turn and for weeks there would be nothing but a blank darkness.' Another political insider simply took to referring to Kitchener as 'the Sphinx'. Asquith began to realize that Kitchener, in fact, was not the man he could count on, and began to theorize how he might jettison this still enormously popular figure without alienating the general public. As matters turned out, the Germans took care of the problem for him. On the stormy night of 15 June 1916, Kitchener boarded the HMS *Hampshire* as it set off from Scapa Flow in the Orkney Islands, bringing the field marshal to an inspection trip of Russia. That was the last anyone heard from him, or some six hundred other people. The *Hampshire* most probably struck a mine in the North Sea, though some experts felt a torpedo might have brought her low, even if no submarine captain ever claimed that credit. Certainly the general public was shocked to its core, though among people in the know Kitchener's death occasioned nothing more than (according to Esher) 'a great many crocodile tears'. Rumours abounded throughout the rest of the war that Kitchener had survived and was a P.O.W. in Germany, but as momentous events and indescribable carnage enveloped western Europe for the next three years, people's fascination with the great general's fate ebbed away. Like his famous and long-drawn-out silences, Kitchener simply and quietly faded from men's minds.

The trip to Russia, of course, had been a ruse (one fully recognized by Kitchener, now considered 'the extinct volcano') to get him out of London. He knew his star to be in decline, that he had lost the confidence of the prime minister and, even more significantly, the Conservative Party cabinet members whom Asquith had brought into his coalition government in May 1915. Asquith had created a new position to advise the government on military matters that would, in practical effect, replace the secretary of war as the fountain of martial wisdom, called the Chief of the Imperial General Staff (CIGS). This appointee would replace Kitchener, which was what everyone desired, but in choosing Sir William Robertson to fill this position, Asquith dealt himself a character even more obstreperous and uncooperative than even Kitchener.

Robertson was a rarity in the British army, a man who had reached the very top of the heap from the far, far nether world of the common ranks below. The son of a tailor, he had no aristocratic lineage of any sort to rely on (not even as the bastard son of some wayward duke), and had entered the workforce as a manservant before joining the fashionable 16th Lancers as a trooper (fashionable, that is, to those who were its officers). Additional grave deficits were that he had rarely heard a bullet fired in anger, had never participated in a cavalry charge and in fact had almost no wartime experience. He had climbed the organizational ladder without having led men in great numbers, commanded armies or paid anything other than lip service to understanding campaigns or grand strategy. He made up for all this, however, by having an unparalleled organizational and administrative mind. Details did not discourage or overwhelm him, he grasped the technical aspects that total war required (from the army's perspective, if not the politician's) and he was tenacious. Furthermore, he was not a stupid man. Known as 'Wully' to his friends, it did not take long for the politicians to dub him 'Wooly', as in 'sullen', 'truculent', 'gruff' and 'xenophobic'. He was all those, and more.

The tandem of Robertson with Sir Douglas Haig has been described by more than one historian as the equivalent of the von Hindenburg/Ludendorff partnership that would soon assume dictatorial powers in Imperial Germany. After two years of war, generals of the German staff had realized that this was truly to be a fight to the finish. They had no interest in a negotiated peace, having not achieved their fullest military aims, and they thwarted civilian politicians in Berlin who made several tentative approaches to the allied powers to inquire about terms that might end hostilities. The vainglorious kaiser they just brushed aside, much to his astonishment. This was no time, after all, for amateurs.

Sir William Robertson, like just about every high-ranking British army officer, had nothing but contempt for those he considered true amateurs – politicians – a trait Asquith might have enquired about more deeply before agreeing to appoint him (Henry Wilson wrote, 'We soldiers think they are all rotters', an appreciation shared by the navy as well, Admiral Beatty referring to Lloyd George as 'a dirty dog'). Not only that, Robertson made no effort to disguise his feelings. At his very first meeting at Downing Street with the 'twenty-three blind mice', he walked off with Carson and asked whether 'he had been attending a cabinet or a committee of lunatics'. Whenever pressed on a question, Robertson often replied with inarticulate or gravelly grunts, sighed continuously when queries struck him as beyond the pale, rolled his eyes, groaned, wrinkled his brow or sat 'silent and sullen'. It was not uncommon for him to begin whatever it was he had to say with the words 'Every fool knows …'. Military affairs should be left to the military was his unwritten conviction; politicians had to provide the means, equipment and money necessary to enable the generals, and in no current sphere in English public life were 'the frocks' failing more miserably than in the question of manpower. Conscription, not operational until January 1916 and full of unconscionable 'exceptions', was a political issue whose volatility men like Robertson did not understand.[5] He had an actuarial and statistician's mind when it came to assessing the populations of the various combatants: who had the most serviceable men and in what numbers, how many replacements in the 18-year-old bracket could each adversary expect to field each spring, who was going to run out of bodies first? Robertson detested the quaking fear with which a Mr. Asquith approached the subject. Men were the lifeblood of armies, 'war was a bloody business', more British soldiers meant more dead 'boche', and why shouldn't Ireland be dragooned for conscripts? The influential war correspondent Charles Repington, a good friend of the general, often dropped into headquarters for 'a good growl with Robertson'. One afternoon he found the CIGS angry 'about Smuts saying the war was won. Robertson thought it was not won, and that it had to be won in England'.[6]

The whole game came down to numbers, and Robertson was better than most when it came to counting. Translating these considerations into a conceptualization of what all this meant on the western front, with its maze of trenches, machine gun nests, artillery positions, endless casualities and mud, mud, mud was beyond both his comprehension and his interest. Britain had gone to war, and it was his business to see it through no matter what.

His foil was David Lloyd George, prime minister beginning in December 1916, a polar opposite in personality, skill, disposition and manoeuvrability. Where Robertson was dogmatic, Lloyd George was all over the map. Where Robertson was 'massively reticent', Lloyd George wore his heart on his sleeve. Where Robertson often struggled to express himself, Lloyd George overwhelmed his listeners with oratorical brilliance. Where Robertson was 'sternly orthodox', particularly when it came to army tradition, Lloyd George put little stock in standing pat over anything. Robertson was stodgy, Lloyd George mercurial. When Lloyd George became prime minister, the two were almost immediately at loggerheads, which surprised no one. Each represented an ethos and approach to the issues of the day that guaranteed the other's antipathy. Each represented just about everything that the other loathed.

David Lloyd George, born in 1863, was a fiercely individualistic Welshman of tremendous vitality. A member of parliament for the Liberal Party since 1890 (a seat he would hold for close to six decades), he was a champion of the underdog and a pacifist at heart. No one ever questioned his intellect, passion, capacity for hard work or the inbred contempt that he had for establishment figures. It was amusing, he thought, that royalty treated him with genuine wariness, 'as they would a dangerous wild animal whom they fear & perhaps just a little admire for his suppleness & strength'. His nimble mind, and the expressiveness of his vocabulary and speaking skills, were certainly a challenge for many of the dimwits with whom he had to deal. 'He talks an awful lot', wrote one well-established hostess, 'and he gave me the impression his tongue works faster than his brain, though it goes pretty fast'. In many ways, George was an individual of faint moral stature, whether it came to issues of politics, marital vows, personal friendship, his 'word of honour' or anything else that stood in the way of something he wanted. But he was a man many stood in thrall of, however deep their distrust.

Lloyd George had entered Asquith's Liberal government as chancellor of the exchequer. With the war progressing in ways few expected, it became apparent that this was to be a struggle between the big guns (nearly sixty percent of casualties suffered in World War I were the result of artillery fire),[7] and the question of ammunition became all-encompassing, particularly the means whereby factories formerly employed in the manufacture of ordinary domestic goods could be transformed, and quickly, into production lines churning out shells. Kitchener had failed miserably in this arena, so much so that Sir John French, the first commander of the British Expeditionary Force, had initiated a 'shell scandal' with judicious leaks to the British press, complaining of shortages at the front which had seriously undermined operations. The ensuing uproar saw Lloyd George given the portfolio minister of munitions, which he undertook with his customary efficiency.[8] This was Lloyd George's first initiation into the realities of war on such a scale, and deeply dissatisfied him with the approach, both languid and yet timorous, exemplified by Herbert Asquith, an attitude shared by many contemporaries, most especially those of the Conservative Party. Sir Henry Wilson, for example, railed against the prime minister. 'Wars cannot be won by indecision', he wrote in his dairy in December 1915; 'so long as we keep Asquith as Prime Minister we run a serious risk of losing the war'.[9] Three months later, again in exasperation, he noted, 'There is only one solution to our impossible position, and that is to get rid of Asquith. He will lose the war if he possibly can, by simply doing nothing. No ammunition, no trench mortars (big ones), no rifle grenades, no anti-aircraft guns, no sausage balloons, no recruits, no huts, no light railway, no *war* ... no *going to war*, no *intention to go to war*'. Lloyd George thought the same and, when combined as it must be by considerations he took into account involving his own advancement, he began a series of complicated calculations that eventually resulted in the fall of Asquith and his own elevation to 10 Downing Street. In his disingenuous memoirs, Lloyd George disclaimed any intention of wishing the prime ministership for himself, but as the Canadian Max Aitken wrote, 'Mr. Asquith once described Bonar Law as "mildly ambitious". Strike out the epithet "mildly", and you have Lloyd George.'

In order to reach the pinnacle, however, Lloyd George had seriously tied his hands behind him. The only way to achieve office had been to deal with the devil, i.e. powerful figures of the Conservative Party – men like Carson, Law, Curzon and Lord Milner.[10] These were individuals congenitally sympathetic to generals, admirals and the king (described by Lloyd George as 'a very jolly chap, but thank God there's not much in his head').[11] When a man like Robertson complained, they listened. When the conservative press published stinging critiques of politicians interfering with the commanders in the field, or 'puffed' generals like Haig with comparisons worthy of Wellington, or exaggerated the accumulations of a few worthless yards into victories the enemy could not survive, the ability of the prime minister to enforces changes anywhere in the military sphere were constricted. He had no one from whom he could expect political support. Certainly not from his former Liberal colleagues, still smarting from his treatment of Asquith, nor from Conservative backbenchers who, 'loaded with a legacy of Tory hate', according to Aitken, detested him. While Lloyd George exaggerated the possibility, expressed in his memoirs, that Robertson and Haig might have joined to establish a virtual dictatorship of Britain, the fact remains that, however much he disparaged both men, he could not replace them. Had he dismissed the pair, his government would have collapsed, and one thing Lloyd George enjoyed being, more than anything else, was prime minister.

Haig Takes Command

'I divide my officers into four classes: the clever, the stupid, the industrious and the lazy. Every officer possesses at least two of these qualities. Those who are clever and industrious are fitted for high staff appointments; use can be made of those who are stupid and lazy.

*The man who is clever and lazy is fitted for the highest command;
he has the temperament and the requisite nerve to deal with all
situations. But whoever is stupid and industrious is a danger and
must be removed immediately.'*

Unidentified German Officer

Douglas Haig was born into comfortable circumstances in 1861, his family
being engaged in the whiskey business.[12] He attended the proper schools (at
Oxford he was tutored by Walter Pater), but his primary interests centred on
horseflesh. Haig was a cavalryman, first and foremost, as were far too many
of Britain's higher echelon officers at the start of World War I (in the opinion
of Sir Arthur Paget, himself a skilled rider, though most of his commands
were of infantry units). Even after two years of dreadfully stagnant and
mechanical conflict, the goal of breaking through enemy lines and exploiting
open country behind with thousands of cavalrymen remained the all-
too-common, if outdated, ambition. In the four years of war, in fact, some
700,000 horses were shipped through Southampton for service to France.
Most of these cavalry mounts ended up dragging artillery and supplies to and
fro, though significant numbers (along with their forage, grooms and stable
hands) were earmarked for recreational purposes. Haig seldom let a day go
by without taking a ride somewhere. If his staff knew the route, arrangements
were made to dump lorryloads of sand along it, to prevent his horse from
losing its footing.[13]

He decided on a military career early on and, with single-minded
dedication, studied all facets of his chosen profession, to the exclusion of
everything else. Many considered him a drudge, but others saw organizational
abilities that were second to none as he plodded from one assignment to
another. Long years were spent overseas, especially in India, and he saw
action in the Boer War, where his doctrinaire views on strategy and tactics
were at times outclassed by the 'irregular' talents of the guerrilla *Afrikaners*.
Promotions came along slowly, but Haig was a patient man. He was not
going 'to settle down into a turnip grower in Fife', and was determined 'to
belong to the few who can guide or command our great Empire'. In 1909
he finally received important general staff appointments, and two years later
was placed in charge of Aldershot garrison, Britain's most important military
base and the home of its expeditionary force. These promotions were not
universally admired. His disdain for 'the mediocrities' with whom he often
had to deal at the War Office was returned in full measure. He and his staff,
many of whom had formed his military 'family' in India, were known as 'the
Hindoo Invasion'.

Haig brought pluses and minuses to his résumé. He was a determined researcher. Manuals, chains of command, organizational charts, professional etiquette and all the things that make armies run were his forte. The great campaigns of the past were familiar to him, and innovations did not offend his sensibilities (unlike one of his early commanders, Sir Redvers Buller, who is best remembered for saying that in military matters there was 'nothing new under the sun'). Under wartime conditions he did not object to commoners rising in the ranks, and he pioneered the introduction of women into the armed forces, however serious his doubts as to their physical capabilities. When he saw that aeroplanes 'worked', he wanted more. It took longer for him to appreciate the merits of tanks, as evidenced by the disastrous aftermath of their concentrated use at the Battle of Cambrai (20 November 1917), but he came around to recognize the potential they represented and encouraged their use.[14] He wanted bigger, better and more modern artillery pieces, machine guns, mortars and poisonous gases, an indication that he occasionally understood the realities of trench warfare. Like both Robertson and Lord Kitchener, he recognized that the war would be a long one and that demands for manpower would arise. Lord Haldane, responsible for many prewar reforms, considered Haig a real thinker, a 'scientist' in the art of campaigning, a man who had 'a first-class General Staff mind'. On top of that he was handsome, the very picture of a warrior, who was abstemious in his personal habits and remained fit and trim all his life. His wife, whom he first met during a royal weekend at Windsor (on the golf course), and to whom he proposed two days later (again on the golf course) said he had beautiful hands.[15]

Haig's obsessional doggedness, however, made for a dry personality, to say the very least. He had no sense of humour, little gift for small talk and few interpersonal skills, in keeping perhaps with his dour Scottish origins. A near fatal flaw was his inability to communicate. Perhaps no major figure among the many who populate the annals of the First World War were as inarticulate as Haig, which proved a humbling experience indeed when he was forced to deal with people like Winston Churchill and Lloyd George. Examples abound. After army manoeuvres in 1912, wherein Haig had been seriously outgeneraled, he gave a speech at Cambridge University in the presence of the king and many senior commanders, from which he decided on the spur of the moment to deviate from his printed text. The result was a rambling, incoherent flow of disconnected sentences that made no sense and led some in the audience to question his state of mind. Many fell asleep and snored, an offence to the royal sensibility. In another, a presentation to a victorious team of cross-country runners, Haig offered the following *bons mots*: 'I congratulate you on your running. You have run very well. I hope you will run as well in the presence of the enemy.' A war correspondent, hearing Haig discourse with a group of French officers, noted that his proficiency in foreign languages was about equal to his command of English. Margot Asquith, an indefatigable conversationalist, wrote in her diary that he was 'handsome and Scotch, and though a very fine soldier a remarkably stupid man to talk to'. While such examples can be taken out of context to merely mock the man, the fact remains that this deficiency did him little good when it came to butting heads with more skilled rhetorical opponents. Lloyd George tried to give Haig a bit of a breather when it came to the field marshal's often inept presentations but, as he tartly observed, 'in my experience a confused talker is never a clear thinker'.

Haig could not have cared less what Lloyd George thought of him. As Charles Repington of the *Times* noted in his diary, 'Haig said that he only regarded P.M. as *x*, and did not care who he was so long as he was a white man and had no axe to grind, and no political game to play.' His inability to express himself coherently, moreover, should not be taken as a sign of irresolution or lack of determination, for Haig was, if anything, a man of his convictions. Once an idea became fixated in his mind, it became almost impossible to budge him from it. Dogmatic, unbending and impervious to argument, Haig's sense of superiority was, unfortunately, buttressed by intense religious conviction (sturdy, albeit conventional) and by an optimistic turn of mind. The former trait allowed him to view with equanimity the disastrous military failures that marked his tenure as commander in chief – it was his cross to bear, but God believed in him; the latter resulted in his surrounding himself with staff officers who were 'pernicious sycophants' and camp followers, consistently generating false intelligence and 'optimistic slosh' (Lloyd George's characterizations) that were often at odds with actual battlefield results. As Haig himself noted to his sister, 'All I require [around me] are people of average intelligence who are keen to do their work properly'. As the war progressed, he lived in a kind of cocoon, isolated from conditions at the front, shielded by his staff who fed him what Lloyd George called 'cock-and-bull stories', protected in London by Robertson and immune from the growing unease that rising casualty figures were causing in the salons and dining rooms of the political elite. These latter were people Haig generally shunned, however, so their views meant nothing to him. Haig was not a creature of fast-moving high society. His idea of fun was to go shopping with his wife and children, then take a cab to the Alhambra Theatre to see *The Bing Boys* revues, after which home for early bed.[16] But his wife's background (a maid of honour to two queens) gave him access where it counted, to the king, and far from being the clod that Lloyd George and his other critics suggested, Haig knew how to play 'the political game' as well as anyone.

Haig's diary, which runs to thirty-eight typewritten volumes, some 750,000 words, is ample demonstration of his character. Devoid of emotion, detached from the idea that the civilized world was being destroyed in front of his eyes, and barren of any intellectual insight, it also betrays the man's ambition and self-deceit. Though often couched in pompous self-abnegation when it came to the political realities of backstabbing and petty schemes ('I hated intriguing'), he was in fact unashamedly thrusting when it came to his own career. This was a war on the grand stage, and he knew it for the once-in-a-lifetime opportunity it represented. On the very first day of hostilities, Haig made it perfectly clear to the king that Sir John French, the expeditionary force's initial commander, was unfit for the job, and left little doubt whom he thought was a better man. When Kitchener's absolutism seemed threatened, Haig chimed in with the suggestion that he be shipped off to India, leaving an additional (and welcome) vacuum at the top. He consistently bypassed normal chains of communication to write privately to important personages in London, the results of which never helped the individuals whom Haig disparaged ('From what I have written, you will gather I have no great opinion of [Lloyd George] *as a man or leader*'). The king, when he heard that Haig was writing confidentially to Kitchener, upbraided the secretary for war, saying 'If anyone acted like that, and told tales out of school, he would at school be called a sneak.' Kitchener replied by suggesting that the king grow up; this is how the game was played. George V, while not the most intelligent individual, caught the drift of this advice and, in turn, invited Haig to write to him! (As far as Lloyd George was concerned, if anyone was a 'squalid intriguer', it was Haig.) Members of the press corps, particularly anyone associated with Lord Northcliffe and his chain of conservative newspapers ('Hands off the Army'), could always count on Haig's headquarters for the latest and most optimistic news, including more often than not suggestive innuendoes from the man at the top that smooth-talking politicians in London were not supporting the troops.[17] Lloyd George warned both Robertson and Haig not to start a press war with him. 'Two could play that game', Repington reported the prime minister saying to him, 'and he, L.G., could do it better than most.' Haig, who considered Lloyd George 'shifty and unreliable', was not frightened by such threats. If he could handle several million German shock troops on the western front, he could handle the little Welsh weasel.[18]

The western front, of course, was the knuckle of their dispute. In just seven weeks the war had bogged down in Belgium and France. 'We have come to a deadlock sooner than anyone could have expected', noted Reginald

Esher. Nineteen-fourteen had been bad enough, but the gallantry of British troops at Mons and during the subsequent retreat of that late summer had not generated, from the public's viewpoint at any rate, the spirit of dejection that first stuck its ugly head with the disaster at Loos in October 1915. This calamity cost Sir John French dearly. French, who had begun the war with breezy predictions that he would soon 'round the Germans up', was now hopelessly befuddled by battles that could not feature his beloved cavalry. The atmosphere around his headquarters was no longer that 'of a picnic' (the words of Frances Stevenson, Lloyd George's mistress), and French's perception of the battlefield drifted into delusion. At one point during the 'race to the sea', French thought his troops were attacking, when in truth they were being pummelled and hanging on for dear life. He 'seemed tired of the war', in Haig's view. 'In his opinion we ought to take the first opportunity of concluding peace, otherwise England would be ruined'. Haig thought French was losing his mind. French was created a viscount, bestowed with other honours and appointments, then shipped home to England, where 'his failing energy' could be restored in some meaningless command. Haig took his place. From that moment on, the Somme became inevitable.

While many politicians in England stood aghast at the casualties generated by these early battles in Belgium and France, the fact remains that British losses, when compared to those of the French and even the Germans, were not yet at a catastrophic level. That would soon change. The 1916 Somme offensive in Flanders, entirely Haig's idea and preceded by a huge artillery barrage, lasted for over four months and chiefly resulted in the extermination of Kitchener's 'New Army'. Haig's objective had clearly been for a dramatic breakthrough in the German line, achieved through a direct frontal attack against entrenched German positions, through which reserve forces could plunge in mopping-up operations. His confidence was so high that he discussed with Reginald Esher that he and the poet John Masefield might write what would be called the *Chronicle of the Somme*, a title resonant of medievalism and chivalry, an English-language *Chanson de Roland*. This was in utter contradiction of what men 'on the ground' thought. The poet Robert Graves, billeted with a French farmer, found himself given a pamphlet entitled *Comment Vivre Cent Ans* ('How to Live a Hundred Years'). 'We already knew of the coming Somme offensive', he wrote in *Good-Bye to All That*, 'so this seemed a good joke'.[19]

Unfortunately, nothing even remotely approximating a victorious outcome occurred. Indeed, no battle in the war caused more British casualties, an astounding 57,470 on the first day alone. The 1st Newfoundland Regiment, consisting of 810 men, was nearly wiped out. In ninety minutes, every one of its officers had sustained a wound or been killed and most of the foot soldiers were dead within 250 yards of their jump-off point. Six hundred and sixty men went down; only 68 survived unscathed. It is said that parish priests in Newfoundland were overwhelmed by the number of homes they had to visit twelve days later when news of this disaster crossed the Atlantic. Today, at Beaumont-Hamel on the Somme, the Newfoundland war memorial stands as the most moving monument of any World War I battlefield. It depicts a wounded stag calling out in pain, a cry never heard at command headquarters ten miles behind the lines. The distinguished military historian Liddell Hart, a combat veteran of the war, went so far as to write that Haig's ponderous assaults reminded him of Frederick the Great in the eighteenth century, men attacking 'in waves, not more than a hundred yards apart, shoulder to shoulder'. In Frederick's day, volleys of musketry would thin out the approaching enemy; in Haig's, the continuous, non-stop fusillades of countless machine guns, firing hundreds of bullets a minute, would do more than that – they would obliterate his 'fine fellows' in a charnel house of death and slaughter. Repington despaired. If the French were constantly looking for the next Napoleon, the English were looking for the next Wellington, but no candidates seemed willing or able to assume the legendary mantle. Haig, he wrote in a letter, 'will never be a commander. I have watched his operations in peace and war, and have never observed in him any talent for command'. What was coming next confirmed his gloomy thoughts.

A shift in Haig's operational thinking soon became apparent. Gone for the moment were projections such as 'I thought we could walk through the German lines in several places'. Instead the word 'attrition' began circulating with far greater frequency in the various memoranda passing between the front and London. The objective of the continuing Somme campaign was now 'to wear out the enemy's forces with a view to striking the decisive blow later, when the enemy's reserves are used up'. This was seen by men like Lloyd George as the evasion it was, an attempt to justify horrific losses with the mathematical justification that the allies had more men and could outlast the enemy. 'Military art remained dumb', added Churchill. 'The commanders and their General Staffs had no plan except the frontal attacks which all their experience and training had led them to reject; they had no policy except the policy of exhaustion. No war is so sanguinary.' Victory, as he saw it, 'was to be bought so dear as to be almost indistinguishable from defeat'. Robertson, sitting in London, was deaf to such arguments. When asked what it was he needed to win, he bluntly stated, 'every available man'.

Such actuarial obsession with manpower reflected the professional opinion of Haig and his compatriots in the upper echelon of British command.

While it is true that they embraced, to some degree, the modern elements of the battlefield which emerged very quickly as determinant factors in the outcome of any battle – tanks, machine guns, aeroplanes, trench mortars, and so on – these were all regarded as 'sideshows' to the main weapon at their disposal, the infantryman. Even the beloved cavalry were secondary to the footman. Artillery would soften a position, but it was the task of the infantryman to actually take it. Once he did, the cavalry could exploit any success achieved and spread terror and panic among the enemy. And what animated the 'Tommy' was his moral character, his discipline, his courage and his steadfastness under fire. This romanticized belief in the moral force of the bayonet, and the man behind it, led generals such as Haig to feel that dense formations of troops would always turn the tide of battle, no matter the formidability of whatever defence that stood in their way. 'Defence' was a considered 'negative', 'offence' a morally superior and almost religious 'positive'. When huge numbers of men failed in their attack, the response of Haig and others was always 'more men'. At some point, or so went the rationale, nothing could stand up to them. One officer of the Coldstream Guards wrote three years before the war that 'masses of men in sufficient lines one behind the other will go through anything'.

The Germans, though in admiration of the doggedness of their enemy, were impressed neither by English tactics nor by declarations of victory by the London press corps that greeted every advance of a few metres. Crown Prince Rupprecht of Bavaria wrote that 'Our losses in territory may be seen on the map with a microscope. Their losses in that far more precious thing – human life – are simply prodigious. Amply and in full coin have they paid for every foot of ground we sold them. They can have all they want at the same price.'

1917 – More of the Same?

'It is deplorable the way these politicians fight and intrigue against each other. They are my great difficulty here. They have no idea how war must be conducted in order to be given a reasonable chance of success, and they will not allow professionals a free hand.'

Robertson to Haig, 5 January 1916

Sitting in London as the Somme campaign floundered, Lloyd George stewed. From the very beginning of the war, his mind had been made up as to the character of this conflict. Writing a letter to his wife in October 1914, he had said, 'I went to the English headquarters. Had a great time. Gave me a new idea of what is happening. It is stalemate. We cannot turn them out of their trenches & they cannot turn us out.' The Somme, 'horrible and futile carnage' as he termed it, simply proved the obvious. When Repington had lunch with the prime minister at 10 Downing Street ('Only a maid to wait. The simplest food – cutlets and vegetables, milk pudding, and French plums'), Lloyd George launched into a tirade; he was 'not prepared to accept the position of a butcher's boy driving cattle to the slaughter, and that he would not do it'. What particularly offended his highly tuned mind – 'I am like a beetle in a glass case or a tiger in a menagerie. There is no nerve relaxation for me' – was the refusal of either Robertson or Haig to admit any failure whatsoever in the petering Somme operation. In fact, Haig had the nerve to call the great battle a success. He had killed thousands of Germans, destroyed artillery beyond counting and delivered a crushing blow to enemy morale. The amount of territory captured became a matter of little relevance when compared to the fighting strength of his enemy, now seriously eroded. It was only a matter of time. Lloyd George couldn't tolerate this thesis, which seemed as stale to him as well-trampled history from Napoleonic times. Edmund Burke, after all, 'was always indulging in prophecies of victory as a result of France's exhaustion. The war with France went on for twenty years.' If Germany's manpower losses were devastating, what of England's? Haig's apologists, however, argued with more scientific detachment. The real question, as his official biographer Duff Cooper inappropriately put in eighteen years later, was 'whether life [had] been sold at market value'.[20] In Haig's opinion, the answer was a resounding yes. The English people must accept the fact that 'we must fully spend all we have, energy, life, money, everything .... Three years of war and the loss of one-tenth of the manhood of the nation is not too great a price to pay in so great a cause.' As a follow-up for the next year's campaign in 1917, Haig proposed more of the same. Lloyd George quailed from the very thought of it, and Viscount Esher despaired, answering in his journal his own question, 'What [does] trench warfare mean? You cannot get a decision from any fight.'

Lloyd George, of course, was a civilian. He was 'soft'. Most soldiers, while not devoid of human feelings, could handle the notion of men dying in large numbers ... very large numbers ... with far more equanimity than the 'frocks' could. Sir Henry Wilson, for example, when confronted by a politician wondering if all the casualties were worth it, replied that 'the loss of men might have been a good reason for not entering the war, but a bad reason for not fighting when in the war.' Wilson had a lively intelligence and a quick tongue – he was, after all, Irish – but like many officers he was prepared for slaughter. In considering what should be done in 1917, he noted in his diary that if 'we don't get sufficient men, in sufficient time, for next year's fighting – if we are not in a position to take punishment of *at least a million between April and October* of next year and still have our divisions full up to the brim – it seems to me that we really *shall* have reached a condition of stalemate, in which case the war is lost.'

The prime minister, however, was not 'soft'. A contemporary, in talking about his character, said Lloyd George had 'no hesitation, no tenderness; make up your mind swiftly, and hit hard'. With each new setback on the continent, with the attendant casualty lists, some quarters of English public opinion were opening up to the idea of peace talks. 'We are going to lose this war', wrote Esher. 'A stalemate and a peace that is only a truce. No flattening out of Germany or reinstatement of Belgium is possible.' Lloyd George was desperate to stem this sort of defeatist sentiment, but he needed results, as he told his secretary: 'success is the only criterion'. What he wanted to see was verve, imagination and victories. None of these were anywhere visible on the western front, which was why Lloyd George was always hankering for operations elsewhere, placing him in the 'eastern' camp, a bad place to be after the Dardanelles fiasco. His philosophy, borrowed from Sir Ian Hamilton, was that 'no general should attack his enemy where he is strongest. He holds him where he is strongest and attacks him where he is weakest.' This was absolute heresy to the majority of the British officer corps. Robertson scorned the notion of draining forces from the west only to squander them in one 'cess pit' after another far from the front that mattered. Haig believed that weakening his force in such a manner 'would be the act of a lunatic'. General Hubert Gough disdained the prime minister's desire for 'an easy and cheap way to victory'. Wilson said, 'The way to end this war is to kill Germans not Turks.... If we beat the Boches, all else follows.'

At this juncture of the war the French had relieved Marshal 'Papa' Joffre of his command, and replaced him by a far junior (and relatively unknown) officer, Robert Nivelle, an artillery specialist. Nivelle had acquired his reputation by a stunning victory on a narrow section of the Verdun battlefield in October 1916. A man of considerable charm (he spoke perfect English, and was a Protestant to boot), Nivelle now floated the idea of transferring the lessons of his small success to a broader arena. He promised surprise, a quick advance, few casualties, a breakthrough and the willingness to cease operations on the instant if negative conditions warranted it. This was not the tired old 'lumber' of Haig and Robertson; this was a fresh approach that took into account the desirability of limiting casualties. 'Nivelle had proved to be', Duff Cooper said, 'the first and last person capable of persuading Lloyd George that victory could be won on the western front'. Lloyd George, to his regret, let himself be talked into it. Not only that, but with a speed and deviousness that only confirmed Robertson's and Haig's distrust of the prime minister, Lloyd George arranged for the British Expeditionary Force, which was to support Nivelle on his left, to be placed under the Frenchman's command. When Haig heard about this at a conference at Calais in February, he virtually choked (one of his aides, the smooth and urbane Philip Sassoon, called this Lloyd George's 'coup de théâtre'). No more egregious insult to the honour of the British army could be conceived, particularly given the ingrained hostility that many officers held for foreigners. Haig's diary is full of disparaging remarks about all manner of nationalities: Italians, Portuguese, French, Canadians, Australians, even Americans, and Robertson, according to the prime minister, scorned everyone except Germans. 'In the order of his distrust came Frenchmen, first and deepest of all, then Italians, Serbians, Greeks, Celts, and last of all – if at all – Germans, [of whom] he had a very high opinion and no dislike.'

This slap in the face brought Haig into full bloom. Always a stickler for protocols, regulations and appropriate etiquette (he took the time, in the middle of battlefield operations, to upbraid a general or two 'on the lack of smartness, and slackness of one of its Battalions. In the matter of saluting when I was motoring through the village where it was billeted').[21] Haig now launched into a blizzard of memoranda, hen-pecking details that might make such an arrangement feasible, attacking points where he refused to take responsibility and generally creating a blizzard of obstructions and deviations from the intent of a unified command. He wrote furiously to his supporters back home, and suffered indignities when Nivelle issued him peremptory commands (the French, in Haig's opinion, were not gentlemen). Lloyd George was delighted at Haig's discomfiture. He had removed from his top commander's hands, or so he thought, the ability to launch another bloodbath. Unfortunately for him, however, he had placed his bet on the wrong horse.

Besides being well in over his head, Nivelle's great scheme was compromised at the very start by a variety of factors. General Ludendorff, the new German commander of the western front, had been deeply concerned over his positions after the Somme. Attrition may have been a ghastly word in Lloyd George's vocabulary, but there can be little question that Haig's blunt attacks, though burdened by his own revolting casualty list, had indeed managed to thin Germany's resources in manpower. Ludendorff's staff found the British army to be 'strategically clumsy, tactically rigid, but tough'; if attrition was to be the game, however, it was having the effect Haig and Robertson wanted. But if such was to be the nature of coming battles, Ludendorff was prepared to accept this reality and concentrate on a defensive strategy. Let the English and French come, he would be ready for them. Liddell Hart, the military historian, admired Ludendorff's adaptability. He 'had the moral courage to give up territory if circumstances advised it'.[22] In a skillfully executed retrenchment, enemy troops withdrew some twenty-five miles to a much stronger position, centred on what came to be known by the British as the Hindenburg Line. Everything left behind was scorched and destroyed, turned into 'a desert' in the opinion of one observer, where 'nature herself seemed to have given up trying to mend matters'. The Germans coded this withdrawal *Alberich*, after the vexing dwarf in Wagner's opera cycle *Der Ring des Nibelungen*, and indeed, this manoeuvre entirely changed the dynamics of the battlefield facing Nivelle. Had he been less impetuous, and less wedded to his initial scheme, Nivelle would have cancelled the attack or reoriented his plans, but he would not. The tactic of surprise, moreover, was entirely lost. Preparations that had taken so little time in his successful attack three months before in Verdun, now took weeks with the greater front to be attacked, which required exponentially more supplies and divisions. German airmen easily spotted increased activity, and security as to the attack's aims and timetable were irrevocably compromised with the capture of French plans which detailed the offensive. A change in the French government also weakened Nivelle, as new politicians in charge, and not a few fellow generals, snipped, critiqued and then volubly deprecated the coming campaign (Pétain was said to be 'openly incredulous'). But as was so often the case, which Lloyd George would experience with the Passchendaele campaign, once such gigantic operations began, their inexorable grind forward became impossible to thwart.

Nivelle's offensive commenced in April 1917 and was an immediate disaster; but rather than cease when all odds began stacking up in the enemy's favour, Nivelle abandoned his pledge to stop the bleeding. He had too much at stake – his entire career – to call a halt, and the results were a shambles of continued futility. The attacks finally ceased three weeks later and, as Haig observed in no doubt grim satisfaction, 'Nivelle will disappear'; and not only Nivelle, as matters turned out, but the fighting spirit of French foot soldiers, the famous *poilus*. Mutinies broke out throughout the French ranks, as men refused to participate in any more futile attacks. Paralysis gripped the French high command. Some recommended wholesale and seemingly random executions – at least 2,000, one general suggested – but the new commander in chief, Philippe Pétain, chose a more conciliatory approach. Pierrefeu, at French headquarters, summarized Pétain's thinking: 'Look to the example of Caesar: execute the ringleaders, distribute corn to the rest'. While statistics are sketchy, only a handful of French soldiers were shot. Considering the extent of disturbances, this was a minuscule response. Starting in June, Pétain, the 'army doctor', made it a point to visit between 80 and 90 front-line divisions, promising better food, more leave and an end to pointless, wasteful attacks. In 1917 his operations cost France 190,000 men; Joffre, in 1915, had lost over double that number, 430,000. Pétain salved the sore, but for the moment the French army was shelved as far as offensive operations were concerned. This internal turmoil was at first little known to outsiders. Certainly the Germans were unaware of it, nor the British public and its leaders. Haig was incrementally informed, to the point of exhilaration. There was now only one army that could win this war, and it was his.

The Nivelle fiasco was a personal reflection on the quality of Lloyd George's judgment. In Robertson's view, this was what happened when you put amateurs in charge of military affairs. He began referring to the prime minister as 'Napoleon', a nickname he invented not so much to reference Lloyd George's military acumen, but for his slight physical stature and his arrogance. The prime minister's credibility within the war cabinet was also severely strained. Haig now had several arguing points at his disposal as he geared up for the spring and summer of 1917. In May he wrote in his diary that the French, obviously, were currently but 'a broken reed'. There was no one left in the field to apply pressure on Germany but Britain. 'Great Britain must take the necessary steps to win the war by herself, because our French Allies have already shown that they lacked both the moral qualities and the means for gaining the victory.' In order to protect the French from disintegrating; in order to prevent Germany from replenishing her stocks of manpower; in order to give the Royal Navy time to defeat the German U-Boat menace; and last of all, to achieve glory on the battlefield – no respite must be allowed the enemy. 'We ought to have only the one thought now in our minds, namely, to *attack*.' With calm resolution, the dour Scotsman turned his attention once again from where it had never really strayed: Ypres.

Passchendaele

'Haig the Hammer'

Headline, The *Daily Express*, 1917

The ancient Belgian wool capital of Ypres, which sits just twenty-five miles from the North Sea in the monotonously flat landscape of Flanders, was soon to be universally referred to by hundreds of thousands of English-speaking soldiers as 'Wipers'. It stood as the anchor of a 'salient' or bulge that poked into the German lines, the result of the first few weeks of war in 1914 when the fighting lines were stabilized into a series of offsetting trench systems that stretched some 470 miles from the Belgian coast to Switzerland. Ypres would prove to be the heart and soul of Britain's commitment to the war. Verdun forever resonates with imagery of France's sacrifice. With Britain and its coterie of colonialists, it would be Ypres.

Salients have some tactical advantages but many liabilities as well. They can be enfiladed on three sides by enemy artillery, their access routes to the front lines are usually well established and thus easily identifiable artillery targets and, in the case of flat topography, they are mortally endangered if the enemy monopolizes whatever high ground there may be. In the case of Ypres, slight ridges to the east of the city in a broad semi-circle, some only a few dozen metres in height, took on exaggerated military importance. Over time, as weeks stretched on and casualty rates rose to monumental proportions, the huge psychological implications of obscure hillocks and mounds of misshapen earth, several identified cryptically as 'Mound C' or 'The Pimple', obsessed the thoughts of would-be strategists. Many officers, especially in the high command, lost all perspective. Their world view, while expansive – they knew the location of Germany – was gradually constricted to a few hundred yards. To take a ridge became, for some, the equivalent of taking Berlin, though in practical terms the achievement meant nothing. As Lloyd George wrote in his memoirs sixteen years later regarding what occurred at Passchendaele, 'The *Times* has two leading articles on successive days on the Broodseinde victory, as it was called. Who remembers the name now? (Try it on one of your friends.)'

Contradicting the alleged importance of such objectives, at least for men in the trenches, was the growing numbness of a barren landscape. Explosives of previously unimaginable destructive power obliterated villages, features of the countryside, woodlots and anything that might remind a person of normality. To march forward into a death zone full of machine gun bullets and heavy ordnance, and to win a trench no different from the filthy, rat-infested hovel you had leaped out of a few minutes (or hours) before, was an irony not lost on exhausted, disillusioned and often shell-shocked infantrymen. Many of these soldiers hardened to the task, becoming as vicious and resolute as their German foes. Others just shrivlled up and died.

Ypres had already been the scene of two formal battles, along with innumerable and squalid scuffles that took any number of lives but which did not qualify as distinct or identifiable engagements. Haig was a firm believer in trench raids and minor operations intended to annoy the enemy. He called them 'winter sports', intended to keep the troops amused and in tiptop shape. Ypres and its surroundings, in the meantime, were reduced to a pile of rubble.

It is a testament to Haig's 'indomitable will' that he should obsess himself once again with Ypres. One of the temptations that salients invariably dangle in front of a general's eye, especially when viewed from a map, is their propensity for encouraging the notion of breakthroughs. One is, by definition, already engorging yourself on the enemy's entrails; a bit more push, and the rupture ensues. As battles became bigger, and the industrial might of the various combatants geared up accordingly, Haig came to realize, as did most of his compatriots on the high command, that the 'more' of everything at his disposal – 'tangible support! Men, guns, aeroplanes!' – must surely turn the tide. Every incremental advantage that he wrung out of London would help crack the German wall. This was a war of firsts, after all. Never in the history of mankind had such explosive power been made available to generals, and to concentrate an overwhelming percentage of it to a relatively narrow front would be the sledge that even the Germans, with all their resolve, energy, discipline and training, could not resist. The blunt application of every single resource was the most obvious course of action that Haig could think of. He began as early as the autumn of 1916 to plan the operation.

As his own thoughts jelled, he later instructed his field generals to prepare battle plans in the area around Ypres with which he tinkered for several weeks, demanding alterations, revisions and rethinking where necessary. As various tactical scenarios began to emerge, the prospects Haig truly wished to accomplish became fixed in his mind. Being, as he himself admitted, an optimist, he proposed a breakthrough of startling magnitude. He would pulverize the enemy with a barrage never yet witnessed, seize the low-lying heights ringing Ypres to the east which were anchored by a village called Passchendaele, then break through to the Belgian coast. Once in open country, the Germans would be flanked, broken up and turned out of Belgium. If that were to happen, the war would be over.

When Robertson saw these goals, even he blanched. Haig, in his opinion, was promising considerably more than he could possibly deliver. Being a 'strict communicant of the great Western Church', however, gave him little choice in the matter. While privately urging Haig to show some restraint, he nonetheless endorsed the overall plan, though when arguing for its acceptance, he fell back along the usual attritional lines. 'In every great battle, a time of extreme stress arrives and the side which sets its teeth the hardest usually wins. Again, before any considerable success can be gained in battle, the enemy's reserves have to be exhausted. This used to be a matter of hours, now it is a matter of weeks and months. The Commander with the last reserves usually wins.' When the king of Belgium got wind of the upcoming campaign, he sent his chief of staff, General Ruquoy, to confer with Haig. This poor gentleman expressed the king's wish that somewhere else might be considered for the coming battles, his majesty being somewhat tired of seeing great swaths of his kingdom destroyed. A more 'indirect' plan to liberate the country was to be preferred. Haig wrote off Ruquoy. 'I formed a poor opinion of the man as a soldier and of his determination as a man.'

At a war cabinet meeting in June, called to discuss what to do next, an important psychological element was thrown into the mix which immeasurably assisted Haig. The first sea lord, John Jellicoe, dropped a 'bombshell' on the conference table. The submarine menace, he declared, if not brought under immediate control, would starve Britain of foodstuffs and essential war materials, and effectively bring her to her knees. This 'startling and reckless declaration' stunned the civilians present. Lloyd George, who on a previous occasion had muttered that he found Jellicoe a 'madman', relates that he 'hotly' rebutted the admiral's assertion and sought to calm everyone's nerves, but the damage had been done. Haig, who also disparaged Jellicoe (he considered him 'an old woman') nonetheless must have found comfort in the admiral's sombre assessment. Haig's plan to reach the Belgian coast, after all, would eliminate submarine bases in Ostend and Zeebrugge, and thus double the intended effects of his summer campaign. To whip the German army, and deprive the enemy of important naval posts, truly would win the war. Haig held the upper hand. What good was taking Jerusalem or some other 'eastern' objective if U-Boats starved Britain into an early truce or a half-baked peace? Conceptually, the operation went forward.

Certainly there were doubting Thomases behind the scenes, even within the military. Repington, for instance, was entirely in sympathy with slugging it out with the Germans in the west. However, we should 'not play the game the [enemy] wanted, namely of constantly losing heaps of men against their prepared positions', but instead turn the tone of battle into a contest between the big guns. Anywhere was fine, he suggested, except Flanders. Before the war Repington had been a military attaché to the Low Countries, and he knew the topography well. The pastures surrounding Ypres were essentially 'reclaimed', having been drained and cultivated by industrious peasants for centuries, their crisscross patchwork of farms and fields delineated by a complex network of sluices, drainage ditches, canals and wetland controls that required annual attention and maintenance. Ypres had already endured months of intensive fighting that had, as a consequence, destroyed many of these agricultural works, and the idea of another major campaign in such poor and wet soil alarmed Repington. World War I had become an artillery war. Hundreds of cannon, large and small, were required to soften up the enemy, destroy his barbed wire, pulverize his trench systems and crush morale, in the process of which the proposed battlefield would be churned up and drastically rearranged more than it already was. During rainy season, Repington foresaw what could happen. In May 1917 he extensively toured the front, where he picked up 'a good Boche steel helmet' as a souvenir. Upon returning to London he met with Wully. 'I reminded him of our past failures in the low-lying lands, and urged him to keep away from them. He listened so attentively that I think some operation in this [sense] may be in the wind.' In June Repington's suspicions were confirmed by an interview with Haig himself. 'I gave him my views about the ground and the inundation ... and that I hated the idea of thrusting the Army into such a daedelus of mud and water.... Haig thought ... that even if he got forward a little bit, it was all to the good.'

Whether the commander in chief wanted to go forward a few hundred yards or several miles to the coast was in many respects a moot point, so fixed in his mind was the notion that German forces would crack under the strain of the coming attacks. His intelligence officer, a fellow Scot, John Charteris, had consistently misinterpreted both evidence garnered from captured prisoners and battlefield reports in order to present the most advantageous picture that he could of imminent German collapse. Haig bought into these assessments with a full heart even as others shook their heads in disbelief. Haig's chief of staff 'thinks the hun is weakening and may give way at any moment', Repington recorded, rolling his eyes; when Charteris again ticked off the catastrophic losses suffered by German forces, 'I could not believe him', many of these assertions taking on the characteristics of 'an extraordinary hallucination'. Even the French were bemused by the optimism emanating from general headquarters. Pétain told Repington that 'Charteris killed off Germans too quickly'. This French general, famous for his pessimism, 'foresaw great difficulties when he discussed these matters with Haig. He thought that our people were very tenacious of their ideas, kept a straight course, but ran in blinkers – and he held up his hands to his face to show what he meant'. As far as Pétain was concerned, 'he did not believe in another Somme'.

Haig, however, was a man who did not cherish dissent, and who did not let reality stand in his way. Indeed, as the former prime minister Asquith had put it, army headquarters made 'spin' a specialty. They 'kept three sets of figures, one to mislead the public, another to mislead the Cabinet, and the third to mislead itself'. It was therefore counterintuitive to expect that he might choose as appropriate battlefield commanders men who might disagree with him, or doubt in any way the means he conceived to attain his ends. In General Sir Hubert Gough, Haig had a man who, like himself, was not afraid to move forward come what may.

Gough, only forty-four years of age and already a lieutenant-general, was resolute, oblivious of personal danger, quick-spirited and full of dash – just what you'd expect of a cavalry officer. Born in 1870, he came from a distinguished Anglo-Irish military family who had, collectively, spent many years fighting in the colonial theatres of India and Afghanistan. He had been educated at Eton (an indifferent student) and Sandhurst, where he excelled. Being a natural soldier and a natural horseman, making his assignment to a cavalry regiment proved preordained. There he mastered the tools which, at the time, were considered indispensable to the profession (and honour) of arms: the lance and the sabre. His aggressiveness was also fostered by a life-long obsession with blood sports. In Ireland's County Tipperary he rode with a famous hunt known as the 'Tips', and in India he enjoyed 'pigsticking' which, as its name implies, entailed chasing boar through thick and thin and spearing it to death. Gough was a wild and rambunctious character, and the Boer War came around at just the right moment to display, for the last time in the history of warfare, the talents of men in the saddle, which overshadowed to some degree major faults in his personality and temperament. In an 1899 assessment, for example, his commanding officer jotted down the following traits:

Field Movements – Good but hasty
Judgment and tact – impulsive
Temper – quick

These indifferent marks were well displayed on the battlefields of South Africa, where Gough struggled under the restrictive commands of old fogies. When he received orders he did not agree with, he crumpled the papers and threw them to the ground, proceeding on his own dangerous larks. In one encounter he spotted a small number of irregulars camping on the svelte. Without bothering to reconnoitre further, he waited for dusk and then charged over several hundred acres of open ground where, to his surprise, he found himself face to face with over one thousand of the enemy. In the short melee that followed he was unhorsed and captured. Two-thirds of his command were also taken prisoner, wounded or killed. Gough redeemed himself to some extent by escaping (as had Churchill two years previously on another occasion in this war), and Lord Kitchener himself, mindful of the man's pedigree (his father had been a decorated general) and respectful of youthful panache, personally absolved him of any responsibility for the blunder.

World War I, when it began, found Gough a brigadier general in command of a cavalry brigade. He performed well under fire at Mons, Loos and several other engagements, earning spectacular promotions. In March 1916 he was placed in charge of the Reserve Army, over 100,000 men, which later became the Fifth Army. Many officers far senior in service were aghast at being passed over with such unseemly haste by someone so raw, and several awkward situations, as well might be imagined, accrued in the many staff, divisional and corps meetings which now took up so much of his time. Gough, a 'fighting' general if there ever was one, chaffed at the bureaucratic nature of his new position. He liked nothing better than to get up to the front lines himself, both to see what was going on and to mingle and inspire his men, which came easily to him (and which was generally appreciated). Gough was not a 'château' general, but he quickly learned that in modern war, commanders, in the reverse of the old cliché, were to be heard, if not seen.

Gough was a major figure in the bloody and muddy mess that had been the Somme in 1916. In his own war memoirs, published in 1931, he complained that it was ever so easy for commentators fifteen or so years after the fact to ridicule those operations as a futile debacle that had sent thousands of young men to the slaughterhouse. In fact, the Somme was 'one of the foundation stones on which the advance to victory in 1918 was built', the typical Haigean argument. 'The Somme shook the German Army to its foundations', he argued, where no other strategy could. He claimed that he was not blind to the casualties – many dear friends and his own brother were among the dead – and he denied that he was indifferent to the mortal danger his orders placed so many troops in. 'Though we may not be infallible', he wrote of himself and others on the general staff, 'we are by no means stupid.'

The very magnitude of the fighting, however, did tend to blur lines of judgment and the ability to be shocked, especially as battles became bloodier. Gough, better than many, tried to keep abreast of battlefield conditions and paid attention to remarks from the front that made it to his desk. Other commanders did not. The pyramidical structure of an army demanded that reports from junior officers in the field, passing through brigade and battalion commanders, be received and processed by the staff of army commanders like Gough, and funnelled to him more or less correctly. Even Haig realized at times that these lines of communication were not functioning properly. The 'fog of war' was a terrible burden on men at the top. Telephone lines were routinely cut by artillery barrages, messengers sent to the rear were often killed en route, and the use of carrier pigeons was a mode of reporting back to headquarters so obsolete as to be ludicrous (birds, often encrusted in the all-pervasive mud, could not fly; or were too terrified or disoriented; or were just pulverized in the mayhem of shrapnel fire). Often men like Haig and Gough had not the slightest idea what was going on, particularly if aerial reconnaissance was unavailable because of weather conditions. Many times during the Somme, Haig thought he was winning the struggle decisively. It often took three or four days to realize that nothing, in fact, had been achieved. It is a macabre reality that when headquarters saw minimal losses reported, they concluded that no worthwhile objective had been won. Entries such as 'total casualties for the last two days' heavy fighting are just 8,000' are routine in Haig's diary. Add to this the hesitation felt by many subordinates who had to bring unfortunate news 'to the top', and you have the picture that critics of the army so often carped about: commanders removed from reality, unaware of physical conditions at the front (usually many miles away from headquarters) and hopelessly imbued with an ethos of 'glory' that had no relationship to the horrific character of trench warfare as experienced by common, ordinary conscripts. Haig admired 'fighting generals', but most of the fighting many of these men did were at headquarters rearranging coloured lines on maps. The future hero of World War II, Bernard Montgomery, was a twenty-nine-year-old junior officer at the time in the trenches around Ypres. In his first action, he had led a charge waving his sword, the first and last time he ever employed that particular weapon. 'Fighting generals' to him meant 'those who had a complete disregard for human life'. Aside from being sent home for wounds, Montgomery spent the entire war on the front. 'I never once saw the British commander in chief, neither French nor Haig, and only twice did I see an Army Commander.'

During the several-month Somme offensive, Gough searched for 'a howling success' somewhere, but it eluded him and everyone else. The capture of a few yards here and there, often highlighted in the press as 'victory', tended to cloud the thinking not only of the British public but of the generals themselves, especially since tactical objectives often proved no further than their artillery barrages could cover. It really did seem 'a victory' if a few obscure pillboxes could be captured, given the expenditure of shells and men that were required to take them. For better or worse, Gough was a 'thruster', and Haig wanted his generals that way; Hubert 'had never lost his head, was always cheery and fought hard'. Men who were 'mad keen to kill Germans' were all that mattered to him.

Unfortunately, a good many Germans were mad keen to kill Tommies, and Gough gained a reputation as a general who took needless chances, gambled excessively, oversaw shoddy staff work, sloughed off insurmountable obstacles as minor inconveniences and relied too often on luck. He seemed to many a 'toff', too imbued with 'tallyhosis', as though battle was merely another day in the saddle chasing down animals. Gough, in his turn, felt that the industrial life of the new Britain had sapped a primal life force out of the nation's manhood. Many of the recruits in Kitchener's Army had shocked him by their appearance – 'poor physique, bad teeth and other outward and visible signs of insufficient nourishment and fresh air in their youth', all negative signs of 'town life' – what these boys needed was a good fox hunt. James Edmonds, official historian on the British Army in this war, recorded a revealing episode involving Gough:

> I heard him complain that his troops had no 'blood lust', the officers no 'spirit of the offensive'. Whilst I was having tea in the 'B' Mess of his headquarters he came in and said, 'I want to shoot two officers'. There was an astonished pause, and the A.P.M [Assistant Provost Marshal] said, 'Beg your pardon, Sir, there are no officers under sentence'. Gough looked at him as if to say, 'you fool', and explained, 'Yes, I know that, but I want to shoot two officers as an example to others'. And he got them.

To Gough and his Fifth Army was given the primary role in attacking the village of Passchendaele. This had been preceded by what Lloyd George called 'an *aperitif*', the capture of the adjoining Messines Ridge by the Second Army under General Herbert Plumer in an unusual and seldom-repeated feat of arms. The Messines vantage-point, to the south-east of Ypres, was another German strongpoint that dominated the lowlands surrounding the city. Beginning the previous year, a series of twenty-one mining shafts had been tunnelled beneath the German trench system; they were packed with almost a million pounds of gunpowder and detonated at ten minutes past three on the morning of 7 June 1917. Nineteen of the twenty-one explosive packages blew (leaving two, undetonated to this day). Something like 10,000 Germans died in just a few seconds, and Plumer's men easily took their positions. Typically, however, there was no substantial follow-up to take advantage of what must certainly have been a shocking situation for German troops in the vicinity. Plumer had doubted whether the operation could really succeed, so novel was the scheme, and whatever advantages had been gained were squandered later in the afternoon as enemy forcers rallied. Messines, however, had been won. The idea now was for Gough, with Plumer at his right wing, to complete the strategic picture by taking Passchendaele, north-east of Ypres. Instead of a quick follow-up, however, Gough's artillery barrage beginning the attack did not start for another month.

There were a variety of reasons for the delay, many understandable, but the fact remains that precious time (and decent weather) were frittered away. Gough used the interval to train men and refine plans, which were still in a state of flux. Plumer's failure to exploit the Messines success was explained away as a successful 'bite and hold' operation, meaning short but violent attacks to capture strictly limited objectives. Plumer seemed to suggest in his approach to the Passchendaele situation that the same philosophy be applied. He recommended short bursts in order to take 500 yards, then another 500 in a following attack, so on and so forth. Gough disagreed. Sitting at his headquarters with the map before him, neatly marked with the black, blue and green lines that signified various intermediate objectives, he dismissed the notion of restricting his goals. His army would advance 5,000 yards on the first day, about a third of the way to Passchendaele. There were no sufficiently fresh approaches to the attack that made it very much different from campaigns in the past; indeed, as he himself admitted, 'This plan had some similarity to the operations carried out in the Battle of the Somme.' That alone should have given most commanders reason for pause.

The Battle Begins

'A porridge of mud'

A British engineer

By early summer, gossip around London dinner parties was all about the coming offensive. If the Germans were surprised (they were not), certainly no one at the Café Royale or the Senior Club or Claridges proved to be out of the loop either. It was the talk of the town.[23] Repington visited friends of his at the sumptuous country estate of Great Hallingbury, just outside of London. 'Had some delightful rides in the forest and good golf [and] croquet. Wonderful weather. The country looks splendid. I never saw such a show of buttercups. The garden looking beautiful. Is there a war?'

Lloyd George knew there was. Sitting in Downing Street some 130 miles across the English Channel from Ypres, he could hear the thunderous cascade of artillery that inaugurated Gough's great thrust, the largest artillery barrage yet undertaken by any army anywhere in the world. Haig himself was shaken out of a sound sleep at 4:15 a.m. that same morning. He was nineteen miles from the front, in a private railway car. The barrage lasted for ten days, and reputedly consumed shells worth £22,000,000.

The Germans, however, had changed their approach to this particular battlefield. Instead of confining themselves to rigid trench systems, they developed a scheme of mutually supportive strong points that resembled more a chessboard than a straight line. These were machine gun nests for the most part, many in reinforced concrete shelters and pillboxes, all scientifically positioned to cover each other's flanks. The skills of Colonel Friedrich von Lossberg, one of Germany's foremost defensive specialists, were applied day and night on the slopes leading up to Passchendaele, creating a veritable hell hole that survived relatively intact the terrific fifteen-day bombardment unleashed by Gough, over four million shells. (Even Gough admitted to the new system's formidability.) Following a creeping barrage that advanced at a predetermined rate, the Fifth Army went over the top on the morning of 31 July, at 3:50 a.m. Before Field Marshal Haig had had time to rouse, dress and avail himself of his traditionally meagre breakfast, men under his command were being mowed down in Flanders Fields just as they had been the previous year on the Somme. Their progress was equally negligible. More ominously, and again replicating the pattern of the previous year, it began to rain. It would continue raining for the next week.

The literature of Passchendaele, of course, is characterized by a single word – mud. It is the telling descriptive, the most heart-wrenching photographic image and the universal lament. Mention Passchendaele and its stories blend into a seamless pastiche of familiar tales: pack mules sliding off duckboards into shell holes filled with mire, there to drown under the weight of their loads; wounded men suffocated in the mud; stretcher bearers, numbering five or six men, required to slog through the muck to bring a single comrade back to a dressing station, a trek that could take five to six hours; artillery sunk in the muck up to their axles; men toiling like oxen to drag cannon from one sinkhole to another; the inexpressible exhaustion marked on men's faces. In sum, the futility of it all.

The mud was predictable. With its drainage system destroyed by incessant shelling, the high-water table of the Ypres salient merely came to the surface and flooded whole swaths of the landscape, especially during the latter part of the campaign in autumn. The soil, a heavy clay, turned to sludge. Not only did it gum up every mechanical apparatus in sight, whether it be a rifle, machine gun or artillery piece, it proved bottomless. A man's foot could sink three feet and keep going. Soldiers burdened with packs that might weigh

80 pounds, found themselves exhausted after just a few minutes' slog. The greatest fear was to trip or, even worse, fall wounded into a shell crater; rising water would finish the job that German bullets hadn't. Some men, fighting to retain a position, found themselves up to their waists in a sloshy brew. The most incredible fact about the entire evolving mess, however, was that most men still found the will and determination within them to continue the mission, to continue the fight, to continue the advance. The great French 'Tiger', Georges Clemenceau, noted what he thought were the determinant characteristics of the various principal nationalities in arms. 'The English took their punishment in silence', he said; 'the French made too many *gestes* and grimaces; the Boche were like dogs, who come to heel when kicked and always would.' In the grim atmospherics of August below Passchendaele, even the human spirit could not, it seems, be vanquished.

The rain discouraged Gough but not enough for him to cease ordering attacks. As word crept back to Haig that things were not going as planned, the commander in chief advised Gough to 'have patience', but this had no effect on the headquarters of Fifth Army. The poor weather hampered effective artillery fire, and deteriorating ground conditions prevented the infantry from moving about efficiently. Fierce German resistance created conditions of mayhem, some units suffering half their number in casualties. The 16th and 36th divisions especially earned Haig's initial censure. 'The men are Irish and apparently did not like the enemy's shelling, so Gough said.' Gough's petulance continued as the battle progressed. The mud, he complained, 'was in German pay'. He took to blaming his men as irresolute and timorous. Tanks were ordered up in support, but proved useless when tossed onto the field in haphazard operations. Tank commanders had never approved of Passchendaele as an area that might reward their newly developing weapon; as a matter of fact, they saw no hope for the foot soldier there either. One noted that 'from an infantry point of view, the Third Battle of Ypres may be considered comatose. It can only be continued at colossal loss and little gain'. This did not restrain Haig, always on the lookout for finer weather and more opportunities, but even he had to admit by mid-September that Gough and the Fifth Army were irrevocably used up. He then turned to Plumer and the Second Army, especially as an interval of dry weather commenced.

It is part of Passchendaele lore that Plumer, unlike Gough, was a more sensitive commander and less inclined to throw his soldier's lives away as though they were bits of confetti at a wedding. One of his many nicknames was 'Daddy', which somehow conveys a more paternalistic attitude. But this view is seriously askew. Plumer was an advocate of limited movements, 'bite and hold' operations, not because he was concerned about excessive casualties but as a matter of common sense. Casualties were a fact of life in war, and it was foolish not to conserve supplies of men where and when possible by pursuing less ambitious objectives. In particular, he stressed the point that overly optimistic goals usually meant that soldiers might 'outrun' their artillery support. This made them vulnerable to enemy shellfire and the inevitable counterattacks that met each British thrust. Best to gain and capture 500 yards than fail to advance 3,500. This in no way diminished the ferocity of what was planned, nor the enormous expenditure of artillery shells, some three and a half million on a front considerably shorter than Gough's. If Plumer believed in one thing to protect his men, it was sufficient artillery support. In three separate 'battles' which Plumer initiated, achieving incremental advances to the village of Passchendaele sitting on the ridge overlooking them, Second Army suffered greater numbers of killed, wounded and missing than had Gough. When the autumnal rains began, he continued battering on, stubbornly, and often ignoring his own premise on the necessity of adequate artillery support. But each baleful spot captured … Polygon Wood, Broodseinde, Poelcappelle – came to signify to headquarters and the conservative press back home a victory. 'What makes troops trust their Chief?' Jan Smuts was asked in London. 'Success', was his reply. Lloyd George couldn't believe it. Plumer was 'about as stupid as Haig'.

When Repington made his rounds through Flanders in October, he heard the generals radiating optimism. 'I found Plumer heart and soul for the Flanders campaign', he noted in his diary, and 'Haig as firmly set upon the offensive as possible'. Back in London, however, a cabal of cashiered officers, beginning with Sir John French, were sniping at Haig. The Somme had been bad enough, was 'the game worth the candle?' he asked. 'The army is being ruined without any commensurate results.' The king finally had enough, and told French, in effect 'to shut up'. Unfortunately, the chief of army intelligence at Whitehall, Major General Macdonogh, chimed in as well, questioning Haig's assertion that German morale was shattered. The commander in chief was furious. What could you expect, he wrote in his diary; Macdonogh, after all, was a Catholic.

If Haig believed in anything, it was the idea of 'structured' battle. Events moved inexorably from one state to the next: the artillery softened up the enemy, destroyed his barbed wire and demoralized him; the infantry attacked, fully knowing that horrific casualties awaited them 'over the top', but because of their moral superiority and 'training' they would achieve their goals; when the weak point in enemy lines was perceived, the inevitable breakthrough would follow. Any deviation of such a schedule was deemed an 'aberration' and not particularly seen worthy of study. This mindset pretty much ruled Haig's GHQ for the entire war.

Lloyd George, who had previously been unaware of the topographical nightmare that was the Passchendaele battlefield, unleashed an epithet of scorn on Haig for this operation. More space in his memoirs is devoted to it than almost any other battle of the war. When Lloyd George visited Haig in September, he was astounded at the air of 'exaltation' that emanated throughout headquarters. General Charteris, for instance, 'glowed with victory', and General Kiggell, Haig's chief of staff, openly ridiculed the prime minister 'as a stupid civilian who knew nothing about war'. Lloyd George's worries over the weather were met by his insouciant reply that 'battles could not be stopped like tennis matches for a shower'. As for Haig, he was 'radiant' and forgiving. The victory was won, Germany would crumble despite the many obstacles that men like Lloyd George had strewed about his path. Unlike the pope at Canossa, however, he would not humiliate the prime minister in this moment of vindication. Haig was in control.

Lloyd George concluded that the field marshal was 'demented'. After weeks of desperate fighting, Passchendaele was still 1,500 yards away. Where was all the talk about submarine ports and sweeping up the Flemish coast? It no longer mattered anymore, apparently. Haig said he was 'using up the Boches'. The general 'was essentially self-centred', Lloyd George asserted in his memoirs. 'There was no other task but his, no other army than the one he commanded; no other use for the youth of Britain than to make up his losses. No victory was thinkable except in battles he planned. His camera only took in a limited circle of the scene right in front of him, and it was too constricted and faint to take in any other landscape'. In his most prescient observation, Lloyd George wrote that Haig reminded him of the blind king of Bohemia at the Battle of Crécy.[24]

The 'revisionist' theory of many younger historians today is that the war cabinet, and Lloyd George in particular, patently shirked their responsibilities by allowing Haig and Robertson to continue their pointless succession of 'billy-goat tactics' (the prime minister's phrase) at Passchendaele, 'proceeding in a succession of sickening thuds'. To a limited degree they are right. Lloyd George never hesitated to heap scorn on his two top generals, both to their faces and, in less inflammatory language, during parliamentary debate. His distaste for their unimaginative tactics and utter disregard for loss of life animated him to the very heights of eloquence, and probably contributed to his plethora of schemes to put British armies in action where their success might be more probable: Italy, the Balkans, Turkey, Palestine – just about anywhere that 'a clear, definite victory which has visibly materialized in guns and prisoners captured, in unmistakable retreats of the enemy's armies, and in large sections of the enemy territory occupied' might be the tangible result. Men like Haig deplored such short-sightedness; grinding away at German strength was their current position. But what Haig, Robertson and revisionist historians themselves fail to take into account was the political dimension of this war: the home front, and what one British general disparagingly called 'the breath of public opinion'.

Certainly Lloyd George could have sacked Haig, even though he confessed that he saw no particular general who was any better, a decidedly negative and sweeping assessment of the officer corps. He did force Robertson out of office in February 1918, but in a generally polite fashion. What Lloyd George could not do in 1917, however, was ruthlessly purge this duo, which would have carried the stigma of failure to monumental proportions, and risked the unmistakable possibility of plunging Britain into a vast psychological slump. Lloyd George might have had pacifist feelings before 1914, but three years later he was wholeheartedly into prosecuting the war. He was not in favour of the peace initiatives many of his colleagues recommended in 1915; he was not for letting Germany off the hook; he was in no temper to treat with the kaiser who, after the war, he wished to hang. To have admitted publicly, by firing Haig, that his attacks in Flanders had been 'useless slaughter [where] men had been smothered in mud and blood' would have, at this stage of the war, stunned the British people, fed as they had been by misleading newspaper accounts and the specious rhetoric of soldiers and politicians alike. Repington, for example, felt that the man in the street was ignorant about the state of affairs at the front. 'The country has been chloroformed', he wrote in his diary.

As the months streamed by, however, though horrific details were still suppressed, the mood had changed. Labour unrest, rationing, dissatisfaction with conscription, the submarine onslaught, the example of Russia, whose army had disintegrated and turned against the state, were all ominous signs of what any reasonable man might consider possible for even a more stable Great Britain. The casualty figures were now such that every family in the empire realized that the situation was not propitious in any way. Haig's public removal would have undoubtedly sapped confidence in all facets of British public life, perhaps touching the royal house of Windsor itself. Lloyd George recognized the potent possibilities of popular discontent, Haig and Robertson less so. Civil unrest of any sort would have been treated by them as the tsar and his generals had in 1905 near the Winter Palace in St. Petersburg, where troops opened fire on demonstrators. By this point, of course, the tsar was a prisoner. But Haig was, if anything, 'old school'. He believed executions stiffened the army's resolve and discipline. The Australians, who forbade any executions of their soldiers, were soft in his opinion.

Arguments have been made that Lloyd George was never in danger of losing his position as prime minister, no matter what he did. Using the same rationale as regards Haig – there was no one better – could also be applied to Lloyd George. Who would have replaced him? Who constituted a threat to his leadership? All well and good that there was no one waiting in the wings, sufficiently popular, to supplant him (though his cabinet would have resigned and a new government be formed had he dismissed the generals). That being said, however, his job was certainly more nuanced and difficult than even that of the generals who showered him with their contempt. Their portfolio was simple: smash the Germans. Lloyd George's was significantly more difficult: smash the Germans by providing the generals with the men and material they constantly craved, while convincing the public that it was all worth it. Haig and Robertson had no genuine conception of this perplexing aspect of the prime minister's portfolio. His restraint, in fact, kept both these men in office when they no longer deserved to be there. Even Repington, a strong supporter of the army, noted the opinion that 'L.G.'s place in history may be higher than we thought, when all his difficulties are considered'. But as his cabinet secretary noted, there was a price to be paid. 'Ll. George has aged in the last twelve months. His hair has turned almost white.'

The Village

> *'The corps delivered the goods.'*
>
> Major-General Arthur Currie,
> Commander, Canadian Corps

With the rains coming down and the battlefield a sordid squalor, Plumer found that the backbone of his attacking forces, the Australians, were all done and incapable of any further effort. Haig continued to insist on the advance, no matter the odds or weather. That being the case, Plumer turned to the Canadians and their commander, Arthur Currie.

Currie had come a long way since his ghastly initiation to fire during the Second Battle of Ypres two years before, the first time artillery gas canisters had been used on the battlefield (initiating many more ghastly innovations, such as flame-throwers), a progression in ability that no one could have foreseen. Units on either side of Currie's positions had broken and run for it on that awful day, but nearly all the Canadians, despite the utter confusion of the moment, held their positions. Currie, however, had committed a breech of military etiquette when he left his post to secure reinforcements in the rear, the only course he felt open to him to prevent an impending rout. He was greeted in Ypres with a bitter harangue from a senior British general, who told him to 'get the hell out of here'. Currie did, but not before rounding up a few strays to fortify his line, which did not break in three days of bitter fighting. He soon became the epitome of the dominion officer: respectful of authority, willing to follow orders, but deeply resentful of British condescensions.

A Canadian militia officer before the war, Currie, had demonstrated no particular ability in any of the tasks assigned him on the home front. As a matter of fact, his career there held a great dark secret. In order to pay off debts accumulated in real estate speculations, he had misappropriated (a polite word) almost $10,000 from regimental funds, which he did not attempt to repay until it became obvious that he was making a name for himself on the western front. In the words of a biographer, Currie was a 'prewar nobody'.

A large man with an unsoldierly appearance (he was described as 'pear-shaped'), he did not inspire much of a reaction from anyone he met, whether general officer or ordinary soldier. He did not have the common touch, did not engender any particular affection and seemed a more or less stolid individual of no great imagination or style. His rhetoric, if issued to inspire the men during difficult times, produced the opposite effect. His letters and diaries rarely verge from the commonplace. Bumping into men during situations that required small talk produced nothing but clichés. But when the shells started flying, he found his calling. Whereas British officers at Second Ypres had viewed his withdrawal there as unprofessional, it in fact showed Currie for the soldier he would become. Seeing everything dissolve around him had not foisted in his brain the notion of retreating; rather it had spurred him to search for and implement solutions that might have a chance of working. He learned a great deal that day, both as a man and as an officer, refusing to be awed by either Germans or Englishmen.

As more troops from Canada and the other dominions continued to land in England and France, friction arose in areas of command and authority that continued to vex Haig and Robertson. They wanted these men integrated into other British units. They had no wish to see semi-independent battalions that insisted on fighting together and, more annoying, were less inclined to acknowledge British superiority in either ability or experience. Haig could not really believe it. The 'colonials' were 'ignorant' and 'conceited'; they needed the most rudimentary assistance to carry out operations and attacks. In 1915, only seven Canadian officers were deemed competent to handle staff work. At the bloody battle of Festubert in May 1915, 'The Canadians seldom were where they said they were. I had to send an aeroplane to look for them.' To Plumer, they were 'very cock-o'-hoop' men who 'know everything'. They needed a bloody nose to learn their lesson. Canadians, whether rank or file or officers, saw things differently. Leslie Frost, a young officer from Ontario, wrote home that 'I am in favour of the Canadian Expeditionary Force being run by Canadians. Imperial officers do not understand us and it will cause perpetual friction to have it go on. At the present time, our officers have the greatest respect for Irish and Scottish regiments but nothing but dislike for the English officers … who think we are backwoodsmen.' Political and actuarial realities led Haig to act more discreetly with these newcomers.

The various dominion prime ministers now had representatives in London (and often at the front) who were the eyes and ears of their governments. Haig had to assuage their growing lists of questions, concerns and often outright rebelliousness, which often taxed his powers of self-control, recognized by even his critics as the strong suit of his personality. (When two high-ranking Canadian officials visited him at GHQ –'well meaning but second-rate sort of people' – their complaints prompted a tirade from the normally composed field marshal. 'These remarks of mine at once made [them] shut up … I sent them off to start lunch, while I went upstairs and washed my hands.') Haig's casualty lists were so appalling, however, and his needs to fill up the ranks so imperative, that he swallowed his pride on many occasions just for the sake of getting bodies into the line. As a result, the Canadians learned from experience. By the time of Passchendaele, nearly all their administrative and staff positions were filled with fellow Canadians. At the top of the heap stood Currie, now commander in chief of the corps, some 100,000 troops. With this added honour came the added weight of his opinions.

Currie soon developed the growing reputation at GHQ of being 'a fighting general', and his men, as even Haig observed, now 'so smart and clean'.[25] The field marshal soon came to be one of Currie's strongest admirers. That does not mean the Canadian general wasn't difficult to deal with. He was. Stubborn and growingly opinionated, he objected to advancing on operations that guaranteed heavy losses or whose goals seemed unattainable. He refused to buy into the notion of dramatic breakthroughs, opting instead for 'bite and hold'. Above all, he would not do what Plumer, in frustration, had done during the early autumn of 1917, repeat attacks against entrenched enemy positions without adequate artillery support. Currie's equation was simple –

no artillery, no attack – and he was not afraid to say so. This should not blind anyone, in attempting to assess the character of World War I generalship, to regard a man like Currie as anything but what he was, a determined and tough officer. Casualties were acceptable to him if he had done all he could to guarantee that men under his command had a good chance of success. So long as he had done all that he humanly could, he had fulfilled his duty and was willing to shoulder the results, however messy. Losing men was inevitable in war, and the balancing act between what were tolerable losses, weighed against progress, if any, were always elements in his decision. This made him considerably different from a Gough or a Plumer who sometimes appeared indifferent. Gough, in fact, was such a loathful case of 'mad ideas', recklessness and 'derring-do' that Currie made it short and sweet to Field Marshal Haig: he refused to serve under Goughie's command. This sort of gall made a man like Haig wince, but he had no choice. He needed the self-confident Canadians more than they needed him. They had become one of the truly crack units under his command, the equivalent of the German *stosstruppen*, or stormtroopers. Currie and the corps were transferred to Plumer's Second Army, but, once there, Leslie Frost and his men caught a warning from an 'older and more experienced officer, who had been in the area before, [who] warned us not to be enthusiastic and said of all the places in the world, he would not want to leave his bones in Ypres'. In Frost's company of 226 men, 69 percent would end as casualties.

Canadians, while revelling in their reputation as the force of last resort, saw the other side of the coin as well. Some did not appreciate being the 'last and forlorn hope', and many were chagrined at the sheer slaughter that enveloped them. Canadian memoirs after the war often alternated between bravado and amazement that anybody, or anything, could survive the experience. 'We went through the works at the double', wrote one young officer. 'The Huns did not tarry when they saw the kilts and the bayonets coming.' Within a few sentences of all this comes something a bit different in tone. 'My company commander, Capt. Hutcheson, had both his eyes torn out by a splinter of a shell which landed between him and me. I was about three yards from the burst, but it only blew me into a shell-hole'. 'I'll never forget the 4th of October, 1917, when we went over the top', wrote another; 'seven of us had grown up together, went to school together, played soccer together, joined the army together and only two of us came out alive. That hurts.'

Currie was never so distant that he proved unaware of these tragedies, and when he was given the Passchendaele assignment, he was not happy. Currie, who had a temper, exploded when he heard the news. 'Passchendaele', he exclaimed. 'Let the Germans have it – keep in it – rot in the mud! There's a mistake somewhere. It must be a mistake. It isn't worth a drop of blood.' He predicted that the last 1,500 yards would cost 16,000 casualties. He was off by 346 men. When he went to see Haig, the field marshal grew opaque. 'Some day I will tell you why, but Passchendaele must be taken.' Currie never found out the real answer. Haig would later intimate that he had to relieve pressure from the French, whose dire state he meant to keep under wraps, and that's why he continued the drive, to keep the Germans occupied. The real answer seems more perverse: Passchendaele had become, like so many other largely symbolic objectives, a point of pride. Haig would not stop until he had it.

The weather by this time was consistent rain, the ground a perfect muck. Dry intervals were too short to effect any appreciable improvement in the terrain. 'The depth of a spade in that soil reached water', wrote one officer; 'splash and fill in'. It is said, perhaps apocryphally, that a general from GHQ actually made an appearance to take a look at the battlefield. 'Good God,' he is alleged to have said, 'did we really send men to fight in that?' Yes, time and time again.

Currie insisted on sufficient artillery to support a three-stage assault on Passchendaele village, each jump-off to win 500 yards, and to be separated by intervals of three to four days. The point of 'a creeping barrage' was for shelling to precede the advancing infantry. Calculations were based on how many yards the men could advance in certain predetermined increments. The ground was such a quagmire, however, that troops often 'lost' their coverage slogging through the bog of mud, and the artillery outraced them; or, in many instances, the full bore of cannon throw-weight could not be applied owing to the difficulty of effective and continuous fire. Many artillery pieces, after just a few rounds, found themselves either hopelessly befouled with mud or else driven into the muck by the force of their discharge. 'A' gun, according to artilleryman Ferguson, 'has sunk to a depth of three feet', and just shifting a piece from one firing spot to another became a logistical nightmare.

Passchendaele ridge was essentially won by individual pieces of heroism and small group actions. The gently rising slopes were a killing ground of machine gun nests and pillboxes that stood impervious to anything but a direct hit from a 'heavy'. The mud simply absorbed many shells like quicksand, the resulting explosions reminding some of underground volcanic eruptions. The fighting was vicious and sanguinary, each enemy strongpoint attacked individually, the position then consolidated, counterattacks repelled and the next pillbox approached in the same manner. The Canadian 85th (known as 'Novies' because they were from Nova Scotia), after slogging four miles single file – '"a long, long trail a-winding" but not to a land of pleasant dreams' – were thrown into the maw on 29 October, 'deeper and deeper in the tongue of a sharp bow or salient which had been steadily pushed by hard fighting into the German lines'. These men found themselves 'completely surrounded by fire; our own guns flashing in the back and those of the enemy on both sides'. With Lewis machine guns, trench mortars, Mills bombs and Lee-Enfields with bayonets affixed, they spent a grim week indeed approaching Passchendaele. The company history is a litany of bravado and heroism, and the first to fall were the officers. Twenty-three out of twenty-six company commanders were knocked out of action, thirteen killed. Captain McKenzie was shot through the stomach; Captain Christie, a bullet through his leg, was sitting at an aid station when a shell scored a direct hit, killing both him and his batman. In such dire circumstances, NCOs, then corporals, and in some cases privates took command of individual groupings of soldiers and continued the fight. 'Not a man faltered', according to the official history. Sergeant Alexander McDonald, wounded twice, refused to be moved to the rear. Only after being hit a third time was he evacuated, again, presumably, against his will. At one point a sweep was made of all previously non-essential Novies back in the rear: 'bandsmen, cooks, orderlies, batmen, hostlers, shoemakers, tailors, blacksmiths'. These men filled the diminishing ranks, and in so doing 'the honour of the 85th was sustained'. It is a notable statistic that during the war only one member of this regiment was ever captured by the enemy. One hundred and thirty-six died, 280 were wounded. After the action, Currie came himself to thank the 85th. Some may have thought to cheer their general but the entire unit, who had been gassed so often in the past week, were stricken with 'gas laryngitis' and temporarily had lost their voices. In all, nine Victoria Crosses were awarded to Canadian soldiers during this phase of the Passchendaele battle. The village was finally captured on 6 November 1917.

There is a legion of Canadian literature in the form of memoirs, diaries and letters home which describe the Passchendaele experience. None of it makes for cheerful reading, and at times seems almost monotonous given the similarity of impressions, the overriding of which could be summarized in a single sentence: 'We lived in the water'. Private Bill Hennings, a machine gunner, stressed the desert-like aspects of the terrain. 'The Germans looked right down on us. One day he looked down too close. Some German fighter plane dived on us with machine guns blazing. At the same time their artillery was directed our way. Inside of a couple of minutes we had almost six or seven casualties. What could we do? There was nowhere to run. There wasn't a tree left in the area. We had to wind our way in and out of our position in the trenches. There was a pillbox overlooking us. Otherwise there was no building at all.' Captain Walter Moorhouse bemoaned 'the absence of cover … everyone stumbled in the open. The bad footing lent a sort of aimlessness to one's gait and added to the general inanity of the scene. In no other campaign of the war was one so conscious of an insistent tone of helplessness.' Gunner Ferguson remembered thinking that 'this war is getting far too rough for me'. Passchendaele was a 'hell hole'. He didn't like the British either. He and his battery mates were thrown out of the bivouac they had created in a ruined laundry; they were replaced by horses. 'This last show was about the hardest due to the weather conditions, etc., that we ever engaged in', Major A. G. Moody wrote, 'and nothing but the indomitable pluck and grit of everyone in it got us through.... None of us will ever forget the Ypres salient.'

On 20 November, Haig formally ended the Passchendaele offensive (also known as the Third Battle of Ypres). He had not succeeded in capturing the entire ridge, so that in effect he was now looking at a salient protruding from a salient, a position his own staff condemned as an 'unsatisfactory defensive position'. Later in the war it would be abandoned without much of a fight. None of this prevented him from being 'as cocksure as ever'.

Could the battle plan have worked without the dreadful weather? Most historians doubt it. 'His plans', wrote one, 'required a drought of Ethiopian proportions to ensure success.'

Bernard Montgomery was disdainful of the Canadian effort. They had lost their minds, he thought, in the futile and bloodthirsty advance. It didn't matter to him who was giving the orders – Haig, Plumer or Currie – 'the whole art of war is to gain your objective with as little loss as possible'. He wrote to his brother that 'the Canadians are a queer crowd, they seem to think they are the best troops in France and that we have to get them to do our most difficult jobs .... I was disappointed in them. At plain straightforward fighting they are magnificent, but they are narrow-minded and lack soldierly instincts.'

Haig's two enormous campaigns in Flanders have generated nothing but controversy, and there will likely never be a 'last word' on the subject. Liddell Hart, a harsh critic, was most disappointed by the inability of general staff officers to recognize that anything had ever really changed in how to wage war. 'Battles, however great the scale', he wrote, 'had [usually] been a matter of hours. With the World War the standard became months – because the battles had usually become sieges, without being recognized or scientifically treated as such. Quantity does not imply quality. Long battles are bad battles.'

Chapter 10

Ireland: 'That sad, beautiful, bitch of a country'

'Ulster will fight, and Ulster will be right.'

Randolph Churchill (father of
Winston) 23 February 1886

In many ways Randolph Churchill had no right to compose these belligerent words, released in a public letter to whip up packs of howling Orangemen in 1886. He was not Irish, he had neither vast estates in that benighted country nor a long rent roll there of impoverished Catholic tenants from whom he could squeeze a shilling every month for a few spades of earth barely large enough for a pig and a garden. He was, in fact, playing politics, or what he called 'the Orange card'. William Gladstone, the great liberal, proved willing to enter into a pact with Satan himself, Charles Stewart Parnell, the latest in a long line of great patriots from Ireland who happened to be Protestant. The goal? Home Rule for Ireland, a bill Gladstone promised to introduce and support. For conservative nationalists, no matter where they lived in Britain or its dominions, Gladstone's various (and complicated) proposals were anathema, daggers to the heart of the imperial identity, and a betrayal of three centuries of history. The diehard Protestant settlers first introduced *en masse* to the northern province of Ulster by James I in the seventeenth century were the bedrock of support for King and Country. No constituency in Britain was more loyal, more steadfast, more willing to draw their swords than these hard men. The very idea of Ireland set adrift from the control of London, and thereby falling under the political sway of an overwhelmingly Catholic south (in other words, the pope) was not only blasphemy but treason. Churchill understood the passion, and preyed on it.

Gladstone never managed to pass Home Rule, but liberal legislation was enacted that oversaw an immense transfer of property in Ireland, from landlords (many absentee) to peasant farmers, which had been for most of the later nineteenth century a key goal of Irish nationalist thought, agitation and political action. The great dynasties of Anglo-Irish landlordism began an irreversible drift into financial ruin and irrelevance, a trend bitterly resented and fought. At the forefront was a talented, emotional and dogged advocate,

Edward Carson, born in Dublin but, on his mother's side, a Lambert from County Galway, a background as stereotypical as it was entertaining. Fox-hunting, the Big House, small Protestant chapels tucked into the corner of baronial estates, education at Trinity College (Protestant, naturally), elaborate winter soirées at Dublin Castle, the epicentre of British power in Ireland – all these were treasured aspects of an elite lifestyle that would, with any kind of political concession to papal 'Celts', inevitably lose its pre-eminence. During the Land League agitations that convulsed Ireland as the nineteenth century drew to its close, Carson, as a crown attorney in Ireland, fought rearguard actions against those who would overthrow the system and way of life that he treasured. He even defended the Fifteenth Earl of Clanricard, known by the nickname Clanrackrent, who was probably the worst landlord not only in County Galway, where he held vast estates, but in the entire island. In doing so, Carson earned the hatred, but never the contempt, of his opponents. They all knew him for the intelligent and stalwart man that he was, though that hardly saved him from being the target of nationalist doggerel:

> Sir Edward Carson had a cat
> That stood upon a stool,
> And every time it caught a mouse
> It shouted: No Home Rule!

Carson was first and foremost an Irishman, something that must never be forgotten when discussing the complicated question of Irish nationalism. The fact that he and his ilk (Yeats being a prominent exception) did not savour the mythic past of Celtic totems such as Cú Chulainn and Queen Maeve, or wallow in the garish sentimentality (as they saw it) of Deirdre of the Sorrows, did not mean they loved their native land any less for ignoring them. They had heroes too (William of Orange, for one), but their affections were far wider than that: the pantheon of traditional British notables whom they reverenced no less deeply, the Wellingtons and Nelsons of a glorious past. They saw, unlike their Catholic brethren, little distinction between loyalty to Britain and loyalty to the land of their birth. The two were one, indivisible. Home Rulers saw it differently: they wanted a free and independent Ireland and, despite all their talk to the contrary, looked forward to the day, with great relish, when they could return the favour, and turn the screws into their Protestant counterparts in the same fashion as they had endured since the seventeenth century. Men like Carson knew that all too well.[1]

As the battle for Home Rule intensified, Carson took a central role, however complicated it became for him to rationalize. Carson was a figure torn in multiple directions. The man of 'the Big House' could find no legitimate or powerful political support from his own societal base, decreasing in influence with each passing land bill, forcing him (in his Irish context) to rely on unionists from the north, in Ulster, for whom temperamentally he had no particular affection. Their intransigence and utter inability to even countenance the word 'compromise' was not a rigidity that he found appealing, no matter his own belief in 'eternal standards'. Overarching everything was his fierce loyalty to the British Empire. Unlike the rabble of Catholic Ireland, which detested just about everything to do with imperial Britain (no matter how many Irishmen had fought and died over the centuries towards its establishment and spread), Carson was devoted to it with it every fibre in his body. Home Rule was conceptually alien to him. What was Ireland without Britain? What it deserved to be, a parochial backwater.

Many contemporaries did not see the situation in such terms. The astute political commentator A. G. Gardiner felt Carson was really a man without any centre. 'The dawn is up in Ireland, but he will not yield to it', he wrote. 'He prefers to go down in the darkness…. His sincerity is the sincerity of the fanatic, but his passion is not the passion of patriotism, for he has no country. He has only a caste. He does not fight for Ireland; he does not even fight for Ulster; he fights for a Manchu dynasty.' This point of view had merit, if perhaps too subtle given the primal passions that each side brought to bear on this issue.

Although not from the north of Ireland, Ulster became Carson's central power base. Protestants in the south, his own kind, were too feeble to threaten anyone, but the demographics in Ulster were entirely different. Protestants ruled the roost in the north, and the sympathies of London generally lay in their direction. Only the contortions of English politics could change the equation and in 1910, unfortunately for Ulster, such became the case. Herbert Asquith, a liberal trying to form a government, found he could not do so without the support of the Irish nationalist members of parliament (mostly Catholic, and led by two able and tested parliamentarians, John Redmond and John Dillon); without their votes, Asquith could not proceed. The concession extracted by Redmond, in the tradition of Parnell, was Home Rule. Members of parliament from Ulster, who were always in the conservative camp, were of course diametrically opposed to any of this. As a newspaperman said, they rarely if ever were inclined to leave their 'Tory cave'.

Describing political alterations in the ebb and flow of this divisive controversy would not advance our narrative here in a constructive fashion. It is a complicated story, to say the very least, and has been well documented by many learned academics. Ireland was the pig's knuckle that no one could swallow. It remained an indigestible item so wrapped in discord, bitterness, religious bigotry and copious amounts of bloodshed that the notion of give and take became a black joke, as well as the termination of more than one promising political career. As Redmond said to C. P. Scott, the sympathetic editor of the *Manchester Guardian*, to propose an idea to Carson that the other might even listen to, or vice versa, was a recipe for political suicide. It was an irony not lost on just about anybody that the British Empire could fight a controversial and at times humiliating war with the Boers in South Africa between 1899 and 1902, yet grant that colony full powers of self-government only eight years later. A similarly smooth transition for Ireland, however, was out of the question. In Redmond's opinion, only a course of action 'IMPOSED' on both parties by London could work. That meant, as he implied, coercion, and Carson was not about to be coerced by anyone, even the king of England, to say nothing of Herbert Henry Asquith.

Asquith was not the man of the moment in this situation, as the sequence of events since known as the Curragh Mutiny demonstrated. In March 1914, in a series of confused and highly charged contretemps, officers in the British army camp at the Curragh, outside Dublin, essentially revolted en masse. Led by General Hubert Gough, referenced earlier in this narrative, 57 officers, mostly of Irish birth, unequivocally stated they would resign rather than lead any punitive expedition north meant to impose Home Rule by force on Ulster. Gough and a delegation were ordered to London where Sir John French, also familiar to readers from earlier chapters, proceeded to muddle and confuse the situation even further. Asquith attempted to rein in the malcontents and impose some sort of order and discipline into the round of meetings that ensued, but the impression that onlookers, the press and, (most importantly) Irishmen across the Irish Sea came away with, was that threats from London to force Ulster into anything were a dead letter. Gough returned to Ireland a hero to his men; he was cheered as he re-entered the Curragh camp. Carson was delighted.

One month later, the turmoil was exacerbated by a major provocation staged by Carson and his unionist allies, a gun-running operation that landed 25,000 rifles and ammunition in the seaside town of Larne, just a few miles north of Belfast. Carson's angry rhetoric, described by a reporter as 'so crude, so raw', heated the atmosphere almost to boiling point. He seemed to be encouraging an armed rebellion … what most people would consider treason. The landing and distribution had gone unimpeded by local police forces, suggesting to Catholics and anyone else interested in the subject that Britain had actually approved of the operation. Not only was Home Rule categorically rejected, but also the only plausible compromise, the exclusion of northern counties from its proposed jurisdiction. In response, two private yachts, one piloted by Erskine Childers of literary fame (*The Riddle of the Sands*) did the same thing at Howth, outside Dublin, to aid the nationalist cause. 'I think an Orangeman with a rifle a much less ridiculous figure than the Nationalist without [one]', as Patrick Pearse said, even if the rifles in question, only 900 antique Mausers, were offloaded more as a publicity stunt than anything else. The point was: if Ulster was going to arm itself, so would the south. A group of Scottish soldiers who responded were pelted with stones and heckled by a crowd fast assembling; they grew tired of that and opened fire, killing three civilians and wounding three score more. One unarmed man was bayoneted to death. Asquith dithered, as usual, trying to find some middle course. The dilemma was acute. In parliament, he was mocked by Tories. Ulster has behind it 'the God of Battles', one cried. 'I say to the Prime Minister, "Let your armies and your batteries fire! Fire if you dare! Fire and be damned!"' Asquith cringed, but in one of the great ironies of the period, World War I landed on his doorstep and saved him.

'When Pearse summoned Cuchulain to his side.'

William Butler Yeats

As the summer 1914 advanced, Ireland was on everyone's minds in the halls of parliament, the opinion pages of newspapers all over Britain and in nearly every community hall, parish council room and local bar in Ireland, to say nothing of the next parish over (meaning America). Kaiser Wilhelm's preparations for war, the noisy threats emanating from Vienna, events in a town called Sarajevo that most people had never heard of, paled in comparison to what was happening in Ireland. In Asquith's cabinet meetings, as Winston Churchill related, the ministers were stuck 'in tedious and bewildering debate', toiling 'around the muddy byways of Fermanagh and Tyrone'. They were deadlocked and vulnerable, since neither side in the Irish debate would give an inch or relent its pressure. People all over that country were arming, the integrity of the army had been undermined and civil war seemed imminent. 'Ulster will fight, and Ulster will be right'. Churchill's father might have said it two decades before, but in Carson's mind it now seemed inevitable, whether he wanted it or not. The entire situation was a proverbial tinderbox. Woodrow Wilson, at the Paris Peace Conference four years later, said the solution to the entire mess was a simple one, though a step he knew Asquith did not have the courage to take. Edward Carson, he said, should have been arrested, tried for treason and hanged. 'The problem', he said, would then 'have been very materially solved'. Instead of which, as Carson's career trajectory proved, he was essentially embraced, appeased and placed at the epicentre of power. His reward, if you want to call it that, was a place in Asquith's cabinet (as attorney general – what, support the law?); and later on, a place in Lloyd George's cabinet (first lord of the Admiralty). Roger Casement was executed as a traitor for pretty much doing what Carson had done in 1914; Casement went to the scaffold at Pentonville Prison, Carson died in his bed nineteen years later.

World War I not only destroyed over 49,000 Irishmen, approximately a quarter of all who signed up during the war, it also annihilated any constitutional hope of solving the Irish conundrum. Asquith squirmed off the Irish hook, convincing Redmond that if his constituency held off agitating for Home Rule, and totally supported Britain in the developing war, then some sort of semi-independent or dominion status would be guaranteed after the end of hostilities (as Yeats put it in his poem 'Sixteen Dead Men', 'You say that we should still the land/Till Germany's overcome').[2] Redmond agreed, more or less spontaneously, to the amazement of his many supporters. 'He swore Ireland to loyalty as if he had Ireland in his pocket', as the writer James Stephens put it. 'He pledged Ireland to a particular course of action, and he had no authority to give this pledge, and he had no guarantee that it would be met.' Redmond, in other words, had let his emotions get the better of him, encouraging Irishmen to join up and serve the king. (John Dillon would have none of that, telling Lord Kitchener, who lusted for men wherever he could get them, that he would not become a recruiting sergeant.) Carson also chimed in, freely committing Ulster to the war effort. Those 25,000 rifles and ammunition landed at Larne would be used against Germans, not fellow Irishmen.

But whereas the Ulster commitment was genuine, that of the south was soft. Radicals at home were dissatisfied with Redmond. Glacial progress for Home Rule, his easy life in London hobnobbing with duplicitous English politicians (he used to 'take the waters' at the Pump Room in Bath!), all left a sour taste in the mouths of men impatient for change. Dying for Britain seemed a poor bet indeed to achieve the long-sought-for freedom that was perennially out of reach. Shouldn't the great European war be used to Ireland's advantage? Distracted, in a fight for its survival, its gaze on Flanders, wasn't this the time to stab Britain in the back, in its moment of weakness? Members of Sinn Féin (from the Irish, 'We Ourselves'), at first an obscure semi-underground organization but now a public alternative to Redmond's Nationalists, began asking these difficult questions. At first, no one paid them much mind – Dillon called the early leaders of this bunch 'fools and mischief-makers' – and looking over their roster, and the backgrounds of other notable separatists, what were they indeed? Arthur Griffith (journalist); Éamon de Valera, Patrick Pearse, Thomas MacDonagh (all teachers); Eoin MacNeill (university professor); Thomas Clarke (shopkeeper and perennial political prisoner); James Connolly (Marxist, labour leader). These were not people who commanded the interest of Herbert Asquith or anyone else of importance in London. But Redmond did sense their threat, and vied for control of the military organization that Sinn Féin began putting together, but he felt secure that he could control things. The Easter Rising of 1916 caught him flat-footed. In just a matter of weeks he would become little better than a footnote to Irish history, something he never expected.

'We serve neither king nor kaiser.'

Banner placed by James Connolly outside
his union headquarters in Dublin.

Although war news from the front distracted Asquith (as much as he could be distracted), Ireland remained a weighty concern, enough so that he handed off its resolution to the more energetic David Lloyd George. Lloyd George tried to hammer out a specified schedule for Home Rule, and a laundry list of specifics (or generalities when the items were too touchy) about what the future relationship might be between the two islands, but fairly quickly all such talks collapsed. On 10 May 1915, Frances Stevenson recorded that Lloyd George had had enough. 'I've *done* with Ireland', he said. Asquith wouldn't leave it at that. The next question was universal conscription, one of the most volatile of all issues (except, perhaps, Lloyd George's passionate campaign against that great devil, drink). The demands for more manpower seemed to make enforced conscription a necessity. Recruitment in southern Ireland, for instance, was not doing well. 'Remembering Belgium and its broken treaty led Irishmen to remember Limerick and its broken treaty', wrote George Bernard Shaw.[3] Were Redmond's pleas being ignored? Were Sinn Féin agitators making headway out in the countryside, arguing that recruits were being duped, that conscription, if it came, was a purposeful

British strategy to thin out the Irish? Asquith squirmed, but Lloyd George did not. Conscription was a dire necessity, he argued in parliament, and once England and Scotland were combed for fresh levies, so too would Ireland. Asquith congratulated his minister for not 'wetting his feet' when it came to delivering tough news, which is one reason Asquith would eventually fall and Lloyd George replace him. Conscription so roiled the Irish question that Dillon, at least, argued for more concessions. The substance of Home Rule now, he argued, not later. Events would rapidly outrun him.

The question of how to approach or even deal with Germany was debated back and forth in Dublin. Some were for active solicitation of military assistance, others said no; the very appearance of collaboration with the enemy would deeply offend moderates in the south and alienate any possible support in Ulster. 'Neither king nor kaiser', was James Connolly's opinion, which seemed the most implausible of all strategies. Could the Irish really shake off British rule without help? Could they realistically hope to defeat one of the great military powers of the world without foreign guns, foreign ammunition or foreign soldiers? Realists said of course not, but the future brains behind the Easter Rising were not realists, they were dreamers. Patrick Pearse was ready to die for Ireland, even happy to do so. He saw no chance of a military victory, and called the blood he intended to shed 'the red wine of the battlefield'. What he wanted was a public martyrdom. That was, after all, an act completely in tune with a Catholic vision of this world. Sir Roger Casement thought so as well, and he wasn't even Catholic.

Casement

Banna Strand on Good Friday 1916

'Both mad and bad.'

T. P. O'Connor, Irish member
of parliament, on Roger Casement

Of all the beauty spots in Ireland, a country with an abundance of them, Banna Strand in County Kerry stands out as one of the more special, seven miles of pristine beachfront facing the Atlantic, bordered by high dunes covered with wind-driven sea grass. Rarely have I seen it in a placid state, or as a suitable place to go sunbathing or swimming. More often than not it is a tempestuous scene indeed. On Good Friday 1916, Roger Casement landed on Banna Strand in pitch darkness with two comrades, launched from a German submarine offshore. 'Landed' is something of a misnomer; in actuality, they were thrown ashore in a wild wrack of waves when their small launch was overturned. Wet, miserable, shivering, they struggled along a slimy outlet stream until climbing up on a dune, a rampart actually, the remnant of an ancient Celtic earthwork known as MacKenna's fort. Casement's companions separated from him there. One tried to sink the boat so as not to leave a trace of their arrival, but could not, then joined the other to search out the nearby town of Ardfert to find help. They needed to get to Dublin as soon as possible, to ward off catastrophe. The projected rebellion was doomed; it was their goal to stop it.

It is difficult to say whether the Easter Rising, if all had gone as planned, could have succeeded. Probably not is the reasoned answer, but it certainly would have come off better if circumstances, communication and just plain luck had played out more in the rebels' favour than that of His Majesty's imperial forces. In the end, however, the failure of the rebellion actually furthered the cause far more than a prolonged bout of combat (actual hard street fighting in Dublin lasted only four days). Pearse was right: martyrdom was just the ticket to success, and the English played right into his hands.

In terms of bad luck, the unfortunate experiences of Roger Casement revolved around the morning of his return to Ireland on that Good Friday, three days before the rebellion was to begin. He and his compatriots on the *U-19* were not the only German presence that night off the wild coast of the south-west of Ireland. The plan had been to land in tandem with a separate freighter, the *Aud*, dispatched from Lübeck with a cargo hold full of guns and ammunition. What followed was a comedy of errors. No one was around at the right time and the right place to greet the *Aud*. Prearranged signals of flashing green lights were misunderstood, ignored or just plain missed. A car with two telegraph experts, intended to commandeer a British wireless station, botched a turnoff, went down a lonely country road and drove straight into the Atlantic from a fish pier, drowning everyone inside. What could be worse? Only a lonely penitent walking along a deserted beach in the middle of the night, pondering the state of his soul and the impending resurrection of Jesus Christ. This man found the boat that Casement had used to reach shore from *U-19*. He ran off to inform the local constabulary. Only in Ireland could such a confluence of circumstances so affect the course of history.

Roger Casement, at first sight, did not seem to be a man who might involve himself in such a harebrained venture. Born to a respectable Northern Irish Protestant family, he had served the crown in various consular posts in remote parts of the world. Dogged, principled, a man with a full and generous heart, he became embroiled on two separate occasions with the dreadful plight of indigenous peoples reduced to near slavery in first, the Belgian Congo (King Leopold II again), and then along the Amazon in South America.[4] The atrocious conditions endured by the gatherers of a natural latex (the sap of a particular species of trees, then boiled down, reduced and processed into rubber) were of such extreme cruelty that the commissions that Casement either participated in or led could not at times believe the testimony and evidence they assiduously gathered, which often made Harriet Beecher Stowe's *Uncle Tom's Cabin* seem a nursery rhyme. Casement's sense of justice resonated from these obscure corners of the world, where his health grew uncertain and his emotions scrambled, igniting the social conscience of Britain which, giving credit where it is due, has often been aroused in that great country where issues of human dignity and essential freedoms have been invoked. For his work Casement was knighted in 1911; at about the same time he became involved (some might say mired) in the rhapsodic world of Celtic myth and romance. These revolved around the Irish language revival, a topic where Sir Roger grew passionate (he could neither read nor write it, however), which with effortless ease grew entangled with the political struggle for Irish independence, radicalizing him in ways many of his friends could not understand.

When war broke out in 1914, Casement became a fervent Germanophile: the kaiser was a great and misunderstood man, Ireland's salvation lay in Berlin and so on. He helped to organize and finance the Howth gun-running operation, and in 1915 took the dangerous course of travelling to Germany as the semi-official representative of Sinn Féin. His mission was to obtain guns and men; the guns were the easy part, more or less, the men less so. In an act that could only be described as treason, Casement arranged for the Germans to segregate Irish prisoners of war from their British comrades. In a specially designated camp, Casement then tried to persuade volunteers to return with him to fight for Ireland in the anticipated rebellion. He had expected to recruit hundreds, but only fifty-two signed on. His reception, in fact, had been a startling revelation. Most of these Irishmen were army 'lifers', many born in the slums of Britain's industrial cities, Liverpool, Manchester, Glasgow and the like. They were not conscripts, nor were they the impressionable young men who were then rushing to join Kitchener's New Army. They were 'regulars' to whom the British Army was home. These POWs jeered, hurled abuse at Sir Roger and at times he was manhandled. 'These were not Irishmen, but English soldiers', he complained. 'All they wanted was tobacco.' German support turned tepid when they saw no groundswell of support, as Casement had promised, a humiliating denouement. An English woman married to a German aristocrat spelled it out for him in Berlin. The Irish cause was nothing to the Germans. 'I told him that Ireland was like a little terrier biting at the heels of two great mastiffs.' The army finally offered 20,000 rifles, Russian models salvaged from the battleground at Tannenberg, to be sent over in the tramp streamer *Aud*, and a submarine to return Casement to Ireland, but nothing more. If the Sinn Féin leaders in Dublin were depending on German support for ultimate success, it wasn't coming. Casement, despondent, realized he had to return home, not to join the rebellion but to prevent it from breaking out.

What he did not understand was that the success of his mission had become immaterial. A split within the leadership of those planning the revolt, about which Casement knew nothing, had rendered his role meaningless. As Easter Week approached, the mainstream commanders of the Irish Volunteers, men like Eoin MacNeill, grew hesitant and indecisive. Should the operation be 'a go' or not. At almost the last moment, MacNeill decided 'no', and issued orders accordingly. What he did not realize was that zealots like Pearse, Clarke, Connolly and others were determined to proceed no matter what, in manic desperation. About eighty percent of the projected rebel force obeyed orders and stayed home on Easter Monday; those who did turn out occupied central Dublin, the rebel headquarters being the magnificent General Post Office on Sackville Street.[5] By the time Pearse began the rebellion, however, reading a passionately written declaration in front of the post office, Casement was already under arrest, and his doom foretold.[6] Constables had tracked him down at MacKenna's fort, his responses to questions posed him were incoherent or contradictory and a crumpled ticket from a Berlin train was found in his pocket (incriminating, to say the least). It did not take much time for Casement to throw in the towel. He was a rebel, he admitted it. By Sunday he was in England, imprisoned in that storied bastion of repression, the Tower of London, a place that people accused of treason rarely left alive. It was not until after ten days that he was given a clean set of clothing. In all that time he wore the same gear he had landed in at Banna Strand, caked with salt water, grime and mud, one of the most humiliating homecomings to the ould sod ever witnessed. On his way, in handcuffs and looking bedraggled, he was spat on by women in the street as his convoy drove through Tralee. Their menfolk were fighting in Flanders; they let Sir Roger know how they felt.

As for the *Aud*, British patrol boats soon rounded it up. Approaching Queenstown in County Cork, under escort as it were, the *Aud*'s captain blew a hole in its hull and abandoned ship.

❦

Executions

John Dillon: 'A bloody ruffian.'
Lloyd George: 'No, a bloody ass.'

An exchange over the behaviour of
British General Sir John Maxwell

The real fighting in Dublin began on the Wednesday of Easter Week, when a British gunboat and other artillery pieces began bombarding rebel positions. It took just a day for many of the uprising's leaders to recognize the inevitable – in the words of one, 'It's a hopeless case.' The rebel holdouts, now isolated from one another, were subjected to everything the British army had, from grenades to artillery shells firing shrapnel and incendiary shells, to incessant machine gun fire. The GPO caught fire, as did adjacent buildings. The centre of Dublin was now, in the truest sense, turning into a pile of rubble. Patrick Pearse, having achieved his goal (or so he thought), called the whole thing off on the Saturday. He was wise to give up the struggle when he did. The GPO, its roof about to cave in, had had to be abandoned. In their flight, the rebels were astonished at the state of downtown Dublin, now in ruins. About the only thing still standing was Nelson's Pillar.[7] Had it been worth it? Of course it was worth it, he rationalized to a comrade, but it would take time for the nation to soak it all in. 'After a few years people will see the meaning of what we tried to do.' Pearse was wrong about that. The moment his body was riddled with bullets from a firing squad on 3 May, his deification began, far ahead of schedule. A previously obscure and unknown teacher of the Irish language, he soon emerged, with the sanctity of a choirboy, as a fallen angel. According to an Irish member of parliament, miracles were soon attributed to his intervention, and those of others brutally executed. They were no longer foolish boys who had caused unnecessary death and destruction; they were no longer traitors who had betrayed their own; they were no longer socialists, anarchists or syndicalists. They were heroes.

Pearse and the others, probably no more than 1,500 men and boys, had been overwhelmed by British forces that soon came to number almost 20,000, three-quarters of whom had been rushed over the Irish Sea from Britain (many of these, green conscripts, had no idea they were going to Ireland; when they disembarked outside Dublin, many thought they were in France); among their officers was the new commander in chief, General Sir John Maxwell. Asquith had declared martial law for Ireland, and Maxwell was to be the military governor. Just the previous month, Maxwell had been finishing a lengthy tour of duty in Egypt, overseeing the transport of troops to and from Gallipoli and defending the Suez Canal from a Turkish invasion. What qualified him to step in the middle of an immensely more complicated situation has never been satisfactorily explained. Perhaps he was the only senior general available who had not as yet disgraced himself in the muck of Flanders. One member of parliament described him as 'a wooden-headed soldier full of stupid little airs'.

With more or less absolute power, Maxwell operated in a vacuum, some of it his own making given his limited intellectual capacity. He received no real direction from Asquith. Despite having served in Ireland for several months, beginning in 1902, he had no genuine familiarity with the local political scene, its major participants, whom he could trust and whom he could not; nor any background on why the rebellion took place or the most prudent way to handle its aftermath. He was a soldier, pure and simple, sent to Dublin to clean up the mess as quickly as possible. Known to his friends as Conky, Maxwell's mind was a blank; military matters were what concerned him, any nuance could be left to others. Unfortunately for British policy, the 'others' (such as Asquith) wanted to be removed from the equation, left alone. Maxwell, 'left alone', then proceeded to bungle the entire situation. His approach was simplified by a single thought: Ireland was not to be treated with a velvet glove.

Order was soon restored. Looting had been widespread throughout Dublin, with many arbitrary street-side executions by soldiers reported. Civilian deaths were disproportionately high, and several unarmed constables had been dispatched by the rebels (Countess Constance Markievicz, one of the more histrionic rebels, allegedly killed one of these with three bullets in the head, gleefully shouting 'I shot him! I shot him!'). Bodies had to be gathered up and buried, over a thousand prisoners were in captivity, the police were rounding up and interning a few thousand more, the state of the countryside was still uncertain. Hasty trials were convened for 'these infernal rebels' under the auspices of martial law, from which over ninety death sentences were passed. It was up to Maxwell to decide how to proceed with these. On 3 May, he authorized three executions. According to his daughter, who commissioned a lachrymose biography of her father, published after his death in 1929, Maxwell agonized over signing the warrants. Perhaps this explains the greatest mistake he made, dragging out the process over nine days, in dribs and drabs as it were, as eleven more were shot ('a fresh batch each morning for breakfast', as Lloyd George's private secretary complained – 'intolerable!'). Crowds gathered outside dreary Kilmainham Jail, waiting to hear the latest news about loved ones or friends. This soot-begrimed holdover from a less enlightened past, a goal where Irish patriots from Emmet to Parnell had been imprisoned, seemed a brute reminder of evil times long thought past. The ominous carvings over the main portico, serpents (meaning traitors) stinging themselves to death, did not hold much hope for those who craved it, milling about in dispirited groups before the gate.

The executions themselves were tawdry affairs, by British standards, on top of the drumhead trials. Kilmainham Jail, which had been closed six years before, was a filthy mess. Soldiers running amuck had at first brutalized some of the prisoners, and the final meetings of those condemned and their loved ones were often unsympathetically arranged and supervised. When Connolly was killed, the last of the executions in Dublin (though no one at the time knew it was to be the last), he had to be strapped to a chair, so serious had been his wounds from the GPO that he could not walk. The entire back of the chair was disintegrated by the volley from his execution squad. By contrast, the dignity, selflessness, patriotism, religious piety and courage of those shot soon became propaganda fodder for the nationalist press. It did not help that Maxwell had all the bodies dumped in grave pits and covered with lime, which outraged many people not at first sympathetic to the Rising. But Maxwell was right on this issue: individual funerals with their inevitable orations, the solemnity of religious services, the burial processions and continued sagas of wives and children spilling tears by the gravesides were scenes to be avoided.

And so the Irish Rising, like all the rebellions in that country's troubled past, was quelled in blood ... in real blood, as James Stephens put it, who was stunned seeing dead bodies lying in the streets of Dublin. While reaction to the entire business was mixed, everyone at least was united by the shock of it all. Carson called the rebellion 'a nail through his heart'. What came after, according to Shaw in the preface of his short play *O'Flaherty V.C.*, was stereotypically British, 'the usual childish petulance' that undoes in one week a century's worth of goodwill. Some Ascendancy types, such as Frederick Wrench, were discomforted that the 'old spirit and friendship' that he had enjoyed with his Catholic tenantry 'vanished overnight'. He couldn't understand it. On the day of the Rising, he had just sold a short horn bull for 900 guineas in the grounds of the Dublin Horse Show. How could life be better? That a few fools had 'come out' didn't bother him until he saw Sackville Street a few days later. The staunchly conservative *Irish Times* saw no reason to criticize Maxwell – the more executions the better ('martial law has come to a blessing for us all', it editorialized; John Dillon considered its stance 'bloodthirsty and wicked'). But to the traditional Home Rulers, all they saw was disaster, not only from the Rising itself but from Maxwell's heavy-handed response. Dillon in particular was aghast. Not only was Home Rule, which he had seen crawl within inches of becoming law, blown to pieces, but his own career stood to be a shambles as well. C. P. Scott had 'never seen a man look so black with suppressed passion'. In a speech riddled with anger and emotion to the House of Commons on 11 May, when it seemed that Maxwell would never cease with his firing squads, Dillon nearly lost control of himself. 'This is a horrible business', he said. The Irish rebels, 'duped', 'foolish' and 'misguided' though they were, had fought bravely against overwhelming odds, and should be treated as prisoners of war, not cattle-driven to the slaughter house. After four years of bloody civil war in America, Abraham Lincoln had not seen fit to hang a single 'traitor', yet in the present instance 'there is no government in Ireland' and the prime minister was content to leave it that way. 'You are doing everything conceivable to madden the Irish population and to spread insurrection.' As for the rebels, 'I am proud of their courage, and if you were not so dense and so stupid, as some of you English people are, you could have had them fighting for you, and they are men worth having.'

> In this rebellion, for the first time in the history of Ireland, at least nine out of ten of the population were on the side of the government. Is that nothing? It is the first time in the history of Ireland where you had a majority on your side. It is the fruit of our work [i.e. the Home Rulers]. We have risked our lives hundreds of times to bring about the result. We have been held up to odium as traitors by those men who made this rebellion, and now you are wasting our whole life work in a sea of blood.... This series of executions is doing more harm than any English in this house can possibly fathom.... I do most earnestly appeal to the prime minister to stop these executions now.... When we complain, what is [his] answer? We must rely on the well-known high character of Sir John Maxwell.... Talk about the well-known high character of Sir John Maxwell? I confess that I have never heard of him before in my life!

As was usual in parliamentary debate, many of Dillon's remarks were greeted with jeers and heckling, and James Connolly, with a comrade, were shot the next day. But Asquith was suitably alarmed that he left for Dublin on 12 May; after his inspection trip, he proposed that Home Rule not be delayed but put on the statute books immediately. The spat of executions in Ireland were finally stopped, though Asquith's wife complained 'not at all too many for what they have done'. That left Roger Casement, and the problem of what to do with him.

'Sun 27. Returned to Buenos Aires. At Station & sailors again.'

Roger Casement, diary entry 1910

Roger Casement (his 'Sir' was stripped from him on 30 June 1916) was the only leader of the rebellion formally tried in a real court of law, in front of a jury, represented by counsel and allowed to make a public statement, dutifully recorded by press accounts, before being condemned to death. Casement's mental state, given the stress of the preceding few weeks, led to a muddled defence strategy that focused on semantic interpretations of treason that baffled most observers and seemed to widely miss the point regarding his intent and subsequent actions, which might have curried more sympathy than he ended up receiving. The verdict, preordained, was followed by the sentence, also preordained. The question became: would mercy be extended to a man of known humanitarian worth, whose values and career deserved some respect in the final analysis and, after all, a reprieve might in some way be a valuable sop to public opinion in John Bull's Other Island. The answer to that question was a resounding no.

The atmospherics of war news from France and Belgium undoubtedly hardened people's hearts in Britain. The whole Easter Rising was considered to be a German plot, those involved in it had betrayed their country in its moment of supreme danger and Zeppelins were dropping bombs on London creating, in the words of one historian, a 'ferocious public mood'. Casement could go to hell. To make sure he did, British authorities resorted to the gutter. In their sweep of Casement's lodgings, they came across the infamous 'Black Diaries', so called to distinguish them from the 'White Diaries', a more or less contemporaneous journal that Casement meant to be 'official', or what he intended as factual notations that would be the basis of formal governmental reports necessitated by his investigatory expeditions in distant colonial countries. The 'Black Diaries' were something more, personal notes on all sorts of everyday events which included, unfortunately for Casement, numerous references to homosexual activity. These were not only undeniably graphic ('Deep Screw & to hilt', 'saw Andokes bathing. Big <u>thick one</u>, as I thought' and so on), but deeply predatory (love, for instance, never reared its romantic head). Casement, hitherto considered to be a pillar of society, was revealed to be an insatiable habitué of a dark and seamy underbelly, trolling through public parks after nightfall for sailors, waiters, hustlers or anyone who would take his money for illicit sex. In Africa and South America, these unsavory obsessions were compounded by the clearly stated fact of his desire for young attractive boys, and his corruption of them seemed especially heinous, akin to something known today as 'sexual tourism'.

For a full half-century and longer, controversy has concentrated on the theory that the 'Black Diary' entries were forged. There seems little academic doubt today, however, regarding their authenticity. Casement was a practising homosexual, often voracious in his appetites and, stereotypically, deeply ambivalent and guilt-ridden about his 'terrible disease'. What certainly is not disputed is the use to which these private notes were applied, to blacken Casement's reputation and to douse any groundswell of support for a pardon or commutation. Copies were made, passed around like a dirty magazine (surreptitiously, in private, 'in confidence') to anyone deemed important enough to see them. It shut their mouths pretty quickly, and suppressed any urge to add a helping hand to the defendant who was not only a traitor, but now revealed as a hardcore sex offender.

It is difficult at times to think of Edwardian England as naïve, despite High Anglican cant to the contrary. People are people, sex is sex, and homosexuality has never been exactly unknown. But it may be a fact that an individual's particular response to proof of homosexual behaviour in that era required, by public necessity, shock and outrage. If they were not appalled, why not? Were they deviant too? John Redmond, when shown excerpts from the diaries, perhaps reacted as he felt Catholic Ireland (and its bishops) expected him to. The Archbishop of Canterbury reacted as his position required: he refused to read them or even touch them, and had an underling do it for him.[8] George V? How could he behave otherwise; he was a family man, a role model for his country. Very few public figures could be expected to brush the news aside, as would certainly be the case in the twenty-first century. To those acquainted with Casement, the diaries were a complete surprise. Casement was no Oscar Wilde, wildly flamboyant and *outré*. Quite the contrary. Some of his defenders, such as Arthur Conan Doyle, felt these sordid notes were a manifestation that Casement was slightly insane, and a good argument for the commutation of his sentence. Very few others shared his opinion, and Casement was hanged on 3 August 1916 within the dreary confines of London's Pentonville Prison. A crowd of munitions workers gathered outside, and cheered when the prison bell rang, signifying that Casement was dead. Then it was back to the factory, win the war. A doctor was brought in to examine the corpse for signs of homosexual activity which, after examining the anus, he confirmed. Casement's friends were denied his body, which, instead, was buried in a sort of potter's field inside the prison walls in an unmarked grave. When I visited the place in 2001, courtesy of Her Majesty's Government, the yard was nicely landscaped with a pleasant green lawn. Perfect for a game of croquet. When Éamon de Valera was a prisoner here, he fell to his knees and prayed in this yard for the soul of Roger

Casement. The executioner was paid £2.22 for his work, but had to wait two weeks for the cash.

Once the diaries had done their job, they were removed from public view and filed away in sealed archives, quite a contrast to the earlier freedom of their passage from hand to hand. That officials were generously spreading their contents around was common knowledge to many observers outside the government. The *Times* noted on the day after Casement's death the widespread diffusion of 'inspired innuendo' that it considered 'irrelevant, improper and un-English'. It would have helped matters to publish this opinion on the day before Casement's death instead of the day after but the *Times*, along with many other publications, apparently felt the sentence was a just one no matter what. In fact, it might have better for all concerned if Casement 'had [just] been shot out of hand on the Kerry coast'.

Ireland has often had a problem with some of its heroes. Too often they have been Protestant, or strayed from the canons of Catholic morality. Wolfe Tone slashed his throat, a suicide, regarded as a mortal sin. The rumours about Casement never died away, and made his public rehabilitation sometimes problematical, especially in the ultra-conservative aura of the 1920s and '30s in Ireland. Nevertheless, he has always been well considered in the heroic literature of the Rising. In 1965, the British government finally acceded to the wishes of their counterparts in Dublin to return Casement's body to Ireland. He was reinterred in the hallowed ground of Republican Ireland, Glasnevin Cemetery in Dublin. De Valera, an old man of eighty-three, was sick in bed that miserable March day, and told to stay there, but he had not been called a 'man with a closed mind' for nothing. He had to be there, and he was, hat in hand, in the rain, to deliver the principal funeral oration. For the next several days, an estimated half a million people walked past the grave as a token of respect.[9]

Chapter 11

The Great War at Sea

'What was it that enabled Jack Johnson to knock out
his opponents? It was the big punch.'

Winston Churchill

F or ten weeks, beginning with the declaration of war in early August
1914, the world's attentions were largely focused on the evolving
fortunes of huge armies as they manoeuvred through both the Belgian
and French countrysides, as well as the eastern zones of conflict in faraway
Prussia. Millions of men were on the move, the battlefields were fluid, no
one was ever quite certain just what was going on and newspaper sales were
stupendous, however inaccurate their reporting.

For those of a reflective nature, or those with a strategist's eye, the major
unspoken anxiety revolved around what they were not hearing, namely any
information of a maritime nature. The great emotional high point of the
naval war was expected by both combatants to be an immediate Trafalgar, the
only question being how long it would take before the two fleets could build
up sufficient steam to hoist anchor and head off to sea for their confrontation.
This was to have been the climactic, head-to-head event, the moment of
truth as it were, the epochal, armour-piercing exchange of heavy guns that
so many naval officers on both sides had been anticipating and training for
during the preceding fifteen or so years. It was the logical denouement of
the world's most expensive and all-consuming arms race, and would either
make men heroes or send them to the bottom. No one had expected that this
deadly exchange would not take place for another two years, and when it did,
in the waters of the North Sea at what came to be called the battle of Jutland,
that it would end in a fog of confusion and stalemate.

For the German imperial fleet, anchored in Kiel on the Baltic and
Wilhelmshaven on the North Sea coast (linked by a sixty-one-mile-long
canal), the coming Armageddon was couched in some foreboding. Under the
leadership of the formidable Grand Admiral Alfred von Tirpitz, Germany had
deliberately challenged the world's greatest sea power, Britain, by embarking
on a stupendous programme of ship-building in 1898. Intensely nationalistic,
egotistical and skilled in the arts of bureaucratic in-fighting, von Tirpitz had

showed no restraint, his natural inclination always being to go for the throat. Given Britain's vast experience at sea and venerable pride in her maritime supremacy, he knew that only at huge cost and acrimonious political debate in Berlin could the goal be met, both of which he was prepared to tackle. As the naval 'race' progressed during the first decade of the century, with tensions persistently mounting, he was also aware of another grave challenge, the threat of which, again, was well within British naval tradition: would the imperial fleet be 'Copenhagened' in a pre-emptive attack, just as Nelson had done a century before in Danish waters? Von Tirpitz was willing to run that risk as well. And so he plied the corridors of the Reichstag pressuring politicians, distributing position papers, justifying expenses as they spiralled upwards in any number of annual naval bills and appropriations. The only impediment before him was a physical one, the capacity of the Kiel Canal, the great connector. In the earliest stages of this maritime competion, even Tirpitz could not imagine ships too big to pass through it.

One pillar of strength (yet also the source of continuous problems, many of an emotional nature) was the kaiser. If there was one thing Wilhelm II liked more than goose-stepping grenadiers or cavalry charges, it was the simultaneous barrage of heavy naval guns from a row of battlewagons steaming in formation. Von Tirpitz was an accomplished propagandist who knew what sent a thrill up the kaiser's spine. When the matter of the Kiel Canal became urgent, Wilhelm told his admiral not to worry: the huge cost of widening would be borne by the interior department, not the navy. Its justification could be pronounced as peaceful; it would benefit, after all, the agrarian economy. With Wilhelm's support came his considerable baggage, all of which was tiring for those who had to deal with him, friend and foe alike, one British diplomat remarking that Wilhelm 'is like a battleship with steam up and screws going, but with no rudder'. Tirpitz always had to proceed cautiously where royal vanity was concerned. The kaiser, in several spasms of creativity, delighted in producing detailed sketches of warships that he wanted built, or interfered in technical matters of design that were quite beyond his limited expertise (when possible, warships should have an additional smokestack added for cosmetic purposes, thereby creating the illusion of formidability; he also concocted the vision of an amoured cruiser top-heavy with armaments and torpedo tubes, fancifully christened the *Homunculus*).[1] What the grand admiral did not expect, when it came down to it, was Wilhelm's pusillanimous nature. Tirpitz was creating his naval monster to fight a gigantic battle at the mouth of the Thames. The last thing he expected was that his warlord would refuse to risk any such encounter.

Unfortunately for Tirpitz, his opposite number across the English Channel, Admiral of the Fleet 'Jacky' Fisher, was more or less his equal in volatility, determination, self-regard and competence. Fisher, in effect, more or less accepted Tirpitz's challenge.

The life story of Fisher is almost a parody of British naval history; indeed, C. S. Forester, in his famous Hornblower series of novels, actually follows much the same timeline, his erstwhile hero, beginning as a mere midshipman, leading a staggering life of excitement as he winds his way up the mast, as it were, to an admiral of the fleet in the West Indies fighting pirates, Napoleonic villains and interfering women through eleven books. Fisher, like Hornblower in the saga, learned to depend on himself early on. His father, an impecunious army officer stationed in Ceylon, packed him off to England at the age of six to be raised by distant relations (almost a cliché in the annals of English upbringings); the two never set eyes on each other again. At thirteen Fisher joined the navy as a cadet, recommended to the service by the last of Horatio Nelson's captains still alive, a bridge, as it were, from the past to the present. Nelson was Fisher's great hero – 'out and away the greatest man who ever lived' – as indeed he was to every sailor worth his salt in the Royal Navy, but that was about the extent of Fisher's dedication to mouldy tradition. If there was ever a man to break china in the wardroom, it was Jacky.

His first station was a ship of sail. He saw tidbits of the Crimean War (actually, heard them, distant reverberations of artillery fire), and spent five years in China where he distinguished himself in various obscure actions. Over the course of his young manhood, he both saw the world (a virulent dose of dysentery picked up in Egypt took four years for a full recovery) and witnessed the technological transformation in naval design, ordnance and custom that one either purposely rejected in its entirely as a matter of principle, or joined. Ever excitable, Fisher joined. He became expert in the evolving science of gunnery, wrote treatises on electricity and the development of mines, spearheaded the development of 'destroyers' (he coined the name) and was fascinated on a trip to Japan by their experiments with a torpedo, an artillery shell that could be fired underwater. He served on a multitude of ships, his first command (as a nineteen-year-old, and only for four days) a paddle wheeler on the China station called HMS *Coromandel*, one of his last the battleship *Renown*, a vessel his naval reforms would condemn to obsolescence just twelve years after its launch. Everywhere Fisher went he inspired, in no particular order, fear, loathing, adulation, reverence, devotion, awe, shock or any combination thereof. His rhetoric was usually extreme, his sense of tact often non-existent. He made friends and enemies in equal number. His roughish character and flamboyant tongue endeared him to people who counted, including Edward VII, who once had to admonish him not to wag his finger in the king's face. Over the last eight years of his active service, he was undoubtedly the most important naval figure in the country, perhaps the world, filling every important position, capped in 1905 by his promotion to admiral of the fleet. By then the naval race with Kaiser Wilhelm (King Edward's first cousin) was going full bore.

Fisher was a complicated man. Though he often expressed himself intemperately – Maurice Hankey wrote to Admiral David Beatty (who would play a critical role at the Battle of Jutland) that Fisher was 'a crank', and Viscount Esher called him 'a Son of Thunder' – he had a cool and surgical view of the geopolitical world around him, and knew very well, in his own mind, whom to worry about and why. France, the traditional enemy, he gradually dismissed. Despite provocations, Imperial Russia did not particularly monopolize his attentions either. It was Germany who mattered. Fisher made this very clear at the Hague Peace Conference of 1899, a peculiar affair that was the brainchild of Tsar Nicolas (another first cousin of Edward's). The tsar, in a semi-mystical frame of mind, organized the event after he read, and was disturbed by, Ivan Bloch's book *Is War Now Impossible?* which, despite its title, seemed to predict the exact opposite in a sort of doomsday approach, buttressed by an avalanche of graphs and statistics. Bloch was not interested in 'frontier brawls' (as he called them), but on the real thing, a generalized conflagration that would engulf the entire continent. The tsar saw the Hague affair as a way to short-circuit what he feared was a drift towards general European war; in retrospect, perhaps, a precursor to the Versailles conference of 1919 and the establishment of the League of Nations. Most of those attending arrived 'in a spirit of hopeless scepticism', according to an American delegate (Kaiser Wilhelm said, 'I shit on the whole affair'), and the choice of Admiral Fisher as a member of the British mission proved an odd addition at best. Fisher charmed many of the international cast of characters who participated, but issued bellicose warnings to any and all within earshot as well, mostly directed to German aspirations for *Weltpolitik*, which translates as 'world politics'. One observer noted that Fisher 'was a bit of a barbarian who talked like a savage at times' with commentary such as this: 'What you call my truculence is all for peace. If you rub it in, both at home and abroad, that you are ready for instant war with every unit of your strength in the first line, and intend to be first in, and hit your enemy in the belly, and kick him when he is down, and boil your prisoners in oil (if you take any), and torture his women and children, then people will keep clear of you.' These remarks were delivered with some 'impatience', as though too obvious to bother saying. C. P. Scott, editor of the *Manchester Guardian*, wrote in his diary that he had 'never seen such a ferocious sea dog'.

Of the many operational reforms initiated under Fisher's watch, the two most important were aimed at Germany. The first involved the reorganization of the fleet. Nine squadrons showed the flag throughout the world, a collection of several hundred ships, many so obsolete that they 'could neither fight nor run away', according to Fisher. These 'parasites' squandered men, money and attention from the theatres that now mattered most: home waters and the North Sea. Fisher abolished many of these (including the North Atlantic squadron, much to the regret of Halifax, Nova Scotia) and sharply reduced many others. Along the way he offloaded over 150 ships, either to irrelevant navies around the world or to scrapyards, and initiated his second great design, an ambitious, to say the least, programme of modernization, the centrepiece of which was the dreadnought. Other changes, also controversial, further embroiled opinion within the service, about which Fisher cared little. The navy was full of deadwood; it had to be purged. In the new super class dreadnought he saw an opportunity to enhance Britain's naval superiority at Germany's expense. No 'fossils', '*old ones*', 'mandarins', 'duffers', 'cads', 'dull dogs', 'scoundrels', 'idlers', or 'naval Rip van Winkles' would prevent him from doing his duty as only he saw fit.

The dreadnought was one on those weapons that made everything around it instantly outdated. Heavily armoured (at least in theory), relatively fast and abundantly equipped with big guns and only big guns (with ranges of over eighteen miles), it was intended to be the immediate bully of the high seas, a vessel that could stand afar and deliver punishing blows without sustaining the same in return. When the first of these slid down the ways on 10 February 1906, witnessed by rapturous crowds and the king himself, von Tirpitz despaired. As rumours of its performance during sea trials spread abroad, despair turned to depression. Five hugely expensive German battleships just constructed were suddenly of no tactical use whatsoever, entirely vulnerable to the dreadnought's fire power, superior armour plating and speed. The kaiser, essentially a spoiled child, demanded that von Tirpitz build a dreadnought in response. Hence the enormously expensive widening of the Kiel Canal, begun in 1907. At first Tirpitz was stunned at the prospects before him, but then he took a calmer look at the arithmetic. Fisher had taunted him with the launch of HMS *Dreadnought*, but when looked at dispassionately, it turned out to be a blessing. Britain and Germany were suddenly on an even keel. By gambling on a super ship, Fisher had essentially placed both powers on a more or less equal footing. The Royal Navy's enormous superiority in surface ships suddenly seemed insignificant in the face of this new maritime weapon because, according to a British officer, 'the *Dreadnought* automatically made more British ships obsolete than those of any other nation' – a few German dreadnoughts would be wolves in the chicken house if it came to that. Tirpitz rethought the problem and rechecked his statistical analysis with typically Germanic thoroughness. He began looking to establish a relative parity of dreadnought-type ships that would put the British fleet within an acceptable 3:2 ratio, everyone's calculation for a winnable battle by either side. Over twenty years of shipbuilding, in fact, he estimated that Germany could launch sixty capital ships. Britain, to maintain its edge, would have to counter with ninety, a prospect Tirpitz refused to believe a democracy could successfully achieve. If the gap was proportionately narrowed, superior German ship construction and gunnery would, he thought, bring the battle that everyone knew was coming into a theoretical realm of success.

In Britain, the evolution of the dreadnought delighted nationalists, especially those in the mouthy press who always pandered to emotions of the moment. When Russian warships passing through the English Channel mistakenly attacked British trawlers, sinking one and killing two fishermen (they thought they were firing on Japanese torpedo boats), the cry from Fleet Street was for immediate war. In 1909 there was a seriously destabilizing 'Naval Scare'. These sorts of periodic alarms were helpful, convincing the general public and various parliaments to accept the expenditures necessary to outbuild the Germans. Unlike a Haig or a Robertson, tripping over their own tongues and furious at the venality of journalists, Fisher cultivated them with his eloquent arguments and mountains of insider information. He was famous for his admonitions to 'burn and destroy' his confidential reports to important correspondents, which they took to mean 'publish as widely as possible, but don't give me away'. Fisher knew full well that both navies were beginning from the same starting line, and every contact that furthered the cause of rearmament was to be cultivated, over and over again as necessary. The soul of journalism, after all, was 'repetition'. Through furious lobbying and scheming of his own, and with the help of naval imperialists, such as Churchill, Britain equalled and surpassed the Germans ship by ship ('Jacky was never satisfied with anything but *Full Speed*', as one of his officers noted). By the war's beginning, in the glamorous dreadnoughts alone, the Royal Navy had twenty-four ready for sea, as opposed to Germany's seventeen. These, as Churchill referenced, would deliver 'the big punch'. Fisher also maintained the edge in battlecruisers, the kind of attack dog he liked best, fast and heavy firing both. Quality was often sacrificed, especially regarding armour plating (giving the lie, to some degree, of a favourite Fisher aphorism, 'Armour is vision'), but in terms of gross tonnage Britain maintained its lead. At a naval review held just a week before the invasion of Belgium, Admiral Sir George Callaghan paraded a fleet under his sole command that numbered an astonishing 460 vessels. On the very eve of war, this grand fleet was sent north to the anchorage at Scapa Flow in the Orkneys, running the Straits of Dover at night, lights dimmed, in a line that stretched for eighteen miles.

'We believed the fleet by itself constituted sea power.'

Vice-Admiral Wolfgang Wegener,
German Imperial Navy.

German strategy by August 1914 relied more or less on the notion that Britain, failing to restrain itself at the beginning of hostilities, would immediately blockade the German coast and goad the kaiser's fleet out of its lair, the large, watery embrasure or bay known as the Heligoland Bight, protected by a small, heavily fortified island of that name some thirty miles offshore, behind which lay several anchorages stretching from the Kiel Canal south to Wilhelmshaven.[2] Nelson had followed just this strategy during the Napoleonic wars, blockading French ports (over one stretch of time, he did not set foot on shore but once in almost two years). Behind heavily mined approaches, patrolled by German torpedo boats and moored lines of submarines, von Tirpitz and his commanders devised several scenarios as to how and when the imperial fleet might emerge and engage. Tirpitz, like the great army strategist von Schlieffen with Hannibal's battle at Cannae, was obsessed by the notion of a single determining battle in the North Sea; he had planned and designed his ships accordingly, to the point, for instance, of allocating very little physical space for crew's quarters – the men would not have to travel far, he reasoned, to fight the British. Tirpitz's dilemma, however, as the weeks passed along with but one sight of the Royal Navy, was contained in a single lament: 'What will [we] do if they do not come?'

The original British plan had been exactly what von Tirpitz was expecting. In the summer of 1911, during one of the several war scares that convulsed the major European capitals, Prime Minister Herbert Asquith had convened a war council to consider his various military options.[3] Admirals in attendance related the traditional course of action, the 'close' blockade of the North Sea German coast, followed by the invasion and eventual capture of Wilhelmshaven by the army (none of whose leaders had been previously briefed on such an operation). Asquith, no military expert, was appalled at these 'puerile' suggestions, as was Winston Churchill, then home secretary, who opined that such plans were 'surely out of the question', posing as they did enormous risks to the Royal Navy's precious capital ships. As a result of this conference, Churchill found himself installed as first lord of the Admiralty a month later, with instructions to clear the cobwebs. By the eve of war, a more realistic general strategy had been formulated. British sea power would strangle German commerce by employing a 'distant' blockade. If the German fleet came out to fight, it would be engaged, but otherwise a waiting game would ensue. Such conservatism was a damper to more ardent spirits, what Fisher called the 'bow and arrow party'.

By August 1914, von Tirpitz found his cause, and thus his star, in decline. A series of diplomatic fiascos in faraway places, none engineered by him, had thrown doubt on the wisdom of *Weltpolitik* that had formed the very heart stone of his 'big navy' approach, based as it was on the theories of an American naval officer then in vogue, Alfred Thayer Mahan.[4] 'Big Navy', of course, translated into big money, to the point where defence expenditures approved by the Reichstag were nearing a fifty/fifty par between the army and its relatively upstart counterpart headed by Tirpitz. Germany had always been a land power, traditionally obsessed with its physical location 'in the middle of the European house' with enemies, real and imagined, pressing in from both east and west. The idea of worrying about a far distant naval base in China (the very thought of which gave the great strategist von Schlieffen nightmares), appeared an irrelevance when everywhere one looked Germany's immediate neighbours seemed bent on armaments and modernizations: Russia vastly increasing its army and improving rail connections towards the west; France spending more per capita on its forces than even Germany; and Britain, its dreadnought programme handily outpacing von Tirpitz. Within the imperial navy itself, von Tirpitz, owing to his penchant for ruthlessness, had steadily accumulated more than his share of critics, many referring to his strategic theories as only so much 'cant', particularly the notion that at some preordained moment in the future, Germany would confront Britain at sea, defeat her forces and then feed on the spoils, its empire. Just looking at the numbers gave little hope that that would ever happen.

As Britain's industry and naval spending outpaced German efforts, critics pointed out huge disconnections in von Tirpitz's strategic vision. By failing to create the hammer that could destroy Britain's control of the seas, von Tirpitz had basically created a fleet that could inflict only 'pinpricks' on the future enemy. It was not sufficiently powerful to force the issue at hand: to interdict Britain's supply lines to and from the dominions and the United

States, on whose food and raw materials the island must depend in case of war. As Sir Walter Raleigh had said four centuries before, there were only two ways to defeat England, one by direct invasion, 'the other by impeachment of our Trades'. Without the power to break out into the Atlantic, 'interdiction of trade' was impossible. Wolfgang Wegener, a career naval officer whose speculations often landed him in trouble with his superiors, excoriated the gaps in von Tirpitz's vision both during the war and after. 'England found herself in a brilliant strategic position' in 1914, he wrote. 'The arteries of her commerce lay in the Atlantic, unreachable by the German fleet from the Elbe. The German trade routes, on the other hand, could easily be severed in the channel and off Scotland. The North Sea, through which no trade route any longer went, became a dead sea.... England saw no reason to fight. One does not need to fight for the command of the seas that one [already] possesses.... We never sought anything in the Atlantic.' Without fleet parity, the apocalyptic battle that formed the centrepiece of a decade-long arms race was foredoomed to failure. 'The navy's manoeuvres and war games presented the same picture. Blue [Germany] always lost as soon as opposed by superior forces in battle.' The kaiser's christening of the imperial fleet in 1907 as the *Hochseeflotte*, or High Seas Fleet, was absurd. In point of fact, his treasured ships were 'nailed fast to the pedestal' of Heligoland Bight, 'a strategically worthless rock', its operational radius confined to the North Sea. The *Hochseeflotte* was little better, in Wellington's memorable phrase from a century before, than 'a damned big rat in a damned small bottle'.

'One of the best five brains in the navy.'

Fisher referring to John Jellicoe

No account of the early days of warfare in northern waters would be complete without a discussion of John Jellicoe, commander of the Royal Navy's grand fleet, a protégé of Fisher's and anointed by him as the appropriate man to handle Britain's helm when the climatic day finally came, nicknamed by the Germans as *Der Tag*, or 'Day of Judgment' (in 1907 Fisher had predicted the date, September 1914).[5] Jacky, being the temperamental and mercurial figure he was, confounded his contemporaries by his choice of Jellicoe, because, aside from their unimposing statures (Fisher was relatively short and stocky, Jellicoe stood barely five feet tall), they seemed to have little in common.

Fisher had a temper, Jellicoe did not. Fisher was ruthless in his contempt for inefficient officers and purged them when he could, Jellicoe often coddled mediocrities and put up with 'deadwood' out of friendship or fear of upsetting naval tradition. Fisher valued initiative and new ideas; Jellicoe often recoiled from the implications of both. Fisher could be rash and immoderate, Jellicoe was neither. Had Fisher been in command at the famous battle of Jutland, his impetuosity, especially with ships whose inferiority in design he had helped perpetuate, might well have resulted in disaster. With Jellicoe in charge, a man well aware of deficiencies within his own fleet (perhaps morosely so), the great Trafalgar-like victory expected from the Royal Navy was probably impossible of achievement. On the other hand, he could be trusted not to sustain a devastating, Trafalgar-like defeat, as the French had in 1805, which in many ways won the war for the allies, a recognition seldom accorded him.

Like Fisher, Jellicoe started his career on the seas at a tender age (thirteen), and spent much of early adolescence seeing the world. Born in the great port city of Southampton in 1859, his lineage was appropriately maritime, his father the captain of a packet boat plying to and from the continent, and, through his mother's line, a direct relation to Admiral Philip Patton, present at the capture of Louisbourg in French Canada, 1758. Jellicoe was an alert, conscientious and inquiring student who did well in the various service schools he attended, especially in subjects generally shunned by more intellectually challenged colleagues, such as mathematics or anything of a technical nature. Gunnery became his specialty. In 1889, when Britain began a vigorous modernization programme for its fleet (authorizations for 52 new ships were put into the production pipeline), Jellicoe was at the heart of figuring out logistics in gun calibres, armour plating and the assortment of nuts and bolts required. He became something of an indispensable cog, or so Fisher felt, especially when the latter was named first sea lord of the Admiralty in 1904. By then Jellicoe had served on a wide variety of ships and been exposed to every issue of any importance within the service, along the way receiving the coveted distinction of being wounded in battle (on land, ironically, during the Chinese Boxer Rebellion in 1900 when he was shot in the left lung, the bullet of which he carried within him for another thirty-five years). On the eve of hostilities, he was in the place where he was supposed to be, second-in-command of the grand fleet. With its current commander in chief, Sir George Callaghan, expected to retire in December of that year, Jellicoe was in line to replace him. Unfortunately for Callaghan, a respected and experienced officer, Germany started the war four months too early. Sixty-two years old and deemed by Churchill, the civilian first lord of the Admiralty, to be over the hill, Callaghan was chagrined to say the least when

Jellicoe reluctantly boarded the *Iron Duke*, riding anchor in Scapa Flow, to take over command. Jellicoe had spent the entire preceding night in a sleeper car heading north from London through the wilds of Scotland, depressed over the entire situation. A more self-centred man, a man like David Beatty for example, would have gone to sleep salivating about his prospects. Jellicoe brooded instead, sensitive to the mores of naval tradition and aware that many in the service would regard him as disloyal, devious and disrespectful of his elders. He would keenly sense what Fisher called the 'mutinous threats' of his fellow officers and, in fact, he shared their feelings that Callaghan had been unjustly ousted, perhaps too much so for his own good. Jellicoe was, if anything, an honourable man and, according to Fisher, 'totally lacking in the great gift of insubordination'. Forty-two years in uniform can do that to a person.

Refusing to delegate authority to subordinates he would not trust, Jellicoe sought to transform the grand fleet into a soulless machine controlled by a single man, himself. A vast 'playbook' of ship manoeuvres, contingencies, battle plans and minute instructions was assembled and passed along to every captain. They were instructed to follow 'the form' without deviation; to watch at all times the flag signals emanating from the *Iron Duke* (radio silence being preferred during battle), and never to dream an independent thought. Jellicoe was the supreme micro-manager, and as such often lost himself in a maze of technical minutiae which, aside from stifling creativity, exhausted him both mentally and physically. One subordinate claimed that Jellicoe, immersed in some detail or another, reminded him of a 'glorified gunnery lieutenant'. For all his professionalism and sound appreciation of the coming naval struggle with his opponent, whose skills and superiority in many phases he acknowledged and respected, the fact remains that he was not an inspiration. His mindset was one of continuous caution. Fully aware of the tremendous burden he carried, Jellicoe thus agreed with the Admiralty position that no battle with the German imperial fleet should be commenced except on grounds of overwhelming numerical superiority. He was not a reckless man, and endorsed the initial plan to enforce a 'distant' as opposed to a 'close' blockade of the German coast.

For the kaiser's fleet to emerge into the open Atlantic, only two courses were open to it. The first, or southern route, was to push its way down the North Sea past Dover, only twenty miles to its nearest counterpoint in France, there to break out into the English Channel. The northern route, more expansive, would require passing between the Norwegian coast and the outer Scottish islands of the Orkneys and Shetlands, a gap of 200 miles at its minimum width. Based in Scapa Flow, almost 500 miles from Heligoland

Bight, the grand fleet was responsible for sealing these northern approaches, and early on the British government declared the entire area a war zone subject to search and seizure of food, raw materials, fertilizers and anything else destined for Germany. This illegal act did much to inflame and harden the attitudes of German military leaders (as well as those of American and Scandinavian carriers), despite their own disregard of international law by the violation of Belgian neutrality in August, a 'scrap of paper' conveniently ignored. Just a month into the war, the Royal Navy did instigate an enthusiastic foray into the Bight, largely the brainchild of junior officers (abetted by the equally enthusiastic and inexperienced first lord, Winston Churchill),[6] that was so poorly planned that Jellicoe, barely informed, had little idea what was going on. His impromptu decision to back up what was, in effect, a massed destroyer raid, saved the situation when things degenerated into a confused melee that drew several heavier German ships into action. These vessels were engaged by Jellicoe's even heavier battlecruiser squadron, commanded by David Beatty, which inflicted considerable losses on their enemy. This proved to be the pattern of future engagements, the attempt by one side to lure the other into a trap or a situation where the heavier firepower of one element of fleet action could overwhelm its opposite number if it consisted of inferior vessels. The action on the Bight, for example, could have turned into disaster if German dreadnoughts anchored in Wilhelmshaven had entered the fray. They did not only because of tidal conditions, the new behemoths being so heavy that at low water they were unable to clear the bar, a galling and unexpected impediment provided by mother nature.[7]

The Battle of the Bight, as it came to be called, embarrassed both sides. Churchill called the action 'brilliant', but less biased observers felt that whoever had authorized the scheme 'would have to be certified on the spot'. Fisher wondered, partially in jest (though no one could be sure) why no admirals had been court-martialled and shot as an example to all. For Jellicoe, the lessons from this 'most enormous muddle' were obvious: grotesque failures of communication, impulsive actions and lack of fleet control were all antithetical to his organized, methodical ways. It was, in effect, far too dangerous to plunge the grand fleet into precipitous and dangerous conditions within eyeshot of the German coast, far far away from English ports. It was fortunate indeed that several badly damaged British ships made it home at all. In direct contravention of the country's naval tradition, in fact, Jellicoe wondered if an engagement was even worth the risk, given what he believed was their relative parity in battle strength. Such hesitancy was not exactly Nelsonian.

For the Germans, the fight was a material and psychological disaster. German field forces were engaged in titanic land battles, both inflicting and receiving heavy casualties, and here was the imperial fleet thrashing about in a dishevelled mess at sea where it lost four ships and some 1,084 seamen (plus a rear admiral) to no British vessels sunk and only 35 dead. In these early days of the war, Kaiser Wilhelm still maintained the final say in military matters. Astounded by such losses, he in effect grounded the fleet, forbidding it any offensive action without his specific approval. As the kaiser's emotions were usually volatile and unpredictable, this in effect 'muzzled' the navy, in Tirpitz's phrase, from undertaking any movements or openings that a sudden development might offer. He and the entire officer corps were both mortified and demoralized. Certain ancillary events, however, at first scarcely noticed, would subtly alter the situation both within the German naval service and, more crucially, within the mind of Admiral John Jellicoe.

'In the beginning, [Tirpitz] thought them toys.'

Perhaps the last semi-modern military conflict that produced few technological surprises was the American Civil War of 1861–65. True, there was the exchange of broadsides between the first ironclads, the *Monitor* and the *Merrimack*, along Hampton Roads in March 1862; and submarines of varied sorts also saw their debut in southern waters (one Confederate boat sank the USS *Housatonic*). But, aside from the monumental casualties, the largest ever seen to that date in contemporary warfare and a harbinger of things to come in the twentieth century, many military experts saw little to learn from the engagements themselves, which progressed on more or less traditional lines. Some British army officers refused to study the war at all, seeing it mostly as a series of large-scale 'skirmishes'. The German general staff felt the same way, Helmuth von Moltke the Elder saying, 'I am not interested in a contest between armed mobs'. World War I was entirely different, with every component of combat taking on surprising evolutions in very short time-frames. The aeroplane is just one example, and the submarine another.

Before 1914, submarines and their potential were barely noticed, aside from a few zealots. Inventors and entrepreneurs pursued the vision of underwater warfare with scattered levels of success and from a variety of inspirations, some idiosyncratic. One of the more ingenious, John Holland, was an Irishman whose motivations were an intense hatred of Britain, hence the desire to sink her ships (his first working model was christened the *Fenian Ram*). Early boats were relatively primitive and none of the great powers, other than France, devoted anything more than cursory funds to their development. By the time Germany launched a working model, Turkey and even Portugal already were at sea with versions of their own. The world's focus when it came to sea power was generally based on big ships, speed and guns. Ocean liners competed to establish records for transatlantic crossings in peacetime, often breathlessly reported in the press. At the turn of the twentieth century, naval manoeuvres proved equally popular, with much attention given to comparative measures in tonnage and firepower. Gun calibres increased accordingly, 6-inch to 8-inch, then to 9.2-inch, 10, 11, 12, 13.5, finally to reach 15-inches by 1914.[8] The shells they lobbed over the sea could weigh nearly a ton, a full broadside almost sixteen thousand pounds. There didn't seem to be anything that a modern warship could not do; they were not dubbed 'Invincible' for nothing. This bravado lasted a bare month or so into the autumn of 1914.

There were 24 working U-boats in the German imperial navy in September of that year (the term U-boat comes from the German *Unterseeboote*, or 'underwater boat'). These were, on average, small, clumsy and uncomfortable vessels displacing 669 tons when surface cruising, approximately 212 feet long with a beam, at their widest, of twenty feet.[9] Carrying 110 tons of fuel, they took on average 85 seconds to dive. Generally crewed by twenty to thirty men and four officers, they were not user-friendly machines. Cramped quarters, the barest of sanitary facilities, a continuous stench of oil, body sweat and other unmentionables, were barely offset by tweaks that a submariner might enjoy (more chocolate rations, for one). Considering that prospects of survival if hit by shellfire or rammed by a surface vessel were not overly bright (when a sub went down, it usually did so with all hands), there wasn't much about the service that proved appealing, particularly to the common seaman, which explains why many ratings were conscripts who had no choice in the matter. Certainly U-boat armaments were not impressive. Some of the early models lacked surface guns, rendering them largely defenceless when on the surface. Those running on oil-fueled motors trailed a column of conspicuous smoke when they cruised, making them easier targets, and their speed of sixteen knots was generally slower than the pursuit vessels that were hunting them. Underwater, powered by electric batteries for perhaps twelve hours at a time, they could reach ten knots, at times barely adequate to achieve a decent firing position when tracking surface ships with greater propulsion or practising evasive manoeuvres. Only capable of carrying six torpedoes, they did not seem a formidable offensive weapon at all, especially considering that their range and durability in rough seas was deprecated, though as yet not truly tested. In the earliest days of the war their tasks were purely defensive: to guard the approaches to Heligoland Bight. Their talents for the kill, it was thought, could be applied only when a quarry was brought to them, as in destroyers, pretending to flee, might lure heavier cruisers into torpedo range. U-boats were so lightly regarded by the *Admiralstab* that being attached to its service was almost considered something of a demotion. Floating mines (also ill-considered by traditionalists) seemed a more productive weapon than submarines. A commodore in the Royal Navy despaired early in the war about the German practice of laying mines. 'It will be months before the North Sea is safe for yachting.'

The stalemate of the great fleets, however, gave U-boats their chance to impress. In fact, their first great 'strike' might well have been illusory. On 1 September, the sighting of a periscope in Scapa Flow, never authenticated, set off a wild shooting spree among the anchored battleships. Several local farmers were startled to find their crofts under fire as errant shells hurled through the air. An almost panicked fleet fled into the open ocean where Jellicoe felt safer. Scapa Flow, with no protective mechanisms in place, was thereafter deemed too dangerous, and was assiduously avoided where possible for several months until a variety of anti-submarine defences could be installed. Thus began Jellicoe's near obsessive fear of this novel underwater menace. He, for one, never underestimated its threat, which was reinforced three weeks later when a single submarine, *U-9*, sank three British cruisers in just ninety minutes off the Dutch coast. Two of these vessels were dispatched as they conveniently clustered around the first sinking ship to pick up survivors. No easier targets ever presented themselves, and they went to the bottom in quick succession, with a cumulative loss of over 1,400 men. Soon thereafter the Admiralty issued unusually heartless instructions that in similar circumstances neighbouring ships were to run for it, leaving men to their fate in the cold North Sea waters. No wonder the British considered U-boat commanders heartless pirates worthy of the gallows if caught.[10]

Jellicoe eventually deserted the North Sea as a base for the grand fleet, preferring the remoter anchorages of Mull in Scottish waters, and then Lough Swilly on the north-west coast of Ireland. The mere threat of U-boats had, in fact, delivered Germany its first tactical victory, though they hardly realized it, as the Royal Navy in effect abandoned its post. To make matters considerably worse, as the fleet steamed to Lough Swilly, the modern dreadnought HMS *Audacious* was fatally struck by what Jellicoe and everyone else assumed was a torpedo. After twelve hours struggling to stay afloat, she sank. This was such an astonishing blow that Jellicoe attempted to suppress the news, but unfortunately the passenger ship *Olympic*, sister to the once proud *Titanic*, had attempted to tow *Audacious* to shore. American passengers, in untold numbers, recorded its sinking using another twentieth-century innovation, Eastman Kodak's Brownie camera. It later turned out that *Audacious* had struck a German mine, but no matter. A British warship displacing 23,800 tons, one of the finest afloat, was sitting on the bottom of the ocean, done in by an insignificant, inexpensive, elusive and cowardly weapon that no one had even thought about a year or two before. The now-retired Fisher, for one, howled in pain. The war was only two months old and the Royal Navy had 'more men lost than by Lord Nelson in all his battles put together'.

Many German admirals, including von Tirpitz, were not overwhelmed by these sporadic successes, but the voyage of *U-20* in October turned their heads. *U-20* had been sent south to the Straits of Dover to attack troop transports, but a mechanical failure with diving gear essentially trapped the sub on the wrong side of the straits. Her captain, considering the odds, figured it would be impossible to retrace his steps home on the surface by the same route, so he chose to circumnavigate the British Isles. Cruising in broad daylight, he ran the Irish Sea, curled around the head of Scotland, entered the North Sea and successfully made it to the Bight after an eighteen-day-voyage. Vice-Admiral Reinhard Scheer was amazed. With the imperial fleet stuck in port, he suddenly saw in the *Unterseeboote* the potential for 'a very effective long-range weapon'.

The targets, at first, were a miscellaneous collection of anything that floated. Tramp steamers, coal barges, slow or aged Royal Navy ships, even fishing trawlers were all indiscriminately attacked. Newer U-boats (now usually powered by diesel engines and equipped with deck guns) would surface when possible if the victim was non-military, ascertain the vessel's nationality, sometimes check the cargo, give the crew time to abandon ship, then either sink by gunfire (torpedoes were precious), open the cocks or place a charge of explosives on board. Ships began to go under in alarming numbers, which made more expansive and previously unimagined hypotheses somehow realistic. Enthusiastic U-boat advocates suddenly saw a quasi-religious goal shimmering on the horizon, the idea being to literally strangle their enemy into submission. Britain relied absolutely on the outside world for survival, as evidenced by her enormous superiority in commercial tonnage, nearly fifty percent of everything that floated. In purely military terms, the switch from coal to oil as the fuel of choice for the Royal Navy immediately made her dependent on overseas shipments, particularly from the Middle East.[11]

Artillery shells were now being predominantly supplied from Canada, as well as vital shipments of raw materials, foodstuffs (particularly wheat), armaments and, over time, troops. Britain was preventing trade from arriving to Germany, violating neutral shipping and trading partners whose ports were far from the war zones. Why shouldn't Germany return the favour? These seemed irresistible arguments, summarized by a phrase called the 'retribution principle', especially to members of the German high command who were facing the possibility of no immediate decision on the western front. These men, of a generally unreflective disposition, were united in their opinion that if stalemate was to be broken, the unfettered use of U-boats must be pursued. The difficulties of such a course, however, proved immediately apparent and essentially reflected what were, in several instances, a decided deficiency in the weapon itself.

U-boat warfare opened an entirely new dimension on what constituted acceptable international behaviour. The boats were small, vulnerable in many respects and of limited utility when considered from (admittedly old-fashioned) notions of legal behaviour. U-boats could do only one thing: destroy their targets. They could not take ships as prizes of war (they did not carry sufficient crewmen to man captured vessels); they could not, in most cases, pay much attention to the lives and safety of enemy sailors (there was no room to accommodate captives on board their submarines); and, as Britain built more sub-chasing destroyers and small pursuit craft, they could not linger on the ocean's surface to examine at leisure a ship's papers or cargo (the development of aeroplanes created additional constraints to their surface activities). Everything of a moral nature designed to differentiate what constituted legal acceptability in naval warfare conspired against their most effective utilization, and this does not even extend to the adverse public relations aspect of submarine warfare which seemed to dwell on its ruthlessness and seeming disregard for the life or death of innocent civilians. The early defensive responses of Britain to this new threat also encouraged what many considered cold-blooded German policy. So-called British Q-ships soon put to sea, innocent-looking merchant steamers that, when confronted with submarines rising to the surface, suddenly revealed hidden deck guns manned by professional gunners who would then open fire. British ships, many loaded with munitions and war gear, routinely flew neutral colours to deceive the enemy. And, lastly, the merchant fleets of the empire took to mounting an arsenal of open deck guns for self-protection, which prevented U-boat commanders from rising to the surface to examine papers or warn crews off their ships before attack. These measures and counter-measures all encouraged extremists in the German navy, Tirpitz at the fore, to recommend unrestricted warfare against all shipping entering the war zones (meaning no warnings), whether British or neutral, the inevitable result of which was the *Lusitania* disaster of 1915, when that great unarmed passenger vessel was deliberately torpedoed off the southern Irish coast with enormous loss of life. The U-boat captain who ordered the attack was amazed at the speed with which the *Lusitania* went down. Survivors had noted, however, that very quickly after the torpedo struck, a second explosion occurred. This was, allegedly, caused by a cargo of munitions, some 173 tons, that the *Lusitania* was illegally carrying, which in hindsight seemed to justify the German attack.[12]

The first half of the Great War at sea was generally marked by perplexity. Britain had superior ships, but the U-boat menace essentially crippled its intended application. Jellicoe was so confused that he barely understood what course to take for the fleet's protection. Imbued with the offensive spirit, both his subordinates within the fleet and the Admiralty all urged aggressive attack forays, 'packs' of ships that would search the North Sea waters high and low to unearth their prey (naval officers, like their counterparts in the army, were often avid devotees of fox hunting). These were universal failures, exhausting to the men, hard on the ships, morale-sappers and with few 'kills'. U-boats had no desire to confront capital ships or even destroyers in head-to-head combat. They were skulkers, preferring to lurk underwater and stab their opponents in the back. When the value of destroyers became apparent as a guard for merchant tramps and coastal shipping (essentially a passive or reactive deployment), Jellicoe fought long and hard to monopolize the majority of these suddenly valuable craft to defend the grand fleet, sitting in inert isolation (Lloyd George called it 'cold storage') either at Scapa Flow or in the wastes of the North Sea. Churchill deplored what he considered to be Jellicoe's excessive caution, but the burden this solitary individual carried was nearly insupportable, as even the first lord conceded. The admiral's position, after all, was unique among allied commanders. He was the man, in Churchill's memorable phrase, who could lose the entire war in a single afternoon.

For the Germans, confusion also prevailed, much of it induced by the quivering kaiser. Hardliners wanted a ruthless U-boat campaign: no warnings, attack every vessel in sight, 'send [crews] to the bottom with their ships'. In short, a war of terror. In order to justify a course of action they knew would be internationally condemned (especially by the United States), they promised exaggerated results within impossible time-frames. When the kaiser demanded immediate returns within six weeks, Tirpitz blithely agreed. 'A silly question deserves a silly answer', he noted. In fits and starts, the campaign began in February 1915, but throughout most of its entire course restrictive conditions the kaiser imposed on the service impeded their performance. Every month, it seemed, new orders, often countermanding others issued just weeks before, tied the hands of U-boat commanders. On some missions they could attack whatever they wanted, on others neutral ships were exempt, or passenger ships, or only this class (with a warning) or that (with warning or no), judged exempt. The situation became a legalistic nightmare, compounded by the kaiser, pulled back and forth by his various coterie of advisers. True 'unrestricted warfare' was not permitted for another two years, and the immediate results were enormously painful for the allies: in three months 977 ships were sunk. The U-boat fleet, constantly evolving with newer and more proficient models, had grown to 105 boats. The approaches to the south coast of England became 'veritable death traps' according to Sir Edward Carson, a later first lord of the Admiralty, an absolute mercantile graveyard. One in four ships leaving English ports never returned. Neutral shipping trapped in England refused to leave the safety of its ports, clogging piers, anchorages and harbours. Haig noted in his diary the unbelievable conclusion that 'We have lost command of the sea.' Fisher plaintively asked, in so many words, 'Can the army win the war before the navy loses it?'

These dreadful shipping losses were dramatic though deceiving, a conclusion no one at the time really understood. Masses of statistics seemed to indicate that Britain could indeed be starved into a compromise peace, but complete figures, correctly understood only after the war's end, pointed to two conclusions. Though gross tonnage sunk was appalling – almost two million tons from February to April 1917 – new ship construction and timely repair to damaged vessels, if given the necessary priority, might be expected over a broader timespan to at least keep even. On the German side of the equation, realistic estimates as to how many submarines would be required to impose a real death rattle (two hundred and twenty) and the length of time required, were so beyond Germany's capacity to sustain that a final projected victory seemed chimerical at best. Several German admirals realized this and resisted von Tirpitz and the hardliners, one adviser to Wilhelm saying bluntly, 'Believe me, gentlemen, you will not scratch the whale's skin [meaning Britain's] with your U-boat war.' This assessment, however, did not calm anyone's nerves across the English Channel in 1917.

That was the year, and June the month, when Jellicoe had dropped his 'bombshell' at a war cabinet meeting that unless the war could be successfully won in the next few months, Britain would have to seek what Clemenceau had disparaged as '*une demi paix*'. The U-boat war was going that badly. By this time, it can be argued, Jellicoe had become England's version of Philippe

Pétain, a confirmed defeatist. Exactly twelve months before, Jellicoe had, at long last, been able to confront the German imperial fleet in open battle seventy miles off the coast of Denmark. This encounter, since called the Battle of Jutland, was the fight every sailor on both sides of the North Sea had craved, though the preconditions were not ideal for either. The Germans, in particular, fully aware of their numerical inferiority, wanted a confrontation only on their own terms. They did not desire, according to Vice-Admiral Reinhard Scheer, 'a decisive battle being forced upon us by the enemy'. Given their inferiority in numbers and large calibre gunnery, their strategy was to slice off a manageable portion of the grand fleet, preferably its heavy cruiser squadron, and deal with it independently of the main dreadnought force. Such a scenario was plausible given certain conditions. As for Jellicoe, he could formally concede that the whole point of the grand fleet's existence was 'to achieve victory', but his actual mindset was more reflected by a proverb that he and his subordinate, Beatty, often tossed back and forth between them: 'When you are winning, risk nothing.' The blockade of Germany was having the desired effect. In peacetime, Germany imported more than half its food requirements from abroad, and was growing ever more desperate for essential raw materials to feed its armament requirements. Imports from Scandinavian countries on the other side of the Baltic were insufficient to meet these many needs. The job was not glamorous, but Britain maintained its supremacy on the sea. Should it lose the grand fleet, however, or see its strength seriously diminished, that balance could be tipped the other way. Fisher's summary was simple and to the point: 'The British Empire ceases if our Grand Fleet ceases.'

Jutland

'*The English thought that they controlled the sea; the Germans, that they were invincible on land. Each side is losing where it thought itself strongest.*'

Walter Page, American ambassador to England

In late spring 1916, one clear British superiority – that of wireless intercepts – gave Jellicoe (or should have) the edge he so desperately wanted. From the earliest days of the war, Britain had been able to decipher many German fleet wireless messages to and from both its U-boat flotilla and its various warships.[13] At the end of May unusual activity indicated to British intelligence that the imperial fleet, or significant portions of it, were raising anchor. This was neither the first nor the last time that such warnings had been issued to Jellicoe. On 30 May the grand fleet put to sea, more or less as a precautionary measure, with Beatty and his battlecruisers, emerging from their base in the Firth of Forth, to rendezvous at the suspected area where they thought elements of the imperial fleet (under the command of Reinhard Scheer and Franz von Hipper) might appear. In neither camp was it suspected that the entire strength of both fleets were steaming towards each other (gross incompetence at the Admiralty did not inform Jellicoe of this possibility, confirmed by Room 40; he steamed south at a leisurely pace. Scheer and von Hipper were also sailing 'in the dark'). At 2:18 p.m. on the next day, a hazy afternoon with pockets of sea fog on the water's surface, Hipper and Beatty came into contact about seventy miles off the Danish coast. A junior officer on the light cruiser *Southampton* watched in awe as a running battle commenced, Beatty's battlecruisers reminding him of 'monsters, following in each other's wake, emerging one by one from the mist and flashing past like express trains. Not a man could be seen on their decks; volumes of smoke poured from their funnels; their turret guns trained expectantly on the port bow eager for battle.' No more eager, it should be said, than their commander, but Beatty's enthusiasm was soon tempered as German ships inflicted heavy damage on his squadron. Two modern battlecruisers, the *Queen Mary* and the *Indefatigable*, disappeared in just minutes after direct hits, enshrouded in huge mushroom clouds of smoke, and Beatty's flagship, the *Lion*, was nearly incapacitated. 'As I watched [the *Lion*]', wrote the *Southampton*'s officer after the battle, 'I saw a tremendous flash amidships as she was hit by a shell or shells. I saw the whole ship stagger; for what seemed like an eternity I held my breath, half-expecting her to blow up.'

These dreadful and wholly unexpected events elicited from the admiral's mouth a torrent of frustration, including his famous remark, 'there is something wrong with our bloody ships today', blurted out to a subordinate.[14] Beatty, famous for his impetuosity, fulfilled one aspect of his intended role in such a battle, however, though he failed miserably in another. After taking a beating on what was afterwards called the 'Run to the South', he reversed course and, chased by Hipper, began his 'Run to the North'. Hipper was overjoyed. A segment of the British fleet – not all of it, he did not want that encounter – had been detached, beaten to a pulp and was fleeing. He pursued, with Scheer and the imperial fleet right behind him. As the ships ran into and out of the mist, though, Hipper remarked, 'something lurks in that soup. We would do well not to thrust into that too deeply'. These were prophetic words. Beatty was, in fact, leading the Germans right into the path of the approaching grand fleet. The problem was that he failed to communicate any of this to Jellicoe.

It was a very near thing for the grand fleet, and lucky for the British empire, its king, royal family, institutions, allies and way of life, that John Jellicoe was the man he was. Douglas Haig disparaged Jellicoe – 'I should not look at him as a man of great power or decision of character' – but Haig was never put on the spot as Jellicoe was at 6:15 p.m. on 31 May 1916. In one of those supreme moments of absolute, soul-searing tension, Jellicoe was forced to make the single decision on which the fate of what everyone believed would be the climactic naval battle of the war might hinge. Two hundred and fifty vessels from both sides, spread over a battlefield that measured some 400 square miles of the North Sea, with approximately 100,000 men engaged (nearly 10,000 of whom would die), their victory or defeat was decided in a mere thirty seconds. Operating in a near vacuum of information –'I wish someone would tell me who is firing and what they're firing at', Jellicoe said on his own bridge – he finally sensed what he was facing: the entire German fleet. Beatty had brought them to his doorstep, even though Jellicoe was uncertain as to the enemy's specific course, formation, intention, composition and present strength after their fight with the cruisers. Sailing in and out of fog, Jellicoe couldn't see a thing, though the air around him was full of reverberations and gunfire. He knew the confrontation was coming, he knew he had to manage and position his fleet to its best advantage in relation to firing position, where the sun was (important for spotting and directing salvos), where the Bight was (he wanted to be between it and the German fleet to cut off the enemy's escape), what course Scheer and Hipper were currently maintaining and how long it would take to manoeuvre his own ships into line. There was also the matter of enemy destroyers with their torpedoes, always a threat he took to heart. All these details were swirling through his head. It was one of his virtues that Jellicoe was able to compartmentalize each, sort them in order of priority, calculate one in relation to the other and calmly consider his options. The various diaries, memoirs and letters of his staff who were present at that moment on the bridge of the *Iron Duke* are united by one commonality as they recalled these few seconds: their admiral's imperturbability. One could state the obvious, that all Jellicoe's naval training, expertise, technical know-how and sense of reassurance were meant to coalesce at this particular moment; such might be a cliché, but it is true nonetheless. Running calculations of amazing complexity through his mind –'The difficulty of ascertaining *at the time* what was going on was just immense', as he later wrote – Jellicoe calmly gave his orders that set the entire line of battle in one single sentence: 'Hoist equal-speed pendant south-east.'

'Would you make it a point to port, sir, so that they will know it is on the port-wing column?' asked his signals officer.

'Very well. Hoist equal-speed pendant south-east by east. Dreyer, commence the deployment.' Seven miles of battleships heeded this command, which took about ten minutes to complete. At this point, Jellicoe had not put eyes on a single German ship. The lay of the land, so to speak, was entirely in his head.

The small span between 6:30 and 6:40 p.m. was undoubtedly the high point of Admiral Sir John Jellicoe's career. When his German counterpart, Scheer, emerged from the mist, he was confronted with an appalling sight, the entire heavy strength of the enemy in a solid line 'crossing his T', the naval expression whereby one fleet is able to cruise with its full broadsides firing against the enemy's approach in single file, only bow guns able to train on its enemy. The overwhelming superiority of massed gunfire by the British (each dreadnought capable of firing broadsides weighing eight tons per salvo), that was unable to be answered effectively, was by contrast the low point of Scheer's career, and he barely stood up to it. At 6:40 he issued his own signal, *Gefechtskehrtwendung nach steurbord*, 'Battle-turn to starboard', which saw his entire line, in perfect precision, turn an abrupt about-face back into the mist. His ships had been punished – several with only one gun turret in operation, others with gaping holes in their hulls, gorging on tons of onrushing sea water – but Scheer had escaped annihilation, at least for the moment. His main concern now was no longer that of a greedy predator looking to pick off strays from the enemy fleet, but one of the hunted rat with nowhere to run, 'a very nasty hole' as one British officer put it. The rest of the afternoon and ensuing night was spent in several desperate measures by the imperial fleet to break through the British line and somehow crawl back to the Bight. This was successfully achieved by the next morning but at considerable cost, and only after one or two instances of near suicidal action.[15]

Jellicoe had expected to resume the battle by dawn of the next day, but when the sun came up he found himself alone on North Sea waters, now strewn with the melancholy sight of dead bodies (both men and fish), acres of floating debris and the sight and stench of oil slicks stretching as far as the eye could see. His glow of satisfaction then turned sour. He had had his chance, but missed it; by 2:45 p.m. on 1 June, Scheer was safe in the Bight. Beatty called this 'one of the saddest days of my life'.

Perhaps the one explanation for Scheer's survival was Jellicoe's caution, for which the British admiral was forever held to task, particularly by more flamboyant types like Beatty, who sought to deflect well-merited criticism of their own role in the battle by pointing the finger at Jellicoe. As was the case with arguments over command decisions within the various allied armies, the postwar years saw a deluge of memoirs from the admirals, most of them concerned with 31 May 1916. These were wounding to the individuals involved; Jellicoe would never be allowed to forget Jutland.[16]

Certainly his actions left him open to critique. He could have pursued more vigorously, especially at 6:30 p.m. when Scheer first retreated into 'the muck'. But the admiral's policy had always been to avoid potential traps, especially when the enemy might be feigning withdrawals only to leave torpedo attacks and mines strewn in his wake. He might have been more innovative in his thinking as to how Scheer planned to return to base, and been more keen to cut him off with night actions. Jellicoe did not trust his fleet to go into action after nightfall, however (a fear Beatty shared), and thus misinterpreted the firing he heard to his rear as minor collisions of enemy forces, whereas it was Scheer punching through behind his destroyers. He might have done several things differently, in fact, but it must always be kept in mind that many of his commanders did little to communicate what it was they were seeing or believing. Jellicoe in many ways was behaving within a vacuum of information. On 2 June he steamed into Scapa Flow, nagged by the feeling that he had failed.[17]

The next day, forewarned by the noise of guns and the wafting odour of cordite fumes, beachcombers on the Danish coast began seeing dead bodies wash up on the shore, a ghastly procession that would continue for almost a year.[18]

Britain had expected by genetic right that when the two fleets engaged, Jellicoe would emerge the undisputed victor. This did not happen. The Admiralty did not help matters with its first communiqué describing the battle, which many commentators described as an apology. One of Jellicoe's official assessment orders after the battle was to upgrade the importance of 'locate and report'. This was given equal importance to the more traditional 'attack and destroy'. Again, this did little for the fleet's sense of manly importance. Some crew members, when they reached shore, were actually jeered as they walked the streets or went into pubs. The press had a field day, the *Weekly Despatch*, as one example, wringing its hand in public: 'We have learned to trust the Fleet.... Then what went wrong last week? ... The Germans succeeded in giving battle to a part of the Fleet with their full strength.... and then returned to their ports before our main fleet could force a decisive action. Why did we fail? The fight itself was mismanaged.... It is not what we expect.... Give the Fleet over to younger men.' Beatty, for one, grew flummoxed with fury. 'Don't believe the bloody papers', he wrote a friend, 'they are all wrong. We gave them a damned good hammering.'[19]

Germany exulted in the material difference in respective losses: fourteen British ships had been sunk (including three heavy cruisers) to eleven German (one battlecruiser), and the Royal Navy suffered three times as many lost men. German ship construction had proved markedly superior, her gunnery, discipline, courage and 'dash' the equal. Wilhelm was delighted. Scheer was not. The kaiser appeared at Wilhelmshaven and distributed the usual cartload of medals, but Scheer had only to look at the royal shipyards to see the real cost of Jutland. His dreadnoughts and cruisers had been thoroughly battered, and many would remain in dry dock for months being repaired. The battle had not been a victory, it had not even been a draw. Germany was too far behind in heavy ships to challenge Britain on the high seas. Scheer would attempt three sallies into the North Sea during the last years of the war, but never with the intent of beating the full grand fleet. He realized the odds of ever winning such a head-to-head confrontation were practically nil. As a New York newspaper put it, 'the German fleet had assaulted the jailer and was [now] back in jail'; or, as a despondent German officer wrote after the battle, the imperial fleet had been 'put on ice'.

For Jellicoe, the aftermath was painful, exacerbated when Lord Kitchener and nearly all hands on the *Hampshire* went down three days after the fleet's return to Scapa Flow, a humiliating loss that further stunned the nation. Jellicoe's stamina and health, now precarious, were strained to breaking point and, almost as a mercy, in November 1916 he was transferred to the Admiralty headquarters in London as first sea lord. Beatty replaced him as commander in chief of the grand fleet. Fellow officers in the army, battle-tested over two long years of constant war, were bemused. The fleet had finally seen action, and been baptized. 'Our navy is just beginning its course of instruction', wrote Henry Wilson in his diary. 'Very expensive, but very necessary. This will wake up the English people and do a lot of good, and put a long Whitsun Holiday in its true perspective.' But Jellicoe's nerves were hardly calmed by what was now put on his plate. With Lloyd George, ever impatient for results in 10 Downing Street, Jellicoe was given his mandate: solve the U-boat dilemma, and quickly.

'U-boat warfare is the last card.'

Theobald von Bethmann Hollweg,
German Chancellor, agreeing to
unrestricted submarine warfare,
9 January 1917.

Stealth attacks by an enemy vessel barely considered a viable offensive threat just a year or two before left British authorities flat-footed in their response. One common characteristic was universally shared by the efforts cobbled together to meet it, however: they were all failures. Some were comical. Harbours and coastlines were patrolled by a variety of hodgepodge vessels, from private yachts to broken-down fishing trawlers to tramp steamers, some of which had men on board who, when a periscope was spotted, were to jump into the water with hammers to batter the lens or to tie a black hood over the mechanism to 'blind it'. Thousands of man hours were spent with primitive hydrophones patrolling infested waters, hoping to pick up tell-tale propeller echoes. In theory, this was a promising idea; in practice, it did not work. Minefields were proposed, and often laid at crucial and known points of U-boat passage, such as the Straits of Dover, along with booms of floating nets and other anti-submarine obstacles, patrolled incessantly by small craft with mounted search lights. Beatty, for example, had the idea of sealing off the Heligoland Bight with 80,000 mines, the issue being that British stockpiles at the time barely added up to a thousand, compounded by the fact that shoddy workmanship and design rendered many of these useless – they usually failed to explode when hit by anything.[20] There was not an effective British mine developed until 1917, when a German model recovered in the North Sea was taken apart over time, examined, and then precisely copied. The tethering mechanisms used to station mines often failed as well, Holland complaining as hundreds of British mines washed up on its shores and beaches. As for booms and nets, they were vulnerable to tides, storm surges and the generally tempestuous condition of rough seas which tore everything apart. Depth charges, in the early stages of research, were still primitive and untrustworthy. The most important goal for many vessels that used them was to get away as fast as possible after the charges were dropped overboard, for fear of being blown up themselves. As Jellicoe began wrestling with these problems, his first response was resignation. Nothing seemed to work and he had no fresh ideas as to what the navy could or should do. His only suggestion was to hint that perhaps a negotiated peace treaty with the enemy might not be the bad idea that everyone thought it was.

Jellicoe's new appointment to the Admiralty coincided, unfortunately for his nerves, with Germany's final determination to unleash unrestricted submarine warfare against both allied and neutral shipping which began, as referenced previously, in February 1917. Jacky Fisher had predicted this before the war even started. His realistic appraisal seems obvious in retrospect: when you have a lethal weapon (the U-boat) that can bring an enemy to his knees (economic starvation), then you use it without scruples. Germany's decision was fully warranted by stalemate on the western front and by the mounting effects of the naval blockade on its own civilians, now feeling the pinch. After the armistice of 1918, Douglas Haig made it perfectly clear that he had personally won the war, but in fact the unheralded sea struggle – not Jutland, but the final defeat of the U-boats – was surely the determining factor. German resistance was not broken in the trenches, nor was it 'smashed' at sea (U-boat commanders were more than willing and able to prolong hostilities). It was broken on the home front by factors that can be summarized by events such as the 'turnip winter' of 1916/17, when that unglamorous food product became the staple on most German dinner tables, which were also characterized by, among other things, scant heating. Had resolve behind the lines remained unshaken, Germany could have held out beyond 1918, for another two exasperating years at least.[21] But as Ivan Bloch had predicted two decades earlier, 'Your soldiers may fight as they please; the ultimate decision is in the hands of *famine*.' She might never have had to rely on the disastrous Operation Michael, Ludendorff's 'gambler's throw', but could have remained an effective opponent, relying solely on defensive warfare. But Germany did quiver, did relent, and socialist rot, as Ludendorff termed it, began insidiously to destroy the national character. When riots and mutinies spread across the land from Wilhelmshaven to Kiel to Berlin, the war was indeed lost.

There was certainly no secret weapon that foiled the U-boats at this critical juncture of the war. True, depth charges – a truly effective anti-submarine device – and their delivery systems evolved into a key component, but their development did not inspire newspaper stories or wide publicity. No one ever printed a headline that featured a depth charge. Nor was the final victory the result of some confrontation like a Jutland. The U-boat war was a cumulative affair rarely dramatized by singular events; in fact, its progress was often overshadowed by what seemed to be, at first glance, devastating failures. Monthly shipping losses, when surveyed on a sheet, seemed powerful indicators that the tide of battle was going against Britain. Jellicoe thought so. When a visiting American admiral came to visit him in London, he was shocked at the current news:

'It looks as though the Germans are winning the war', I said to Jellicoe.

'They will win unless we can stop these losses – and stop them soon', the admiral replied.

'Is there no solution for the problem?' I asked.

'Absolutely none.'

Convoys

'We are sitting on top of a volcano which will blow the Admiralty and the Navy and the Country to hell if we don't pull ourselves together.'

Admiral David Beatty,
29 April 1917

Sir Joseph Maclay, a shipping magnate from Glasgow, was one of several important civilian experts whom the government recruited to fill specialist roles with which professional army and navy officers were either unfamiliar or incompetent to perform. Sir Eric Geddes, for instance, a businessman with extensive experience in railways, sorted out the logistical mess created behind the lines in Flanders by the sudden influx of men, munitions and supplies which threatened to overwhelm the French transportation system. In the German army an entire section of the general staff was devoted to such issues; in the British army, blundering about was the keynote. When Geddes was finished with that task, he was made first lord of the Admiralty, given a uniform and appropriate title, and instructed to clean up the navy as well. For Maclay, the mandate was equally sweeping. His job, as minister of shipping control, was to organize the shipping industry for war: increase merchant ship construction, streamline port efficiencies, make certain that ship owners and the government were coordinating with each other.

Lloyd George, in keeping with his distrust of Haig, Robertson and their minions in the high command, now settled his sceptical gaze with equal disapproval on the command structure of the Royal Navy, an even more ossified nest of fossils than the army, if such was possible. In Lloyd George's view, shared by Churchill during his tenure as first sea lord, the navy was a closed circle of antiquated attitude and tradition, jealousy guarded by a clique of admirals and senior officers who regarded any innovation to custom as anathema. The chain of promotion, for example, was deemed to be carved in stone; advancement due to ability rarely contemplated, more attention paid to precedence and one's position on the naval list being the primary consideration for stepping up the ladder. Outsiders, in particular, were viewed with deep suspicion; individuals who bucked the system, with contempt. Some naval custom was so enmeshed in dry rot that operational blunders of a farcical nature often ensued. One unwritten maxim was: never contradict a superior officer or question his motives for an order. On a summer's day in 1893 off the shores of Tripoli, the commander of the Mediterranean Squadron gave a fleet command during sea manoeuvres that an entire coterie of junior officers knew to be technically incorrect. As the admiral's own flagship, the HMS *Victoria*, arced into a collision course with another, HMS *Camperdown*, no one on the bridge dared countermand the original order or suggest that evasive action might be in order until the ships were a bare twelve hundred feet apart. The aftermath was *Victoria* sitting on the bottom of the Mediterranean, along with 358 of her men. (At the time of the incident, John Jellicoe was in his berth on the *Victoria* with a raging fever. He was lucky to survive and, given the many courts martial that resulted, also lucky that he was not on the bridge at the time and thus accountable.)[22] Jacky Fisher spent much of his career trying to weed out such deadwood and encourage fresh thinking. His protégés, Jellicoe among them, were called the 'Fishpond' behind his back, and he marked them for speedy promotion, causing, as one might expect, considerable resentment. Even so, the majority of senior officers remained entrenched in both position and state of mind. Lloyd George could not stand it. The only advantageous difference between Haig and the admirals was that when admirals made a mistake on the high seas, they generally went down with their ships to a watery grave. That was one way to make them pay the price for stupidity.[23]

Lloyd George's memoirs, published well after the war had ended, between 1933 and 1937, is often an exercise in self-congratulation. The idea of countering the U-boat onslaught with massed and well-guarded oceanic convoys is claimed as his idea, and his idea alone, pushed through despite the united and stubborn opposition of admirals and sea lords, Jellicoe most of all. There is some degree of truth in these assertions, but the situation was not as black and white as Lloyd George claimed.

It is certainly true that Jellicoe was at his wit's end. Worn out, somewhat despondent and baffled by this fresh challenge to Britain's naval supremacy, he seemed rudderless. Civilians like Maclay were making inroads into matters usually considered immune from outside interference. The admirals pushed back. Maclay, and then Lloyd George, argued that convoys be given a chance, their deployment having had a long and generally successful pedigree in past wars. Jellicoe and his staff wrote memos in opposition: pooling ships made them that much more an appealing target (with vessels steaming about 900 yards apart, a good-sized convoy could take up a ten-square-mile blog of sea); merchant ship captains could not hold course in unison, or maintain speed or follow orders; the speed of a convoy would be fatally hampered by the slowest vessel in it; the Royal Navy did not have sufficient numbers of destroyers to waste on convoys, they were mostly required, as everyone knew, to guard the grand fleet. These conclusions were presented with a sense of lofty infallibility which might have been impressive had any been proven correct. In fact, aside from the accepted value of destroyers, none of them would hold up, which did not prevent endless wrangling and disagreements from continuing. Things became so bad that Maclay informed his friend Beaverbrook that 'the confidence of our mercantile marine in the Admiralty has been frittered away and does not now exist'.

While the idea of trying out convoys to see if they might diminish the ghastly monthly losses in tonnage was not solely Lloyd George's idea, he certainly encouraged the notion that anything promising should be investigated. Jellicoe was slow and resentful in his response, partly out of pride, partly out of his own sense that he knew what would work and what wouldn't and partly because he was now mentally prepared to throw in the towel. He was, in many ways, a defeated and demoralized man, and remained defensive about convoys for the rest of his life. In one of his memoirs, he castigated the notion that amateurs knew anything about initiating convoys on an enormous scale, such people being 'without any knowledge of the seas or naval matters'. He eventually signed off on a proposal to try out the convoy idea, but without enthusiasm. His colleagues began writing him off. On Christmas Eve 1917, Geddes unceremoniously dismissed him from office.[24]

Several 'trial' convoys, however, were set in motion, the first of any significance from Gibraltar home for England. No losses were recorded, even though the average speed was a plodding six and a half knots. On 24 May 1917, another convoy of twelve ships, guarded by a single cruiser, set sail from Hampton Roads, Virginia, average speed nine knots. Approaching the Irish coast, eight destroyers deployed to meet them. As a united convoy, no ships were lost, though a slower and more decrepit vessel had to drop out to make its own way to port. This ship was promptly torpedoed. There was a lesson to be learned from that occurrence.

What was it about convoys that discomforted submariners? Most crucially, the escorts who accompanied merchant steamers made life miserable for their hunters. More eyes searching the horizon from any number of crow's nests and bridges made detection that much more probable. U-boat commanders, in setting up their torpedo attacks on a single, unaccompanied ship, had time and leisure to pick their perfect spot for firing; not so in convoy formations, with many ships taking up a lot of space and practising, more or less in unison, evasive manoeuvres. Any attack on a convoy would additionally give away the sub's position, and escort vessels were quick to pounce. The concentration of vessels with the convoy system meant, correspondingly, the concentration of torpedo boats and destroyers. With better depth charges, now catapulted not only from a ship's stern, but projected laterally to either side of the destroyer, using a new propulsion unit called a 'Y' launch, the arc of attacks with these weapons increased exponentially, and thus their deadliness. Admirals had deprecated convoys by the argument that they were such inviting targets; they failed to see the other side of the coin – that convoys lured U-boats to the honey pot, where hunters awaited them.

The other consideration was the breadth of the Atlantic Ocean. It is a huge open space, just as likely to 'hide' a single ship as it might a convoy of sixty. This was a difficult notion to conceptualize at first, but the odds were equally stacked that if one vessel could slip by, so could the massed assemblage of many more. Added to this equation were the relatively modest numbers of U-boats prowling about. At any one time during the unrestricted phase of U-boat warfare, approximately fifty submarines would be on station, mostly at the northern and southern approaches to the British Isles. Those identical zones saw the same concentration of destroyers and armed trawlers when a convoy turned up, there to counter the threat. A young submariner named Karl Dönitz, who would achieve considerable fame (and infamy) thirty years later during World War II, saw an immediate change once the convoy system went into effect: 'The oceans at once became bare and empty.'

Encouraged by these first results, the convoy system was slowly inaugurated. In three months, 21 transatlantic conveys crossed the ocean, some 354 ships. A mere two were lost. The total number of vessels convoyed over the same time frame (coal shuttles to France, Mediterranean trips, the Norwegian and Dutch trade) – an impressive 8,894 vessels – saw U-boats account for the loss of only twenty-seven. Figures for unescorted vessels, however, stayed very high – 356 sinkings – and monthly totals of lost shipping continued to be discouraging, but for those who examined the figures closely, like Sir Eric Geddes, the former railway baron, the trends were obvious and enormously favourable to the convoy system.[25] Geddes had imported an entire cadre of civilian statisticians to the Admiralty, their task being to analyze the numbers. By March 1918 he became, according to Hankey, 'very cheerful about submarines'. New ship construction for that year was estimated to be 1,800,000 tons, which would not be sufficient if losses approached 1917 levels. In fact, owing to the convoy system, lost tonnage figures had dramatically decreased, so much so that Geddes predicted a surplus of available merchant capacity for the coming year. His detractors within the Admiralty scoffed. Sir Henry Oliver, later to become an admiral of the fleet himself in 1928, decried the mounds of 'paper' that Geddes generated. 'We have been upside down here ever since the North Eastern Railway took over', he wrote. 'Geddes is mad about statistics and has forty people always making graphs and issuing balance sheets full of percentages etc.' Attitudes such as Oliver's helps explain why the Royal Navy was as ill-prepared for World War II as it was for World

War I. Hankey shared Geddes's optimism. 'So long as we can build ships as fast as we lose them, I for one remain confident of ultimate victory.'

It certainly became clear that new ship construction, previously weighted towards heavy cruisers and dreadnoughts, should be redirected towards the floating 'platform' that worked best, the relatively inexpensive and quickly constructed destroyer, a highly manoeuvrable ship loaded with depth charges and torpedoes and capable of speeds of up to 34 knots. Though the big-ship era of the early period of war was tactically over, the fact remains that by 11 November 1918 a little over five percent of Royal Naval vessels were engaged in convoy protection, an astonishingly meagre number when considering, as Liddell Hart did in 1930, that the Atlantic 'front' was the most important of the war.

Germany countered in typically ingenious ways. She built better subs, bigger subs, subs that were capable of carrying the war well beyond the Irish Sea. *U-155*, a long-range boat, made itself a nuisance off the Azores in the summer of 1917. At sea for over one hundred days, she cruised 10,220 miles (all but 620 on the surface), sinking seventeen ships totalling 52,000 tons. She carried eighteen torpedoes and had two substantial deck guns, fore and aft, of 5.9 inch calibre, making her an offensive beast with enough firepower to battle any Q-boat. In the three months from May to July, the ratio of sunken ships to U-boats lost was a very favourable fifty-three to one. Fifteen subs had not returned to port, but twenty-two new boats had been launched during the same quarter.

Actuarially speaking, the U-boat war would be decided on four levels: for the British, rates of construction for new merchant shipping and for augmentation of destroyer fleets and escort vessels; for Germany, rate of construction for new U-boats, and the ability to replace experienced crews lost at sea with complements of equally skilled and dedicated men. Make no mistake about it, submariners were a special breed of warrior. Thirty of these calibre of men drowned in a sunken U-boat were certainly more valuable than the machines in which they died.

This entire transitional period was difficult to live through if you happened to be a British admiral or a first sea lord. The press played up every ship sunk, especially if the German enemy behaved like a heartless beast, allowing woman and children to drown or killing neutral citizens. Convoys arriving safely into port, however, were stories journalists knew nothing about, given their lack of drama or even publicity because of censorship. The tide of the naval war turned imperceptively to most observers. Beyond the lurid headlines, people failed to understand that the U-boat campaign was not achieving its goals of sinking 600,000 tons of shipping a month, that British industrial might was rebuilding inventory at a satisfactory rate and that the calorie gap between what was being served for dinner in England was ever widening when compared to the 'turnip' fare on German plates. U-boat losses were mounting, and by the last quarter of 1917 the ships-sunk to U-boats-lost ratio had declined by half, 21 to 1. Figures supplied by Geddes showed that in the same time frame only 26 ships were lost out of 2,552 that criss-crossed the Atlantic in convoys. The allies, in fact, were winning the war. As Hankey noted in his diary, 'the blockade, the dreadful weapon of our sea power, is accomplishing gradually and unseen its inevitable purpose; gnawing the vitals and relentlessly sapping the strength of our foes. Germany is hungry; Austria is starving! We have great difficulties of our own, but nothing to compare with these, thank god!' General Ludendorff realized this as early as August 1917, and Operation Michael was the result, that elusive search for the climactic and final breakthrough.

U-53
Life on a U-boat

> *'The whole sea is a powder barrel.*
> *For all this there is only one remedy – nerves!'*
>
> U-boat Captain Edgar Freiherr von Spiegel.

In 1917, Kaiser Wilhelm's official marine painter, the artist Claus Bergen, finagled his way aboard *U-53* on one of its war cruises, during the course of which he observed and sketched the dangerous life these self-styled 'band of brothers' led. Many of his studies were turned into larger-scaled paintings once Bergen arrived back to shore, and these proved enormously popular. Admiral Scheer invited Bergen to join him on a cruise with the imperial fleet, firing off salvos with blanks so the artist could get the feel for what Jutland had been like, several scenes of which he promptly painted (*Hipper Emerges from the Mist* was a typical subject). After the war he also jotted down a narrative of the submarine trip, which had proved to be the highlight of his war experiences, and collected reminiscences from several other U-boat veterans as well, from officers right down to able seamen. It, along with other memoirs, presents a fairly accurate picture of what life was really like in a combat environment where most of its participants did not expect to come back alive.

U-boats were complicated and ingenious devices, 'steel cigars', in the words of a British submariner, 'in which every cubic foot was occupied by some piece of machinery and which was a kind of spider's web of pipes, valves, gauges, pumps, engines, air-bottles, and electric leads, amongst which officers and men somehow managed to sleep and eat'. In general terms, the bow of the boat was the forward torpedo room with two tubes on either upper side. Spare torpedoes, nicknamed 'smoking eels', were stored there as well. This was also the crew's quarter, slung with hammocks or crude platforms usually shared by several men, often wet and clammy after deck watch. Behind them, separated (as were all the various compartments) by a watertight bulkhead, were bunks for the officers and a small, separate cabin for the captain. In the centre stood the control room with its steering mechanisms, navigational gear and mechanical controls for diving and surfacing. Above this area was the conning tower, the egress through which, one at a time, men could scamper either above or below deck. Following in succession aft were the diesel engine room (for surface propulsion), the electric motor room (underwater propulsion), a small galley and finally the rear torpedo room with another two tubes. Along the exterior hull were long water tanks: when filled with sea water, the boat would submerge, when cleared with compressed air, the boat would surface. Attached to these, both bow and stern, were a set of horizontal rudders. The eye of the boat was the periscope, attached to the conning tower and fitted with complex German optical gear. When enemy aircraft became a security risk, these were outfitted with an ingenious adaptation that allowed a skipper to scan the skies before coming to the surface. The rudders and periscope, so essential to the operation and safety of the boat, were also its most fragile components, easily disabled by collisions with underwater obstacles or when fouled by steel nets or drags. Submarines were isolated when under water, their wireless sets functional only on the surface.

Technological adjustments to the wartime capacity of the boats improved each month. Every skipper had a recommendation about something mechanical after a tour, and these were often incorporated in newer designs and models. One thing that did not change were creature comforts. Life aboard the boat was miserable. Hygiene was non-existent. The clothes you came on board in were generally the ones you wore every day and night. Men did not bathe, fresh water was too precious. Beards and hair went long. Sleep often proved impossible (U-boats lacked stability on the surface, they pitched and rolled in any kind of fresh weather). When drenched (which was constant), one hoped for a sunny interval when the metal hawsers stretched from bow and stern to the conning tower could be used as a clothesline. After just a few hours underwater, the air grew stale and fetid. Grease and oil were everywhere: in your food, on your hands and body, all over your clothing. The diesel room, in particular, was a remembrance of hell and its awful temperatures, as nearly all memoirs attest, including that of seaman Waldemar Schlichting:

> Before I lay down I swallowed a little tea, and glanced into the engine room; an appalling burst of heat flung me backwards; the thermometer stood at nearly 45 Celsius.[26] The men were standing over their engines in the bare minimum of clothing, and their drawn, gaunt faces, smeared with oil and filth, looked like skulls. The air was unbelievable; the thudding combustion-engines exhausted such fresh air as could be pumped through the ventilators, and what remained of it was not enough to lighten the prevailing atmosphere. Hot whirling eddies of vapour hovered over the engines and drifted to other parts of the ship; the men were continually mopping their foreheads, and now and again one of them would moisten his lips with a drop of repulsive lukewarm tea, which, like all the food and drink in the boat, tasted strongly of oil.

Improvisation was a key to U-boat survival. The chief engineer was probably the most important individual on board. If the diesel motors were off just a bit, he was expected to notice, despite the overwhelming clatter of the engine room. If a part malfunctioned, someone on board could be counted on to fabricate a replacement. Likewise, if someone was injured. Bergen saw an officer fashion splints from a disassembled cigar box to set a broken arm. During emergencies, everyone was expected to keep their heads and concentrate on a solution. The most dramatic episode in Bergen's book relates the appalling situation of *U-88*, when a boat it had sunk actually pinned the submarine to the bottom of the sea floor, threatening to entomb them all. This might seem an appropriate denouement for people seen as not much better than pirates, but *U-88* actually managed to wiggle out of its predicament in one piece.

The spirits of the crew required special attention. Social barriers between officers and men, rigid in the imperial navy from destroyers right on up to dreadnoughts, were extraordinarily relaxed on submarines. The valued captain was the man who treated his men like family or stressed the fraternal bond that danger and isolation often generate in wartime. 'To pass the time', a wireless operator related to Bergen, 'the Commander was playing the flute to us in the men's quarters, I was accompanying him on the concertina, and the boys were singing. The atmosphere grew positively gay.' Whenever there was something to celebrate, many captains produced a welcome bottle of schnapps to pass around. Birthdays were generally remembered, and when possible Christmas was spent quietly on the ocean bottom, the gramophone playing 'Stille Nacht, heilige Nacht'. If a doomed merchantman seemed likely to surrender some loot, captains rarely interfered with his scavenging crew. Boarding parties sent to plant explosives on a ship to sink her (torpedoes and artillery ammunition being precious) often came back with fresh food, especially valued. In one instance, 'a large fat pig was wandering about the sailing ship's deck; we shot it and hauled it into a dingy. [The cook] appeared on deck armed with soap, brush and razor, and in a thrice, though we could hardly trust our eyes, the pig was soaped and shaved. "Pork and beans", announced the cook!' When circumstances allowed, salvage and floating barrels were often hauled on deck after a ship went down and eagerly hacked open. These might contain anything from salted fish to cocoa to English marmalade to 'pure American hog's lard – We swam in fat!' Food bonanzas reminded the crew of why they were there: to exact revenge on their enemies.

The war of terror for most German U-boat men was considered thoroughly justifiable. Women and children on the home front were 'supporting life on vile, injurious, almost uneatable food substitutes and their watery turnips' owing to the illegal allied blockade, so what were they to do? Not retaliate? 'What the enemy did, it must also be our right to do', wrote Bergen. The sentiment of innocent victims back in the fatherland purged their conscience from any guilt felt watching sailors jumping overboard to their deaths, ships splitting in half and plunging to the bottom with 'a death gurgle', even hundreds of transport mules and horses screaming death agonies as they drowned. Steel was an ingredient that not only fashioned their boat, but hardened their hearts.

Cruises could last for over a month. From their several lairs around the Bight, submarine crews would gather on board the deck to hear an impassioned speech from whichever admiral was about, followed by three cheers for the fatherland. Comrades and sometimes girlfriends gathered on the breakwater, waving them out of harbour. Escorted by patrol boats guiding them through protective mine fields, they would then cast off alone, 'under orders for the next world'. The goal was 30,000 tons of enemy shipping sunk. Anything less than that and no bands would greet them upon their return, nor would their admiral welcome them home with a warm salutation.

Life was tough on a U-boat. On the surface, in tempestuous weather, even the most hardened seaman could find himself the victim of *mal de mer*. The conning tower, which reminded Bergen of a Roman war chariot, was the nucleus of activity. Men dressed in motley gear, 'fur caps, jerseys, sea-boots, sou'westers and leather coats', served four-hour shifts as lookouts, often lashed to the boat with straps to keep them from being washed overboard – usually a death sentence. This was critical duty, since the temptation, once a target had been sighted, was always to look in that direction. Many German boats were lost when enemy sub chasers slipped up unobserved while U-boat crews were busy with the matter at hand, sinking something else.

When submerged, tensions and anxiety often ran high. Probably nothing was feared more than mines. Areas known to have been heavily laid with what U-boaters considered 'dirty traps' laid by 'a bunch of murderers', had special nicknames such as 'The Witch's Kettle' or 'The Caviar Sandwich'. It turned men's legs to jelly when they heard the drag of a mooring cable run the entire length of the boat or, even worse, 'the ominous iron grating sound of a mine' against their hull, just waiting to explode. In such cases, and a battle cruise rarely escaped such occurrences, 'the bony hand of death had come too near'. As film-goers know all too well, depth charge attacks (a favourite staple of submarine films such as *Das Boot*) were very trying. Even seasoned captains could crack under the strain. After repeated attacks, one was reported to have thrown his charts on the floor and screamed '*Es ist alles Mist*', which roughly translates as 'This is a dog's life'. Such lapses were not edifying for the crew.

Attacks on enemy shipping, especially when in convoy, were laborious, frustrating and often futile affairs. Submarines spent much of their time chasing targets, frequently finding themselves too slow to keep up or unable to position themselves for a good shot, all for the lack of an extra half-knot of speed. Anti-submarine vessels, whether destroyers, armed trawlers or torpedo boats, made life dodgy. When under attack, if a vital component was damaged, commandeers found themselves operating in the dark, literally and figuratively. Karl Dönitz, his periscope shattered, was forced to surface 'in the blind', having no idea – other than a dark suspicion – of what might await him on the surface. For Dönitz, it was disaster. His U-boat was sunk, and he himself was lucky to be picked up in the water. He spent the rest of the war in a POW camp, time well spent, he claims, developing wolf pack tactics that would be the keystone of the World War II German submarine campaign two decades later. Easy pickings were wonderful sport. Captain Spiegel of *U-202* sank fifteen unarmed fishing boats in just two hours, and tramp steamers of only 1,000 tons were common fare. He described the experience as being 'a wolf in a flock of sheep' with no shepherd around with his dog. A really big catch could be the highlight of a cruise (or a career), as described in the dispatch of a 13,000 ton steamer by *U-54*:

Two tremendous detonations followed, and the great ship began to sink. In a last defiance her bow reared up at almost right angles out of the water. Strange smouldering flames burst out of her; we made off at top speed. Suddenly a column of fire and smoke shot up like an erupting volcano, and with a terrific explosion the entire ship was blown to pieces. A blaze and a flash, and then – nothing. The sea was scattered with falling fragments, and a vast tidal wave rose up and nearly engulfed us. We stood as though turned to stone, watching that tremendous drama of destruction.

At such moments, U-boat crews felt themselves all-powerful. They revelled in the notion of being 'the hunter', prowling the wastes for wild animals to chase and pull down, often in fiery spectacles, as just described. They were also capable of lachrymose self-pity when, instead of hunting, they, in their turn, became the hunted. Then the memoirists would compare themselves to poor wretched rabbits, mercilessly hounded by packs of dogs loaded with lethal weapons. At times these 'multiple personalities', usually expressed with considerable vehemence, betray a glaring lack of perspective. To see oneself as a dashing pirate one minute, then a helpless victim the next ('Once more we must imitate the hare and make a dash for safety') was truly self-deceiving.

One common denominator that united almost all the U-boat men was their sense of comradeship, unique in all the services for its intensity. Aviators tended to be individualistic: the great air aces, for instance, were sometimes intensely lonely individuals who, for whatever reason (often psychological) stood apart from their compatriots. Old army units that had once celebrated their regimental lineage often had no long-termers left after a few tours in the trenches to remember any of it, and Kitchener's 'pal divisions' stood largely hollowed by war's end. Sailors in the grand fleets often held strong allegiances to their ships and, at times, to the reputed dash of their commanders, but a dreadnought's crew numbered over a thousand men, and no captain could (or would) know all of them. U-boats were different. The intimacy of danger in cramped quarters, the hazards of the job, the inherent loneliness of a station far from shore and any human comfort, tended to forge a close-knit union of spirit that every observer noted. As Bergen said, it was 'an iron bond'.

Their isolation had another effect. 'We were utterly convinced we would win the war'. Returning to Heligoland and its 'familiar red rocks' after a cruise, to be greeted as heroes by comrades and sometimes even by the kaiser himself, somehow made the carnage and defeatism of the western front a long way away. No one was more stunned by the mutinies that ravaged the German imperial fleet in 1918 than the submariners. We 'have been doing all the Navy's work in [this] war' said a U-boat officer to some captured Americans; 'the battleships and cruisers of the High Seas Fleet have been doing next to nothing.' Another said, '*We* weren't the ones who had lost the war; we had done our duty.' They greeted the armistice of November 1918 with a combination of both incredulity and relief. [27]

Victory at Last

'A sorry prize.'

Lloyd George on the peace
achieved in November 1918.

Awareness that erosion on both the German military and home fronts had become catastrophic was signalled on 1 October by the kaiser's appointment of Prince Maximilian of Baden as the new Reich chancellor, his specific instructions being to begin negotiations for an armistice. Prince Max attempted to use American President Woodrow Wilson's famous 'Fourteen Points' as the basis for a truce and then a permanent peace agreement, to the fury of many British, French and Italian politicians and officers, who had neither been consulted nor had anything to do with its drafting. (Sir Henry Wilson's diary is full of disparaging remarks on 'that ass Wilson.... He really is the limit.... [should be] put in his proper place.... His 14 Points (with which we do not agree) were not a basis for an armistice, which is what the Boche pretend they are.... Wilson is acting on his own.... the war is *not* over, the 14 Points are *not* an armistice, an armistice is not *peace*.... Everyone angry and contemptuous of Wilson.... a dangerous visionary.') One of the preconditions established by the president was an end to U-boat warfare. He did not want any more events such as *U-86*'s exploit of 27 June, when it torpedoed the fully loaded Canadian hospital ship, *Llandovery Castle*, then rose to the surface and machine-gunned survivors. It must be said that German conduct on so many fronts generally had the effect of hardening international opinion against its cause, with submarine warfare heading the list. The desire to 'hang the kaiser' at war's end was not the idle threat or slogan it may seem today.[28]

On 20 October 1918, twenty-two days before the armistice was formally announced, all U-boats were recalled to base, though their service was not finished. Officers of the naval high command, wishing to redeem their honour, designed a dash into the North Sea to confront the Royal Navy's grand fleet in one final and allegedly glorious finale. This impulse has been described by more than one commentator as the equivalent of Wagner's 'Ride of the Valkyries.' Fortunately for the lives of several thousand ordinary seamen, mutinies broke out on the imperial dreadnoughts. Red flags were hoisted up the halyards, officers were murdered, socialist contagion spread through the fleet. Admirals turned to the only service they could trust, the U-boats. Many were ordered out to sea again to prevent contamination, others were told to line up torpedo tubes to sink their own ships in harbour if necessary. In effect, however, the fleet was lost, and the officer corps, to their eternal sorrow, realized the game was up. When Lothar von Arnauld, Germany's premier U-boat ace, pulled into his berth in Kiel, he simply went down to his cabin, changed into civilian clothes, and walked out to catch a tram for home, hoping not be recognized by rebellious seamen. This was, he later wrote, 'the bitter end'. He and his U-boat colleagues had sunk an incredible 5,282 allied vessels, representing some 12,000,000 tons of shipping. Over 5,000 of his friends, shipmates and comrades had perished in 178 boats; 114 surviving *Unterseeboote* were surrendered to the British. When inspectors found an additional 62 in home waters, and 149 being constructed in German shipyards, they insisted these either be surrendered or broken up. Over one hundred enemy boats ended up being tethered to one another in the broad estuary below Harwich on England's east coast. At night, fishermen and scavengers rowed out and looted all they could, 'clocks, chronometers, hack watches, barometers, sextants, binoculars, precious metals, handy little motors', and anything else that came under the category known as 'etc'. Germany, by the Treaty of Versailles, was forbidden ever again to construct or maintain a submarine arm. It would take only 22 years to prove how ineffective this prohibition turned out to be. World War I veterans such as Karl Dönitz were full of ideas as to how their performance could be improved and, unlike their leader in World War I, the feckless kaiser, they would have a commander in Adolf Hitler who thought nothing of restraint or international opinion. The dogs of war would be unleashed as never before in naval history.

Scapa Flow Today
A Watery Grave for the Imperial Fleet

At the end of the war, Germany's proud fleet, beset by mutiny, rebellion and socialist contagion was ordered to sail to Scapa Flow, the vast, 120-square-mile watery embrasure of the Orkney Islands in Scotland. What a sight that must have been, the defeated enemy, humiliated, steaming single file through Hoxa Sound into the enormous anchorage. Nine months later, when rumours of the draconian terms of the Versailles peace treaty spread from ship to ship, the commanding admiral of the fleet, in full-dress uniform with all appropriate awards and decorations, ordered battle flags hoisted on all his ships, and then for his men to open the cocks on every vessel. Most slid to the bottom before their British wardens actually realized what was happening. Several ordinary and unarmed German seamen were machine-gunned to death as British patrol boats opened up on figures scurrying around on the decks of the various warships, or seen rowing away from sinking vessels. Not much of a fuss was made about them.

Taking a ferry from the Scottish mainland to Scapa Flow has few if any reminders of how critical a station this was (in both world wars) to the fortunes of the storied Royal Navy. Entering the Flow, one sees a few old shore battery emplacements, and several of the small islands are now linked by causeways (some known as Churchill Barriers) that were constructed in the 1940s to block the many separate channels that course into and out of Scapa Flow, many of which were boldly used by German submarines to infiltrate the anchorage. The feat by *U-18* in 1915 to slink into the Flow was more than replicated on 14 October 1939, when the battleship HMS *Royal Oak* was torpedoed by *U-47*, killing over 800 men. A small buoy marks the spot, as well as a perennial oil slick that will probably continue to the end of time. Otherwise this great body of water looks pretty much today as it did when the Vikings first came here in the eleventh century: empty, lifeless, supremely beautiful.

An ingenious engineer by the name of Ernest Cox bought the licence to salvage what German destroyers he could for £250, most of which lay in about 100 feet of water. Between 1924 and 1926, he refloated twenty-six of them, and for the next six years, seven battleships as well. Most of these were towed, keel up, to scrapyards on the mainland. When the great general strike of 1926 cut off Cox's coal supply, he merely sliced open the bottom of the battleship *Seydlitz* and scavenged what was left from its fuel bunkers. None of his remarkable ability to improvise saved him from financial ruin, however, and after his bankruptcy another firm took over the enterprise. By the time it was finished, World War II came around the bend, just in time to start over all over again with newer wrecks.

The Hebrides have their fair share of tourists each summer, drawn here by birds, one or two mysterious stone circles, and splendid scenery everywhere you look. There isn't much else. When I spent three days there in springtime, the place was utterly deserted. One of the lonelier spots is a peel tower high on a cliff overlooking the Atlantic, easily mistaken for some local ruffian's stronghold from the sixteenth century, but it is not that. Put up in 1926 by Orkney stonemasons, it honours Field Marshal Kitchener, who went down on the HMS *Hampshire* on a stormy night in 1916, a little over a mile offshore. A plaque on the tower's wall states it was built here to be 'nearest to the place where he died on duty'.

Kitchener was not the only one who perished in these waters. The rocks, shoals and horrific weather in this part of the world have claimed many lives. On 12 January 1918, two destroyers patrolling for mines were pulverized in heavy weather and dashed to pieces on ocean rocks within sight of shore. Every man but one went down, the lone survivor rescued from a tiny 'islet' within sight of land a few days later, dazed and all but dead from exposure. The ships could not be salvaged; they both remained for several winters visible to the eye, but a few more years of stormy weather knocked what was left to pieces. Local farmers who habitually combed the shore for seaweed to fertilize their fields had to desist for several years, when human remains were continually being found ensnared in the wrack.

Chapter 12

'Halifax Wrecked'

The Halifax Herald

'Nova Scotia's Win-the-War Newspaper'
7 December 1917

The morning of 6 December 1917 was clear, pleasant and not overly cold. As the city of Halifax, Nova Scotia, awoke to another busy day, coal and wood stoves were lit, children were dressed for school, breakfasts were cooked and eaten, men hurried to work, mostly on the waterfront with its many industrial sites. The harbour was congested, as it had been throughout the three years of war. Dozens of substantial vessels were either at anchor or tied to wharves. The port itself, which in 1913 had handled some two million tons of goods, was now being swamped with a seven-fold increase. In 1917 alone, 2,000 merchant ships had come and gone from Halifax. Its anchorage was also the primary demarcation point for troops being shipped to the European war zone. In some irony, the *Titanic's* sister ship, the *Olympic*, had been a frequent visitor, her luxury accommodations stripped bare, her ornaments and fine china removed for safe-keeping. Photographs of her on the Halifax waterfront show a vessel pretty battered and in need of much more than a paint job. For some 56,000 Canadian boys over the course of four years, Halifax would be the last sight of home they would ever see. Most lie buried in France and Belgium.

The harbour is really two bodies of water. Inland sits Bedford Basin, a neatly enclosed twenty-one square miles of perfect, deep-water anchorage. Convoys generally gathered here before setting off into the Atlantic. A passage informally called the Narrows, a channel about 1,500 feet wide, connects the Basin with the wider reach of Halifax Harbour. On one side of the Narrows is Dartmouth, on the other side a working-class suburb of Halifax called Richmond, named after the seven-storey Richmond Sugar Refinery that stood on the waterfront. Once past the Narrows, and then George's Island, curtained by anti-submarine nets and covered by coastal artillery, the passage leads past McNab's lighthouse into shipping lanes for Europe or the United States.

At a little past 8 o'clock in the morning, two ships approached each other in the Narrows. Leaving the Basin was the *Imo*, 5,000 tons and twenty-eight years in service, built in Belfast for the White Star Line where she carried passengers under the name *Runic*. Sold to a Norwegian whaling concern, she was operating now under contract to the Commission for Relief in Belgium, headed by Herbert Hoover.[1] Prominently displayed on both her sides were huge signs, BELGIUM RELIEF, an attempt to persuade ruthless U-boat captains that she carried humanitarian supplies and nothing else. The Germans often refused to believe such blandishments. However callous, the fact remains that the famous *Lusitania*, despite protestations to the contrary, was probably carrying munitions for the beleaguered British Army when she was torpedoed off the Irish coast two years before, taking 1,198 civilians to the ocean's bottom. The safety of a ship like the *Imo* often came down to whether a U-boat wished to conserve its torpedoes for a target of more importance. Entering the Narrows in the opposite direction was a munitions ship, the *Mont Blanc*. Unlike the *Imo*, she was fully loaded. In between the two was an American streamer, the *Clara*, which had preceded the *Mont Blanc* twenty minutes earlier on its way into the port. All three ships carried veteran local pilots.

The *Mont Blanc* was little better than a tramp steamer. Requisitioned for war duty, she had survived multiple crossings over the Atlantic, but for her December voyage from New York, she carried a cargo that was new to her: 2,300 tons of picric acid, the prime ingredient of a powerful explosive agent known as lyddite, as well as shipments of TNT, gun cotton and, for good measure, some thirty-five tons of benzol fuel, strapped to the deck in metal drums. The key to victory on World War I battlefields was no longer cavalrymen, however much generals of the British high command might wish this to be the case, but the brute club of an artillery barrage. Before the Battle of the Somme in 1916, for example, almost two and a half million pounds of explosive shells were fired by the Allies on German positions. The *Mont Blanc*'s cargo was therefore a prime cog to the war effort, and the largely French crew had a right to be nervous. Their ship was a floating bomb. Too slow to keep up with the convoy then leaving New York, she was ordered to follow the New England coast to the Bay of Fundy, then steam directly to Halifax. From there, it was likely that she would proceed, again without escort, to her home port of Bordeaux.

The captain of the *Imo*, annoyed at a refuelling delay that had prevented him from shipping out the previous afternoon, was impatient to be off, an attitude his pilot, William Hayes, was aware of. Having negotiated the passage of vessels into and out of Halifax hundreds of times, Hayes felt no disinclination to err on the side of caution. The *Imo* was doing seven knots as she began entering the Narrows.

The catastrophic event that was to follow was mostly caused by the *Imo*'s consideration of the approaching *Clara*. Standard procedure within the shipping lane was for vessels to pass each other port to port; in other words, the left side of each ship passes the left side of the other. But the American vessel, wanting to tie up in the city's dockyard more quickly, exchanged whistle signals with Hayes on the *Imo*, indicating its wish to reverse standard procedure by switching lanes, enabling the *Clara* to reach its berth in Halifax expeditiously. After the vessels had passed each other, starboard to starboard, Hayes noticed a tug with two barges, also in *Clara*'s lane, but instead of switching back to his normal position, he remained in the incorrect channel. At about this time the *Mont Blanc* came into view, about 450 yards away.

The pilot of the *Mont Blanc* sensed immediately that the *Imo* was ploughing ahead on the 'incoming' road, and he ordered a one-whistle blast of warning and decreased his speed to 'Dead Slow.' For some inexplicable reason, the *Imo* responded with two blasts, an indication that she intended to exaggerate her course even farther to the left, a move so astonishing that the *Mont Blanc* went into a 'Dead Stop' mode. Ships, however, cannot halt their forward progress at a moment's notice. The *Mont Blanc*'s pilot, seeing a collision in the making, called for his ship to steer hard to port, coming up on a parallel course with the approaching vessel. Hayes, his counterpart on the *Imo*'s bridge, the situation unfolding rather too quickly for comfort, blew three blasts, indicating 'Full Reverse.' This had the unfortunate effect of turning the *Imo*'s bow dead right. These several exchanges of whistle horns caught the attention of several seamen and officers on other ships. One grabbed his binoculars and was heard to say, 'Boys, there's going to be a head-on here'. The *Imo*'s momentum had slowed, but not quickly enough, and she ploughed straight ahead into the now stationary *Mont Blanc*'s starboard bow. Sparks flew. On an ammunition ship, sparks can be deadly. In this particular instance, as one chronicler of the events described it, the result was 'the greatest man-made explosion before Hiroshima'.

The primary culprit was the highly volatile picric acid, spilled bits of which ignited into small fires, rather like the head of a wooden match. Ruptured drums of benzol on the deck released fumes that fuelled combustion. Greasy smoke began to pour out of the *Mont Blanc*'s ruptured bow, and she began drifting towards the Halifax shoreline at Richmond. In the space of a mere ten minutes, seeing the situation as hopeless, the *Mont Blanc*'s captain gave the 'Abandon Ship' order. Forty or so men scrambled into lifeboats and frantically pulled for the Dartmouth shore. They were probably the only people in greater Halifax who knew what was coming.

The fourteen or so remaining minutes in the lives of some 2,000 people were, for many, rather exciting. They had the spectacle of a first-rate fire to watch, having no idea at all as to the volatile munitions that the *Mont Blanc* was carrying (she was not flying, as was customary, a large red flag that would have signified its dangerous cargo). The Fire Department was called out, but largely from fear that burning embers from the vessel might ignite wooden buildings and wharves. A tug tried to tie on to the disabled ship, thinking to tow her into deeper water where she might sink. Crowds materialized on the waterfront. Men left work for a look, their wives stood at kitchen windows, taking it all in. On the Dartmouth side, the French sailors of the *Mont Blanc* had beached their boats and were running for their lives. Some witnesses claim they gave no warnings, but few people in the area spoke French, so there's really no telling. One sailor, finding himself charging through a squalid Micmac Indian camp, grabbed a baby out of its mother's arms and kept on running. She chased after him. At the railway yards down by the water in Richmond, a telegraph operator named Vince Coleman heard a sailor yell something like 'Everybody out! Run like hell!' He did but then stopped, remembering that the overnight train from St. John, New Brunswick was due to arrive in just a few minutes. He returned to his post and telegraphed the following: 'Stop trains. Munitions ship on fire. Approaching Pier 6. Goodbye.' It was 9:04 a.m. Thirty-five seconds later, the *Mont Blanc* exploded.

There is no mystery as to the exact moment. Museums in and around Halifax have collections of watches that were found on victims or recovered from houses. The hands all stop at 9:04. The first explosions were of the fuel drums, heated by fires in the hold, which blasted off from the deck like mortar shells. They detonated in the air or when they fell to earth. Following them came the rest of it: the picric acid (both dried and liquid), the gun cotton, the TNT. Everything on board, as one writer has noted, 'was engineered to blow up'. The first thing people might have noted would have been the sound, estimated at speeds of 13,320 miles an hour; then the overwhelming blast of air pressure – people standing next to windows were later found beheaded, blinded or horribly maimed by the flying glass. Many were stark naked, their clothes and shoes having been torn right off their bodies. A fireball came after that, then a rain of deadly debris; finally a wave estimated at twenty feet high which sucked some 200 people to their deaths on its recoil. Underwater divers working on the hull of a ship suddenly found themselves roiled about and their oxygen lines tangled. Only two quick-thinking men topside saved their lives. A steeplejack, Karl Norgan Pettersen, an immigrant from Norway, was working on a fifty-foot Marconi tower on Geizer's Hill, overlooking the city. He related to his grandson the interesting experience of suddenly looking at the ground, just a few metres from his face, as the tower was bent to earth. It then flipped up again to its original position. Securely strapped, Pettersen was not flung away like a stone from a slingshot.

The *Mont Blanc* was obliterated. The shank of its anchor, weighing some 1,140 pounds, was found over two miles from the blast sight, one of its cannon barrels three miles away. The *Imo* was thrown up on shore by the tsunami. The Richmond Sugar Refinery simply disappeared, as did most of the wooden houses in the neighbourhood behind it, some 300 acres in all. About 25,000 people, in the space of a few seconds, were suddenly without shelter. Fires spread throughout the north end of Halifax as coal and wood stoves, knocked over, ignited their surroundings. Flimsy shacks in Africville, a shanty town where poor blacks lived, were shielded from the direct blast, but nonetheless not much was left standing. Trees and poles were levelled. The sailor from the *Mont Blanc* who had grabbed the baby, sensing what was right behind him, dove to the ground, covering the child with his own body. Both survived. The train from St. John, with some 300 passengers aboard, stopped in time. The telegraph operator who saved them perished. A giant black mushroom cloud, estimated by a captain at sea who saw it to be some 12,000 feet tall (an exaggeration; the plume was considerably lower than that height), loomed over the city. Greasy black debris covered everything and everybody. Many people staggering about the ruined streets were taken for negroes. The helmsman of the *Imo*, who survived (its captain did not), was arrested as a German spy, his accent and a letter in his pocket being identified as Germanic. It took some time for him to establish that he was, in fact, Norwegian. That night a blizzard dumped sixteen inches of snow. Some survivors, trapped in the wreckage of their homes, froze to death as the temperature plummeted to 16 degrees.

The enormity of the explosion was most apparent to Canadian soldiers who had returned from the Western Front in Europe, and were now stationed in Halifax. Although they were certainly used to seeing destroyed cities, such as Ypres, and were relatively immune to the sight of dead and decayed corpses, the civilian casualties were a profound shock. Oral recollections, assiduously collected, repeat over and over again that decapitated children, women hanging dead out of windows or strung from poles in ghoulish poses, were almost the last straw. They really had seen everything now.

Scientists have calculated the force of the Halifax explosion with equations undecipherable to laymen. Simply put, the consensus is that at 9:04 the *Mont*

Blanc generated the equivalent energy of 3 kilotons of TNT. *The Little Boy*, dropped on Hiroshima in 1945, created five times that force, 15 kilotons. While these figures pale in comparison to the hydrogen bombs of the 1960s (the Soviet *Tsar Bomba* tested at 50 megatons), the fact remains that until 7 December 1917, there had been no bigger man-made explosion witnessed by anyone on earth. Some 2,000 people died (600 of whom were children), 9,000 required medical attention, thousands were made homeless and an estimated $35 million worth of damage had been incurred.

Although communications with the outside world were drastically curtailed, news of the catastrophe, much of it passed along by railway telegraphers relaying Vince Coleman's initial message, spread quickly – so quickly, in fact, that stocks plunged on the New York Stock Exchange that very afternoon. The Germans, it appeared, had bombed North American soil for the first time. Within just three hours, the Governor of Massachusetts sent the following telegraph to his counterpart in Nova Scotia, who at that point had no way of receiving it: 'Understand that your city in danger from explosion and conflagration. Reports only fragmentary. Massachusetts ready to go the limit in rendering every assistance you may be in need of. Wire me immediately.' By 10 p.m. that night a relief train had pulled out of Boston's North Station loaded with supplies, medicine, food, doctors and nurses. It would take two days to reach Halifax, ploughing through snow drifts and stopping at many stations to pick up more volunteers. Joining other trains from mainland Canada and throughout the Maritimes, it arrived to find a situation even more calamitous than had been feared. The place 'looked like some blackened hillside which a farmer had burned for fallow in the spring'. The next several days in Haligonian history were a tale of endless work (almost 6,000 eye injuries alone), incredible hardship, human tragedy of enormous proportions and one or two miracles. The dead were everywhere, lives, bodies and spirits had been shattered. Photographs in papers all over North America showed babies lined up in rows, their parents and siblings all gone. One 23-month-old baby girl, Annie Walsh, had enough good luck to last a lifetime. The blast levelled her house, killed her mother and sister, and blew her under the sturdy cook stove, which remained standing, its embers in the ash tray still warm from breakfast. These kept her alive in the frigid weather for twenty-six hours, when she was finally discovered by a soldier. Thereafter she was called 'Ashcan Annie'. On Day 6 of the search and rescue effort, the last surviving Haligonian was found in the rubble; the last recovered body not until a year later.

Supply trains funnelled essential needs into the city: food, blankets, clothing (4,000 women's underwear), tents, medicines, bedding, coffins, embalming supplies and, most importantly, thousands of window panes. It was, after all, winter. Five emergency hospitals were set up and also temporary morgues. Having some experience with the *Titanic* disaster, city officials had a system quickly in place to register bodies and their characteristics, in the hope of establishing names and addresses. Even so, ninety-five were never claimed or identified. These were buried in a potter's field. Rumours, of course, took a while to settle down, but one that persisted dredged up memories from the old colonial days when most whites feared and loathed Indians. It was said that a handful of Micmacs still living in Dartmouth had rowed their canoes over in the middle of the night to loot the ruins of Richmond. Army patrols were beefed up for added security. For many, especially in the United States which had just joined the European conflict, these many stories, some true, some false (as is the case for any disaster), were the first real glimpses of 'war' they had ever experienced.

The relief trains also brought into Halifax various teams of lawyers. An official inquiry was convened a week after the explosion which took on the atmosphere of a lynch trial. Owners of both the *Imo* and the *Mont Blanc* were involved (they would end up suing each other before all was said and done), and the two star witnesses, the captain and pilot of the *Mont Blanc*, were both grilled as though on trial for murder. Racial animosities were barely concealed: a connection was palpable between the French captain and French-Canadians in general, who were all regarded as traitors in English-speaking Halifax for refusing to serve in the war with more enthusiasm. This was a slight disconnection in logic, but people's nerves were frayed and everyone was looking for a scapegoat, especially since the Germans, for once, 'hadn't done it'. These two gentlemen from the *Mont Blanc*, along with an officer of the nascent Royal Canadian Navy, were all eventually indicted for manslaughter, though only one actually stood trial; he was acquitted. The civil suits lasted for several years, winding their way up to Canada's highest court and, after that, the privy council in London. The conflicting testimony about who blew whistles when, and how many, and what the intended messages were to oncoming vessels, grew so inordinately complicated that even naval men could not figure out the exact sequence of events. It was finally decided to split the blame. Both the *Imo* and the *Mont Blanc* were judged to have been delinquent in the proper etiquette of manoeuvring in the Narrows.

As for Richmond, it was bulldozed, redesigned as a model community and had its name obliterated from the municipal records. Many current Haligonians have never heard of it or know of its historical whereabouts. The next year, in gratitude to Massachusetts, which had not hesitated a second in its efforts to assist, the city of Halifax shipped south a fifty-foot Christmas tree as a holiday gift. In the 1970s, with the fisheries in decline, the coal mines teetering, industrial manufacturing a thing of the past and Halifax, 'Warden of the North', a virtual footnote, proponents of Nova Scotia's newest export commodity revived the tradition. Each year the industry association that represents Christmas tree growers and wreath-makers in Nova Scotia sends a big beauty to Boston, where it is erected on the Common as an official symbol of the holidays. A pleasant reminder of a ghastly event.

Who would have imagined that the biggest detonation of explosives during World War I, a four-year span where hundreds of thousands of tons worth of shells were launched and blew up, would not occur on the ghastly Western Front of France or Belgium, but in a place three thousand miles away, a city of which few Europeans were even aware of.

Chapter 13

Manfred von Richthofen

The Last Knight?

'le diable rouge'

Perhaps no significant and new weapon saw more technological progress in design, effectiveness and utility than the aeroplane. True, tanks were a shock when they first appeared on the field of battle, but they remained pretty much what they were for the duration: slow, clumsy, awkward behemoths that frequently found themselves stuck in the mud, easy targets and death traps for anyone caught inside. The Germans saw little use for them at first, and lagged far behind the allies in production and, more importantly, appreciation. Many of their tanks were retrofits, machines captured from the British or French, repaired, repainted and relaunched against their former owners. German proficiency with amoured vehicles would have to wait until 1939.

The same could not be said for aeroplanes. Originally, they were conceived as replacements for cavalry scouts, their mission to see from the sky what mounted soldiers generally observed from hilltops – the movement of enemy troops, the location of artillery and ammunition dumps, the divination of intent on the part of their opposite numbers. In the static world of trench warfare on the western front, cavalry had been reduced to obsolescence; generals and intelligence officers saw reconnaissance flights as the only means possible, other than spies or interrogating captured soldiers, of gaining information.

The first scouting planes were fairly primitive. Generally crewed by two airmen, one to fly, the other to observe, they usually flew low to the ground and attracted rifle fire from soldiers below ('one can hear every shot', a flyer wrote; 'it sounds like chestnuts snapping in a fire'). This was the greatest danger to their security. During the initial stages of the war, with the sky becoming more and more crowded with aircraft, semi-comic duels might occur, where pilots or observers fired pistols at one another or, in Manfred von Richthofen's case, a hunting rifle; over time, these were replaced by machine guns, usually mounted on a swivel, whereby the observer, in either a front or rear cockpit (depending on the type of aircraft), might fire at an opposing plane, generally without effect. Some enterprising warrior-pilot, itching to fire a gun of his own, decided to mount a machine gun overhead, on top of his wing, to avoid hitting the propeller. This was awkward, to say the least, an aviator having to control his plane with one hand, and stretching the other over his shoulder to fire the machine gun (quickly replaced by a lanyard attached to the trigger which the pilot pulled in order to fire his weapon). This was largely a 'hit or miss' proposition. The solution seemed to be placing the machine gun (either one or two) on the hood of the engine, the problem here being the propeller. Early designs lined the propeller edge with metal or something called 'a deflector wedge', so that spurts of gunfire would not shred it into splinters but, unfortunately, ricocheting bullets could be redirected back to the pilot, hardly the desired result. Ingenuity, however, trumps every difficulty. A 'delay' was invented, whereby the machine guns fired only when the propeller blade did not obstruct it. This development transformed the original 'scout' plane into an offensive weapon which, when organized as companies, became known as *Jagdstaffel*, or 'hunters'. Observation planes, more or less in an instant, became highly vulnerable. Pilots and observers, looking down at the ground, could suddenly find themselves attacked from above, hundreds of bullets screaming all around them, ripping the clumsy fabric stretched along their aircraft's wooden frame into shreds, severing strut wires holding wings together, knocking out or stalling engines or, even worse, inflicting mortal wounds. Flying solo observation flights became a near suicidal occupation, and these pilots were gradually sent aloft only with 'fighter planes' to protect them. The result were wild aerial melees, pilots engaged in duels, sometimes 'packs' of ten to fifteen planes on each side being involved. Midair collisions became a fact of life. The first great German ace of the war, Oswald Boelcke, died in the middle of a dog fight when his plane brushed into that of a comrade, tearing his wing off (Boelcke, whose word was 'gospel', liked to tell his acolytes, Manfred von Richthofen included, that every day for breakfast he would shoot an Englishman).[1]

With each passing month, newer, faster, deadlier planes flew from the sketching board of designers such as the Dutchman Tony Fokker, into production lines, resulting in speeds unheard of just a few months before, which generated all kinds of structural issues with their flimsy 'crates' (as the aviators liked to call them). It was not unheard of for pilots to see one of their wings begin to flutter or, even deadlier, shear away, just from the structural stress of a high-speed manoeuvre. These aircraft were not so much 'crates' as they were coffins.

Even so, they attracted their devotees, men so enamoured with the deviltry of it all that they ignored the actuarial odds regarding survival.

War on the ground did not excite their interest; it had devolved into a meat grinder devoid of glamour, devoid of the opportunity to demonstrate one's courage in a highly public fashion. What modern general ever saw one of his subordinates lead a charge, the usual prerequisite for winning a decoration or commendation? In the muck and slog of a mud-filled battlefield, in terrains devoid of colour, feature or life of any sort, and dominated by weapons that were fired from miles away by an enemy one never saw face to face, how was a man to stand out? For some, the answer to that question lay above their heads in the clean and unencumbered sky.

It was an easy leap to go beyond this simple illusion of purity, and propagandists from both sides generally did, equating the pristine environment of the heavens with a gloss of more imaginary bent. As war aces from both sides accumulated their kills, an aura of chivalry was hypothesized to satisfy the ever-growing appetite of a popular press that was, over time, becoming numbed and depressed by war. Pilots were seen as medieval horsemen, aerial combat as duels; the obsequies paid to aviators killed in combat – elaborate funerals 'like that of a reigning prince', opposing pilots dropping commemorative wreaths over enemy lines, the creation of Teutonic and Arthurian imagery (when von Richthofen died, he was called Siegfried, after Wagner's opera) – all these presented a colourful alternative to the dull, drab, dreary news from the trenches. These were 'clean' fights, not the butchery of modern, industrial war. By imputation, motives were that of the knight-errant, hearts purer and ends nobler. Not surprisingly, this represented a serious distortion of what these earliest fighter pilots really felt about their chosen mode of battle. At the very least, this was certainly true for Baron Manfred von Richthofen, who shot down the incredible number of eighty enemy planes in a career that lasted a mere twenty months. Motivated as he certainly was by glamour and the thirst for fame, von Richthofen's primary obsession was bit more pedestrian. He was a pathological killer driven by blood lust. Nothing made him happier than shredding a fellow human being from 50 metres away, machine guns blazing. Unlike many men below him in the trenches, he had the pleasure of seeing his opponents die. When they did, he often landed next to their wrecks, if he could, to grab a souvenir from the rubble. If not exactly an Indian looking for his totem scalp, one wonders how different in substance von Richthofen's motivations really were.

*'Victory would belong to him who was calmest, who shot best
and who had the clearest brain in a moment of danger.'*

Von Richthofen was born in the Silesian town of Schweidnitz to a 'small
estate' *Junker* family. His father was a retired army officer, one of the few
military men in his dynastic tree. When they served the state, they did so
mostly as administrators or civilian office-holders (we 'always lived in the
country', Manfred wrote later). The most significant person in his life
was his mother, a strong-willed and determined figure who was far more
intimately involved with her children (two other sons and a daughter) than
her more distant husband. Although they lived in a handsome townhouse,
the von Richthofens were minor gentry: reasonably prosperous, but hardly
on a lavish scale. Aristocratic titles – the famous 'von' – were no passports
to wealth, however important to personal vanity. The only brush this family
ever had with culture, and it was distant, proved to be a far-removed cousin,
Frieda von Richthofen, who ran off with the impoverished British writer D.
H. Lawrence, cheerfully leaving behind a husband and three children. It is
doubtful whether any of the von Richthofens read anything Lawrence ever
wrote.

Manfred was an ordinary student who rarely pushed himself in anything
that did not interest him, something he freely admitted. 'I did just enough
work to pass', he wrote. 'In my opinion, it would have been wrong to do more
than was just sufficient', a revealing statement on the merits of efficiency,
given his later career. Of medium build, he was a decent athlete and learned
to survive the harsh discipline of the cadet schools that his father insisted he
attend. His only passion, and it was real, was the hunt. When given his first
weapon as a seven- or eight-year-old, an air gun, he immediately went out to
his grandmother's garden and killed as many tame ducks as he could before
adults intervened. He plucked feathers from each one as souvenirs, and held
on to them his entire life. The habit of taking trophies never left him.

Young Manfred was an enthusiastic horseman, and the thrill of the chase in
open fields neatly corresponded with his penchant for blood lust. The cavalry
was a natural career path for his military profession, but the early days of the
war proved disappointing. He saw more quickly than most that the days of
horse charges were over, and he finagled his way into flight training, first as
an observer and, over time, into fighter planes. This did not come naturally to
von Richthofen. He crashed on his first solo flight, and was never more than
a pedestrian pilot. His disdain for loops and fancy manoeuvres in the air was
mostly a disguise for the fact that he proved incapable of extreme techniques
of his own (he was contemptuous of flashy French pilots – they reminded

him of bottled lemonade that, once opened, went flat pretty quickly). He more than made up for this deficiency by an aggressive spirit and something that he called 'hunting fever', which spelled the doom of over one hundred allied airmen. When he saw some hapless target in the sky, his first thought was, 'He must fall'.

Von Richthofen was no ordinary Prussian. He had disliked the harsh discipline of his various military schools, and did not take kindly to orders with which he disagreed. The very newness of the flying corps, without tradition and unburdened by decorum, appealed to his individuality. Up in the sky, he was his own boss; he paid attention to the lessons that early war aces passed along, but, as he processed these, he adapted what he learned to his own skill set. He had a keen eye, patience and a clear mind when bullets began flying (the sound of his machine gun, he wrote, relaxed him). However clear the objective (to down the enemy), he kept one thing foremost in his mind: it was important that he survive, not only for himself, but for the war effort in general. He frowned on unnecessary risk-taking. If his odds in any given encounter did not look favourable, he never hesitated to withdraw, unlike British pilots against whom he was usually arrayed. They were largely 'stupid' and 'foolhardy', in his opinion, never refusing a fight no matter what, reminding him of his more reckless younger brother, Lothar, who 'does not know how to run away'.[2]

The extreme youthfulness of the early cadres of pilots certainly made them looser. Ernst Udet, who survived the war with sixty-two kills to his credit, was only eighteen in 1914. Like so many of the others, he was brash, without fear and eager for the *Pour le Mérite*, Germany's most distinguished wartime decoration. He liked to thumb his nose at the enemy; his rear wing and elevator assembly had the inscription 'You and Who Else?' painted on them. Von Richthofen had the same bravado. In a provocative gesture, he had his plane painted bright red, which made him stand out in the sky. It signified, as Lothar admitted, 'a certain insolence. Everyone knew that it attracted attention. Consequently, one had to perform.' In imitation, all the members of his squadron painted theirs the same colour, as though to say (as von Richthofen did) 'Go on shooting. You won't hit me.'[3]

Von Richthofen methodically added to his 'bag of machines', which reached a daily peak during the battle of the Somme (an 'El Dorado' he called it, the 'happiest hunting ground'; the British had another name for it, 'Bloody April'). Von Richthofen downed twenty-one enemy planes in April alone; on the 24th, four in one day. His reputation grew accordingly. The French gave him a nickname, *le diable rouge*, or 'the red devil'. His quarters became cramped with souvenirs from his victims: an engine that he had transformed into a candelabra, machine guns, propeller blades (one of which was carved into a walking stick), identification numbers removed from assorted fuselages (Udet had one sprayed with a pilot's blood, especially evocative). After sixteen kills, he was given command of his own *Jagdstaffel*, a promotion so swift that infantry officers looked on in astonishment, a trajectory never even possible in their own careers. Von Richthofen's arrogance increased accordingly. He lectured aeroplane manufacturers on the deficiencies of their designs, and disputed more senior officers. 'It does not matter to me that [enemy aircraft] are shot down in my [sector]', a general whose front von Richthofen flew over daily said to him; 'rather that you ... barricade the air', [and allow no one to view my operations]. 'This was not at all my view of military aviation', von Richthofen wrote, 'I did not go to war to gather cheese and eggs.' The only object of a pilot was to engage in combat, not to waste time in petty patrols. He could get away with such moments of contempt. He was, after all, a hero.

Manfred received his *Pour le Mérite* in January 1917. Being handsome, photogenic and undeniably brave, he was removed from combat to go on tour, as it were, to sustain morale on the home front. He met most of the famous men of Wilhelmine Germany, including the kaiser, who spent most of their time together spouting off in his accustomed monologues. As a memento, Wilhelm gave von Richthofen a gigantic bust of himself, a self-portrait as it were, the imperial warlord looking suitably fierce, carved from marble and adorned with bronze motifs. It was so heavy that two servants were required to carry it into the dining room. Von Richthofen had it crated and sent home to his mother. When he wasn't busy at public functions, he went hunting on princely estates: grouse, wild boar, elk, bison, what did it matter what he killed? All he liked to do was 'fly and shoot pigs', as he wrote in his book. According to Udet, von Richthofen 'was the least complicated man I ever knew'.

'I no longer know any mercy.'

One of the more famous German fighters in mid-war was the Albatross, in its various permutations. A biplane (i.e. 2 wings) it weighted approximately one ton, was twenty-eight feet long, and powered by a 160 h.p. Mercedes engine, top speed around 110 mph. It took about fifteen minutes to climb 9,000 plus feet, but was not noted for its manoeuvrability in a tight corner. It made up for that with speed and firepower, mounting two air-cooled Spandau machine guns that could each fire 400 rounds per minute. Like all mechanical contraptions, the guns could often jam. Richthofen carried a small hammer in his pocket that he used to bang the weapons when they did so. Fuel capacity often limited patrols to 90 minutes or so. If the weather was right, it was not unknown for von Richthofen to fly four combat missions a day, interrupted only by lunch at midday (on occasion, oysters and champagne).

Von Richthofen's 'bag' of eighty kills, like that of all the other aces, was inflated by the quality of his victims. Germany's more or less defensive posture on the western front, especially after the Verdun debacle, presented obvious advantages to German hunters. Haig's obsession with frontal attacks necessitated up-to-date reconnaissance, and British flyers aggressively infiltrated German airspace to get it. This meant easier targets, be they observation planes flying low to the ground, or clumsy variations on a new category of plane, bombers, whose first forays were ludicrously primitive (pilots often tossed their payloads over the side by hand, hoping for a lucky hit).[4] The adjective most used to describe these planes was 'lumbering'. Tactics were relatively simple: von Richthofen rarely flaunted his approach, he wanted to gain the advantages inherent in full surprise. He liked to attack from above, when his victim's attentions were focused in the opposite direction, towards *terra firma*, and often led his pack from a V formation ('He was the steel point', Udet said), which protected him from being attacked from behind. He preferred to have the sun at his back on a first approach, blinding his opponents, and he wanted most of his fighting to take place over German lines, not British, where ground fire could be a problem, to say nothing of superior numbers of enemy aircraft. With outclassed opponents, von Richthofen showed no mercy. He usually held his fire until the last minute, to get as close as possible to the target, and then poured all he had into him until the outcome was certain (in one of his kills, he closed to within thirty feet of his victim). To make certain, one followed the falling opponent right to the ground (but only on the German side of the trenches; if the enemy managed to get across, let him be). Manfred was infuriated when his brother Lothar, having set a British plane on fire, greedily broke off his combat to chase another target that caught his eye. The first plane, as things turned out, managed to limp back to its own line, and survived. Lothar wasn't being serious, Manfred thought; he seemed to be on a lark. Hunting was not something Manfred took lightly. You stalked an enemy until you killed him. Richthofen was a bird of prey 'who picked off lame ducks', according to a British flyer, and feasted on the inexperienced.

This is not to say that he was a slouch when it came to confronting veteran fighter pilots. He was not. His famous dogfight with the British ace Major

Lanoe Hawker, lasted over thirty minutes, beginning at about 10,000 feet in altitude and ending at 150. 'After the usual waltzing', Von Richthofen had manoeuvered himself into the favoured position, on his opponent's rear end. It was Hawker's job to try and break away … no one wanted their 'crate spit into from behind'. Circling each other over and over again (at one point Hawker waved at von Richthofen, who noted later his thought that 'I was not meeting a beginner'), the Englishman found himself running out of both altitude and fuel. After a few desperate loops and other evasive manoeuvres, he finally took his chance and headed flat out for the British lines, but von Richthofen could not be budged. Hawker wasted time and speed with a few zigzags, which shortened the gap between himself and his pursuer. At this point the two planes were flying at about 100 mph, and only a hundred feet above the ground. Von Richthofen, running out of ammunition, took a last careful aim and fired his final burst. Hawker, struck in the head by a single bullet, lost control of his plane and it crashed a mere 150 feet from British trenches. Richthofen had the machine gun removed as a trophy, and the serial number from Hawker's tail rudder cut off. He sent these home to his mother in Schweidnitz in celebration of his sixteenth kill. He also continued his habit of commissioning a small silver cup, suitably inscribed with date and type of aircraft downed, to mark each of his victories. This collection came to a halt after the sixtieth cup, when his jeweller in Berlin said that silver was no longer available.

What made Manfred von Richthofen special? This is a hard question to answer because von Richthofen was neither a scholar nor given to introspection, and had not been gifted with an eloquent pen. His book, mostly dictated to a secretary, was 'written' reluctantly, on orders in fact from Berlin, and heavily reworked by censors looking to enhance image over facts. Whatever newspaper interviews he gave were likewise unrevealing, as were recollections by family members, particularly his mother, whose interest in her Manfred after his death was mostly as a burnisher of reputation (it was she who spread the legend that her son was romantically involved with an unknown sweetheart, refusing to marry because he believed himself doomed. Von Richthofen had no interest in women). The true indication of Richthofen's skill must therefore be found in his body of work, the techniques he used (as gleaned by his instructions to newcomers, and stray remarks remembered in the mess), and the hints he gave, perhaps unintentionally, when discussing the habits of other pilots. It is certainly true that it did not take long for young Manfred to tire of the notion of glamour when it came to his chosen profession. Once his appetite had been sated with commendations, medals, meeting the kaiser and more or less instant fame, he appears to have sought shelter in the perfection of his craft. Killing became mechanical, 'my former excitement had gone'. He became controlled, cold, wary.

Richthofen should probably be remembered best as the consummate technician, a surgeon, a man always steady in trying circumstances. In combat, he said, one should think 'quite calmly and collectedly, weigh[ing] the probabilities of hitting and being hit. The fight itself is the least exciting part of the business, as a rule. He who gets excited in fighting is sure to make mistakes.' Lothar, for example, was little better than a 'butcher' in his brother's opinion, a stuntman who showed off in the cockpit, did not assess the pros and cons of any prospective action and lacked the patience necessary for the prime prerequisite of success – stalking. Manfred von Richthofen was a stalker, a man used to sitting for hours in a tree blind, all night if necessary, for the opportunity to get off a single, fatal shot. Lothar was a brawler in the air, looking for trouble at every turn. Von Richthofen was a tactician who studied the odds; if a situation smelled wrong, he would turn away. If it looked promising, he would go for the jugular. In the later stages of his career, he resembled a robot.

As the war went steadily downhill for Germany, pressure mounted on von Richthofen. Allied production of war material began outstripping Germany's. Numbers of new enemy aircraft were arriving daily on the battlefront, some of which, like the Sopwith Camel, were more than competitive with the Fokker Dr.I, a triplane that von Richthofen was now flying but which was plagued by mechanical and design problems, many of which were never resolved. Fokker delivered only 320 of these to the front; nearly 5,500 Camels were manufactured in Britain for war service during the same time frame.[5] More ominously, von Richthofen only had to look around to see the ranks of his friends and colleagues irrevocably thinned by constant combat in the air. At twenty-five years of age, he was now the 'old man' of the service. What were his realistic chances of surviving the war? How much longer would that old German saying, *Glück muss man haben*, apply to him?[6] Both he and Lothar had suffered crash landings, requiring extensive stays in hospitals and numerous close calls. There is a frightening picture of Lothar, in fact, his jaw wired and face contorted in a pose worthy of Frankenstein. Surely the hourglass was running out on them both. On 21 April 1918, it did for Manfred.

'All I could do was try to dodge my attacker. I noticed it was a red triplane, but if I had realized it was Richthofen, I would have probably passed out on the spot.'

Lieutenant Wilfrid May
Manfred von Richthofen's prospective kill (Number 81)

Wilfrid May had no business being in the air on 21 April. He was green, raw, and one of but hundreds of British flyers that were being thrown into combat with almost no experience under their belt. They were, as one commentator noted, 'easy meat' for people like Manfred von Richthofen. May's superior officer, Canadian Captain A. R. Brown, was a different sort, a veteran and something of an ace himself with ten kills. But he was a self-confessed burn-out, suffering combat stress, ulcers and premonitions that his time was up. A fellow pilot had noted in a letter that Brown 'had lost his nerve' (as he said himself, he lived on milk and brandy). Be that as it may, Brown went up as usual on that April morning. He put May at the rear end of his formation; he told him to stay out of trouble, observe what was going on and not to get in a dog fight. Von Richthofen, heading a hunting group of thirteen, spotted May as the dance began. Before May had much of a chance to adjust, he found von Richthofen on his tail. May did what anyone in his spot would have done, he headed for home as fast as he could, but von Richthofen wouldn't be shaken off. The German ace was thinking, as he had on so many other occasions, 'Here comes number eighty-one.'

Luckily for May, his superior officer saw the spot he was in, and broke off to give a hand, heading for von Richthofen from a right angle and letting off a burst of fire which may (or may not) have hit the red triplane. Then he sheared off. From available evidence, it seems that von Richthofen was not deterred, but continued his pursuit of May ('very close on my tail', as the young man put it). May, flying at low level along the Somme river, felt that von Richthofen 'had me cold ... I knew I had had it'. But in looking over his shoulder he suddenly saw the enemy's plane spinning half over and then, to his immense relief, crashing. Brown seemed to be, in May's mind, in the immediate vicinity, and appeared to be the man who pulled the fatal trigger, but later evidence seems to be that von Richthofen was felled by rifle or machine gun fire from ground troops. He had ignored his own cardinal rule about chasing an opponent into enemy territory where, as he knew, his chances of being in the crosshairs of exponentially greater numbers of enemy guns (especially flying at the low level he was) were alarmingly higher. Blood lust, it seems, had got the better of his judgment at long last. A single bullet entered his body under the right arm, pierced his heart, and exited via the left nipple. He was probably dead before his plane hit the ground, and Wilfrid May, a lucky man indeed, lived for another thirty-four years.

Once the news spread about that the wrecked Fokker Dr.I triplane had been piloted by Manfred von Richthofen, now plainly deceased, it was picked apart as clean as a chicken carcass by souvenir hunters (Brown ended up with the Fokker's pilot seat, which he donated to a museum in Canada). Von Richthofen's body was hauled away on a corrugated sheet, photographed and autopsied, as authorities tried to figure out who actually had fired the fatal bullet. Brown, who went to see the corpse, came near to throwing up. He wrote his father that 'It is a terrible thing if you think about it that they should examine a body to see who should have the credit of killing him. What I saw that day shook me up quite a lot as it was the first time I have seen a man I know I have killed.' Although the body was badly mangled (von Richthofen's teeth had all been knocked out from the impact of the crash), Brown remained smitten by the angelic appearance of his foe. 'He appeared so small to me, so delicate.' The next day *le diable rouge* was buried with full military honours. The whole business was so stressful to Brown that he more or less collapsed nine days later, invalided out of the service as a result. When he returned to Canada after the war, he chose a quieter profession, becoming an accountant.

German pilots, to say nothing of public opinion, were immeasurably depressed by the grim news of 'Siegfried's' death. It was something of a black mark to be shot down by ground fire, and not considered the 'beautiful death' that so many of these men often morbidly sought in aerial combat. Von Richthofen's walking stick, symbolic of command for the *Jagdstaffel* he had led, was inherited by the next in line who, inevitably, died in action soon thereafter. The last man to wield it was Hermann Göring, of later World War II notoriety. His final act as head of the unit was to threaten socialist rabble who attempted to commandeer his planes when the armistice was declared.[7] Lothar von Richthofen, after yet another crash, was hospitalized until the end of the war.

Ernst Udet, like many fighter pilots of World War I, had a difficult time adjusting to civilian life. On a trolley in Berlin late that November, a burly revolutionary, seeing Udet's *Pour le Mérite*, called it a piece of tin and attempted to rip it off. In the ensuing fistfight, joined in by bystanders and a conductor, the miscreant was finally thrown out at the next stop, cursing and screaming. Udet's sense of dignity was momentarily restored, but not his sense of place. After a long barnstorming career, Udet, now an alcoholic, finally found a place in the resurgent Luftwaffe. He had a great deal to do with the development of the stuka dive bomber which so terrorized civilian refugees in the first days of World War II. He succumbed to depression, both personal and professional, in 1941, when he committed suicide. Göring died five years later, by his own hand as well, taking a fatal dose of cyanide just before he could be executed as a war criminal.

Chapter 14

St. Petersburg ... then Petrograd ...
then Leningrad

'Cosmopolitan in its leanings, but Russian in its recklessness.'
Grand Duke Alexander, referring to St. Petersburg

Unlike all the other major European capital cities, St. Petersburg was a relatively new creation, founded in 1703 by Tsar Peter the Great, who named it after his patron saint. Although Berlin did not attain significant stature until the reign of Frederick William the Elector in the seventeenth century, historians have found mentions of that place since the thirteenth century. But when Peter first saw the future site of his imagined city at the mouth of the river Neva, there wasn't a soul in sight other than a few fishermen. The Swedes, with whom he waged fierce and dreadful campaigns for control of the eastern Baltic, had built a fort five miles upstream (which he overran after a short siege); neither they, nor anyone else, would have settled where Peter chose to. But, then again, he had a mind of his own, and no one dared contradict it.

When the Neva approaches the Baltic, it loses its singularity of form, breaking up into a marshy delta full of streams, rivulets and low-lying islands. It is not a place where many people would have dreamed of building a major city. Like Venice, water commands everything, and the site was often deluged with gale-driven storm tides, suffering flood after flood. Its many islands required bridge-building and, later, canals to pull it all together as the town expanded. No one wanted to live there. The climate was horrific, the surrounding land so unproductive that food supplies had to be imported from far away and building materials, meaning stone, were locally scarce. The ancient capital of Moscow consisted mostly of wooden buildings; Peter decreed that he and the nobility who followed him to the new site (by imperial fiat) were to construct their town houses, and later palaces, in masonry. This alone made the place different from anywhere else in Russia.

The story of its initial decades of existence is a telling reminder that Russia is like nowhere else, and provides an insight into what being an 'autocrat' truly means. Peter the Great was a larger-than-life character. He decided to create the city primarily because of his desire to be a European, not some

Manufacturing floor, Krupp Iron Works, Essen, Germany. Touring the Ruhr Valley in 1909, the newspaper baron Lord Northcliffe ominously viewed the landscape. 'Every one of those factory chimneys is a gun pointed at England', he said to a companion.

The uniform Archduke Ferdinand wore on the day of his assassination. The car in which he and his wife were killed appears in the background.

George Bellows's *The Barricade* (1918), painted in response to reports of German atrocities during the invasion of Belgium. Bellows depicted innocent villagers in the nude, and in poses reminiscent of medieval imagery depicting martyrs such as St. Sebastian.

Claus Bergen's watercolour, *The Battle of Jutland* (1916), depicts the German battlecruiser SMS *Seydlitz* in action, several of its guns already silenced by enemy fire. The cacophonous atmospherics of the battle are realistically portrayed: the noise, smoke, near misses, flying spray. The *Seydlitz* fired 376 salvos during the battle, of which ten hit a target.

Closing Up, by George Davis (1919), depicts British biplanes re-forming to beat off attacking German Fokker fighters. Davis was a prolific painter and illustrator, for many years at *The Illustrated London News*, to which he contributed over 2,500 images. He served in the Royal Air Corps during World War I, drawing up training manuals on manoeuvring for novice pilots, many of whom were woefully unprepared for aerial combat.

The tone of propaganda posters evolved as the war dragged on. Early versions were often chivalric, typified by the Austrian example (right), captioned *Protection of Austria, Guaranteed by Habsburg Throne.* The 1917 image (below), also Austrian and more sombre, was captioned *And You?*

A watercolour of Tsarina Alexandra Feodorovna, wife of Nicholas II, leaving church services, by Valentin Serov (1901).

Portrait of Muttar il Hamoud min Beni Hassan, one of T. E. Lawrence's bodyguards, by Eric Kennington (1920).

With the war ended, chaos ruled in several major European societies. In Berlin, the KPD, or Spartacists, forerunners of the German Communist Party, for several weeks threatened to overthrow the post-war government. The poster on the left, depicting a worker with rifle, states, 'Who protects us against collapse? The armed proletariat!' The Austrian painter Maximilian Florian's work *The Revolution* (below) shows an Amazonian female warrior dragging a wounded comrade from a street battle with right-wing forces.

William Orpen's *To the Unknown British Soldier in France* (1923, modified 1927). The original version (right) was deemed unacceptable by the Imperial War Museum, which had commissioned it. After Orpen excised the skeletal Tommies and the cherubs, then dedicated the painting to Douglas Haig, the museum relented.

The Resurrection of the Soldiers by Stanley Spencer (1928). Looming over the main altar in a private English chapel, Spencer's huge idiosyncratic painting depicts soldiers emerging from their graves, greeting and embracing comrades also rising from the dead, then proceeding to deposit their crosses with Jesus Christ, dressed in white, centre background. This is one of the few representations of Christ in art history where the saviour is beardless.

Flower of Death – The Bursting of a Heavy Shell – Not as It Looks, but as It Feels and Sounds and Smells (c. 1919), by Claggett Wilson, an important 'modernist' portraitist, landscape painter and muralist. Wilson lived several years in prewar Paris and exhibited in the Salon, the annual exhibition sponsored

by the Académie des Beaux-Arts. Serving as a lieutenant in the American Expeditionary Force, he was wounded twice, gassed and earned several decorations. He painted many works depicting battlefield scenes.

The Menin Gate, Ypres.

boyar sitting in Moscow, a place practically in the middle of nowhere. He was a visionary in many respects. Believing in sea power, and having visited several thriving European port cities as a young man, he saw the merits, both commercial and cultural, of having great fleets that could communicate and trade around the globe. He wanted a new capital that had access to the sea in most weather, and that would be so close to the established continental nation states that some of their enlightened traditions might rub off on his own backward, illiterate and blockheaded people. As much as Peter might admire western progressiveness and technology, however, he was a tsar to the marrow of his bones. St. Petersburg was built by brute, conscripted labour; peasants were brought in from all corners of the realm, lured by inducements little better than crumbs or by force, there to live and work under the most squalid conditions. Camp fever, dysentery, scurvy and malaria periodically swept through the wretched camps, the weather discouraged even the hardiest of peasants, and Peter's ruthless drive for results made the place a virtual hell. In Peter's mind, Russians were used to all that; they were there to do his will. It is not known exactly, but it is thought that between 30,000 and some 100,000 workers perished in the city's construction. Peter called the place 'paradise'.

St. Petersburg became a 'western' city. Its architecture, much of it baroque or neoclassical, was often built to the plans of Italian and Dutch designers; the city was excessively decorative and had little in common with parochial Russian art or custom (the interior of churches excepted). The skyline was dominated by the church spire of Sts. Peter and Paul, which could have passed for being anywhere in Germany. The boulevards, lined with extravagant palaces, were wide, spacious and orderly, unlike the jumble of medieval Moscow, full of twisting alleys and side streets crammed with shops and dingy taverns. Its canals, in flights of fancy, could be compared with those of Venice, though the notion did not often come to people's minds in the midst of winter (latitudinally, the place was the equivalent of Hudson Bay in the wilds of Canada). As the city grew and spread, and the tsar's court became an established fixture there after Peter's death in 1725 (when the temptation to desert the site and return to Moscow was entertained, accomplished but then reversed), the aristocracy took root and fulfilled Peter's expectations. The boyars of old, with beards to the floor and dressed in heavy embroidered robes, gave way to French and German fashions – clean-shaven, wearing suits of satin and dresses made in Paris. European grand tours became *de rigueur*, classical statuary and old master paintings were purchased from dealers in Athens and Rome, the official language of the court became French, manners thoroughly continental and court etiquette as stuffy and stilted as anything in Vienna. French wines, cuisines and chefs dominated the dining rooms of the cosmopolitan wealthy; after meals of many courses, habitués of the night could resort to gypsy dens and drink vodka until dawn, in keeping with the notion that they *were* Russian. And, of course, beneath the veneer of European culture, they were Russian. As Turgenev wrote so eloquently, 'The Slav soul is a dark forest.'

The army attempted to follow Prussian norms. Many German officers served as mercenaries in Russian forces and remained in St. Petersburg for their entire careers (their descendants staying afterwards), earning decorations, rewards and hereditary positions in government. The Germanic influence in the city cannot be overestimated, though Slavs could be as snobbish as anyone else. Nothing was worse, as Count Witte put it at the turn of the twentieth century, then the 'mediocre intelligence of a Baltic German'. At the start of the war, these hunnish associations became an embarrassment. A large number of official court sinecures and office-holders were identified by German phraseology; many noblemen had the aristocratic 'von' in their names and titles; even the name of the city itself was German (*Sankt* and *burg*, both offensive), so much so that Tsar Nicholas II found it expeditious to exchange St. Petersburg for Petrograd as more Slavic-sounding. This did not appease most people. 'I spit upon it,' one Russophile had written in criticizing Peter the Great. 'You repudiate Moscow, and away from your people you build a solitary city.' As far as he was concerned, Peter was a traitor. The French Ambassador, Maurice Paléologue, recorded in his memoirs a conversation he had with a patriotic Muscovite in 1917, who kept referring to the capital as Petersburg. He asked him why. 'Because "Petersburg" is its real name; it's a German city and has no claim to a Slav name. I'll call it "Petrograd" when it deserves it.'[1]

Rasputin: The Holy Fool

'Many of the visitors looked upon him as a great saint and ascetic, although they knew that he was crazy. But it was just his craziness that attracted them.'

Fyodor Dostoyevsky,
The Brothers Karamazov

A gray sameness characterizes many of the personalities who figure so prominently in the annals of World War I. Unimaginative generals by the dozen; members of what George V called '*the* Club' (crowned heads of Europe, largely blood-related, united mostly by medieval and retrograde political ideas); politicians and diplomats by the dozens, blind, deaf and dumb to the ramifications of their often absurdly complicated, back-room machinations; millions upon millions of nameless soldiers from the four corners of the earth, dressed in plain or khaki uniforms, fed into the maw of dehumanized war that cared little for individual heroics. Amidst this flood of anonymous conformity, a man like Gregory Rasputin stands out like fireworks lighting up the sky. This is an amazing comment to say about an effectively illiterate peasant, raised hundreds of miles from anywhere of political significance.

Rasputin was born in the Siberian village of Pokrovskoye. Period photographs of the place present an idyllic picture of life on the frontier: a few timber buildings sloping down to a riverside, a handful of cattle, horses and free-wandering pigs, a large slightly dilapidated-looking church, painted white, dominating an agricultural crossroads. Life could be harsh, with scorching summers and bone-numbing winters, the steppes a long vista without a single feature that, if anything, encouraged wanderlust in those who wanted something more from life. Rasputin spent his formative years as a drover, hauling goods and produce from place to place, sleeping under his wagon at night or in the company of peasant girls who, like himself, had no future, no sense of destiny and no respite from the drudgery of daily life other than what vodka and random promiscuity might provide. Rasputin was different in one respect, however: in his long days and nights in the solitude of his work, he had developed an ear for God. However it came to him, whether in the wind or through the sounds of animals or in conversation with wandering mystics tramping the rutted Siberian roadways and going who knows where, he came to like what he heard.

Rasputin's eldest daughter, Maria, wrote long after her father was dead that he had an incredible memory: bits of scripture, oddments of folkloric insight, catch-all phraseology that seemed reflective of peasant wisdom – once recited, he remembered it. Refined through visits to nearby monasteries, where Rasputin would often live for weeks, he developed the persona of that commonplace in the vast Russian landscape, the *starets*, or 'holy man'. Neither monk nor priest, he more resembled John the Baptist from the Old Testament who had abandoned the norms of society, both secular and religious, to find his God on the edge, on the extreme. A character in Dostoyevsky cries, 'You see those two branches? In the night it is Christ holding out His arms to me and seeking me with those arms. I see it clearly and tremble.' Some commentators could not tell the difference in these 'eternal pilgrims'. Were they 'haggard and ragged' saints wandering 'ceaselessly from monastery to monastery', or were they simply vagrants, indulging in that distinctly Russian trait of 'nomadism?'

At about thirty-one years of age, Rasputin left Pokrovskoye, his wife and family, for a 2,000-mile trek to Mount Athos in Greece, the most renowned centre of spirituality in the orthodox world. What he saw there shocked him (he suggested that he witnessed homosexual behaviour among the monks), but the impulse to keep on the saintly road never left him. Although somewhat conjectural, he is thought to have then walked from Greece to the Holy Land, a trip he definitely replicated a decade later in 1911. As coincidence would have it, he was in Jerusalem exactly when T. E. Lawrence was there. What a strange meeting that might have been had these two exotic individuals crossed paths. When Rasputin returned home nearly three years later, it is said that his wife did not recognize him. In her eyes, the man who stood before her asking for a bowl of milk and a piece of bread was just another stranger taking advantage of the hospitality for which Russians are famous. She became used to his disappearances and returns. Come spring, he would walk away from the front door, with a walking stick and a bundle; come winter, he would be back. 'Gregory has turned a pilgrim out of laziness,' said his father, which was only half-true. He had a genuine calling; he was restless, he had what one observer called 'the itch'; his buoyant spirit could not be satisfied by the constraints of making a living, ploughing a field all day or delivering goods to market. He was meant for something more in life, whatever that might be, and he knew it. That his mission in life would extend beyond a spiritual arena, however, would have surprised him more than anyone.

This wild and unconventional man was more than just a religious dreamer. He had a backwoods quality about him akin to faith-healing and second sight. Along his journey's road, where he begged for supper and lodging in the barn, he captivated his gullible audiences with what for them was entertainment: stories from the bible, primitive teachings, rough and ready spiritual advice, the sights and sounds of faraway places that he had visited, a look into the future. In any agricultural community, a shaman's capacity to deal with what matters most, its animals, is always high on the list. Rasputin often treated livestock; he knew horses very well, for example, and even cured a dog owned by a grand duke that had been given up for dead. It did not take long for the power of his prayer to be applied to humans as well, a sick child here, a dying man there; or blessing those with a need, a woman desirous of a child, an invalid wanting to walk. An immediate healing could often be delayed (conveniently) by a forecast into the future: you will be better, you will have a boy, your future is assured. Whether it came true or not didn't matter, Rasputin would be long out of sight by the time of any resolution to the request he had been asked to pray for (if it happened to come true, so much the better). Rasputin himself rarely took credit for anything. God worked through him, a humble vessel. He never asked for any reward.

Rasputin has been called many things by many people: a charlatan, a whoremonger, a quack, a cheap hypnotist, a religious fraud. There are elements of truth in each of these indictments. He was also, however, a truly sympathetic man who abhorred sin, cruelty and war, who had a genuine desire to do good, had little interest in money or worldly goods and always offered a helping hand when he could, often without thought of remuneration or even thanks. When a disturbed woman stabbed him in the stomach in 1914, screaming aloud that she had killed the Anti-Christ (which she very nearly did), Rasputin, holding his entrails in his hands, saved her from being caught up and hanged by an angry mob.[2] He did not give that impulse to forgiveness a second thought. He was, in his heart, a religious man. Like all human beings, conflicted as they generally are, he was a sinful creature as well. He has been remembered almost universally for his sins; the comfort he gave has been largely forgotten.

Physically formidable – well-built and strong – he had a piercing gaze that he often used to rivet people to himself. Some have called this a cheap theatrical stunt meant to overawe those weak-minded enough to fall under his spell (mostly women), but so many others have commented on the magnetism of his energy field that it seems impossible, in fairness, to dismiss it out of hand. Contemporaries could often misidentify, for instance, the colour of his eyes – some said blue, some said gray, some said green 'like a viper' – but few could dispute their power. In his earliest career as a St. Petersburg celebrity, he was noted for his vagabond appearance: greasy peasant clothes, long tangled hair and beard, overgrown dirt-encrusted fingernails, the pungent odour of an unwashed body. He really was a man of the desert, straight from a cave, muttering words of holiness (often incoherently). One or two ecclesiastics of real standing embraced Rasputin as a genuine *starets*, but the question remains: if Tsarina Alexandra Feodorovna, the consort of Tsar Nicholas II, had never borne a son with haemophilia, would she have met Rasputin, or likely ever heard of him? The confluence of their lives, an incongruity to western eyes, was surely a twist of fate that no one involved could have foreseen; but then again, as one observer noted, 'It is impossible to understand Russian history if one judges Ivan the Terrible and Peter the Great – or even Stalin – as if they were Englishmen.' The same could be said for Rasputin if not, ironically, for Tsarina Alexandra.

Rasputin was initially taken up by important members of the orthodox church, comforted as they were by John of Kronstadt's imprimatur, rather than by individuals of less saintly inclination, primarily Militsa Nikolaevna, the wife of Grand Duke Peter (a first cousin of the tsar), a 'superstitious, gullible, excitable' woman. Her influence over Tsarina Alexandra was baleful. A habitué of séances and other spiritual exercises of uncertain legitimacy – but fashionable nonetheless – she was a mainstay in St. Petersburg's high society, the daughter of a king herself, Nikola I of Montenegro. This sort of 'royalty' could in some cases be the cause of ridicule – Wilhelm II had referred to her father as little better than a horse thief – but the fact remains that his five daughters had irrefutably married into important dynastic unions, earning him the nickname, 'father-in-law of Europe'.[3] When a particularly charismatic or appealing spiritual figure appeared within the city, Militsa and her sister (also married to a grand duke), usually made sure to meet, appraise and, when appropriate, recommend that person to their friends. Rasputin was one of many 'remarkable men [that] they dragged to the imperial palace', where he made a more lasting impression than most.[4]

His primary 'conquest' was the empress, Alexandra, whose experience with a previous dubious character, known mysteriously as Maître Philippe, perhaps explains the potential for harm that introducing such men as these was capable of producing. By 1903, Alexandra had been married for nine years. She had, over the course of six of these, produced four children, all girls, but not the all-important male heir that was expected of her. Militsa Nikolaevna steered Philippe to the empress in 1901. As a means of denigrating his persona, Philippe is usually described by unsympathetic historians as the son of a butcher from Lyons, France, but his pseudo-hypnotic powers and sinuous soothsaying were powerful enough to fool the empress. Philippe apparently convinced his 'patient' that she was indeed pregnant with a male child. She developed, under the power of suggestion, symptoms of pregnancy – a swelling girth, fuller breasts and so forth. She took to wearing maternity clothes; her husband was delighted. At some point, however, physical developments ceased progressing and real doctors were called in, whose verdicts were damning to Philippe's reputation. The empress was not pregnant, the whole thing had been a psychosomatic fantasy – Philippe had made a wager on Alexandra's fertility, but had guessed wrong. He was handsomely paid off, under a condition of silence, and returned to France. This episode was just another in a long list of complaints about the empress that contributed to her cascading esteem in the eyes of just about everyone. This was a woman who, in the widest sense, could please no one. Unbeknownst to her, however, was the fact that several months later during a church service, the *starets* Rasputin was heard to say that the empress's plight would soon be over; she would become pregnant, and deliver a male heir. As for haemophilia, a disease about which he certainly knew nothing, not a word.

The Tsar

'He wanted to be alone. Alone with his conscience.'

A. A. Mossolov, tsarist official, in reference to Nicholas II

It is fashionable to describe Tsar Nicholas II as a political incompetent; people thought so at the time, and continue to do so today. This is generally offset by generous praise for his qualities as a human being; he was a superb and conscientious parent, a deeply affectionate husband and literally a saint when it came to the last eighteen months of his life, a series of tribulations he endured with humility and distinction (at least according to the Russian Orthodox Church Abroad). Nothing in these pages will dispute either set of generalities. He was an incompetent and he was, in many ways, a saintly man.

Few dispute the fact (nor did Nicholas himself) that he was utterly unfit to lead his country on the premature and unexpected death of his father, Alexander III, in 1894. Nicholas was barely twenty-six years old, had done nothing in his life with any distinction, either intellectually (in his studies) or militarily (in his career as a cavalry officer), to prepare him for the solitary and, ultimately, lonely role that any autocratic ruler must shoulder.[5] He did not share the thrusting personality of his cousin, Kaiser Wilhelm, who relished the opportunity that total power presented (however inadequate to the task he happened to be), nor did he ever view his position as anything other than a burden. He did not enjoy the respect of other Romanovs. His mother doubted his fortitude, and his uncles (the elder grand dukes, there were several of them) so often treated him with disdain and 'well-rehearsed bellowing' that Nicholas 'dreaded to be left alone with them'. The example of Nicholas's father was also problematic. Nicholas inherited his predecessor's work habits, tendencies towards absolutism and a deep, spiritual belief in Mother Russia. What he lacked was his father's ferocious resolve and arrogance. When it came to making decisions, Nicholas proved irresolute. When it came to taking advice, he often found the presumption of those giving it, offensive. When it came to hearing bad news, he rarely understood the ramifications or potential for harm, either to himself or to the country. In far too many instances, the tsar found himself with nowhere to go, nowhere to turn and no one he felt sufficiently competent (given his regal stature) in whom he could confide, with one important and fatal exception – his wife.

Nicholas ruled the old-fashioned way, by himself. The fact that he was conscientious barely disguised the sad truth that he could not handle the tasks of governance. This is no particular slight on him; one must question, given Russia's size, diversity and the host of problems facing it, whether any single individual could possibly have given a decent account of himself under such trying circumstances. The fact remains, however, that the tsar's single-minded devotion to the theory of regal autocracy tied his hands in ways he did not understand. Unlike many emerging constitutional governments, Nicholas had no cabinet structure in place, or anything approximating a secretariat that could assist him in sifting through information, forming coherent policy objectives or providing a relatively unjaundiced assessment of current trends and needs. Instead, Nicholas received his reports from entirely separate governmental entities, all of which, following the bureaucratic incentive, refused to interact or communicate with the others. War, agriculture, foreign affairs, police – the leaders of these and all the other offices of government reported individually to the tsar, who often made his decisions based more on the personality of each of the various ministers (whether, for example, he or his wife liked him or not), than on the merits of the issue at hand. A decree made one day affecting a single department could often be later found to have entirely undermined the thrust of another's policy, to the resulting confusion for all concerned. Buried in paperwork (he did not even have a private secretary; he licked all his envelopes himself), Nicholas could not keep his affairs in harmony; fawning ministers generally refused to contradict his inconsistencies – the tsar, they would say, knew best. When discord did arise, he often found himself overwhelmed with the complexity of it all, agonizing as to which course to take, that often resulted in the usual syndrome of following the advice of the last person consulted. Little wonder that after a long day of boring, laborious and time-consuming agonies of conscience, which often left him 'worn out, subdued, disillusioned' and burdened with headaches, he delighted in hiding himself away at night ('our time', he called it) in the banalities of family domesticity and reading novels aloud, in English, to the empress. The French ambassador put the matter succinctly in one of his diary entries: 'I forget who it was said of Caesar that he had "all the vices and not one fault", Nicholas II has not a single vice, but he has the worst fault an autocratic sovereign could possibly have – a want of personality.' Caesar, he said, really wasn't the appropriate analogy, Louis XVI was more like it, the inept, weak character who ended up losing his head on the guillotine.

Nicholas generally shrugged when faced with the complexities of supreme rule, and hid himself in the wrap of Christian fatalism. God, in his inscrutable wisdom, had many options to reward or punish his creations and he, the tsar, would live with the consequences. Nicholas II was not a person who could, or would, change the course of history. When comparing him to men like Trotsky or Lenin, he is inevitably found wanting. No wonder, in the face of such collective ruthlessness, that he and his family were swept away like so much pollen in a sharp wind.

'I would give my life a thousand times, not just once.
Russia must be free.'

Ivan Kalyayev, assassin

As a symbol of oppression, one couldn't do much better than Grand Duke Sergei Alexandrovich, one of Tsar Alexander III's three surviving brothers, and thus Nicholas's uncle. Appointed Governor General of Moscow in 1891, he came to the position full of autocratic hauteur: opinionated, aloof, arrogant, cruel and oblivious of any democratic impulse, he managed the affairs of Russia's greatest city with dictatorial disdain. If a mob needed dispersing, Sergei would never hesitate calling out the troops to maintain order and obedience. A few dozen corpses bleeding to death in a snow-covered square would not roil his conscience. He was a cold-hearted fellow indeed, as witnessed by one of his first acts, the expulsion of every Jew from Moscow. This may have satisfied his deepest prejudices, but on a larger scale it proved to be, in keeping with Romanov standards of incompetence, a stunning blow to the city's commercial vitality, some 25,000 Muscovites losing their jobs in now-defunct Jewish businesses.

In affairs of the heart (if indeed Sergei had one), he had preceded his nephew's inclination towards the German house of Hess by marrying Tsarina Alexandra's older sister in 1884. Elizabeth (familiarly called Ella) was, like Alex, an extraordinarily beautiful woman and, again like her sister, deeply attracted to orthodoxy, which she fully embraced and, indeed, relied upon when her world came crashing apart in the years of revolution. A jaundiced, though apparently accurate portrait of Ella was provided by her niece, Maria

Pavlovna, whom the ducal couple 'adopted' in 1902. This young girl of thirteen was mesmerized by Ella's refinement, bearing and magnificence (especially when covered in jewels), but repelled at the same time by her coldness of heart. This may have had something to do with the questionable nature of the marriage itself. Sergei was not only the undisputed chief of Moscow, he was also the not-to-be-contradicted head of his household, every member of which was held to the highest level of performance. Sergei treated Ella, Maria wrote in her memoirs, 'as if she were a child. I believe that she was hurt by his attitude and longed to be better understood, but it was as if she were being driven deeper and deeper within herself for refuge. She and my uncle seemed never very intimate. They met for the most part only at meals and by day avoided being alone together. They slept, however, up to the last day of their life together, in the same great bed.' Rumour had it that Sergei was homosexual. The couple never had children.[6]

On New Year's Day 1905, the grand duke resigned the city's governorship, though retaining his military command. In retrospect, he should have relinquished both offices, for by remaining a powerful governmental figure, his attraction as a target for assassination stayed as high as ever. Six weeks later, riding in his conspicuous carriage, he was attacked as he entered the Kremlin by a dedicated socialist/revolutionary, one Ivan Kalyayev, who had spent weeks 'stalking the grand duke like a shadow, invisible yet, like fate, inevitable' (as a comrade put it). Standing just four feet from the coach, he tossed a bomb right onto Sergei's lap, an act he expected to be the last of his life. No one was more surprised than Kalyayev that he survived the explosion. Certainly Sergei did not (nor his coachman).

Ella, the windows of her palace having been rattled by repercussions from the bomb, rushed into the square, oblivious of the danger that other killers might be looking for additional victims, and what a gruesome sight greeted her eyes. Sergei Alexandrovich, or what was left of him, was scattered in bloody pieces around the wreckage of his coach. Part of his head here, a bit of torso there. Showing considerable fortitude, she collected what she could on her knees, and had a military cloak cover the assembled, gory pile. Sergei had enjoyed wearing rings; from a severed hand, she removed what she could and put them in her dress pocket (another hand was later found on a nearby roof; its rings were recovered as well and returned to the grand duchess). Not once did she lose her composure, an indication perhaps that aristocratic breeding can often result in admirable traits of character, despite many signs to the contrary. In an act of both courage and compassion, she later visited Kalyayev in his jail cell, an act that stupefied the other Romanovs. She told her husband's killer that she forgave him, and would pray for his soul. She left behind, for comfort, an icon. In a poem he wrote later, Kalyayev noted that 'her frock was so black and it smelled of the grave'. He, of course, was unrepentant. Two months later, sentenced to death by hanging, his execution was botched, whether purposely or not is unknown. The rope, it appears, was too long, and instead of having his neck broken by the sudden fall from the gallows, he was left, feet on the ground, slowly choking. Three attendants eventually hauled the rope higher, and Kalyayev finally died.

Sergei's funeral was largely unattended by members of the extended family, by order of the tsar. When his casket was buried in the crypt of the ancient Chudov monastery, located within the walls of the Kremlin, only a handful of his immediate family were there. It was deemed too dangerous for any of the Romanovs to be seen in public, with passions running so high; Nicholas remained ensconced in Tsarskoe Selo, an assemblage of royal palaces thirteen miles from St. Petersburg, guarded by one of his elite regiments. None of this was a good omen for the rest of 1905. In fact, that fateful year would be, until the beginning of the Great War itself, the most disastrous of his reign.

Ella, in the four years she spent recovering from the shock of it all, finally decided to withdraw from the world, in keeping with her growing sense of religious conviction. Selling all her precious jewels and everything else of personal value, she established a convent and devoted all her efforts to the poor of Moscow. Not even her gold wedding band was spared. Though now attired in nun's garb, 'she still inspired profane passions', according to one admirer. When war came, she tirelessly cared for the wounded, who were often just dumped on the platform of the central railway station and left to fend for themselves. Vladimir Lenin did not take any of this into consideration when he came to power. In June 1918 he ordered his secret police to round up as many Romanovs as they could find. Ella was arrested, and shipped off to the Siberian border. Being something of a fatalist, she probably had a pretty fair idea of what awaited her there. In Moscow, after all, workmen 'accused her of starving the people' and she dared not leave her convent's walls.

Tsarina Alexandra Feodorovna

'An unhappy neurotic.'

The marriage of Alice of Hess to the handsome Nicky in 1894 was, on the surface, the stuff of fairy tales. They first met when they were twelve and sixteen years of age respectively, and it was immediate love on his part, a passion that he carried within himself their entire life together. They were enthusiastic bedmates, helpmates and parents. Their flood of letters to each other, full of endearments, familiarities, pet names and obvious terms of affection reflect the genuine happiness they shared. The brutality of their deaths simply enhances, with dramatic intensity, the tinge of dark pathos to their story. If it were not for their exalted rank and the pivotal parts these two individuals played in the collapse of the imperial order in Russia, no one today would be any more interested in their lives than they would in those of some other outwardly contented married couple, no matter the inevitable minor flaws of character. A person can be a neurotic, self-centred hypochondriac, obsessed with any number of insecurities large and small, without having them affect a larger political or social order. In this particular case, such defects of personality wrote huge in the tangled unravelling of a 300-year-old dynasty. They bare scrutiny on that account alone.

Alice of Hess was the sixth of seven children born to a German ducal house. Her mother was Queen Victoria's third child. Unbeknownst to anyone at the time, Alice inherited, through both her mother and grandmother, what came to be called 'the English illness', haemophilia (passed along only through the female line). This was to have tragic consequences far beyond the bounds of mere family life. Her mother died of diphtheria when Alice was six. In keeping with the usual Victorian standards of ghoulishness, Alice's father kept his wife's room shrouded in black until the day he died, which he did in 1892, collapsing in front of his daughter at the dining room table, dead before he hit the floor. Alice spent much of her youth with her maternal grandmother in England, where she witnessed even more outlandish ceremonies of mourning. Queen Victoria, dressed in black for four decades, insisted that her dead consort's bed be turned down every evening; even his chamber pot was washed daily.

Such morbidity had its effects on Alice's personality. An emotional girl, sometimes given to jittery nerves and phobias, she nonetheless was highly schooled in the arts of aristocratic hauteur, liberally taught by Victoria, obsessed in her own right with etiquette and the appropriate deportment that all royals under her supervision were expected to display. Suppression of emotion was highly prized by the aged queen; she drilled it into her granddaughter day after day. A person might experience a variety of feelings at any given moment, but in public an icy, indifferent, aloof demeanour was best suited when dealing with strangers, inferiors, hangers-on or members of the aristocratic hierarchy. These lessons Alice took to heart, as they segued nicely into the kind of girl she was – shy, withdrawn, emotionally private. She was not a people person.

Her marriage to Nicky was strewn with obstacles. Queen Victoria had nothing against Nicholas, but she worried about Russia. The throne there, in her opinion, was unsteady. Nicholas's parents were not thrilled either. Alexander III disliked Germans, even though Alice, whose first language was English, struck many people as more at home at the bucolic Balmoral Castle in Scotland than the Neues Palais in Potsdam, full of noisy, strutting Prussians. Alexander, however, mortally ill, decided to accept the union. Since he was weakening fast, the nuptials were rushed; Alexandra arrived by regular railway, not the imperial coach, to the summer palace in the Crimea just in time for her father-in-law to die. This naturally put something of a pall over everything that happened next. With the court in mourning, certain liberties were taken to make certain everyone attending the royal wedding could avoid wearing black. Alice had to be formally admitted as a convert to the orthodox church (Nicholas had sent his private confessor to England to give her instruction; a Russian teacher went as well) and had her name changed to Alexandra Feodorovna. The new and strange religious ceremonies that she underwent must have amazed her by their idiosyncrasies, frequency and duration. She spent her honeymoon, according to one of the grand dukes, 'attending two masses a day and receiving visits of condolence'. He found the entire situation 'grotesque'. As if to make matters worse, the coronation ceremonies later in Moscow were marked by tragedy, wherein several thousand revelers were trampled to death in outdoor festivities where gifts and free beer were to be distributed to common folk. A great ball that evening went on as planned; revolutionaries, anarchists and even many lords and ladies thought the resulting image distasteful, the royal couple dancing in celebration, as it were, on the graves of their people.

Alexandra made a poor impression on just about everyone. Undeniably beautiful, she had the unfortunate trait of never smiling. There are few contemporary photographs of her that this writer is aware of that show even a flicker of warmth; instead, the image of an ice queen is generally presented. She appeared stiff and distant in nearly every public appearance, which most onlookers ascribed to the arrogance thought so typical of Germans. In fact, this studied persona was actually a mask, a disguise, a role that any actor in her situation might have been expected to perform – a queen being a queen (and just as Victoria had taught her to be). Beneath the exterior of frigidity stood a lonely and frightened girl of seventeen, painfully shy and overwhelmed by the rush of events. Russian high society, an especially venomous institution, would be unforgiving. They mocked her Russian (marked by an English accent), seized on every minor lapse of courtly etiquette and perked their ears to allegedly disparaging remarks made of her by the dowager empress, Nicholas's mother, which circulated through dinner parties and salons as delicious gossip. It is ironic that the dowager empress, herself a foreigner (she was Danish), should have been so unsympathetic to Alexandra's plight, having been through it herself, but this strong-willed woman was deeply jealous of Nicholas's affections, and did little to disguise it.

As Alexandra Feodorovna grew older and a bit more settled, she returned the collective enmity. Her pride, as she wrote to her husband, prevented her from 'letting others see the knife digging into' her back. Always prim and very proper (except within the intimacy of her close-knit family and the marital bed) she disparaged those who disparaged her. St. Petersburg society was, in her opinion, close to degenerate, a sycophantic collection of drunks, gamblers, fornicators and adulterers. She dreaded the formal social occasions expected of the imperial court – balls, receptions and galas – and made no effort to disguise it. She preferred spending time at Tsarskoe Selo, south of the city, serviced by a private train. Her friends could see her there, but there were few of them; her closest, Anna Vyrubova, was a very ordinary woman, adding to the collective ridicule that society heaped upon the empress.[7]

Very little of this would have mattered had Alexandra produced a healthy male heir to the throne, but she did not. The Tsarevich Alexei, born a decade into their marriage after four daughters, was a haemophiliac. Any simple fall or nosebleed could be a life-threatening occurrence, and the agonies suffered by the little boy as he passed from crisis to crisis was understandably heart-wrenching for his parents, who spent their time huddled about the sick bed at all hours of day or night as circumstances demanded. Physicians called in could only shake their heads; the boy came close to dying time after time, and the medical science of the day was helpless to do anything about it. Here, the royal habit of keeping up appearances, of maintaining a stiff upper lip, did them actual harm. The affliction was at first kept under wraps for as long as possible; no one was to know, which denied the royal couple a huge dose of sympathy that would have done them good on the troubled road ahead. It certainly would have softened the widespread public perception that Alexandra was unapproachable, elitist and divorced from everyday pain; most people, after all, have an interest and consideration for private tragedy, no matter the social standing of those involved. It further alienated the empress from any desire to mingle in society or to indulge in the sort of superficial hospitality that was the usual fare of a tsar and his court, the purpose of which was supposed to make them the centre of St. Petersburg's life; but no, the gap between the royal couple and those who should have been their staunchest allies – intelligentsia and the aristocracy – was thus further exacerbated. Finally, it physically isolated the empress, who now focused her entire energies on the well-being of Alexei. Tsarskoe Selo became, more than ever, a domain separate from the rest of the world where she and her husband would struggle with this domestic misfortune more or less on their own, as a private ordeal imposed on them by God. This was not conducive to establishing a healthy or positive atmosphere, especially for the fragile empress. Always strong-willed, she became ever more dogmatic, especially in seeking for answers in religion; ever emotional, her mood swings began verging into uncontrollable fits of crying; ever possessive, her attentions became fixated on Alexei and, more significantly, on her husband, a more passive and reflective person 'in need' of her strength. As she once said to him, 'How I wish I could pour my will into your veins.' This might have been well and good within the close-bound confines of their apartments and oriented towards family issues, but when it spilled into political considerations affecting the nation at large, the ramifications would prove deadly.

Members of the extended family grew concerned as the years passed, particularly by the incessant atmosphere of 'chronic melancholy, vague sorrows, the see-saw between elation and despondency' that characterized Tsarskoe Selo. Grand Duke Alexander wrote in his memoirs that 'Life lost all meaning for the imperial parents. We were afraid to smile in their presence. When visiting the palace, we acted as we would in a house of mourning. The Emperor buried himself in work but the Empress refused to surrender to fate. She talked incessantly of the ignorance of the physicians. She professed an open preference for medicine men. She turned toward religion, and her prayers were tainted by a certain hysteria. The stage was ready for the appearance of a miracle worker.' Into this feverish atmosphere strode Gregory Rasputin, 'God's fool', as the tsar called him, 'a simple peasant.'

1905

'Afterwards Nicky told us that he had said to the Japanese that Russia wasn't just a country – but a part of the world, and that in order to avoid war, it was better not to try her patience, or else it could end badly.'

Grand Duchess Xenia Alexandrovna, the tsar's sister,
14 January 1904 [8]

Nicholas first mentions Rasputin in a diary entry dated 1905, a period fraught with hardship not only for the tsar, but for Russia. The Russo-

Japanese war, the result of friction between these two nations over spheres of influence in eastern Asia, had been a disaster from its very first day, 8 February 1904. Nicholas, like every other of his generals, thought the conflict would be nothing but a cake walk, both by land and sea. The tsar referred to the Japanese as 'monkeys', and officers at headquarters considered the enemy's armed forces 'a colossal joke'. That would not prove to be the case. The tsar's Pacific fleet was largely destroyed before and during the siege of Port Arthur, the primary Russian land base on Chinese soil. Initiating hostilities in a surprise attack, uncivilized behaviour that would be replicated in 1941 at Pearl Harbor, the Japanese initially disabled three of the most powerful ships anchored beneath its walls, and during the course of the city's siege they destroyed what was left. Nicholas unwisely dispatched his Baltic fleet halfway around the world in a spirit of revenge and to teach his enemies a lesson.[9] The result was another ignominious sea battle at Tsushima, wherein some Russia ships actually struck their colours, the last time in the history of naval warfare that an actual capitulation on the high seas would take place ('The word "surrender" tortures me,' a nobleman wrote in his diary, 'do Russians surrender?').[10] By land, the results were equally dismal, the Russian high command proving itself hopelessly inept when it came to outfitting and directing operations of such magnitude and so far away. A war initially thought to require 400,000 troops with 100,000 horses, spiraled into 1.5 million men and 200,000 mounts. Some observers estimate that seventy percent of the illiterate soldiers in the tsar's army had no idea who or what the Japanese were. ' "How far away is the front?" they all asked their officers. "Seven thousand miles". "Seven thousand miles!"' After nineteen months of ferocious fighting and approximately 150,000 Russian casualties – during which Europeans awoke to the fact that Japan was now a formidable (and industrialized) modern power – Nicholas finally sued for peace, accepting Theodore Roosevelt's offer to broker a treaty, negotiations taking place in Portsmouth, New Hampshire (for which the American president received the Nobel Prize).[11] Nicholas sent an experienced politician, Count Witte, to make the best of a bad situation, which he accomplished with considerable aplomb, if mordant humour. 'When a sewer has to be cleaned, they send for Witte,' he told an acquaintance. On a more serious level, Witte considered the tsar a man of 'intellectual and moral weakness'.[12]

During the course of 1905, trickling news from the front remained all bad and deeply corrosive to the reputation of the tsar and autocratic rule in general. France, Germany, Britain, even Russia … these were the countries advancing the borders of civilization, usually by force. They had the moral imperative, backed by their culture, arts and intellectual acumen, to tell the rest of the world what to do, particularly when the people they subjugated or manipulated were racial inferiors. Defeats at the hands of 'barbarians' such as the Japanese began being seen as litmus tests, a forerunner of Oswald Spengler's 1918 blockbuster, *The Decline of the West*. Embarrassing military reversals, all unexpected, had one direct result: political agitations for reform, now reaching new heights, the implications of which Nicholas steadfastly ignored. On 22 January, his troops opened fire on a peaceful demonstration that was congregating in front of the immense Winter Palace to present him with a petition. It was led by a priest, and several participants were carrying icons and portraits of Nicholas. Several hundred (no one knows the exact number) died in the snow that late morning, since known as 'Bloody Sunday' (the *New York Times* called the incident 'butcher's work'; the ballet dancer Vaslav Nijinsky found himself caught up in mobs of fleeing people, and was nearly trampled to death).

Ordinarily, such repression was the more or less standard response on the part of any tsar of the moment; Russian history was so full of monstrous atrocities that Bloody Sunday hardly merited a footnote when considered in comparison. Count Kokovtsoz wrote that the tsar 'viewed the internal tumult indifferently, he attached no particular importance to it'. This singularly unnecessary event, however, galvanized not only the general public but many of the upper classes as well, besides students and professors. Worker strikes paralyzed the economy, dancers at the imperial ballet refused to perform, men like Trotsky and Lenin agitated ceaselessly, Sergei Alexandrovich was assassinated in Moscow. In May news of the Tsushima disaster reached St. Petersburg, and the next month saw the famous *Potemkin* mutiny, a battleship of the Black Sea fleet where several officers were murdered.[13] The tsar floundered. Beset by concerns over the tsarevich, ill-equipped to handle fluid situations – and ill-disposed to grant concessions – he nonetheless found himself backed into a corner. A constitutional government along the lines of a Britain was utterly abhorrent to him. His paternal instincts warned him that Russia could not handle freedom. They were 'his children', he was 'their father'; the fact that a few hundred had been shot in front of the Winter Palace did not shake his resolve that he was the all-knowing soul of Russia. He wore simple blouses around the house; to the despair of his chef, he preferred basic, old-fashioned peasant fare, borscht and the like, not French *haute cuisine*. He 'knew' the people and understood their 'dense ignorance'.

Nonetheless, under constant pressure and faced with economic paralysis, the tsar finally gave in and issued the October Manifesto, a limited grant of constitutional government. A parliamentary and elective Duma was established, and though its scope was severely restricted (the tsar retained appointive powers regarding ministers, the Duma could 'advise' but not rule and so forth), it seemed to most a powerful step in the right direction. The tsar of Russia was no longer a genuine autocrat, a reality that made both Nicholas and his wife sick to their stomachs, as it did the more reactionary members of his Romanov family and members of the aristocracy. 'We all wore our full-dress uniforms, the ladies of the court displayed their jewellry', wrote one grand duke on the occasion of the Duma's opening session, but 'deep mourning would have been more appropriate'. The tsar's mother did not help things when she burst into tears at the humiliation of it all. 'This frightens me greatly,' she said, looking out at the assembled members of the first Duma, 'dressed as if intentionally in workers' blouses and cotton shirts'. She could not get over the obvious hostility in their eyes. 'They looked upon us as enemies ... an incomprehensible hatred for all of us.'

Nicholas, unsurprisingly, immediately did as much as he could, through his ministers, to undermine, frustrate and neuter the new arrangement. After only three months he maladroitly dissolved the Duma – it was 'too' democratic, too full of 'talkative professors' – and rewrote the eligibility of those who could vote in order to ensure a more conservative and cooperative assembly on the next go-around (also futile – it was quickly dissolved). Trotsky, in particular, was bemused at the chaotic scrambling of monarchists, reactionaries and the petty bourgeois. The October Manifesto, and everything that came in its wake, was merely 'a police whip wrapped in the parchment of a constitution'. Nonetheless a third, and even more feeble Duma, managed to stay in being between 1907 and 1912, then another, into the war. Its procedures were generally contentious, ill-humoured and discordant, a raucous assembly arguing back and forth. One of Nicholas's premiers complained that dealing with this body 'was like drowning or getting stuck in a bog'. Another yelled out in frustration, 'You want great upheavals – I want a great Russia.' From the monarchy's point of view, the perpetual agitation and constant attacks on autocracy 'can be expressed in two words: Hands Up!' In the background, the tsarist police state, full of spies, informants and the usual instruments of dictatorship, kept a watchful eye on subversives. In 1906 alone, some one thousand individuals were executed after trials of questionable legality. The tsar's chief minister at the time, the generally competent Peter Stolypin, had no hesitation about that; everyone knew what the term 'Stolypin's necktie' meant, the hangman's noose. Assassinations and murders of undesirables were also undertaken by right-wing death squads, loosely called the 'Black Hundreds', and when the situation called for it, pogroms were unleashed. The French ambassador, who was disgusted at the anti-Semitism that permeated all ranks of Russian society, felt that pogroms were a deliberate policy meant to revive 'old popular virtues'. The tsar's letters, like others of his ilk, reflect the same spirit. For the man in the street, hostility to the status quo gathered momentum, even if an appreciation of what lay on the other side seemed obscure. Konstantin Nabokov, a diplomat in the tsar's service (and the writer Vladimir Nabokov's uncle), 'asked a coachman if he had any sympathy for revolution. "None" was the reply. Who would he vote for? "Revolutionaries". Why? "Because the only way to keep awake a beast is to have it disturbed by flies. As soon as they cease to buzz, all is quiet and we get nothing."'

For the next decade, as Nicholas wrestled with both himself and his empire, trying to regain the authority he lost in 1905, Rasputin wandered in and out of the royal household. At first his presence was unobjectionable, an occasional guest who amused the children with stories of his many wanderings, charmed their parents with his profound, though often inarticulate spirituality and who seemed a true connector with the stolid peasant virtues of orthodoxy and tsarist fidelity. Where he truly took hold, however, was in the sickroom of the tsarevich. There, he performed miracles.

The first on record occurred in 1912, and was long distance by nature. Alexei, in torment for over a week, was all but given up for dead; the doctors expressed no hope of recovery, the last rites of the church were administered. Exhausted and in the throes of utter despair, Alexandra sent for Rasputin. Too far away to help, he sent a telegram. The boy would be fine, dismiss the doctors, he was praying. For some inexplicable reason, Alexei survived the immediate crisis. No one could believe it – doctors, Nicholas, Alexandra, anybody. The physicians attributed the recovery to luck, but Alexandra, and to a lesser degree her husband, said that Rasputin had done it. In December 1915, during another crisis, Rasputin entered the boy's room, hugged the tsar and Alexandra in the familiar embrace of Russian peasants, and went to the bedside. Gazing at the 'moribund' boy, he fell into prayer, made the sign of the cross, then turned to his parents. According to Anna Vyrubova, he simply said ' "Don't be alarmed. Nothing will happen." Then he walked out of the room and out of the palace.' As before, the danger passed, the boy recovered. If the tsar had reservations by that point, they simply vanished thereafter. He joined his wife and put complete trust in Rasputin, saying at one point, 'I have survived only because of his prayers.'

What powers did Rasputin really have? This represents, beyond the numberless questions involving Rasputin, the core of all the mystery surrounding him. He had, quite clearly, a calming air about him when called upon during these frightening episodes. He radiated assurance and, perhaps more importantly, the confidence that faith often nourishes in individuals so inclined when extreme situations present their bleakest face.

The people he helped were believers: in God, orthodoxy, the possibility that divine intervention might produce a miracle; to those who did not believe, Rasputin's efforts usually fell flat. Stolypin was the subject of a bomb attack in 1911, where the front of his house was blown off and two of his children seriously injured. Alexandra begged him to seek Rasputin's help. 'He ran his pale eyes over me', Stolypin told an acquaintance, 'mumbled mysterious and inarticulate words from scriptures, made strange movements with his hands, and I began to feel an indescribable loathing for the vermin standing over me.'[14] Anna Vyrubova, on the other hand, an adoring acolyte to say the least, was seriously injured in a dreadful railway accident in 1915, incurably so according to the doctors. Rasputin rushed to her bedside where she was moaning convulsively. 'Annushka, look at me', he said holding her hand. 'Gregory, thank God', she replied, and her physical comeback began from that moment. The susceptibility, or gullibility if you will, of those for whom Rasputin intervened may explain some of his success, but to dismiss entirely his effectiveness is to deny the historical record. Call him a faith healer, a quack, a layer-on-of-hands, any or all the above, but the fact remains that he was a man of considerable ability when it came to soothing other people's pain. How he did it we shall never know. Rasputin himself, speaking with one of his female admirers, pointed out the simplicity of their relationship. 'If you could see their lives now', he said, 'even if they are tsars, you wouldn't want to live like that! He is alone and she is alone, there is no one they can trust, everyone is willing to sell them out, but I caress and comfort her, and she becomes calm. Is my affection disinterested? My affection is like no one else's, it's such as they have never known, nor ever will again. Do you understand, darling?'

With each successive feat with the tsarevich, Rasputin's influence at Tsarskoe Selo increased exponentially. Alexandra came to rely on him almost completely, and why not? He was the only person alive who could help her son. As the tsarevich's tutor wrote years later, Rasputin gave Alexandra 'hope, as a drowning man seizes an outstretched hand'. Between constant prayers and vigils in her private chapel, and ever-increasing consultations with Rasputin (often held at Vyrubova's quarters near Tsarskoe Selo), the empress came completely under his thrall. She even began imagining that a telepathic connection existed between their two spirits. 'He always senses when I need him', she said. Count Vladimir Kokovtsov, a politician and deeply suspicious of Rasputin, found 'the peculiar, mystic nature of this woman' unsettling.

Alexandra's impulsive and emotional nature led her to several indiscretions. A series of letters that she wrote the *staretz* somehow found their way into general circulation. If read in isolation, and without knowledge of the tsarina's flowery and exaggerated style, they could on the surface be easily taken for love letters, as indeed they were interpreted throughout Petrograd. With Rasputin's increasingly outrageous private life becoming the talk of the city, Alexandra's reputation began being dragged through the mud as well. She was sleeping with Rasputin at Tsarskoe Selo, some of these 'revolting comments' alleged; not only that, he had seduced the daughters as well. The tsar was a pathetic cuckold; perhaps he just stood there watching. Vyrubova was also smeared, so much so that she requested that a doctor confirm and publish the fact that she was a virgin. The old adage that Caesar's wife must be above suspicion never looked more brutally true, however. By the time of the great war, the tsarina had no reputation left to defend, and it was an easy jump to the next, and decidedly more serious slander, that she was in fact a German spy.[15]

In his colloquial and familiar way, Rasputin energized the illusion held by the imperial couple that St. Petersburg and all it represented was actually a barrier between the country at large and themselves, almost an alien entity. 'Only quite lately I was still thinking that Russia hated me', Alexandra said to a visitor in January 1917. 'I know now that it is only Petrograd society which hates me ... the whole of Russia – the real Russia, poor humble, peasant Russia – is with me.' This was but another misperception. Before the war began in 1914, two events full of ceremony became highlights of the social calendar: the commemoration of Napoleon's defeat in 1812 (1912), and the 300th anniversary of Romanov rule (1913). The many festivities associated with each again deceived the tsar and his wife into thinking that the masses of this great empire still revered him and his style of rule. Applause from bystanders, peasants kneeling in the streets as they passed by, the ever-persistent approval (and blessings) that he received in lengthy church ceremonials, convinced him and his wife that a deeply patriotic Russia was behind them. Some observers could not believe such self-delusion, however, Count Kokovtsov noting his impression during a royal progress that the crowds were disappointingly small and lacking enthusiasm, attracted only by a 'shallow curiosity'. Minor episodes, some embarrassing, inevitably disturbed the outwardly idyllic picture. At Kazan Cathedral, on St. Petersburg's most famous street, the Nevsky Prospect, Rasputin appeared for one of the many tercentenary celebrations. He took a seat reserved for members of the Duma; when the president of that body, Mikhail Rodzianko, saw Rasputin in his place, he furiously upbraided him. Rasputin fell to his knees in prayer. Rodzianko responded by assaulting 'this disgusting libertine' and 'pervert', punching and kicking him, yelling he would 'drag you from the cathedral by your beard'. Like a dog being whipped, Rasputin slunk away, professing forgiveness for the sins being committed on his defenceless body. In his memoirs, Rodzianko denies that he kicked Rasputin, claiming that he only 'nudged him in the side'.

It cannot be said that the tsar knew nothing of Rasputin's dreadful reputation, his wild drunkenness, innumerable seductions, continued visits to bath houses, solicitation of prostitutes, public exposure of his privates, even his occasional urination on church porches. The tsar did not have at his disposal a network of spies in the thousands for nothing. These reports disturbed him; occasionally Rasputin was forced to confess his failings to 'father', and occasionally he was told to go home and straighten out his life, and not to return to Petrograd unless summoned. But there was always another crisis ahead, another nosebleed, where he would be urgently needed. Alexandra's will on such occasions could not be denied. Rasputin's influence, one foreign observer said, 'recalls the tenth century rather than the twentieth'.

'You do not seem to trust your friends anymore, Nicky.'
'I believe no one but my wife.'

An exchange between the tsar and his brother-in-law,
Grand Duke Alexander

Russian soldiers, if well led and equipped, could be counted upon for exemplary courage and stubbornness on any battlefield, and they proved it during the first year of war. Although the Tannenberg fiasco was deflating, Russian forces more or less held their own along an ever-shifting front that gradually extended from the Baltic to the Black Sea. Casualties were horrific, but manpower was never a problem; losses could be replaced from an enormous population pool of over 150 million people. It was to be the armaments of war that would be lacking.

The industrialization of Russia had progressed dramatically since the Russo-Japanese war of the previous decade, but it was nowhere near the match of imperial Germany. The same nonchalance and overconfidence of the Russian high command that had marked 1904/05 proved equally endemic as great battles surged back and forth over the plains of Poland in 1915. It is said that after sixteen months of war, nearly a quarter of all reinforcements sent to the front had no rifles, no ammunition and no adequate training to speak of. When rushed into combat, they were instructed to scavenge what weapons they could find from dead comrades on the field. German superiority in heavy artillery was never challenged, and Russian dependence on its allies for machine guns, shells and just about every necessity for modern war, were greatly hampered by the paucity of adequate, all-weather commercial ports and an overwhelmed railway system. There was also the unquestioned divide that existed between the officer class (many educated and from the elite) and those they commanded (mostly illiterate peasants). Discipline was harsh and often arbitrary; if an officer pulled out his revolver and shot one of his men or beat him senseless, there was no recourse but to shrug and bear it. The abstruse variations in political dialogue that obsessed Petrograd made no impression on the common conscript, but as the war stretched on and defeats piled up, a sense of hopeless resignation in the ranks became quite apparent to many observers. The British army attaché, Alfred Knox, who had been present at the Tannenberg disaster three years before, was a man of indefatigable optimism, but he felt the average soldier, though 'sound at heart', was fatally 'tired'. Harvests had been missed, a peasant's village seemed hundreds of miles away (which it often was), he missed his wife and children, the Jews were behind everything. As weeks and months passed, this enormous human assemblage would become a ripe forest of discontent, susceptible to agitators, dissidents and ideologues of every stripe, though in the end most soldiers wanted only one thing – to go home.

The tsar, his generals and professional diplomats in Petrograd never sensed the impending bombshell that would soon burst over their landscape, the physical and psychological disintegration of the army. Grand Duke Nicholas, the tsar's uncle, a towering man well over six feet tall and every inch the picture of a soldier, was the commander in chief. He had, at first, determination to his credit, and some strategic skill, but he was as incapable as everyone else on the scene to comprehend fully or control the enormous task at hand, and grew discouraged as the weeks and months passed by. 'The grand duke', as one Duma member put it after visiting army headquarters 'did not possess sufficient energy.' Most observers dismissed such defeatism, relying on an almost inarticulate faith in the endurance of the common Russian soldier, the 'steamroller' of history, the ethos of 1812. You won't see a repetition of that miracle, a nobleman told the French ambassador. The Napoleonic 'campaign was very short. Six months at the outside. It's easy to persevere when you're winning'. As a Romanov, the grand duke also worried about the tsar's political situation, and knew perfectly well that his name was being bandied about as a possible regent if his nephew was deposed. He was contemptuous of Alexandra's influence over Nicholas, and shared the bitter hostility toward Rasputin. When Rasputin announced that he would travel to the front and bless the troops, the commander in chief replied that he was welcome to do so. When he was finished with the soldiers, however, he would be hanged on the spot.

With the war not going well, Tsar Nicholas made the last of his ruinous decisions: he decided to assume personal command of the army. In his childish way, he saw this move as a gesture of ultimate sacrifice, his personal undertaking, for good or ill, of ultimate responsibility. The tsar considered himself, after all, a soldier; he had wanted to follow the same course during the war with Japan. Had he done so, he probably would have been removed from the throne then instead of in 1917, which might have saved Russia considerable bloodshed, and the world at large a much less turbulent twentieth century. He was talked out of the notion in 1905, but no one could change his mind this time. Alexandra and Rasputin encouraged the move. The tsarina in particular distrusted Grand Duke Nicholas; she distrusted his motives – he was too popular with the troops and should be more subservient and humble in his posture towards her husband. Almost everyone else was aghast. The tsar would be several days' travel away from Petrograd, virtually irrelevant should fast-moving events require his presence in the capital; further erosion on the battlefield would, additionally, be blamed entirely on him. It was one thing to sack generals; could he sack himself and still retain the throne? Ten out of his twelve ministers begged him not to do it; Rodzianko considered the idea 'insane'. He ignored them.

From the moment Tsar Nicholas boarded the imperial train and left for army headquarters almost 500 miles to the south-west of Petrograd, the fate of his reign stood sealed. One might argue, as many have, that had he not shouldered this immense burden, had he not, in effect, deserted the capital city, events might have played out in less calamitous a fashion. Perhaps Nicholas could have finally accepted the sort of constitutionally inclined government that the times made so obvious a requirement, so obvious even he might have recognized its necessity; perhaps by being more experienced than his poor wife, whom he left in charge of governmental business, he could have avoided the embarrassing and politically explosive mismanagement that she oversaw; perhaps he could have short-circuited the train of events that opened the crack of opportunity for Trotsky and Lenin, beyond which there lay no hope for the Romanovs. History is a catalogue of such whimsy, the 'might-ifs' that never happened. Leaving for the front (a euphemism, of course; the tsar was a titular commander in chief and nowhere near actual fighting – he spent a good many hours just playing dominoes), an act he equated with the Passion of Golgotha, was merely the last in a series of dreadful miscalculations on the part of this hopelessly befuddled individual. In attempting to save his vision for Russia, he in effect destroyed everything that he held dear.

By the late autumn of 1916, Nicholas was essentially estranged from all his extended family. Isolated either at army headquarters or at Tsarskoe Selo (which he visited when he could), his thoughts seldom strayed from his wife and daughters, united with them on the commonality of their love and concern for the afflicted Alexei. The young tsarevich, as his Swiss tutor correctly observed, 'was the centre of this united family, the focus of all its hopes and affections'. The fact that Rasputin appeared to be their only reed of hope in terms of alleviating the young boy's present pain and his uncertain long-term future, exacerbated their sense of loneliness. One after the other, over the course of almost eleven years – from his mother, sisters, brothers-in-laws; indeed, whomever had the nerve to even broach the topic – the tsar and his wife had been urged to sever their relationship with the man nearly all of them considered to be an out-and-out charlatan. In 1912, the dowager empress, saying 'it's either me or Rasputin', advised the royal couple 'to send him away now'. They would not. Alexandra's sister Ella, the widow of Sergei Alexandrovich, made a special trip from Moscow in the dead of winter, 1917, with the same plea, as recorded by the French ambassador:

> The Emperor and Empress gave her a very frigid reception; she was so amazed at it that she asked:
>
> 'Perhaps it would have been better if I had not come?'
> 'Yes', replied the Empress drily.
> 'Then perhaps I'd better go?'
> 'Yes, by the first train', replied the Emperor.

On her way back to the Petrograd station, Ella stopped to see Felix Yusupov. 'She entered the room trembling and in tears', he wrote. "She drove me away like a dog!" she cried. "Poor Nicky, poor Russia!"' This proved to be the last time these sisters ever met. Grand dukes, friends, politicians, whether gently in some cases or more forwardly in others, begged the tsar to take action. His general response? 'I allow no one to give me advice.'

It is a very easy thing to paint the Rasputin epic in garish colours. The man was larger than life in some respects, and his mark on Russian history so direct and decisive (given his origins, background and level of education) that it almost demands a sense of awe in the retelling. But simple facts must not be ignored or swept into the background just to make way for more vivid highlights. Beneath the almost oriental grandeur that marked everyday routine in the life of the tsar and his wife – the Winter Palace, for example, 'a place of depressing magnitude' whose bedrooms reminded one visitor of an 'American convention hall' – the fact remains that Nicholas and Alexandra were human beings, beset with the usual infirmities of both character and mindset that characterize us all, and afflicted by a family tragedy involving their much-beloved son. The simple *starets*, Gregory Rasputin, alleviated their collective pain, whether through sorcery or simple psychology (when it came to the tsarina) we shall never know, but in terms of the two of them together, we do know: he was their friend. Perhaps they saw in him an idealization of Russia, its soul and capacity for generosity; perhaps they saw in his religious simplicity a glimpse of the Holy Land, Christ unfiltered. As the ranks of collective Russia closed their door on the imperial family, from the drawing rooms of St. Petersburg to the affections of his closest relatives (whose motives the imperial couple saw as base), perhaps Rasputin was a symbol of disinterested solidarity, a man who had no motive in life other than their well-being. Of the many negatives that can be ascribed to Rasputin – his legion of moral failings, above all – he was not mendacious. He died as he was born, in a peasant's blouse. While it is true that the coarse fabric of his earliest shirts were replaced by the time of his death by a silken version, embroidered by the empress herself, it was, in the end, merely an ordinary shirt.

After Rasputin's murder, Ambassador Paléologue recorded an incisive remark by an old friend, a Russian arch-monarchist, who expressed sympathy for the imperial couple in a very revealing way.

'You know what I thought of Rasputin', he said, 'the mystical and filthy rake always filled me with unutterable loathing. I only met him once in a decent house into which I'd strayed. He was going out as I went in. The ladies present were watching him make his exit with languishing glances. Speaking personally, I had an irresistible desire to kick him through the door. So you see I'm not exactly in mourning for him. But all the same I think it was a great mistake to kill him. He had won the confidence and affection of our beloved sovereigns. He inspired them, encouraged and amused them, consoled and exhorted them, and was a general tonic. In the intervals of his fornications he gave them advice for the good of their souls and the government of the Empire. He often made them cry, as he didn't shrink from brow-beating them. He sometimes made them laugh too, for when he kept out of his mystical drivel, he had no equal in broad humour. They couldn't get on without him. He was their mainspring, their toy and their fetish. He oughtn't to have been taken from them. Since his departure they haven't known which way to turn. I expect the wildest follies from them now!'

'Oh Majesty. I see Christ behind you!'

Alexander Protopopov, Minister of the Interior,
addressing Alexandra Feodorovna,
December 1916

These were the kinds of words Alexandra Feodorovna liked to hear. They reinforced the self-imagery she had both of herself and her husband, two divinely inspired figures doing their best for Mother Russia in a crusade of sorts, embellished by the spiritual profundity of the orthodox church, itself deep and mysterious. Icons, incense, the incredible beauty of the liturgy, the miracle of communion – these sustained and nourished her, strangely so considering her Lutheran upbringing. The former prime minister Sergei Witte saw it differently. He felt that the tsarina's religious piety was superficial, that she had no genuine understanding of dogma, doctrine or the essence of orthodox religious teaching ('a sealed book to her'). She was, in his opinion, an 'orthodox pagan'; in pre-Christian times she would have been overwhelmed by bonfires on distant hills, the reading of entrails, the sacrifice of lambs.

Being a Christ-like figure sustained Alexandra as she more or less ruled Petrograd in her husband's absence. She certainly knew that her hiring and firing of numberless ministerial figures (often advised by Rasputin) would be seen unflatteringly throughout the city, especially given the nonentities she replaced them with, chosen for their autocratic loyalties or, too often, merely on whim, but the empress never looked back. As the political climate lurched into an atmosphere of literal poison, she remained defiant, infallible, oblivious. She certainly never realized that Rasputin, 'my only friend', as she described him, had slid into the final, and most reckless, chapter of his remarkable career.

After eleven tumultuous years in and out of St. Petersburg, and in and out of influence with the tsar, an overconfident Rasputin seemed finally to lose his footing. Always careless, he grew more so now that Nicholas was hundreds of miles away and the tsarina alone, an ideal set of circumstances from his point of view. He made no effort to moderate his behaviour, and took no account whatsoever of how his political interferences might endanger him down the road. Rasputin always was a fatalist – he constantly predicted his own assassination – but in fact he walked straight into the valley of death on his own two feet. His apartment could be visited by from 80 to 100 petitioners a day, mostly people with private agendas whose only concern was their own advancement. Money changed hands by the minute; Rasputin could receive a bribe in one hand, and give it away with the other. Financial gain was not important, but being at the centre of attention was. The empress approved nearly every request that Rasputin made of her; bureaucrats who received his scrawled and barely literate notes demanding an office or a favour from the petitioner standing in front of them, generally dared not refuse. Few if any of these multifarious decisions had much to do with policy; Rasputin, while not apolitical, had no genuine motivations other than a loyalty to the Romanovs. He had an interest, naturally enough, in matters concerning the church (where his influence was deeply resented by incumbents), and his antennae concerning 'the people' could be keen (he once urged the tsar to give railway priority, for at least three days, to ship in food supplies to a complaining city, a festering psychological situation to which Nicholas had not a clue). But moderation was never a prominent feature of Rasputin's character. He never knew when to stop, whether praying to an icon so fervently that, when finished, he could be drenched in sweat, or in his multitudinous sexual exploits which, if believed, would be the envy of most adolescent males. He also grew impervious to danger, which turned out to be his biggest mistake.[16]

Polite society in Petrograd was fast becoming anything but polite. Disdain, and even downright hatred of 'the German woman' reached feverish proportions. Ambassador Paléologue was astonished at the loose and treasonable talk that surfaced at nearly every dinner party that he attended, where disposing of not only the empress, but the tsar as well, was openly debated. On 5 January he went to a salon where, 'helped by champagne, the company painted the situation at home in the blackest colours, with that riotous pessimism in which the Russian imagination delights'. The plots were simple. The tsarina, 'a lunatic', would be kidnapped and sent far away to Siberia, there to be confined to a convent for the duration. For good measure, that other German, her sister Ella, would be sent there as well to keep her company. Nicholas would be deposed, violently if necessary, and be replaced by a regency in the name of his son. 'He would do well to reflect on the fate of Paul I', as one remarked, a reminder of the viciousness that has often marked Russian history.[17] Four days later, he went to another affair, hosted by a prince for his mistress, an event 'bathed in the aroma of Moët and Chandon, *brut impérial*, which flowed in streams'. There, 'with the servants moving about, harlots looking on and listening, gypsies singing', schemes to overthrow the tsar were thrown about with drunken abandon. These upper crusts of the Russian social network were keenly aware, as the imperial couple seemingly were not, that the entire structure of their way of life was tottering in dangerous ways, and that only drastic action could possibly redeem the situation at this last moment ('Unless God himself intervenes, it is physically impossible for the state not to collapse'). The French ambassador, and his English counterpart as well, were habitués of the gilded world in which these aristocrats abandoned themselves. Champagne-inspired talk could be dismissed as just that, but Paléologue recorded many conversations with more sober and discreet individuals whom he respected for the soundness of their judgment. Here too he could be shocked.

> I believe I have frequently remarked on the casual way in which the Russians – even the most ardent devotees of tsarism and reaction – admit the possibility of the Emperor's assassination. No one minds talking about it in my presence. The only limit is that they slightly cloathe their meanings in the sketchy veil of euphemism or allusion. As I was strolling on the islands this afternoon, I met Prince O——, a typical old Russian nobleman, of haughty manners, broad and cultured views; a proud and glowing patriot. We walked and talked together. After a long and pessimistic diatribe he casually enlarged on the death of Paul I. I understood what he meant and betrayed some surprise. Then he stopped, crossed his arms, and looking me full in the face, blurted out: 'What do you expect, *Monsieur l'Ambassadeur!* Under a system of absolute power, if the sovereign goes mad, there's nothing for it but to put him out of the way!'

The very proposition of regicide, from the mouth of a man supportive of an established system three centuries old, was certainly 'scandalous ground' in Paléologue's opinion. It reminded him of the saying, 'Though I might have to admit the right to kill Nero, I should never admit any right to judge him.' This indeed, as Paléologue suggested, was the dichotomy of autocracy.

The dominant suspicion was that the empress and Rasputin were part of an organized *camarilla* or cabal, influenced by German agents, who were seeking to undermine troops at the front, oppress the population and do away with all constitutional or democratic concessions that had previously been granted. Tsar Nicolas would be restored to the unfettered pre-eminence of his father and grandfather. No Russian would dare look him in the face or speak to him without his head bowed. Aside from the alleged pro-German bias of Alexandra (totally false), the rest of the charges were largely true, though to accuse her of having a coherent political position or programme 'materially exaggerates and contorts' the true picture, according to Paléologue. The tsarina, in his opinion, was 'too impulsive, wrong-headed, and unbalanced' to be the kind of conspirator that all Petrograd suspected. She was, in point of fact, mostly in the grip of religious fantasies, and carried along more by hysteria and emotion than anything else. She had no true grip on just about anything that was happening.

'I'm going kill him like a dog.'
Vladimir Purishkevich, regarding Rasputin

Before attacking the imperial couple directly, Rasputin was targeted. His murder, undertaken by aristocrats and monarchists, was not a sign, as many have argued, that the removal of this evil influence was intended to show support or concern for Nicholas and Alexandra, to in effect 'save them from themselves'. It was meant to save the system, not the current rulers; desperate, emotional, passionate and depicted as an act of true devotion to Russia, it was instead a reactionary effort – and far too late – to preserve a life of privilege that the Great War, with all its unanticipated centrifugal energies, was fast undermining. The three assassins were Prince Felix Yusupov, a cross-dressing dilettante, 'slight and effeminate', who was heir to the greatest fortune in Russia; his family's palace, complete with a private theatre, is synonymous with surfeit luxuriousness (Yusupov liked to boast that his family sent their dirty laundry to Paris to be washed). Grand Duke Dmitri Pavlovich was Yusupov's second, twenty-five years old. Both these men were blood relations to the tsar and, it has been alleged, lovers. The third was an older and more sinister character, Vladimir Purishkevich. 'Reactionary' is an adjective almost too mild to describe his political views. He was involved in several right-wing political groups, had carried out pogroms against Jews with pathological intensity and detested Rasputin for the discredit and opprobrium that he had smeared on the royal family. On the wintry night of 30 December 1916, Yusupov picked up Rasputin at his apartment. In greeting him, he gave Rasputin, in the Russian fashion, 'a resounding kiss on the mouth'. Rasputin allegedly said, 'Heavens! What a kiss, boy! I hope it isn't the kiss of Judas!' Yusupov took him to the family palace. In a basement apartment he claims that he fed the *starets* poisoned cakes and wine, enough, or so he had been advised, to kill an ox. He strummed his guitar and sang songs for Rasputin, filling his glass as necessary, delightedly thinking to himself, 'What had become of his second sight?' Didn't he know that his host was going to kill him?

Steady nerves, however, were not Yusupov's forte. As the evening wore on, nothing seemed to affect his victim. Was the potassium cyanide not working? Was Rasputin getting the last laugh, mocking death in the face? Rasputin grew restless; where were the girls? Yusupov, in a panic, left the room. What was he to do, he said to his fellow conspirators, nothing was working? Purishkevich put the matter bluntly. He gave Yusupov a revolver and told the weakling to shoot him. Close to hysterics, Yusupov did as he was told, firing a single bullet into the evil creature's back, watching him crumple to the floor. The job was done, the doctor who had supplied the poison checked his pulse and said so … or was it? As the others left to gather up something in which to wrap the body, Yusupov was stunned thirty minutes later to see Rasputin struggle to his feet, foam spurting from his mouth, to grab him by the shoulders. Yusupov shook himself free and, panic-stricken, ran from the place screaming. Purishkevich, hearing the commotion, grabbed his own gun and rushed outside into the courtyard. There he saw Rasputin running at full speed for the gate. 'I couldn't believe my eyes', he later remarked. He lifted his pistol and fired four shots; two hit their target just as he was about to reach the street. He walked over and kicked the body several times. Yusupov reappeared and, in something of a maniacal, almost fetishistic fury, repeatedly pummelled Rasputin's head with a rubber truncheon or blackjack. Post-mortem photographs of Rasputin show the gruesome effect; the snow in the courtyard was covered in blood. Prince Dmitri then appeared with his car. The body was rolled up in a curtain – of what design or fabric or cost we do not know, but possibly silk – and put in the back; chains to weigh down the corpse were loaded up as well, and the car driven off to a prearranged dumping site, under a bridge crossing a canal that had had a hole chopped in it beforehand. The body was hauled down to the river and pushed under the ice. Goodness gracious, they had forgotten the weights! Those were thrown as well, to what effect we shall never know. When the conspirators returned to the car, parked on the bridge, they found one of Rasputin galoshes in the back seat. They threw that onto the ice, and then left. When police investigators saw the boot, they figured out the connection and discovered the corpse within three days. A hurried autopsy, abruptly cut short when the empress sent a nun in her service to prepare the body for burial, found water in the lungs, indicating the possibility that Rasputin, after all that had happened to him, might have died from drowning. No trace of potassium cyanide was discovered.

The murder was Petrograd's worst kept secret. Purishkevich boasted of the deed almost immediately, and the identity of the other two was common knowledge within twenty-four hours. A policeman, hearing the shots that night, had made inquiries at the Yusupov palace, but was told merely that a pet had been killed in a drunken mistake. Yusupov was furious when, in order to corroborate this story, he had to shoot 'one of my best dogs' later that night. So many rumours and wild stories criss-crossed the capital over the next several days that, even now, it is difficult to sort through hyperbole to find the truth. One of the more lurid (and preposterous) involved Tatiana, the imperial couple's second daughter, allegedly molested by Rasputin, who observed the entire crime disguised as an army officer; not content with Rasputin's demise, she ordered him castrated, while still alive, as a final punishment. These grotesque embellishments disturbed Paléologue. One of his confidants said the previous evening's exploits reminded him of the Borgias, but Paléologue disagreed. 'Magnificence in lust and villainy is not given to everyone.' Yusopov's inspiration, he felt, belonged more to the realm of an Oscar Wilde.

Certainly the memoirs of those who committed the deed are of dubious veracity in many of their details, so much so that a completely verifiable record is probably impossible. Conspiracy theories remain in vogue to this day. One of the more recent alleges that officers of the British army, attached to the embassy, were in on the kill, allegedly to foil the empress in her treasonable urge to remove Russia from the war. These fly in the face of reality, but one never can be sure. The empress handled the news with surface calm. She urged Nicholas to return from army headquarters to assist her in this dreadful hour of need. When suspicions arose concerning the young princes, she ordered them confined to house arrest. Prince Dmitri's father was so astounded that his son might be implicated in such a sordid affair that he confronted him with an icon and a picture of his deceased mother, asking him to swear his innocence. For the love of Russia, Dimitri denied any involvement.

'We are on the verge of a catastrophe, there is no more coal or food, we are living from day to day, everything is in complete disarray.'
Grand Duke Alexander Mikhailovich,
brother-in-law to Nicholas II
28 February 1917

Four days after his death, Rasputin was surreptitiously buried, in the middle of the night, on grounds directly adjacent to Tsarskoe Selo. The empress handled all the details, completely ignoring the *staret*'s family (they were not invited to attend the final service). Had the Romanovs retained their crown, plans would have proceeded to build a chapel over the grave, in keeping with Russian tradition when it comes to commemorating the assassinations of important people. Such was the case of Nicholas's grandfather, the murdered Alexander II, and such would be the case regarding the tsar as well (a church on the site of his death, and another one where his mutilated body was dumped). Aside from the royal family, a mere handful of witnesses and the officiating priest were present. Alexandra left a handwritten note in Rasputin's crossed hands, addressed to 'my dear martyr'. The site was directly visible from the main thoroughfare from the capital to Tsarskoe Selo. 'Many a time I have passed it', wrote one diplomat; 'it can be seen from the road through the trees. At this time of year, under a winter sky and lost in the immensity of the fog-bound, icy plain, the place is mournful and melancholy. It was a very proper setting for yesterday's scene.' Meanwhile, necromancers and conjurers had a busy time, holding séances where Rasputin 'spoke' from the grave.

Of more immediate concern was the fate of his murderers, which lay to the discretion of the tsar. The three culprits seemed to have expected mercy; they were, after all, the darlings of the moment in high society, if not at Tsarskoe Selo. Yusupov, in particular, was cocky. 'He believed in his lucky star and counted upon the protection of public opinion', said a friend. He also relied on his family, the grand dukes, and all their compatriots, many of whom, after 'running around, conferring, and gossiping', aggressively lobbied the tsar to act with discretion. Harsh penalties, they said, would further roil popular feelings against the royal couple and aggravate an already tense political situation. 'It was the will of the family that the whole matter should be quietly dropped', wrote Anna Vyrubova.

Nicholas's brother-in-law could not believe it. Did they honestly expect 'the tsar of Russia to decorate his two relatives for having committed a murder?' 'I am filled with shame', Nicholas remarked to Vyrubova. 'He [then] expressed himself as being entirely through with all of them.' Notwithstanding, Yusupov was treated leniently, sent to live in comfort on one of his hunting estates 600 miles from Petrograd. He was unrepentant to the day of his death in Paris, an exile, in 1967. Prince Dmitri was sent to the Persian front, about as far away as humanly possible. His family was horrified, and begged Nicholas to change his mind. The poor boy 'is physically ill and deeply shaken', he would never survive the place. In actuality, the sentence saved his life. During the purges ordered by Lenin, wherein Dmitri's father was executed along with several score of other Romanovs and their entourages, he was busy travelling to Teheran, from there to Bombay and from there to England, courtesy of the British army and navy. Had he remained in Petrograd, he too would have been shot.[18]

This personal tragedy completed the isolation of Nicholas and Alexandra, both from the nation at large, their capital city, their family and, most damaging of all, from reality. The empress 'is in a state of complete and incurable delusion', wrote one close observer, 'her main argument was that everyone needs to be brought to heel, and put in their place'. Alexandra said it more bluntly to her husband: the people 'must learn to fear you, love is not enough', she wrote in a letter to him. Russians 'want to feel the whip'. Nicholas, by contrast, lost all his fire, if indeed he ever had any, and regressed into a shell of passivity and resignation. 'Perhaps a scapegoat is needed to save Russia', he had said, 'I mean to be the victim. May the will of God be done.' (Contrast this with the resolve, willpower and bottomless energy of his enemies; as Alexander Solzhenitsyn said of Lenin, 'A single wasted hour made [him] ill.') On edge, at times unable to sleep, Nicholas consulted a well-known 'Mongolian quack' who prescribed a blend of herbs to settle his nerves, rumoured to be a combination of hashish and henbane. Shortly after Rasputin's funeral, the former minister Count Kokovtsov had what turned out to be his last interview with Nicholas. He was shocked at the tsar's appearance, the many wrinkles on his face, sallow colouring, lack of vitality in facial characteristics, an inability to concentrate, 'a forced, mirthless smile fixed upon his lips'. He was, to all intents and purposes, 'almost unrecognizable, [a man who] was profoundly unsettled and hardly knew what was happening around him'. Kokovtsov, on leaving the room, burst into tears.

Nicolas returned to army headquarters, Alexandra continued her maladroit administration of affairs. By this time the government's ministers were in total eclipse, leaders in the Duma openly wondering if the tsarist regime could last another day. Only a spark was missing, and it was struck by the usual and familiar causes: bread lines, a lack of fuel in a cruel winter (temperatures in the city were thirty degrees below zero), discontent in the barracks, a barrage of rumours, all dire. The city was buried, as one grand dame put it, in a 'strange mood of constant, if repressed, unease'. One army general was incredulous at the mutinous condition of the Petrograd garrison, now bloated to 170,000 men. These soldiers should be dispersed to the front, he advised, with the caveat, if they could be forced to. With 40,000 good men, and 20,000 bloodthirsty cossacks, he could handle anything, but the Petrograd units were cannon fodder for the most part, untrained boys, conscripts, replacement troops, all demoralized and susceptible to rabble-rousing ('The barracks are being flooded with pamphlets', the French ambassador noted with unease; in 'shops and cafés, it is openly said that the "German woman" is about to ruin Russia and must be put away').[19] On 8 March 1917, bands of hungry residents broke shop windows, looting food and other items; crowds grew bigger and more hostile. People were heard yelling for bread; in a few days they would be yelling more sinister slogans, 'No More Romanovs' and 'To the Ditch with Them'. Police units could not handle the situation over the course of several nights, and troops were brought in. When first given the order to fire, some units obeyed, killing an estimated 200 people, but they were embittered to be called upon to do so. Given time, most of them either refused or shot their rifles into the air. Some officers who persisted in 'doing their duty' were murdered. Ensconced at Tsarskoe Selo, Alexandra wired her husband that the disturbances were minor, only a 'drawing room revolt', nothing to worry about. Nicholas was reassured; just another instance of 'excitement in Petrograd'. Three days later he received a cable from the president of the Duma, Mikhail Rodzianko, a man Nicholas considered a 'fat' lout. Unless the tsar made immediate concessions to popular feeling, he wrote, only 'anarchy, elemental and uncontrollable', would result. In response, the tsar sent a general with four front-line regiments to take care of the situation, and dissolved the Duma. It was, of course, far too late.

British General Alfred Knox was visiting the Russian ministry of artillery, located on a wide boulevard, Liteyny Prospect, where he witnessed the point of no return on 12 March. Standing on the second floor with senior officers, he saw the street suddenly empty, pedestrians and a few officers having caught sight of something that Knox could not yet see, and now running for it as though for their lives. In ten minutes, a huge wave of armed soldiers surged down the street and both sidewalks, sweeping away anything in front of them. There was no noise, no commotion, only the tramp of several thousand booted feet. 'What struck me was the uncanny silence of it all', he noted. 'We were like spectators in a gigantic cinema.' Soon a few shots rang out, and the doors to the ministry were forced open. The officers with whom Knox had been meeting all ran for it out the back doors, but Knox was not that sort of man. He walked down to the ground floor through the mob, now stealing everything in sight, went to the cloak room and, in fluent Russian, asked for his coat. One of the insurgents helped him put it on, as a proper orderly should. Knox then left the building out the front gate. What he witnessed there was the utter breakdown of order.

With the government (in Rodzianko's words) 'completely paralyzed and totally incapable of restoring order', the Duma took control, in effect seizing the reins of authority from the tsar and his ministers. This was not, despite what monarchists might later say, an act of treason, but more the case of occupying a vacuum. Rodzianko, for example, had no desire to supplant the tsar, but he had no choice, an associate telling him 'Take the power … if you don't, others will.' Throughout the absolute chaos of the days and weeks that followed, one thing was now certain. The tsar was finished. When it finally dawned on Nicholas that the situation was perilous, he attempted to return to Petrograd, but his train never made it. Insurgents took control of the line, and the tsar's progress was short-circuited to a siding near the Estonian border, some 160 miles from the city. There, effectively alone and cut off from any sort of power base (in other words, combat units that might possibly have retained their loyalty) he was more or less bullied into abdication, not that it took much effort. Five days later, he was formally put under arrest.

Even after years of reflection, several of the Romanov family and those of their faithful retainers who survived the revolution, and later wrote their memoirs, remained stunned that the tsar, 'who had never been able to make up his mind' on just about anything, could have 'so quickly consented to abdicate'. Nicholas had repeatedly said in the past that Petrograd and Moscow were merely 'two needle-dots on the map of our country', with a population of only a few hundred thousand. Compare that to the nation as a whole – 168 million people, covering a sixth of the globe – and what did it matter what a handful of hooligans or mutinous rabble did in a few city streets? 'A twenty-four-hour battle in the suburbs of St. Petersburg would have restored order', said one grand duke in 1932, but Nicky did not have the stomach for it. It really was as simple as that. Though it broke his heart, he was, in the end, relieved. He was not, as it turned out, his father's son.

The news of the abdication was so catastrophic that no one at Tsarskoe Selo dared tell the empress. Nicholas's uncle finally made his way to the empress but, inarticulate with grief, he could only stand before her silently, kissing her hand. 'The tsarina's despair almost defied imagination' wrote one witness, but Alexandra steadied herself after a few moments. Courage was never an attribute she lacked. She wrote her husband a series of cables –'I *fully* understand your action – my own hero!' – but these were returned, marked 'Address of person mentioned above unknown'. This would be but the first of an enduring stream of indignities that Alexandra would soon suffer, which would include the dreadful finale, the atrocity of her eventual murder.

⁂

Figuring It Out, Not Always Easy

'If we had known how thin the sides of the volcano were,
we would never have provoked an eruption.'

Prosper Duvergier de Hauranne, French politician,
discussing the revolution of 1848

The pivotal days of 1917 are generally divided into two sections, and both were arguably the most crucial moments of modern Russian history. The first were the March Days, wherein the tsar was overthrown and the Duma, followed by a provisional government, took over the reins of power. They were from the first in a deadly competition with more extreme leftist groups, operating 'soviets' or working committees within the ranks of both industrial workers and the Petrograd garrison. These insidious 'organisms' (as they were often described by constitutionalists or those seeking a western-style democracy) soon appeared in all the major cities, Moscow and Kiev especially, and began making inroads through the countryside as well, disingenuously appealing to a peasantry desperate for one thing, and one thing only, land. At the far left of the left, and a largely minority voice, stood the bolsheviks, most of whose principal leaders had long since been deported as the disruptive menace they were. Leon Tolstoy, for example, was an émigré in New York. When he tried to return home, after hearing the exciting news from Petrograd, he found himself interned in Nova Scotia, of all places, in a POW camp. He used his time there to harangue captured German storm troopers on the efficacy of social revolution. Vladimir Lenin was an exile in Zurich, who feared his day would never come. He could barely believe it when German agents negotiated with him the offer of an unobstructed passage to Petrograd. What fools these people were, he said to himself. The famous Ten Days of October, when the bolsheviks, in a nearly bloodless coup, toppled the provisional government, represents the second historically portentous phase of the 1917 Russian saga. Over the Winter Palace the double-eagled standard of the tsar no longer flew, replaced by an enormous solid red flag. The world would not be the same again for another century.

In the immediate uncertainty of these initial weeks, it became clear to most astute observers that their dire predictions over the past decade were coming true. Agitators, well-intentioned or not, had battered the tsarist system, subjected it to ridicule; but now, with power in their hands, if they were unable to move forward in a way that most people saw as competent, they would in their turn find themselves ousted in a revolutionary avalanche of instability. Everything familiar in Russian society would be undermined.

Count Kokovtsov, with the benefit of hindsight, thought the real culprits to his country were not so much bolsheviks or anarchists, but the well-intentioned liberals and Petrograd progressives who had insidiously destroyed all confidence in the governmental status quo (that it deserved it was another matter). If the new breed of leaders could not come up with something more authoritarian than 'a parody on Western European parliamentarism', the country would disintegrate. Another conservative politician put it more directly in November 1915, with these prophetic words. 'In the case of genuine revolutionaries', he said, 'you know where you are at any rate; you see where you're going ... or will go. But these others – whether they call themselves Progressives, Cadets, or Octobrists is all the same to me – are traitors to our political system and leading us hypocritically into the revolution, which will certainly swallow them up on the first day. It will go a long way further than they think, and its horrors will be worse than anything known.'

The provisional government did not help matters from its very inception, making the colossal mistake of continuing the war. The legations of their allies, France and England, were delighted, but sceptical when they saw socialist reforms within the army. No more corporal punishment (What, officers could no longer strike their men?); abolition of the death penalty (What about deserters?); doing away with saluting (Discipline?); electing their own officers (Impossible!). Knox, a stickler for protocol within the ranks, was appalled when he read the usual, and almost daily, proclamations issued by the Petrograd Soviet of Working Men and Soldier Deputies. This was no way to run an army. Rodzianko tried to reassure him. 'My dear Knox', he said to him, 'you must be easy. Everything is going on all right. Russia is a big country, and can wage a war and manage a revolution at the same time.' Such confidence ensured that Rodzianko would end up fleeing to Serbia where he died, penniless, in 1924.

The linchpin of the provisional government, an entity that would last for eight months, was Alexander Kerensky, a little 'half-Jew lawyer' according to Knox, and a former member of the Duma. He was an impressive man, superb orator and full of both energy (he went full bore on only four hours of sleep a day) and revolutionary zeal (though Trotsky disparaged his socialist credentials, likening them to a 'little red silk handkerchief'). Kerensky was a man who shed no tears for the tsar, whom he considered 'a simpleton'. He was also full of himself and overly confident. The 'soviets', he told Knox, were already 'losing ground'. In a week or so he would have them under control, and the war effort on sound ground once again. None of this took place. Perhaps a victory on the field of battle might have helped things, but in the summer of 1917, after a disastrous Russian offensive, the Russian soldier began voting, in Lenin's famous phrase, with his feet. The front stood in danger of a complete collapse.

'We can always find enough strength to bear the misfortune of others.'
François de la Rochefoucauld, *Maxime 19* (1665)

Maurice Paléologue continued making the rounds of his aristocratic friends. He had suffered a few close calls himself during the tumultuous days of March. His car was sometimes surrounded by hostile mobs who had no idea what an ambassador was, and even less comprehension that a France existed somewhere to the west. Paléologue stopped trying to explain that his country and theirs were allies in a common cause against Germany; the war was so unpopular, it was best left unmentioned. In his arch way, he found it amusing to see and hear the sidewalk harangues that sprouted up on every street corner. 'What an artless and affecting sight it is when one remembers that the Russian nation has been waiting centuries for the right of speech!' But the rhetoric, which he termed an 'open gale', was unnerving, especially for a person well versed in the vitriolic excesses of the French Revolution, and what they augured for the future.

The town houses and palaces he visited, those that had not been ransacked, were full of nervous people. 'We shall not get out of it *this* time', said one grandee. 'What will we do without our rent rolls?' Paléologue found little if any sympathy for the tsar and his wife. In fact, some were hoping that the fury of the new state would focus, and thereby restrict itself, to the royal couple. The tsar will lose 94 million hectares of land, he heard one magnate say; they don't need ours. The ambassador noted that 'everyone consoled himself' at that. In a more poignant moment, he noted rather sadly a brief vignette from another house call.

As I reached the upper landing, through the open door of the drawing-room I caught a wonderful view of the Neva, the Cathedral of SS. Peter-and-Paul, the bastions of the fortress and the state prison. Seated in the embrasure of the window was the lovely Mademoiselle Olive, maid of honour to the Grand Duchess; she was lost in thought and gazing out at the Fortress. She did not hear me come.

I broke in on her reverie: 'Mademoiselle, I've just guessed the direction of your thoughts, if not your thoughts themselves. You seem to be looking at the prison very hard!'

'Yes, I was looking at the prison. In these days one can't help looking at it.'

As she turned to my secretary, she added with her delightful laugh, 'Will you come and see me, Monsieur de Chambrun, when I'm lying on the straw in a dungeon there?'

Lenin

'In twenty years of life and struggle, Lenin had experienced every kind of opponent – the haughtily ironical, the sarcastic, the sly, the base, the obstinate, the stalwart, not to mention the spluttering-rhetorical, the quixotic, the effete, the slow-witted, the lachrymose, and other miscellaneous shits. With some of them he had wrestled for many years, and not all of them had he overcome, flattened with one blow, but he had always been aware of the immeasurable superiority given him by his clear view of the situation, his firm grip, his ability sooner or later to down any of them.'

Alexander Solzhenitsyn, *Lenin in Zurich* (1976)

Unlike Gregory Rasputin, Vladimir Ilich Ulyanov, who at thirty-one years of age adopted the pseudonym 'Lenin', was no illiterate peasant chained to the estate of some absentee landlord, and thus mired for life in the drudgery of mind-numbing manual labour. His father was an educational administrator, his mother a well-read, intelligent and versatile woman who capably led their family when Lenin's father died unexpectedly in 1886. Both believed in the Enlightenment values of good schooling, a progressive society (within limits), hard work and loyalty to god (in his father's case, at any rate), country and tsar. No one was more shocked than Lenin's mother when their eldest son, Alexander, became involved in left-wing politics while attending university in St. Petersburg; and no one was more horrified when he was implicated in a conspiracy to assassinate Tsar Alexander III. The boy was arrested, tried and condemned to death in 1887. The tsar had a chance to commute his sentence, but he signed the death warrant without hesitation. Bright university lads were common enough and, after all, the young traitor had expressed no remorse for his deeds. Young Vladimir neither forgot nor forgave. In time, he would order the execution of the tsar's son, Nicholas, in an act of fitting revenge.

He was a fine student. In an incredible piece of coincidence, his headmaster during secondary school was Fyodor Kerensky, the father of Alexander Kerensky, a figure against whom Lenin would butt heads in the famous days of 1917. Kerensky Senior was full of praise for Vladimir's work habits, intelligence and prospects. He did note, as negatives, the boy's 'excessive reclusiveness' and 'unsociability', which demonstrates that teachers whom young people often detest are sometimes not lacking in perceptiveness. He possessed exceptional language skills, could read, with full nuance, both French and German, and without outside instruction he mastered English as well. His education in the town of Simbirsk, where he was born in 1870, gave him a good though narrow introduction to the classics, which he perfected over a long life of serious reading. But when Lenin followed his brother's footsteps to university life in St. Petersburg, he pretty much replicated the poor habits of that unfortunate young man: he immersed himself in radical politics.

As a neophyte intellectual, Lenin fell in love with Karl Marx, more so than he ever did with any woman. As an exercise, he began translating *The Communist Manifesto* into Russian when he was only nineteen; the master's work, full of certitude, authority and moral righteousness, and often expressed in abstruse language that was exciting and dangerous in its mental challenges, left a mark on Lenin that has been likened to a branding with a white hot iron. Marx was god and, aside from Friedrich Engels, perhaps no man ever mastered the labyrinth of Marx's thinking, or expanded it so thoughtfully, as did Lenin.

He certainly had the time for it. Expelled from university for his dangerous dalliance with subversive activities, he was sent by his mother a thousand miles away to a family farm near the river Volga to manage affairs there (a task that did not interfere with reading or study). Over his entire life, this was probably Lenin's only experience with Russian peasants; he created policies that affected the lives of millions not so much from his direct exposure to their lives and conditions than from books, pamphlets and Marxist ideology. This is but one of many contradictions that the career of Vladimir Lenin presents. Theory propelled and guided his political convictions far more persuasively than facts on the ground.

One thing that allowed Lenin's extreme political ideas to survive was that nearly everyone in the socialist 'opposition' wanted the Romanovs gone. They were united by their detestation of the system, so much so that differences of approach and dialectical arguments, though often violently expressed, did not undermine their mutual determination to destroy the status quo. 'Old Russia' had to go. In its place would be western (specifically German) social standards of scientific 'progress'. In the views of most, these would be achieved peacefully (after the tsar's removal, by whatever means). Lenin's belligerence, intransigence and tendency towards authoritarianism were largely written off as the ravings of a crank. He was, however, an ally in the common struggle, and therefore tolerated. Most of those involved in the complicated politics of the early twentieth-century revolutionary struggle seriously underestimated this intense and fiercely driven man.

In looking at Lenin's career retrospectively, it is clear that he was an intellectual before becoming a man of action; a bookworm before becoming a revolutionary; an economist before becoming an executioner. Two personality traits that never left him, however, were a smouldering self-confidence and a combustible inner rage that never subsided, though an optimism that great events would inevitably shake the foundations of capitalist Europe within his lifetime did waver. He wondered if he might ever see the day when the 'carrion crow' of the Romanov coat of arms (double eagles, in fact) would ever crumble into dust during 'the next rising of the tide'. To use Alexander Solzhenitsyn's phrase, he lived in Switzerland frustrated and pent up, 'as if in a corked bottle'. It was written of Lenin at about this point in his life that 'he couldn't take a joke'.

Solzhenitsyn, exercising the usual novelistic rights, wrote imaginatively on Lenin's character. How much he made up, and how much is intelligent supposition, remains for his readers to decide. Lenin, unlike Trotsky, perhaps, but more in keeping with Stalin, never left any truly personal writings behind that might elucidate any of the hidden corners of his mind or personality. Trying to get to know the 'real' Lenin is therefore very difficult. Over the course of the twentieth century, Soviet historians compiled almost daily accounts of his political doings – over twelve dense volumes – that are so monumental that they shame any Vatican exercise in anointing someone a saint. Lenin is a canonical figure, to be sure, but unknowable at the same time. He no doubt intended it to be that way. The novelist Arnold Zweig asked in wonder, 'How did this obstinate little man .. become so important?'

'I'm a Marxist! The world's best Marxist is me!'
Maxim Gorky, in annoyance, speaking of Lenin's arrogance

In the world of day-to-day events, and the practicalities of current politics and their ramifications, Lenin was frequently just a bystander. The disturbances of 1905 had seen him in Geneva, far from St. Petersburg and rather isolated from events there. He heard sketchy details about Bloody Sunday by hanging around a local café where Russian émigrés ('compulsive revolutionary windbags') were accustomed to congregate, but the news was stale and outdated by the time he heard it; when he finally made it back to Russia, he quickly realized that only arrest and prison awaited him there, so he decamped to Finland, trying to keep his hand in the action from there. Nine years later, the outbreak of World War I also came as a surprise. He had paid little attention to the panoply of indications, readily reported in daily newspapers all over Europe (which Lenin read at no charge in public libraries), that war was coming. He was too mired in pedagogical disputes (once disparaged by Stalin as 'storms in a tea cup'), usually argued in letters, pamphlets and obscure socialist newspapers, to pay much attention to anything else. And in the final irony, the man who incessantly argued that revolution was right around the corner, was caught flat-footed by the February revolution that saw the fall of Nicholas II. For thirty years, ever since his brother's execution, Lenin had let his hatred for the Romanovs fester; it was astounding to him that in the course of just three weeks, the entire monarchial edifice collapsed and that none of it had been his doing. The speed and significance of what had happened was at first so overwhelming that he was simply too stunned to react – what was true, what was just rumour, how could he tell what was really going on? But the orderliness of his mind, the steadfastness of his resolution and the years of dedication to the cause soon got him back on track. The mission now was to somehow interject himself into the chaotic maelstrom of St. Petersburg's evolving disintegration (so that he could contribute to its further spiral); to propel himself into the middle of events as disruptively as possible; and to gain control over not only his own small and splintered party, but somehow to brush aside larger, better financed and more organized rivals from the moderate centre in order to seize the entire apparatus of power himself. These were not modest goals, and they could be achieved only at a price: indiscriminate and at time inchoate violence … violence almost for the sake of violence. For perhaps the first time in his career, Lenin would be forced to put into action what he had merely written about in his dingy apartments or in scattered reading rooms in far-flung libraries. He had always talked a great game when it came to 'liquidating' institutions, whole classes of people, the entire apparatus of conventional government. Could he really do it when theory now had the opportunity to transform itself into reality? Unlike many dreamers who had come before him, Lenin stood the test, with both good and evil results.

First things, however, first: how to get himself back to Russia? How to get himself back to Petrograd? Many fanciful schemes were debated, several involving disguises, false papers and assorted gimmicks. His wife, Nadezhda Krupskaya, a practical woman, discounted most of these. When Lenin was hypothetically dozing in a crowded third-class compartment (even great men needed sleep), she argued that Vladimir would probably mutter aloud as he was dreaming, something to do with eradicating mensheviks, and he would be uncovered. In the end, after negotiations as speedy as they were complicated, seeds planted years before came to fruition. German diplomatic authorities in Switzerland had been well aware for several years of the Russian émigré community settled in that country. Their ambassador, Baron Gisbert von Romberg, actually knew of Lenin and was reasonably familiar with his activities. A 'pact with the devil' was concocted between the two, and Romberg formally cabled Berlin regarding the feasibility of shipping Lenin and a few other provocateurs into Petrograd. Erich Ludendorff stated in 1937 that he had never heard of Lenin – why should he have? – but anything that might help Russia leave the war was music to his ears. The kaiser, who had delighted in the news of the tsar's overthrow, seeing therein no possibility of anything even remotely similiar ever happening to him, felt the same. What harm would it do to throw a few more destabilizing smoke bombs into the political maelstrom of Russia's capital city? He signed off on the whole scheme, and never once expressed any regret for doing so, in keeping with his habitual inability to admit a mistake. This manoeuvre goes down as the most maladroit in the political history of the twentieth century. As one Russian aristocrat was to write in her memoirs, 'They sent us the bolsheviks as they might have sent tanks or poison gas.' James Joyce, in Switzerland at the same time, likened the whole thing to the Trojan horse.

The railway trip itself was an exhausting seven days. Thirty-two men and women, including one four-year-old boy, had assembled on a railway platform in Bern on the morning of 9 April 1917. Lenin wore a knapsack, heavy with books, his wife had a pile of pillows and blankets, a basket with food; all the travellers carried the usual assortment of beat-up suitcases. No one watching this shabby mélange could ever have imagined the portent that this journey, with such a complement of obscure figures, would hold for the world at large. Lenin himself was clearly the leader, from devising schemes that would prevent any appearance of collaboration with German imperialists to organizing how the only toilet was to be used (too many smokers monopolized the facility, spending inordinate amounts of time locked in – something had to be done to accommodate those with weaker bladders!). As the convoy snaked its way north, troop transports, equipment trains, even the private train of the crown prince were shuttled aside to make way for Lenin and his cronies. A dreadful, storm-tossed ferry trip to Stockholm followed; once disembarked, Lenin was talked into going to a shop to buy more appropriate clothing, the idea being that he should 'resemble a human being' if at all possible. A train to the Finnish border, which had to be crossed by sleigh in the early morning hours, and then another train; at every stop, at every customs barrier, papers had to be checked, with anxious moments for all concerned. The latest newspapers were bought, the reports therein only infuriating Lenin, not appeasing him with hopeful tidings. Members of the bolshevik party, including one Joseph Stalin, had pledged their support to the Duma's provisional government. Lenin fumed: the provisional government was just as bad as Tsar Nicholas – he would soon take care of them. On 16 April, the final leg of this momentous journey began, locomotive # 293 departing Helsinki for Petrograd.[20] At or around midnight on the 16th it arrived at that city's Finland Station. A crowd of thousands were waiting. What they heard confused just about everyone.

This should have been a moment of triumph for Vladimir Lenin, the occasion for a bouquet of roses, perhaps, and celebratory speeches. It was not. Lenin was in a mood of sullen resentment. The provisional government was nothing but a bunch of lackeys. This was no time for rapprochement, a joining of hands, a moment for national reconciliation, the chance for all to revive a great and noble country. No, that was all cheap sentiment. This was a time for revolution, full-scale upheaval and no second chances for anybody. Standing on the top of an amoured vehicle, Lenin harangued the crowd. Never let it be said that he deceived anyone with what his plans were for the immediate future. His wife shook her head. Lenin, a man of limited social skills, had clearly misunderstood the moment at hand. She feared he had lost his mind.

The next weeks were frenetic. Lenin frustrated all attempts to unify the various splintered Marxists under one tactical roof. He continued to heap scorn on every faction, the mensheviks most of all. His strident calls for more revolution and more disruption gained him few allies. Lenin appeared to have become, said one socialist, 'the universal apostle of destruction'. What no one could argue with, however, was the man's single-mindedness and his ferocious energy. This was his moment, and he knew it. He would never return to the drab existence of a Zurich if he could help it. In the heady days of April and May he also became more comfortable within himself. Never a first-rate orator, and used mainly to addressing small audiences at the prewar (and puny) socialist conferences that he attended, Lenin now found himself giving impromptu speeches all over Petrograd, and sometimes to several hundred people at a time, few of whom, unsurprisingly, were intellectuals of the sort he was used to addressing (to be honest, how many beyond the first few rows who could actually hear what he was saying was also problematic). Lenin, however, found his stride. He developed a considerable stage presence, radiating supreme confidence, no matter the outrageousness of whatever it was he was talking about. People saw more than they heard, and what they saw was a bulldog, a man of resolution, force, vigour and infallibility. It was not unusual for Lenin to give impromptu harangues from the balcony of his headquarters, the former mansion of Mathilde Kschessinska, once the tsar's mistress, at any or all hours of the night. The very force of his personality soon ensured that he became the indisputable boss of the bolshevik party.

He worked himself to near exhaustion. Being an academic at heart, he arranged his hectic schedule in such a way as to give him some time, at the very least, to write. In May alone, he published nearly fifty articles for the party news sheet, *Pravda*. Many of these are unintelligible to today's reader (and probably to those who perused them then), but they represent a treasure trove of research material for scholars searching for clues as to the evolving nature of Lenin's ideas as he faced immediate and practical problems.[21] He was not, in many ways, the doctrinaire figure of legend; if a position needed softening to overcome an immediate or threatening spate of opposition that could endanger the larger struggle, he was often willing to accommodate, if only superficially. Realpolitik ruled the day. The future prime minister of Israel, David Ben-Gurion, who idealized Lenin, and travelled to Moscow in 1923 hoping to see him before he died, noted that 'he is not afraid of rejecting today what he required yesterday, and requiring tomorrow what he rejected today; he will not be caught in the net of platitude, or in the trap of dogma'. Lenin had a fine memory for those he despised, and often merely changed a point of view solely for the sake of appearances. The most important thing was: he knew that he knew best.[22]

Trotsky

A 'son of a bitch, but the most famous Jew since Christ.'

Raymond Robins, a member of the
American Red Cross Mission to Petrograd, 1917

Vladimir Lenin was a fortunate man indeed to have by his side the estimable Leon Trotsky (one of several pseudonyms employed by Lev Bronstein, though

'Trotsky' stuck). In 1917, Trotsky was a thirty-eight-year-old professional revolutionary. Born into a moderately prosperous Jewish family (his father was an entrepreneurial farmer), he followed the usual rebellious route of so many Russian youths: romantic, idealistic, too smart for his own good, handsome, dynamic, an excellent student, unruly when it came to authority figures and drawn to danger and intrigue. During his young manhood he was arrested, detained, questioned, found guilty of various offences and sent off to the Arctic rim of Siberia or other 'prisons' on multiple occasions. The miles he travelled when shipped off to various detention centres numbered in the thousands (his first, from Moscow to Siberia, ran to 3,400 miles). Along the way he jettisoned his first wife and family for another, and escaped one tsarist jailer hidden under a pile of cattle fodder, one of his more famous adventures. For several years he travelled the Marxist underground circuit throughout Europe, eagerly meeting the giants of his cause, and earning his keep largely with a pen, writing articles and pamphlets for socialist newspapers and journals. He arrived in London unannounced in the autumn of 1902, largely to meet Lenin, about whom he had heard much. Arriving at Lenin's apartment by cab, he hadn't a ha'penny to his name (Lenin's wife had to pay the fare). Lenin was immediately drawn to this gifted and dedicated young man, nine years his junior. Though differences over Marxist dogma (about which Trotsky could be elastic) and tactical disputes between the various splinter groups often brought them at loggerheads, Lenin made certain never to allow a permanent breach between them. Trotsky was too valuable to alienate.

Trotsky was a man of passion. A potent and inspirational writer, his oratorical abilities matched those found on the printed page (reams and reams, as it turned out. Neither Lenin nor Trotsky made much of an effort to edit themselves). At times he could be a coarse rabble-rouser, and appeals to gutter emotion came naturally to him if he saw them having an effect. 'We shall not enter into the kingdom of socialism in white gloves and on a polished floor', he once said. But he was more than capable of refined appreciations. During his flight from Siberia in 1902, he read Homer's *Iliad* for relaxation; when imprisoned in 1905, he ploughed through Shakespeare. But in revolutionary matters he was direct and results-oriented. His superb oratorical gifts, his flair for dramatics and skewering the opposition, were not the sort of 'parliamentary eloquence' that might distinguish a Disraeli or a Palmerston, both of whom he mocked. To trample the existing order required demagoguery; it required the ability of a man to jump on a soapbox, on any corner of any street, and throw one's listeners into a rage. Trotsky had that kind of skill, better than any man alive. When the tsar issued his October Manifesto in 1905, many Russians of a liberal persuasion seemed satisfied;

progress was being made. Trotsky would have none of that. Addressing students at the university from a balcony, Trotsky, in his own words, 'shouted' invective on the tsar and his concessions. To reinforce his point, he tore the Manifesto into pieces and hurled it into the wind.

Revolution also required more abrasive skills than just talking; it required steely nerves and the application of terror when needed. In the moment of struggle, worrying about law or justice was some sort of middle-class 'fetish' that could be jettisoned without qualms. Lenin and Trotsky were at one on that subject, in truth an ideal team. Lenin was the cerebral intellect, 'the prophet of the creed', as a Frenchman put it, Trotsky 'the man of action', but both were hard-hearted when it came to procedure. Trotsky called Lenin 'Maximilien' behind his back, a joking tribute to Maximilien Robespierre. If Lenin was indeed Robespierre, then Trotsky was Danton. In the dramatic and dangerous days of winter 1917, he did not hesitate to fan the flames. 'I tell you', he said to mutinous sailors during one speech, 'heads must roll, blood shall flow.... The strength of the French Revolution was in the machine that made the enemies of the people shorter by a head. This is a fine device. We must have it in every city.'[23] Lenin saw no reason to delay. On 6 November he ordered the uprising. Trotsky was the man who carried it out; there was no fear or hesitation in anything he did. Kerensky ended up fleeing for his life.

The Fall of the Provisional Government

> *'Ah, these Russians, they are original! What a civil war!*
> *Everything except the fighting!'*
> French military attaché, Petrograd, 10 November 1917

Kerensky, the 'soul' of the provisional government, had gambled hugely by keeping Russia in the war, but the failure of his summer offensive, and the refusal of his ministries to redress deep-seated social problems with anything but words (particularly those relating to industrial workers and the peasantry), paved the way for Lenin's growing willingness to force the issue. Kerensky can be faulted for allowing hostilities with Germany and Austria-Hungary to continue, but undue blame for Russia's internal deterioration, arguably beyond his power to stem, is perhaps unreasonable. It did not help having a man of Lenin's predispositions waiting in the wings, searching without respite for any sign that the moment of supreme weakness had come, and with it the signal to revolt. Bolshevik inroads to the all-important Soviet Petrograd increased by the day; two parallel instruments of governance – the soviet and the provisional government – could not coexist indefinitely. Workers and soldiers in the city, by now saturated with revolutionary sentiment and overwhelmed by inflammatory (though often indigestible) rhetoric, stood like dry tinder awaiting the match. Kerensky's inability to soften the tone of political debate, and to convince the population of Petrograd that times would improve for the better, stood little chance when compared to the endless stream of propaganda churned out by the extreme left, especially as defeatism regarding the war reached acute proportions. Dissatisfaction among radical workers, the soviet and the Petrograd garrison peaked in July, and again Lenin missed his cue. The time was not perfect, he concluded. He went to Mathilde Kschessinska's balcony and dampened the fire. Kerensky pounced. The bolsheviks were a pack of Jews (there was some truth to that, enough to arouse the usual anti-Semitic hysterics); the bolsheviks were being financed from Berlin (there was some truth to that as well); the bolsheviks were German spies (unlikely). A crackdown was ordered, many bolshevik leaders, such as Trotsky, were imprisoned, and Lenin was forced to flee (Stalin shaved off Lenin's moustache, and a wig was purchased for the trip back to Finland which, while successful, had several farcical episodes). But the check was only temporary, thanks again to another dreadful botch by Kerensky.

Though he considered himself a revolutionary socialist, Kerensky lacked the hardened discipline of Lenin, especially so when he attempted to position himself as a centrist. He believed, and perhaps rightly so (if one wished to think in conventional terms), that governing Russia required at least a minimal acquiescence of the middle class and, more importantly, conservative elements in the command structure of the armed forces. He was also a patriot, something Lenin never claimed to be; as Kerensky put it, Lenin 'did not regard the bourgeois motherland as his own and felt himself bound by no obligations towards it'. Lenin, of course, was contemptuous of all such considerations, practical or otherwise, but then again he had never governed anything. Kerensky sought to bring order to Petrograd, which involved deradicalizing both the garrison and the soviet. He enlisted the commander in chief of the army, Lavr Kornilov, whereby supposedly loyal front-line units would be transferred to Petrograd, and stability thus restored. This manoeuvre was irretrievably ruined, both by the principals themselves and, more importantly, by the go-betweens they used to communicate with one another. Kerensky came to believe that Kornilov's approach to Petrograd was, in essence, turning into a coup against himself. There is some reason to believe that this paranoid suspicion was, in fact, true. Kerensky, thoroughly rattled, appealed to the left, bolsheviks included, to 'save' the revolution and defuse the approaching crisis. Provocateurs and propagandists descended on the approaching units, infiltrated their ranks, and the enterprise floundered in a wave of speechifying and arm-twisting. Kornliov was arrested, imprisoned, then more or less allowed to escape. Kerensky survived, but his days of power, and that of the provisional government, were now on a death watch. By turning to the bolsheviks for help, he had legitimatized them in the eyes of the public. Trotsky and others were released; Lenin returned to Petrograd, in disguise, aboard the same train from Finland that he had first travelled on, # 293. Ensconced in a safe house, he plotted for the next appropriate moment, which came about a month after his return from Finland in October 1917.

In retrospect, the following week and a half, among the most momentous in history (made famous by John Reed in his stirring, and often fictitious book, *Ten Days that Shook the World*),[24] was in fact more noisy than it was violent. Very little fighting took place. Red Guards and bolsheviks under the command of Trotsky seized various government buildings without undue opposition, a short siege forced the Winter Palace into surrender (the cruiser *Aurora*, anchored on the Neva, fired the symbolic first salvo), and Alexander Kerensky more or less disappeared into the oblivion of academia (after living for some time in Paris as an émigré, he taught at Stanford University for several decades at the end of his career). One observer remarked that his government 'was overthrown before it could say ouch'. Kerensky's attempts to organize loyal army units to march on Petrograd were doomed to failure. There was no such thing as a 'loyal' army unit anymore. Nonetheless, the days were frantic. Lenin presided over meetings day and night, wrote manifestos, outlined a platform on which the new government he intended to lead would function and outmanoeuvred all his leftist rivals. By the time he was finished, his once minority bolsheviks stood more or less in control of Petrograd, and yet even now he was, outside of revolutionary circles, relatively unknown (in the many thousands of words that Nicholas and Alexandra wrote to each other, Lenin's name is not mentioned once). Very few of those who did know of Lenin realized that he was no more a socialist than he was a tsarist, that in fact a totalitarian, single-party system was what he had in mind. Reed wrote idealized, romantic accounts of proletariats and members of the soviets listening attentively to speeches around the clock, avidly reading every tear-sheet and pamphlet in sight, dissecting the various streams of political nuance that were being spread throughout the city, but in fact the universal desire was quite simple: bread, peace and a slice of the pie (if not all of it).[25] Lenin moderated his rhetoric accordingly so as not to disturb these aspirations, but his goals were far more drastic. After only three days, in fact, he closed all opposition newspapers, suppressing freedom of speech as successfully as any tsarist flunky. A few weeks later, he enthusiastically authorized the creation of a secret police, more or less a clone of the familiar tsarist tool of repression. As Trotsky had predicted in 1904, the 'dictatorship *of the* proletariat' would evolve into a 'dictatorship *over* the proletariat'. In his bitterly expressed arguments behind closed doors with his bolshevik comrades, Lenin's language and expressions were often extreme and vitriolic. At times almost drunk with fatigue, he could also be caught up in contradictions, especially regarding Marxist doctrine, which he seemed to be altering as circumstances demanded (one of his more astute biographers called him 'a monumental opportunist'.) Some of his proposals, he was told, did not square with reality. 'So much the worse for reality', he replied, before addressing the next problem on his list.

Reality, of course, can seldom be evaded. Would the boshevik government, of which he was now the head, last any longer than Kerensky's? Would it last longer than the Paris Commune of 1871 (64 days)? Would it last out the week? The odds were not promising, no matter what the timeline. Trotsky laid down the challenge facing them when he said, 'We've won the power; now we must keep it!'

'The first principle of an hereditary monarch is to survive.'
Kenneth Rose, biographer of King George V of Britain

Physical similarities between first cousins George of England and Nicholas of Russia were apparent to everyone who saw them together ('the image of him', said a British lady in waiting in 1896 about the visiting Nicki, if only a somewhat skinnier version). The two monarchs-to-be enjoyed each other's company when the circuits of royal obligations (usually weddings or funerals) brought them together, and felt themselves natural allies after 1914 in the shared struggle with their other first cousin, 'Willie'. When George V heard about Nicholas's arrest, he immediately cabled the tsar, reassuring him that 'I shall always remain your true and devoted friend'. He began backpedalling within days.

Lloyd George, an anti-monarchical type all his life (when the king asked him to carry the sword of state in front of the royal personage on a ceremonial occasion, Lloyd George refused –'I won't be his flunkey', he told his mistress), had initially welcomed the Romanov's overthrow. He saw the Russian revolution as an inevitable path to democracy and publicly said as much, to which King George, given his autocratic prejudices, took umbrage. But when the matter of what to do with tsar and his family became a rather urgent matter – the provisional government in St. Petersburg wanted Nicholas and his family out of the country immediately, and the tsar had openly expressed a preference for England – it was the king who quailed, not his 'republican' prime minister.[26]

It has generally been accepted by most commentators on the reign of George V that he was not the most perceptive individual ever to sit on the British throne. His political views were generally retrograde, his judgments of individuals more swayed by genealogical considerations than anything else and his familiarity with the majority of his subjects remote, to say the least. As Margot Asquith once said bluntly to his face, 'You see, sir, you only see fashionable Tories and not very clever ones' at that (the king, a man full of resentments, was annoyed by this remark). But in terms of self-preservation, his antennae were finely tuned. His family's background was German, and ever since the beginning of the war he had seen dreadful examples both at home and abroad of irrational prejudices taking precedence over people's common sense. The first lord of the Admiralty, Lord Louis of Battenberg (later changed to Mountbatten), as loyal a royal servant as ever there was, had been forced out of office just two months into the war because of scurrilous rumours regarding his allegiances – as Asquith had said, 'our poor blue-eyed German will have to go'. The king's solicitous regard for another deposed king, Constantine of Greece (whose wife was the kaiser's sister) had also unleashed a barrage of negative publicity. It seemed that British warships were routinely in the business of rescuing the detritus of European royalty wherever a popular uprising against autocracy raised its ugly head, and the cumulative effect on popular opinion was proving unsettling in the drawing rooms of Buckingham Palace as the daily newspapers were perused for signs of unrest. Even the king himself had been suspected of Germanophile leanings, which angered him tremendously. George was, after all, the first crowned head of Britain in over seventy years who did not speak the native tongue with a 'foreign' accent. These ominous portents, as well as the inescapable fact that the red 'contagion' was spreading everywhere, convinced a nervous George V to put his foot down. Tsar Nicholas needed a helping hand? He would have to look somewhere else.

The king, through his mouthpiece, Sir Arthur Stamfordham, his ultra-reactionary private secretary best known for his nickname 'Better Not', raised a barrage of practical obstructions in his back-and-forth notes with the prime minister. Where was Nicholas to live? (Certainly not Balmoral. Too chilly in the wintertime.) Who would pay for the living expenses of such a numerous family, plus staff, supporting a lifestyle to which monarchs were entitled? (Not George V; let the Russian provisional government foot the bill). How would the public perceive his willingness to help yet another deposed monarch? (not well, argued Stamfordham; King George's position might be fatally 'compromised'). By early April, the offer of asylum had been formally withdrawn. This did not prevent the king from sending a battleship to the Black Sea port of Sevastopol two years later to evacuate the tsar's mother, her inevitable trunk full of jewels and any number of other Romanovs to the safety of Malta.

'God! He is our only recourse.'

Citizen Romanov, former tsar, 22 March 1918

The days of pondering where he might be spending the rest of his life ended fairly shortly for the tsar; in direct correlation, in fact, with the deteriorating condition of his captivity. Confined to the grounds of Tsarskoe Selo at first, he remained dumbstruck at his fall from grace, but contented nonetheless that he was finally freed from the responsibilities of rule. He had done his best and been found wanting; he would concentrate now on what gave him his greatest pleasure – domestic life with his wife and family. He spent time in his study, selecting which books he planned to take with him into exile; he also burned many letters and private papers, just to be on the safe side. He had been loosely accused, after all, of being in touch with the German enemy. Snippets of war news angered him, and the political chaos in Petrograd was abhorrent; the attitude and behaviour of his guards, often insulting, lewd and gratuitous, proved difficult to stomach. Nonetheless, these were the crosses that the almighty had inflicted on him and his family, to be borne with the dignity with which his birth endowed him. Gradually, however, even his sang-froid could not ignore the fact that with each passing day the perimeters of daily life were contracting. Fewer privileges, fewer contacts with friends and family, diminished opportunities for outdoor recreation, a decrease in the quantity and quality of food, a gradual siphoning away of retainers and servants, growing disrespect from detachments of soldiers assigned to the palace (when two officers were seen kissing the hands of one of the princesses, they were arrested for counter-revolutionary behaviour).

Whenever the family was allowed out of doors to garden, chop wood or take walks, crowds would gather to watch and yell catcalls, an atmosphere Nicholas likened to 'being thrown to the wild beasts'. The tsarevich's little boat was smeared with faeces; soldiers repeatedly pushed the tsar around, or gave him their middle finger. Commissars, investigatory committees and Kerensky himself often blew through their quarters at inconvenient hours to either question or hector the tsar. He began hearing rumours that he or his wife – maybe the two of them – were actually going to be tried in the city. What could possibly be the charges, he wondered, and the consequences if found guilty? His wife's affection and respect for Marie Antoinette, whose portrait used to grace her drawing room, suddenly seemed pregnant with implication. Nicholas found cause to be wary; he began wondering what sort of trouble might lie ahead.[27]

Kerensky, at first contemptuous of the tsar, became more solicitous as his own problems mounted, and considerably less confrontational. Kerensky was a deeply intelligent man, and it did not take him long to realize (as did Lenin) that a climactic denouement lay just over the horizon, with the future of Russia at stake. He understood, as Nicholas had not, that the battle to come had nothing to do with the thousands of acres, tilled by millions of obtuse peasants, that lay stretched forever eastwards. It would be fought in the streets of Petrogard with just a few thousand people on each side. Whoever controlled the city, and its apparatus of government, would control the country. Amid the chaos of revolutionary rhetoric and wild emotion which surged through the city, so brilliantly conveyed by Reed, Kerensky saw his own future with growing apprehension. The bolsheviks were just looking for their moment. Lenin, headquartered in the palace of the tsar's former mistress, was clearly plotting, waiting his chance. As Kerensky said to Nicholas, the bolsheviks 'are after me, and then will be after you'. As Nicholas wrote in his diary, 'The seed of all this evil is in Petrograd itself.... What a mess!'

On 11 August, genuinely concerned for the tsar's safety ('I refuse to be the Marat of the Russian Revolution', he later wrote in his memoirs), Kerensky decided to move the family east ... far, far to the east, in the city of Tobolsk, situated at the foot of the Ural mountains. A further winnowing of retainers followed, a further restriction on what they could bring and what they could not, a further humiliation of being paraded in front of glowering crowds of bystanders as they left Tsarskoe Selo, and later during the progress of their trip. In her luggage, Alexandra packed the shirt Rasputin had worn on the night he was murdered, a bloody talisman that she hoped would bring them a blessing. The tsar, as usual, tried to put the best face on this truly unsettling journey into the unknown. He proved to be the rock of his family. When they finally reached Tobolsk after four days of travel, they were settled in 'a dirty, boarded-up, smelly house consisting of 13 rooms', where children and servants slept mostly on the floor. Kerensky still controlled events in Petrograd on the day of their arrival, but when they left Tobolsk eight months later, he no longer was. In the stunning events of the October Days (7–17 November 'new style'), Lenin, Trotsky and the bolsheviks seized power in an almost bloodless coup. Almost immediately they sued for peace with Germany. Nicholas called this initiative treason. It was also his death warrant. Wilhelm was tempted to make the repatriation of the Romanov family back to Germany a condition of the following peace negotiations (Nicholas was horrified, and his wife said she would never leave Russia). That settled matters for Lenin and, indeed, the mob. It proved that the tsar was actually pro-German, and he would pay the consequences.

Tobolsk was not considered a reliably bolshevik stronghold, especially so with counter-revolutionary 'white' forces prowling about in the vicinity. Civil war was now a reality in Russia. In April 1918, a special commissary from Moscow appeared unannounced, 'an evil portent', the Swiss tutor wrote in his journal, 'vague but real.... Everyone is restless and distraught.' Three days later, the family was again uprooted. The tsarevich, little Alexei, again afflicted with severe bleeding episodes, was deemed too sick to travel. In a wrenching moment, Nicholas and Alexandra were forced to decide who would go and who would stay behind until the boy was better. The royal couple decided they should remain together, and, taking one daughter with them, said their goodbyes. 'The servants were assembled in the large hall. Their Majesties and Maria took leave of them. The tsar embraced every man, the tsarina every woman. Almost all were in tears.' The tutor, Pierre Gilliard, never saw any of them again.

Between Tobolsk and their new destination, Yekaterinburg, lay over ninety miles of rough country (not that the tsar was ever told where they were going; he thought perhaps Moscow). There was no imperial train, no horse-drawn royal coach, certainly no automobiles or trucks to convey them – only a few rough farm carts, all but one open to the weather. Straw was thrown on the dirty floors, and the royal party ordered to board. The roads were abysmal: dusty, pitted or, alternately, drowned in mud. They once changed horses, incredibly enough, in the village where Rasputin had lived. 'We saw the whole [of his] family looking through the window', Nicholas noted in his diary. The imperial caravan often travelled well past dark, the only light for miles around provided by a full moon. The carts crossed numberless streams and rivers, 'the horses up to their chests in water'. Wheels came off, or were jammed, meaning the wagons were actually dragged along the road. After several days of difficult travel, they finally saw their new quarters, a two-storey house in the dreary mining town of Yekaterinburg. A rough wooden fence had been thrown up surrounding the building; it came to be known around town, ominously as things turned out, as the House of Special Purpose. For the first few nights, no bedding or furniture was provided.

A routine of daily humiliations commenced. Some guards were respectful and considerate, others were not. Petty house searches, guards at the toilets, meagre food, a minuscule yard in which to exercise – tended to depress the royal family. All their windows were whitewashed, eliminating views and sunlight. 'It looks as if there is a fog outside', the tsar jotted down. 'It has become gloomy in the rooms.' When Nicholas complained, his keepers informed him that they wished to create a 'prison regime', and he had better get used to it. At one point, the entourage were ordered to produce any money they had, and to note the amount on a piece of paper (to be stamped as their receipt). The former Tsar Nicholas and the former Tsarina Alexandra both wrote 'nothing'.

The tsarina wrote twenty-one letters to her children in Tobolsk. It is unknown how many reached their hands. In a month the family was finally reunited, but the routine seldom changed. Thirteen-year-old Alexei, who also kept a diary of sorts, wrote several entries saying over and over again 'Everything the same'.

'Two of the Lets backed out – they didn't have what it takes.'

Yakov Yurovsky, executioner

During the course of these July days, 45,000 Czech soldiers had steadily advanced from the east towards the town of Yekaterinburg. Their odyssey gives some clue as to the almost formless turmoil that was roiling the countryside, now being criss-crossed by armed bands of sometimes unknown allegiances. These men had been members of Franz Joseph's Austro-Hungarian army, taken captive on the fields of battle after more than three years of war. Rearmed by Kerensky, it had been his intention that they fight in the Russian army against their former allies, all with the questionable objective of 'liberating' Bohemia. The bolsheviks, concluding their peace talks with Germany, wanted nothing to do with these troops and made arrangements to repatriate them in perhaps the most logistically wearying exercise ever conceived by man; they would be shipped via the Trans-Siberian railway all the way to Vladivostok, then put on board ships to be taken back in the direction from which they had just come, ultimately to France. There they could join the allies and perhaps disappear in the meat grinder of front-line trench warfare. What this had to do with Czechoslovak 'freedom' is somewhat difficult to fathom. Not surprisingly, the Germans had no desire for these soldiers to reach the western front; they threatened to abrogate the Treaty of Brest-Litovsk if Trotsky did not immediately stop their transit and disarm the Czechs. When Trotsky attempted to do so, the Czechs began fighting, and essentially commandeered vast swaths of the railway line, severing the only avenue of communications from east to west. Joining with other counter-revolutionary forces, they began pushing across Siberia towards the Urals, with what objective in mind it is hard to say. By 12 July, these tough men were only days from Yekaterinburg.

Millions of words have been written trying to affix responsibility for what happened next. Did Lenin personally order that a sentence of execution be passed on the Romanovs? Did he know about it in advance, did he sign any papers, did he look the other way or did he just nod his head in silent assent? A trail of evidence does not exist to prove anything for certain, but circumstantially it is hard to conceive that Yakov Yurovsky, an *apparatchik* of the secret police, would have dared to fire a bullet into Tsar Nicholas II's head without the sanction of Lenin's approval. Vladimir Lenin was no sentimentalist. During one round-up of Romanovs, the liberal and patriotic Grand Duke Nikolai Mikhailovich, a historian, a man of culture and entirety sympathetic to the struggle for everyday freedoms in Russia, was arrested and sentenced to death. The writer Maxim Gorky, among others of Lenin's associates, pleaded that he be reprieved. 'The revolution does not need historians', was Lenin's reply, and he signed the death sentence without a moment's hesitation.[28] No one wanted Nicholas and his family to be rescued by 'whites'. No one, apparently, wanted to go through the bother of transplanting them yet again, except perhaps for Trotsky, who had visions of a great public show trial where he, as the main prosecutor, could humiliate the tsar during cross-examination. No one, frankly, wanted anything more to do with the royal family. They were an anachronism, ideal candidates for liquidation, and Yurovsky was the cold-blooded man of the Soviet future to do it, just about every aspect of which he botched.

Eleven men were assembled, more or less one executioner for each victim. Everyone knew what the task entailed. One of the myths perpetuated in the years that followed was that Yurovsky plied his men with vodka to steel their spirits, but this has never been confirmed. At the last moment, two of the squad refused to participate. 'They didn't have what it takes', Yurovsky would later write. At 10:30 on the night of 16 July, Yurovsky went upstairs to awaken the royal party. The Czechs were threatening the city, he told them; it was time to move. The family and the four remaining retainers all dressed and were led to a small room in the basement; incredibly small, only 11 x 13 feet. Two chairs were brought in for the tsarina and young Alexei. 'The squad were ready in the next room', according to Yurovsky; 'the Romanovs did not suspect a thing'. The men filed it with revolvers, Yurovsky blurted out to the tsar that he and the family were to be executed, and he shot Nicholas in the head, killing him instantly. This set off a disorganized fusillade from the others, so wild and indiscriminate that Yurovsky himself was almost hit, and another soldier was actually wounded. Bullets ricocheted off the brick walls, the room filled with smoke, screams added to the mayhem, the floor grew slippery with blood. With all the magazine clips emptied, the shooting stopped and Yurovsky finally established order, only to realize that many of the victims were still alive. One, a maid, was chased like a rat from corner to corner, bayoneted some thirty times before she died. Others had their skulls smashed with rifle butts or boots. Even the pet dog of one of the children was killed. Yurovsky himself put two more bullets into Alexei's skull to make sure the deed was done. After reading the details of this butchery, the idea that one of the tsar's daughters, Anastasia, might have survived (several imposters claimed to be Anastasia after the war) remains delusional.

Yurovsky was upset when he surveyed the brutal scene before him. He had not taken into account that the result would be so untidy. The bodies were dragged out to the courtyard, and several men assigned to clean the room. Investigators, however, who accompanied the Czechs when they entered Yekaterinburg a few days later, had little difficulty identifying this as a place of slaughter. Yurovsky's instructions regarding the disposal of the corpses had been clear (at least to him); they were to be stripped, mutilated with sulphuric acid, burned if possible and buried somewhere far from the sight of men. The best that can be said is that Yurovsky tried.

The initial idea had been to dump the bodies in an abandoned mine shaft, far off the beaten track and known only to a few. On his way to an agreed-upon rendezvous where trucks, which could go no farther, were to be replaced by horse-drawn carts, he was disappointed to find it full of armed men, many drunk, who had mistakenly been told they were to be the executioners. In the confusion that followed that night, jewels were found hidden on the various bodies, unleashing a desire on the part of just about everyone there for loot. Yurovsky, to his credit, browbeat the crowd into turning over whatever they had found thus far – he threatened to shoot anyone on the spot who was found with valuables in his pocket. Local peasants began showing up too, attracted by the tumult. The situation was beginning to turn into a carnival. With tremendous difficulty, Yurovsky managed to order most of this disorderly mob back to Yekaterinburg; with just a few men whom he could trust, he continued with the grisly 'funeral'. The mine was eventually found, the bodies partially burned, then dumped down the shaft. Unfortunately, this repository was flooded and the corpses did not sink. A few grenades thrown down did no good. Fiasco stood staring Yurovsky in the face. The Czechs were coming, the bodies had not 'disappeared'; perhaps he saw his own execution for incompetence as a distinct possibility.

Yakov Yurovsky did not get a moment's sleep for fifty hours. The bodies were hauled out of the shaft, shifted to the carts, then reloaded onto the trucks. A relentless sequence of mishaps followed: trucks breaking down, horses falling over on their riders (Yurovsky injured his foot and could hardly walk), his men exhausted and fed up, inquisitive peasants suddenly appearing when least expected. Almost at the point of giving up, Yurovsky finally had several shallow trenches dug in wilderness settings; more bonfires and the application of sulphuric acid, depositing remains here and there. Trucks were driven back and forth over the pits to trample the disfigured earth. Many of these remained undiscovered until 1979.

The purge of the Romanovs continued the next day, ninety miles away. Grand Duchess Elizabeth (Ella), the widow of Sergei Alexandrovich, and now a nun, along with five others, were driven to another mine shaft, hands tied behind their backs and blindfolded, then thrown in alive. Their killers expected them to die in the fall, but instead they heard splashes, the shaft, again, being unexpectedly full of water. They did not drown. Grenades were tossed in, to no avail, because Ella could be heard singing a hymn below. Timber was then thrown down, in the hopes of crushing those below. Dry brush was collected and pushed into the declivity, then set alight. Surely they would either burn to death or be choked. Evidently not. It is thought that most, if not all, of these Romanovs died miserably over the course of several days from hunger, general exposure or pure exhaustion. We shall never know exactly how. The last recorded words of Grand Duke Sergei Mikhailovich were a plaintive confession of bewilderment. 'Tell me why?' he asked the head of the squad before his death. 'I have never been involved with politics.'

'I was shown into the dining room, where I had often dined with Princess Obolensky, the wife of the last Prefect of Petersburg. This once beautiful room, where the elite of Petersburg had gathered, was now filthy, its floor covered in spitting, and its furniture broken and dusty: it was a picture of what Russia had become. The only witness of its brilliant past was an old, thin, melancholy usher, who recognized me and said sorrowfully in a low voice: "What times, mon Dieu, what times!"'

Countess Marie Kleinmichel, 1918

When Countess Marie Kleinmichel wrote these words, she was well into her seventies, having lived (until she was sixty-eight) in the wealthy, rarefied and immensely privileged world of the Russian nobility. Nineteen-seventeen had seen that world collapse; from her perspective, at the end of her mortal coil so to speak, she could view the ashes with some degree of detached aplomb. As chaos, cruelty, anarchy and fierce whirlwinds of revolutionary turmoil swirled around her, she on more than one occasion said that she feared nothing and was ready to die if it came to that. During the interview described above, where she had come 'face to face with a little Jew, rather handsome, with a clever cynical face, who seemed to be seventeen or eighteen' (he was actually twenty-one), she found herself confronting a not untypical dilemma. Certainly she could have her papers signed, her passport stamped and an exit visa provided ... but only if she revealed the hiding place of one of her aristocratic friends whom the bolsheviks wished to arrest. Her guile and sang-froid, however, oiled by years of experience wending her way through the social and political Byzantium of life at the tsar's court, provided the wits required to survive with her sense of honour suitably intact. She would betray no one, to the annoyance of her juvenile interrogator, and ultimately managed to escape the country that she, and her kind, had loved, defended, abused, pillaged and tyrannized for centuries.

Countess Kleinmichel had presided for two decades over one of St. Petersburg's most influential salons, specializing as it did in rumour and politics. She was a 'pretty and clever' gossip, as a contemporary observed, a specialist at wheedling information out of generals, counts, diplomats and various family relations of three tsars in succession, the Alexanders II and III, and then Nicholas II. She witnessed everything that happened to them from a first-row stall. On 13 March 1881, for example, she milled beneath the rotunda of the Winter Palace with other stalwarts of the *ancien regime*, having come there when she learned that yet another attempt had been made on the life of Tsar Alexander II. She had first heard the news with little emotion. In fact, her trip to the palace by sleigh had been a mere formality, to congratulate the tsar on having survived yet another attempt on his life (the fourth); as one of the tsarinas had said, after all, *Je suis tellement accoutumée à ces choses'* – a weary 'I am so accustomed to these things'. This time, though, the situation was different.

'The Tsar is wounded', said some.
'One of his legs is torn off', said others.
'There is hope of his recovery'.
'There is no hope; both his legs are cut off.'

'Thus words followed and contradicted each other', she recalled. The tsar's cloak was displayed to the noble audience. 'It was torn, and covered with mud, blood, bone splinters and pieces of his flesh. Many knelt down, crossed themselves and sobbed before that relic. Valets de chambre carrying basins full of reddened water came out of the bedroom and passed down the corridor. People stopped them and dipped their hands or moistened their handkerchiefs in that precious blood.' The tsar's morganatic wife entered the chamber; her screams could be heard outside the doors. The royal doctor, assessing the dreadful and mutilated body, said he had fifteen minutes to live before bleeding to death. Alexander's confessor announced the inevitable demise, after this medical diagnosis, to the agitated crowd. Everyone fell again to their knees, 'and the Reaction began'.

The 'reaction' was the pullback in liberal concessions that Alexander II had initiated. His son, a retrograde man of little finesse, had witnessed his father's death and had no desire to suffer the same fate, as conspiracies against his own life multiplied like a virus. Among those caught up in the resulting secret police dragnets was the brother of one Vladimir Lenin, who paid the price when he was summarily hanged. Countess Kleinmichel weathered these crises without seriously considering their ramifications. The ship of state, in her view, was steady, despite these ominous rumblings of discord. Her mind changed in 1905, the beginning of a twelve-year slide until 1917 when, unimaginably, the tsarist system would crumble into so much dust. The countess was first made aware when touring her rural properties during the summer months, dealing with managers, estate agents, engineers and the businessmen who negotiated contracts for her produce. She wrote to a friend that 'most of them are very well-bred people, but their children are abominable. In every one of these families I see a little Marat of fourteen, and a Théroigne de Méricourt of thirteen, who are growing up and are very disquieting'.[29]

On one of the tempestuous nights of early March 1917, people of this ilk battered down the back gate of her elegant palace in St. Petersburg with rifle butts, shot or stabbed her doormen, and proceeded to ransack the place, looking for spoil, the wine cellar and Countess Kleinmichel, and not necessarily in that order. She and her dinner guests fled down the main staircase and then into the icy, snow-filled streets. Instead of serving hors d'oeuvres, soup, a fish course, an entrée, dessert, cheese tray and a savoury to an elegant company of like-minded grandees, her servants fed a motley collection of drunken soldiers and sailors of the proletariat. From across the street, she could see her liveried staff, now wearing red bows on their arms, bringing bottle after bottle of fine Bordeaux wines for the delectation of the mob. The French and British legations, usually safe havens for respectable people seeking refuge during insurrectionary times, would not receive any of them. Sir George Buchanan, King George V's ambassador, who had been a frequent guest of Countess Kleinmichel, now stated that he would 'not meddle with Russia's internal affairs, that he had renounced his right to shelter fugitives'. The countess and a young friend, the Princess Cantacuzène, finally found sanctuary at the Chinese legation, where they slept on a sofa for three nights, but armed bands soon stormed in to haul the two away. The countess, it was said, had placed machine guns on the roof of her palace, giving instructions to open fire and murder the populace; she was also accused of telephoning the kaiser in Berlin, betraying army secrets to the enemy (the countess, being of an older generation, explained that she did not have a telephone, but no matter). Her companion, the princess, was a more mundane villain, merely an enemy of the people, but that was sufficient to earn arrest as well. 'You are too old to walk far on foot', one soldier said to Kleinmichel; 'we will find a car for you'. One of his comrades disagreed. 'The old hag can jolly well walk.' As their argument ensued, Princess Cantacuzène, being a more sprightly girl than Countess Kleinmichel, managed to slip away into the crowd gathering outside, and 'vanished from sight'.[30] The countess, with a revolver pointed to her head, was taken away for interrogation.[31]

The next several months were harrowing times for anyone with a title, whether in St. Petersburg or Moscow it hardly made a difference, with scenes straight from the French Revolution of 125 years before. Many grandees fled to their country retreats, hoping to ride out the storm. Some of these found their properties occupied by peasant 'soviets', and consequently in even more danger than before. Others were summarily collared by officials whose legitimacy, though suspect, could not be effectively challenged. Count Kokovtsov, after several adventures, found himself in custody. 'On Tuesday I was photographed', he wrote, 'so my picture is now side by side with those of pickpockets, robbers and such'. Countess Kleinmichel flitted through various stages of arrests and releases; during moments of relative calm, she was allowed the use of a room in her former palace, now pillaged, along with six or seven servants upon whose loyalty she could not be sure. Her elegant dining rooms, salons, sleeping chambers and dressing rooms were commandeered by seemingly nomadic groups of revolutionaries, whose doctrinal disagreements often degenerated into brawls and random shootings. Liquor fueled these contretemps, adding to the volatility of tempers and trigger fingers. Occasionally summoned for further questioning, the countess often reported to grand addresses that had formerly been among the very best in St. Petersburg. They were now full of detainees and people awaiting drumhead trials. 'The vast rooms of the *Palais de la Tauride*', she remembered in her memoir, where festivals, balls and receptions had been so often enjoyed, 'witnessed anew, and for the last time, the gathering of all the distinguished people of the metropolis: aristocrats, society peoples, and high civilian and military officials.' She witnessed the former Minister for War, Vladimir Sukhomlinov, 'pushed into the room. His uniform was ragged, his decorations had been torn off, and the insignia of his rank had been stripped from him. Some very young men, or rather boys, in officers' uniforms, came up to him and struck him.' Outside, 'the yells of the mob were like the roar of the tide'. There was no platform or guillotine waiting out there for Sukhomlinov and his compatriots, only bloodthirsty people ready to beat him to death with fists, sticks, cobblestones … anything that was handy.[32]

Countess Kleinmichel was one of the lucky ones. She finally squirmed her way of out Russia and found refuge in Germany. There, in another year, she would watch the disintegration of the Hohenzollern dynasty as well. These were not good times for royal families anywhere. Occasionally her path would cross those of other émigrés, 'fragments from the same shipwreck', anticipating that among these fellow travellers the word would soon pass from mouth to mouth that 'Old Countess Kleinmichel has died in Baden'. She wanted all to know, when that moment came, 'that I shall not carry resentment into the grave'.[33]

'In the military sense, we were a zero.'

Lenin, referring to the wartime situation,
November 1917

The bedrock of Lenin's entire strategic purview had been the potential contagion of revolution. Once undertaken, as it had been in Russia, the spark would travel and ignite somewhere else, certainly in Germany and perhaps in France (even boring Switzerland, he thought, was subject to an upheaval). The outbreaks would be spontaneous and more or less contemporary with events in Petrograd. This was the sure way to peace, with imperialist governments falling all over Europe. Then negotiations could bring a cessation to war, without any true victor, annexations or spiteful reparations. After peace, everything else would fall into place: the abolition of private property, the collapse of capitalism, the establishment of bolshevik clones all over Europe. Lenin was, if anything, a universalist who, as an American perceptively noted, 'lack[ed] any sentiment of nationality'. Russia mattered, but the universe outside its borders more so (as a French diplomat said at the Versailles Peace Conference, Lenin 'meant to conquer the world'). It was probably the biggest surprise of his life that none of this ever happened.

There was no general collapse of the existing governmental system in Europe. That meant no support from proletariat soviets in other countries that would join Russia in laying down its arms. Instead, Lenin and Trotsky faced unpleasant possibilities. There might be a peace but, ironically, one negotiated among the other warring combatants and ultimately aimed at the destruction of Russia's newborn revolutionary movement. The downfall of the Romanovs and the resulting near anarchy pervading Petrograd (as it mostly seemed to outsiders) was described in most European capitals in terms associated with disease. Bolshevism was a plague, and like the plague it had the potential of spreading fast, so fast that in a blink of an eye the condition to which any country, but most especially one sick of war or suffering privations on the home front, might well succumb.

At the very beginning of hostilities, initiatives for a peaceful resolution to the conflict had been proposed by any number of individuals and organizations. The industrialist Henry Ford personally chartered an ocean liner in 1915 to cross the Atlantic with a heterogeneous collection of peace advocates, including himself, thinking that the publicity might force the various belligerents to stop fighting and start talking ('War to End Christmas Day, Ford To Stop It', ran a headline of the *New York Tribune*). The Lord Lansdowne proposal, suggested by a man of impeccably conservative credentials, had disrupted the cabinet of Asquith in November of that year. He was a man whose ideas were not casually ignored.[34] After Emperor Franz Joseph's death in Vienna, (November 1916), his successor immediately began investigating avenues towards concluding a separate peace, no matter what the attitude of his generals. Jane Addams, a well-known agitator for peace, even found a receptive audience at the foreign ministry in the Ballhausplatz of all places. 'I have no doubt you are saying to yourself at this moment, this American woman is quite mad', she said to the Austrian premier. 'Mad', he replied? 'Do you see that door? Every hour of the day and far into the night men come through that door and say to me: "We want more men for the trenches – we want more guns – we want more ammunition, more money." Mad, indeed? You are the only sensible person that has passed through that door in a long time.' In Berlin, Catholics and socialists in the Reichstag began agitating for peace in July 1917. The pope preached for an immediate resolution in August 1917 and, most famously of all, Woodrow Wilson with his fourteen points, laid the basis for beginning negotiations where no victor would be anointed. These were, as an amalgam, powerful indicators that influential people and movements were sick of war. Peace at any price was a sentiment shared by many.

With stalemate on the western front, and few military solutions in sight, what was there to prevent Germany, France and Britain from concluding their own separate agreements with one another, and then turning with a vengeance to crush a movement in Russia that most foreigners viewed as a malignant threat to their own social order? In such a scenario, Russia stood almost naked. Her army was finished, to all intents and purposes. Lenin had ordered an end to any offensive operations, which was a good thing since few, if any, units would have obeyed orders to attack. But even on a defensive footing, could Russia withstand any sort of attack put together not only by Germany, but by the other allied countries as well? Thousands of Russian soldiers were deserting the front lines. There was land to be had for the taking back home, or so they were told, and they did not want to be left behind when it came to dividing up the vast estates of landlords and aristocrats (little did they know that Lenin's real objective was not peasant ownership of individual plots of land, but a huge system of 'collective' farms). As Lenin summarized the situation later, he put it bluntly: 'In the military sense, we were a zero.'

When pushed into a corner, Lenin was generally pragmatic. He issued instructions to the commander in chief at general headquarters at Mogilev, some 500 miles south-west of Petrograd (where the tsar had wasted so many weeks in idle preoccupations) to open negotiations immediately with his German counterparts. This officer, Nikolai Dukhonin, unwisely refused. He did not feel the pressure or urgency that Lenin did, saucily dismissing the bolshevik government as a pack of opportunists, without legitimacy. Lenin immediately dispatched one of his minions, 'Ensign' Nikolai Krylenko, a man of little military experience, to replace him, along with a motley assortment of naval personnel as a sort of bolshevik shock group. After the obligatorily long railway journey, Krylenko arrived at headquarters to take command; Dukhonin mocked his alleged replacement, counting on the loyalty of troops stationed at Mogilev as his personal guard. Krylenko might have lacked the practical experience of soldiering, but he had more than enough resolve to settle this jurisdictional dispute, ordering his men to execute Dukhonin immediately, which they did. Dukhonin was bayoneted and stomped to death outside his own office; his body, stripped and further abused, was then trussed up outside to a post, a cigarette put in his mouth, and then shot to pieces in target practice. So much for niceties. The German high command was then immediately contacted, negotiations commenced and a three-month truce agreed. Some forty German divisions were thereby freed up for duty in Flanders.

As was usual with Lenin, he had many different reasons for initiating peace talks. One that loomed large was the army itself; he wanted the war over, and the army disarmed and demobilized, so that it could no longer be used as a threat (or instrument) that could overturn his own government. Kerensky had been an example, a man who had attempted (and, thankfully in Lenin's eyes, failed) to do just that. He also thought the example of 'the people' actually ending the war – as opposed to the tsar, Kerensky or any number of others associated with the tainted and corrupted past – would be an object lesson for the oppressed proletariat and conscripted soldiery of Germany, France, Great Britain and Italy. Russian soldiers had decided to lay down their arms; so could all the others. Lenin's original pronouncement, called the 'Decree on Peace', was not addressed to Kaiser Wilhelm, President Poincaré, King George V or the Italian prime minister, Vittorio Orlando. It did not travel through the generally discreet channels of diplomatic communications, but was broadly announced to, more or less, the general public. This step, along with just about every other that Lenin undertook in his first days of power, alienated the conventional European establishment. Suddenly the initial sympathy, and in some cases enthusiasm, for the overthrow of the tsar's tyranny, turned into bewilderment, then suspicion and finally hostility. What the new government was doing smacked of base treason. Russia was no longer seen as a reliable ally; it was seen instead as a rogue nation, renouncing its treaty obligations and actually abetting the common enemy, Prussian militarism. And, most importantly, Lenin's open appeal for a peace without conditions mostly disturbed those who held the truest tools of power – the professional soldiery of Europe.

Erich von Ludendorff was interested in only two things: military triumph and the humiliation of his foes. His counterparts in London felt the same way: without a victory parade through the streets of Berlin, the whole war would have been a waste. Marshal Foch thirsted to put his foot on the neck of the Boche. George Patton and Douglas MacArthur were champing at the bit; would they be too late to hear the roar of cannon, to go over the top, to strangle Germans with their bare hands? None of these men was interested in peace, none was interested in the naïve, desperate and surely duplicitous overtures of a government whose ideological roots they detested. Given the disastrous events of the twentieth century, how different that saga would have been had the focus of all these countries been turned more to Russia than to the western front?

Many of the principals in this long and intriguing story often referred to the Russian people as children. Tsarina Alexandra wallowed in the notion: Russians were too stupid, too ill-educated, too docile to be anything but serfs. They needed her husband to be their 'father'. The American ambassador in Petrograd called them 'an infant class', who, when it came to basic democratic precepts, would need 'kindergarten material' to find their way. They had no idea of the kind of man Vladimir Lenin was. After the fall of Nicholas, the allies had just assumed that Russia would remain in the war. When they began entertaining doubts, they resorted to threats. An American commission to Petrograd after the first revolution put the matter succinctly. The Russian treasury was without operational funds to all intents and purposes, and America was willing to help, with one condition: 'no fighting' meant 'no loans'. This was, as Lenin noted, a typically capitalist ploy. He responded by repudiating the entire catalogue of tsarist bond obligations entered into with foreign governments, banks and shareholders. This ended up bankrupting thousands of ordinary Frenchmen who had invested in railway bonds, among other offerings, but Lenin did not care. He wiped the slate clean and never looked back; any pretence that bolshevism was in any way 'democratic' evaporated in just a few months.

Despite several moments of brinkmanship, bravado and bluffs, ended only when the German army responded with renewed military operations on the eastern front, Lenin and Trotsky finally agreed to a humiliating peace treaty with Imperial Germany, whereby Russia lost the Baltic states and vast portions of Ukraine, some of it the richest in the land.[35] The hated bourgeois governments of Western Europe were not falling, help from abroad for the revolution was not, it appeared, forthcoming. This was a particular shock to Lenin, whose vision was the whole world. The struggle now became to maintain the bolshevik pulse in Russia itself, where counter-revolutionary foes of all stripes, aided and abetted by foreign money and, later, troops, were coalescing into formidable opposition. The 'mask', if you will, of international bolshevism was falling off. Lenin and Trotsky focused on Russia, as a dreadful civil war commenced. He achieved peace on the great world stage of World War I, but merely substituted in its place squalid, pitiless and ruthless bloodletting within his own borders. The American secretary of state predicted that the brutality of the French Revolution would pale in comparison. Lenin would have replied, what did he expect? This was a true fight for survival in which the weak could not survive. Lenin had no interest in Freud, but Darwin was a different matter.

'Baboons.'

Winston Churchill, referring to
bolsheviks in general

The Russian civil war that raged about the country as the Versailles conference straggled to its end was a vicious, sanguinary, merciless and confused series of manoeuvres and battles. One of the more famous images was Trotsky's amoured train, bristling with machine guns, which he used to rush from one embattled front to another, and immortalized in Pasternak's *Doctor Zhivago* ('In three years', he wrote in his autobiography, 'we circled the earth five and a half times'). During these tumultuous months, 'I had practically unlimited power'. Lloyd George regarded Trotsky's ability to organize a Red Army 'without munitions or factories or transport … one of the greatest achievements of the war'.

Bystanders hoping to stay on the sidelines found such an impulse dangerous, as one aristocrat sagely observed. 'In a civil war', he wrote, 'there is no such thing as neutrality. All that happens is that eventually both the protagonists are apt to consider you a potential traitor, to be dealt with accordingly.' Counter-revolutionary 'white' armies were formed, armed and commanded by a variety of interesting individuals, all loosely united only by their anti-bolshevik fervour and the personality of whomever was in charge; troops of varied nationalities, including about 7,000 Americans, often had no idea what their role was supposed to be. Their general, William Graves, made decisions on the spot, based mostly on his like, or dislike, of the various characters who crossed his headquarters threshold. The thousands of men in the Czech Legion, referenced earlier in this narrative, were no closer to home than ever. Still armed and still dangerous, they operated in a political no-man's land, uncertain what to do or whom to trust. They, in their turn, were viewed as imperialist scum by Trotsky and Lenin. These misadventures paled beside the doings of Edmund Ironside, a British general sent to Archangel to sort things out, if such a proposition was even possible. A protégé of Winston Churchill, Ironside had the appropriate imagination, verve and gumption to deal with the nefarious collection of characters who were, in effect, roaming in a confused power vacuum, but even his staunchest defender could label the ensuing accumulation of political gaffes as nothing better than an *opera bouffe*.[36]

Churchill, surprising no one, had been all in favour of British military intervention on the grand scale. A few more years of bloody battles did not bother him, so insidious a threat did he consider the communist virus (he referred to Lenin and Trotsky as 'baboons'). Very few people in London were willing to put up any longer with his warmongering schemes; as Lloyd George said during the Versailles peace conference, 'Winston is in Paris. He wants to conduct a war against the bolsheviks. That *would* cause a revolution!' Admiral Alexander Kolchak, a polar explorer and veteran of the Japanese war, found himself in Siberia with the 'whites'. Through machinations too complicated to describe in detail, he became a de facto head of state and advanced eastwards for Moscow. General Graves, in particular, had no use for Kolchak, characterizing the men under his command as 'brigands and murderers' responsible for numberless atrocities and pogroms. Kolchak, in his turn, thought American troops were mostly 'Jews from the east side of New York'.[37] Early successes of the 'whites' soon gave way to a multitude of defeats, however, and, like so many monarchists in the past, Kolchak found himself fleeing, a safe passage in his pocket on the only train line there was, the Trans-Siberian Railway, sections of which no one knew who controlled. The Czechs eventually arrested him, turned him over to local revolutionary parties, who ended up transferring him to the bolsheviks (who had called him, in print, 'a reptile') in exchange for who knows what. His fate was sealed. On 7 February 1920 he was taken into a courtyard, given the last rites by an orthodox priest (they would soon disappear from the scene as well, when the 'reds' had consolidated their position countrywide) and stood before twelve soldiers. He took a large, jewel-encrusted case from his pocket, a present from Tsar Nicholas II, and counted out how many cigarettes he had left, thirteen in all. 'Just enough for every one of us', he said. He had a smoke and was then shot, dying 'like an Englishman' or so it was said at the time. He shared one posthumous indignity with the hated Rasputin; his body was taken to a nearby frozen river, a hole chopped and the corpse wedged beneath the ice, not to reappear again until the next spring.

Events in the chaotic years following 1917 in Russia were not conducive to social niceties. Rasputin's body was dug up, kicked around and burned to ashes. The corpse of former commander in chief Lavr Korniliv was similarly abused. After his escape from prison, Kornilov had fought in the civil war with the 'whites', where he distinguished himself as a vicious, predatory and indiscriminate killer. His headquarters were hit by a random artillery shell, which he did not survive, and when bolshevik forces later overran the position, they took it upon themselves to dig up his body, which was dragged to the local dump and, after several indignities, it too was burned.

The Cruiser *Aurora*

In 1924, after Lenin's death from the effects of a stroke, the city was renamed once again. Stalin modelled the former Volgograd after himself (Stalingrad) the next year. After World War II, the ancient East Prussian city of Königsberg would change to Kaliningrad, after one of his cronies. St. Petersburg/Petrograd was christened Leningrad, an appropriate choice given that's city's pre-eminence in the revolutionary saga. Lenin, like other bolshevik leaders, had been worried that if Ludendorff resumed operations on the eastern front in 1918, Petrograd would inevitably fall, German forces being, after all, only a hundred miles from the city centre. Lenin hastily moved the seat of government inland to Moscow in March 1918 as a precaution. Some say he panicked by doing so, though it is hard to imagine, after all he had been through, that anything but ice water flowed through his veins. But the Brest-Litovsk treaty was signed, and hostilities were not resumed with Germany until 1941, two decades later. Leningrad that time around was attacked, encircled and besieged in the famous battle that lasted for 872 days. Over 750,000 men, women and children of the civilian population perished during those ghastly weeks, most from starvation, but the city did not fall.

In 1991, with the collapse of the communist system, the city became where it had begun in terms of nomenclature, St. Petersburg. Visiting the city today is a peculiar experience. Peter the Great is now, touristically speaking, the centre of attention; it is impossible to avoid his presence. Whether stuck in traffic, walking about or just perusing thousands of brochures and tour guides, his image is everywhere. The *de rigueur* experience is to visit the Winter Palace, with its vast art collection, the first paintings assembled mostly by Catherine the Great, beginning in 1764. Like many of the palatial town houses and palaces, this specimen is garishly painted in bright, Italianate colours, undeniably blinding given the building's enormity. It reminds me of a birthday cake. While these structures radiate wealth and sumptuousness, they lack a sense of refinement. The Yusupov Palace, in particular, scene of Rasputin's murder, is heavily ornate and radiates an aura of undigested culture. Long corridors, cold rooms full of heavy accoutrements and clunky candelabra, call to mind the most famous of all the Romanov artefacts, Easter eggs designed by Fabergé. The English diplomat Harold Nicolson best summarized their overall effect. 'These costly trinkets appeared to me symbols of tsarist Russia', he wrote. 'Inside that warm and brilliant shop the silly enamelled eggs would be laid out upon a black velvet napkin; outside the frost gathered slowly on the coachman's beard'. Nabokov put it even more bluntly, calling many of Fabergé's ingenious constructions nothing less than 'monstrosities'. A tour of the palace's basement rooms is more in touch with reality, though it too is marred. A display of mannequins representing the principals on that bloody night of 30 December 1916 leaves an unfortunate impression, the whole episode being reduced to the status of a cheesy melodrama. Poor Rasputin, one thinks. In a nearby sex museum run by one of Russia's new breed of entrepreneur, the reported penis of the *starets* is preserved in a jar of formaldehyde. It is more than a foot long, and is probably that of a horse, but how is one to know for sure?

Having no desire to join endless lines outside the famous Hermitage, and no desire, to be truthful, to stare at several hundred Titians, I spend much of my stay in St. Petersburg walking its long, long streets, full of ornate town houses and ducal seats. Though begrimed with tons of soot, they are certainly an intriguing collection of architectural styles, but mostly impressive by their sheer number. Vladimir Nabokov's family residence, adorned with pink granite (again, barely distinguishable under layers of dirt), is now a school of some sort, and depressing beyond belief. Its once elegant foyer is illuminated by strings of fluorescent lights, where a custodian or janitor of some sort is doing crossword puzzles at a battered desk. She is not exactly welcoming to visitors. The Nabokov family employed fifty servants here and at their country house forty miles outside the city. The sort of *noblesse oblige* of this 'extinct' (as he called it) family is deftly sketched by him in this short passage from his marvellous book, *Speak, Memory*, begun in 1947. 'Not only were the kitchen and the servants' hall never visited by my mother, but they stood as far removed from her consciousness as if they were corresponding quarters in a hotel. My father had no inclination, either, to run the house. But he did order the meals.'

The bridges crossing the Neva to the fortress of Saints Peter and Paul, begun by Peter the Great in 1703, are choked with traffic. More long walking ahead. In front of a rebuilt Finland Station is the obligatory statue of Lenin, overcoat flapping in the wind, fists clenched, screeching out some revolutionary diatribe. A museum dedicated to the revolution is located nearby in Mathilde Kschessinska's mansion, where the tsar dallied with his mistress, and which Lenin used as his headquarters. There is no one here to speak of except for that staple of Russian institutions, matronly women in every room watching you closely for any sign (one could imagine) of counter-revolutionary behaviour. This dearth of visitors surprises me. I cannot say if this is because Vladimir Lenin has ceased to be the pivotal figure of world history he seemed to be just three decades ago, or whether tourists today, through a fog of inattention or poor schooling, just have no idea who he was. The display cases are superbly organized and their contents fascinating. Lenin's study reminds me of a monk's cell in some remote and distant monastery. Warming up to him would be a severe test.

My last stop is to visit the battlecruiser *Aurora*. It fired a blank shot from its forward gun towards the Winter Palace, the signal to storm the building. 'The Shots Heard Around the World' might be a suitable descriptive if it hadn't been appropriated at Lexington and Concord over two centuries before. The *Aurora* was severely damaged during the disastrous battle of Tsushima in 1905. Contemporary photographs show gaping holes in her hull. One of her damaged amoured plates was removed and cut down to accommodate the photograph of a senior commander killed in that engagement, his visage staring out from the shell hole with its jagged, sharp edges. For some reason, I am quite engaged by this strange tribute. Up on deck, people have their pictures taken by the famous forecastle gun. I await my turn, but the guide deflates me by saying that it's not the real thing. In perfect English he explains that, in the 1941 siege, all the *Aurora*'s artillery pieces were stripped from the ship and hauled to the trenches, embedded there, and more or less lost to history. 'They certainly killed more fascists than they did Japanese', he says. Hearing that, I'm less inclined to take its picture, but I do anyway.

Chapter 15

T. E. Lawrence, 'of Arabia'

'T. E. was an intuitive, affectionate, Galahad-like man of action who became a frightful crash before his War was over, and is to be judged thereafter as a broken hero who tried to appear whole and made the best of it.'

Robert Graves, 29 June 1954

British general Edmund Allenby, who ended his career as a field marshal with a vivid title, first Viscount Allenby of Megiddo, said T. E. Lawrence 'was perhaps the most interesting product of the Great War', an understatement if ever there was one, matched by a second observation that he was 'a character difficult to know' (one might substitute the word 'difficult' with 'impossible' to gain a more perfect description). When Lawrence first came to Egypt in 1914 – a region in turmoil and about to be invaded by Turkish forces – he was pretty much a nobody, working on assembling and updating topographical maps for military use (the northern stretch of Sinai, for example, was practically unknown).[1] Slight of build, barely 5' 5" tall, modestly spoken for the most part and often described as 'shy', he did not stand out in social company or during routine meetings. More an academic than a soldier, his disdain for military protocol, attire and deportment was at first hotly criticized by professional officers and NCOs, when they came to notice him at all; one officer wondered, in fact, just who this 'pipsqueak' was. Once Lawrence became indispensable, however, such hostility had to be sullenly muted.

The assets Lawrence brought to the fore in 1914, and which first served to make him valuable, were both linguistic and intellectual. He had a more than passable proficiency in Arabic, and a more than passable familiarity with the people who spoke it. Both talents were in short supply, especially among the hierarchy of British headquarters in both London and Cairo where, according to Lawrence, there was not a trace of 'ethnological competence'.

Military intelligence was usually equated with groping in the dark. The clearly bright and inquisitive Lieutenant Lawrence was assigned to intelligence duties, and later to a bureaucratic operation formally called the

Arab Bureau. His task was to sort through the Who's Who of the Arabian labyrinth.

Lawrence was enthusiastic and insatiably curious in his work, a reflection of an upbringing that was disciplined, yet receptive to individual – one might say idiosyncratic – discovery. But contradiction marked Lawrence in just about every facet of his life and character. His mother, a fierce Evangelical Christian in the Scottish mode, imparted in her sons a strong abstinent streak: hard prayer, hard work, little room for frivolity, no adolescent interaction with the opposite sex, a disdain for opulence and its manifestation in fine food, drink, tobacco or dress (Lawrence complained years later that his mother was always 'hammering' him). It showed in his early lifestyle: he affected vegetarianism for much of his youth; he disliked group sports as a youngster, although he was a fine athlete in anything solitary: bicycling, hiking, running; and he could immerse himself in academic subjects to the point of pedantry.[2] It must have been a shocking discovery when he learned that his parents were not, in fact, married. 'Mrs. Lawrence' had been a nanny in 'Mr. Lawrence's' estate in Ireland, where he had fathered four children with his legitimate wife, living the casual lifestyle of a well-to-do baronet on a considerable landed estate ('who is said never to have written a cheque or read a book', nor would it ever have occurred to him 'to earn his living'). The seduction of hired help on the semi-feudal premises of country squires was certainly nothing new; eloping with the hired help and siring a second family of five children, while living an 'undercover' existence, certainly was. How Lawrence reconciled the truth of his family history with his mother's religiosity will never really be known, as is the case with many aspects of his life. That he disliked formal religion on the basis of its hypocrisy was probably one result, and nostalgia for a noble bloodline, which he affected, perhaps another. But as he said reproachfully when considering his bastard upbringing, he was but 'a flea in the legitimate prince's bed'.[3]

The abstraction of asceticism appealed to him throughout his life: the hermit living removed from society and its distractions; the knight errant on solitary expeditions into the unknown where demons lay (Malory's medieval saga, *Le Morte d'Arthur*, was one of Lawrence's favourite books); the self-inflicted mortifications that early Christian saints endured in order to gain paradise; the improbability of so many individual Crusaders and their exploits, many unrecorded or noted by anybody. When Lawrence first experienced the barren landscapes of the Holy Land, beginning in 1909, these strands of extreme impulses found a perfect arena for their expression. As a friend later noted, 'Had he been born on the fringe of a desert, he would have become a prophet; had he lived in the Christian Middle Ages, he would have become a saint. He had the instincts and negations of both, without their faith.' War just pushed additional emotive fuel to the mix: energizing, exhilarating, primal.

Lawrence initially came to the Middle East as a student from Oxford, first in studying castles built by European invaders during the Crusades, then as an archaeologist who for four years worked on a site in northern Syria,[4] the Hittite city of Carchemish ('the mounds are enormous'), during which, incidentally, he met Gertrude Bell, an eccentric British woman who would later be an influential policy-maker, particularly in the postwar creation of Iraq. Their initial interchange was not particularly successful; she criticized the digs as amateurish and 'prehistoric', and Lawrence and an associate, in their turn, attempted 'to squash her with a display of erudition'. Lawrence, certainly not for the first time, and certainly not for the last, was never a man to cower in the face of Establishment figures, especially if his protagonist displayed airs or proved condescending. Bell left, somewhat abashed, with the comment that Lawrence was 'a pleasant boy'.

Be that as it may, the years between 1911 and 1914 were transformational for Lawrence. Often left unsupervised on the site, he gained valuable experience interacting with both area Turkish authorities, who had only an obstructionist interest in what he was doing, and the local populace, from whom he hired workers, bought supplies and interacted with on a daily basis, honing his language skills, which were considerable, and gaining insights into Arabic customs and what, to outsiders anyway, seemed their often inscrutable behaviour. One thing Lawrence did not at first spend much time considering in and around Carchemish was any notion of an Arab awakening, or a desire for 'freedom' or 'independence'. It did not take him too long, however, to sense a restiveness not far below the surface of daily life. He saw a peasantry burdened by poverty, illiteracy and a generally bleak outlook on life, which tended to obliterate any thought or hope for a future under Ottoman rule. This would stand in stark contrast to the Bedouin lifestyle of the Arabian desert that would so enthral him after the onset of war in 1914.

More importantly, being 'in charge' gave Lawrence an opportunity that few individuals ever achieve, the fulfilment of adolescent fantasies. The digs around Carchemish became for him the equivalent of taking control over a feudal kingdom. The British Museum, which funded the excavations, spent years purchasing as much of the site itself as possible, with some adjoining parcels as well, always in the face of reluctant landowners, Turkish authorities and, finally, German engineers, commissioned to build a railway bridge over the Euphrates; their outbuildings and equipment threatened portions of the dig. The museum property became an enclave that Lawrence was determined to defend. He treated workers on the site benevolently, as though they were Saxon serfs tilling his seigneurial property. He was their knight errant come from far away; they deserved his concern and protection. He even more or less adopted a boy named Dahoum, who served him as a surrogate squire. To Dahoum, he dedicated his famous book, *Seven Pillars of Wisdom*, beginning with the words 'I loved you', indiscreet perhaps, but Lawrence did not care. What other people thought of him rarely mattered.

Often accompanied by Dahoum, Lawrence undertook several adventurous excursions, some of which were dangerous, given the volatility of the various peoples he encountered, Kurds, Armenians, Turks and Arabs. He generally carried a pistol with him; his first, a Mauser, weighing three pounds, gave way to lighter American models. The friends usually travelled in subsistence mode, eating whatever the locals did, drinking the often fetid water, sleeping out in the open. Lawrence's frugal nature and hardy constitution served him well, though at times he was felled by dysentery ('the great bugbear of the European traveller') and other regional ailments. Dahoum was there to care for him. Being the intellectually curious man he was, Lawrence could not help but familiarize himself with the political currents that were beginning to unsettle the region. Everyone sensed that Ottoman rule was shaky, the state of its army weakened, especially later on after horrendous losses during the Gallipoli campaign. It has been estimated that over a third of its strength was now composed of Arabic peoples, mostly conscripted, whose loyalty was largely maintained by the threat of a whip. Lawrence realized all this and took it seriously, though many of his conclusions and opinions seemed often at cross purposes with each other.

If war had not broken out in the summer of 1914, Lawrence would probably have led the life of an academic archaeologist: writing grant proposals, supervising digs, composing travel books, teaching now and then, annoying co-workers during interdepartmental meetings. Not many people outside of Oxford or the British Museum would ever have heard his name.

The Arena

There are lands of mystery in this world that have fascinated Europeans for centuries, some by their very inaccessibility (Tibet comes to mind), others by enigmatic custom or social mores that stand utterly foreign to normal Western outlooks (China and Japan). But the Middle East is in a class of its own. Beginning with Egypt, a land dominated by the river Nile, and ruled for centuries by pharaonic God kings whose megalomaniac burial tombs, the pyramids, astonished all who heard or read about them, one could then metaphorically gaze north-east across the forbidding Sinai desert to what has traditionally been called the Levant: the Mediterranean coastlines of today's Israel, Lebanon and Syria. Beyond that lay the relative fertility of Mesopotamia (Syria and Iraq), with its ancient civilizations along the Tigris and Euphrates rivers, birthplace of the first written language. On the eastern edge lay Iran, traditionally known as Persia. Most important was the region's centrality to the three greatest monotheistic religions – Islam, Christianity and Judaism – each of which made claims and counterclaims (theological, historical, geographical) that generally put them diametrically at odds with one another, with enormously complicated and often sanguinary results.

To the uninitiated, the region seems synonymous with wasteland: scorching sun and extreme heat, hundreds of square miles of barren desert sparsely inhabited by nomads – 'these forbidding solitudes', as Winston Churchill hyperbolically put it, 'their endless sands, their hot savage wind-whipped rocks, the mountain gorges of a red-hot moon'. As generalizations, these ignore reality. The Mediterranean coast, the Nile Valley, the Mesopotamian heartland, were all productively farmed, with great, complex metropolitan centres established throughout the region, citadels of scholarship that advanced human knowledge in multiple disciplines. It should never be forgotten that poor wheat harvests in Egypt meant food riots in Rome.

The time frame of our narrative finds a region somewhat in flux. In the mid-19th century, Egypt was essentially a self-governing state within the Ottoman Empire, called the Khedivate. Since the construction of the Suez Canal in 1869, foreign control of the debt-burdened Egyptian government had grown apace, much to the resentment of the local hierarchy, which culminated in rebellion, 1882, easily crushed by English forces. Egypt became a de facto protectorate controlled by Britain, though still ostensibly a part of the Ottoman 'mosaic'. With the outbreak of hostilities in 1914, the figurehead khedive, Abbas II, foolishly declared that Egypt stood with its co-religionists, the Ottomans, upon which he was immediately replaced by London with his more compliant and pragmatic uncle. Britain then more or less annexed Egypt as a formal, rather than shadow, possession. Control of the government and the army lay in the hands of the British military governor, in 1916 General Archibald Murray.

Though details clearly differed, the Sudan, south of Egypt, also came under British control after Kitchener's overwhelming victory at the Battle of Omdurman on 2 September 1898, crushing the Mahdist revolt and, incidentally, avenging the loss of General Charles Gordon at Khartoum thirteen years earlier. It essentially became a British colony, in 1914 governed by another British general, Sir Reginald Wingate. Wingate's area of interest included the opposite side of the Red Sea from Sudan, the Arabian kingdom of Hejaz.

These background details matter because they encapsulate what most concerned British authorities in the Middle East as the Great War commenced, the Suez Canal. The Canal was vital to just about every facet of its war plan: control of the eastern Mediterranean, more direct access for troop transport from Australia and New Zealand to the combat zones of France and then Gallipoli; the lifeline to India and the Far East, integral cogs of Empire; and, just as vital, war morale. To lose access to the Canal would be a catastrophe no one wished to think about.

Proceeding in the north-easterly direction from Egypt, present-day Israel, Jordon, Lebanon and Syria were all under Ottoman control in 1914. The holy city of Jerusalem held intense psychological importance, but strategically the control of Damascus was the goal of most war planners, and from there farther north to Aleppo. France and Britain each had their eyes on various pieces of the Levant, the French in particular for Lebanon and Syria. Their rivalry for influence there and in Iraq, farther east, was of keenest interest as well to India, though once oil reserves there were discovered, the country gained the acquisitive eye of all the western powers.

The arc of these countries might roughly be described as a horseshoe (familiarly known as the Fertile Crescent). Like a horseshoe, the centre space, seemingly empty, could be said to describe the Arabian component of the region (today's Saudi Arabia, Kuwait, Bahrain, Qatar, United Arab Emirates, Oman and Yemen), approximately 1,200,000 square miles, three-quarters of which is desert, the largest in the world after the Sahara. This entire diamond-shaped peninsula was also technically under the control of the Ottomans, but, practically speaking, authority was unevenly administered by six regionally powerful warlords. Some paid lip service to the sultan in Constantinople, and were suitably rewarded with subsidies and weapons, but others did not bother.

The vast spaces of central Arabia, however, were essentially ungovernable, a free zone contested by a wide variety of individualistic clans who fought among themselves continuously, often pursuing blood feuds many generations long. These often-nomadic tribes, known as Bedouin, were reputed great warriors; they exacted tribute where they could, spent considerable efforts raiding their neighbours and were callous enough to rob pilgrims bound for Mecca during the annual Hajj pilgrimage. Others settled near watering

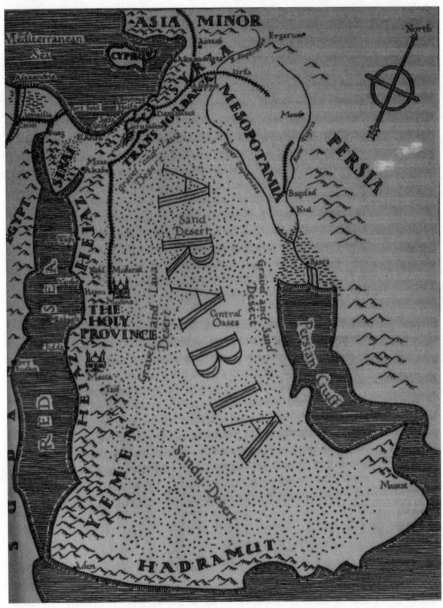

Heather Perry (also known as Herry Perry), drew this map of Arabia for Robert Graves's 1927 book, *Lawrence and the Arabs* (London, Jonathan Cape).

holes, which were possessively guarded from strangers (unless willing to pay). Routes of passage, caravan tracks, logistical details were usually determined by the availability of water stops. Bedouins were notoriously independent; their greatest contempt were for 'town Arabs', men who enjoyed 'the cloying inactivity of Ottoman rule'.

Important desert clans could oftentimes generate 500 fighting men when encouraged to assemble for an expedition (usually with money, promises of camels or the prospect of loot). Smaller clans, many associated with villages surrounding a well, might be good for only thirty. They were led by a variety of leadership types, but most commonly on the local level by a sheik. Theoretically, they owed ultimate allegiance to the Sharif of Mecca.

None of this Bedouin culture would have been possible without the ubiquitous camel, which could work, on average, almost a week without water, and travel distances of twenty-five miles a day were standard. This incredibly adaptive animal was a Bedouin's most valuable possession: transport (sturdy pack animals), food resource (meat and milk), its dung (fuel and manure). They are long-lived (a lifespan of half a century is not unusual), and in military usage, speeds up to 40 mph in short bursts were possible. Breeding camels was an important industry; like any animal, certain pedigrees or types were more highly valued than others, depending on their proposed utility (pack animals on one extreme, racing camels on the other).[5]

Kut

By the spring of 1915 Lawrence had been in Cairo for nine months, his map-making tasks gradually augmented by intelligence duties. The Arab Bureau was ridiculously small, comprising a handful of mostly academic specialists, but its portfolio was huge: figuring out the landscape of the entire Middle East and, correspondingly, endorsing policy measures for London to consider, a job description that frequently saw it in competition with a much more influential and established entity, the bureaucratic machinery of the British Raj, meaning India.

The importance of India to the British Empire (as opposed to the Middle East) cannot be exaggerated, nor the character of the East India Company, which for about a century effectively monopolized its economy – Adam Smith called this operation the 'plunderers of India' in *The Wealth of Nations*, and he was not far wrong. It is easy to see why. India was not only a major supplier of raw goods to Great Britain (cotton, jute, tea, indigo, coffee, varied natural resources), but in return proved to be a major market for the finished products made from them. By 1913, twenty percent of British trade goods were sold in India. Out of £33.6 million sales for heavy machinery, for instance, £4.5 million ended up in India; railway engines and train cars, likewise – £7 million in gross sales, £2.2 of which went to India (the country's rail grid went from 200 miles in 1858 to 35,000 by the beginning of war). Again, using 1914 as a benchmark, India's population included over eighty million Muslims alone, dwarfing that of Egypt, the most populous of the Middle Eastern countries. At the start of World War I, India had by far the largest army in the Empire, all of which was paid for and maintained by Indian tax revenue. In terms of balance of payments, this was a classic example of colonial exploitation.

Over the three centuries of India's inclusion in the imperial scheme of things, certain administrative evolutions had seen important decisions left in the hands of local British officials in India (many of whom had spent their entire bureaucratic careers there), regarding domestic policies but also foreign ones as well. Some of these policies saw Indian decisions that diametrically contradicted aims espoused in Cairo and, at times, in London. The results, as one officer put it, were often 'inconvenient'.

Lawrence, from his perch in Cairo, was having his disdain for convention and military decorum reinforced on a daily basis. 'We think the staff above the rank of captain are shits', he wrote to George Lloyd, one of his closest friends. An early scheme of his ('my invention', he called it), a naval landing at the Turkish port of Alexandretta, was shelved, largely the result of the Gallipoli fiasco which soured many military men on amphibious landings in general. In late 1914, a largely Indian army, of course under the command of a British general, Charles Townshend, had seized the soon-to-be important oil fields of Basra at the head of the Persian Gulf, and then, 'bursting with confidence', advanced northwards with no particular goals in mind, given that enemy resistance was proving slight.[6] Victories were so 'cheaply' achieved, in the words of one critic, 'that the prestige that could be won by capturing Baghdad proved irresistible'. India had long entertained colonial dreams of its own in this region, seeing in ancient Mesopotamia a vast breadbasket to be exploited, and an outlet for its ever-growing population. But five months later, Townshend found himself ultimately stymied at the approaches to Baghdad, and forced back down the Tigris some hundred miles to the insignificant town of Kut, where he was surrounded and besieged. Three relief forces, again commanded by British officers, were monuments of incompetence. In just two weeks, 10,000 men (the relief force numbered 20,000) were either killed or wounded in repeatedly inane frontal attacks on entrenched Turkish positions. Meanwhile, 12,000 men in Kut itself began starving to death.

To meet this developing catastrophe, a desperate scheme was hatched. If the garrison at Kut could not be militarily rescued, why not 'indirect means' (Lawrence's tactful description)? Why not bribe the Turks with a huge cash settlement, in this case £1 million, in return for the release of troops trapped inside the town? A good dose of racial condescension lay behind this scheme, dreamed up by Lord Kitchener himself; the consensus in London seemed to be that Turks were venal, devious, corrupt, self-serving and cowardly – they would welcome the easy way out, a cushion of gold coins. Incredibly, the hitherto obscure T. E. Lawrence was entrusted with the mission, a courier, as it were, from the War Office on Whitehall to the dusty, cholera-riven hovel of Kut. To elevate the tawdry nature of the proposed transaction, Lawrence was promoted to captain, so as not to unduly offend both the officer cadre of the British-Indian forces – about as hidebound a group of men as any Lawrence ever dealt with – and the Turkish siege commander. After a voyage down the Red Sea, then around the Arabian Peninsula into the Persian Gulf, followed by a gunboat trip up the Tigris River, Lawrence arrived at Kut with two other officers. Together they emerged from British lines under a white flag and strode halfway across a no-man's land and stopped. There they waited several hours in the intense heat, surrounded by the bloated bodies of dead men. At last escorted, blindfolded, to Turkish headquarters, their offer of gold was dismissed without a second's hesitation. Townshend surrendered the next day, approximately four months after the Gallipoli withdrawal. In the long history of the British Army, two more humiliating debacles so close together had never been recorded, and the lesson was not lost on Lawrence. As far as he was concerned, the traditional structure and leadership of the British army had ossified into a creaking and decrepit relic of former glories. The thousands of dead men that littered the road from Basra to Baghdad were the most obvious manifestation of the rot that Lawrence saw so keenly. To most of the British-Indian generals, of course, the losses, while bad, were not hopelessly so. Most of the casualties, after all, being Indian, were certainly replaceable.[7]

The Hashemites

Of the six predominate warlords who vied for control of vast, semi-deserted Arabia, one stood higher than the others, if only because his title, Sharif of Mecca, had immense honorific importance considering the centrality of that city to Islamic consciousness. Mecca is 90 miles east of the Red Sea in the previously noted region of Hejaz.

Provincial Hejaz parallels the Red Sea for most of its eastern shore, running north/south from Aqaba, an insignificant village at the tip of the gulf after which it is named, that veers north-east off the Sea; to about 200 miles south of the holy city of Mecca, the Islamic Jerusalem. The word 'Hejaz' translates as 'The Barrier', a reference to the virtually unbroken run of sharp hills and heights which separate the coast from the trackless desert to its east. Various small towns line the seashore, for no apparent reason, there being no ports, harbours or obvious benefits for shipping. Nonetheless, they were of some usefulness as landing spots for the delivery of supplies. The cities of most importance in Hejaz were Mecca, of course, along with Medina, two hundred miles away. A British intelligence officer sent to assess the economy of Hejaz in 1916 concluded there wasn't one to write about.

The honorific title of sharif is literarily meant to designate a man with direct lineage to the prophet Muhammad, and generally restricted to clans that legitimately could claim that link (genealogists were highly valued, as might be expected). Sultans in Constantinople were free to appoint a sharif to the most important position of all, that of Mecca, from a pool of suitable candidates, which were often considerable. In 1909, Hussein ibn Ali, a Hashemite, was so chosen, making him the most important political figure in the region, if not the most powerful.

Sharifs were traditionally nurtured in the environment of the Bedouin desert. They were expected to spend large swaths of their youth embedded with various tribes, learning the harsh skills of survival which it took to mould a true leader. Many were also exposed to life in the sultan's court, far away in Constantinople, to absorb the more Machiavellian lessons of kingship. Hussein, in fact, was born there. Most such men were given considerable doses of religious instruction, since they were quasi-clerical figures who commanded great respect among all elements of Arabic society. More importantly, sharifs were inculcated into the incredibly complex network of family ties, allegiances and political intrigues that determined every step of a man's decision-making process. No world was more treacherous, be it the polished corridors of the sultan's various palaces in Constantinople, or sitting by a fire in the middle of nowhere in the Arabian desert. Very few felt 'secure on the throne'.

In practice, Sharif Hussein of Mecca did not command absolute authority, either in his kingdom of Hejaz, and certainly not in the peninsula at large. Local sheiks could, and often did, defy his wishes; Hussein could plead, cajole, threaten – send clansmen of his own to enforce obedience – but often he was reduced to being a supplicant, bribes in hand, to achieve his ends. Bedouins had, to put it mildly, a wilful streak that was often hard to handle. Hussein's pugnacious rival was Ibn Saud, of the Saud dynasty, whose base lay in the town of Riyadh, in the middle of the desert. The Sauds had a long, torturous history. At one time, their reach had included Mecca, but local rivalries and long conflicts with Egypt had seen their influence wax and wane over the 19th century. In one respect, Ibn Saud certainly represented the typical Bedouin profile: he detested, as a matter of nature, anyone who could be seen as a more consequential figure than he and, in that vein, he detested Hussein. Secondly, he had no genuine interest in anything other than his own and his family's political and military fortunes. The idea of a united Arab entity, especially one under the aegis of a hated rival, was of no relevance to him. This is one reason, as will be explained later, that British-India favoured Ibn Saud in his perennial intrigues against Hussein who, ironically, would be supported by the British Cairo establishment and later, by London. Such were the difficulties of a Victorian empire too large and defuse for its own good.

Sharif Hussein's familial situation was complicated, not unusual given his four wives and eight children. Sons whom he considered important received educations largely resembling his own, a combination of Constantinople atmospherics with long sojourns in the desert. The eldest, Ali, was followed by Abdullah, his father's favourite. The third son, Faisal, took precedence over a half-brother named Zeid, considerably younger than the others, whose mother was a Turk. This 'formidable family group was admired and efficient', according to Lawrence, 'but curiously isolated in their world. They were natives of no country, lovers of no private plot of ground. They had no real confidants or ministers; and no one seemed open to another, or to the father, of whom they stood in awe.' In many ways, Lawrence saw them all as more or less blank slates; the question he asked himself, privately, was which one could he most decisively influence – which one had the 'capacity to carry a revolt to the goal I had conceived for it?' The solution would not be a simple one. Each of these young men rarely let down their guard, mostly from a sense of self-protection. They were generally conspiratorial, reserved, equivocal and often purposefully enigmatic. They took after their father in that respect.

Negotiating anything with Sharif Hussein was considered a purgatory to the English officials who had the misfortune of dealing with him, in particular his British liaison officer, one Colonel Cyril Wilson. Hussein, after interminable haggling with Cairo and London, had finally been persuaded to launch the 'Arab revolt' in June 1915, largely on the basis of a promissory note (the only adjective that fits) that pledged financial support, equipment, supplies and a limited number of advisers. More importantly, the McMahon-Hussein Correspondence, as it was later dubbed, held out as the ultimate enticement to the sharif that after the war (and depending on who won) an independent Arab state consisting of Arabia, Syria and Iraq would be established, with Hussein, of course, at its helm. Hussein dismissed the original offer of just an independent Arabia; he set his eyes on the true prize, the Levant and Mesopotamia. The war news was so dismal everywhere that London gave in and granted Hussein what he wanted ... or so he thought.

Hussein, generally difficult, did not want foreign troops on Arabian soil: the presence of Christian 'crusaders' would do nothing but inflame the local population and undercut his position as an opponent to the sultan's claim to the caliphate.[8] Hussein launched the revolt from his palace in Mecca, whence was fired a single shot into the sky from an ancient musket, whereupon the Turkish garrison was attacked and quickly overcome. Hussein did not bother to inform Cairo that he had crossed the Rubicon. Lawrence reported that 'few people had really believed the sharif would fight'; his decision 'took us by surprise'. Mecca's fall was about the only good news to come from the first several months of the rebellion.

Lawrence respected Hussein, exasperating as he could be. 'Ambiguity covered his every communication', he noted on Hussein's good days. When the sharif was difficult, which was most of the time, he proved 'obstinate, narrow-minded, suspicious'. He was also controlling, particularly with money, which in effect leashed the sons to their father, none of whom enjoyed his full confidence. He established two of them, Ali and Abdullah, in towns along the Red Sea, with Faisal positioned in mountainous terrain to the east. None of them had independent means to operate on their own. They mostly stood about awaiting orders from Hussein, or else spent hours consulting with area sheiks over dinners of mutton and rice served by slaves.

Sykes-Picot

Leon Trotsky must have chortled with delight when news was related that researchers going through tsarist papers and documents in Moscow had found copies of what later became known as the Sykes-Picot Agreement, hashed out between representatives from England and France, to which Russia had agreed, and signed in May 1916. Without any scruple whatsoever, Trotsky released these sensitive, to say the least, documents in *Pravda*, the official communist paper, from where the *Manchester Guardian* picked them up and subsequently published on 26 November 1917. A more damning example of imperial arrogance would be hard to find, nor a greater propaganda weapon with which to expose the self-serving venality of capitalist behaviour; for in these several pages, the Tripartite powers insolently carved up the entire Middle East, assuming conveniently that the Ottoman Empire would soon cease to exist. In broadest terms, Russia would finally occupy Constantinople and its waterways to the Mediterranean; France would gobble up Greater Syria and the Lebanese coast, and for Britain, Palestine and the oil fields of southern Iraq. There might be a few crumbs here and there for Arabs – they could have Mecca and the wastelands of Arabia – but whether by direct or indirect means, practical control of this vast region, with millions of mostly Islamic peoples, would devolve to Christian nations practised in colonial rule: free to pillage natural resources, free to suppress local, antagonistic impulses (with force when necessary) and free to dominate political and military affairs. The baleful consequences of such hubris have infected the world stage ever since, with no true resolution in sight.

'A holiday and joyride in the Red Sea.'

As Lawrence ruminated over the disjointed fiasco that the Kut expedition represented, he picked out its cardinal sin of omission: the refusal of British-India authorities to consult, recruit and utilize indigenous Arabs to further its goal, the eviction of the Turks from Mesopotamia. The reasons were two-fold: racial prejudice was one – the Arabs were deemed to be disorganized rabble who could not be incorporated into a traditional military structure, and thus were inherently peripheral; and secondly, India had its eyes on the region as a possible colonial acquisition of its own – why excite Arab 'nationalists' with notions of freeing themselves from Ottoman control, when British-India simply intended to replace one master with another?

How Lawrence insinuated himself into the very centre of the Arab Revolt is perhaps the most intriguing aspect of his career; indeed, the key to understanding the element of idiosyncratic genius that lay at the heart of his character. His own narrative of its progression in *Seven Pillars of Wisdom*, which he began after the war, is also illustrative in many important ways. The description, while largely correct chronologically, is really a highly tailored and deceptive rendition that disguises what really transpired and, ironically, diminishes Lawrence's role and elevates that of Faisal. This is typically Lawrentian, and well in keeping with the cross-currents that so often tortured him. He desired more than anything else to be a hero, but was satisfied if no one else truly realized it but him. Many times over the next decades of his life, he enjoyed and relished being in the spotlight, 'to keep ourselves a legend', as he put it, but when the blaze of recognition became too bright, he shunned it as unworthy and corrosive. He was happy enough to take pleasure in his own recognition that, without him, the Arab Revolt would have come to nothing.

In October 1916, with the rebellion going nowhere, Lawrence's superior in intelligence duties, Ronald Storrs, who also spoke decent Arabic, was ordered to find out the state of play in Hejaz. He set off by steamer from Cairo and headed south into the Red Sea, where Hussein's men controlled several towns along the southern Hejaz coastline. Lawrence, bored sitting at his desk, managed to wangle a ten-day pass and impulsively joined the mission – without orders of any kind, without a mandate or authority, without, in fact, anyone really knowing where he was going or what he was doing. Lawrence was on a 'joyride', as he put it, accountable to no one, not even Storrs.

The only way to interpret *Seven Pillars* on its recounting of what transpired is to acknowledge Lawrence's emotional debt to his favourite reading matter: the Arthurian legends with their knights of the Round Table. Lawrence was the wandering knight errant, looking for the man who could draw Excalibur from its rooted stone, the man to whom he could attach himself like a faithful Lancelot or, perhaps more germane, like Merlin, the man with magical powers. In Jeddah, their first stop, Lawrence met and studied Abdullah, but found him wanting. Next was Rabegh, where both Ali and Zeid were stationed. Neither fitted the job description (Ali had no 'force of character' and seemed 'rather tired', whereas Zeid, who 'had been brought up in the harem', appeared 'pleasant' but was clearly too young and inexperienced to be 'the born leader of my quest'). The next to be inspected was Faisal, encamped in hilly terrain in the desert one hundred miles to the east. Storrs had returned to Cairo, but he was instrumental in urging Abdulla to allow the fact-finding trip to proceed inland. Permission proved to be difficult. Having Christians milling around about the shore was one thing, allowing even one of them access into the desert was quite another. At Storr's urging, a reluctant Abdullah had called his father in Mecca (dialing him directly: his number was Mecca 1), and it had been an argumentative conversation, but ultimately the old man agreed. Ali and Zeid garbed Lawrence in Arabian robes to cover his uniform and told him not to interact with anyone encountered on the trail (he ignored that entreaty very quickly). The party left by night so as not to attract notice, and bypassed populated areas when they could. His guide was sullen, and at first refused to engage in any meaningful conversation; and Lawrence's rear end soon grew sore in this, his first extensive trip on a camel (it was easy enough to ride without falling off, he wrote, but the curious gait of the beast was hard to accommodate for anyone more used to horses; and the spine of a camel was thin and bony enough to make riding one, even with a saddle, akin to balancing on a thin steel rod). In two days of hard travel, they arrived at Faisal's encampment.

Seven Pillars now takes on a messianic flavour. Lawrence was in attendance to Faisal barely over a day, yet the impression he gives is one of complete ... and here I use a word Lawrence might well have ... enchantment. Faisal radiates an almost otherworldly glow, and in some of the most vivid and exotic words that Lawrence ever wrote, he describes his shimmering presence: 'Faisal looked very tall and pillar-like, very slender, in his long white silk robes and his brown head-cloth bound with a brilliant scarlet and gold cord. His eyelids were dropped; and his black beard and colourless face were like a mask against the strange, still watchfulness of his body. His hands were crossed in front of him on his dagger. I greeted him.' What we have here is the Perfect Arab, 'the man I had come to seek'. After lengthy meetings, Lawrence departed camp the next day, eager to report back to Cairo.

What He Was Thinking? His Conclusions

The next week or so were crucial to Lawrence's evolving plans for the Arab Revolt, and more importantly his prospective role in it. Guided to the port town of Yenbo, he found himself, once there, without transport. Looking up and down the Red Sea, he saw no Royal Navy steamers going to and fro on which he might hitch a ride, and no information as to when he could. He was stuck there, for five days as it turned out. He passed the time by composing a substantial report on his mission, which gave him the chance to settle his mind, to draw his own conclusions as to what he had seen and heard and to plot strategy. This is probably the interlude, despite what he later wrote in *Seven Pillars*, when he decided conclusively that Faisal could be the man of the hour, that Faisal was clever enough to see that relying on Lawrence was his best chance to both break away from his father and to forge his own destiny as leader of the revolt. This would be a co-dependency, but one inevitably balanced towards Lawrence. Faisal had complained bitterly to Lawrence about everything that he lacked: machine guns, decent artillery pieces, ammunition and, most of all, money. Lawrence promised all these, and more. Keenly aware of Arabian suspicions about foreign (and Christian) interference in their affairs – Faisal had pointedly referenced Sudan: Britain hadn't originally wanted it, but after killing 10,000 Sudanese at the battle of Omdurman, it ended up running the place to its own benefit – Lawrence pledged a 'hands off' approach for the future. He had no authority to make such a pledge, but he knew what Faisal wanted to hear; in fact, he agreed with it himself. His first problem was to channel his military superiors to the same conclusion.

It is fascinating to watch Lawrence, an utterly obscure subordinate with no experience of war or politics, worming his views into the highest echelons of the British command structure, and from there into cabinet discussions in London. Self-confidence was not something he lacked. His objectives were twofold: to encourage direct material support for Faisal's 'army', but also to forestall the growing inclination of professional officers like Colonel Wilson to land British troops in Hejaz to join up with Faisal. In order to achieve these goals, he saw the necessity of pumping up Faisal in British eyes and, by extension, making a convincing case that Arab 'nationalists' would join the Hashemites in their struggle. In his reports and presentations, Lawrence patently distorted details of the Arab landscape that did not validate these arguments.

There was, for example, less than widespread support among many sheiks and emirs for Sharif Hussein and his sons' pretensions. Though Lawrence had been impressed by the variety of clans he had seen in Faisal's camp at Wadi Safra, these were outnumbered by chieftains who either actively opposed their ambitions, or else were waiting for more proof that the Hashemites could actually prevail against better-equipped Turkish forces. Secondly, he was less than candid about Faisal's weaknesses, which were many. Faisal was not judged a competent military leader by professionals (Wilson, in fact, considered him cowardly), and even Lawrence, three years later in *Seven Pillars*, listed a variety of character weaknesses: 'impetuous','hot-tempered and sensitive', 'unreasonable' and so on (in his private correspondence, he did call Faisal 'an absolute ripper'). Thirdly, he vigorously argued that Arab desire for independence from Ottoman rule was a national, popular movement, there to be exploited. This was an exaggeration. Arabs, and certainly Bedouins, disdained the Turks to be sure, but the notion of armed rebellion was motivated from the top down, not the other way around. Hussein and his sons were largely interested in their own dynastic ambitions. If the British could further such aims, so much the better; but if the Turks had better offers, Hussein was willing to listen, as both he and Faisal did several times during the war, the generality of which Lawrence was aware of, though the complexities of their intrigues gradually came to 'shock' him: Faisal was 'definitely "selling us" [out]', he noted in a letter after the war. As far as simple tribesmen went, they did as they were told by their sheiks. Fourthly, Lawrence misrepresented what truly motivated Arab fighters. Plain and simple, it was gold and loot. He also downplayed the extremely retrograde views that Hussein made little effort to hide. His adherence to medieval Sharia law would not have made him a particularly attractive figure to London.

Instead of proceeding to Cairo when a ship finally docked in Yenbo, Lawrence steamed in the opposite direction, ending up across the Red Sea in Sudan, then travelling inland to Khartoum, there to confront General Wingate, its governor, whose military authority covered Hejaz. Wingate, with long experience in the Middle East, was a potential ally to Lawrence in one respect: he acknowledged Arab prowess as a disrupting, irregular force, and respected the notion that they could play a militarily important role. Counterbalancing this helpful support was his conviction that British forces must be landed in Hejaz immediately to form the backbone of offensive operations there. Colonel Wilson vehemently agreed.

What exactly Lawrence said in his briefings with Wingate proved murky in the retelling. Once again, Lawrence told Wingate essentially what Wingate wanted to hear, and once in Cairo, misrepresented to General Murray the tenor of their discussions. Certainly not for the last time, Lawrence coloured the dialogue to suit his needs and opinions. Murray, for example, was adamantly opposed to diverting significant numbers of troops to the Hejaz. They were needed for the coming attack being planned for the Levant – Jerusalem, and then Damascus. But unlike Wingate, Murray had no genuine respect for Arab fighters. What had they done for the cause, he wrote Robertson, the chief of the Imperial Staff back in London? They had been supplied with over two million rounds of ammunition and all they had to show for it were a measly 2,000 dead Turks. Consequently he was delighted with Lawrence's argument that Faisal should go it alone, yet be adequately furnished with enough support to annoy the Turks, and, he hoped, keep them bottled up in the south. Robertson agreed as well; he wanted nothing to do with siphoning off troop strength to peripheral operations. Gallipoli had been bad enough. He explained to the prime minister and cabinet in London that he supported delivering supplies and gold coins to Faisal, based on the reports of his man on the spot, 'said to have intimate knowledge of the Turks and the Arabs'. Robertson, of course, had never heard of Lawrence. Why should he have?

The result of all this interdepartmental back and forth saw Lawrence the winner, ordered to return to Yenbo yet again, this time as the official British liaison to Faisal, at first a temporary assignment until a more 'suitable' officer could be found. In one of the classic misstatements found in *Seven Pillars*,

Lawrence claimed a reluctance to accept the posting. 'It was much against my grain, I urged my complete unfitness for the job', but in fact he was delighted.

Lawrence brought many qualities to the assignment. The first was an unquenchable belief in the Arabs themselves. Yes, they were troublesome, yes they were excitable and yes they were unreliable when it came to formal warfare, but he had faith in them as irregular fighters. Lawrence was a born intelligence officer. He saw things that more hidebound officers could (or would) not comprehend, and applied them directly to what he perceived to be Arab strengths in both the field and in their character. His keen eye for geography was especially useful, and his physical ability to handle the difficult climate, even more so. Add to this an open personality and exceedingly ingratiating manner – servile and obsequious when necessary, but genuinely supportive – and what resulted was not only the perfect liaison officer, but the perfect courtier as well.[9] Faisal recognized these qualities, and in just a few weeks Lawrence's posting became permanent. Not everyone was pleased. Colonel Wilson, in fact, was apoplectic, and not just because of his subordinate's sloppy attire and unmilitary bearing. 'Lawrence wants kicking and kicking *hard* at that.... I look at him as a bumptious young ass who spoils his undoubted knowledge of Syrian Arabs etc. by making himself out to be the only authority on war, engineering, HM's ships and everything else. He put every single person's back up I've met'. Wilson's rant was ignored; several observers, in fact, thought Wilson was having a nervous breakdown.

The Hejaz Railway

The first several weeks of Lawrence's attachment to Faisal's entourage, the beginning of two solid years in his service, were not propitious in any way. Faisal had concocted several ambitious forays against the Turks, involving simultaneous movements on the part of his three brothers, but these had proven comically inept; in several cases, Arab forces had dissolved into formless flight not because of Turkish firepower, but from the mere rumour of their proximity. This did not bode well for the future, especially since several British officers in attendance witnessed and reported back to Cairo what they had seen. Lawrence's first efforts were thus limited to public relations and damage control.

The Turkish dilemma was actually more acute than realized. From their southernmost base, the city of Medina, their ultimate goal had always been

Mecca. But any drive to the Holy City was subject to flank attacks, mostly from the west, originating from the string of coastal villages up and down the Red Sea concurrently occupied by the rebels and easily resupplied from Egypt (at first, according to Lawrence, with 'old rubbish thought serviceable for the wild Arabs'). Turkish efforts to reclaim these towns were arduous affairs, for they were generally about 100 miles from the major communications corridor that they controlled, the vital Hejaz railway, a narrow-gauge single track that ran 810 miles from Damascus to Medina. Disembarking from the rail line, Turkish forces faced daunting struggles to even approach their targets: dreadful terrain, no roads to speak off, water always a concern, with attacks from an enemy skilled in guerrilla warfare, who often took no prisoners 'if their blood was hot'. Lawrence estimated, regarding one of these Turkish expeditions, that the enemy lost forty camels and up to twenty men a day from sneak attacks. Morale under such circumstances plummeted; without control of these Red Sea towns, the Turks were forced to concentrate troop strength in a defensive line encircling Medina, just far enough to put the city out of artillery range. To all intents and purposes, Medina was the southernmost outpost of Ottoman rule in Hejaz. Its only link for supplies, reinforcements and encouragement was the railway. Significant manpower (several thousand out of Medina's standing garrison of 13,500 men) was drained away to defensive positions all along the track, to protect bridges, depots and small forts, which became, as a result, natural targets for Arab marauders. With each Arab advance north along the Red Sea coast – from Jeddah to Rabegh to Yenbo and, by winter of 1917, to Wejh – more miles of the railway became subject to attack.[10]

Lawrence very quickly ingratiated himself into Faisal's inner circle, frequently sleeping in the emir's tent each evening after long sessions over strategy, supplies and, most importantly, money. Money was the essential lubricant, without which the rebellion could not continue. Faisal may have been the dispenser, but Lawrence became the conduit, controlling the money bags from Cairo that Faisal used to buy the allegiance of ever-fickle clans, many of 'dubious loyalty'. In becoming the paymaster, as it were, and also the argumentative advocate for more and more gold sovereigns from Cairo, Lawrence consciously strengthened and weakened his 'master'. Faisal's doling payments to his followers diminished his father's control of his son, and thereby bypassed Hussein in the purview of British authorities in both Cairo and London. Faisal became the man who mattered, not the Sharif of Mecca. At the same time, Faisal recognized that Lawrence was essential to all his schemes and machinations, some of which were extraordinarily complicated. Lawrence became, as Lawrence intended, his 'omnipotent adviser', the man

Faisal could not do without, which had the added benefit of increasing T.E.'s independence from staff headquarters, which he succinctly described in one of his letters: 'The atmosphere of being one's own master ... is pleasant.'[11]

Faisal soon urged Lawrence to dress in Arab gear so as to not stand as 'the Christian' during interminable meetings. Being constantly in Faisal's presence also gave Lawrence the opportunity to further assess Faisal's strengths and weaknesses, the former to buttress, the latter to compensate for. He learned quickly enough that Faisal was no soldier, that his special talent, in fact, was more important: the ability to control the disparate clans. In one instance that Lawrence reported to Colonel Wilson, 'there was a fight three days ago between 300 Ageyl and 400 Hadheyl over a question of camels.[12] About a thousand rounds were fired, and two men killed and six wounded. The fight was checked by Faisal himself, who went out bare-headed and bare-footed, as he happened to be, and made peace at once ... a good illustration of his personal prestige among his followers.' Faisal 'labours day and night at his politics', he added.

The more embedded Lawrence became in the hierarchy of Arab leadership, however, the more conflicts faced him. The dilemma produced inside his energized mind by the Sykes-Picot Agreement was acute. He evidently had become aware of this secret agreement in June 1916, a full seven months before the *Manchester Guardian*'s scoop, and it immediately compromised just about everything he thought he was doing for the Arab cause and, indeed, threw him emotionally off the edge. He thought it right, for example, that newly independent Arab states begin their existence under the eyes of competent colonial experts (so long as they were British, and not French). Yet he feverishly encouraged his Arab friends to pursue unfettered independence, which many times he promised them would be theirs should they follow his guidance. The Balfour Declaration of 9 November 1917 was another example of two irreconcilable positions heading for an online collision. Britain favoured a homeland for Jews in Palestine, a position Lawrence grudgingly accepted, knowing full well that such a proposition was bound to unsettle Arabs and alienate them from a British sphere of influence. A full century later, the difficulty of reconciling these divergent pathways remains as intractable as ever.[13]

Despite much that has been written about Lawrence over many decades, one truth must be pointed out: he was an Englishmen, as patriotic as any other John Bull, and had no ingrained hostility to any of his country's hallmark traditions or institutions. He was disdainful of convention, it is true, and equally so for people he found incompetent, whether soldier or politician. But British interests were ultimately his interests. As his later friend the novelist E. M. Forster put it, Lawrence 'was intensely patriotic, lived for the Empire, and believed he could serve her best from beneath'.

But he was also fast being 'Arabianized'. His affection for Faisal, his notions of freedom and independence from mongrelized elements of modern society and his romantic conception of Bedouin (or Arthurian) heroics, made the goals of the Arab rebellion more or less his own, at least publicly. The basic incompatibility of the McMahon Agreement, Sykes-Picot and the Balfour Declaration were not lost on him. On his 30th birthday, after Edmund Allenby replaced Murray as commander of the Egyptian Expeditionary Force, Lawrence summed up where he stood mentally: 'Here were the Arabs, believing me, Allenby trusting me, my bodyguard dying for me: and I began to wonder if all established reputations were founded, like mine, on fraud.'

Aqaba

'It is not known what are the present whereabouts of Captain Lawrence.'

British intelligence officer, Cairo
5 July 1917

Aqaba was not a place most English strategists in London either knew about or paid much attention to. What did an out-of-the way, utterly obscure and insignificant fishing village mean to them? Amidst the quite small, numerically speaking, working groups on Arab affairs in Cairo and some of their military superiors, the matter was of considerable importance, though, as usual, opinions ranged far and wide.

Taken at face value, Aqaba, in isolation, was not worth much; but in light of both Lawrence's operational scheme of things, and the rivalries between those great imperial powers, Britain and France, it was of prime importance. Sitting at the head of the Gulf of Aqaba, it was a spearhead aimed directly into the gut of Syria. Any force occupying it, if properly supplied by sea from Egypt, was in a perfect position to achieve several important goals: further disruption of that Turkish lifeline, the Hejaz railway; obstructing over 16,000 Turkish troops bottled up in Medina from relieving the main Ottoman army that would soon be attacked by British forces from Egypt; protecting the British Army's right flank as it advanced up the coast towards Jerusalem and Damascus; and, most importantly, giving the allied powers a foothold in the postwar Levant that would probably thwart Arab desire for independence (what little of it that remained after a prolonged crackdown in Syria, 1915 and 1916, where the Turks ruthlessly executed nearly three dozen 'nationalist' plotters). Lawrence was aware of these possibilities and juggled the myriad consequences that lay over the horizon through his own often conflicted lens. He concluded that Aqaba must be an Arabian 'show' and no one else's.

Lawrence began arguing that taking Aqaba was not important. As was becoming deliberately frequent with him, he was lying. As a friend later wrote in a reminiscence, Lawrence 'possessed all the qualifications for success, including, it must be admitted, the faculty of unscrupulousness in the interest of his main objective'. He never 'hesitated to exceed his instruction(s)', or, in fact, to ignore them. 'Most of my opinions were strong', he later wrote in *Seven Pillars*; what he did not admit is that he often kept them to himself, especially when in the presence of superiors, like Wingate, Murray and later Allenby. Allenby, in fact, found him 'quiet and unassuming'.

What Lawrence really wanted was Faisal sitting alone in Aqaba. All the British need do was supply the Arab irregulars with guns, ammunition, specialist advisers, food and, most importantly, gold sovereigns ('the all-powerful persuader' – after only one year of war, the British government had already paid out over one million pounds to its Arabian surrogates). Some British generals favoured such an approach, others did not. The Arabs, many felt, were not disciplined enough to go it alone from Aqaba. They would need British troops to provide the backbone, and British troops were required elsewhere for the main push from Sinai to Jerusalem, not wandering around the desert. But French interest in an Aqaba expedition of its own worried them more; a successful French foothold in Aqaba would solidify their efforts to get feet on the ground for Damascus – it seemed best that Britain be there first. As for the enemy, if the Turks did not sufficiently value control of the little village, the Germans did; teams of navy personnel were spotted preparing to lay mines along the approaches to the port ... shades of the Dardanelles! A quick naval strike dispersed this effort.

Lawrence decided, very much on his own, to take Aqaba with Arab forces alone. This was a tremendous gamble on his part, but, as he later told a friend, 'It gives one great power to be always on the edge of something.' A successful operation would require London to further its support of Faisal's army and, by extension (in Lawrence's opinion, anyway), to keep its word regarding the future of the postwar Middle East. He was correct in the first assumption, but wrong in the second.

On 9 May 1917, Lawrence set off from Wejh with a small retinue of about forty Bedouin. The initial goal was to reach a string of wells in a two-hundred-mile long valley called Wadi Sirhan (in present-day Jordan), there to camp and, he hoped, entice area sheiks into joining the expedition to Aqaba. Leading the party was the roughish Auda Abu Tayi, sheik of the fearsome Howeitat clan. Auda was the epitome of Bedouin indomitability, a fiercely independent freelancer whose only true loyalty was to himself and his clan, and the very definition of the stereotypical desert brigand. He grew fond of Lawrence, and served the cause more or less faithfully, but in the end it was hatred of Turks and the lure of loot that mattered most.

Some of Lawrence's best writing in *Seven Pillars* is descriptive, and his narration of this long and arduous trek is among his best, some of it through the dangerous El Houl desert of northern Arabia: long passages of observation, things he saw, descriptions of terrain, the rigours of travelling miles in the hot sun and frigid nights, the delights of being with companions whose lives he saw as Homeric (an admiration rarely shared by his English co-workers). In the course of these travels, among other things, his linguistic skills improved. 'At the beginning', he wrote, 'my Arabic had been a halting command of the tribal dialects of the Middle Euphrates (a not impure form), but now it became a fluent mingling of Hejaz slang and north-tribal poetry with household words and phrases from the limpid Nejdi[14] and book forms from Syria. The fluency had a lack of grammar, which made my talk a perpetual adventure for my hearers. Newcomers imagined I must be the native of some unknown illiterate district; a shot-rubbish ground of dissected Arabic parts of speech.'

Wracked by a bout of fever, and beset with boils, Lawrence finally arrived at Wadi Sirhan, where he endured days of what could only be described as wrangling, i.e. the Arabian version of diplomacy. Behind it all, he became obsessed by a sense of guilt, the whole deception that British authorities, and by extension he himself, were perpetrating on the Arabs. 'Can't stand another day here', he wrote in his journal. 'Will ride N. and chuck it.' In a hasty note to his superior at the Arab Bureau, he jotted down the following: 'For all sakes try and clear this show up before it goes any further. We are calling them to fight for us on a lie, and I can't stand it.' In early June he and only two companions set off on a daring (some might say foolhardy) reconnaissance trip northward into Syria, at one point almost to Damascus itself. The point of this project, as indeed, was true for so much of Lawrence's self-guided mission, was to get some sort of grip on what important people were thinking. The term 'important', of course, was often relative to the setting. An insignificant headman in an insignificant village was worth talking to, even if he could provide only ten men, but in a larger sense, was it really? The point was to collect tribal intelligence, who's in, who's out. The attitude he mostly found was Wait and See.

The usual result of 'persuasion' in Arabian wartime negotiations of the type pursued by Lawrence during this 400-mile trip was stalemate. Very few sheiks or clan leaders, particularly as the theatre of hostilities approached Syria, wanted to commit to the revolt unequivocally, especially 'town' Arabs whose interactions with Ottoman authorities had often been administratively acceptable. What did 'independence' mean to them? Onerous taxation, conscription, the depredations of Turkish forces ... what was the difference who the oppressor was, Turk or Arab? Townspeople were also keenly aware that disloyalty or treason could have harsh consequences, more so for them than for the footloose and elusive Bedouin. News of Armenian massacres ordered by Constantinople in the spring of 1915 were well known; Turkish reprisals were generally gruesome affairs; it was wiser to give no offence. Faisal and Lawrence knew full well that many would straddle the fence until the outcome was more fully guaranteed. Lawrence returned to Wadi Sirhan more determined than ever to put things right by the Arabs who had placed their trust in him.

In his absence, the camp had seen an influx of volunteer Bedouin arrivals, swelling their numbers to about 500 fighters. Compared with Flanders, Gallipoli and even the British forces in or around Cairo, about to launch the long-awaited attack east towards Jerusalem (some 150,000 men), the numbers under Lawrence's command seem ludicrous. The scale may have been absurd, but the result would not only make T. E. Lawrence an important figure within the British command structure – more so than any minor officer might hope for – but would also change the entire character of the Arab Revolt into something more momentous for the future of the region than that of a petty 'sideshow' (Lawrence's term).

For two weeks, Lawrence and Auda marched to and fro through south-western Syria conducting a series hit-and-run raids designed to confuse the Turks as to their ultimate goal. To some degree the strategy worked: Turkish officers responded with 'relief' columns, emanating from the important railway town of Maan (garrison strength some 7,000 men), which resulted in several massacres of innocent villagers, and the dynamiting of important wells. Incidents of the former served little purpose other than to inflame Auda and his men; incidents of the latter were serious impediments to Arab mobility, but in most cases on-the-spot repairs were sufficient to provide the necessary water to keep them on the move. On 1 July, Lawrence felt that the subterfuge had done its work: he headed for Aqaba.

The retrospective figures, which Lawrence did not know at the time, were puny. Aqaba was defended by about 300 men; what embedded defences it had were mostly directed towards the waterfront, installed to prevent a landing from the sea, whence any attack was expected. Lawrence and Auda were advancing from the interior. One or two lightly defended strongpoints lay landward, in mountainous terrain that had to be negotiated before reaching the Aqaba plains. Lawrence soon learned that a column of 500 Turks were marching to bolster the garrison. Auda's scouts caught up with them on 1 July, when they discovered the enemy encamped by a stream in the hollow of a valley, overlooked by a series of higher ridges. The Turks could not have chosen a worse defensible site. To add to the picture, they also failed to post night guards around their perimeter. Unimpeded, the Arabs occupied the heights, and next morning, the beginning of a brutally hot day, they began firing on the Turks below.

Lawrence wrote a graphic account of the battle in *Seven Pillars*, the resolution of which, if he is to be believed, came as a result of an exchange of insults between himself and Auda. As the day had progressed, and overcome with heat, Lawrence had crawled into a rivulet in search of a trickle of water, where Auda came up to him. Saying something to the effect of, see how my tribe fights, Lawrence replied, 'By God indeed, they shoot a lot and hit a little.' This infuriated the old warrior into a tantrum. Ripping off his headgear and screaming oaths, 'he ran back up the hill like a mad man' and told his followers to mount up. 'Get on your camel if you want to see the old man's work', he yelled. Lawrence did as he was told, and watching from a height, witnessed what was, in effect, a charge of medieval knights, fifty men on horseback riding wildly helter-skelter toward the Turkish centre. After a ragged volley, which brought down two of Auda's men, the Turks ran for it. That was the signal for Lawrence, and his 300 men mounted on camels, to attack the Turkish flank, now a disorganized, panic-stricken rabble. Lawrence, in the forefront, pretty much lost control of his camel, plunging downhill at full gallop. Firing his pistol right and left into the fleeing mob, his mount suddenly toppled, 'as though pole-axed', hurling Lawrence into full airborne flight, knocking him nearly unconscious when he hit the ground. Lying there, he expected to be trampled to death by the camel horde thundering down behind him. By the time he gathered his senses and looked about, the battle was over, though not the slaughter. In a paroxysm of blood lust, the Bedouin massacred some 300 Turks, taking only 160 prisoners. One of these Lawrence interrogated, roughly by his own account. Maan, he learned, could be easily taken; this appealed to the Arabs, sensing that more plunder would be there than at Aqaba, but Lawrence, and not for the last time, managed to turn their heads in the direction he wished. They set off that night, but not before Lawrence toured the battlefield. In one of the more ghoulish descriptions in the entire book, he marvelled at the aesthetic beauty of all the naked corpses lying in the moonlight, having been stripped of everything by the Arabs. He also discovered that his dead camel had not been brought down by enemy fire; Lawrence, it appears, had himself accidentally shot the beast in the back of the head during his wild charge down the hillside. Aqaba easily fell four days later.

The important thing now was to inform Cairo as quickly as possible, so that crucial supplies could begin arriving for Faisal in Aqaba. Lawrence considered his options and decided on the most arduous, but most direct, course of action, a 150-mile camel ride across the Sinai desert to the village of El Shatt, on the canal, directly opposite the port town of Suez. Following the ancient pilgrim route, they made it in forty-nine hours. An exhausted Lawrence (now weighing less than a hundred pounds) 'rang up Suez headquarters and said I wanted to come across (having) urgent news for headquarters'. Their reply? 'They were sorry, they had no free boats just then. They would be sure to send first thing in the morning ... and rang off.'

The Bull

Having repulsed the Turkish effort to reach the Suez Canal in August 1916, General Archibald Murray laboriously organized an Allied riposte, the intention being to head east for the fortified town of Gaza first, then on to Jerusalem. Murray was hindered by the mindset in London that the Western Front was all that mattered; he was continuously having his troop strength drawn off to the wasteland of attritional warfare in France, and then by the Gallipoli operation. But advance he did, seven months later. He had little time to think about Lawrence and his guerrilla operations along the Red Sea.

The first action in and around Gaza was initially deemed a success, which Murray unfortunately conveyed to London prematurely, triggering hysterical headlines in the British press announcing, at last, a victory somewhere. Unfortunately, this was not to be. The Turks, well led by German officers, were in solid defensive positions, fought stubbornly and repulsed the later attacks. A second offensive likewise ground pointlessly to a halt. Murray found himself recalled, replaced by Edmund Allenby. Lloyd George, newly ensconced as prime minister, told Allenby he expected a present by Christmas:

Jerusalem (an 'amateurish demand', according to one military historian); he didn't get it, but Anglo-Indian forces, following up on the debacle at Kut, produced Baghdad on 11 March 1917.

Like several of his contemporaries, Allenby first saw action during the Boer War, where he distinguished himself from many other officers by avoiding any glaring mistakes. He was a solid soldier, did as he was told and gained some appreciation for the irregular tactics employed by the Boers, which predicted in some ways how he would deal with Lawrence in the future. He was a stickler for detail and was not above indulging in titanic displays of temper, often on matters of trivial importance. To be chewed out by 'the bull', as he was known, 'was like being blown from the muzzle of a gun'. In the first two years of war on the Western Front, he was involved in several actions of the type favoured by Haig, with corresponding losses. Having 'no ideas' to speak of, as Hubert Gough noted, he soldiered on regardless, and the gruesome casualty count of the unsuccessful April 1917 assault on Arras was a check to his reputation. His relationship with Haig deteriorating, he sought a fresh start somewhere, and was given command of the Egyptian Expeditionary Force in June. Arriving in Cairo, one of the first things that greeted him was news that his only son had just been killed on the Western Front.

Then, of course, there was Lawrence. For a stickler of protocol, the image of Lawrence, whom Allenby later described as 'a little bare-footed skirted person', must have been something of a shock. So too his news: the entirely unexpected capture of Aqaba. Could he believe it? As Lawrence admitted, Allenby had to decide whether the shoeless and weirdly dressed junior officer in front of him was a 'genuine actor' or a 'charlatan'. Lawrence helped him out by a quick exposition with map, and Allenby decided on the former opinion, promising to provide Faisal with all the help he could. The fifty-six-year-old British general may have been unimaginative in many respects, but he did clearly see the advantages of 'marrying war with rebellion'. Aqaba, serving as Allenby's right flank, was only one hundred miles from British forces that would soon be driving once again for Gaza, and from there Jerusalem. Allenby 'cared nothing for our fighting power' – 'three men and a boy with pistols in front of Deraa' was all he wanted from the Arabs. But Allenby saw the disruptive potential very clearly, and so noted to London. Lawrence was beginning to be noticed.

Sensitive matters now had to be dealt with. Strategically speaking, Palestine and then Syria were now to be the war theatre for Arab operations. Medina, 800 miles south, diminished in importance, as did even Mecca for that matter. Sharif Hussein was no longer the man of the hour, but his son Faisal.

Lawrence was summoned by the 'obstinate, narrow-minded, suspicious' sharif to explain the current situation; he shipped down to Jeddah for what was certainly a delicate conversation.

Despite Lawrence sometimes denigrating the intelligence of the sharif in *Seven Pillars*, the old man was no dupe and realized perfectly well that the Allied powers were using him to their own ends, and undercutting his position with regard to his sons, particularly Faisal. Complicating the situation was that the sharif had just been visited by Sir Mark Sykes and François Georges-Picot, the negotiators of the imperialist Sykes-Picot Agreement referenced earlier, who had attempted to obfuscate its more egregious conditions. The sharif would have none of it, according to Lawrence. Syria and Iraq 'were Arab countries, but I will neither take them myself nor permit anyone else to take them', the sharif told him. 'They have deserved independence and it is my duty to see they get it'. As far as Hussein was concerned, Hejaz (he was now calling himself King of Hejaz; later, as his hopes expanded, King of the Arabs) and the other elements of a Greater Arabia, were one in culture, religion and interests; to carve out alien (and Christian) European enclaves was unacceptable. 'The Hejaz and Syria', for example, 'are like the palm and fingers of one hand, and I could not have consented to the amputation of any finger or any part of a finger without leaving myself a cripple'. Herein lay the dilemma that Lawrence himself could never quite reconcile in his own mind, but he said enough to calm Hussein, who drifted off, 'as usual, without obvious coherence', into religious discursions.

Gaza & Jerusalem

'I'm not going to last out this game much longer: nerves going and temper wearing thin, and one wants an unlimited account of both.'

Lawrence, September 1917, from Aqaba

Allenby's campaign for the next three months was ironic enough that even he might have noticed. The movements he originated (largely the plans of his predecessor, to be sure) were largely conventional and involved the sort of manoeuvres, feints and flank attacks that any student of military history would have recognized in an instant. Perhaps not Napoleonic in their conception, but certainly workmanlike. Even cavalry sweeps played their part, a refreshing reminder to horsemen like Allenby that perhaps the old days were not dead and gone. In effect, Allenby conducted operations that many officers, British and German alike, had thought would be in play three years previously, when war first broke out. Many had believed, conventionally, that the whole thing would be over in a year. No one had predicted the Western Front.

Turkish forces usually fought stubbornly in defence, but they were seriously outnumbered as Allenby began his campaign into Palestine. A move towards Beersheba on 31 October, twenty-five miles to the east of Gaza, surprised German headquarters. When the town fell in just a day's fight, a pathway to Jerusalem opened up, and Gaza faced the prospect of being encircled, forcing a Turkish withdrawal six days later. More fierce fighting took place as the Turks retreated, but their front was crumbling. In just a month Jerusalem would fall.

As Allenby's campaign unfolded, Lawrence's more or less came apart. Since his dramatic capture of Aqaba, the little fishing village had been transformed into a formidable depot of tents, latrines, supplies, Rolls-Royce amoured cars and tenders, acceptably Muslim soldiers (Egyptian and Indian) and many British advisors. Added to that were streams of Bedouin, who came and went as they wished, lured by the possibilities of looting expeditions and killing Turks. The place became a maelstrom of activity, presenting problems of organization and coherent planning that Lawrence was ill-trained to control. He took refuge by plunging into a series of quixotic expeditions, some aimed at destroying sections of the Hejaz railway, others of a more information-gathering character. Both were often conducted on the spur of the moment, as many observers noted, and he was often gone for weeks at a time. It was wondered by some if Lawrence was suffering a breakdown of some sort; or did he, in fact, have a death wish?

Destroying the railway was extremely popular among the various Bedouin clans, since it was a threat to what most of them did for a living. They either robbed pilgrims on their annual Hajj pilgrimage to Mecca, or they extorted protection money to guard them from other Bedouin. The Hejaz railway was potentially a much safer route to the holy city for pilgrims, as well as being dramatically shorter and cheaper; a few days on the train, as opposed to weeks of dangerous, tiring travel overland. One visitor to the camp, just before a raid was to commence, noted the pandemonium of the atmosphere: there was Lawrence, wearing a 'whimsical expression', surrounded by 'swarthy desert warriors, restless, unable to stand still, constantly shooting and indulging in all sorts of antics. It seemed unreal – almost an Arab "phantasia" ... ceaseless movement, much shouting, din and noise'.

Lawrence's attacks on trains and bridges were a keystone to the strategy he had outlined in several conferences with Allenby. These were intended to both isolate Medina, preventing the transfer of troops to the defence of Gaza and Jerusalem, as well as occupy the attention of large numbers of enemy soldiers required to protect the railway. Lawrence often insisted on leading these raids himself, generally undertaken after long and arduous trips through the desert, in the process of which he suffered several wounds and was lucky not to have been killed. In some instances he led groups of only sixty tribesmen in forays against Turkish units numbering in the hundreds. In others he brazenly walked about in the open prior to attacks; once he waved to Turkish soldiers passing by on a train, with his detonator, disguised only by a bush, more or less in plain sight. One of his detonations saw him inexcusably close to the railway, as he graphically detailed in *Seven Pillars*:

> The explosion was terrific. The ground spouted blackly into my face, and I was sent spinning, to sit up with the shirt torn to my shoulder and the blood dripping from long, ragged scratches on my left arm. Between my knees lay the exploder, crushed under a twisted sheet of sooty iron. In front of me was the scalded and smoking upper half of a man. When I peered through the dust and steam of the explosion the whole boiler of the first engine seemed to be missing.[15]

But none of these remotely approached in peril the reconnaissance mission he undertook to the important Syrian junction of Deraa. It stands apart in more ways than one.

Accompanied by two Bedouin, Lawrence left their camels behind and walked into the town alongside railway tracks. The three were stopped by a suspicious soldier, but only Lawrence, due no doubt to his light complexion, was detained. That is about all one can say with certainty; the rest has been debated by historians, soldiers, writers, personal friends, film directors and the general public for the last hundred years. No one will ever know the truth.

According to Lawrence in *Seven Pillars*, he was interrogated, beaten within an inch of his life by a variety of sadistic Turks and, by implication, raped by an officer. Much of this (but not the rape) is described in prose that seems at times to luxuriate in grim details, giving the narrative a sadomasochistic edge seemingly confirmed, in hindsight, about what we know about Lawrence's behaviour well after the war. Did he make the whole thing up in some sort of hallucinatory trance as he wrote *Seven Pillars* in 1919? Was putting this on paper some sort of deferred wish fulfilment for something that did not happen but that he hoped had? Did he write so intimately about all this just to confirm for readers his honesty, by implication vouching that everything in the book could be believed (when in fact much of the narrative was misleading)? Again, the verdict is unclear. Charlotte Shaw, George Bernard Shaw's wife, and one of Lawrence's most important postwar correspondents, was frequently exasperated. Lawrence was such 'an INFERNAL liar', she said to her husband, but Shaw disagreed. 'He was an actor'.

It is probably true that Lawrence was pushed around, perhaps beaten to some degree, by his captors. But the explanation of his 'escape' is unconvincing (he climbed out of the window in the unguarded room where he was kept and just walked away). Certainly no one noticed anything out of the ordinary in his physical condition when he returned to camp at Aqaba, nor did he speak to anyone immediately after about what may have happened. What people did begin to notice was a growing moodiness on his part, an emotional see-saw between despondency and the sudden urge for 'action' that might dispel it. He also impulsively surrounded himself with a private bodyguard of about sixty Bedouin, some unattached to any specific clan and regarded as outcasts. As always, he was constantly 'working' the Arabs to get things done: buying 'mangy camels' for meat, distributing booty, compensating the relatives of those killed, treating the wounded (urine used as a 'rude antiseptic'). He grew exhausted. 'For a year and a half I had been in motion, riding a thousand miles each month upon camels: with added nervous hours in crazy aeroplanes, or rushing across country in powerful cars. In my last five actions I had been hit, and my body so dreaded further pain that now I had to force myself under fire. Generally I had been hungry: lately always cold: and frost and dirt had poisoned my hurts into a festering mass of sores'. He was cheered, though, by a summons from Allenby to join him immediately. Jerusalem was there to be had.

On 11 December 1917, Edmund Allenby entered the Holy City through the Jaffa Gate, the culmination of over a month's worth of fighting and some 18,000 casualties (numerically about nine times more men than Lawrence and Faisal commanded at the time). It has been calculated that he was the thirty-fourth man in history to conquer Jerusalem. Lawrence was in his entourage, dressed this time in a British army uniform, not Arab robes. The entire party was on foot, there were no triumphal flags or bands, in deliberate contrast to Kaiser Wilhelm who, nineteen years before, had arrived on a state visit in full military gear on a war horse. Crusader Redux!

After a few hours Allenby left, just as he had come, with Lawrence in tow, but the restrained taste the general exhibited was not emulated in the Western press, which rejoiced in the victory with evangelical fervour. The *New York Herald* injudiciously ran a banner headline, Jerusalem had finally, after centuries of Muslim occupation, been 'rescued'. And *Punch*, not to be left behind, ran a cartoon of Allenby gazing at Jerusalem spread out at his feet, dressed as Richard the Lionheart.

The remainder of the campaign, which culminated in the fall of Damascus ten months later, was remarkably different in character from the almost whimsical capture of Aqaba. Lawrence's ragtag collection of Bedouin tribesmen had been seriously augmented by regular Commonwealth soldiers. He no longer rode camels dozens of miles per day or night, but instead was being carried about (often at speeds of over 70 mph) in a Roll-Royce tender, christened 'Blue Mist', driven by a British army mechanic (who claimed they drove over 20,000 miles together). For conferences with Allenby or Faisal, an aeroplane was regularly put at his disposal. Cairo, Aqaba or wherever Allenby happened to be, Lawrence could often be found there as well. His forces blew up train rails and bridges almost at random, and harassed fleeing Turks mercilessly, more or less turning the enemy into a formless mass of demoralized refugees. Directed by Lawrence, who showed little remorse – indeed, he dutifully described the worst incidents – hundreds of these men were deliberately massacred. Any Turk or German soldier thinking to surrender took a real chance that his attempt would be ignored.

'He must accept the situation as it was.'

Allenby, as regards Faisal,
Damascus, 3 October 1918

For Lawrence, Damascus was everything. All the confusion over the myriad of possibilities that lay ahead in the postwar Middle East would be substantially clarified by the simple reality that possession is nine-tenths of the law. Faisal and the Arabs in Damascus meant that France was not there, nor the British for that matter, without whom, as even T. E. realized, Faisal would not be either. Be there first was his mantra.

In the end, technically speaking, he wasn't there 'first'. Australian cavalry units had passed through Damascus proper at dawn on 1 June, seeking a shortcut directly through the city in order to block fleeing Turkish forces. At about the time they left Damascus, two hours later, Lawrence was driven to the city centre in his 'Blue Mist' tender. He was accompanied not by Bedouins on camels, but an Indian cavalry unit. No matter, he essentially claimed the city for Faisal, and smooth-talked Henry Chauvel, an Australian general who arrived right on their heels, into sequestering his men away from important municipal buildings associated with civic rule. Unfortunately for Lawrence and Faisal, this essentially left a vacuum, administratively speaking, in Damascus, one that neither man had the ability or resources to fill (Faisal wasn't even initially there himself). Anarchy became the state of play for two full days: widespread looting, the collapse of police authority, the indiscriminate execution of Turkish stragglers – the situation veered out of control. Chauvel, realizing he had been misled by Lawrence, asserted his authority by 2 October, and Australian forces paraded through the city.

These initial days of chaos had found Lawrence at about the end of his strength, and no wonder. The past months had exhausted him in every way. Constant physical privation, emotional turmoil, the stress of being in charge under impossible conditions, the drain in trying to keep volatile and often venal Arabians within his circle in some sort of unity –- all this in the end undid him. His skills in diplomacy, put to the test almost hourly, in some ways emptied his soul. He could not mould the disparate personalities into a single course of altruistic action; what passed for Arab 'unity' in effect splintered in front of his eyes. Interspersed with hours of argumentation, Lawrence could be found wandering the city almost aimlessly, trying to find solutions to the myriad problems in front of him. One of these involved hundreds of Turkish wounded who were languishing in so-called hospitals under conditions so squalid that an Australian medical officer, accompanied by Lawrence, whirled about and struck him in the face, so outraged was he at the disgusting scenes presented him. In another, again in the presence of an officer, the two men came up to scenes of Bedouin tribesmen murdering defenceless Turks. The officer was appalled when Lawrence 'asked them in a gentle voice to stop'. When they continued their 'nasty' behaviour, the officer drew his revolver and shot them, upon which Lawrence said, 'For God's sake, stop being so bloody-minded'.

None of this mess was adequately described in *Seven Pillars*, which Lawrence deceptively described as a largely Arabian triumph, adequately, but not critically reinforced by Allenby's conventional Commonwealth army, a reversal of the truth. But all the charades ended very quickly with Allenby's arrival on 3 October. Faisal might say what he wished, and Lawrence could mutter here and there in protest, but Allenby laid down the law, pretty much what the Sykes-Picot agreement had mandated. Syria would be administered by Hussein, not Faisal, and under a French mandate (meaning control). Lebanon and Palestine would be directly governed by Britain and France. Any modifications to these arrangements, such as what to do with today's Iraq (Britain would take it) could be negotiated after the war at whatever peace conference was convened. One year later, when just such a conference was called to order in Paris, Faisal, who essentially outmanoeuvred his father to take control of the movement, was originally not even invited to attend, nor was any other important Arab leader, though he ended up, temporarily as events turned out, as the titular 'king' of Syria.

Lawrence told Allenby he would not work with any Frenchmen, and requested leave, which the general granted, perhaps pleased to be rid of this peculiar individual now that his usefulness had largely passed. Lawrence left the city for England on 4 October, never to return to the Syria he had so loved. 'I was tired to death of these Arabs'.

Chapter 16

Berlin: Black Hours in a Red Tide

'New Year's Day, which throughout Germany and the whole of the world has been greeted as the year of peace, began with a cold and dreary day.'

Admiral von Müller, diary entry, 1 January 1918

In September 1914, barely a month into the great war, Helmut von Moltke the Younger allegedly told the kaiser, 'Your Majesty, we have lost the war'. He was referring to the collapse of the great scheme to envelop Paris, thwarted by the French in truly dramatic fashion at the desperate Battle of the Marne. Von Moltke realized that the ambitious gamble involving the violation of Belgian neutrality (which ensured Britain's entry to the war) and the necessity for a stunning, quick victory, had been lost. Two years later an American businessman visiting Germany related the following conversations he had had with well-placed officers of the imperial army. 'They admit that they cannot win the war, or succeed at sea, or win the economic struggle against England, but they think that their army cannot be beaten and that the war will end somewhere in the region where the respective armies are now situated.' If the then-present commander of German forces, Erich Ludendorff, had, in seeming contradiction, both curbed his ambition and not lost his nerve, that scenario might well have worked, and a negotiated settlement, instead of Germany's utter defeat, might have transpired. As 1918 began, however, Ludendorff essentially lost faith in the German people. Perhaps the lesson of tsarist Russia frightened him; perhaps he understood too well the pernicious character of socialist and revolutionary viruses that could strike a people down when they were subjected to economic and psychological hardships. Remaining on the defensive was certainly the appropriate strategy to follow in 1918, but Ludendorff could not bring himself to believe in it. Instead, he decided on another 'gambler's throw', a stupendous attack that would brush aside whatever stood in its path, achieve that ever-elusive breakthrough and scatter the enemy in two directions, one to the sea (the English), the other towards Paris (the French). Once again the persistent desire for open country lured him on, and the implacable belief that he could not be stopped, overruled what should have been a more cautious, but potentially successful, strategy. Operation Michael would destroy the German capability to prolong the war.

Churchill, in a postwar analysis, was scornful of Michael. 'The reader will now observe how low the art of war had sunk', he wrote, and indeed, Ludendorff himself did not consider the proposed battle as anything particularly subtle. He would 'chop a hole. The rest follows'. The hole, however, was to be a big one, created by some 6,000 pieces of artillery concentrated on only forty-three miles of front, most of it occupied by General Sir Hubert Gough's Fifth Army, or what was left of it after Passchendaele. In only two days, 21 to 23 March, as Pétain rightly noted, 'this army [would] no longer exist'.

Despite the many instances of Gough's deficiencies in high command (related earlier), he was not without determination, experience and some intelligence. He knew he would be attacked, and correctly predicted how the German offensive would unfold – 'a short bombardment up to about six hours, and the most strenuous efforts to obtain surprise' – and the probability that 'these efforts I cannot be sure of defeating … in view of the state of my defences'. GHQ replied with a variety of scenarios in reply to his bleak assessment, most involving a fighting withdrawal and the necessity of giving ground, however grudgingly, if he was attacked. Gough disliked the condescending tone of his instructions. It reminded him of teaching grandmother how to suck eggs. Though a specialist, as he saw it, of the offensive, he never doubted his ability to conduct an adequate defence, but even he admitted that 'I was unaware of the magnitude of the coming attack'. No one else was either.

Douglas Haig had had a difficult several months following Passchendaele. Lloyd George took pleasure in condemning that battle as an 'utter fiasco' and now energetically looked for ways to shackle his commander in chief from undertaking any further campaigns along similar lines. Once again the prime minister became interested in unifying the command of allied armies under a single generalissimo – anyone but Haig. In November 1917 he helped insert a new layer of strategic responsibility, a supreme war council that would be stationed in Versailles. Sir Henry Wilson, Haig's avowed enemy (Asquith had called him 'that serpent'), was eventually selected as the British representative, an insult to the field marshal, who thought of Wilson as an incorrigible opportunist and intriguer. Whenever Wilson came in contact with someone who might do him a good turn, it was said, he got an immediate erection. At first this body exercised little real threat to Haig's position (as Repington recorded in his diary, 'The Versailles soldiers sent in a few memoranda, mostly general principles, such as two and two make four').

But soon these gentlemen were given supreme control over allocating reserve divisions – where and when they would be deployed – and this very critically undercut the field marshal's authority. The next month he was forced to fire Charteris, his intelligence chief, and the month after that Kiggell, a right-hand-man if there ever was one. The final blow came in February of the new year when Lloyd George removed Robertson as chief of the imperial general staff, replaced by, of all people, Henry Wilson.[1] Haig made perfunctory efforts to save Robertson, but in fact he barely lifted a finger for the man who had done so much infighting for him in London, and the former CGIS was understandably bitter. After the war he was heard to say over dinner at the Senior Service Club, that 'I'll never go farting with Haig again'. But the field marshal had other things on his mind, such as salvaging his own career. He could be excused if he felt that he was the next to be purged, but the German enemy saved him by distracting everyone's attention with Operation Michael.[2]

Certainly this campaign, launched in March, did not come as a complete shock. Most intelligence reports indicated that something was afoot, but where exactly the onslaught would fall was not clear. At first Haig felt he would be attacked along his northern fronts, near the coast; then he thought perhaps not. One thing is certainly clear: Ludendorff picked the weakest and most vulnerable front of all for his main thrust, Gough's. In retrospect it is hard to believe that Haig left the Fifth Army so exposed, especially given his foreboding that something big was coming (as he wrote his wife at the end of February, 'I feel in the words of 2nd Chronicles, XX Chap., that it is "God's battle and I am not dismayed by the numbers of the enemy"'). The Fifth had the longest front of his four armies, the weakest trench system and embedded defences, inadequate labour battalions to assist in making roads, laying cables and improving dugouts, and perhaps the most demoralized and thinly positioned troops under his command. In one conference, Haig informed Gough that many divisional generals refused to serve under him, and that common soldiers considered the Fifth unlucky. The commander in chief came to understand this fact of life only because the secretary for war, Lord Derby, had told him so. The antipathy to Gough, Derby wrote to Haig, 'is almost impossible to describe to you'. Gough was astonished to hear the news, and somewhat offended. The battering he had subjected his men to at Passchendaele seemed to have escaped his notice.

Gough certainly tried to make his front presentable, but he lacked the resources. 'We must make the best due with what we have' was his common rejoinder when pressed by subordinates for whatever it was they requested; he could not wave a 'fairy wand' and make things happen by wish. Still, he thought everything was in control. On St. Patrick's Day he entered two of his horses in a riding competition, and came in fourth out of 120. Wellington, after all, had attended a grand ball before Waterloo. A little past five in the morning four days later, the stupendous German barrage woke him up. Initial reports indicated that his entire line was under bombardment. He 'issued a few orders', then went back to bed. 'By 8:30, shaved, bathed and fed', he did the only thing men like Haig, Plumer, Charteris, Kiggell and he could do at such as moment. He stood by the telephone and waited.

Over the next forty-eight hours, the Fifth Army disintegrated. This is not to criticize in any fashion the courage and skill with which most of its men met the overwhelming assault of Ludendorff's striking force, which outnumbered the Fifth by a margin of eight to one, but many Canadians reported that they had seen British conscripts 'bolting in no sort of formation'. The fighting was some of the heaviest and most desperate of the war, and the German attackers paid a dear price as they advanced. But advance they did. It is one of the ironies of this war that in the futile attacks of 1916 and 1917, allied armies wore themselves out attacking defensive positions and never broke through, whereas in 1918 the Germans sliced through allied lines as though they were butter, advancing some forty miles (in World War I terms, an inconceivable distance). Gough lost 350 field guns and 150 heavies in just the two days. Fog obscured the battlefield so thoroughly that return fire from British guns (those that were left) was done 'by the map' instead of based on observation, thus diminishing their effect (many allied soldiers thought they were shelled by their own men). Ludendorff's orders had stressed speed: 'The fastest, not the slowest, must set the pace.' Allied resistance points were often bypassed, to be mopped up later, and though such pockets poured enfilading fire into the German storm troopers, the fact remains that huge incursions were made all over the Fifth Army's front. Gough, in his thoroughly delusional memoirs, credits the Fifth's defence as a victory of sorts. 'A retreat', he wrote, 'is not necessarily a defeat.' His withdrawal, he claimed, 'was a clearly defined manoeuvre foreseen months before it took place'. He told Repington, in fact, that the Fifth was never 'broken' even though he had lost sixty percent of his force. When Haig held an emergency conference five days later with all his army commanders, Gough was not instructed to attend. He and his command were now irrelevant. One day after that, he was sacked. Haig muttered a few words in his defence, but a scapegoat for what appeared to be an unraveling of the entire front was required. The field marshal gave a few minutes' reflection that perhaps he should take responsibility for the unfolding debacle himself, but this inner rumination was short-lived. 'I was conceited enough to think that the army could not spare me.' Gough was certainly bitter when he left his post, 'not at all sure where I was to get a bed or dinner that night'. Not only had he been deserted, in his view, by his own compatriots, but he had had to suffer the indignity of being dressed down, to his face, by Marshal Foch. He claimed that the only panic he had observed was from London and GHQ.

At German headquarters, the early mood was ecstatic. First reports had been better than anything that could have been hoped for. The enemy 'had taken a terrific pasting', read the initial assessment, and the kaiser, once more in his 'hurrah' mood ('well in the saddle once more', as an aid put it), ordered champagne after disembarking from his private train (but not before yelling at a startled guard an impromptu greeting at the top of his lungs, 'The battle is won, the English have been utterly defeated!'). Such good news would not last, however, this was truly the last throw.

The next several days were fraught with tension. Haig issued an uncharacteristically florid declaration to his armies: 'With our backs to the wall ... there is no other course open to us but to fight it out.' This text was greeted with both pride and incredulity. According to the acerbic historian A. J. P. Taylor, 'this sentence was ranked with Nelson's last message'. However, 'at the front, the prospect of staff officers fighting with their backs to the walls of their luxurious chateaux had less effect'. To many, the war, in a sudden instant, seemed lost. Lloyd George felt Haig seemed 'rattled', George Riddell, that Haig 'has lost his head'; a still embittered Lord French said that both Haig and Robertson both should be 'court martialed, taken out into a square, and shot'. The prime minister went to church but found little solace in prayer, especially the plea 'O Lord, make haste to save us', saying to himself, 'Hurry up or You will be too late!' An emergency meeting of allied politicians and commanders at Doullens on the 26th finalized Lloyd George's campaign to disenable Haig. Marshal Ferdinand Foch, rehabilitated to some degree from his disastrous performances in the beginning of the war, was given command of all forces in the field. This was certainly a moment of utmost peril, and he greeted his new position with words that will long be remembered. 'It is a hard task you offer me now: a compromised situation, a crumbling front, an adverse battle in full progress. Nevertheless I accept.'[3]

Foch was saved by the stiffening resistance of all the allied forces (except, perhaps, for the token Portuguese troops, who must have wondered what they were doing there in the first place; these men broke and ran whenever the going was tough). In fact, the Herculean efforts of Ludendorff in launching the heaviest attack of the war were beyond the capability of his troops to sustain and, at a critical moment, he himself lost his bearings and missed a critical opportunity to push for complete success. Like sand running out from an hourglass, the tide of battle turned. In a series of counterattacks, which turned into full-scale offensives against the enemy, the Germans were repulsed, pushed back and then placed utterly on the defensive themselves. In heavy fighting over the next three months (known as the 100 Days), the entire complexion of the war changed. Though never routed, German troops were harried and pressed to the point of sheer exhaustion, many losing heart and surrendering (two-thirds of all German losses from Operation Michael to the end of the war were battlefield captures). Leading these attacks, in great measure, were dominion units, and most particularly the Canadians under Currie. The foe were often tenacious, however, fighting like 'a cornered rat' as he put it, and twenty percent of total Canadian casualties were suffered during this period; but the end, miraculously, seemed in the opinion of some to be in sight, so much so that Henry Wilson, the new CIGS, felt compelled to warn Haig against futile attacks against prepared positions that might cause unnecessary (and unpopular) casualties. People at home were worried that the field marshal was more than capable of launching 'another Passchendaele'. Haig considered this advice an impertinence. He also felt fully vindicated, having predicted since the Somme that the Germans would collapse. That, of course, had been two years and thousands of deaths ago.

'War is like this. Here is an inclined plane. An attack is like this ball running down it. It goes on gaining momentum and getting faster and faster on condition you do not stop it.'

Marshal Foch

Over the gloomy summer and early fall months, depleted German units stood battered as French, British and freshly arrived American forces (well over one million of them) launched relentless attacks along the western front. The military historian Liddell Hart described them as 'beating a tattoo on the German front'. According to Lieutenant-Colonel Bernard Montgomery, 'We really have the Bosche on the hop.' Germany's allies were not faring much better. In Austria-Hungary, 1916 saw Emperor Franz Joseph finally gone (pneumonia), succeeded by a young man of twenty-eight whose childhood personality had been marked by 'an exceptional sweetness of character.' This was not a trait, otherwise commendable, that would equip him to deal with the collapse of his empire. Karl I of Austria (crowned Karl IV in Hungary) was a well-intentioned and reasonably bright individual, but his situation was desperate from the very beginning. Only two years into the war, Austria-Hungary had suffered casualties of over two million men, and whatever enthusiasm had once existed for continuing the conflict was evaporating by the day, most particularly on the civilian front where scarcity of food and household basics had reached crisis proportions. Galicia, for example, produced over a quarter of the empire's grains. Now overrun by armies marching back and forth, and further damaged by poor weather at harvest time, the agricultural output of the empire had dropped by half in just two years. Bread was leavened with sawdust, Vienna's soup kitchens served 54,000 people a day, the workweek was extended to 66 hours, all abyssal conditions that would extend well after armistice day. When Freud sold an article to a Hungarian journal, he asked for payment in potatoes.

The contagion of social unrest infected the workforce, now wracked by strikes. Raw materials ran scarce. Church bells were melted down, as were door handles. The customary distribution of photographs showing the new emperor and his wife, Queen Zita, dressed (as the occasion warranted) in the royal robes and crowns of either Austria or Hungary, did little to assuage an increasing anger in the populace. If anything, it illustrated the growing divide. Continued reports of military failures generated 'an increasingly hostile mood towards us', reported a German diplomat, 'as if [the Austrians] are shedding blood for *our* war'. Sarajevo seemed a generation earlier, for all that it mattered.

The new emperor, 'young, very earnest and rather disconsolate', was outspoken on the need to find a way out – any way out – that might bring the war to an end. Emperor Karl had given up any notion that his empire might survive; he would be happy to retain Vienna and the Germanic portions of the old dominions if he could. As he sent out frantic feelers to initiate a separate peace, a process he secretly began just a month into his reign, his 'flabby' attitude was heartily condemned at general headquarters in Berlin when rumours started flying that Austria was squirming to get out of the war. The kaiser called him just 'a boy, weak-kneed and easily led'.

Some of the allied powers responded with lukewarm replies to his overtures (Emperor Karl requested a personal meeting with Woodrow Wilson, which the president ignored) but the emperor lacked the necessary forcefulness to push his genuine desire for peace into effective political action. Owing largely to his background, he relied on old tools of diplomacy, such as private emissaries recruited from the aristocracy, who were to initiate negotiations among their own in either the hushed backrooms of private clubs or through royal go-betweens such as the king of Spain. This was far too genteel, considering the circumstances. 'Mr. Lloyd George said he wanted no diplomats', reported one of these courtiers to the emperor in Vienna. 'Diplomats were invented to waste time.' On the other end of the spectrum were members of the bureaucracy and army, along with his German allies, who were constantly agitating that the emperor remain firm. His assurances to them that he would were considered at face value as lies and evasions, especially when Karl, as 1918 rolled towards its end, agreed to all sorts of desperate concessions to constitutionalism and federalism, whereby components of the empire would be granted autonomy within their own borders. By that point, those very peoples were declaring themselves independent republics, and being recognized as such by the various allied governments. The emperor would later rue his decisions. 'I first tried to rule autocratically, and then democratically', he told a British liaison officer; 'both were errors, but of the two the latter was the greater.'

Turkey was in even worse shape, thrashing about for any way to sidestep complete dismemberment, and 'the main object of the Bulgarian king is to avoid assassination', as von Müller put it. King Ferdinand, the gentleman in question, was reported to have muttered a melancholy farewell when he left Mannheim after his annual taking of its medicinal waters. 'Au revoir. Next year, I shall be back again for the cure as a private gentleman.' The kaiser and he 'have both outlived our time'.

In Berlin and many other cities, strikes were now commonplace and revolutionary rhetoric at dangerous levels. Ludendorff's blithe enabling of Lenin was now back to haunt him. The Russian embassy in Berlin, flying a huge red banner, was a hothouse of agents, spies and clandestine operatives whose mission in life was to undermine the reactionary regime of Wilhelmine Germany.[4] Berlin, as a relatively 'new' metropolitan entity when compared to other European capitals, was not so much a collection of antique housing and ancient palaces as it was an important industrial centre with a largely working-class population. This proved to be prime recruiting territory for socialist provocateurs. Going on strike was presented as a way to support the troops, punish warmongers, bring the battles to an end and hasten the demise of the Hohenzollerns. Even the kaiserin grew alarmed. Hearing of a proposed strike, and the kaiser being absent, her handlers rushed her to a restive factory to mingle, cajole and sympathize with the workers. She handed a particularly ornate medal to one of the shop stewards 'which, as evil tongues affirm, he promptly hung around his dog's neck which accompanied one of the processions next day'. At the front, things were even worse.

By September, everyone in the know, including Ludendorff, realized that the German army 'was obviously at the end of its tether'. Ludendorff had what many considered a sort of nervous breakdown on the 28th. Thereafter he oscillated between desperate appeals for the politicians to arrange an armistice at any cost, to violent pledges to fight a scorched-earth strategy to the very end. Unfortunately for him and Hindenburg, the puppet chancellors they had more or less ensconced in office (Georg Michaelis and Count Georg von Hertling) were inferior men incapable of resolute action, incompetents who had lost whatever governmental cohesion or control there might once have been over the Reichstag. There, opposition deputies ratcheted up the volume excoriating the continuing war, described by Oskar Cohn, a socialist, as 'a family affair of the Hohenzollerns'. Through all this, Wilhelm remained isolated, 'full of lust for battle' at one moment, but 'ill and depressed' at the next. When members of his government in Berlin called for guidance or some sense of direction, he continued his habit of refusing to come to the telephone. Visiting headquarters or anywhere near the troops, he would instruct conveyers of bad news to 'leave me in peace'. One evening, von Müller noted that 'the kaiser said at dinner that he was now at the front, and at the front he refused to speak to any civilians'. When in Berlin, his wife shielded him from the slings and arrows of an ungrateful nation. The kaiser, she warned, needed rest. When occasionally cornered, he often spewed more bombast. He had the country and the army behind him. If there was any trouble from the deputies, his chancellor has 'my final decree, the revolver, in his pocket'. This continuing contempt for politicians pretty much sealed his fate. On 25 October, Ludendorff threw in the towel. 'There is no hope. Germany is lost.' This ruthless individual 'was like a cat on hot coals', said one observer. At any moment his front was liable to collapse like a dyke surrounding flat Dutch countryside. If that happened, he and Hindenburg could guarantee nothing but chaos and revolution.

'It is a pitiful sight to watch the death throes of a great nation.'

Evelyn Mary Stapleton-Bretherton, born to a family of English gentry in 1876, was not the anomaly that on first appearance she might seem. In 1907 she married the fourth Prince Blücher, a German aristocrat and direct descendant of Count Gebhard von Blücher, the crusty Prussian field marshal whose timely arrival on the battlefield of Waterloo in 1815 had sealed the Duke of Wellington's victory over Napoleon. The famous painting by Daniel Maclise depicted their handshake, on horseback, when the two met at a Belgian crossroads as night fell on 18 June, the Prussian cavalry already embarked on their merciless harrying of the retreating French. In grateful thanks, Blücher had been awarded a magisterial estate known as Krieblowitz in Silesia with hundreds of acres, serviced by indentured peasants living in adjacent villages, clustered around the obligatory and palatial castle. Evelyn's new father-in-law, however, having inherited the generic Prussian trait of inflexibility, had quarrelled with domestic authorities in the fatherland and, in a pique of annoyance, he rented Herm, one of the Channel Islands, and removed himself there to raise, what else, kangaroos. Having argued with just about everyone, including his son, Evelyn had few dealings with the man. She and her husband lived in the convivial milieu of well-to-do aristocrats in Edwardian England, visiting county houses, hobnobbing with the rich and famous of London's café society and generally not having a care in the world. The war changed all that.

In just about every capital of the various warring countries, nationals of the enemy were treated with immediate vitriol and suspicion, regarded as vermin, potential spies, the killers of innocent children and other exaggerated offences. London was certainly no different. In the space of just a few days, Evelyn's life was turned upside down. Her husband was ordered out of the country (as was her father-in-law, whose presence just offshore France offended authorities there), and she suddenly found herself on a railway platform with German Ambassador Prince Lichnowsky and the entire embassy legation, some 250 people. The atmosphere was funereal, 'as if a dead man was being borne away'. Despite the fact that Evelyn would have four brothers in British uniform during the course of the war, one of whom would die, and another be crippled, along with a whole assortment of cousins and relations also in uniform, she found herself an exile because her husband was a German.

Amid the confusion of war, this entourage of diplomats and castaways arrived safely in Berlin, having passed (by her count) sixty-six separate troop convoys going in the other direction, an extraordinary display of 'absolute order and expeditiousness'. Berlin was not as comforting. No one would cash her cheques, they were without funds for over a week, they were crowded into lodgings at the International Hotel, a magnet for the dispossessed amalgam of émigré foreigners who had, by ill chance, married foreigners. One of Evelyn's friends, a princess, was typical: half-Dutch, half-English, and married to a German. They were surrounded by people, many threadbare, all in the same pickle and constantly aware that everyone's eyes were on them (particularly the hotel's staff). Evelyn and the other 'guests' from England had to be certain never to speak their native tongue either in public or over the telephone. Politics was a subject rarely broached in mixed-nationality dinner parties (of which there was a constant stream), and 'anti-German inclinations' were to be avoided at all costs. Police authorities were a constant nuisance. Despite his noble pedigree, her husband was frequently harassed and embarrassed on account of suspicions directed towards Evelyn. As the military governor of Berlin said to him, 'I mean to teach German princes not to marry English wives.' Through all this Prince Blücher, now safely ensconced in his ancestral castle at Krieblowitz, did not offer them either a reichsmark or a sanctuary.

Evelyn's diary has proven a treasure trove for historians interested in the day-to-day mood swings of the Berlin populace. She was, by and large, an astute and generally impartial observer, though many of her entries are a wearying recitation of tea and party dates with their social ramifications. Counts, generals, aristocrats of every stripe, subservient butlers and even Roger Casement parade through her pages, along with commentaries on the usual and often banal Red Cross activities for which she and her set volunteered. For whatever reason, she maintained a generally sympathetic feeling for the kaiser throughout the war. Her pity for him in the autumn of 1918, when the entire Wilhelmine era came crashing down, makes for painful reading. She was, of course, mourning the demise of the world she loved.

As early as 1916, Evelyn was aware of trouble on the home front. 'Austria wants peace at any cost', she notes. 'Men coming home from the front are beginning to murmur.' Food shortages due to the British sea blockade, after only two years of war, were beginning to appear. The well-known propensity in Germany for the swelling girth of its men and women 'has become a legend of the past'. The kaiser had become 'a pathetic figure', often discussed with 'scorn'. Some were saying that one of the emperor's six sons should be sent to the trenches and 'sacrificed', just to show him the private agonies that too many German families were experiencing. Not many people were parading through the streets any longer crying 'Ave, Caesar!' when referencing the kaiser.

War news, heavily censored, was disbelieved. 'Every advance of the enemy [is portrayed] as an elastic bend in the German line.'[5] The submarine campaign was seen by just about everyone as Germany's 'last card'. Debate in the various levels of the parliament, to which her husband belonged, was no longer civil or united behind the war effort. Whenever the chancellor of the moment appeared, members of all political persuasions were 'ready to tear his speech to rags', turning the assembly into a cacophony of discord. 'As for the mood of the people, the heroic attitude has entirely disappeared.' The 'turnip winter' of 1916/17 was merely a portent of even worse conditions one year later (over the course of the war, it was estimated that German civilians lost half a million tons of weight). Not only food, but clothing, shoes and coal (the last 'seems suddenly to have disappeared from the face of the German

Empire', according to our diarist, resulting in 'pipes bursting all over Berlin') now became scarce and precious commodities. Things were to be no better in the countryside, as the suddenly elevated Princess Blücher would discover.

In September 1916 old Prince Blücher fell from his horse and subsequently died. His son, as heir presumptive, now succeeded to the title … and everything that came with it. In a scene that the widow of every titled scion must have dreaded, the estranged son turned up at the doorstep of Krieblowitz and oversaw his father's wife's removal, along with her entourage, from the princely splendours they were used to enjoying, to be replaced by Evelyn as the new chatelaine of the household. Evelyn could not believe her good fortune. 'It is not easy to describe the difference which suddenly took place in our lives', she wrote. 'After having existed for more than two years in a bed-sitting-room in a hotel, we all at once found ourselves in possession of several beautiful castles and estates, a palace in Berlin, and many rich acres of land in the country. In fact it all seems like some new phase of the *Arabian Nights*.' This sense of good fortune soon evaporated. Food remained scarce. Over eighty farm workers had been drawn away by the war, replaced by Russian prisoners who sullenly brought in a meagre harvest. Food on the table was whatever Prince Blücher could shoot in the woods. Good servants were impossible to find. 'The fowls are exasperating and will not lay any eggs.' Evelyn wants a pig slaughtered, but political reality steps in the way: 'The whole province of Silesia [would] watch the act with hungry faces, counting how many mouthfuls we appropriate.' In Berlin, occupying the luxurious Blücher mansion, within eyeshot of the Brandenburg Gate, butlers soon must draw the shutters and disguise the family's presence. At Krieblowitz, it was the peasantry whom one had to fear; in the city, the proletariat. This was not a time 'for timid people'.

'*I'll tell you something. Unless the war ends within three months the people will end it without their governments. I can't have a wager with you because should this happen it will be impossible to pay the debt.*'

Count Ottokar Czernin, Austro-Hungarian Minister to Romania

Three months? How about three days. On 3 October, thrashing about for a new chancellor, the kaiser's attention was directed towards a mildly liberal monarchist, Crown Prince Maximilian of Baden, as possibly the only choice left to lead a government that would have no option but to seek peace without a moment's delay. This was such an unappealing diktat that no one bothered to ask the chancellor-to-be if he would accept the appointment. They just assumed he would do his duty. As the prince later wrote in his memoirs, he felt like a man who had just awoken from a deep, deep sleep, only to remember that he was about to be executed.

Never had a man faced more dire complications than Maximilian of Baden (to his friends he was just 'Max'). His appointment had not been universally well received. Ludendorff said with considerable understatement (rare for him), 'We had not much in common', and another general dismissed him as 'an arrogant ignoramus, incapable of any work at all'. On every level (except perhaps the civilian population, currently starving on diets of 1,000 calories a day, who sensed that the war was lost), Prince Max dealt with dizzying levels of incomprehension from just about all sides. First there was the kaiser. His nerves frayed and genuinely exhausted from four years of 'war', the All Highest was numb to the ominous portents that clouded his future. He knew Germany faced defeat, but he failed to recognize with any seriousness what this meant for the Hohenzollern dynasty. Some advisers with fortitude had warned Wilhelm of the coming dangers for his family, some more forthrightly than others. The shipping magnate Albert Ballin told the kaiser that if he did not initiate peace feelers soon, 'revolution will break out', with obvious personal consequences. Admiral von Müller stated in April 1917, 'I was able to say to him for the first time during this war that he was fighting for his throne.' The result, recorded in the admiral's diary, was that the kaiser grew 'very excited' but otherwise remained oblivious. A few minutes after any bad news, he could revert to his 'well-known, impossible Victory mood'. Müller despaired. 'Once more a rich dinner', he wrote, 'with the same bunch of idlers' whose main purpose in life was to shield the kaiser from depressing reality. Ballin went so far as to complain that Wilhelm lived in 'Cloud-Cukoo-Land'.

Certainly one ominous sign was perfectly obvious. For over two years, according to innumerable observers who noted such things in their diaries, Wilhelm had been regarded with near universal contempt by average men in the street. They considered him to be the originator of their collective miseries, and were no longer susceptible (if indeed they ever truly were) to his bombastic, outdated and highly charged rhetoric. His naval adjutant, among others, deplored the fact that the supreme war lord had no contact to speak of with his subjects, that he had no idea what ordinary people were either thinking or experiencing. Nights at the kaiser's headquarters were scenes of surreal detachment. When the kaiserin was present (to the despair of everyone) and arrived at the dinner table 'in full regalia, studded with pearls and diamonds', a collective groan could almost be heard from around the table. The kaiser was to be relied upon for pep talks to the troops, usually mitigated by the generous distribution of medals, but oftentimes these speeches were 'excessively long' and 'incomprehensible to his audience'. In front of civilian workers, his talks generally fell flat. In one address at a munitions plant, he was greeted, before and after, in complete silence. Prince Max knew what all this meant, but Wilhelm did not. For nearly two years the word 'abdication' was on the lips of too many people for the implications of such loose talk to be ignored. The kaiser, however, lived in some other world.

Until the end of September, the generals too had remained insensitive to reality. Their contempt for the political process remained keen. Ludendorff and Hindenburg, virtual dictators since their successful campaign to oust Bethmann Hollweg, the last chancellor Wilhelm ever appointed who had a glimmer of intellect (aside from Max), translated this contempt into the self-assurance that they understood such things as economics, parliamentary politics, public relations and the entire gamut of processes that make civil government work. In fact, they were rank amateurs, used, as Ludendorff put it, to 'banging their fists on the table' in order to be obeyed. This was not the way to get things done, aside from sending men over the top in yet another costly attack. When Woodrow Wilson announced his famous Fourteen Points, the generals wilfully miscalculated the American president's intent. These were not starting points over which diplomats might dispute, argue and negotiate, as Ludendorff chose to believe. He saw them as a breather, a respite, a tool behind which – as the useless politicians, a pack of chatterboxes, haggled with their equally inept counterparts from Britain, France, America and Italy – the general could rest, repopulate and rearm his army before restarting the war machine in six or eight months.[6]

Max regarded such thoughts absurd. The Fourteen Points, as he recognized from the start, were non-negotiable. They constituted a demand for surrender, pure and simple. With momentum on the enemy's side, with the German army on its heels, with the home front teetering, how could anyone think differently?

The third oblivious entity were politicians back in Berlin, particularly leaders of the Social Democratic Party. Prince Max must have wondered at their capacity for realistic thought. The world was now their oyster. Most Reichstag members had been shocked into near speechlessness when Ludendorff had announced at the end of September that the war was lost (the news of which had leeched throughout the Reichstag by the next day), but many in the socialist camp had howled with delight. 'Now we have got them!' one said, referring to the generals, and the fate of the kaiser was seen as not far behind. As much as Max hoped to save the monarchy, he quickly understood that such an option was almost unattainable. The facts spoke for themselves; as Gustav Noske, a man of common sense, put it, 'if the kaiser goes, we will get a better peace'. This pained Max. He was royalty himself, after all – Wilhelm was his first cousin – but the matter was effectively out of his control. He had to end the war, undercutting the generals if necessary; he had to transfer the reins of government to leaders the people would trust and follow in order to avoid almost certain anarchy. With significant courage, his aims clarified, he turned to the only party he could, the Socialists. To his astonishment, they had no idea what do to with this glorious opportunity, the culmination of their life-long dreams. They lacked the ruthlessness of the man who was watching all this very closely from the other side of the border, Vladimir Lenin.

The German Social Democrats (SPD) controlled a third of the Reichstag seats. With all the right-wing, nationalistic deputies in severe disrepute because of the dire news from the front, they were the only significant party left standing who had a sense of cohesion and some rapport with the discontented elements of German civilian life, so demoralized and rebellious that law and order stood threatened. But the SPD was, in fact, far from united. No political ethos has been so riven by ideological discord than socialism, and such was certainly the case within Germany. Theoreticians had been busy for thirty years dissecting, analyzing and arguing about the works of Karl Marx (himself a German), but no consensus had ever been universally accepted. The SPD was split into three basic, and ever shifting, schools of thought. The majority adhered to the fundamental tenets of mainline socialism: better conditions for the working class, a redistribution of wealth, the nationalization of key industries, the abolition of the monarchy. As war descended on the nation, however, they reverted to a strain they had generally condemned, namely nationalism: yes, the war was monstrous, a fulfilment of Marx's theory that capitalists would continuously foment conflict for the sole purposes of profit and power. But who would do the dirty work? Workers, of course, fighting in trenches and killing other workers on the other side. But when the kaiser appealed for war credits in 1914, the SPD put aside its long-standing principles and voted in favour. Germany was threatened, after all, so how could good Germans not support their own? Lenin, sitting in Zurich, could not believe it. Here was the beginning of everything he hoped for, the final death rattle of capitalist society, and the SPD was supporting the war machine? In typically dismissive language, Lenin called them a pack of whores.[7]

Splinter groups emerged within the SPD. An 'independent' group, small in number and joined together in a somewhat amorphous fashion, adhered to the Leninist line that coming revolutions were international in character and not to be characterized as 'Russian', 'German' or 'French'. The unifying element, regardless of nationalities, was to be the oppressed proletariat. To these men, supporting financial credits to fund the war was hypocritical, and they rejected voting for any measures that might enable or prop the crumbling edifice of free market capitalism. The Independents generally supported the SPD in most of their political manoeuvres, but they could be shifty and touchy on matters that undermined Marxian fundamentals. The third element, typically, were the extremists, few in number but strident and doctrinaire, disrespectful of mainstream socialists and seemingly as intent on destroying them as they were in bringing down the monarchy. Their scorn and contempt knew few bounds. In the political maelstrom that swept Berlin and the other major German cities beginning in late September 1918, they were shrill and bellicose voices for radical change. In Berlin they were led by two firebrands, Rosa Luxemburg and Karl Liebknecht.

Luxemburg, forty-seven years old, was an intelligent, educated and well-travelled revolutionary, having agitated in, and fled, a variety of countries. Like Lenin, she had found herself for periods of time in the relative security of Switzerland, but when the call to the barricades came, she honed in to the heart of things, Berlin. Her main vehicle of expression was in the pages of the *Die Rote Fahne*, or 'The Red Flag', which she largely wrote, printed and disseminated throughout the city. She was the resident intellectual of the movement. Liebknecht, a former deputy of the Reichstag, forty years of age, bespectacled, slight, with the looks of a Heidelberg professor, was the son of one of Marx's great friends. While often personally disorganized and dishevelled in thought, there was one ability he possessed that few were able to equal. He could light up a crowd. Thrown out of the SPD for his outrageous behaviour, arrested and jailed for subversion, he became both a martyr and a hero. Prison did nothing to moderate his views. When released in one of Prince Max's general amnesties (undertaken to assuage the workers), he yelled to the adoring crowd waiting for him outside the walls, 'Two years ago I went into prison a socialist. I have come out of it an anarchist. I will tell you the reason why.' During the chaotic days of Max's hurried deliberations, Liebknecht was all over Berlin, driven to and fro from one mass meeting to another on commandeered army trucks flying the red flag of revolution. He was becoming an unstoppable force. As far as Max was concerned, Liebknecht was an issue the SPD had to resolve, as he stated plainly to its leader, the long-time socialist Friedrich Ebert. Ebert did not have to be told this bleak news, he knew it already.

'The bitterest moment of my life.'

Erich Ludendorff, 26 October 1918

With a sigh of relief, no doubt, Prince Maximilian turned over the government of Germany to Ebert on 9 November. In doing so, he realized that his own role in the public life of his country was over. He would never inherit, as was his hereditary right, the crown of Baden. He would never be a monarch. His mansions, estates and wealth might, in fact, evaporate if the socialists had their way. But he had fulfilled the mandate he was given to do, no matter the wretched results for the social caste he represented.

Max was one of the few individuals between 1914 and 1918 who 'bearded the lion in his den', as Sir Walter Scott had once put it. On 25 October he had issued the kaiser with an ultimatum: either Ludendorff had to go, or Max would resign. The latter was unthinkable; even the kaiser realized that immediate revolution would be the result of such a resignation, which would be seen by everyone as the 'price' for Ludendorff's retention of power. The very next day, at a meeting in Berlin described as 'icy', the kaiser told the once mightiest man in Germany that he was out. 'I was no longer capable of astonishment', Ludendorff later said, this was 'the bitterest moment of my life'. Wilhelm, who never developed any feelings of gratefulness or appreciation for the services of others, said not a word of thanks to his crestfallen soldier, but merely dismissed him from his presence, Hindenburg looking on in relative silence. Out in the courtyard, the generals whom the kaiser had ridiculed as the 'siamese twins', parted acrimoniously. These three men would never meet together again. Ludendorff returned to headquarters at the front, gathered up his things and went to the station for a return train to Berlin, where he would take refuge in a rented room, fearful that radicals might crash through the door at any moment, haul him out into the street and shoot him. Generals more famous and talented than he (Marshal Ney comes to mind) had suffered just such a fate 'There I stood in Spa', Ludendorff later wrote, 'in the prime of my life, at the end of my military career.' No one wept to see him go.[8]

Exercitus facit imperatorem
'The army makes the emperor'

Old Roman saying

Max was thus unburdened of one liability, but he had another to go – the kaiser himself. While once hopeful that a regency might be established under the aegis of the still-popular Hindenburg, in which one of the crown prince's least objectionable sons could be named the heir presumptive to the Hohenzollern throne, he soon gave up that notion. Berlin, in a real ferment, would not hear of such a thing, nor in all practicality would the enemy, to whom Max was in the process of sending a delegation to discuss an armistice. The kaiser, who refused to make a decision about his future, would have to be pushed. When Max picked up the telephone to convey this news to Wilhelm, however, he was shocked to find that the kaiser was intent on fleeing Berlin. With the army, or so the logic went, he would both be safe from a seat of government fast turning 'red', and be at the head of an armed and loyal force that, once an armistice was declared, could be marched back to the capital as a reactionary hammer to crush his insubordinate subjects. The unfortunate similarities between the kaiser and King Louis XVI of France, whose pathetic attempt to escape Paris in 1791 had ended ignominiously at Varennes (and then two years later at a guillotine) was not considered. The only person more surprised by this move than Max was Hindenburg, sitting once again at general staff headquarters in Spa, Belgium. The last person he wished to see stride through the doors was Wilhelm.

The normally quiescent empress was apparently the instigator of this desperate move. She realized that her despondent and sometimes easily persuadable husband might well yield to Max's importuning for an abdication, but she was of stronger heart than Wilhelm.[9] She refused to consider any notion of surrendering the crown, and urged him on to Spa. She stayed behind to prepare for the worst, gathering together her valuables in case a sudden escape was required. Max was considerably disheartened at this development, especially as the kaiser continued his habit of refusing to take incoming telephone calls, no matter how urgent. With time running short, and Marshal Foch disrespecting the German peace delegation in a forest outside Paris, Max put an end to five centuries of Hohenzollern rule. On 9 November, he announced the abdication of Kaiser Wilhelm II. Then he resigned. This ignited a royal temper tantrum at Spa. Max was denounced as a traitor by his now ex-royal master, who was 'convulsed with rage'.

The ninth of November was probably the longest and most painful day of the kaiser's life. The imperial army and its officers had pledged their oaths of allegiance not to Germany or the German people, but to the kaiser. He was perfectly prepared to take advantage of that faith to unleash their power on the nation itself. The day saw much loose talk about artillery, bombs, poison gas, machine guns – the entire panoply of war – that he was prepared to launch into Berlin. As a socialist delegate had said earlier, Wilhelm 'wanted to make his subjects love him by means of a stick'. Also percolating in his ever-fertile mind was the notion that Britain could still be approached to side with Imperial Germany in a scheme to depose the Americans. Did King George V really think that American troops would return home once the war ended? Of course not; they would be used to topple the British Empire. Wilhelm proposed a 'European Monroe Doctrine' that would spell out to Washington and Wall Street that their ingenuous presumptions would not be tolerated. The kaiser envisioned that Japanese troops, detraining in Serbia, would help Germany and the British to expel these presumptuous newcomers back across the Atlantic. But as these wild schemes were debated, 'taking up a good deal of time' in the words of one aide, German units were fading from sight, men here and there slipping away through the woods to join thousands of other loiterers behind the lines, spreading rebellion and socialist propaganda along the way. It was suddenly apparent at headquarters that the situation was deteriorating with a rapidity no one could have expected. Even troops assigned to protect Spa, allegedly loyal to the core, were disappearing, those remaining on duty refusing to salute their officers. Not only could Hindenburg no longer guarantee his kaiser's safety, he was surely now thinking about his own. At late morning and early afternoon conferences, interspersed with walks in the gloomy, rain-soaked park surrounding his quarters in Spa, the kaiser, Hindenburg and Ludendorff's successor, quartermaster general Gröner, met in funereal circumstances, surrounded by advisers. Many of these argued that the kaiser should indeed lead his troops to Berlin and reconquer the fatherland. An admiral present scoffed at that idea, since it bore 'no relation to the realities of the moment. I openly declared before His Majesty, and before all present, that His Majesty had no need of an army in order to take a walk. His Majesty needed an army which would fight for him', and such was manifestly not presently the case. Gröner informed Wilhelm that the home front was a shambles; supply lines to the front had been broken by revolutionary elements; there was no place for the army to turn. Wilhelm replied, 'In that case I shall place myself at the head of the units that remain loyal and I shall restore order'.

'That would mean civil war, Your Majesty – and war within the army itself in addition', replied the general.

'I don't believe that!' the All Highest retorted. He then demanded the loyalty of his army. Gröner replied that, in reality, the kaiser no longer had an army. Wilhelm reminded his two generals about the oath that every soldier gave to follow the orders of their emperor without question. Hindenburg squirmed, stuck in a swamp of inarticulate grief, leaving it to Gröner to apply the coup de grâce. 'Today', he told the kaiser, 'oaths are but words'.[10]

At 5 a.m the following morning, the kaiser's train departed Spa, headed for the Dutch border, but it did not get far. Revolutionaries had taken over the railway yards in Liège. Even though the train was garrisoned with at least twenty well-armed troops, the notion of gunning their way through to Holland was ridiculous. Wilhelm was transferred to a motorcade and, taking back roads, the retinue appeared at a minor customs station at about dawn, to the stupefaction of local authorities. The kaiser spent most of that day pacing along a train station platform smoking cigarettes, waiting for some indication as to what the Dutch government planned to do. Belgian workers, who could see him across the border, spent several hours, according to a witness, 'staring, pointing, hooting and jeering'. When arrangements were finally made, he was transferred to a nobleman's estate who lived nearby. Upon arrival, he asked his host if he was a Freemason. When assured of the man's Protestant piety, he then ordered a cup of English tea.

As for the empress in Berlin, she was beyond shocked by these developments. Arrangements had previously been made regarding the safety of the crown jewels; she now turned her attention to packing away as many other precious goods as possible for the trip to Holland, largely arranged by Dutch authorities. Queen Wilhelmina, for instance, was of the opinion that Dona should be by the kaiser's side more or less immediately, to give the state of exile 'a more private character', as opposed to the perception that the kaiser's retinue of military officers might just be a male cabal plotting the downfall of the newly formed German Republic. One uncharitable observer made the following comment on Dona's unseemly preoccupation with material possessions: 'The loss of her throne had not affected her so much as the possible and eventual loss of her wardrobe.' Before dawn on a frigid winter's morning she was driven to the railway station, accompanied by only two attendants who had refused to desert their mistress. A solitary conductor escorted her to an appropriate compartment, lighting the way with a lantern. The station was crowded with soldiers returning from the front lines, all armed and loaded with equipment. Street battles and bloody riots with socialists, anarchists and workers awaited them. No one recognized the kaiserin as she departed to join her husband. When next she returned to Berlin three years later, it would be in a casket.

The Forest of Compiègne

'What is the purpose of your visit? What do you want from me?'
                    Marshal Foch, to the German peace delegation

With these condescending and contemptuous remarks, Marshal Ferdinand Foch greeted the German peace delegation on 8 November 1918 at a railway siding in the middle of the vast forest of Compiègne, once the hunting grounds of French kings in search of deer and boar. Now it was the Germans who were to be skewered. The assembled diplomats from Berlin, only one elderly soldier among them (as though to advertise their peaceful intent), were probably the most dishevelled and depressed group of men in the German empire, and their mission the most thankless. To some degree, the initial German proposals for peace during the preceding month had been adroitly handled. Exchanges of proposals and notes had been directed to Washington, to the desk of President Woodrow Wilson, whose Fourteen Points seemed a promising basis for the launch of negotiations. Berlin obsessed over the word 'negotiation', implying as it did the give and take of talking points as opposed to being presented with ultimata. It also had the agreeable byproduct of avoiding discussions with France, Britain and Italy, which promised to be far more acrimonious. With typical obtuseness, however, German military leaders refused to call off military operations or create a lull that might be conducive to measured discussions. In particular, the continuing U-boat campaign could do nothing but poison the atmosphere, especially on 10 October when the RMS *Leinster*, an Irish mailboat, was torpedoed, sending over 500 mostly civilians, many women and children, to the bottom. Wilson's attitude certainly hardened as the month of October dragged on. He was unfamiliar with the persona of Prince Maximilian, and unaware of the problems with which Max was dealing. As far as Wilson was concerned, it seemed pretty clear that the kaiser and his thick-skinned generals still ran Germany, and he could not believe anything they proposed for a minute.

As far as the other allies were concerned, fury with Woodrow Wilson was percolating at a high pitch. They did not want the American president to communicate with the enemy without their consultation; they did not want their war goals diluted by someone who had been, through most of the war, almost removed from the process. Britain had lost close to a million men, France 1.3 million. If anyone was going discuss peace terms, it would be London and Paris, and by 'discuss' they meant 'demand'. In their minds, Wilson's pre-eminence in the negotiating procedure undercut their role and threatened what most of them wanted – the destruction of Germany as a world power. In order to do that, generals like Haig insisted on a crushing military victory, one so thoroughgoing that Germany would have to accept 'an ignominious peace'. (Sir Henry Wilson's diary is full of disparaging remarks on 'that ass Wilson ... He really is the limit ... [should be] put in his proper place ... His Fourteen Points (with which we do not agree) were not a basis for an armistice, which is what the Boche pretend they are ... Wilson is acting on his own ... the war is *not* over, the Fourteen Points are *not* an armistice, an armistice in not *peace*'.) Wilson and the other generals, like the American president, had no idea that Ludendorff and Hindenburg regarded the war as lost. Foch, for example, was depressed by the realization that fighting would probably continue throughout 1919, though he had no doubts about the ultimate decision. 'Materially, I do not see that victory is possible,' he had said, though 'morally, I am certain that we shall gain it'. The enemy presented few signs of giving up; they 'accepted battle everywhere'. He was mildly surprised when told that Germany was serious about peace. Hearing the news, however, did not give him joy and relief, only a sense of resolve. Despite the fact that allied armies would not be occupying Germany or marching through Berlin in triumph, he would make certain that their ability to rest, recover and fight another day would be denied them. His heart, and certainly that of his premier, Georges Clemenceau, was hardened to the fate of Germany.

Max's peace delegation arrived at 7 a.m on the morning of 8 November in considerable secrecy. Compiègne, forty-seven miles north of Paris, was a 35,000-acre preserve, deeply forested and remote. The German train pulled in to a small switchyard, the other side of which was Foch in his train. He sat in passenger car # 2419-D, soon to be the most famous in world history. The seats had been removed, and a conference table erected in the middle, with chairs facing one another on either side. Here the marshal received the enemy.

In reply to Foch's question as to what they wanted, the German spokesman at Compiègne replied with the obvious answer, to be given 'the proposals of the Allied Powers towards the conclusion of an armistice'. To this Foch said, 'I have no conditions to give you.' That was followed by a long period of awkward silence. The delegate then brought up President Wilson's last received note, which Foch dismissed out of hand. Nothing Woodrow Wilson had to say mattered at this particular moment. Foch was not sitting in the middle of these dreary woods to discuss or negotiate anything. 'Do you wish to ask for an armistice? If so, say so – formally.' The delegates then began to realize that, in the old French phrase, *'les jeux sont faits'* – the game was up.

Prince Max, and the entire German foreign office, were looking for a Congress of Vienna style of conclusion to the war as their best-case scenario. In 1814, the victorious powers who had defeated Napoleon met in the Austrian capital to rearrange several borders and to settle their nations' differences. Restoring the decrepit French Bourbons to the throne was one of the several items on their agenda. Lord Castlereagh of Britain had arrived with a retinue of just fourteen advisers. Any disagreements would be settled in the familiar company of gentlemen with similar backgrounds and persuasions. In the forests of Compiègne, however, any pretence of reciprocity proved non-existent.

Foch laid down the allied terms for an armistice. They contained nothing about armies remaining in place until peace treaties could be signed, nothing about 'peace without victory', as Wilson had once trumpeted. The German army, though not technically defeated, would be treated as though defeated. The Germans would immediately evacuate all foreign soil; they would leave behind huge stockpiles of weaponry and ammunition; the entire fleet would steam to British ports for internment and, obviously, confiscation; likewise all U-boats; German forces would abandon their positions on the west bank of the Rhine; not only that, at three German crossing points they would surrender 'pockets' on the eastern bank amounting to thirty kilometres each, which would be occupied by allied troops. This last provision guaranteed that Germany surrendered her last geographic advantage. In the event of reneging on any articles of the armistice, the allies would have a foothold in Germany proper from which to resume offensive operations. And to make matters even worse, the allied blockade that was starving Germany would continue indefinitely, a staggering proposition that would only encourage civilian unrest (Foch didn't care, that was Germany's problem). None of these items were subject to negotiation. Not only that, Berlin had a meagre window of but seventy-two hours, or until 11 a.m. on 11 November, to accept or reject. This was pretty much a demand for unconditional surrender, and as yet none of these articles had even mentioned the most dreaded (and inevitable) word, 'reparations'. The delegation asked that fighting cease while they communicated with Berlin, in the hopes of saving lives, a curious consideration since the previous four years had witnessed more occasions possible to count where human life had been frittered away as so much chaff. Foch refused, got up, and left the room. He was very pleased with himself.

By now, of course, Prince Max was no longer chancellor. Friedrich Ebert had taken his place in a process that was, as a matter of law, illegal since no one in any constitutional authority had actually appointed him. That mattered little at the moment. Things were devolving into such chaos that he saw no choice but to end the fighting immediately. At 8 p.m. on 10 November a message sent in the clear that Berlin accepted all conditions. Fighting would cease at 11 a.m. the next day.

10:58 a.m., 11 November 1918

The enemy withdrawal still presented many bloody battles, and the Germans, with customary ruthlessness, disregarded several conventions of war. Without warning they bombed a hospital behind the lines at Les Éparges in a night attack. Attracted by the fires, more warplanes repeated the assault. With explosives falling, the operating theatre continued full bore. Sixty persons were killed, including some nurses, and eighty were injured. Adding the *Leinster* to the list of atrocities was also bad publicity for Germany to overcome. Scenes such as these did not put allied troops in a very forgiving mind. Nevertheless, by 7 o'clock the next morning an official communique was issued by Haig to the men under his command. At 11 a.m. an armistice would begin. The war, it seemed, was finally over. Only five hours to go. This interval would be disastrous for Canadian General Arthur Currie and his postwar legacy.

The Canadian Corps under Currie, who had so distinguished themselves during countless bloody battles, was now attached to British General Henry Horne's First Army. Horne was an old-school Haigean, a not very bright or original soldier, a man Liddell Hart dismissed as 'stupid'. He did not lack for courage, of course; few of these men did. He had been in charge of the rear guard during the British Expeditionay Force's retreat from Mons in the first days of the war and, as he wrote his wife on 8 November, Mons was a stain he wished to efface. 'It would be a great satisfaction to me to take [it] … I am pushing the troops' (10 November).

Much has been made of the fact that Horne could have marched into Mons anytime after 11 a.m. on 11 November. It was a condition of the armistice that German forces withdraw to certain positions, and to leave places like Mons behind. Horne would have entered the city, bands playing, in complete triumph. He preferred, however, the more satisfying course of taking the place by force of arms, and the Canadians, as was usual for the 100 Days, were to clear the path.

Horne, by this point, had had enough of Arthur Currie, confiding to Haig that the Canadian was 'suffering from a swollen head'. Horne disliked Currie's penchant for arguing over orders, his preconditions before setting off to accomplish the tasks given him (more artillery!) and his somewhat sullen attitude. Currie, for his part, was tired of the British. They rarely gave credit when credit was due, they took the Canadians for granted, were indifferent to their losses and, even after three years at war together, their condescension was as marked as ever. Mons had been a mythic element in the mythology of World War I (the 'Angels of Mons' had appeared, mirage-like, to foil the Germans in their 1914 attacks), but Currie did not think it was worth any men to recapture. Currie was 'old school' in his own fashion, however. Orders were orders, and he obeyed them. He was taking a bath at his headquarters at 7:50 in the morning of 11 November when he heard about the armistice, to begin at 11 a.m. No instructions were given to ease off during the interval. Instead, the Canadians continued to advance, showing their customary 'dash'.

It is a matter of confusion (and argument) how many Canadians fell on 10 November and early on the 11th as they captured Mons; far less than critics imagine is probably true. But at 10:58 a.m., Private Henry Price, born in Falmouth, Nova Scotia, and drafted into the army just the previous year, was shot through the heart by a German sniper as he and his compatriots were clearing a house of retreating enemy soldiers. He was the last of some ten million soldiers to be killed in this conflict. Two minutes later, the Great War officially ended. Private Price would not live to hear the pipes of the 85th Canadian Novies as they paraded down the main street of Mons to the cheers of Belgian civilians. He would join what were estimated to be some 11,000 needless casualties who fell wounded or dead in the final hours of the war along the western front. Some of these, incredibly enough, were suffered at Mons when a cavalry charge, of all things, was actually ordered to take a bridge over a canal. These men were mowed down by German machine guns. Was there ever greater folly? Fifty years later, Private Price's comrades made a trip to Belgium, and unveiled a small plaque on the spot where he had fallen. That house has since been demolished, and the memorial re-erected somewhere else in the town, though no one at the visitors' centre, when I visited Mons, knew anything about its location. Price is buried in a small military cemetery outside the town, next to nine other Canadians and several Germans.

In the streets of the allied capitals, pandemonium ruled as mobs of celebrants paraded through the streets, many inebriated. The writer Katherine Mansfield, friend of D. H. Lawrence and Virginia Woolf, was disgusted. There they were, she said, 'singing the good old pre-war drunken rubbish'. Georges Clemenceau wrote in his memoirs, suitably entitled *Grandeur and Misery of Victory*, that he sat down and burst into tears.

'There are reports current here to the effect that King Ferdinand is going mad and is subject to fits of melancholy and weeping. This, I presume, we may class with the rest of the reports of this nature, according to which all the remaining monarchs in Europe should have been long since dead or in a mad-house; although the responsibility for this war is enough to send anyone into an asylum.'

Princess Evelyn, Berlin

Everywhere in Germany, minor revolutions were replicating events in Berlin. Ludwig III, king of Bavaria, was toppled, igniting much agitation in the Catholic south that Bavaria should secede from the empire, or at least what was left of it. There was no love lost for those 'pigs of Prussia' who had destroyed the country. King Frederick Augustus of Saxony fled Dresden, along with most of his family, helter-skelter into the countryside. His eldest son hid out in an apartment in Breslau, but because he was afraid to identify himself, he lacked the necessary ration card to buy even bread. His sister found herself running across farm fields with nothing in her pockets but a toothbrush and a hankie. The crown jewels of the principality, worth two million reichmarks, were smuggled out of Dresden by that royal caricature, the ever-loyal family servant, who dressed himself up as a Red Cross official. When he made it to safety, the jewels were trundled off to a hiding place in a wheelbarrow. The king ended up at one of his remote castles in the forests of Silesia, but he was ordered out by a delegation of reds, who at least had the courtesy to offer him a ride to the railway station. He refused to get into a car waving a red pennant, however, and indignantly ordered everyone off his property, an injunction met with laughter.[11]

Princess Blücher offered him a suite of rooms at her own castle at Krieblowitz until he could get his feet back on the ground, but no one with a title was safe there for long. Evelyn and her husband made the rounds of tea parties in Berlin, hobnobbing with émigrés in various stages of destitution, until it was too unsafe to walk about outside. Mobs would strip the fur collars off their elaborate winter coats, or steal any pair of shoes that looked at all new. Many of Evelyn's friends found themselves walking home barefoot in the early winter chill. Officers were especially vulnerable to the ill whims of the crowd. Epaulettes could be torn off, and decorations stripped and thrown to the ground. Admiral von Müller was issued a regulation revolver to carry about for protection when he took long walks in the Tiergarten in his uniform. He overheard people saying things like, 'They won't be strutting about like that for long.'

As November slid into December and beyond, the street scene in Berlin became wilder. Rosa Luxemburg and especially the rabble rouser Liebknecht were 'the people of the hour', but as Evelyn noted in her diary, 'We are all very unclear as to what exactly he wants.' This was an extremely unperceptive observation; it was clear to just about everyone in Berlin, and certainly those who read the millions of broadsheets that were scattered about hourly from passing trucks, that Liebknecht and the radicals, known as Spartacists, were planning a coup against the Social Democrats, an uprising that would copy the example of St. Petersburg just thirteen months previously. Ebert, trying desperately to retain control of the government, saw himself in the same unenviable position as his Russian counterpart, Alexander Kerensky – a middle-of-the-road parliamentary liberal too radical for the army and the arch right wing of the junkers but, alas, a pathetic milksop in the view of Liebknecht and the mob. The only question in anyone's mind was when Liebknecht, the Robespierre of Berlin, would figuratively pull the trigger.

Princess Blücher eventually got the message. On 5 January 1919, some 50,000 Spartacists marched through the main fares of the city, parading by, among other places, the Esplanade Hotel, the address for many a royal refugee. The future was pretty clear. Liebknecht and his crowd, when they hit the streets for real, reinforced by armed sailors from Kiel, would begin 'by plundering the big private houses'. Many watching this massive demonstration knew they had to run for it. Prince and Princess Blücher eventually made their way to Holland, then home (at least for Evelyn) in England. Germany was finished for her.[12]

She undoubtedly took pleasure in the events of 5–15 January, but one cannot know for sure, because she stopped keeping a diary. For once in his career, Liebknecht had botched his timing, the Spartacist attempt to seize power having begun on the 5th more or less spontaneously by radical workers whom he made little effort to control. Once things started, he refused the entreaties of Luxemburg, among others, to push back the throttle into neutral. Rosa feared, quite rightly, that the moment had not yet come, that the uprising was premature and would force Ebert into a corner. As even Marx had said, communist uprisings would inevitably 'be answered with cannons'. Like the rat he was, Ebert did what Luxemburg predicted. He turned to the army.

As is generally the case, an impending disaster can often make for strange bedfellows. Ebert was no revolutionary. He believed in order, just not the monarchical variety that Germany had suffered through three decades of Kaiser Wilhelm II at the helm. He telephoned Quartermaster General Gröner at army headquarters and put it to him. Would the army support the government at this moment of bolshevik peril? Gröner replied that it would. The question was, however, what kind of army had Gröner at his command?

The Germany of 1919 was full of disillusion. Army units had marched home after the armistice in good order, but then had more or less dissolved. The average private or corporal had had enough of war; all he wanted was a train ticket home. If he could, he might sell his weapon to someone on the street for some spare change, but beyond that he was fed up. That was not true, however, for every soldier.

The war had brutalized millions. Some could readjust to the quiet life of peacetime, but others could not. Whether out of intense nationalistic allegiance, a feeling of betrayal perhaps or just for the nihilistic thrill of war, some veterans stayed in uniform, kept their discipline and did what they were told. Many joined informal units centred on a particularly charismatic officer, or simply milled about their former barracks with like-minded comrades 'from the old days', keeping their weapons at the ready. They remained contented as long as they were fed. In some respects, resembling a militia, they stood to guarantee law and order just for the sake of it; in others, they were motivated by intense feelings of hatred for those behind the front line who, they were told, had stabbed them in the back. Officers played on these emotions, being largely unreconstructed reactionaries. They no longer retained much affection for the kaiser (whom many disparaged on the grounds that his flight to Holland was an act of cowardice), but they did feel that Germany must be governed, as it had for centuries, by might. Gröner and Friedrich Ebert turned to these officers and their units, since famously known as the *Freikorps*, to crush the Spartacists, which they proceeded to do with a vengeance.

The *Freikorps* were stormtroopers for the most part, professional soldiers in their training and methodology, but with one important distinction from the years 1914–18. They were, as presently constituted, an 'unleashed' body of freebooters – not mercenaries or soldiers of fortune, but essentially freed from restraint by the ordinary conventions of military behaviour. They most closely resembled the Black and Tans, discharged British veterans who were to dragoon Ireland a year later. When the *Freikorps* went into action against the Spartacists in the first two weeks of January, they outclassed their opponents in firepower and cohesion. They showed no hesitation shelling public buildings, turning them into ruins; they showed no hesitation killing unarmed workers or those who attempted to surrender; they showed no hesitation when Rosa Luxemburg and Karl Liebknecht fell into their hands after most of the fighting was over. On 15 January, Luxemburg and Liebknecht were both pushed around, slapped, punched and generally abused by *Freikorps* soldiers at their temporary headquarters at the Eden Hotel (a misnomer if there ever was one). There the decision was made to execute the two of them. Liebknecht was led out to the back where he was savagely hit on the head with a rifle butt. Taken to the Tiergarten by six officers, he was shot multiple times and left dead on the grass. Luxemburg was also struck to the ground by a rifle blow, which may in fact have killed her. Driven to a frozen canal, she was shot in the head and her body dumped over the side of a bridge, where it lay unretrieved for five months. In May, when the ice had melted, her corpse was finally recovered. These judicial murders went largely unpunished, the price Ebert had to accept for his retention in power. The *Freikorps* would be a continuous thorn in the new republic's eleven years of existence, a hotbed of political intrigue, coup attempts and a breeding ground for the communist-baiting Nazi street gangs that did so much to propel Adolf Hitler into power. When Ebert was faced with another crisis, however, these same troops again proved useful, killing at least another 1,000 workers during their uprisings throughout the Ruhr industrial basin in 1919. In one of Rosa Luxemburg's last editorials in the radical press, she mocked the emphasis on 'Order', but it was this single-minded Germanic obsession, more than anything else, that made her a 'marked' woman and caused her violent death.

Chapter 17

Versailles: Where It All Ended
(or Should Have)

'What sort of peace would the Americans have imposed if a German army had been encamped for four years within fifty miles of New York?'

David Lloyd George

Several weeks before the actual Armistice Day of 11 November 1918, Marshal Ferdinand Foch called a meeting of the allied military commanders to discuss peace terms should the Germans ask for them. The handwriting was on the wall, in Foch's opinion; it was only a question of when. 'We are dealing with an army that has been pounded every day for three months', he noted with complete satisfaction. General John J. Pershing of the United States deferred to his French and British colleagues in the order of their remarks. He felt it only appropriate, given the discrepancy of their collective sacrifices, that he speak last. Haig, for once, squarely faced reality. Britain was done: she had no more men, no more money, no more resolve to go on. In his opinion, France was finished as well. As for the Americans, they were 'ignorant of modern warfare' and, in his opinion, 'cannot be counted on for much'. (These remarks were so intemperate that he afterwards apologized for making them in a note to Pershing, who replied that he appreciated the 'official correction'.) Peace terms, in Haig's opinion, should be generous enough not to encourage the Germans to resist any further. The time for fighting was over. Pershing, however, saw things differently. Nothing less than unconditional surrender would satisfy him. He had visions, it appears, of marching down the Unter den Linden in a victory parade.

Pershing caught flak for these remarks which, not helping matters, he had put in a memo for circulation. The civilian politicians all caught a collective whiff of ego and presumption from their military counterparts, and they quickly snapped the whip: the soldiers were technicians, advisers to their presidents and prime ministers. When it came to peace terms, they could keep their opinions to themselves. Clemenceau dismissed Pershing's remarks as 'theatrical'. Here was Caesar, just at the moment when a Caesar was not required. Others remarked that Pershing was getting 'the big head'; the

Germans were a beaten foe, and here was the American who wanted the glory of putting them away when the enemy's capacity to resist had been severely cramped. Again, to quote Clemenceau (and his resentments), the United States had reserved its strength so as 'to throw her full power for the supreme victory on the last battlefield'. Pershing was not anyone's idea of an evil genius, but a grain of truth lies somewhere in the bombast of post-hostilities' assessments. The general realized that his performance, and that of his men, had been uneven, often through little fault of their own (which was something he refused to admit in his memoirs). It was not an unnatural ambition to add lustre to a chequered battlefield performance, and marching triumphantly into the very heart of Berlin would go a long way to cleaning up the record. President Wilson was not impressed. He thought Pershing had gone 'glory mad'.

'My ancestors were troublesome Scotsmen.'

Woodrow Wilson

Thomas Woodrow Wilson, the 28th president of the United States, was arguably the most morally engaged man ever to hold that office. He may also hold the distinction of being the most stubborn, an attribute he certainly inherited from his ancestors. On both his maternal and paternal sides he was descended from Presbyterian Covenanters, followers of Luther, Calvin and John Knox, bred hard in their religious beliefs by years of exile, war, strife, persecution and long exposure to the rigours of living in climates that bred isolation and character (for better or for worse). Scotland and Ulster, two festering, rebellious sores that contributed to Charles I losing his kingdom and his head, haemorrhaged its peoples to the new world by the thousands for over three centuries, the Wilsons and the Woodrows among them. America did not soften their enthusiasm for religion. The president's father was a minister, his mother the daughter of a minister; the woman he married in 1885 was Presbyterian as well, her father likewise a preacher. The atmospherics of family life was thus totally resonant of the 'ould kirk', an outlook that stressed predestination, the personal direction by God of a man's life, the notion of a covenant, or pact, between the Almighty and his chosen people. It did not permit of disobedience or lack of faith, and could often be a hard, inflexible road indeed.

Wilson was a southerner. He grew up largely in Virginia, and retained vivid memories of the Civil War years and their thoroughly unpleasant after-effects. He never forgot the squalid intrigues of Ulysses S. Grant's administration, which was remarkable for a boy not yet in his teens, but an early sign that his interests included current events and politics. Despite all the clichés of strict Covenanters and their rigid mores, Wilson had a lively temperament and enjoyed life. He was not dour, despite his diligence as a student, and certainly harboured ambition, both romantic (which he did not indulge until his twenties) and professional. He was interested in the law (but not in being a lawyer) and government (he loved writing constitutions, with rules and regulations, the first of which he authored at seventeen years of age for a theoretical Royal United Kingdom Yacht Club). Attending Princeton University (his room was near that once used by Edgar Allan Poe), he was a middling student but a fine formal orator, debating clubs taking up much of his time. Pursuing an academic career (he was a popular professor of government and the author of several books), he reached a pinnacle of sorts by being selected president of Princeton in 1902, authoring several important initiatives at that school intended to raise its intellectual and democratic character (he was successful in the former category, but failed in the latter, which encouraged his resignation).

More or less handpicked by powerful local bosses to run for governor of New Jersey, a state then dwarfed in most ways by neighbouring New York, Wilson surprised everyone, including himself, by winning handily. He quickly repudiated the unsavoury characters who had initially supported him, men like party boss 'Sugar Jim' Smith, and proved the sceptics wrong by proposing and pushing through several pieces of progressive legislation. Flashing a sense of humour, he said that anyone who could master the politics of being a college president could easily handle whatever came his way at a puny state capital in New Jersey. Being something of a fresh-looking success story, he found himself in the thick of things from 1911 on, when he manoeuvred himself (with a great deal of help) into the swirl of presidential politics. He was a talented speaker, a very bright man with ideas, incorruptible and with high expectations both for the country and for himself. Taking advantage of former president Theodore Roosevelt's rash decision to run as a third-party candidate against the man he had previously anointed as his successor, the incumbent Taft (thereby splitting the Republican vote), Woodrow Wilson, at fifty-two years of age, squeaked into the White House, as remarkable a turn of events as it was unexpected. If World War I had never happened, he would likely have been one of the more successful and self-satisfied presidents in the nation's history.

That being said, Wilson had his share of opponents who could not stand the sight or sound of him. No one really enjoyed Wilson's addresses to Congress: to some it reminded them of schooldays, a teacher lecturing his students. Others reacted more viscerally, that the president was acting like a king, his speeches compared to addresses from the throne. His progressive values galvanized opponents, conservative Republicans and big business interests, who viewed the president as a self-righteous prig, and who resented his constant preachiness and high moral tone (Henry Ford called him 'a small man'). Wilson had nothing but contempt for them; Republicans, he said to his doctor, gave him gas attacks, enough to poison anyone within range. He came across, to those who did not like him, as doctrinaire, unyielding, smug and humourless. This was a public persona that he never really shed.

While Wilson could seem remote and chilly in manner, he was, when among intimates, 'witty and genial' company. Fond of limericks, *double entendres*, singing, corny jokes, golf (a game he was truly miserable at) and, unfortunately, 'negro' stories (full of the 'n' word), he found tremendous domestic comfort within the circle of those whom he felt he could trust. These included both the women he married (his first wife died in August 1914, distracting him, to say the least, from the events that led to the world war in August of that year; he remarried sixteen months later); his personal physician, Rear Admiral Cary Grayson, and his alter ego, the deferential Colonel Edward M. House. Other than these few individuals, the president, as an observer noted, 'seems to have almost no intimate friends'.

Colonel House (the title was purely honorific, having something to do with Texas, where he was born) proved to be the éminence grise of Wilson's circle. Independently wealthy, he was passionately interested in politics but saw no future in it for himself. Of diminutive stature, a pedestrian speaker, with a reserved, almost shy persona, he seemed the antithesis of a cheap, backroom pol (of the sort, for instance, who put Wilson in the governor's mansion). Though self-effacing, soft-spoken and 'colourless', he was a superb behind-the-scenes operator, a political 'Merlin' according to one observer, who smoothed the way, shouldered the burdens and did whatever proved necessary to further Wilson's career path and various agendas, two items that the president considered as one with a sort of missionary zeal. Since their first meeting in 1911, where the two men hit it off instantaneously, House proved indispensable. The president, in point of fact, relied on him almost exclusively, barely consulting his cabinet on the matters he considered of most importance. House did not seek glory or credit for himself. His devotion to Wilson appeared supreme. But behind the featureless façade, Lloyd George, for one, perceived the tinge of self-interest that actually motivated the Colonel:

> Wilson was his idol, but his in the sense that it was House who had picked him out, shaped him as a politician, built the altar for him and placed him there above it to be worshipped. As a party leader Wilson was not the creator of House, but his creation. All the same there could be no doubt of House's genuine admiration and worship for what was the work of his own hands. He recognized that he had chosen first-class timber. [1]

Colonel House, in effect, became Wilson's de facto secretary of state, a status that William Jennings Bryan and then Robert Lansing, who had thought the office and its duties theirs, quickly came to understand.

The Great War in Europe put Wilson to the test. He wanted nothing to do with it, a sentiment most Americans shared, but, as an enlightened humanitarian, the leader of a nation with enormous untapped industrial resources on which the combatants looked with envy, he saw his duty to act as a mediator from the position of strength as the most powerful neutral nation on earth. House was sent on missions to the various European capital cities where his interviews provided the president with up-to-the-minute bulletins on where matters appeared to stand. These were, practically speaking, fruitless when it came to actually formulating a peace through private channels. In Berlin, House found jingoism running mad; in Paris and London, a commitment to see things to the end, no matter what. Despite these conversational dead ends, in December 1916 Wilson made his first formal offer of diplomatic intervention, pointedly asking the combatants just what it was that they were fighting over. No one could give an adequate answer to that question because there was no answer. As A. J. P. Taylor wrote, the war had no aims other than mastery, mingled up with the urge, pure and simple, to fire guns and kill the perceived or traditional enemy. The old 'balance of power' equilibrium had been thrown out of joint, and the only resolution that a small body of statesmen and generals could think of to restore it was waging war. This was so shocking an admission that it was generally camouflaged, according to that great cynic, George Bernard Shaw, by the 'crude melodrama' of making the kaiser, the tsar or anyone convenient, a villain. 'The common soldier', he wrote, 'is never trusted with the truth'. For Woodrow Wilson, the situation was the stuff of tragedy, a specifically European tragedy that he was intent to keep the United States out of. When the *Lusitania* went down in May 1915, the president practised restraint, as he would in the face of many other provocations as well, using the words that he (and Americans in general) were 'too proud to fight'. Senator Henry Cabot Lodge of Massachusetts, who detested Wilson, called this 'the most unfortunate phrase that he ever coined', and the very remark gave Lodge's friend Teddy Roosevelt a metaphorical heart attack. Fuming, sputtering, 'beating himself to pieces against a wall', Roosevelt very nearly called the president in public what he frequently called him in private, a 'lily-livered skunk' and 'an abject coward'. This did not deter Wilson. In his state of the union speech before congress on 22 January 1917, he called for 'a peace without victory', and first floated the idea of a League of Nations. In his opinion, the only solution to the war was a stalemate, a situation where no one could claim a battlefield triumph and dictate peace over a drumhead. It would be best, in other words, if no one won.[2] This was anathema to hardliners in both Germany and Britain. As Lloyd George put it, if Wilson's offer of mediation was accepted, a truce might be declared, and 'once the war was stopped it would [be] impossible to resume it'. In other words, a fate worse than death.

Getting Ready

Certainly America did not want war, and neither Germany nor Britain wished to see the United States enter the conflict on the opposing side. Yet neither combatant could desist from provoking the president into a declaration that he would. Wilson's nerves were strained to the maximum. Britain's seeming arrogance on the high seas knew few bounds; its blockade over the entire northern European approaches from the Atlantic, intended without a blush to starve civilians and to force Germany into a surrender that could not be achieved on the battlefield, was an arbitrary and borderline illegal act in its effects on neutral shipping (not only the merchant marine of the United States, but those of other important maritime countries as well). To many Americans, this strategy smacked of colonialism, another reminder of Britannia Ruling the Waves as she saw fit (her savage treatment of Ireland after the Easter Rising adding another layer of resentment in America). But poor British behaviour paled alongside that of Germany, which retaliated to the blockade with submarine warfare on a grand scale, which it ran with varying degrees of ruthlessness, reflecting an ongoing tug of war in Berlin between hardline militarists who would not, as the British newspaperman C. P. Scott put it, tolerate being starved to death, and those moderates (usually civilians) who thought provoking the United States to be a ridiculous blueprint for final victory. German policy regarding submarines went through several gyrations, more or less in response to American howls of indignation, the *Lusitania* fiasco being only the most sensational. Wilson's campaign slogan in 1916, 'He Kept Us Out of War' (which he personally felt very uncomfortable about using), reflected his success on one occasion, after yet another outrage on the high seas, of extracting concessions from Germany without recourse to arms. But in April 1917, extremists represented by the likes of Ludendorff took yet another of their high-risk gambles, and removed all restraints from their U-boat commanders, who were permitted to attack just about anything afloat without warning. Wilson, in effect, had no choice but to go to war. The insouciance in Berlin that year matches that of twenty-four years later, when Hitler returned the favour after Pearl Harbor as he too, almost by whim, added the United States to his lengthening list of opponents. The result would be the same in both cases. What were some of these people thinking?[3]

The man Wilson selected to lead the expeditionary force to Europe was an experienced Indian fighter, Major General John J. Pershing (as a young man, Pershing had pursued the Apache chief Geronimo, and then 'General' Pancho Villa).[4] In June 1917, the fifty-seven-year-old Pershing arrived in France with the first contingent, which by the end of the year would total some 146,000 men. Nearly two million more would follow, numbers that would never have been possible without a draft law, always controversial in any democracy (the speaker of the house of representatives condemned the measure, saying a conscript was nothing more than a convict). One hundred thousand of these Americans would never return home alive. Pershing visited the ornate tomb of Napoleon; he was encouraged to unsheathe that great general's sword, in the hopes that a shred of genius might rub off on the rough-hewn American. On 4 July, he was led to the tomb of the Marquis de Lafayette, and had his photograph taken saluting the man who had given his all to aid the American Revolution, but who had been lucky to survive its French successor. He was reported to have uttered the memorable phrase, 'Lafayette, we are here', and he later mourned the fact that he had not, as it became an instant classic back home (an aide had said it). Then he delved into war matters which meant, of course, bickering with those he had come to help.

ҫ∕∕ᴆ

Clemenceau

'The old Jacobin.'

Foch, referring to
Georges Clemenceau

Georges Clemenceau was a good hater. He hated his many political enemies (President Raymond Poincaré in particular), he hated Germans, he hated most army officers with whom he had to deal (some with more forbearance than others). He hated anything to do with Napoleon III, he hated idealists who had no idea what was going on around them, he hated defeatists. About the only thing he loved in life was France, which took precedence over everything.

Clemenceau, however, was not a run-of-the-mill nationalist; for most of his career he was deeply involved in radical politics of one sort or the other, and when out of office (which was not all that often as he aged) he owned, wrote and edited leftist newspapers and journals, the most influential of which was *L'Aurore*. Born in 1841, he was an old man by the time the Great War broke out. This led many people to believe, correctly as it turned out, that most of his frames of reference when dealing with governmental affairs after 1917 when he became, for the second time in his career, the prime minister, would be tinged by the past as opposed to the future. World War I, for him, was merely an extension of the Franco-Prussian War of 1870: the opponent was the same, the stakes were the same, the dreadful losses, defeats and despair were the same. Nothing much had changed to alter his attitude about anything.

He certainly paid for his beliefs. He had been jailed as a radical, he had been forced into exile for his beliefs (to America, where he met his wife), was often hounded for the various controversial opinions that he never hesitated to publish, and an anarchist fired five shots at him during the Versailles peace conference, one of which found its mark. He was in the eye of the storm during the famous Paris Commune, which could easily have cost him his life (the downfall of Napoleon was one of the highlights of his career); and his long trajectory in French politics during the ensuing Third Republic represented an exhausting catalogue of controversy. He became known by his nickname *Le Tigre* ('the Tiger') as he ruthlessly ruined one ministry after another, seemingly satisfied with destruction for its own sake, as he refused to occupy the ministerial vacancies he so often created, a seemingly sterile strategy for a politician with known personal ambition. The Dreyfus episode, perhaps the most debilitating, long-running and corrosive scandal ever to afflict any contemporary European society (combining as it did anti-Semitism, treason, espionage, cover-ups of blinding crudity and virulent rhetoric almost beyond description) saw Clemenceau at the very centre of public discourse. He ran over 600 articles excoriating the injustice meted out to Captain Alfred Dreyfus by the upper echelon of the reactionary French officer corps, the culmination of which was his publication in *L'Aurore* of Emile Zola's famous denunciation, *J'Accuse!* ('I Accuse'), which was the equivalent of throwing a bomb into a crowded room. When Zola died in 1902, his ashes were removed from their initial burial site six years later and transferred, with great solemnity, to the Panthéon. As prime minister (his first tenure of that office, which lasted for three years), Clemenceau effectively hogtied his top generals and forced them to attend, much to their humiliation. He was a man who brooked no disrespect. Foch called him 'the old Jacobin', a remark that was not offered as a compliment.[5]

Stability in the French government during the early days of the war was not its outstanding feature. Ministers came and went – many old, decrepit and inept – as did governments; generals like Joffre had little time for civilians, and treated them with either contempt or indifference.[6] Clemenceau was different. His long history of republicanism, his distaste for monarchs and the officer corps, his disgust with how the war was being waged, made him strident in making certain that his voice was not only heard, but obeyed. For the first time in three years (he took the oath of office on 16 November 1917), a genuine strong man headed the government, an irony to say the least, as Churchill noted. Clemenceau was the last man on earth that most of the political establishment wanted at the helm, he said, but the old French *chien* was the only figure left of any reputation to whom it could turn at this moment of acute danger. (President Poincaré, who returned Clemenceau's disdain, had selected him with the fatalistic remark that 'so long as victory is possible, he is capable of upsetting everything! Now that everything seems to be lost, he alone is capable of saving everything.') Without allies, without friends, without confidants, Clemenceau shouldered the burden alone. At times he forgot who was in his cabinet, not that it mattered to him since they were barely consulted. The niceties of government did not interest him either, nor anyone's feelings. 'You wish to sleep with Madame Poincaré?' he said to an office-seeker outside his office. 'Ok, my friend, it's fixed.' He didn't care if Poincaré heard the jibe or not.

Clemenceau's entire focus was to win the life-or-death struggle with Germany. Nothing else mattered. His belief in France was primal. Despite everything wrong with his country, it was his first concern, top priority and the graveyard of his early beliefs. Gone were the precepts of his beloved radicalism, gone was his sympathy with socialist mewings for a negotiated peace. He would let nothing bar the way to victory. Press censorship? Fine. Jail men for their defeatist attitudes? Again, fine. Military sideshows like the Dardanelles? Nonsense, the western front was all that mattered. A magnanimous peace for Germany? We'll see. 'My foreign and my domestic policy are ever the same', he famously exclaimed to the Chamber of Deputies in 1919. 'Domestic policy? I make war. Foreign policy? I make war. I always make war.' When Ludendorff's final offensive, Operation Michael, threatened to split the allied front, with Paris endangered, Clemenceau kept his nerves when everyone else could not. The fractured command structure of the separate allied armies was, to him, a recipe for disaster. He ramrodded through his demand for a real *generalissimo*, a man who, like him, would shoulder ultimate authority and responsibility, and he chose Foch. The appointment, a dream come true for that once-disgraced general, had its repercussions later on down the road when, through conceit, Foch let it be known that he had 'won' the war himself. Clemenceau did not hesitate to drop the hammer once more. He did not wish to hear such foolish talk again, he told his general. As a soldier, he should be quiet, do what he was told and respect the fact that civilians were in control of things in France, not peacocks in uniform. Clemenceau was the boss, and Foch had better understand that simple fact.

Clemenceau exasperated Lloyd George much of the time, but the old man charmed him nonetheless. He had the 'powerful and the square brow of the logician', the British prime minster wrote in his memoirs, 'the head conspicuously flat-topped, with no upper storey in which to lodge the humanities; the ever vigilant and fierce eye of the animal who has hunted and been hunted all his life. The idealist amused him.'

Black Jack

Pershing was a spit-and-polish soldier: demanding, strict, hard-working, diligent and concerned over both appearance and performance. He was an excellent leader of men, a thorough trainer, an officer who expected results, and grew exceedingly jealous when it came to his prerogatives and spheres of influence, though not a man who shared either responsibility or power lightly. Pershing had some rapport with his men, but not too much. When ordered to command African-American units, often known as 'Buffalo Soldiers', he did so without a qualm, something that could not be said for many other officers. On returning from the Indian wars to West Point as an instructor, his rigid professionalism alienated many of the cadets over whom he had charge, who called him 'Nigger Jack' behind his back which, as his career advanced, was softened to 'Black Jack'. It is unknown whether he cared about it one way or the other.

By 1917, Pershing appeared to have a great deal in common with the late, lamented Kitchener of Khartoum. Both were professional soldiers who had enjoyed long and distinguished careers. Both had seen combat, ordered men to their deaths and supervised operations in which considerable numbers of their enemies had been swept aside and slaughtered, their bodies left on the field of battle in bloody mounds or thrown into communal graves. This is what you did when you were dealing with heathens or Third-World peoples with few redeeming qualities. In Kitchener's case, his experience was in Africa and India for the most part, and with the civilian Boers of South Africa who, though rough and ready, were for the most part farmers and grazers. With Pershing, it was Apaches and Sioux, then Spanish conscripts on San Juan Hill, followed by Philippine rebels and Moro tribesmen, both halfway around the world. Pancho Villa's guerrillas were next, yet another collection of irregulars who were nothing at all when it came to a formal contest of arms. Pershing, like Kitchener, was well decorated for all his achievements on the field of battle, and had the usual worship for the venerable Anglo-Saxon infantryman, whose superior courage he took for granted. In so thinking, he generally neglected to evaluate the calibre of his opponents. He would soon discover that German storm troopers had little in common with Indians firing bows and arrows, that attacking a remote village in the middle of a Philippine jungle was not the same thing as rushing well-defended trenches and concrete pillboxes. For Pershing, as it was for Kitchener, Europe would present a steep learning curve for which little in his long experience as a military man had prepared him.

The arrival of Americans on the continent had been treated as a miracle, one that was coming none too soon. Pershing was appalled at the 'pessimism' he found in England, and even more disturbed by what he saw in a 'badly hammered' France. The disastrous Nivelle offensive from April 1917 had left French troops 'disaffected' and the populace 'depressed'. Meeting General Pétain ('not especially talkative') gave more occasions for gloom.[7] It became clear to Pershing that the allies wanted American troops in the line as quickly as possible ('trained or untrained', according to Foch, it made no difference); it was also clear that French and British generals felt entitled and eager to exercise more or less total control over their deployment in battle. This predisposition to lord it over 'colonials' did not please Pershing, in much the same fashion as it had not pleased the Australians, New Zealanders and Canadians (no one bothered to ask what that other dominion contingent, the Indians, ever thought). Pershing's troops, as he realized with some mortification, were green: untrained, raw, full of enthusiasm perhaps but unprepared for battle (in 1917, the American aviation corps had only thirty-five qualified pilots; Britain had over 230 'aces' alone). He had been upset in England watching British soldiers, recovering from wounds or conscripted, being hastily trained and then thrown, almost carelessly, into the maw. He had no intention of allowing American boys to suffer the same fate. He was also adamant that American troops, when they were set to go, would do so on his orders and no one else's, and as a recognizably 'American' army.[8]

Pershing, however, was just as green as his troops, and seemed to have learnt little from the fiasco of three years of stalemated trench warfare that he and all the military world had presumably been watching, if only as a courtesy to their joint professionalism. Just as deeply as Haig, Robertson or any of the French officers obsessed with *offensive à outrance*, Pershing believed in the power of the foot soldier, armed simply with rifle and bayonet, who could batter his way past anything. He was equally obsessed with the notion of 'breakthroughs'. After a war correspondent asked him soon after his arrival if such a thing was even possible in modern warfare, Pershing rolled his eyes and snapped off the reply that 'of course the western front can be broken. What [else] are we here for? You may quote me.' Implied in his response was that French and British generals had failed to achieve this result because they didn't know what they were doing. American soldiers were better marksmen; they would finagle their way through German trenches by efficiently knocking off the enemy with superior artillery support and better 'open field' training. Sergeant York, the Tennessee woodsman who could pick a flea off a Boche helmet with a single shot, was Pershing's idea of the perfect soldier. It would take a great deal to convince him of the contrary.

The appointment of Foch to supreme command in response to the all-or-nothing German offensive of 21 March (Operation Michael) did not change Pershing's view that American troops would operate as American entities, and not be homogenized, when needs required, into British or French units. Operation Michael had put the fear of God into every allied heart, however – Pershing found the scenes of panic at a Parisian railway station 'pathetic' – and the emergency forced the general, for the first time in ten months on French soil, to relent, authorizing the entry into 'hot zones' of American troops in significant numbers. In addressing officers of the 1st Division (among whom was Captain George C. Marshall of later fame),[9] he repeated a mantra that could have been said in the first days of 1914, the strangely antique notion that the 'will to win' was in itself sufficient for victory. 'We are a young and aggressive nation', he told them. 'Use your head, and hit the line hard.' It was time to show the Europeans a thing or two about fighting. Four days later, however, the 26th Division (Yankee) was battered by German veterans who overran their line, inflicting the first serious casualties the American Expeditionary Force had experienced. Lloyd George, in an 'I-told-you-so' mood, wrote that this sort of thing 'was bound to occur on an enormous scale if a large amateur American United States Army is built up without the guidance of more experienced [meaning, no doubt, British] general officers'. Pershing, who had a temper, seethed, but he would not be rushed. When American units were slowly integrated into combat situations, their performance improved (the struggle for Château-Thierry, less than sixty miles from Paris, was a good example), but the greatest test would come when an entire 'show' was planned, organized and implemented entirely by Pershing and his staff. The allies were not only eager to see the results, but desperate. The Americans seemed to be arriving, but when would they fight?[10]

While Pershing had his defects (a British diplomat called him 'an able man but not a great one', Smuts of South Africa said he was 'very commonplace', and Haig said he was 'obstinate' and 'stupid'), a genuine feel for administration and organization were not among them. The task he faced was logistically overwhelming, enough to crush any single officer (at one point he promised to provide the allies with 100 fully trained divisions, enough to win the war in 1919). Pershing did not delegate well, and tended to micromanage situations by often dwelling on unnecessary detail. Unlike Kitchener, however, he learned to adapt; the challenges were simply so large that he really had no other choice. He often ignored the strictures of reporting his every move and requisition back to the war department in Washington (hopelessly inept, in his opinion), and had little qualms in sacking senior officers for incompetence. When he gave a man a task, he often left him alone to do it, or fail to do it. The proof would be in the result was his adage. He could, and often did, lose his temper on occasion, rarely minced words and resented people who wasted his time. Franklin Delano Roosevelt, then assistant secretary of the navy, insisted on coming by with a delegation for a visit, which Pershing barely tolerated 'with his tight-lipped smile'. All these people 'wanted was to get shot at' without being hit, 'and to smell dead men and horses', according to one of the general's aides, but Pershing had sufficient charm and presence to handle them. When it came to men like Foch, Clemenceau, Pétain, Haig and all the others, his task was undeniably more difficult.

Clemenceau found Pershing 'friendly but obstinate'. Foch found him just plain obstinate, and the two men clashed repeatedly as the summer of 1918 progressed. Foch wanted constant pressure on the Germans. He had a feeling in his bones that the Boche was weakening, and he wanted no let-up in forcing Ludendorff to run through what reserves he had left, classic attritional strategy. The problem was in the numbers. Haig's 1917 losses had been horrific, and France stood nearly exhausted. The time had come to push Americans into the breach, to follow what Liddell Hart called the 'Brusilov System', or 'getting men killed in order to get the war over quickly'.[11] But Pershing would not be rushed. During several conferences held that summer and early autumn, some attended not only by the generals but by Clemenceau and Lloyd George as well, the exchanges often turned ugly. Pershing was determined not to turn his boys into cannon fodder, especially if fighting under some other country's flag and not as a purely American force. Clemenceau was often enraged, Pershing mulish, while Foch stood in the middle. Discussion among the British and French began taking a conspiratorial turn, to inform President Wilson that Pershing had to go. Smuts wanted to 'squeeze every last ounce' out of the Americans, and Pershing was the obstacle; the 'job was too big for him', he must either be replaced or sent to oversee stevedores in various French ports as they unloaded arriving war material from America. Better yet, he should concentrate on training and leave the war to people who knew something about it. Feelings were running high, teeth were gnashing (as Clemenceau put it).

It is ironic that Foch more or less found himself defending Pershing's point of view as best he could. He thought persuasion rather that face-to-face confrontation was perhaps the best way to get what he needed out of Pershing. Clemenceau couldn't believe it. American forces were not so much unusable as they were unused. Foch should order Pershing to obey. Foch refused. His tactic was subtle. Pershing would have his army – the First American – but Foch would slyly siphon off its strength into French formations. Pershing, blind to his ego, would barely notice. 'It is by manipulation of this sort that I expect to diminish the weakness [in staff work and general inefficiency] of the American High Command, rather than by orders', he wrote Clemenceau. Foch would do whatever it took to keep the ball rolling. Pershing was no fool, however. He told his staff that Foch had only one strategy: to wait for him.

The first real test for American staff work was the St. Mihiel operation, designed to eliminate a German salient south-east of Verdun. Pershing occupied Pétain's old headquarters in the little village of Souilly, and oversaw the planning and implementation of US forces. The coming battle was to be limited in its scope and objectives; the enemy before them were second and third echelon forces, the sector had been a relatively quiet one. Between 12 and 16 September, the First American went into action and acquitted itself well, too well in fact. Exhilaration became the rule, a satisfaction that Pershing shared and encouraged. He spent a good deal of time figuring out decorations. Two weeks later his mood would change. Foch had a sterner task in mind for the Americans.

Secretary of War Newton Baker visited France in September. He had a conversation with Foch about the number of US divisions that would ultimately be required, thinking in terms of Pershing's staggering suggestion of a hundred. Foch was in a good mood. 'I win the war with forty', he said to Baker. In a pantomime of a boxing match, he feigned a battering of the ribs, followed by a few punches to the stomach, then a knockout punch to the jaw. Constant pressure, that was the key to victory. The famous 'Hundred Days' that followed would be the despair of Ludendorff, the low point of which was the very opening round at Amiens, which he described as a 'black day for the German army'. American participation involved what came to be known as the Meuse-Argonne battle, well to the east of Amiens, part of the strategy of hitting Germans all along the front, and it began on 26 September. It, too, would be a black day, but this time not for the German foe.

With so little time between St. Mihiel and the first proposed salvo of the new offensive, involving as it did the stealthy transfer of nearly 850,000 men sixty miles from one sector to another, the burdens placed on staff preparation were crushing and, broadly speaking, poorly handled. Commentators afterwards blamed American inexperience for the confusion that followed, but given the smallest of windows it must be wondered if any general staff could have pulled it off, given the necessary time constraints. By far the more serious obstacle to success, however, was the nature of the countryside that Pershing was ordered to attack. It was, to say the very least, formidable.

Between the at times impenetrable obstacle of the Argonne forest in Champagne, and the heights of the Meuse River to its east, lay a front of some 25 miles, a sort of chute running north-south for another 13. In the middle of the chute were a series of smaller hills and other natural obstacles (dense woodlots, for one), all of which made for a dream scenario for the German general in charge, Max von Gallwitz, short on manpower but long on imagination. The heights on either side were perfect for enfilading artillery fire, the interior geography highly favourable for interlocking defensible strong points. German inventiveness, after four long years of trench warfare, now reached its diabolical apogee. The several lines of defence, named after various witches in Germanic and Wagnerian lore, were a veritable textbook of military ingenuity, a hell's kitchen as it were.

The 47-day struggle that began on 26 September has been divided by historians into three phases, the first two of which were monumental and bloody fiascos. Foch believed the 'immaturity' of the Americans stood fully exposed in this battle: too many men bunched up in the attack lines, clogged roads and supply lines, a reliance on romantic predispositions as opposed to experience. Pershing had fallen into the usual trap of believing that overwhelming superiority of numbers would give the desired and almost inevitable result, a breakthrough (French forces, for instance, would have used half the numbers, given the length of front that Pershing used). When these men rushed forward, to be in many cases simply mown down by cleverly sited machine gun posts, Pershing and his commanders could often think of nothing more expedient then sending more men forward to do the same thing, the 'slugging it out approach' that Haig had made infamous. The front soon devolved into a huge logjam of men and material, often going in opposite directions. Clemenceau, visiting the front, was so stymied in the traffic foul-up that he furiously abandoned his car and tromped over a mile across open country to find a hill where he might catch of view as to what was going on.

Lloyd George was not too happy either, calling the American performance to date 'our worst disappointment'. Atrocious weather conditions contributed to what fast became chaos. After just a few days of this, French General Maxime Weygand characterized the First Army as being in a stage of paralysis, and a liaison officer from Foch's headquarters saw signs of confusion and muddled thinking among senior American officers. When fighting Germans, he noted, battles could not be 'improvised'. The second phase of the offensive, launched on 4 October, was no better – a series of more or less frontal attacks on the well-prepared German positions. The American flier Billy Mitchell, who would gain notoriety between the world wars for his aggressive belief in air power, was incredulous watching it all from a thousand feet, infantrymen just 'knocking their heads against a stone wall. It was terrible for us to look down from the air and see the uncoordinated, not to say disorganized, nature of the combat'. The battle proved 'continuous' for almost two weeks, with little to show for it other than growing casualty lists and mounting frustration. Weather, the terrain, the Germans, flu: everything was conspiring to foil the American advance. A tremendous temper tantrum by Foch only added to the dreadful situation. On 13 October, the pressure on Foch led him to lose his composure. Clemenceau had just composed an insulting letter to his *generalissimo*, saying the problem was not Pershing refusing to obey, but Foch refusing to command. Foch, in his turn, furiously upbraided Pershing at a hastily called meeting. 'No more promises', he reportedly yelled at Pershing, 'Results! The only thing to judge by.… If an attack is well planned and well executed, it succeeds …; if it is not … there is no advance.' Pershing was so stung by this tirade that he omitted mentioning it in his memoirs, which were often exhausting in their day-to-day detail. The next afternoon, in his diary, he jotted down a line that Douglas Haig might have written: 'If we keep on pounding, the Germans will be obliged to give way.' After three weeks of 'pounding', the American advance finally achieved the objectives that Pershing had expected on the first day of battle. By this time the First Army was adjudged by one of its officers as 'disorganized and wrecked'. Pershing split the army into two separate forces, each with a commanding general, while still retaining overall control. It was thought in this fashion to streamline operations on a front that now stretched for nearly one hundred miles.

Fortune sometimes favours the brave; at other moments, it shines where it wishes too, indiscriminately and without prejudice. Had the German army collapsed during the middle of October, the reputation of General John J. Pershing, and the reputation of American arms, would certainly have been judged as tarnished. But the war lasted for another three weeks. The weather finally turned for Pershing and, more importantly, so did the German ability to resist. Even Ludendorff finally realized that the game was finished. The culmination of one hundred days of unrelenting allied attacks had finally reached the point where the Germans were were 'all used up'. The third phase of the Meuse-Argonne campaign, generally dated to 4 November, collapsed the crumbling German front in impressive fashion. The complaints about staff deficiencies and unimaginative tactics generally evaporated in light of the incredible dash and courage of American arms. No one, after all, had ever doubted the bravery of men under Pershing's command, and criticism of their commander in chief found welcome shade in the overall delight with, at last, victory.

The tally sheet was grim, as any visitor to the many American military cemeteries in the Meuse-Argonne region can attest. The First and Second American Armies inflicted over 100,000 casualties on von Gallwitz's forces. They, in turn, suffered 117,000. But the war was over.

The Fourteen Points (or were they Commandments)?

Though Woodrow Wilson had, by necessity, his attention on war, peace was never far from his mind, it being the more congenial topic, given his interests and personality. He had Colonel House working on a general set of principles that might be a basis for possible negotiations with Germany, when the time might be ripe for them, which coincided chronologically with the ongoing exchange of terms between Germany and the bolsheviks at Brest-Litovsk in Poland. Several of Trotsky's sweeping declarations there, mostly regarding a condemnation of aggressive wars and the fate of more or less defenceless small countries, appealed to Wilson's sense of justice, but also forced his hand. It would never do to cede the high ground to this gang of monsters. On 8 January of the New Year, 1918, Wilson presented Congress with his Fourteen Points, a blueprint for any coming peace parley, a set of propositions that he claimed were the reasons that America was in the war. The fourteenth of these, linked insolubly to all the others, was the creation of a League of Nations, a body of all countries, large and small, that would do away with the need for secret treaties and secret alliances, the Old-World model of doing business, precisely the ingredients that had imploded the European world nearly four years before. Wilson had been shocked when Arthur Balfour, the new foreign secretary in Lloyd George's cabinet, paid a courtesy visit to Washington after America's entry into the lists. Balfour had revealed to the president, confidentially, an entire array of previously undisclosed arrangements entered into by the various allies, by which some were bribed (mostly the Italians), and others appeased by an arbitrary division of spoils (German colonies, but other tantalizing prizes as well, the Middle East among them). Balfour called this 'dividing up the bearskin before the bear was killed'. Wilson learned quite a bit from this conversation. It gave him his first real insight into the kinds of men with whom he would have to deal in the future.

The Fourteen Points galvanized world opinion, both positively and negatively. Some saw it as a revolutionary declaration, a break with the past, a needed reform of mouldy European tradition. Comparisons to Luther's 95 articles were common (to John Dos Passos, for one). Others found them presumptuous, interfering, unrealistic and arrogant, comparisons here being to the Ten Commandments (Clemenceau noted that while God had restricted himself to only ten conditions, Wilson, in a greedy splurge, had done Him four better by coming up with fourteen). Some of the points were relatively uncontroversial: the return of Alsace-Lorraine to France; the evacuation of Belgium and other war-torn countries; a commitment to fair dealings with the Soviet Union (though no one knew with whom they were to deal or whom they could trust in that confused part of the world). Others were benign: a League of Nations seemed a sensible idea, though the devil, as always, would be in the detail. Economic provisions regarding the removal of tariff walls and free trade seemed so far out of reach that no one gave them a serious thought; and while mutual disarmament sounded good on paper, was that a realistic proposal given human nature? Freedom of the Seas was another sensible 'principle', but for a power such as Britain to accept unilaterally such a notion was surely unthinkable (Lloyd George noted that old sea dogs in the Admiralty were 'breathing fire' about it). Could high-mindedness overwhelm national, private, self-centred national concerns? Who knew?[12] What all could agree on, however, was the most troubling undercurrent of the entire proposition, its core difficulty: self-determination of peoples. This was a beacon call to oppressed minorities everywhere. Wilson supposed it to be a logical solution to the broken bits of empire that now lay strewn across the map, whether it be Ottoman, Habsburg or tsarist. Far-flung colonial entities grew encouraged, sensing a seismic shift that might, for the first time in many decades, help to achieve some measure of freedom from economic and personal serfdom. An itinerant peasant from Vietnam, Nguyen Sinh Cung, arrived in Paris sometime towards the end of 1917, and quickly submerged himself in émigré and socialist groups, many of whose members grew inspired by the Fourteen Points. With friends, he composed and circulated petitions and manifestos of anticolonial bent and optimistically ordered a formal morning suit for when he would address Woodrow Wilson. That day never happened and Nguyen Sinh Cung, who later changed his name to Ho Chi Minh, began seeking his saviour somewhere else, namely in the works of Lenin (the world would hear from him again). To cynics, of course, Wilson's Fourteen Points were fantasies, and their architect a dreamer. Trotsky called all the talk about self-determination 'dreary palaver'.

Certainly Wilson was not the first man by any means to dream up the notion of an international body, league or congress of nations designed to forestall or mediate potential flare-ups between its members before minor disagreements could fester and lead to something bigger. George Bernard Shaw, for instance, proposed just such an organization well before the war began but he, after all, was a vegetarian and self-described crank, so no one took him seriously.[13] The League was the cornerstone to everything else, however, as far as Wilson was concerned, the engine that would carry the rest of the world's problems to resolution. It conveyed the spirit of the Old Testament Covenant, a human imitation of the divine, whereby men, copying God Almighty, signed a pact that could never be violated. This was so ingrained a notion in the president's world view (and character) that woe betide any man who crossed him on it.

'I will have to do some plain talking when we get on the other side.'

President Wilson, to his physician,
on the day of his departure for Paris

As the man who knew best, or thought he did, Wilson ended up squandering the advantages that seemed never-ending when war appeared won by November 1918. His first mistake, and a crucial one it proved to be, was his decision before leaving for Versailles to lay everything on the line during the by-election of that autumn. Wilson was never a magnanimous man when it came to his political enemies. Opponents of any stripe infuriated him; the Calvinist streak in his Scottish gene pool refused to admit of compromise with those whom he considered beneath him, whether politically, ideologically or morally made no difference. People like the influential Massachusetts senator Henry Cabot Lodge and former President Roosevelt were nitwits, in his view, and he could not believe that most Americans did not share his poor opinion of their intransigence and doctrinaire jingoism, the blind faith in 'conservatism' that even the horrific experience of the Great War had not budged ('Make no changes [in your thinking], and consult your grandmother when in doubt', as he put it). The president accordingly made the oncoming congressional election a litmus test for his vision of the new, postwar world, a decision Lloyd George later characterized as 'a fatal error of judgment'. The desire for a genuine peace, one that would last for the ages, seemed so pre-eminently a good idea that Wilson could not believe for a second that poor wheat prices in the American mid-west or the egregious imprisonment of a few radical socialists without due cause would seriously cost him votes. But cost him votes they did. Republicans gained control of both the house and senate in a stunning repudiation of the president (reminiscent of what befell Winston Churchill after World War II), undercutting his aura and prestige in the eyes of those wily European politicians who were waiting for him in Paris. Whether he recognized it at the time or not, this meant the chairmanship of all congressional committees would revert to Republicans. This would become a disaster when the treaty that Wilson brought back from Versailles six months later for ratification (without which it would have no validity for the United States) was required to worm its way through the powerful Foreign Relations Committee, chaired (as though by some sort of satanic design) by Henry Cabot Lodge. This, of course, inevitably became the graveyard of everything the president had worked and prayed for. It proved to be the death of him as well.[14]

The second fateful decision was made after the 11 November armistice itself regarding American representation at the upcoming peace conference. 'Peace', naturally enough, was something of a misnomer in the autumn of 1918. What the world had was, in essence, a ceasefire. German forces on the western front had by no means laid down their arms; they had stopped fighting, but they remained a formidable military force nonetheless. As for central Europe, the eastern front and within Russia itself, conditions were considerably more fluid. Where formal armies no longer engaged in structured combat, irregular and guerrilla units were active, and outright civil war was igniting sporadically all through the former Austro-Hungarian, Ottoman and tsarist empires. Socialist groups were actively seeking to undermine provisional governments that, in some countries, had only the barest control over events; many countries were equally poised to scavenge on the decrepit corpses of their immediate neighbours (Greece, for example, eyeing Turkey). The threat of chaos loomed everywhere over the immediate horizon of just about anywhere that a diplomat might look. What would, or could, happen next?

In Woodrow Wilson's view, it was up to him to restore Order. Self-righteousness was never a virtue the president lacked. Balfour's revelation nineteen months previously of the private division of spoils agreed to by the various allies for when the fighting ceased, continued to shock him. Here lay the seeds for future wars, here lay all the corrupt self-interest for which the Old World was infamous. If it took a university professor to scold, coerce, reform and re-educate these recalcitrant remnants of a corrupt political tradition, he was the man for it (the British diplomat Sir Robert Cecil would later assess Wilson as 'a trifle of a bully'). The president's coteries of advisers were shocked when they heard that Wilson planned to attend the upcoming peace conference himself. To summarize the opposition, his secretary of state, Robert Lansing – a man Wilson disliked and perpetually ignored – presented a reasoned argument that he delivered in person the day after the armistice:

> I pointed out that he held at present a dominant position in the world, which I was afraid he would lose if he went into conference with the foreign statesmen; that he could practically dictate the terms of peace if he held aloof; that he would be criticized severely in this country for leaving at a time when Congress particularly needed his guidance, and that he would be greatly embarrassed in directing domestic affairs from overseas. The President did not like what I said. His face assumed that harsh, obstinate expression which indicates resentment at unacceptable advice. He said nothing, but looked volumes. If he goes [to Versailles] he will someday be sorry. He will probably not forgive me, and may even decide not to make me a delegate [to the conference]. However I have

done my duty. I believe that I have told him the truth. My conscience is clear.[15]

Looking at things retrospectively, it is easy to find fault with Wilson's personalization of the entire process. He would never have agreed, of course, but the judgment of many participants was best summarized by a member of the British delegation when he wrote afterwards that Wilson's presence in Paris 'constitutes a historical disaster of the first magnitude'. Colonel House agreed. By participating and, in effect, soiling his hands in grubby negotiations, Wilson had come down from his pedestal and transformed himself into nothing more than 'common clay'.

When the president addressed Congress before his departure for Europe on the troop ship *George Washington*, he was given 'an ice bath' by Republicans, 'not even applauding his reference to brave soldiers and sailors', according to one spectator, a 'churlishness' that the current television era would not have allowed. Others tried to put a good face on the situation, praising the president for 'stopping the Republicans on the Marne', but as a portent of acrimony to come, it was 'a bad omen'.

[Prime Minister] lunched at Mr. Balfour's flat to meet with Queen of Romania, & according to everybody, was in his best form. David says she is very naughty, but a very clever woman, though on the whole he does not like her. She gave a lengthy description of her purchases in Paris, which included a pink silk chemise. She spoke of meeting President Wilson on his arrival. 'What shall I talk to him about?' she asked. 'The League of Nations or my pink chemise?' 'Begin with the League of Nations,' said Mr. Balfour, 'and finish up with the pink chemise. If you were talking to Mr. Lloyd George, you could begin with the pink chemise.'

Frances Stevenson, diary entry 10 March 1919

Wilson's reception in Europe was flabbergasting, much to the annoyance of seasoned diplomats such as Lord Derby, who grew sick of seeing the president being 'treated so like a god'. Despite the often dour elements of his personality, Wilson was not without a touch of vanity, and at first he was charmed and thrilled by the generosity of the huge crowds that greeted him– 'the whole population of Paris', according to Cary Grayson, on his arrival to that great city – seeing in all the commotion a universal stamp of approval for his ideas on peace. But the wear and endless festivity wore on his nerves. The ostentation of his quarters in Paris, 'a little palace', as one of his aides put it, annoyed him (but not his wife), as did the rich and heavy French cooking, covered in sauces. He just couldn't 'see any sense', he said, 'in wrapping up food in pajamas'. The obligatory trip to England, full of speeches, receptions and royal protocols, was also tiring for a man who, as Derby said again, 'was very much averse to banquets and entertainments'. At the also obligatory dinner at Buckingham Palace, attended by the usual horde of bemedalled generals and bejewelled *grande dames*, Lloyd George uncharitably commented on Wilson's attire, 'an ordinary black dress suit', a strange condescension by a prime minster who gloried in his own modest roots. Margot Asquith, on the other hand, was fascinated and especially eager to meet the president. According to Mrs. Wilson, who was seated at her table, the wife of the former prime minister ('clever, egotistical, and exceedingly plain') had told the king 'that she did not want his food', only an introduction. She had heard that Wilson 'really had brains', which seemed to her remarkable for an American, since 'she had met many' and never thought any of them were smart. The king, impervious to people with 'brains', thought the president was 'an odious man'.

Perhaps the most touching moment in Britain for the president was a special trip he arranged, 'entirely unofficial' at his own insistence, to the ancient border town of Carlisle, where his mother was born in 1826. Wilson called it 'a pilgrimage from the heart'. In a pouring winter's rain he first stopped at his maternal grandfather's home (the formidable Rev. Dr. Thomas Woodrow); the current residents, suffering from the influenza that would eventually kill roughly 4 percent of the world's population, were too sick to formally welcome the president, and he confined his visit to a short view of the room where his mother had entered this sorry world.[16] Then he was taken to Dr. Woodrow's church and, though loath to interfere in an ongoing service, he was persuaded to offer a few words to the congregation. No other speech, formal or informal, is more revealing of Wilson's character than the charming, intimate and humble remarks that he gave to the parishioners there assembled. After noting that his grim grandfather would have been furious at his appropriation of the pulpit, he then gave a brief précis of his own remembrance of that gentleman's 'stern lessons of duty [that] he spoke to me. I remember also, painfully, the things which he expected me to know, which I did not know.' Wilson then beautifully knitted together the yearnings for peace of common men, in churches as insignificant as the one they were in that day, whose 'moral force is irresistible.... Like the rivulets gathering into the river, and the river into the seas, there come from communities like this streams that fertilize the consciences of men, and it is the consciences of the world that we are trying to place upon the throne which others would usurp.' Wilson's 'covenant' was never better expressed than in this relatively unknown local church which, being unheated, was as cold as a December day could make it. Like everyone else in attendance, the president did not remove his overcoat.

The welcome given Wilson in Rome was even more rapturous (little did the Italians realize that he would be a constant foil to their ambitions for a slice of Balkan coastline and the important port of Fiume). No doubt gritting his teeth, the president paid an official visit to Pope Benedict XV, who was suspected by all of having had preferential feelings for Germany and Austria-Hungary during the war. For a Presbyterian Covenanter to be blessed with the sign of the cross from a Catholic pope, of course, was something that would have made Wilson's forebears turn over in their graves. Wilson cleansed his soul to some degree by visiting a Protestant episcopal church thereafter.

One invitation he initially refused after returning to Paris was to tour the battlefields in France and Belgium, as his hosts were 'hounding' him to do. They could not emotionally blackmail him, he said; he would not judge Germany 'in frenzy'. But he ignored the statistics that such sightseeing would have emphasized, especially for a Clemenceau and a French general public, whose individual calamities had been horrific: the hundreds of thousands of dead men (25 percent of all males between eighteen and thirty); two and a half million wounded, many with lost limbs and, even worse, lost sanity; 6,000 square miles of agricultural and industrial land utterly destroyed; villages and towns (the mainstream of traditional French life) gone without a trace; acres of infrastructure ruined. If one did not know better, it might appear that France was the defeated country, not Germany. Across the Rhine, for example, the war had never been fought, and barely a sign could be visibly seen of any material damage. Several members of foreign delegations, however, disparaged the gloomy recitation of French war losses. The economist John Maynard Keynes concluded that 'the amount of material damage done in the invaded districts has been the subject of enormous, if natural, exaggeration'. British liaison officer Brigadier-General Edward Spears agreed, writing to Sir Henry Wilson that the French public 'is beginning to recover from the state of semi-coma into which it had sunk during the last 18 months of the war. The French are realizing that they are victorious and in this realization of victory are being tempted to exaggerate the part which they have played in the war.' This astonishing condescension reinforced in many French minds their traditional antipathy towards Britain in general. Foch wrote, 'Once Germany had been beaten, England was sure to revert instinctively to her traditional policy of checking the victor – in this case, France – from becoming over-powerful.' As for Woodrow Wilson, the French negotiators met him with intense suspicion, which the early days of the conference did little to dispel.[17]

'For President Wilson the League of Nations meant, if not the whole Treaty, at least the only part of the Treaty in which he was interested. He intended that it should conform to his ideas, and that it should be recognized that they were his ideas and not those of anyone else, be he associate or subordinate. His abnormal confidence in himself and limited confidence in others were largely responsible for his reluctance to delegate his duties. Thus it was that what he could not attend to himself he often neglected altogether. From his own point of view it was a fatal decision.'

David Lloyd George

After what seemed like an exaggerated length of time, the conference finally convened for business on 12 January 1919 (John Dos Passos said the French were happy with the delay: they 'were content to wait while the Germans starved a little more').[18] Grayson was mightily impressed as the American delegation drove to the venue, crossing La Place de la Concorde, 'site of Old Mother Guillotine' from the French Revolution, along to the foreign ministry building along the river Seine. Grayson found the huge conference room stifling, even though it was January, and opened a window. Lloyd George remarked, ever ready with a quip, that 'that was probably the first breath of fresh air let into the place since the reign of Louis XIV'. Clemenceau was not amused, the window was closed, and the French premier proceeded to get into a shouting match with Vittorio Emanuele Orlando, the Italian prime minister. They reminded Grayson of 'a couple of dogs, barking at each other'.

At first, Wilson held all the cards. By entering the war at, relatively speaking, the last moment, he had become the decisive factor in the achievement of victory, and thus in a position of considerable influence when it came to dictating a peace settlement and, from this superior pulpit, arranging the agenda to suit his quasi-religious views. United States forces on the ground were rounding into shape: already, over two million troops were on European spoil, marginally tested but well equipped, eager and immune to the war weariness that infected every other power. American wheat and grains were looked upon to feed a hungry Europe that, in some places, was approaching starvation levels. And, last but not least, everyone owed money to America; too much, in fact, to ever pay back.[19]

But the president was handicapped from the very start by his preoccupation with the proposed League of Nations, almost to the exclusion of everything else. This earned him the immediate contempt of the European leaders, who considered themselves practitioners of *Realpolitik*. It did not help that the president had very few concrete details to share about the League, precisely because he did not have any: as one of his advisers put it, he 'did not know a God damn thing about what the Prez was thinking', and after hearing Wilson in Paris, Lord Derby found him 'vague' and 'hazy'. In Wilson's mind, however, the details did not matter – they could be hammered out later in the process; this implied a willingness (which he assumed) that his colleagues would join with him in fleshing out his general ideas. They were loath to do so. Clemenceau, for example, had three early private meetings with Wilson. He must have been amused at what he heard (and heard he did, as Wilson launched into non-stop monologues). Later, addressing assorted French deputies, Clemenceau noted his favourable impression of the president's high moral values but, knowing Clemenceau, was it possible he was pulling everyone's legs, as was his wont? He used the word *'candeur'* to describe Wilson, but to his hearers this was an ambiguous bit of praise. It could mean that the premier admired the president's candour in discussing how the future peace might look. But in a double entendre, *candeur* can also mean a fool with his head in the clouds, an eternal optimist with no conception of political reality. His remarks engendered a minor flurry of controversy, which Clemenceau casually brushed aside. What was the matter with the president; didn't he have a sense of humour? The official transcript of Clemenceau's remarks, however, replaced the word *candeur* with *grandeur*. [20]

Lloyd George was of the same opinion. He resented Wilson lecturing him with his 'little sermonettes'. According to Lord Cecil, the British prime minister has 'no real interest in the League', and wished to move on as quickly as possible to more realistic issues. The president's rigidity and shows of temper and/or disdain surprised him; he seemed unaware that American feelings, as represented by Wilson, were utterly contemptuous of the Old World and its annoying habit of telling everyone else what to do, how to feel, where to go and whom to salute. He and Clemenceau grew tired of listening to Jesus Christ (Clemenceau's analogy), and his ponderous 'theology'. They were men of the world. So was Wilson to some degree, of course, but with an important distinction that he never fully appreciated. Clemenceau and Lloyd George were creatures of the parliamentary world, where give and take was a way of political life. One had to be fast on one's feet to survive that particular milieu, quick of mind, agile with facts (or what could be projected as facts) and clever at repartee. Parliamentary wrangles generally required a rapier, not cannon, and often reflected a fluidity that made the American congressional system seem sluggish. 'My mind is a one-track railway and can only run one train of thought at a time', Wilson had admitted, but without thoroughly understanding the advantage this gave to his more slippery colleagues. Initial negotiations, torturous in their detail as various drafts were submitted for multiple inspections and editorial changes, inevitably diluted Wilson's intentions, however ill-defined they continued to be. What did become obvious to the president, however, was that the general drift of his formulations were steadily being undermined, distorted and emasculated. He wondered if anything even remotely effective could be achieved. What was coming out in various drafts, he complained, was but a 'skeleton' of his original intent. It is a tribute to his tenacity that, realizing the awkward drift for what it was, he dug in his heels and refused to relent on his core beliefs. Either the League would come into being, or he was finished with Europe. Clemenceau and Lloyd George were taken up short, and gradually they acquiesced on several important issues regarding the League, the most prominent of which linked the League to the actual peace terms. The two were to be united in one document. When Wilson left France on 15 February for a short trip home to attend to urgent matters in Washington, he was content with his progress so far. The other delegations were also relieved. With Wilson gone, however temporarily, perhaps they could finally get down to business. Lord Curzon noted his meeting with the French ambassador to London:

Monsieur Cambon expressed great disappointment and irritation at the slow progress that was being made with the business of the conference, and he attributed this in the main to the unfortunate lead which had been given to the proceedings by President Wilson. Of the latter he spoke in very critical terms. He regarded him as an academic lecturer with considerable literary gifts, but out of touch with the world, giving his confidence to no one, unversed in European politics, and devoted to the pursuit of theories which had little relation to the emergencies of the hour. The business of the peace conference was to bring a close to the war with Germany, to settle the frontiers of Germany, to decide upon the terms which should be extracted from her, and as soon as possible to conclude a just peace. All such questions as the freedom of the seas and the League of Nations … could very well be postponed to a subsequent stage.

In other words, by Old World standards, put aside and eventually buried. There was still time, as Lloyd George said, for Wilson 'to come down to earth'.

As for Wilson's opinion of his opposite numbers, he hit the nail on the head for all three. Lloyd George was 'a man without principle', Clemenceau 'too old to comprehend new ideas', and Orlando little more than 'a damned reactionary'. He was not going to let them have their way.

'We cannot merely sign a peace treaty and go home with clear consciences. We must do something more.'

Woodrow Wilson

Having passed this milestone in the negotiations, Wilson was in a good mood as he travelled home on the troop ship *George Washington* which, despite wandering seventeen miles off course on its approach to Boston Harbour in a dense fog, and coming perilously close to running aground, nonetheless disembarked its passengers on 24 February 1919. Crowds in the street greeted the president warmly. The famous tenor John McCormack sang a version of the *Star-Spangled Banner* that 'that well nigh carried the crowd off its feet', and Wilson addressed the citizenry with his usual arsenal of inspired rhetoric. People like Clemenceau, Orlando, Lloyd George and, indeed, even himself were 'not masters of their people', he said, but 'the servants of their people'. This was true, but not in the ways he meant. Public opinion was for peace and the League, but leaders of all the allied countries were hamstrung by just that, public opinion. French public opinion insisted on the Rhineland, the Saar, breaking up the German nation into parts; British public opinion wanted to 'make them pay', i.e. reparations; Italy wanted Dalmatia and Fiume, as interwar negotiations had promised them as their fee for entering the war. Public opinion in the United States wanted the League just as much as anyone else, but the 'people' didn't want to police the world, be drawn again into the type of general quagmire that seemed such a European specialty, or lose its right to do as it wished in any facet of foreign affairs. These generalized opinions were usually force-fed and endlessly repeated by the press in each country, all outdoing themselves 'in emotional extravagance'. The result, according to the British diplomat Harold Nicolson, was an 'alert but ignorant electorate' that no politician could ignore. 'Democratic diplomacy possesses many advantages', he wrote, 'yet it possesses one supreme disadvantage: its representatives are obliged to reduce the standards of their own thoughts to the level of other people's feelings.' Nicolson referred to the constraints produced by democratic systems as an 'octopus' that strangled intelligent discourse. In many ways, the much-abused and discredited ways of autocracy were to be preferred. 'What we want', he wrote home, 'is a Dictator for Europe and we haven't got one, and never will have!' This was a cry of despair ('I need a holiday', he noted two weeks later); by 1940, of course, his idle thought would become reality, and a disastrous one at that.

While Wilson spent seven exhausting days in Washington sorting through an immense array of problems, largely domestic but with the Peace hovering over everything, Colonel House, back in Paris, felt compelled to face what he considered an obvious fact. It was either bend, or no treaty and no League. He then proceeded to concede ground on major agreements that the president felt, with considerable justification, that he had already won. Wilson, 'setting his jaws' as a newspaper man reported, generally dismissed the objections raised by Republicans and assorted Democrats, at just the same moment as House began to betray him in Paris.[21] Wilson was probably more thunderstruck than at any other point in his life when House reported his negotiating results on 13 March, when the *George Washington* landed again in France. Although House was at pains to emphasize that 'it was sometimes necessary to compromise in order to get things done. Not a compromise of principle, but a compromise of detail', the president would have none of that.

'Betray', of course, is a strong word. Did it truly apply to Colonel House, the quintessential 'yes man' according to Wilson's wife, 'a regular jellyfish', a figure so bland that he seemed, on occasion, to fade into the wallpaper? The assessment of House's behaviour and motivations has been the stuff of academic discussion for decades, and House himself, in keeping with his character, was largely reticent in discussing the almost immediate chill that developed between himself and the president after they met in the French port of Brest. House's generally matter-of-fact diary entries begin showing an uncharacteristic sprinkling of negativities on the president's behaviour, adjectives of the 'stubborn' variety, but he nowhere addressed the nub of the issues between them. The only real account is that of Wilson's wife, who recorded the president's reaction as he entered their railway compartment after leaving House. His alter ego, he said, 'has given away everything I had won before we left Paris. He has compromised on every side. I have to start all over again.' They held hands in a sort of mute astonishment. House continued to play a part in the ensuing negotiations, but his relationship with Wilson, one that had lasted for some eight years in a state of genuine intimacy, was finished. When Wilson returned to the United States after the peace was signed, the two men never saw each other again. The president had become, as Lloyd George put it, 'irreconcilably angry'.

'The plain people are with the president [but]
it is not [with the] plain people we have to deal.'

Colonel House

The first matter of concern for Wilson was Georges Clemenceau. On a wintry February morning, an anarchist had fired multiple shots at the old man, one of which hit him in the back, below the breast bone. Its location was so sensitive that doctors decided to leave the bullet *in situ* where, in his words, it 'was quite happy [to find] a resting place'. A nurse said to him that it was a miracle he had survived; Clemenceau replied, as a good republican, that he did not believe in miracles. Although Clemenceau shrugged off the episode with his usual mordant sense of humour, the attack and its after-effects took their toll. Wilson thought he had aged, was not quite as sharp or focused. John Maynard Keynes said that he now seemed 'a very old man conserving his strength for important occasions'. Secretary of State Lansing drew several sketches of the French prime minster fast asleep during assorted conference sessions.

Entering the second (and crucial) phase of the conference, Wilson now found himself in deep water. The consensus among his colleagues was simple: to take advantage of the progress that had been made in the president's absence and to wrap matters up as soon as they could. House said it best in his diary: 'my main drive now is for peace with Germany at the earliest possible moment'. With that in mind, the Council of Ten was immediately transformed into a Council of Four (sarcastically referred to as 'Les 4 Bigs'); when Italy left in a temperamental fit three months later, it became a Council of Three, most of whose meetings were held in private, oftentimes without even a secretary or anyone available to take notes. This was backroom dealing of the grossest sort, 'TNT stuff' according to an American member of the delegation, the type of imperial arrogance that Wilson had so strenuously condemned in the past, and best described by John Dos Passos as 'three old men shuffling the pack, dealing out the cards'. For Wilson, it was the price he had to pay for retrieving, and then salvaging, the League, which in his opinion was the entire object of the game (as Prime Minister Billy Hughes of Australia put it, 'The League of Nations was to him what a toy was to a child – he would not be happy till he got it'). The bill he gradually paid was steep: the virtual abandonment of his Fourteen Points, the Fourteen Points that had inspired the world.

Wilson did not go down without a fierce struggle, however. In a series of furious arguments that exasperated his opposite numbers while draining what little emotional and physical strength he had left (his physician's diary is full of notations to the same effect, 'the president was completely fagged out this evening').[22] This was entirely in keeping with his character; as he told House, nothing was worth having in this life if it did not involve a fight to get it, and fight he did. Lord Cecil noted the change. 'I found him in a very truculent mood', he wrote on 16 March. The task was made simpler by the blatant provocations he was presented with – it was simple to ignite his ire, so outlandish were the many claims with which the assorted victors wished to shackle their common foe, mostly taking the form of reparations and the settlement of Germany's western frontier. On the reparations issue, the figures bandied about were so crippling that some of the economic advisers present in Paris (whose opinions were generally ignored) wondered why Germany had bothered to give up the fight. According to Herbert Hoover (always 'gloomy', according to House), the allies were 'making it more difficult for Germany under peace conditions than it was under war'. Even Lloyd George, despite intense pressure from home, found the demands on the German economy simply 'absurd'. He noted, in a prediction that sadly came true, that 'injustice [and] arrogance displayed in the hour of victory will never be forgotten or forgiven'. The French, of course, could not have cared less. The Italians may have been simply venal in many of their demands (Churchill called them 'harlots'), but the French had considerably more malice in their hearts. They were not so much 'greedy' as they were 'anxious', viewing European history as 'a perpetual prize fight, of which France has won this round, but of which this round is certainly not the last....The old order does not change, being based on human nature which is always the same' (these points according to Nicolson and Keynes). In such an atmosphere it was impossible 'for even supermen to devise a peace of moderation and righteousness'.

The French were even more demanding when it came to German frontiers and natural resources. The Rhine was an issue; France wanted the entire west bank as 'a rampart' against future aggression, its status to be a demilitarized buffer zone (managed from Paris) that would put several thousands of Germans under the French orbit. Clemenceau also demanded the Saar basin, again, full of Germans, to say nothing of coal. These were direct contradictions to both the letter and spirit of the Fourteen Points (self-determination?), and Wilson exploded. Until that morning, he told Clemenceau, no one had ever heard of the Saar and he would do nothing to split it from where it belonged, with Germany. He also had little sympathy for what the Rhine symbolized to France (Lloyd George unhelpfully wondered if there was a substantial emotive difference between that river and the Rio Grande). Clemenceau, in his turn, stomped out of the meeting, muttering that Wilson was no friend of his; *au contraire*, he was a friend of the Germans. This was certainly a display of temper from both men, but it concealed what a clever tactician the old French dog really was, tacitly recognized by Keynes. Clemenceau, he felt, 'was by far the most eminent member of the Council of Four, and he had taken the measure of his colleagues'. Although he would often 'close his eyes with an air of fatigue', he was ever alert to the possibilities of give and take when it came to serious issues. He allowed the 'most definite and the most extreme proposals' to air (being ever ready to compromise), which put his adversaries (mainly Wilson) 'in a position which they felt as invidious, of always appearing to take the enemy's part and to argue his case'. Wilson fell into this trap, one that his fiercest critic, Teddy Roosevelt, had predicted. If Wilson was going to Paris to act as some sort of neutral umpire, he was not only a fool but a disloyal friend to Britain and France. 'It is our business to stand by our allies', he said. That late morning the president told some of his entourage that 'I am in trouble.... I do not know whether I shall be seeing Monsieur Clemenceau again.... In fact, I do not know if the Peace Conference will continue. Monsieur Clemenceau called me a pro-German and abruptly left the room.' The result proved to be, after more haggling, a victory for Clemenceau, one of many that Wilson was forced to concede, all in the name of preserving the League of Nations. France secured the Saar for fifteen years, and a demilitarized Rhineland was established more or less along Clemenceau's desired lines (though not Foch's). This pattern was repeated over and over again during the ensuing weeks as the Fourteen Points were gradually eviscerated.

So much time had been wasted, and the pressures to wrap up the conference so intense, that portentous decisions regarding all sorts of questions were rushed to resolution (others, of less importance, were brushed aside, such as whether Monaco should be allowed to join the League). Lloyd George, the ultimate trimmer, led the way, hammering out compromises, anxious as he was to return home where a mountain of domestic difficulties awaited him (he would remain in office for another three years, before being defeated at the polls). Being a man largely devoid of principles (according to his enemies), he was smart enough to see that the general political situation throughout the continent did not permit for further delay. Central Europe and Russia seemed to be disintegrating in front of everyone's eyes. Which would come first, peace or total anarchy? Borders were defined and populations moved from one sovereignty to another (some almost by whim), amidst an atmosphere of 'snarling and crawling', according to Wilson. Areas of mixed peoples, sects, languages and religions were akin to 'mangrove swamps, where roots were [irreconcilably] tangled and intermingled'. House agreed, in some despair. 'To create new boundaries is always to create new troubles; the one follows the other'.[23] Mounting evidence that bolshevism was up to no good prompted a gradual hardening of hostility towards its presumed menace as a travelling bacteria, the result being the initiation of tentative military operations against red forces in Russia. (Wilson called the bolsheviks 'poison'.) These and a multitude of other problems resulted in the corridors of the Quai d'Orsay, full of 'vulgar gold and faded silks', being jammed with supplicants of all kinds: Zionists, Armenians, all manner of Slavs, White Russians, Arabs, Greeks, Irishmen, assorted Orientals, Indians – all desperate for appointments to meet the American president or anyone who might influence him. House held his share of conversations with exoticisms, one of whom, the archbishop of Albania, came in full ecclesiastical regalia, a sort of throwback to a medieval orthodoxy little changed since Noah's Flood. Then there was T. E. Lawrence, complete with Arabian headgear, accompanying the equally impressive Emir Faisal, whose joint occupation of Damascus in the waning day of the war was, as Nicolson put it, 'extremely awkward'. (The last thing Britain or France wanted was an independent Arabian state; they wanted 'to divide the swag', i.e. the oil-rich lands of the Middle East; the Suez Canal was another prize worth controlling.)[24] The president summarized the blizzard of minor characters with whom he was forced to deal by a comic reference to his chat with the king of Montenegro: 'Not that I give a damn, but how's your mother?'

The most obdurate of the varied nationalities were the Poles, whom Lloyd George viewed as 'hopeless … very like the Irish', but the enduring migraine concerned the Italians, whose persistence in agitating over the eastern shores of the Adriatic, and the port city of Fiume in particular, proved excruciating to all the Big Three. Everyone grew tired of the often hysterical appeals from Orlando and his delegation who were, internally, wracked with dissent and worried that commotion back home would force them all out of office, which resulted in their refusal to admit to any sort of compromise. Clemenceau dubbed Orlando 'the weeper', and Wilson said 'I'm sick to death' of him. Balfour called the entire delegation 'swine'. Italy's uneven (to say the least) performance during the war excited everyone's contempt; their victories could be impressive (Vittorio Veneto, though against a completely dispirited Austro-Hungarian force), but their defeats (Caporetto) were almost beyond catastrophic. It did not seem to most observers that the average Italian's heart was really 'into the war' with any true resolve. The American general, Tasker Bliss, dismissed them entirely, recalling the scorn that Italian naval officers, in his presence, had heaped on their courageous British counterparts after the fighting had stopped. The Royal Navy had foolishly sallied forth from Scapa Flow to take on the Germans at Jutland, they said, the result being huge casualties and lost capital ships. The Italian navy, on the other hand, had never left port and, therefore, had not lost any ships … a superior actuarial record, without a doubt. 'The Italians are a bunch of cowards', Bliss fumed.

Those most furious with Orlando, however, conveniently forgot that over 650,000 Italians had lost their lives during the war, with nearly a million more wounded, and that some reward was necessary to placate that country's public. Even so, such gruesome casualties were not enough to make Wilson and the others ignore the fact that Italy had, in effect, sold her services to the highest bidder, the allies; that her motivations were not idealistic, but imperialist, to enlarge the territorial borders of a greater Italy at the expense of Austria-Hungary, the Slavs in general and Turkey; and that her claims were inconsistent with the kind of peace that Wilson envisioned. The American president, remembering his enthusiastic reception everywhere in Italy just three months before, took another of his ill-advised gambles. Assuming that he held the moral high ground, he appealed directly to the Italian public to support his repudiation of Orlando's exaggerated demands. The more worldly-wise among the delegations centred in Paris deplored this move, as just another example of Wilson's disconnection from reality, a sentiment Lloyd George constantly caught from Clemenceau, to whose body language the British prime minster seemed particularly attuned. When Wilson went off on one of his idealistic tangents, 'Clemenceau wonders what he means and, metaphorically speaking, touches his forehead as much as to say, "A good man, but not quite all there."' Such was this Italian gesture, which set off such a fury in Rome and other cities that riot police were required to control angry mobs. Posters sprang up all over the country of Wilson wearing a *pickelhaube*, or spiked helmet, the arch symbol of Prussians. On 22 April, the Italians withdrew from the conference and left the city, a move the French press sarcastically dubbed *'Le Voyage' de M. Orlando.* Wilson was stunned. Earlier that month, he suffered what is now believed to have been a minor stroke. It was to be followed by others of increasing severity. People began noticing that one of his eyes twitched, at times uncontrollably. The president was living on borrowed time.

'Do you think', asked Balfour of Clemenceau, 'that there is the smallest prospect of the Germans accepting these terms?'

'They won't the first day, but they will.'

It is hard to say whether Wilson fully understood the enormous gulf that now separated what his earliest visions had been just six months before, and the reality of its shortcomings as embedded in the 413-page document that the Germans were presented with on 7 May (the exact day, four years before, when the *Lusitania* was torpedoed). He was by that date emotionally isolated; the only people whom he now trusted and confided in were his wife and his physician, Admiral Grayson. Everyone else had been shuttered away, their reservations, opinions and advice neither asked for nor, if proffered, accepted. In general terms, the president was pleased. He realized that hundreds of details in the final document were not to his liking (an American called them 'minor injustices'); he also accepted the fact that 'his' League was an imperfect instrument, but his sense of triumph that it now existed rose supreme. It might be vague, it might not be perfect, but it was an instrument that later men could hone and perfect. He never claimed that the League was anywhere near completed, only that its necessity was preordained.

The Germans, initially excluded from the League until they had reformed themselves (and complied with the onerous conditions of the armistice), were horrified. Their delegation, led by the elderly foreign minister, Ulrich von Brockdorff-Rantzau, had been treated little better than prisoners of war when they arrived in Paris after a long, purposely slow train journey (so the Germans could better view the devastated north of France, which had the desired effect; one of the delegation wrote his wife that 'we had seen all we could endure', the experience had 'seared my soul').[25] The delegates transferred to automobiles; bystanders threw rocks at their cars, and spat on the road as they passed by. Their accommodations were surrounded by barbed wire, and combat troops patrolled nearby. The route of their convoy passed captured

German tanks and heavy artillery pieces assembled on the streets as trophies of war. This was not to be a peace between equals, that much was certain.

Brockdorff-Rantzau made a dreadful impression as he received the Treaty terms in a large public ceremony. He 'looked ill, drawn and nervous', Sir George Riddell noted in his diary. 'He walks with a slight limp. His complexion is yellowish, and there are black rings under his eyes which are sunk deep in his head. When he was taking off his coat, I noticed that his face was covered with beads of perspiration.' As a group, they 'compared badly with the Allied representatives'. Palpably nervous, Brockdorff-Rantzau was physically unable to stand as he delivered his response to various remarks by Clemenceau. Most attenders considered this a gross breach of etiquette. Nor were the German's comments well received, a mixture of sullen resentment with occasional doses of bravado thrown in. None of the so-called Big Three spoke or were familiar with German, so they indulged in the customarily prejudicial response that can occur when that guttural, dissonant and seemingly arrogant language is listened to, if indeed not understood. Militarism, Prussians, troop commands, the 'harsh metallic' tone of his address – Brockdorff-Rantzau fulfilled all the necessary clichés to turn his listeners' hearts to stone. Lloyd George was so incensed, he broke his letter opener in two. 'The effect on President Wilson's mind', according to him, 'was to close it with a snap.' Only Clemenceau remained unperturbed. 'We are accustomed to their insolence', he told the British prime minister; 'we have had to bear it for fifty years.'

The question then became: would Germany sign it? And if they did not, what would the allies do? When the terms were revealed to the Reichstag in Berlin, pandemonium broke out among all the political parties no matter what their persuasion. 'The unbelievable has happened', said one member. Another wrote his wife, 'I had believed in Wilson until today.' Whatever had become of the Fourteen Points? Nationalists and right-wingers lost all perspective, reflecting a thought that Marshal Foch had written to his wife in a private letter: the 'Germans do not appear to agree they have been beaten; we did not take the war to their territory, so they are not defeated, they say.' These diehards were all for resuming the war, forgetting the fact that their beloved army harboured but a shell of its former resolve. General Hans von Seeckt, the army's representative to the Versailles delegation (a man, according to Repington, who would not hesitate to shoot someone at dawn) surprisingly counselled restraint. The army was in no condition to withstand an allied invasion, an opinion that von Hindenburg, back in Germany, seconded. Leftists, on the other hand, were caught in a desperate political position. The Treaty was such a ferocious instrument of revenge that any government willing to sign it would be immediately excoriated, condemned as traitors or assassinated, blamed for every current and future ill and thrown out of office (some of which came to pass, as a matter of fact).[26] This would leave a vacuum whereby either extremists of the Trotsky variety might again attempt to seize power or, more likely, a right-wing military coup that would put a violent end to the socialist experiment. The result of the latter would be a crumbling Paris Commune of sorts, with impromptu roadside firing squads weeding out their entire movement. There appeared to be nowhere to turn.

In the seven-week interval between the receipt of the Treaty and its eventual signing, the assembled participants held their breath. Brockdorff-Rantzau's delegation attempted to renegotiate the most egregious conditions, but only Lloyd George was willing to talk further. Wilson and Clemenceau, by contrast, had had enough, and adopted a 'take it or leave it' posture, despite the growing weakness of their own positions. Only the American army under Pershing was ready to go again if hostilities were resumed. The pressure in Britain for early demobilization was enormous, and the French were so weary that sending *poilus* back to the front represented an inconceivable thought (though again, not to Foch, who was planning to hurl forty-two divisions into the heart of enemy territory). Dissension among the allied delegations was also a corroding factor. Young Turks like John Maynard Keynes, Harold Nicolson, William Bullitt and others who had come to Paris with such enthusiasm, had now become 'renegades', as one of them put it, scornful of Wilson, incredulous at the terms of the Treaty, and ready to quit on a moment's notice (especially after a night of heavy drinking, when things invariably looked bleakest).[27] News that mutinous German sailors had scuttled their battleships at Scapa Flow on 21 June further hardened everyone's animosity towards the defeated enemy. They couldn't be trusted to do anything right.

A collective sigh of relief emerged, however, when Germany finally resolved to put the entire matter to sleep by signing the document. Their rationale was fairly simple: the financial penalties were so draconian that Germany would never pay them; the other punishments were such that, over time, they too would prove to be unenforceable. Better to sign and then move on. German industrial might had not been irrevocably disrupted or destroyed during the war, its potential to resume its premier position, in the long term, remained a distinct possibility. It was time for the war to end. With considerable courage, though trembling nonetheless, the current chancellor, Gustav Bauer, a hitherto obscure labour leader, cabled Paris that the treaty would be signed (not, however, by Brockdorff-Rantzau, who resigned in disgust). On 28 June 1919 (another anniversary, this time the day that Franz-Ferdinand was assassinated in Sarajevo, five long and seemingly remote years before), German signatories were called in to the Hall of Mirrors at the palace of Versailles to sign the Treaty, in a ceremony that Sir Henry Wilson and most everyone else of any importance thought was long on display, but utterly short on dignity (women guests mostly chattered away, some attenders asked the Germans for autographs, and so on). Colonel House thought it was disgraceful, reminiscent of the Greek and Roman custom of dragging those vanquished in war behind their chariots in the dust and debris of city streets, to the delight of loutish onlookers. Others commented that the Germans were treated as common criminals, being led from subterranean holding pens into the prisoner's dock. Sir William Orpen, at the time perhaps the most successful and best-known portrait painter in Europe, was in Paris during the conference, wangling an opportunity to paint Woodrow Wilson as one of his projects (not successfully, since the president intensely disliked Orpen's first rendition of his ears; only with difficulty would Wilson consent to further sittings). Orpen painted the ceremony, an encyclopaedic canvas that included nearly all the central characters as they looked on at one of the German delegates bending over the final document and adding his signature. In Harold Nicolson's apt phrase, the poor German, hunched over the desk with his neck facing down, seemed reminiscent of a victim waiting for the onrush of that uniquely French creation, the sharp blade of the guillotine, the most famous victim of which was Louis XVI during the French Revolution. How ironic that Orpen included in his painting a slogan, embossed in gold, carved near the ceiling of the palace wall – *'Le roi gouverne par lui-meme'*, or 'The king governs by himself', a notion the Great War had demolished. When the signing was abruptly adjourned by Clemenceau after forty-five minutes, the fountains of Versailles were turned on for the first time since the war started. The Big Three took bows from a garden overlook, and guns were fired all over Paris. President Wilson immediately departed for Le Havre, the *George Washington* and home. He couldn't wait to leave the city; Lloyd George wasn't far behind. Clemenceau was tired but satisfied. Nicolson's diary entry the next morning summarized that young man's weary attitude. 'Celebrations in the hotel afterwards', he wrote. 'We are given free champagne at the expense of the rate-payer. It is very bad champagne. Go out on to the boulevards afterwards. To bed, sick of life.'

Time of Judgment: How to Explain What Went Wrong

> *'What I seem to see – with all my heart I hope*
> *I am wrong – is a tragedy of disappointment.'*

Woodrow Wilson

It has been frequently written that Clemenceau, Foch and the French delegation in general ('still hot from the fray', as Clemenceau correctly put it), were shortsighted and vengeful when it came to extracting concessions, reparations and military emasculation from the allegedly beaten Germans. It is certainly true that there was little love lost between these two countries and that France, more ferociously than any of the other allied governments (aside, perhaps, from the Italians), were obsessively focused on grinding the Germanic nose into the dirt. France wanted the Rhineland, she wanted the three bridgeheads on that river's eastern bank, she wanted the German coalfields in the Saar, she wanted the imperial army replaced by something little better than a glorified police force (a bare 100,000 men, conscripts with but a year required in service). In other words, she wanted a prostrate Germany. While there is a degree of truth to these damning assessments, there are additional shadings of grey to justify the French viewpoint.

The Franco-Prussian War of nearly five decades' memory was in some respects a model that the French copied. After that disastrous conflict, Germany had inflicted humiliating and draconian terms on their traditional foe. One might almost say that France was returning the favour. Human nature being what it is, could they be blamed?

Secondly, France had borne the brunt of the fighting between 1914 and 1918. She had lost almost 1.3 million men; the war had been fought largely on her territory; along with Belgium, her industries had been destroyed or looted of their heavy equipment, her mines flooded, her railway system degraded, her men dragged away into forced labour pools by the initially victorious enemy. Was Germany to be allowed, after a peace treaty and a pause, to catch her second breath, to simply reignite her powerful economy (essentially undamaged by war) and thereby overwhelm French and Belgian commercial interests still struggling to reconstruct? These are interesting questions not easily resolved by a simple denunciation of French desire for revenge. Could Clemenceau have survived politically if he had fought to stem or divert this national rage? Certainly not (as a matter of fact, his career came to an end anyway). Clemenceau, who did so much to win the war, was comparatively powerless to bring into being the sort of postwar Europe that might have guaranteed a more stable future. He helped to create the only type of treaty that had a chance of being accepted by his countrymen; that it was a travesty did not make it unique in the annals of European history. There was also the question of his personal make-up. As an American put it, 'every question was viewed by him in the light of how it would affect France', and in that spirit 'he suffered from no qualms of indecision'.

It seems undeniable that the entire premise of the Versailles peace conference was immeasurably distorted by Woodrow Wilson, and the unquestioned prominence that his political statements generated throughout the continent and, indeed, the world. It was doomed from the start. As Secretary of State Lansing had prophetically remarked, the president's public declarations of intent 'will raise hopes that can never be realized', which is exactly what happened. Wilson should never be blamed for his high idealism; indeed, any consideration of his moral stature must by necessity diminish that of Theodore Roosevelt, who seemed by comparison nothing more than a circus barker, according to the journalist A. G. Gardiner, 'raising clouds of dust'.[28] But, idealism aside, the practical result was a quagmire, a weakened central Europe, and little more than a blueprint for future war. Nicolson wondered if any other result had ever been possible. Too many architects, he noted in a letter home, 'each designing an entirely different house'. There is also little doubt that Wilson, while intellectually competent and more than able, found himself outmanoeuvred by his amoral colleagues, who proved more supple and pliant when it came to hammering out the various deals and compromises of the conference, the details and ramifications of which they often knew nothing, and cared less about. As Henry Wickham Steed, the knowledgeable editor of *The Times*, saw right away, Wilson was out of his sphere, being 'temperamentally unfitted for direct personal negotiation'.

In terms of domestic politics, the predominant puzzle requiring explanation has largely revolved around President Wilson's inexplicable misreading of both his political enemy's tenacity and the mood of his country. The peace treaty he brought home had barely a chance of passage through Congress, especially given the president's refusal to meet any of his opponents halfway. Perhaps his capacity to compromise had been stretched to the limit by his bitter experiences in Paris; perhaps illness clouded his judgment; perhaps his Calvinist gene pool clicked into gear so wholeheartedly that it overrode the political instincts that had generally served him well over his career. The answer is probably an amalgamation of all three of these explanations. But, fundamentally, the president was caught in a vise of his own rhetorical making: he was skewered in large part by the inherent contradictions of his purposes, especially after America's entry into the war. 'Peace Without Victory' was a fine and noble expression, but could one propose to young men and women going off to war that their intent was not to win the ensuing battles, but to somehow fight them to a draw?[29] Germany was the enemy. Public opinion, except in the socialist press, made no distinction between the militaristic cabal surrounding the kaiser, and those German delegates in the Reichstag who were clamouring for peace. They were all, by and large, the common enemy. Most Americans, whether encouraged by jingoism or simple logic, thought the idea behind any war was to triumph. As Americans died in Château-Thierry, Belleau Wood and the Argonne Forest, the idea of sympathy for Germans, or the notion of a postwar world free of conflict, was too far beyond the mentality of most people to accept. They tended to agree with Wilson's arch enemy, Senator Lodge, that 'the only peace for us is one that rests on … unconditional surrender. No peace that satisfies Germany in any degree can ever satisfy us.' Wilson had nothing but contempt for such narrow-minded aims (he made a remark about Lodge that 'when I get out of this office, I will tell him what I think of him'). He had no idea, as House noted in his diary, how 'war mad' Americans had become. The gap between Woodrow Wilson and the great American tradition of Civil War generals such as Ulysses S. Grant and William Tecumseh Sherman, ravaging their way through the south spreading destruction, was seldom wider. Wilson had never been a soldier and had never wanted to be one. Blood lust or dreams of revenge were, to him, alien concepts.

Lloyd George published his memoirs of the Versailles peace conference two decades after the treaty was signed. In its final pages, he imagined what it would be like to enter the afterlife as a visitor, rather like Dante in the *Inferno*, to ask his compatriots what they thought about the European world of 1939. Clemenceau, he was certain, would say something along the lines of, 'I told you this would happen'. Lloyd George could hear it now, in Clemenceau's 'fierce staccato, that Germany had behaved exactly as he had anticipated.… She was now more powerful, more domineering, more dangerous, more ravenous than ever.' With another world war on the verge of beginning once again, who could have quarrelled with such an assessment? As for Wilson, 'he would not have changed his opinions in any particular'. The League failed, Lloyd George had the president saying, because of Henry Cabot Lodge and other diehard Republican partisans. Looking over the 'agony' of 1939, Wilson would simply have said to the noble senator from Massachusetts, 'This is your doing'. Probably the only man happy with the Treaty, and happy with the League, was a man Lloyd George had never heard of in 1919: Adolf Hitler. During the often ragamuffin years of his early career as a right-wing demagogue, Hitler railed on and on about Versailles. It was the staple of his repertoire, the topic he hammered over and over again. As the 1920s progressed, however, his political trajectory could no longer be viewed with any sort of amusement. He had hit a goldmine, burrowing into a deep seam of resentment, anger, humiliation and a deep-rooted desire for revenge. As Foch repeatedly pointed out, you could never trust a German; they were at heart unregenerate militarists. The shame of Versailles, the 'stab in the back' thesis, the urge to rearm and fight again, all found their germination in the gutters of Munich beer halls and the street corners of every German city where soapbox oratory flourished best. The postwar aims of Foch, Clemenceau and unregenerate Tories such as Sir Henry Wilson was somehow to 'prevent Germans from being Germans'. But their vindictive and vengeful policies failed, ignoring the more enlightened opinion of the South African prime minister, Louis Botha, that the least desirable outcome of the Great War would be the creation of a festering sore in the middle of Europe. The only person who could relish such a condition, and who took full advantage of it, was Hitler.

Chapter 18

Known & Unknown Soldier(s)

'On the day of the funeral procession coffins of cypress wood are carried out on wagons, one coffin for each tribe, with each man's bones in his own tribe's coffin. One dressed but empty bier is carried for the missing whose bodies could not be found or recovered.'

Thucydides, *The History of the Peloponnesian War*

The Last Day of 1918

Lewis, the largest of the outer Scottish Hebridean islands, had sent 6,000 men to the fronts, of whom 1,000 never returned. In perhaps the saddest event of the entire ghastly war, 760 demobilized island veterans were gathered together on the Scottish mainland to take the ferry home on New Year's Eve 1918. Crowds of family and relatives were all gathered in the harbour of Stornoway to welcome them back, alive and all in one piece. There were so many servicemen milling around the ferry terminal at Kyle of Lochalsh, however, that a second ship was required to make the 68-nautical-mile voyage, HMY *Iolaire* (Gaelic for *Eagle*). As it crossed the body of water known as the Minch, it ran into severe weather and, just a mile from the mouth of Stornoway Harbor, it was driven onto a set of dangerous shore rocks known locally as the Beasts of Holm. Of the 275 or so passengers on the *Iolaire* (rated to carry 80 passengers), about seventy made it to shore, only fifty or so feet away. Instead of welcoming home their husbands, sons, brothers and loved ones, islanders spent the next day combing the coast in a search for bodies. Among the many thousands of war memorials that lay throughout the British Isles, the lonely plinth standing on the shore nearest the Beasts is perhaps the most melancholy of the whole lot.

Those 200-plus lost men were not officially designated 'war dead'. Nor was Henry Willoughby Sandham, who died in a military hospital in Greece after the armistice, a bureaucratic exclusion that embittered his sister who, with her husband, built the least conventional memorial to a lost one that exists in Britain. Located near Burghclere, a small village fifty miles west of London, the Behrends (John Louis and Mary) commissioned a strange bird indeed, the artist Stanley Spencer, to paint murals in a small chapel they built in honour of Sandham. Spencer, too, was a veteran of the war, having served in Macedonia. In a series of nineteen separate panels that took six years to complete, he chose as his subjects everyday and mundane experiences that could hardly be called heroic. *Scrubbing the Floor, Sorting the Laundry, Filling Tea Urns* – these were the focus of his semi-abstract, neo-primitive, post-impressionist gaze, and their very ordinariness is, in fact, the key to their impelling effect. Stanley, to use a phrase now common, was genuinely 'weird', and the triviality of his subject matter (in one scene, men smear jam on bread slices for afternoon snacks) are all the more strange when compared to the very large central piece over the altar, *The Resurrection of the Soldiers*, a masterpiece, but, in a brooding sense, the oddest of them all. A sea of crosses clutters the foreground, as soldiers emerge from their graves, greeting and shaking hands with their comrades, liberated from death. Other soldiers converge on Christ, depositing their crosses at his feet. Unlike conventionally religious scenes, Christ is not the focal point of the painting. He is, rare for any depiction of the adult saviour, clean-shaven and marked only by his white cassock; behind him, a Bruegelian tableau of crosses being carried by the resurrected dead. The entire scene, though not depicting warfare or ghastly visions of death in the trenches, is nonetheless nightmarish. It is hard to believe any parent or bereaved relation would gain solace from looking at these images, whatever their artistic merit. Then again, perhaps the Behrends were not looking for solace; perhaps they agreed with John Maynard Keynes, who objected to the 'sentimental purification' that seemed to him to mark so many of the commemorations for those who perished in the great conflagration. The chapel at Burghclere represents, more than anything else, everyday revulsion.[1]

Within a decade of the armistice, most of the warring nations had fastened on the concept of the Unknown Soldier around which to coalesce their national sorrow.[2] The idea was simple: to disinter from the battlefield the corpse of a man about whom nothing was known, except the fact that he was dead. Rank would not matter, social distinction would not matter and the unit or regiment of service would not matter. The only prerequisite was anonymity, the Unknown 'sacrificing even the remembrance of his very name', as Clemenceau put it. The body would be returned home and reburied in his country, reverenced by the nation at large. The single man would become, in essence, everyman, although in most cases the humble origins of whomever was chosen soon stood overwhelmed by the munificence, splendour and meticulous ceremony that were lavished on the deceased. It was also, in the opinion of some, a process that inevitably glossed over the reality of the man's fate, the very waste of his death as it were, replacing it with symbolism that reeked of everything that had caused the war in the first place: imperialism, militarism, the 'glorification' of a heroic death. Not many men, after all, would have their bier followed, on foot, by the king of England, who had placed a mediaeval sword from his 'private collection' on the casket; not many 'ordinary' men would be buried in Westminster Abbey; not many would have thousands file by his grave site over the course of several days in a national outpouring of grief seldom ever seen anywhere (the only modern equivalent in Britain, anyway, might have been the funeral procession of the late Diana, Princess of Wales, in 1997).

George V felt uneasy about the entire Unknown Soldier scenario. He, like the nation at large, was tired of war (at least he could drink again; he had 'taken the pledge' not to touch a drop for the duration, which he mostly honoured). Going through the pathos of yet another burial, this time on a national scale unheard of before, would unnecessarily roil people's memories and cause undue pain. His opinion was brushed aside. On one matter of etiquette, however, he stood firm, refusing to award the British Unknown with the Victoria Cross, England's highest award for heroism. The Unknown, being unknown, had not been witnessed doing anything extraordinary on the battlefield other than being killed, so how was one to know if the recipient was truly worthy? George dug in his heels on this one, and prevailed. It did not help matters that General Pershing later placed a Congressional Medal of Honour on the grave site in Westminster Abbey; when an American Unknown was interred in 1921 in Washington D.C., reciprocity was expected. Surely the king would award a Victoria Cross in return (he would not). As the king's retrograde private secretary explained, the Congress Medal (as he called it) was some nouveau decoration without sufficient pedigree, and nowhere near the exalted plateau of a Victoria Cross. (As is usual in such situations, the facts were otherwise: the Victoria Cross was officially instituted in 1856, the Congressional Medal of Honor only six years later.) This officious display of snobbery threatened to intensify into something of an international incident until the king was overruled by his cabinet, and tempers cooled. The American Unknown received his Victoria Cross, as well as something his British counterpart did not have, an eternal flame. As far as the Belgian Unknown was concerned, however, an inferior decoration, the Military Cross, was deemed 'quite sufficient'.[3]

On Armistice Day 1920, the Unknown Warrior was buried in Westminster Abbey, after a long procession that began on the continent and arrived, in London, at Victoria Station. (William Orpen painted the Unknown's flag-draped coffin as it sat in state in France. On either side were two emaciated Tommies, seemingly out of their minds from shell shock, draped in ragged army blankets. These were later painted over.) The king joined the ceremony outside Whitehall, after which he unveiled the famous architect Edwin

Lutyens's 'cenotaph' (from the Greek for empty tomb; everyone looked to the heroes and historians of the ancient Hellenic past for their inspiration in such matters).[4] Lutyens undoubtedly envisioned, sketched, designed and oversaw the construction of more war memorials than any man who ever lived. It is to be wondered how he retained his sanity (his collaboration with the renowned horticulturalist Gertrude Jekyll, in more pleasurable domestic applications, such as vacation homes, undoubtedly helped to soothe his mind). Britain, to say nothing of France and Belgium, was literally jammed with Lutyens's designs, most of which radiate tremendous emotion, though also, in keeping with British understatement, tremendous restraint. The London Cenotaph, which served as a model (sometimes literally) for several others, is very powerful, very moving and very severe, a series of slightly inward-leaning blocks of diminishing size, on top of which lies the empty coffin. No inscription other than the dates of the war in Roman numerals and the words 'The Glorious Dead' (Kipling's phrase) are carved on the slabs of Portland stone used in its construction. Lutyens refused any payment for his design, which cost a little over £7,000 to build, the equivalent of seven Sopwith Camel aircraft.

At Westminster Abbey, the Unknown Warrior was then solemnly interred just inside the west entrance, covered by earth brought over from the various European battlefields. It is by far the most prominent and centrally located burial in that ancient building. The burial service was relatively brief but most impressive. No nation so revels in ceremony as Britain. In later months a few brief flurries of controversy erupted, to many people's displeasure. The inscriptions around the edges of the burial site, chosen by the dean of the abbey, were unsurprisingly Christian in tone, which offended several Jewish rabbis. The dean was discomforted. What was he supposed to do? he wrote one of these critics; Westminster was a Christian church, he couldn't be expected to satisfy everyone. What about Muslims killed in a British uniform, or poor Hindus for that matter? he asked. The words he designed for the central slab, a piece of stone quarried from Belgium, also came in for comment, especially the lines that commended those in the war 'who gave the most that man can give, life itself, for god, for king and country', among other things. Those disenchanted with war pointed out the obvious: no one 'gave' their lives, they had their lives taken from them. The only person to emerge unspotted in such rhetorical wrangling was Rudyard Kipling.[5] His judicious selection and/ or composition of several memorable lines used at war cemeteries that spread from his native land all the way to the Far East, struck a universal chord. The best-known of these are surely 'Their Name Liveth For Evermore' and 'Known Unto God', the latter generally inscribed on the grave slab of unidentifiable bodies. Countless tons of white Portland stone were shipped overseas to mark every Commonwealth grave. Families were generally given the option of having a biblical phrase, or anything else they wanted, carved on the headstone at a cost of 1 ½ pence per letter. One read SCHOOL WAR DEATH (1 shilling, 9 pence). Many generals and members of the British high command followed suit, as a measure of solidarity, and opted for the same unadorned marker for their own graves. Field Marshal Sir Douglas Haig, since the war's end better known by his new title of 1st Earl Haig of Bermersyde, was buried on the gorgeous grounds of Dryburgh Abbey in Scotland after his death in 1928. He could have commissioned a grandiose mortuarial confection, but chose the simple soldier's slab instead. He had a remarkably humble phrase carved on his: 'He trusted in God and tried to do the right' (4 shillings, 7 ½ pence).

Most of the general public were genuinely moved by all the attention focused on the Unknown Warrior, belying the king's initial concern. There were, of course, exceptions. One survivor of the war was an alumnus of Rugby, the famous public school. In his dormitory of fifty-six boys, twenty-three had been killed in action. He thought it a waste of time to remember the dead; what use was that to them, being no longer alive? He thought the living should be celebrated. So did the poet W. H. Auden, who favoured paying attention to the vertical man, not his horizontal counterpart. G. B. Shaw thought about writing a play on the whole process, the catch being that when resurrected in heaven, everyone would be shocked to learn that the Unknown was a German.

The Cenotaph continues to play a significant role in British ceremonialism. Each year the monarch reviews veterans as they march past Whitehall. Every group, in turn, deposits a wreath of red poppies at the base of the Cenotaph. It is a solemn procession indeed, and takes several hours to complete. Siegfried Sassoon, the most bitter of all the war poets, hated the sentimentality of it all, especially the tripe that apologists like Kipling (called by one historian 'the king's trumpeter') continued to publish.[6] In a poem published in 1933 Sassoon wrote,

> The Prince of Darkness to the Cenotaph
> Bowed. As he walked away I heard him laugh.

Later on in 1933, a German diplomat placed a wreath on the Cenotaph and then gave the fascist salute. A British war veteran came by, took the lilies and laurel leaves away, dumping them in the nearby Thames. Whether it was the swastika on the ribbon that offended him, symbolizing as it did the rebirth in

Germany of 'jingoism run stark mad' or simple detestation for the enemy, was never fully explained. James Sears, the culprit, was fined 40 shillings for 'wilful damage'. He then ran for a seat in parliament. The novelist E. M. Forster noted that he often took long walks during the night through London streets with his friend T. E. Lawrence, 'avoiding the Cenotaph, because he was in uniform and would have been obliged to salute it'.

On the day the Unknown Warrior was laid to rest at Westminster, his French brother-in-arms was interred under Napoleon's Arc de Triomphe in Paris. His body came from the Verdun battlefield. Placed on a military caisson, it was drawn through the streets of that devastated city to the railway station between rows of *poilus* standing to attention. It was a rainy day in Verdun, and the atmosphere unrelievedly dreary. The subversive, anti-establishment Parisian periodical, *Le Canard Enchaîné*, refused to succumb to popular emotion. The best 'unknown soldier' in their opinion was the one who had burned his identity papers and deserted. French graveyards also witnessed their fair share of bitterness. In the famous Parisian cemetery *Père Lachaise*, containing the graves of many an illustrious warrior, a widow had these words carved on her family plot:

> Same prayers
> Same grave
> Same glory
> To the victim of 1870 (father)
> To the victor of 1915 (son)

Rome, one year later, was sunny for its turn. Italy's Unknown was buried in the glaring splendour of the white-marbled *Altare della Patria*, more familiarly known as *Vittoriano*, designed in 1885 to celebrate Italian reunification. This ostentatious, to say nothing of garish, piece of architecture (known to some Italians as 'The Typewriter' for all its columns), is festooned with the usual Caesarian flourishes. The ornate gun carriage carrying the coffin is displayed in a museum within the building.

Ireland presented a special challenge, in keeping with its utterly twisted political condition. After 1923, when the vicious civil war finally ended, the more or less politically correct line from Éamon de Valera and his Republican diehards was that anyone who had enlisted in the British armed forces to fight in France had been duped. Officially speaking (or, more accurately, commemoratively speaking) they simply disappeared from the stage. The Irishmen killed in the Easter Rising (some 450 individuals) were grandiloquently celebrated; the 49,000 or so who died in Flanders fields, were essentially ignored. In Protestant churches in both north and south, parish registers dutifully commissioned books of remembrance, with beautiful calligraphy, which listed the flower of the Anglo-Irish gentry who had given their lives for the king, the naves of same crowded with regimental plaques and fading battle standards, many full of holes; by contrast, in Roman Catholic churches, nothing on the wall except stations of the cross. Committees were established, meetings held and plans projected to create some memorial that might rival that on Messines Ridge in Belgium ('The Irish Peace Park'), but nothing ever materialized, due in large measure to more or less official obstruction.[7] Lutyens was finally commissioned to put together a design, and a site was set aside which, ironically, lies below the hill where the Kilmainham Jail sits in brooding menace. Construction began, in fits and starts, in the 1930s, but the site was not formally opened until the 1980s. The many intervening years had not been kind to Lutyens's conception. At one point, it was virtually taken over by squatters and tinkers with their caravans, camp fires blazing in the winter nights, children sent out each morning to beg for their suppers. The prosperous boom times of the Celtic Tiger saw the place finally tidied up; the buildings repaired, the grounds put in shape, an 'inauguration' staged, but the location is remote, signage dreadful, its very existence still downplayed, and most visitors, aside from formal occasions, are dog walkers and joggers. The layout and design have much to be blamed for this eclipse of interest. Lutyens may have meant well, but his scheme was dreadfully impolitic, a Georgian 'Big House' atmosphere that curiously (but appropriately) emphasized the rear end of the mansion and not its ornate and formal entryway. The visitor feels, wandering around here, as though he's rummaging through the stables, or the dairy, or the smithy or any number of other outbuildings that cluttered the working courtyards of the Master's Anglo-Irish manse. This is a monument to the back door, the place where Irish peasants did the dirty work before they inadvisably signed up to become cannon fodder in the king's army. While they died in France, British artillery turned central Dublin into ruins as reward for their fidelity. The final touch is a snippet of maudlin poetry from Rupert Brooke that lies engraved on the floor of a Georgian cupola or garden folly. Was there anything less appropriate?

In the Soviet Union, the tsarist armies are a dead letter. During the long Stalinist regime no memorials of any real significance to the hundreds of thousands who fell were even contemplated. The very idea would have been enough to send a person to the gulag. Perhaps in the more benevolent twenty-first century some recognition may be made, but to most people in present-day Russia, World War I was a long time ago and best forgotten.

The Turkish memorial to their Unknown, finally completed in 1958, is a huge four-columned monolithic structure that can be seen for miles around, and is perhaps the most fitting of all considering the circumstances. Just about all the Turks buried here and elsewhere on the Gallipoli peninsula are 'unknowns', pushed beneath the earth in mass graves 'without a shroud'. Their families were never sent official telegrams informing them of their father's or brother's or son's deaths (most were illiterate anyway, whether victim or bereaved made no difference); families often just surmised that their loved ones were dead when they never came home after the war. It is hardly an understatement to most Turks, given the enormous casualties they suffered, that a verse written on one of the columns (from the national anthem) can hardly be contradicted: 'You are the noble son of a martyr.'

The German situation has been complicated by the ignominy of World War II. Twenty unknown soldiers from the eastern front were buried in the enormous memorial built in 1924 on the site of the Tannenberg battle, along with the body of Paul von Hindenburg after he finally died a decade later. The vast, mock-Teutonic castle was dynamited as Soviet troops approached in 1945; what was left of the site was rummaged for badly needed building materials during the later reconstruction period (many bricks ended up in a World War II Russian memorial in a nearby town, later, in its turn, bulldozed by the Poles). The process of obliteration is now more or less complete today; the site is practically unrecognizable. German World War I military cemeteries in Belgium and France were and are understated affairs, purposely so to discourage vandalism. In 1931 the disused guardhouse to the Berlin palace of the since-deposed crown prince, known as the *Neue Wache*, was converted into a war memorial. The elegant and rather small neoclassical structure sitting on the Unter den Linden, Berlin's major thoroughfare, featured an oculus or skylight in the centre of its roof. This building was effectively blown to bits in the final siege of Berlin in 1945, but the East German Communist government resurrected the notion of its use as a war memorial, to be dedicated, in rather clumsy language, to the 'Victims of Fascism and Militarism'. Deaf to nuance, and as if to deliberately confirm its own dictatorial bent, the hammer and sickle was prominently engraved on the inner wall. An unknown soldier, but also an unknown resistance fighter were buried inside, urns filled with dirt from various concentration camps arrayed along the walls, and an eternal flame installed. 'Eternal' proved to be a misnomer, however: the flame was extinguished after reunification in the 1990s. Then all hell broke out, in which World War I receded to the background. No issue proved quite as contentious as the controversies that surrounded what the revamped *Neue Wache* might now pretend to be. A memorial to dead German soldiers? A memorial to the people that German soldiers killed? A collective admission of guilt? A memorial to German Jews? A symbol of reconciliation? An object lesson for the future? Or simply a monument to sadness? Opinions were diverse, feelings high and agreement impossible. The present concept centres on a statue by the leftist sculptor Käthe Kollwitz, who lost a son in the first war. It is a pietà of sorts, an enveloping old woman with arms and cloak wrapped around her dead child. It is an almost pyramidal representation that spreads from the mother's head outward to the floor. As Kollwitz wrote in her diary, 'Pain is very dark'. The sculpture sits beneath the oculus, which is open to the sky. It was not universally praised. One critic, boiling with rage over the entire convoluted premise, said the overall impression was one of an outhouse, Kollwitz's pietà nothing more than a tall pile of accumulated bird shit dumped from the hole in the roof. He, like many others, felt that the whole building should be razed. Such are the complications of modern Germany. Crippled in World War I, thoroughly destroyed in World War II, it is now, yet again, the powerhouse of Europe. The ironies of its present wealth allow it the leisure time to contemplate and dispute, as few countries can, the harvest of its contradictions.

One More Note on Death (and how we remember)

Having extensively toured all the combatant nations that participated in this Great War, visited the battlefields and countless historic sites, as well as museums, mausoleums, cemeteries, libraries and monuments, two final comments on the business of commemorating death. By far one of the more melancholy war memorials I saw lies in the northern city of York, near the train station, a Lutyens design built to acknowledge the deaths of over 2,000 employees of the North Eastern Railway Company, an enterprise long since defunct. This is not one of Lutyens's more inspired creations, an obelisk surrounded by two enveloping wings, a rather formulaic statement by his terms. Begrimed with soot, acid rain and the pollution of half a century's worth of passing coal-driven railway engines, the names of those commemorated have gradually been worn away and effaced. A sign nearby explains that cleaning or re-engraving all the names would do more damage to the structure than it was worth, and so several bronze plaques to the side were emplaced with the men again recorded ... lest they be forgotten. For some reason, the place is unrelievedly depressing.

Three hundred and forty-six members of the British armed forces during World War I were executed (only three were officers), 306 for desertion, an act likely brought on in several cases by shell shock, a disorder with which most court martial officers were generally unsympathetic (to say nothing of Haig, who reviewed most capital sentence cases). By contrast, German military authorities formally executed only 48. Lance Corporal William Moon, a Canadian, was a celebrated example. His nerves were finished when an exploding shell decapitated a fellow soldier, spraying the man's blood and debris in Moon's face. After a short stay in hospital, he ran for it when returned to the line. When caught, he was sentenced to death and shot early in 1916. Private John Doherty of the Black Watch, one of the most famous regiments in the British army, hightailed it not once but twice. Medical examiners could not vouch for the cause of his nervous condition, and one morning he and eleven others were formally executed in the foul atmospherics of a French *abattoir*, or slaughterhouse (instead of cattle, men were butchered). Generally speaking, in order to make the examples salutary for their compatriots, firing squads were drawn from units the condemned had fled. This made it more than likely that the executioners in fact knew, or knew of, the men they were shooting.

In fairness, the vast majority of death sentences ordered by courts martial in the wartime army, over 3,000 in fact, were generally commuted, so long as the detainee returned to the trenches and did not 'fill his pants' again. Many of those not pardoned were repeat offenders; given 'a pass' the first time around, they could expect no mercy for the second. Fourteen of these men were found in Britain itself, having no intent ever to return. It is also undeniable, however, that some executions were little better than drumhead justice, administered quickly after pro forma trials where those accused received minimal representation. It is a chequered history, and not a very enlightened one. Several movements in the 1990s, often supported by liberal elements of the press (*The Manchester Guardian*, for one) but opposed by those of a more conservative bent (*The Times*), agitated for a blanket pardon, particularly given that several of those executed were practically youngsters, having lied regarding their age when they foolishly followed the rage to 'sign up'. Members of the House of Lords expressed their disapproval of such a measure, as did Earl Haig, the field marshal's son, who said that many of those judged guilty were 'rogues' and 'criminals' who undoubtedly deserved what they got. The pardons were finally granted in 2006. Some family members had the gravestones of their relatives changed. If a man had been executed on the front, the words 'Killed' were usually carved on the slab, instead of the customary 'Killed in Action'. A few chose to have a new inscription carved, 'Shot at Dawn'.[8]

At the same time as people were arguing over pardons, a London tabloid floated the idea that Haig's equestrian statue on Whitehall, not far from the Cenotaph, should be removed and melted down. Haig was little better than a hack, they argued, his imperviousness to casualties close to criminal indifference. The statue itself, as referenced earlier, had been controversial from the start, mostly in relation to the rendition of Haig's horse by the sculptor Alfred Hardiman. Lady Haig had been furious; the steed looked like a draught horse and not anything the field marshal would ever have ridden. Hardiman, who lost money on the project, retorted that the image was stylized, as in many Renaissance statues, a demonstration of Haig's resolve, the steed (indomitable if not necessarily noble) ploughing ahead no matter the obstacle. Devotees of horseflesh (forget about Haig) mercilessly critiqued Hardiman's depiction of the steed, a 'circus' horse to some, ready to urinate according to others; the horse's head suggested 'Forward!' with his hind quarters just the reverse – 'Back!' Why have Haig on a horse anyway, some newspapers quipped? A modern general should be depicted getting into or out of his staff car, or dictating to his secretary. For better or for worse, the commotion died away. Hardiman's effort stands just where it did on 10 November 1937, when the Duke of Gloucester unveiled it, his brother the king having declined the honour. As Catherine the Great once said, 'Victors are not judged.'

Liverpool

Then, there was the question of religion. Along with millions of people, had God died as well? Was there a shred of divinity to be found in the carnage, cruelty and fractured lives these four years of the most destructive war ever undertaken by mankind? In all the combatant nations, God was felt to be 'on our side', but what were the results? What was the collateral damage? Who constituted the pool of true believers who would still go to church, or pray or put a farthing in the collection box? Aside from all the people killed, there were now 500,000 German widows, 1,000,000 orphans, and 2.7 million men either disfigured or amputees. In Britain, statistics for those disfigured were less, but still an astounding quarter of a million; *The Times*, for many, many months after the war, continued to run a subsection of its obituary columns entitled 'Death by Wounds'. For many, absorbing these gruesome realties, the answer for a God was a resounding no. As a microcosm of the dilemma, there stands the story of the Liverpool cathedrals.

Liverpool, then the third city of England, was a microcosm of commercial success. A stupendous harbour, a gateway to the New World, the nub of progress, wealth, manufacturing and the bustle of business, its enormous customs hall generated more income for the imperial treasury than any other tax-gathering entity in the country. The first consul from the infant United States was assigned to Liverpool, not London, demonstrating the acumen of Yankee traders. Liverpool was a nineteenth-century marvel, the epitome of empire.

As such, its population became a reflection of that empire. In the 1850s, because of the Irish famine, some two million impoverished peasants, many with no English, passed through the city, continuing on to the United States or Canada if they could afford the passage. Many thousands could pay no more nor go farther and essentially squatted in the city centre, turning once fashionable neighbourhoods into slums and contributing to an overall decline in civil order. Many observers found the religious tensions brought on by the Irish influx about as bad as anything they ever saw in Belfast. These destitute mobs were joined by Welsh, Chinese, Jews, Portuguese, blacks (many a Liverpool fortune was made from the slave trade) and transients from all over the world, and the conglomeration of peoples and interests was presided over by the usual hierarchy of business and aristocratic leaders, notably headed by the hereditary earls of Derby, who lived on a palatial estate of several thousand acres eight miles outside the city. Churchill called Edward Stanley, the seventeenth earl, 'the uncrowned king of Lancashire'. When elected as lord mayor of the city in 1911, he sat in a seat kept warm by fourteen predecessors with his name since the sixteenth century.

The main church of the Anglican bishop of Liverpool, an unimposing and insignificant building, had been a perennial embarrassment to the established religion, however appropriate to the numbers of communicants about whom it could boast. Roman Catholics, owing to the influx of Irish immigrants, was the faith of the numberless poor and miserable underclasses, ministered by priests of little education or refinement, however dominant they were as stalwarts of their community. Local politics veered towards a racial divide, with resultant struggles for pre-eminence and power. Derby and others felt their storied Protestant tradition (conservative and unionist) should be buttressed, as it were, by a structure of dominance, and he proved to be the first contributor of any significance towards a fund for a new cathedral, projected from the start to be the largest Anglican Church in the world.[9] In

1902 an architect was selected, a site chosen, plans approved (neo-Gothic, of course) and building begun in just two years. By the time its foundation was laid, however, a nearly six-ton-block of local red sandstone, critics were already decrying 'the hideous waste of money' that such a project would require. Liverpool Cathedral said another, was 'an anachronism even when begun'.

Lord Derby brushed such criticism aside, especially at the opening ceremonies where he had the honour of hosting the king and queen. But war changed all that, and Derby came to have other things on his mind besides cathedrals, though in essence the issues he faced were the same, trying to stave off change and modernity. A fervent believer in bulking up the army, he became one of the most successful recruiters in the country. After all, it was his family's tradition of service; his forbears had done the same thing for Henry V at Agincourt. Derby was not picky about the means (whether voluntarily or by conscription made no difference to him) and he had no problem reaching into Liverpool's slums to recruit Catholic Irishmen, despite their reputation for drunkenness and insubordination. They were first placed in their own company, and in marching off to war they preceded their Protestant bothers-in-arms. For a day, at least, religious prejudices were buried. As the Protestants paraded past, Irish women yelled out words of encouragement. 'Stick [close] to the Irish', they yelled, 'the Irish will see you through.'

In 1917, Derby persuaded his son, an officer in France, to stand for a safe seat in Liverpool, a family sinecure as it were. Much to his shock, an opponent entered the field, a private from the British army (minus a leg) whose platform was the pathetic treatment that maimed soldiers were receiving at the hands of a heartless government at home, particularly a proposed measure that required demobilized veterans to be medically re-examined, with the intention of sending them back to the front. The king begged for recruits, he claimed, but what did he do for them when the fighting was over and they (the crippled ones anyway) had no way of making a living? (A Labour MP was evicted from the House of Commons for an outburst in 1922, when he yelled, 'You are a dirty lot of dogs slobbering over dead soldiers and starving the living ones'.)

Derby first thought to withdraw his son from the contest, given the possibility of an enormous embarrassment should this election be lost to a nonentity, but he soldiered on (with his considerable fortune, he could afford to) and his boy won the seat. Derby then saw it as his duty to begin an association of ex-servicemen called the Comrades of the Great War, benevolent and paternalistic, intended to head off socialist rabble-rousing before it made serious inroads into the ranks of men coming home – disaffected, hardened and trained in the use of arms – finding a landscape without employment or anything different from what they had left four years before. Respect, and a nice pat on the back, was worth more than anything money could buy, in Derby's opinion. As the owner of 68,000 acres and an annual income of £250,000, he could afford to be high-minded. Douglas Haig, who found no meaningful outlet for his postwar energies, became involved as head of the British Legion in 1925, which became the more or less 'establishment' veterans' organization. He was not the man for this task, since most of the members in his portfolio had been conscripts, a category of soldier whose numbers he required but whose political views he distrusted. They were men, as a class, who fostered only 'unrest and discontent; they came forward under compulsion and they will depart the Army with relief. Men of this stamp are not satisfied with remaining quiet, they come from a class which like to air real or fancied grievances'. He was right in that respect. Trade union membership in Britain doubled during and after the war; it jumped 21 per cent in the single year of 1919, as men reentered the workforce. These were returning heroes for whom the Anglican cathedral was meant.[10]

The kingpins financing the cathedral were certainly tone deaf. As the gothic pile inched to the heavens, what were the views from the top? Acres of dilapidated housing, slums of the worst sort, children running about the streets with no shoes, a city centre now reeling as the great depression of the 1920s began in earnest. Triumphalism ran supreme within the building yards, however, few details escaped the notice of the ever-watchful cathedral overseers (the stained glass committee, for example, 'questioned the hair style of a long-dead saint, the size of a camel, the thick knees of a prophet's ankles'). Meanwhile, Liverpool teetered: sectarian and neighbourhood disputes caused endless difficulties, labour and materials doubled in price and the pressing need for more funds never ceased.

The Roman Catholic bishop proved no less ambitious than his Protestant counterpart. Sir Edwin Lutyens was hired to design a counter-Cathedral, (to his eminence's annoyance), to be built on the opposite end of Hope Street where the Anglican project was rising. The diocese had purchased the long-derelict workhouse site, once the home, if one could call it that, of 5,000 inmates (essentially indentured servitude), and about nine acres in size. The Anglicans were so appalled at this initiative that they tried to buy the site themselves before the RCs could come up with the money, but they failed. Lutyens, 'pleased as punch' at the commission, proceeded to draw up an enormous monstrosity, aping St. Peter's in Rome (which he had once

The Tsar

Tsar Nicholas II, in happier times, surrounded by his family and personal Cossack guards.

Nicholas, in confinement, saws wood with his son, Alexei, in the Siberian town of Tobolsk.

The Winter Palace, St. Petersburg, 'a place of depressing magnitude', photographed by Karl Bulla.

Police mug shot of Lenin, 1895.

Lenin the orator, commemorated outside Finland Station, St. Petersburg.

Train 293, 'the first chariot of socialism!'

The forecastle gun of the *Aurora*, aimed at the Winter Palace.

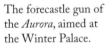

Lenin's office, Kschessinska mansion, St. Petersburg.

Lawrence 'of Arabia'

T. E. Lawrence in British Army uniform.

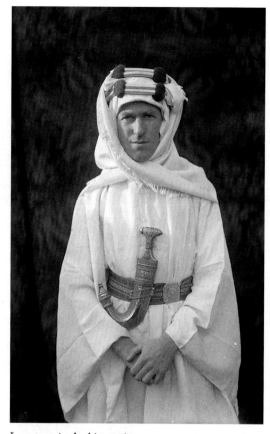

Lawrence in Arabian attire.

Auda Abu Tayi, sheik of the Howeitat clan, an accomplished commander of irregular Arab forces.

War in the Desert

Aqaba, daringly captured by Lawrence on 6 July 1917.

Hejaz railway bridge, dynamited by Arab guerrillas commanded by Lawrence. Note the steel train rails are still in place. Lowell Thomas is among British officers surveying the scene.

'Blue Mist', Lawrence's Rolls-Royce tender.

Jerusalem, 1918. Note the entire city was still contained by its medieval walls.

Faisal, 'king' of Syria and then of Iraq, photographed by Lowell Thomas.

General Edmund Allenby, caricatured in *Punch* as the crusader Richard the Lionheart.

Zeichnet Kriegsanleihe

Die Zeit ist hart, aber der Sieg ist sicher

Above: This 1917 poster of Hindenburg states, 'Times are hard, but victory is certain.' A year later, notions of victory had disappeared, and Prince Maximilian of Baden (right) had the unpleasant task of initiating peace initiatives, which necessitated the abdication of the kaiser.

Peace

Compiègne railway clearing, showing the spot where Foch's train car met the German peace delegation.

Enthusiastic crowds jammed the Place de la Concorde in Paris to welcome President Woodrow Wilson, 14 December 2018. A column of French *poilus* file through the centre, many of whom are broadly smiling, no doubt very happy to have survived the war.

Wilson visiting front-line American troops on Christmas day, 1918, Chaumont, France. To his left are his wife Edith, then General Pershing and the president's physician and close friend, Rear Admiral Cary Grayson.

Freikorps soldiers readying for action. One armoured car is towing an artillery piece, indicative of the disparity in equipment that socialist street fighters faced.

Woodcut by Käthe Kollwitz, 1919, depicting the bier of Karl Liebknecht, murdered in Berlin by *Freikorps* troops in January of that year.

Memorials

Troops march by Lutyens's Cenotaph in 1919, commemorating the signing of the Versailles Peace Treaty.

The Tannenberg memorial, East Prussia. It was destroyed in 1945.

Kollwitz war memorial sculpture, in the *Neue Wache* (New Guardhouse), Berlin.

Memorials

The sepulchre of T. E. Lawrence, designed by Eric Kennington, situated in the village church of St. Martin's-on-the-Walls, Wareham. He was buried elsewhere.

Canadian memorial, St. Julien.

The war memorial to 'The Men of Burwash', which included the son of Rudyard Kipling, killed in his first action, the Battle of Loos, 1915. He had just turned eighteen.

Aftermath

Basement room where the Tsar and his family were murdered, in the Siberian town of Yekaterinburg.

A party of bolsheviks pose at the site of the burial pit where Nicholas and his family were hastily buried. The seated man far right, Peter Ermakov, was a member of the execution squad.

Ray's Barbershop, Gerrard Street East, Toronto. The apartment above it was Grand Duchess Olga Alexandrovna's last address.

Aftermath

Emperor Karl and Empress Zita, in the garish robes of the Hungarian monarchy, 1916. Two years later, the royal family fled.

Ernst Jünger, the enthusiastic author of *Storm of Steel*, gloating over the corpse of an Indian soldier. His book was a best seller in post-war Germany.

After the Armistice, Germany surrendered its entire surface fleet as well as its submarine force. This German sub, *U-118*, beached on the shingle strand of Hastings in the south of England, attracted a host of sightseers. It was eventually cut up on site and sold piecemeal as scrap metal.

Belgian war veterans lay a wreath at the statue of Edith Cavell, in the centre of London, 1934.

Kaiser Wilhelm, in full military dress, as a retired gentleman in Holland.

Victoria removed. Her statue in front of Leinster House, Dublin, was hoisted away in 1948. After thirty-eight years 'For Sale' and 'in storage', it ended up in Australia.

Liverpool

This rendition of Lutyens's proposed Roman Catholic cathedral for Liverpool appeared in *The Illustrated London News*, captioned as a 'prevision'. It was never built. The Anglican cathedral is to the left.

Bricklayer Arthur Brady, with his stepfather. At one point he was the solitary worker on the Catholic site, laying 500 bricks per day.

The Anglican cathedral. Slum clearance and damage from World War II left it with a single neighbour, a house whose owner refused to leave.

The Old Order Gives Way to the New

The grave of Johann Strauss II (d. 1899) in Vienna's *Zentralfreidhof* cemetery. Strauss wrote light opera, popular music and hundreds of polkas and waltzes, the most famous of which is *The Blue Danube*.

The marker of the modernist composer Arnold Schoenberg, 'The Emancipator of Dissonance', also in the *Zentralfreidhof* cemetery. Hounded out of Europe by the Nazis, who considered his work 'degenerate', Schoenberg emigrated to the United States, where he became a citizen in 1941. Still, his ashes were buried in Vienna, near Beethoven's grave.

Private Adolf Hitler, 1915 (seated, with moustache).

disparaged as 'that pimple'), all to be built in 'pinky brown' stone and with the second largest dome in the world. While the bishop could count on a larger congregation than the Anglicans, his parishioners were certainly poorer and no less disillusioned after the war, and Lutyens's creation advanced no further than its enormous crypt. During one depressing interlude a single apprentice, one Arthur Brady, nineteen years old, was the solitary workman on site, laying his customary 500 bricks per day (the crypt alone required around four million). At times, the site was abandoned and filling up with rainwater, a huge hole in the ground swarming with rats. No wonder that the 'God is Dead' movement, usually associated with the 1960s or so, really had its antecedents far earlier. Oswald Mosley, the British crypto fascist, summed it up well after 1918, damning 'these old dead men with their old dead minds, embalmed in the tombs of the past... THIS IS OUR GENERATION NOT THEIRS'.

When I was a child of only seven in 1953, my parents took the family overseas for a Grand Tour of Europe. We travelled on the *Empress of Australia*, once a luxurious ocean liner, then a troopship, then back again to luxury (through not at the same level). I recall seeing Liverpool as we approached and docked, a vast landscape of rubble. During World War II, the city suffered more air raids than anywhere else other than London, and much of the centre was destroyed, turning some 70,000 people into the streets, the neighbourhoods surrounding the cathedral especially hard hit. Urban renewal of the 1950s proved incredibly pedestrian, encouraging urban flight on an unprecedented scale. Even I was aware that something was not right with this place.

Returning in 2013, Liverpool reminded me of a ghost town. The harbour was empty, the enormous system of docks and waterside warehouses were deserted of martime activity, the imperial headquarters of Cunard and other merchant princes largely vacant with hundreds of thousands of square feet for rent or sale all over the city centre. Climbing up to Hope Street, with its twin cathedrals, was an exercise in loneliness, the only sign of life being university students at school here, a refreshing glimpse of youth. It was not until 1965 that a new design, modernist, garish and ugly, was chosen for the Catholic cathedral, and the building successfully started and finished in just five years. Lutyens's crypt was not used as the cathedral's foundation. It now houses an ecclesiastical museum and is available for private parties or wedding receptions (each of its four chambers can hold 500 people). A few minutes' walk away, past handsome row houses, stands its Anglican counterpoise, a throwback to medieval times.

At one point the Anglican cathedral, which took some three-quarters of a century to finish, was threatened with an elevated highway project and associated low-income highrises that would have further isolated an already detached site. The slum buildings and war-related rubble were gradually cleared away, but nothing much replaced them. The cathedral rose in its glory, surrounded by the waste of twentieth-century neglect. The nearby neighbourhood of Toxteth, housing poor black families with little economic future, exploded on three occasions in ugly race riots between 1981 and 2011. When the building was formally declared complete in 1978, it stood as more of an anachronism than ever. Aside from special occasions, only a handful of parishioners attend its daily services.

Expecting to enter the ugliest building in the world, I was amazed to find my visit unusually sublime. Aside from the inevitable gift and tea shop (occupying prime liturgical space), the interior is restrained, soaring, majestical and welcoming, all in the same breath. It is a remarkable accomplishment, all the sadder given the obvious irrelevance of established religion. Somehow this building seems a manifestation of collective hopes, formal and conventional, that died generations ago. To earmark 1914 through 1918 as the end of everything that this cathedral was meant to express seems less the exaggeration than it might seem. I left this building both saddened and exhilarated, two emotions I had never expected.

Chapter 19

Postscripts

'What is the outlook for 1919? Lloyd George ought to last out a year. Clemenceau won't. President Wilson will be discredited. We shall have serious trouble in Ireland, and many wars in many places, and Bolshevism frightens me.'

Diary entry, Field Marshal Sir Henry Wilson

Anger over the pounding his men had taken during the last stages of the war embittered Canadian General Arthur Currie. When his prime minister, Robert Borden, came over the Atlantic for the last time in November 1918 to attend the Versailles peace conference, Currie unburdened himself to his chief in no uncertain terms, as Borden recorded in his diary, giving an 'awful picture of the war situation among the British. Says incompetent officers not removed, officers too casual, too cocksure'. 'Lack of organization, lack of system, lack of preparation, lack of foresight' marked the officer corps. The sad state of affairs before Operation Michael was launched was simply a disgrace. The 'casual indifference and indolence' of the army commanders left elements of the Fifth Army's front effectively defenceless. Instead of laying more and more barbed wire, for instance, some 'men were employed in laying out lawn-tennis courts'. Borden found the entire report 'depressing', and at the next war cabinet meeting he 'did not mince matters', but delivered 'with restraint' an indictment of the high command that shocked his listeners. Afterwards, Lloyd George and the other dominion prime ministers offered their congratulations for an excellent tirade. Borden's disillusionment seemed reflected by some of the public events he was compelled to attend. At a recent speech by the king, he noted the muted response. No one cheered.

Borden would have a trying time of it at Versailles. His legation was put up at the Majestic Hôtel, its French cooks, waiters and maids replaced by an English staff. The results were heavy, stupefying meals and a surfeit of liquor. Borden managed to skip the dinner hour two to three times a week. All he wanted was 'an apple, a glass of water and a long walk'. A Mademoiselle Perret gave him French lessons, a curious thing indeed for a man who had been born in Grand Pré, the home of Longfellow's mythical *Evangeline*. His unfamiliarity with the language did not obscure from him what seemed to be the predominant feature of the conference, the French desire for the ruination of Germany. He found the initial French proposals for peace 'a most astonishing document' which were bound to lead to trouble if implemented. He proved to be right. Lance Corporal Adolf Hitler, gassed at the Ypres salient and now recovering in a military hospital in Pomerania, would see to that.

As a lawyer by training, Borden worked long and hard on many aspects of the forthcoming treaty, and later on documents that set up the League of Nations, but his primary goal at Versailles dealt with Canada. It became clear to him very quickly that without effective lobbying on his part, the council chambers that decided the future of Europe, and with it, world peace, would be closed to all the dominions. President Woodrow Wilson, who in a short period of time managed to alienate just about every allied contingent, greeted the proposal to include Canada with 'incomprehension'. His secretary of state, Robert Lansing, asked 'why Canada should be concerned with the settlement of European affairs?' They were merely an appendage to the British empire, and Lloyd George could speak for them. Borden was stunned. 'I had not come [to Versailles] to take part in a light comedy'; the situation was 'intolerable'. Luckily for him, Lloyd George came to the rescue. Telling the president 'a few home truths', he 'reminded him that both Australia and Canada, with tiny populations, had lost more than America and her 100,000,000. This was a facer.'

After countless diplomatic negotiations, Borden achieved the results he wanted, but little else. The basis was laid whereby future relations with Britain would be more tightly defined and codified which, though often ambiguously understood, really did result in Canadian independence. When Canada joined the empire's cause in 1939, she did so of her own free will. This was a rather large sum to pay for her costly involvement in the first war, whose results really did not matter to the majority of Canadian citizens. Even Borden, a Tory to his heart, sometimes wondered. As he wrote to his wife, 'Canada got nothing out of the war except recognition'.[1]

Borden, like all his Canadian boys, sailed home to a country that was largely perplexed in the aftermath of war. The casualties were considered excessive, people wondered at the cost. Soldiers stuck in France or as occupiers in Germany chaffed at being kept in uniform, a sentiment shared by many a Tommy as well. Bloody riots at Britlish ports broke out when troops returning from leave refused to board transports back to France. Canadian boys in England waiting to go home initiated thirteen disturbances. In one, 800 of them surrounded a police station where two Canadians were being held and laid siege to it. One policeman was killed. Soldiers were heard dissing their officers with taunts such as 'bugger your orders'. Churchill cautioned Haig to restrain himself. The field marshal, once again, felt that a few salutary executions were in order. Borden was unsettled when crowds greeted his car with a hail of stones. This was not the victory celebration he had expected. His reintegration into the provincial world of Canadian politics was also something of a comedown. When the Prince of Wales (the future King Edward VIII) visited Canada after the war, Borden was forced to engage in lengthy correspondence with the young fellow over the advisability of playing golf on a Sunday.

There are photographs of Canadians troops disembarking at Halifax, marching through hastily erected wooden archways festooned with floral displays and Welcome Home signs. But the air is cold and snow is falling. Halifax, recovering from the great explosion, looked in places something like Ypres.

Field Marshal Haig

Douglas Haig's last months of command were full of self-satisfaction, though interspersed with occasions that he perceived as insults to his persona, many occasioned, naturally enough, by Lloyd George. Haig sent Sassoon to negotiate with the prime minister as to an appropriate title for his reward, and was offended when the offer of a viscountcy was suggested. 'I note that when Field Marshal French was *recalled* from the command of the Armies in France for *incompetence*, he was made a Viscount!' He was also infuriated when Lloyd George asked that Haig join a triumphal parade through the streets of London with Foch and other allied officers.

> I heard that I was to be in the fifth carriage along with General Henry Wilson. I felt that this was more of an insult than I could put up with, even from the Prime Minister. For the past three years I have effaced myself, because I felt that, to win the war, it was essential that the British and French Armies should get on well together. And in consequence I have patiently submitted to Lloyd George's conceit and swagger, combined with much boasting as to 'what he had accomplished, thanks to his foresight in appointing Foch as C. in C. of the Allied Forces, to his having sent Armies to Egypt, Palestine, Mesopotamia, Salonika, etc etc.' The real truth, which history will show, is that the British Army has

won the war in France in spite of L.G. and I have no intention of taking part in any triumphal ride with Foch, or with any pack of foreigners, through the streets of London.

On 5 April 1919, Haig officially relinquished his command upon leaving continental shores for the last time. French and British guards of honour lined the quay in Calais, and a band played martial airs. Everything 'very clean and smart'. With his wife at his side, Haig boarded ship and set off into the English Channel, the docks loaded with yelling and waving men, 'a very thrilling sight'. Haig was not often given to emotion, but he could not avoid thinking of the 'anxiety and the glory of the Great War in France' as the ship got underway. Landing in Dover – 'no kind of ceremony' – he took train to London, where crowds of immense size and cheer awaited him. Haig's car had difficulty making its way through the crush. He was finally 'left alone with my family for a little rest and peace, I hope'. For him, the war was finally over. So too was his career, to all intents and circumstances, as Winston Churchill observed. 'No sphere of public activity was opened to him', Churchill wrote. Haig simply 'disappeared into private life'. He died in 1928.

In light of the magnitude of Haig's involvement in the fortunes of the British Expeditionary Force in France – and in view of the magnitude of casualties that his armies both inflicted and received – estimates of his talents or deficiencies have often been as extreme as the events in which he participated. Many of his contemporaries, especially in the army, along with several distinguished commentators and historians, have seen him in the light of the times: an officer who had thrust upon him the almost insurmountable burdens of a great war never before imagined in human history, dealing with numbers of men, equipment, supplies, logistics and a myriad of personalities that no ordinary individual could possibly keep straight. That, in fact, no other choice for a commander in chief was available. Haig had climbed the rung of every important position within his profession, won praise in many, and was to all intents and purposes about as qualified for this post as any other man in England. Lloyd George, his bitterest critic, conceded that fact fairly quickly. He detested Haig, but saw no one whom he thought was better.

The other side of the ledger is bleaker, and often coloured by the magnitude of losses in killed, wounded, missing and simply evaporated human beings who were squandered under Haig's dispassionate gaze. The immense slaughterhouse campaigns that he directed – the Somme and Passchendaele in particular – certainly contributed to what Haig saw as his primary objective: the destruction of Germany's army. No other conclusion could be deemed satisfactory, in his opinion; if enemy forces were not crushed into a more or less total surrender, what was the point of the war, merely to delay the day of reckoning to a later generation? This inviolate objective distanced Haig from the dreadful sacrifices that were to be required, and it was a heavy load that he accepted in his customarily phlegmatic and stoical fashion. The king and politicians at home had entered into this war and, fairly quickly in the process, gave him the command. He accepted their mandate and proceeded to accomplish it (in his words) 'without counting the cost'. Critics could dwell on those costs – nearly a million British dead – and harp on the dismal unimaginativeness of his attacks, but the result did achieve what it was meant to achieve. Germany lost the war on the western front, its will to fight extinguished. Observers who hold Haig in contempt cannot contest the eventual outcome, only the means.

One thing cannot be held against Haig. He was sufficiently alert to the circumstances of modern war to realize that this wasn't South Africa, where he had last seen combat. Yes, he was a cavalryman at heart and yes, it was his fondest dream, still held by him against the realities of trench warfare on the western front until as late as 1918, that victory would finally be achieved when the German defences were pierced, and thousands of mounted cavalry would sweep through and scatter the enemy with drawn sabers. Haig is often held to ridicule when this fantasy arises in the pages of history books on World War I. But that aside, he, almost alone of the earliest allied generals, saw the coming conflict for what it would become: a long and bitter struggle demanding the full and complete resources of every country involved. Sir John French, the first commander of the British Expeditionary Force, was in Haig's opinion a well-intentioned fool, strutting around headquarters making 'reckless declarations', predicting that any moment now his forces would crush the Prussians, whereas, in point of fact, the German enemy was at that moment preparing a bloody kick in the mouth from which the BEF barely emerged intact; they ended up, as Haig noted in his diary, 'retreating and retreating'.

In Haig's view, unreality spouted from the mouths of most everyone in those first days. Unsustainable optimism, unrealistic objectives, an officer corps with too many 'old women', and even a king who had no idea as to 'the grave issues both for our country as well as for his own House, which were about to be put to the test'. Haig's response to these negative portents was typical of him. He put down his pen, went outdoors and played a round of golf with his wife. This sangfroid was probably his greatest strength in the days that lay ahead, and undoubtedly the most damaging aspect of his personality in the eyes of critics, who harp on about his emotional indifference to the bloodletting going on in unimaginable quantities. They read his diary and see little reflective thought on Haig's part to the carnage all around him. If Haig had had a heart, however, he never could have 'won the war'.

Three Other Generals

Sir William Robertson arrived back in London after a tour in Germany as commander of the occupying forces, an assignment he equated to being stationed in Timbuktu. No crowds awaited on him at Victoria Station. 'On a dark and dismal night' he hailed a 'broken-down taxi' and returned to his rented house on Eccleston Square.

Sir Henry Wilson celebrated the end of the war by climbing the imposing Butte du Lion which overlooks the Waterloo battlefield and watched British infantry, again victorious, marching to their billets. He retired from the army in February 1922 and turned to politics, where intransigence on Irish matters led to his assassination four months later by two I.R.A. gunmen who were more or less instantly tried, convicted and hanged. Lloyd George recalls in his memoirs how he and Churchill stared at the two pistols that had done the deed, laid out on the cabinet table at 10 Downing Street.

Arthur Currie, whom Borden considered the finest officer in the Canadian Corps, was greeted very coldly on his return nine months after armistice day. His reception at Halifax city hall, in fact, reminded a local reporter of a funeral. The first years of the war had seen Currie at the front often enough, checking out terrain for himself and looking out for the men; while lacking the common touch, he always argued for and sought tactical angles that would result in the least numbers of casualties for troops under his command. But many considered him a 'château' general by the last days of the war, blindly obeying the constant stream of British orders to attack, attack, attack. Haig, though dim at times over what others might say or do, certainly recognized that tales brought home by fighting men on leave could do a great deal of damage behind the front. Such appears to have been the case with Currie. He inspired little love from the men he commanded; around countless hearths and kitchen tables in Canada there was too much talk of hopeless fighting, friends being killed or maimed and of commanders rarely or ever seen in the trenches. Currie's rejoinder to that would be that a trench was no place for him or any senior officer. War was different now.

The atmosphere was thoroughly poisoned by Sir Sam Hughes, a mythic figure in Canadian politics and the first minister of militia and defence as hostilities began in 1914, an office he was unsuited to hold and from which he was eventually dismissed. He was now an embittered and altogether deranged old man in extremely poor health. Still a member of parliament, a position which protected him from ever being charged with slander, he began a vicious campaign of character assassination against Currie. It is difficult to tell, with such a volatile personality, just what it was that so animated Hughes, but he attacked his former protégé with a thunderous barrage of invective. First in letters, then in speeches in the House of Commons, he called Currie a murderer, an instigator of massacres, an unbridled glory-monger and a man fit only for a court marshal. He should be 'punished as far as the law would allow'. These harangues were met first with startled amazement and, more ominously, silence. Few supporters of Currie rose in his defence. Sir Robert Borden, when he heard about the ruckus, remained conspicuously aloof. Currie arrived in Ottawa on 18 August 1918. Neither Borden nor any prominent members of his government were there to greet him; they were too busy hobnobbing with the Prince of Wales in New Brunswick. Currie was greeted by polite applause when he entered the parliamentary chambers. There would be no rousing ovations, no motions of thanks and certainly no monetary reward. Douglas Haig received £100,000 from a 'grateful nation' and a mansion in the Scottish countryside on his return home. Currie received nothing.

General Sir Arthur Currie, for better or worse, would be tainted for the rest of his life by the innuendoes raised by Hughes and others that his hands were covered in blood. He served McGill University for thirteen years as its president, beginning in 1920, which took his mind off the war to some degree, but ugliness concerning his conduct raised its head time and time again. There was tremendous ill-feeling when various official histories of the war were begun, with proposed drafts circulating on both sides of the Atlantic. Sir James Edmonds, author of the British series, had often been on record concerning Currie's 'unsoldierly behaviour', and his treatment of the Canadian contribution was decidedly lukewarm, much to the indignation of those writing the Canadian version. Currie's fragile digestion suffered accordingly, as he joined the literary fray. Difficulties of a public relations sort were often, and regrettably exacerbated by his own maladroit behaviour. Postwar Canada slipped into economic depression after 1918, now that the need to produce millions of artillery shells had dried up. Many returning and disenchanted veterans began agitation for a $2,000 cash grant to both reward their wartime service and to help tide them over during rough times. Currie injudiciously disapproved of this 'bonus battle', which certainly did not endear him to his former comrades in arms. Instead, he was put in charge of a fund that paid for the funerals of men who died in destitution, a somewhat macabre irony to say the least. In 1927, an obscure newspaper in rural Ontario published a scathing editorial that savaged Currie's conduct at the capture of Mons, stating bluntly that Canadians were blindly sacrificed on the very eve of peace just to satisfy an egomaniacal desire for additional battlefield accolades. 'The men were sent on in front to charge the enemy. Headquarters, with conspicuous bravery, brought up the rear.' Currie immediately sued for libel and a lengthy trial ensued, the 'Third Battle of Mons' as it was called, wherein the general fought perhaps the most difficult engagement of his career, attempting to salvage his legacy. The jury declared for Currie and awarded him a judgment of $500. He had asked for a hundred times that amount. He died in 1933, aged 58, a disappointed man. He had done his best, had obeyed orders – what more did people want from him?

The Council of Four

The government of Vittorio Emanuele Orlando did not survive the conference, so he was not present at the final ceremony. He remained active, on and off, in Italian politics for much of his long life (he did not die until 1952, far outliving his colleagues). An early flirtation with Mussolini did not unnecessary diminish his reputation; he received a magnificent state funeral in Rome, where he was buried. Monarchists immediately agitated that the body of King Vittorio Emanuele III, who sat on the throne during World War I and somehow retained his crown during the postwar chaos of 1918 (though not that of World War II, being forced to abdicate in 1944), be brought back from a graveyard in Egypt where he had fled, a campaign not fulfilled until 2017.

Woodrow Wilson's post conference career was one of utter misery. Depending on how one perceived the man and his politics largely determined the adjectives contemporaries used to describe the torturous road he followed. Wilsonian admirers called it martyrdom; those who detested him thought mostly he got what he deserved through his usual, maladroit combination of obstinacy and intellectual arrogance. In a remarkably mean-spirited and largely inaccurate profile, Sigmund Freud wrote that Wilson was a neurotic 'who in his subconscious was God and Christ'. The truth lies somewhere in the middle of these various extremes.

Certainly the president's failing health contributed to his erratic behaviour once he returned to the snake pit of Washington. He attempted to reason with his opponents who, led by Senator Henry Cabot Lodge, were marshalled to kill the Treaty on the senate floor. Wilson entertained, he met with waffling, undecided and/or moderate senators in his office, and he addressed Congress. What he would not do is agree to changes or modifications to any aspect of the proposed League or to the peace conditions offered to Germany. Closing the door in such absolute terms chilled the hearts of those leaning towards supporting him, and irrevocably hardened those otherwise disposed. The president had made the entire conference a one-man show. He had purposely excluded from the delegation Republicans, such as former President Taft, he had generally ignored the team of experts assembled and brought to Paris to advise him and now he shunned the political expertise of his alter ego, Colonel House. He became thereby the sole individual lightning rod upon which every grievance, complaint, objection and political calculation against the Treaty would strike, and strike it did.

Against an avalanche of negativity, the president once again decided to take his case to the common people. Despite the pleadings of his wife and Admiral Grayson, Wilson embarked on an excruciating cross-country campaign tour. Over the course of twenty-three days, he gave forty speeches (of varying quality), took part in multiple parades and public ceremonies, shook thousands of hands, travelled some 8,000 miles and generally wore himself into the ground. It is a painful experience watching period photographs of the president giving orations before packed audiences, stacked up in rows or on hillsides, and realize that the poor man was probably shouting in order to be heard. There were no public address systems in such venues that could carry his voice as far as it was needed. Wilson's physical condition grew beyond exhaustion; often he could sleep no more than two or three hours a night. Late in the evening of 25 September 1919, he suffered another small stroke. Taken back to Washington, almost against his will, he was then, to all intents and purposes, finally struck down. Grayson informed the public that Wilson was now bed-ridden with a nervous collapse, but in fact a major stroke had left him partially paralyzed and, at times, practically incoherent. For the remaining fifteen months of his presidential term, Wilson lay bedridden and hidden from sight, in the process growing a full beard. At times he received visitors who, by turns, were either shocked (if he was in a bad way) or reassured (if he was more or less lucid). His wife and Grayson assisted where they could, but governmental business was largely conducted by a rudderless cabinet full of men the president had never fully trusted. In such circumstances, the agility and resourcefulness required to navigate the Treaty through Congress was largely lost. Senator Lodge, 'that quintessential stuffed shirt' and 'petrified dandy' of Massachusetts, won his most satisfying political victory. The United States did not join the League of Nations that its president had given everything he had to establish. The election of 1920 saw a crushing defeat for Wilsonian principles, and the election of the thoroughly mediocre Republican, Warren Harding, whose resolve to 'return to normalcy' mostly meant the reinstitution of isolationism as national policy. After his election, the president-elect labelled the League officially 'deceased'. John Dos Passos saw the whole thing as typically American, likening the national mood to that of a baseball game – 'We won, let's go home' – Europe could look after itself, and good luck. Wilson retired to a handsome townhouse in Washington where, in moments of near derangement, he considered whether or not he should run for president again. On Armistice Day 1923, a small crowd stood outside his house and Wilson graced them with a few public remarks, the last he ever gave. 'I have seen fools resist Providence before and I have seen their destruction'. A Covenanter to the end.

Wilson succumbed to his variety of ailments on 3 February 1924. Grayson had warned him that he would soon die. 'The machinery is worn out', he replied, 'I am ready.' These were his last words. His physician and friend could not help adding, as a postscript, that Wilson 'was as much a casualty of the war as any soldier who fell in the field'. Mrs. Wilson, in a personal letter to Henry Cabot Lodge, asked that he not attend the funeral service at Washington's National Cathedral.

Georges Clemenceau decided that his reward for service rendered during the Great War and beyond was to be proclaimed the next President of France, more or less by acclamation. As a veteran, and a gleeful one at that, of more ministerial intrigues and machinations than he could remember, it should have come to him as no surprise that a grateful France was not, in fact, grateful. Seven months after the signing ceremony at Versailles, Clemenceau, his dignity ruffled and his feelings hurt, retired from the political scene after initial voting results did not produce the landslide he expected. Most people (and many of them nervous) waited for the inevitable, the publication of his memoirs, but the old man refused to write them. 'It was enough to contemplate in silence the grandeur of it all', he said to a visitor who came by to see him in his 'bourgeois den', adding 'he did not care what people thought or said. It was all one to him'. This was not true, of course; after he read Foch's memoirs (calling them 'gossip'), he wrote a response of sorts, but he could not get it right, revising his manuscript so many times that it lost, in a measure, its coherence. His book was published after his death in 1929.

Lloyd George lost the general election of October 1922, but left Downing Street convinced that he would return to power one day again, and sooner rather than later. He never did. Throughout his career, 'he aroused every feeling except trust', wrote the historian A. J. P. Taylor. 'He had no friends and did not deserve any'. Though a member of parliament until the day of his death in 1945, his prominence in the political picture of Britain was the story of steady diminishment. It did not help matters that he tended to overlook the Nazi menace and that, in fact, he rather admired Hitler. His acceptance of a title in the last year of his life was an additional blemish to his liberal reputation, though marrying his long-time mistress, Frances Stevenson, was generally regarded as the right thing to do. There is some debate as to whether, at his advanced age (he was eighty-one at his death on 26 March 1945), he actually understood the implications of either decision. Winston Churchill gave one of the better speeches of his career eulogizing his friend, colleague and at times opponent in the House of Commons.

As for Ulrich von Brockdorff-Rantzau, he died in 1928. He asked those gathered around his bed not to mourn for him. He had already been long dead, he told them, ever since Versailles.

Emperor Karl I of Austria-Hungary

Karl, his wife and his family, had slipped away from Schönbrunn Palace on the night of 11 November 1918 by a side gate, heading for a hunting lodge in the countryside. Their entourage numbered about fifty, though they left behind one of the empress's maids in the confusion. This poor woman appeared in the royal bedchambers the next day with an early-morning breakfast tray, and found four thugs attempting to pry open a wall safe, suspected repository of the customary royal jewels. Had they managed to crack it, of course, they would have found it empty. Royal treasure in the early twentieth century had only one meaningful *raison d'être*, a hedge against future poverty in the bitter years of projected exile.

The old family property outside Vienna to which the party fled was not secure. Food was low, there was no electricity (or candles), and gangs of 'reds' were prowling the countryside, posting crude placards on the gates saying they knew who was inside and they meant to hang them all. These were not viewed as idle threats, or so George V believed.

With an irony that perhaps King George was impervious to by nature, he being an individual of ordinary intelligence, the similarities between the plight of Tsar Nicholas and Emperor Karl seems finally to have made a connection. Through the usual clandestine channels of aristocratic communication, he and his wife were made aware of Karl's precarious plight. Whereas the tsar had been an ally, however, what to do with Karl, another of those alleged German warmongers, presented difficulties of a different sort. The king did not relish the opportunity of assisting an avowed enemy of his people, but then again kings were kings, and blood was thicker than water, given the fact that all of them seemed related, however distantly, one to the other. In a first tentative step, an officer was discreetly ordered to visit the imperial 'compound' to assess the situation and to offer the 'moral support of the British government' if need be. Such vague instructions gave the officer in question, a colonel in the Scots Guards, very wide latitude. This gentleman soon gained the confidence of the emperor and took matters more or less in hand. As a royalist himself, he patiently listened to the emperor's troubles over the course of long walks, wherein Karl, 'an eminently lovable but weak man', explained the technicalities by which he should still be seen as the sovereign of his kingdom; such legalisms would have delighted any lawyer ('again and again he repeated that he had not abdicated; "I went into retirement .... I am still the emperor"'). Colonel Strutt also enjoyed tea with the empress, and took her measure very quickly ('the real head of the family'). They would be difficult to move without her consent, but Strutt thought the time had come. When driving in the imperial automobile along a road that ran parallel with a railway track, a troop train full of demobilized soldiers steamed alongside for some distance. Strutt was discomforted by the invective that soldiers yelled at the car, seeing that as a portent of serious trouble ahead. He insisted that the royal family must flee, and made all the arrangements pretty much himself. On a wintry day in March 1919, Emperor Karl and Empress Zita crossed the border into Switzerland, leaving their troubled homeland behind.

Karl's later career, rather short in retrospect, was full of activity, much of it black comedy. He made two attempts to regain at least half his kingdom, Hungary, ruled in his absence after abortive stints of communist regimes by a man he thought of as a supporter, Admiral Miklós Horthy. This in itself is an indictment of Karl's judgement of character, for no more slippery or conniving figure ever strode across the pages of European history than Horthy. Expecting that Horthy would automatically step aside should Karl even set foot in Budapest, the emperor departed his asylum in Switzerland on 26 March 1921. The first impediment, rather mundane it seems, was that the emperor did not possess a passport. After all, as a reigning monarch, why should he need one? This difficulty, it was adjudged, could be sidestepped only if the emperor crossed the French border by himself, on foot, in the middle of the night, by some unknown track, which he did. Arriving in Paris, he took a series of trains under false papers provided by émigré supporters, wearing dark glasses for most of the journey. In a pique of royal vanity, he was astonished that no one recognized him. Crossing into Hungary, he arrived unannounced at a bishop's palace, where a dinner party was in progress. His reception there should have forewarned him. One guest (he saw his political career destroyed, in one instant), nearly fainted in shock, and another, who came later, muttered 'Too soon, too soon'. After a multi-hour journey to the royal palace in Budapest, no one opened the door of his car, saluted or in any way welcomed his appearance. He then bungled his meeting with Horthy by not arriving with a military force behind him, 1,500 of whom had been assembled for just such a purpose. He did not even carry a revolver, which he should have used once he realized (within an hour) that Horthy was betraying him. Had he showed some of the resolve and ruthlessness of a Dragutin Dimitrijević (*Apis*), he would have shot Horthy in the head, strode to the balcony, announced he had returned and lived or died by the consequences. Instead he haggled with his insubordinate regent, tried to bribe him with a few decorations and titles, and then abjectly returned to his car and left the city. The war correspondent Charles Repington called this foray an 'operetta'.

Seven months later, Karl tried again. This time the empress, although pregnant, decided to accompany him, to add a stiffening character to the venture, as it were. Although neither had ever flown in an aeroplane, they hired a six-passenger Junkers to take them into Hungary. This time an army of sorts awaited them, commanded by royalists of alleged resolution. With some determination, Karl could have stormed the capital and toppled Horthy, but his vacillating character failed him again. After a meaningless skirmish in a suburb of Budapest, Karl allowed himself to be outmanoeuvred, both militarily and diplomatically, and this sad Habsburg debacle finally ended. On 31 October, a small British gunboat, the *Glow Worm*, took the royal couple on board, proceeding down the Danube ... past Belgrade, past Moldava ... to rail connections, then another privately owned boat, all under the protection of British soldiers and sailors (the empress recognized one of the dishes served up for lunch, and learned that the chef had once cooked for her years ago at Schönbrunn Palace). Once at the mouth of the Danube on the Black Sea, they were transferred to another ship of the Royal Navy, the cruiser *Cardiff*. It deposited them twelve days later on the shores of Madeira in the Atlantic Ocean, which became for them the equivalent of Napoleon's St. Helena. When Karl died there of pneumonia in 1922, at only thirty-five years of age, the world took no notice. He was buried in the island's only real city, Funchal, though his heart was removed and transported in a small urn to the Benedictine abbey of Muri, founded in 1027 near Basel and a favoured mausoleum for the Habsburg family who first originated (or, to put it more succinctly, were first noticed) in this part of Switzerland.

As for the empire Karl had ruled, it lay in ruins. When the South African Jan Smuts visited Vienna in 1919 on a fact-finding mission, he could not believe his eyes. With a certain sympathy he said, 'It is a world that we cannot imagine – a world gone completely to pieces.' Harold Nicolson, in the same delegation as Smuts, found the place dispiriting and 'unkempt ... paper lying about: the grass plots round the statues are strewn with litter: many windows broken and repaired by boards nailed up. The people in the streets are dejected and ill-dressed: they stare at us in astonishment... I feel that my plump pink face is an insult to these wretched people.' The entourage had a lavish luncheon at the famous Café Sacher, which infuriated Smuts as a 'gross error in taste'. Nicolson, however, enjoyed the meal.

The Empress Zita lived a long life, dying in 1989. She moved constantly, often forced by pinched economic circumstances, war or the exigencies of her large family (she had eight children, one of whom was born after her husband's death).[2] Her list of addresses was a long one: various small villages in Spain, Belgium and Switzerland, the cities of Luxembourg and Quebec, even rural New York State (during World War II). When she passed away at ninety-six, she was buried, by rights, in the Capuchin *Kaisergruft*; the horse-drawn hearse that carried her coffin through the streets of Vienna was the same that had been used for Franz Joseph seventy-three years before. In keeping with Habsburg custom, her heart was removed and taken to Muri Abbey, there to be interred next to Karl's.

The empress had long despaired that any of her children would ever wear the crown of Austria-Hungary, and replaced visions of a resurgent Habsburg dynasty with another, the canonization of her husband, 'the peace king'. This quixotic mission occupied her attentions for decades, and reached a milestone of sorts when the emperor was beatified by Pope John Paul II in 2004 after a miracle was allegedly attributed to his intervention. This immediately opened the stage for ugly arguments as to whether Karl had authorized the use of poison gas against Italian forces in the last months of the war. Certainly Emperor Karl had been, without doubt, a devout Catholic; but then again, so too was that great hunter, Archduke Franz Ferdinand.

As for Admiral Horthy, the emperor's Machiavellian protagonist, his subsequent career defies easy summary. Hungarian politics remained turbulent until the end of World War II, when it became for all intents and purposes a subjugated state under the firm control of Moscow. The brief and celebrated (in the west, at any rate) Hungarian revolt of 1956 was a futile gesture at best, civilians with a few guns being no match for tanks. Hungary did not become the fully independent country it is today until 1989. Through 1944, Horthy played a variety of roles in the governance of his country, at times a ceremonial figurehead, at others (in moments of crisis) a power that no one could ignore. His first decade as head of state was more or less an exercise in constitutional 'monarchy'; later on, showing less patience, he could behave more dictatorially. Genuinely motivated by intense patriotism, Horthy grew steadily more suspicious and wary of everything, from Jews to Germans to communists. Being an admiral in a country that no longer had a navy presented certain problems of dignity, but he was genuinely popular with most segments of the population and grew trusted as a father figure. However, the rise of fascism in general, and Nazi Germany in particular, presented insurmountable difficulties that would prove to be his downfall. Dealing with Adolf Hitler was not the same thing as handling Emperor Karl. Though Horthy's skills at manipulation and intrigue grew wiser with time and experience, he was no match when it came to the cold-blooded usages of power. The führer badgered Horthy into corners where he never wished to be: formally joining the axis powers in 1941, temptations in land-grabbing that, while momentarily alluring, contributed to worldwide condemnation and social instability, the deportation of Hungarian Jews – these were just a few. The situation became so inauspicious by October 1944 that Horthy did the unimaginable, actually concluding backdoor negotiations with the soviets (whom he detested) for a separate peace as the war seemed to him irrevocably lost. When Hitler heard rumours of these he did three things: invaded Hungary, kidnapped Horthy and imprisoned him in Bavaria. Luckily for the regent, Hitler did not pursue the next logical option, Horthy's execution.

Anyone thrown into a cell by the führer generally received a pass when it came to postwar exercises in blame and retribution. Horthy did appear at the Nuremberg war crimes tribunal, but as a witness, not a defendant which, given the dreadful deportation and murder of over 400,000 Jews in Hungary under his regime, was certainly a piece of luck. Horthy still had friends in high places, many of them American and some, such as Pope Pius XII, with the capacity to forgive. He and his family were finally settled in Portugal, where he died in 1957. Thirty-six years later, his body was returned to a free Hungary for reburial, the stipulation in his will emphasizing the word 'free'. This occasioned predictable controversy, especially when members of the then government attended the ceremonies, despite the 'Jewish question'. After all, he was, in the words of the prime minister, a 'Hungarian patriot'.

Atatürk

'Soldiers, your goal is the Mediterranean.'

Gallipoli proved a stunning victory for the Turkish army, but it was really the only one of the war that gained any international recognition, and many observers gave most of the credit to the Germans.[3] By 1918 the predicted grand result finally played itself out: the disintegration of the Ottoman Empire. In a week-long battle in Palestine, in September 1918, General von Sanders and what was left of the Turkish army were thoroughly routed at the hands of the British;[4] the fate of many Young Turks proved disagreeable in the extreme;[5] Constantinople (the Turks preferred calling it Istanbul) was occupied, mostly by British troops; and the sultanate wobbled along with its customary impotence. With ravenous appetites, the allies argued and gorged themselves on what was left, though an information gap of extraordinary proportions existed. The Big Three at Versailles – Wilson, Clemenceau and Lloyd George – matched each other in their ignorance of geography, the situation on the ground and the resilience of the Turks. In the end, the crisis of October 1922, largely the result of Mustafa Kemal's (i.e. Atatürk's) indefatigable resolution, contributed to the downfall of Lloyd George's government. Though he sat in parliament to the year of his death in 1945, Lloyd George's days of influence and power petered away.[6]

The final exercise in map-drawing by the victors at Versailles occurred in Lausanne, Switzerland, in November 1922, which put a stamp (though not one of approval) on what had largely become a *fait accompli*. By then, four years after the war, the Arab territories of the empire in the Middle East had been divided, mostly into mandates controlled by France and Britain, which have largely resulted in the enormous difficulties this region has presented the international community to this very day. The Soviet Union had helped itself to swaths of Turkish lands in the Caucasus, but the bolsheviks were practical in many respects, and joined with the Turks to suppress the ambitions of ethnic peoples on the wild borderlands attempting to establish petty states of their own. These poor Armenians, Kurds, Georgians, Daghestanis and Azerbaijanis had placed too much faith in the promises of the Fourteen

Points, which proved impossible to enforce so many miles from the White House in Washington where they had been conceived. The Italians and Greeks, who had intrigued for great tracts of coastline in Asia Minor, with projected inroads to the fertile lands that lay beyond them until the great (and largely barren) Anatolian plateau, differed in their sense of resolve. The Italians, when they gave the situation a good and hard look, showed the better judgment – they withdrew. As Woodrow Wilson said at Versailles, modern Italians did not remind him of ancient Romans. Greece, on the other hand, through a combination of arrogance, pride and vainglorious appetite, did the opposite. In 1919, they attacked what they thought was a disintegrating front in both the west (Thrace) and east (pushing off from the port city of Smyrna, and eventually reaching 400 miles inland in what Lloyd George called 'a daring and reckless military enterprise'). Greek civilization had enjoyed a long history along the shoreline of Asia Minor; it was one leaders in Athens, to say nothing of sentiment on the streets, could not find within themselves the power to ignore. Almost a million people of Greek descent lived in Turkey, mostly along the Mediterranean coast. Majestic ruins at places like Pergamon still stirred the Greek imagination. Aristotle himself had established an academy in Assos. How could Greece abandon places such as these, redolent of their heritage and contributions to western civilization? And, of course, there was Constantinople itself, whose commercial life was largely underpinned by a vigorous and successful Greek merchant class. There were many reasons to plunge ahead, though a sense of political reality was not one of them. Churchill watched all this in some disgust. The 'war of the giants' was over, 'the wars of the pygmies have now started'.

The attitude of Versailles peacemakers presented Turkish nationalists like Mustafa Kemal with the perfect stimulus. The very existence of their country was publicly put in jeopardy (President Wilson had wondered aloud whether a Turkey should even exist; Harold Nicolson, the young British diplomat, wrote unhelpfully that 'The Turks have contributed nothing whatsoever to the progress of humanity: they are a race of Anatolian marauders'). Control of the Dardanelles and the Bosphorus was a question bandied about with casual largesse: there were many possibilities, but the Turks were not one of them. Constantinople was occupied and foreigners seemed disinclined to leave. The sultan was a figure of ridicule, the caliphate (or spiritual headship of Islam) a disputed point. The Ottomans, after all, had lost control of Mecca in 1916. On the night of 16 May 1919, Kemal and men who would form the nucleus of his general staff, obtained British visas to leave the city, their destination Samsun, on the Black Sea, their ostensible mission to establish law and order in a region falling into chaos. This was, in many ways, the equivalent of the German mission that sent Lenin to St. Petersburg. Kemal's long-term objective was to rally the disaffected to himself, mostly army officers as devoted to the ideal of Turkey as he was; to establish a rival seat of authority to the sultan; to push the Greeks and other foreigners out of Anatolia; and to regain control of the straits. In four years he achieved all these goals, much to Britain's everlasting regret.

Kemal showed the same qualities during this struggle as he had at Gallipoli. Whether in military or political affairs, he was ruthless. Cunning and subtlety were not his trademarks, menace was. Like Stalin, Lenin and any other dictator one could mention, his objective was to sweep all opposition aside. While not impervious to the blandishments of power and office, he remained always loyal to the notion of country, of doing what he felt was in the best interests of Turkey. 'I don't act for public opinion', he said. 'I act for the nation and for my own satisfaction', objectives he felt that ran in the same direction. Firmly secularist, he rejected the pomp and vanity of Constantinople and the sultanate, establishing a competing seat of government in the very centre of Anatolia at Angora (now Ankara). This was not a glamorous site, nor is it today, but it offered a stark alternative to the endless line of venal sultans and the ostentation of Istanbul. On 26 August 1922, consolidated and clearly on the ascendant, Kemal launched a great counterattack against the Greeks. The goal of his soldiers, he said, was the Mediterranean, and by 10 September he was there. In Smyrna, the Greek and Armenian quarters were put to flames, with civilians massacred in unknown numbers by rampaging Turks or drowned at the quayside, pushed into the water by the crush of refugees fleeing the violence. This was all witnessed by British soldiers and sailors sitting offshore in ships that could have helped in an evacuation, but at first did not. Kemal said he regretted this 'disagreeable incident', but his message was clear. By 1924, there were few if any Greeks still living in Turkey, transplanted westwards whence they will never again return en masse except as tourists. When Kemal shifted his attentions northwards, Lloyd George decided he must be stopped before reaching Constantinople. The prime minister was ready to put troops on the ground ('It looked as if we were drifting into another war', wrote Sir George Riddell) and issued the usual emergency call to the dominions. The Australians wouldn't hear of it, all talk of 'to the last man and last shilling' long forgotten, and the New Zelanders only with extreme reluctance. They had been burned here once before.

In October, with many of his objectives in hand, Kemal agreed to a ceasefire and a peace treaty. He sent one of his trusted associates ('trusted' is a misnomer, actually, since Kemal really trusted no one) to the conference table in Lausanne. The British negotiator, Lord Curzon, sneered at him – 'more like an Armenian lace-seller than a Turkish general' – but it was Curzon who was humiliated. 'Hitherto we have dictated our peace treaties', he admitted, but in this case the tables were reversed, Lloyd George recognizing the fact that Kemal 'was now dictating to Europe'. Turkey had troops on the ground, and there was little appetite in Britain for yet another costly, wasteful and potentially embarrassing military adventure. With the British economy suffering a postwar depression, 'everyone was [too] busy scratching for a living' to be interested in yet another imperial escapade. The sultan, in one last futile gesture, had sent an emissary of his own to Lausanne to represent Turkey, but by the time that poor gentleman arrived, Kemal and the parliament in Ankara had formally abolished the sultanate, and the representative of all that was corrupt and decadent was not even allowed to enter the conference hall.[7] Though Curzon banged his fist on the table several times over the next several days, and engaged in other instances of histrionic behaviour, the establishment of the modern Turkish state was formally recognized by the signories in July 1923. The nationalist faction of the Turkish army and of Kemal himself had clearly won the day.

The wreckage that lay behind was formidable. Greek and Turkish populations were exchanged and resettled, an enormous human tragedy. Many Greek refugees, once returned home, were treated like second-class citizens; those who could no longer speak their native tongue earned contempt, few jobs and fewer opportunities. Ernest Hemingway, much of whose experience from the First World War seem concentrated on humbled and retreating armies, described tattered Greek troopers straggling home, 'dirty, tired, unshaven, wind-bitten soldiers, hiking along the trails across the brown, rolling, barren Thrace countryside …. They are the last of the glory that was Greece. This is the end of their second siege of Troy.'

Mehmed VI mutely joined the ranks of deposed monarchs. His fate was so foreordained that he left with barely a whimper. Two British Red Cross ambulances had pulled up to the gates of his palace during a night of driving rain on 1 November 1922. His imperial entourage had by then largely deserted him, so much so that only nine members of his household accompanied this sad and pathetic figure: a doctor, barber, two household servants, the master of the court, two secretaries and two black eunuchs, pulling the inevitable trunks packed with gold and jewels. On their way to the harbour, one of the trucks suffered a flat tyre, with no spare available to replace it. Several anxious moments went by before it could be fixed; had the mob been awakened, the sultan would have been torn to pieces. The Royal Navy, by this point quite expert in the business of evacuating royal personages, steamed to Malta, from where Mehmed travelled on to Italy.

The British captain admired the sultan's cigarette case, and wondered if he might have it as a memento, as it were, to mark the end of the Ottoman Empire. The sultan did not rise to the hint, hoping instead that the ship would go back to Istanbul, now that he was safe, and retrieve his five wives and several daughters who had been left behind in the confusion. He died in San Remo (what Lord Curzon called 'a second-class English watering place') in needy circumstances in 1926, a familiar refrain in the annals of those who are doomed to fade away in political exile.

Under the guise of parliamentary democracy, Kemal ruled Turkey in a dictatorial but sometimes benevolent way until his death in 1938. A heavy drinker all his life, he died of cirrhosis of the liver. The modern, secular republic of Turkey today is largely his creation (though currently in some danger of being Islamicized), in keeping with the adage that good Turks should 'walk from the East in the direction of the West'. It is not uncommon to enter restaurants or hotels throughout the country and find their entire decorative motif centred on Kemal: paintings, pictures (he was a handsome man who photographed well), amateur portraits, all kinds of memorabilia, interspersed with flags, rifles and old swords. Not for nothing has he come to be known as Atatürk, 'Father of Turkey'.

The Memoir Business: Brisk and Busy

> *'What on earth does this mean?*
> *People who write books ought to be shut up.'*
>
> King George V, when he heard that the irascible
> Margot Asquith intended to write a memoir

One thing Arthur Currie never did was write his memoirs, a field of endeavour that many of his English and dominion compatriots entered with glee, seeking to straighten the record, settle scores, propagandize controversial decisions or generally exact revenge (Lloyd George said his bookshelves were 'groaning' with them). On the English side, some were more gentlemanly than others, some more sanitized and alert to the sensitivities of contemporaries who were once comrades in the common effort of winning the war. In other cases, the author didn't give a damn, and let his bombshells land where they might. Lloyd George, for one, danced on Haig's grave. Reading his omnivorous six-volume tome would give one the impression that he never suffered a single lapse in judgment during the war years. 'Some of his friends', wrote his mistress, 'think that he would do better sometimes to admit that he has occasionally made mistakes, and been in the wrong, but he seems to be incapable of doing this'. Lloyd George was merciless in his treatment of the generals.

Henry Wilson, whose assassination robbed him of the opportunity to publish his diaries, was perhaps saved from embarrassment by his editor, who ran roughshod with a red pencil to obliterate Henry's often intemperate remarks. There were enough of these left, however, to confirm the general opprobrium heaped on Wilson that he was a shameless 'humbug' and 'terrible intriguer', out to make mischief.

Haig edited himself. His diary, which he had meticulously compiled, ran to several typescript volumes which he extensively amended, rewrote and 'corrected' as he saw fit, thereby reducing their historical value. They were used by Duff Cooper who, with the endorsement of Haig's wife, wrote an entirely Haigean version of the war. The field marshal's detachment, reserve and blood-chilling diffidence remained intact. When more of his papers, even further edited by a family-approved historian, were published in 1952, Max Aiken declared them a public suicide '25 years after his death'.

Robert Borden wrote a two-volume memoir which, in keeping with his character, was dull, understated and relatively tepid. He had retired from the premiership in 1920. C. P. Scott wrote in his diary that none of the prewar leaders deserved to remain in office; 'no man who is responsible can lead us again', he felt. Alone of the principal allied leaders, Borden had held office from the very start of the war until its finish. The others, and deservedly so, had been swept aside.

Hubert Gough authored two memoirs, largely intended to defend his generalship of the unfortunate Fifth Army. At his dismissal, he had been vaguely promised an official inquiry as to his behaviour, but it never came to be, despite his desperate urge to put the record straight, a course of action his friends discouraged. Viscount Esher told him to 'suffer in silence'. Gough spent many postwar years trying to resurrect his reputation. Haig, perhaps from a guilty conscience, deigned to invite 'Goughie' and his wife for a weekend at their baronial estate in Scotland after the war. This was designed to be seen as a sort of public absolution on Gough's performance; at least that's how Goughie perceived it. He actually served again during World War II in the home guard. He outlived just about everyone else, dying in 1963 at ninety-two years of age.

King George V is recalled from his published correspondence, for the most part, and the observations of others who recorded their exchanges with the royal persona in their own diaries. Writing a memoir, of course, was beneath the dignity of a monarch unless you happened to have been dethroned, forced to abdicate or expelled from one's country, in which case the need for funds might overwhelm a royal personage's more natural sense of discretion. The various diaries of the principals involved offer interesting, if often contradictory, portraits of George V. He comes across as an amiable nonentity in Haig's observations, unable to grasp either strategy or tactics, and more interested in matters that appealed to his notions of majesty, kingship and feudal bonds of loyalty which his subjects cheerfully (in his view) bestowed on him. In exchange, he bestowed on them a variety of medals, titles, regimental standards and the usual ceremonial trappings in which monarchies are so interested. Protocol was his specialty. Although inverately opposed to anything that might alleviate the squalid conditions of the labouring class (according to Lloyd George), he was catholic in his generosity when it came to pinning decorations on a soldier's tunic. All his English soldiers 'are by nature brave', he liked to say. A lack of discernment, however, disturbed people like Haig, who considered himself more than unusually alert to the conniving of the troops. The king approved giving medals to soldiers who had dragged their wounded comrades out of battle to hospitals in the rear as 'justified and beneficial'. Haig responded by describing mobs of the king's subjects running from the front, having cast their weapons and packs by the wayside 'with a look of absolute terror on their faces, such as I have never before seen on any human being's face'. Victoria Crosses awarded to men lugging their comrades to the rear was a dubious proposition, since [ever the clinician] that meant one less rifle on the firing line. Haig, in fact, posted police to prevent the practice, seeing it as an excuse for men to flee when the going got hot. The king didn't know what to say to that.

The overriding visual impression of this particular monarch is a photo of his visit to a munitions factory somewhere in the industrial hinterland of his country, published by Lloyd George in his memoirs. The king, surrounded by vast piles of neatly stacked artillery shells, wears an expression on his face that can only be described as befogged. He does not appear to have the mental agility that could transform, in his own mind, this vast stockpile of gunpowder with the reality of its intended use, and the indescribable carnage that lay just over the English Channel. He appears numb to it all, and emotionally removed. 'What a happy army it is', he wrote Haig after a visit to the front or, at any rate, to a portion of it that was not being shelled, gassed or blown to pieces. Hitler later noted his opinion that kings are 'biological blunders'. He may have had a point.[8]

Pershing

The end of World War I represented the highlight of Black Jack Pershing's career. Ensconced in an elegant château, he entertained the president over Christmas 1918, an array of fine French champagne set out for Wilson's delectation. The president was unmoved by such ostentation. Though not a tall man, Pershing presented a striking figure as he led American troops in victory parades down the Champs-Élysées, and later Fifth Avenue in New York. He looked every inch the conquering hero. The guns having gone silent presented problems, however. Like most conscripts, American boys wanted to go home, the sooner the better, but occupation duties and the demands on allied shipping caused frustrating delays. A commonly heard joke that made the rounds was, 'Lafayette, we are *still* here'. Finally settled in Washington, Pershing busied himself with paperwork, inspection tours and the politics of figuring out what a peacetime army should look like. Promotions were a constant problem. Many of Pershing's protégés were treated shabbily in that respect, much to his anger, and some decorations that he did not recommend also engendered hard feelings (Douglas MacArthur, an egomaniac of the first order, wanted a Congressional Medal of Honour, but Pershing would have none of that).

Gradually, Pershing found himself bored. Like many an American general before and after, he allowed his name to be floated about as a potential candidate for the presidency in both 1920 and 1924, an enterprise his father-in-law, Senator Francis Warren, gently discouraged ('Do not let your head get swelled', he wrote). These clumsy efforts generated more embarrassment than delegates. Naturally, Pershing was disappointed, for there was now little else on the horizon that interested him, or replicated in any way the wild delirium and adrenalin of waging war. In 1924, he retired from the army. Not being a literary man, he did not relish writing his memoirs, but a substantial advance from a New York publisher spurred him on. The two volumes, released in 1931, were both a financial and critical failure. Ten dollars a set was too rich for depression-era Americans to afford, and most readers found the narrative dry and boring. They also seemed to resent the constant focus that Pershing placed on Pershing, one critic suggesting an alternative title, *Alone in France*. Pershing was glad in one respect that he had not been forgotten. Every Armistice Day, his office was flooded with telegrams, letters and cards of congratulation and remembrance, which cheered him enormously. He travelled to France on an annual basis for several years, where he was also universally honoured.

The problem for Pershing was that he lived so long. His conservative views on military affairs dated him. Billy Mitchell, whose notorious trial in 1925 was, on a minor scale, something akin to the Dreyfus affair, fractured the army in many ways, pitting traditionalist versus visionary. Pershing thought Mitchell was a scoundrel, and dismissed his extravagant claims for air power. World War II, which Pershing never thought possible, proved him wrong on this and other subjects. As the years passed, Pershing's physical and mental faculties deteriorated, and from 1941 on he lived at the Walter Reed Military Hospital in Washington. General de Gaulle, leader of the Free French during World War II, visited him during a trip to Washington in 1944. The sight of a French general in uniform sparked a note of recognition in Pershing, long-ago memories of Foch and Pétain. He said to de Gaulle, 'Tell me, how is my old friend Marshal Pétain?' This froze de Gaulle, who gathered his composure and managed to formulate a more or less polite reply, 'The last time I saw him, he was well'. He then left the room. In the autumn of 1946, at eighty-six years of age, Pershing married his long-time mistress, Micheline Resco, a Romanian woman more than three decades younger, whom he had met on his first day in Paris, in 1917. At the time he had been more or less engaged to George C. Patton's sister, but 3,000 miles of separation, thanks to the Atlantic Ocean, had cooled that romance. Resco provided Pershing with warmth during the long, difficult days of his service in France (as did other women), and their relationship continued, sometimes fitfully, until his death in 1948. On his last Armistice Day, only ten telegrams were delivered to the old soldier's bedside.

The Siamese Twins

Paul von Hindenburg's postwar career is well known. He became president of the Weimar Republic in 1925, a man unfit by age, mental health and political acumen to deal with the myriad of problems now facing his shattered country. He thought he could handle the emerging Adolf Hitler, for example ('I'll make him a postmaster, and he can lick the stamps with my head on them', he said), but failed miserably when that man's popularity exploded across the country. He grew senile in office, reportedly signing anything put in front of him, including paper sandwich bags. He died a decade later. His body was dug up, along with his wife's, from the Tannenberg memorial in 1945 as the red army swept west with utter ruthlessness in the face of Germany's collapse. The famous Russian 'steamroller' was exactly that, crushing everything in its path. Considerable mystery surrounds the deceased field marshal's journey thereafter, undertaken in growing furtiveness. During the post-World War II years, Germans saw a generalized disrespect when it came to honouring their dead. Göring, von Ribbentrop and all the other Nazis condemned as war criminals and hanged (those who did not commit suicide, that is) may have been despicable individuals, but did they or their famines deserve to have the cremated remains of their husbands or loved ones dumped from a truck into the river Spree? (Concentration camp survivors would undoubtedly say yes.)

Von Hindenburg, even in death, remained a refugee for years, spirited from one hiding place to another until collective temperatures had cooled sufficiently to reallow a decent burial. In a dark corner of the cathedral in the Hessian city of Marburg, famous for its medieval *Elisabethshrein*, the old field marshal and his wife have a final resting place. On the wall of their crypt is a large painted wooden panel, showing his aristocratic genealogy over how many centuries. It would be more impressive if any of these could be discerned in the overwhelming gloom of the cathedral's shadows, barely illuminated by a few electric chandeliers. The caretaker informed me that the occasional wreath is delivered, but otherwise there are few visitors interested enough in the past to spend any time here.

After the war, Erich Ludendorff went mad, rhetorically speaking. He fled Germany in disguise (blue-tinged sunglasses and a false beard), ending up in Sweden where he tried to regain his sense of worth and balance. Later immersed, through the influence of his second wife, in the netherworld of Teutonic myth, he dabbled in the occult and pursued a writing career, publishing books of astonishing intellectual brutality. One, *Der Totale Krieg* ('Total War') argued, in effect, that nations should live on a war footing in perpetuity; everything in the economy and life should be geared for it; war, total war, was the end in itself, a never-ending treadmill. This might have been extreme even for the likes of Hitler, whom Ludendorff joined in the abortive Beer Hall Putsch of 1923. In that farcical episode (in which, nonetheless, twenty men were shot and killed), Hitler had fled after a volley from one hundred policemen had shredded the Nazi marchers. Ludendorff, a man who feared nothing, continued marching forward. He died in 1937, at seventy-two years of age, and is buried in Bavaria. His grave slab is decorated with a naked sword blade. It is claimed by some that he had changed his ways at the end of his life, had turned to god for comfort. Ludendorff, in effect, had sheathed his sword. This seems hard to believe.

Pétain

Foch emerged from the Great War a national hero, but he remained bitter about the Versailles arrangements. He saw Germany as a perpetual threat. French wives who were now widows, he suggested, had more grief in store for them when their sons would be cut down in a second world conflagration. His own daughter had lost her husband on the western front; in 1944 her son perished as well, in the RAF.

Pétain continued to serve in the army for years and, briefly, as a minister in one of France's many postwar governments. He was appalled by the shrinkage of French military prestige, as reflected in cost-cutting budgets and reduced manpower levels. The army was so bereft of funds that it could not afford annual manoeuvres for two consecutive years in the 1930s. Meanwhile, Germany rearmed with a vengeance. Strategic thinking within *GQG* remained focused on the usual foe, but practical considerations – antiquated models of artillery, tanks, electronics, even the standard infantry rifle – prevented ambitious thinking.[9] On the eve of war in 1939, France did not even have a bomber capable of flying to and from Berlin with a full payload. In the face of such diminished resources, Pétain's ingrained negativity became a driving factor in the eventual decision to once again invest in a huge defensive wall that would bar the way to a resurgent German foe. Fewer numbers of soldiery (the low birthrate continued) seemed to dictate that military tactics be passive. This was the Maginot Line, named after a sergeant by that name who was wounded at Verdun, later to become a successful politician. An impressive statue of Maginot stands on the battlefield today, not far from the ossuary; he is shown being carried, wounded, by two comrades who are hauling him back perched on a rifle between them. It makes no mention of the fact that his line failed miserably in 1939, nor that just five years before a maverick in the French army, Charles de Gaulle, had predicted that it would fail in a book entitled *Towards a Professional Army*. This work sold more copies in Germany than it did in France.

Pétain outlived them all: Nivelle (dead in 1924), Mangin (1925), Foch (1929), Joffre (1931). In the nether reaches of his ninety-five-year-old mind, no longer lucid in 1951, surely Pétain would have wished that he had died as well – long, long ago. In 1931 he retired, at seventy-five, but again and again he was recalled to service, at no time more disastrously than in 1940 during the early stages of the German invasion. Premier Paul Reynaud, in response to the virtual collapse of the French army, turned once again to the marshal, naming him his chief military adviser and vice-premier. 'They only call me in catastrophes', Pétain said. When Reynaud had had enough, the old man succeeded him. Through the course of his life, there had been 107 French governments. He would lead the 108th.[10]

Pétain, like most senior French generals, became severely depressed as war news grew ever grimmer. The climax for them was Dunkirk. If the Marne was the 'miracle' of World War I, its counterpart in World War II was surely Dunkirk. Some 224,000 thousand British soldiers, and then 110,000 mostly French, were spirited from continental shores just as it seemed certain they would be swallowed up by the enemy. The news was bittersweet to Pétain and Maxime Weygand, now *général d'armée*, they gave the British little chance to win the next phase of war, alone as it would be, begging for American help that might or might not ever come. Britain would have its neck wrung like a chicken, said Weygand. Both men were extremely bitter about what they considered Britain's perceived fecklessness in June 1940. France had 109 infantry divisions in the field fighting the Germans, Britain only ten. As the fronts cracked, the British made no secret of their desire to bail out. The Dunkirk evacuation was no victory as far as the French were concerned, nor to the Belgians. Churchill's exhortations that they keep on fighting was interpreted by Pétain and his circle of advisers as thinly veiled devices meant to protect the British army as it tried to extricate itself from France, leaving everyone else to shift about as they might.[11] Churchill made it a point that the Royal Navy should take King Leopold of Belgium across the Channel to safety, but not the king's army.[12] On 11 June, just seven days after the Dunkirk operation had concluded, Churchill flew to France in an attempt to keep the French fighting. He was asked for air support, but the prime minister refused; British fighters were required for the expected Nazi invasion, he said, and could not be spared. The PM helpfully suggested instead that Paris be defended no matter the consequences. 'To make Paris a city of ruins will not affect the issue', replied Pétain. Then Churchill suggested that even if the French army lost its cohesion as a fighting entity, Frenchmen could carry on with a guerrilla war. Pétain, in his icy way, was furious. 'That would be the end for France', he told Churchill.

There were many calls, as the western front disintegrated, for the government and its leaders to continue the fight from the French colonial empire in North Africa. The country still had its fleet, and the ability to transport considerable numbers of troops to Algeria. But Pétain refused. 'I shall never leave France', he said. What caused so much trouble for him after the war is that he made this defeatist remark only seven days following the German invasion. In just a week, Pétain was ready to surrender.

Some said that the old marshal didn't have steel in his makeup any more, but the majority of Frenchmen at the time saw it differently: Pétain was simply being realistic. What was the point? he asked. 'It is easy, but stupid, to talk of fighting to the last man. It is also criminal.' Pétain knew the French army was finished. As he often said, thirty years of Marxism, with skimpy budgets to match, had eviscerated his country's ability to compete on the battlefield.

At eighty-four years of age, he often teetered between reality and fantasy. Perhaps he could negotiate with Hitler, he mused aloud. What nonsense, replied Reynaud. 'You take Hitler for Wilhelm I, the old gentleman who only took from us Alsace-Lorraine [in 1871]. But Hitler is Genghis Khan.' At other junctures, though, a sort of rationale could be found to his thinking. De Gaulle certainly saw it. Pétain would make peace with Germany on the best terms he could. The army would continue to exist, but the Third Republic would not. Its replacement would be a throwback to happier times: a society built on family, faith and hard work, not socialist rot like Liberté, Egalité, Fraternité. In the frenzied days of late spring 1940, Pétain stood solidly for an end to the war. When arguments, which were often and passionate, swirled around to the contrary, Pétain remained silent, as though sleeping. Edward Spears, the British liaison officer to *GQG* during the first war, found himself in the same capacity in the early days of the second, though this time as a general. During one critical meeting, he wrote in his diary that 'Pétain seemed dead'.

It was a calculated risk on Pétain's part to sign the armistice on 22 June 1940. He assumed, as did his entourage, that Britain would soon follow suit, and when she surrendered, given Churchill's rhetorical vehemence, there wouldn't be much of that country left in one piece. In which case Pétain's behaviour would be seen as prescient; otherwise, as a fellow general put it, 'we are criminals', and a price would eventually be paid.

Pétain meet Hitler once, on 20 October. He had little effect on the führer, which surprised no one. France lost two-thirds of its territory to German occupation; Pétain set up shop in the spa town of Vichy, then famous only for its sparkling water, to administer the rest. In his name, men like the odious Pierre Laval actively collaborated with the new German order: deporting Jews, sending Frenchmen abroad to work in German factories, helping fight the Resistance. When the allies invaded North Africa in 1943, Hitler abrogated the Vichy arrangement and sent units of the Wermacht to the south for Toulon, to secure the French fleet. From then until the final days of the war, Pétain was kept more or less a hostage with no say in his comings and goings. On 24 April 1945, the Germans actually did him a favour; in a convoy accompanied by a guard of Gestapo agents, he was moved into Switzerland. Pétain should have stayed there.

Certainly de Gaulle wished he had. De Gaulle was a man of vindictive temperament, but despite radio attacks on his former mentor and heaps of scorn that he poured on the man and his behaviour during World War II, he would have preferred the Pétain issue to go away.[13] He maintained enough respect for the marshal, and his long service to France, that he was prepared to let him die in obscurity somewhere in a neutral country. He was not sympathetic in any way to French communists, with whom he struggled to gain mastery of France in 1945/46; all they shouted was that Pétain should be put against a wall and shot.

Unfortunately, as a man of honour, Pétain returned. He was greeted with flowers by some, but others spat on his railway car. Arrested, confined, interrogated and generally abused, he was hastily put on trial, a long and verbose exercise of dubious propriety. Pétain spent much of the time dozing. In the end, by a single vote, the jury found him guilty of treason and sentenced him to death. Laval was shot by a firing squad, but Pétain, reprieved, ended up imprisoned for life on a remote Atlantic island called Île d'Yeu, ten kilometres off the coast of France in the Bay of Biscay, a better fate certainly than Captain Alfred Dreyfus had suffered half a century before. Île d'Yeu was no Devil's Island in the middle of nowhere in French Guiana. Pétain wasted away for six years, growing senile and incontinent, dying in 1951 at ninety-five. In a moment of delirium, he said to his jailor, 'Cunt, that's all that matters'.

The last (though perhaps not final) twist in Pétain's saga occurred in the winter of 1973. A group of strangers in a blue van came over to Île d'Yeu on the ferry and set up their wares, mostly used clothing, for the weekly produce fair, held on Saturdays. During the night they dug up Pétain's grave and removed his coffin, all of 1,760 pounds; on Sunday morning they returned it to the mainland. Their ringleader, an Algerian war veteran, then held a news conference at a Parisian café. His demand was simple. That Pétain should be buried in the Douaumont ossuary, as the old marshal had requested. He wanted to lie, Pétain had said, 'among those French and German soldiers marked as unknown'. While elements of this escapade were farcical – the body was quickly recovered from a garage in a suburb north of Paris, and reburied on Île d'Yeu – the ramifications were less so. Many people in France thought Pétain should be honoured for the good and decent things he had accomplished for the country, while others, less forgiving, felt his name did not deserve rehabilitation. Many veterans of the Resistance said his body should be dumped in the Atlantic well before Île d'Yeu was reached. There seemed to be, at least in 1973, little neutral opinion, an atmosphere that may well fade as time marches on.

Charles de Gaulle, who himself was mercifully deceased at the time of this unfortunate episode, and thus unavailable for comment on the future resting place of Philippe Pétain, seems to have had the final word, as usual. 'Pétain was a great man', he had said. 'He died in 1925.'

Trotsky, and Those Whom He Helped Destroy

When Lenin died at the early age of fifty-four in 1924, his political will and testament generated only confusion as to who he thought should succeed him. Always an admirer of Trotsky's fluency, both with pen and voice, he nonetheless begrudged his brilliant companion's late arrival into the party's ranks. He did not formally join until September 1917, having had dalliances with various opposition splinter groups over the previous two decades. Was he, in his heart, a genuine bolshevik? About Stalin, there was no doubt about that; he was a party man through and through, and his bureaucratic skills were superb. But Lenin wondered about his personal ambition, his cold-blooded ruthlessness and his tendencies towards conspiracy. Lenin was comfortable with the notion of a dictatorship, but only in the name of the party; a cult of personality was not what he envisioned for an industrial Russia moving forward from monarchical feudalism. By refusing to indicate an unambiguous choice for the individual who would come after him, he set the stage for a vicious power struggle that intrinsically favoured the man who possessed more individual and self-centred ambition, and that man was Stalin. His single-minded desire to eradicate anyone standing in his way had been a trait that disturbed Lenin; it ended up destroying Trotsky.

By 1925, Trotsky became the odd man out, expelled first to Turkey, then to France, on to Norway and finally (in 1936) to Mexico.[14] He was probably lucky to have made it out of Russia alive, one of the few Stalinist moments of indecision on record, and even luckier not to have been assassinated as he wandered abroad. Turkey, for example, was crawling with 'white' refugees and Romanov retainers who would have been happy to settle scores with one of their greatest tormentors.

Had Trotsky remained quiet and unobtrusive, had he accepted his status as an 'Old Pretender' émigré, he might have lingered through a graceful retirement, but Trotsky was never a man to keep quiet. He maintained a continual and subversive correspondence with an ever-dwindling circle of friends and followers in the universal diaspora of displaced Marxist malcontents, and his pen remained as fluid as ever. Aside from John Reed's *Ten Days*, his autobiography is probably the most inspirational book to come out of the Russian revolution (like Reed's magnum opus, Trotsky's is full of misinformation). But as the years flew by, his audience shrank. The English historian A. J. P. Taylor, an extravagant admirer, praised Trotsky's tenacity but noted the pathos of his literary activity. 'He went on writing even when he found no readers.' Trotsky seemed condemned to fulfil his own scathing denunciation of political foes, that they were doomed to end up scattered on 'the rubbish can of history' (as one historian acutely noted, 'should he have expected a different fate?'). Stalin's psychopathic paranoia, reaching its peak in the late 1930s during the great purges, finally squirmed its way into the suburb in Mexico City where Trotsky lived, worked and collected cacti. In an act of crude barbarity, a secret service assassin murdered Trotsky in his spartan study on 21 August 1940. Instead of shooting or stabbing him quickly, this faceless apparatchik battered him with an ice axe, splattering blood and gore all over the desk and floor. After hurling whatever he could lay his hands on to repel the attack – an inkwell, a dictaphone, a table lamp –Trotsky grappled with his assailant. The struggle lasted some four minutes until his wife and bodyguards finally arrived to disarm the assassin, but intervention came too late. He died the next day in a city hospital; a young American writer, Saul Bellow, sat in the waiting room along with other devotees of the great man. For good measure, Stalin ordered several members of Trotsky's immediate family to be assassinated as well, a process that took some years to accomplish. The killer served twenty years in a Mexican jail; when released, he was greeted as a hero in the Soviet Union. The scene of his crime is now part of a museum/ shrine; Trotsky himself is buried in the central courtyard. Visiting the study today is an antiseptic exercise; everything is as neat as a pin.

On the royalist side of the ledger, the last immediate Romanov to die was Grand Duchess Olga Alexandrovna, Tsar Nicholas's sister, the youngest child of Alexander III. This unfortunate young girl was married off in 1901 to Duke Peter Alexandrovich, a notorious rake and gambler many years her senior (she was only nineteen). Why she consented has always been a mystery. The union was never consummated, Duke Peter being a homosexual, a fact she learned early on her wedding night when her husband never appeared (he spent the night at a club playing cards). They lived in a cavernous palace of 200 rooms in St. Petersburg. It is now headquarters of the local chamber of commerce. In an act of mercy, the marriage was eventually annulled, and Olga married her lover, Nikolai Kulikovsky, an officer in the cavalry. Unfortunately, this gentleman was a commoner. When they both joined Olga's formidable mother in the winter of 1920 to share in her exile (the Empress Dowager

Maria Feodorovna had escaped to Denmark), Maria generally refused to be in the same room with him. This made for very lonely family meals.[15]

Finances were precarious. The enormous Romanov deposits in London banks mysteriously disappeared. Nicholas and Alexandra's best-known biographer, Robert Massie, spent considerable effort trying to sort through the tangled morass, but even he gave up. Queen Mary of England, married to Maria's nephew, King George, allegedly took advantage of her distressed situation, paying less than market price for various jewels smuggled out of Russia.[16] But the English royal family did on occasion provide shelter when necessary; Olga's sister, Xenia, lived for years in a home in London provided by the Windsors on the grounds of Hampton Palace, appropriately called 'Wilderness House'.

In the waning days of World War II, Olga and her husband were disconcerted to discover that Joseph Stalin still remembered who they were. Russian troops occupying Germany were just a few miles from the border; requests were made to the Danish government that they be turned over to the Soviet authorities. Fearing deportation, or worse, the couple fled to England, then to Canada, where they purchased a dairy farm. Olga and Nikolai, along with their two sons and the grand duchess's faithful maid, Mimka, cleaned out the stalls and performed all the other menial chores required to keep the place afloat; when they weren't doing that, she maintained a lively correspondence with other Romanov refugees, and dismissed the various imposters who showed up claiming to be Anastasia or any number of other long-dead members of her family. Advancing age and Kulikovsky's death in 1958 left Olga pretty much alone, impoverished and in ill health. Her last address was an apartment in east Toronto owned by Russian émigrés, located over a shabby barbershop called Ray's. She died in 1960.

Moscow's ancient Chudov Monastery, founded in 1358, was razed in the late 1920s on the orders of Joseph Stalin. Some of its reliquaries, manuscripts and icons were saved and preserved in state museums, but others were dispersed as either loot or meaningless religious detritus. It was replaced by a grandiose building, the Praesidium of the Supreme Soviet, during the construction of which many graves and funereal monuments were also arbitrarily bulldozed. In 1990, workmen excavating a section of parking lot uncovered the long-lost crypt of Grand Duke Sergei Alexandrovich, murdered eighty-five years before just a few yards away. He was identified, when the coffin was opened, by his uniform and other personal artefacts inside. If communist authorities from the 1950s had still been in charge, these remains would probably have been tossed into a nearby construction dumpster, but instead the Russian Orthodox Church, beginning a post-Berlin Wall renaissance, arranged for the body to be reinterred at the Novospassky Monastery on the outskirts of the city. This complex of buildings had suffered its share of indignities over the course of the twentieth century – a prison at one point, then for years a squalid collection point for drunks picked up on city streets by police patrols – but at least it survived and was reconsecrated in 1991, a development neither Trotsky nor Lenin ever foresaw.

The mortal remains of Sergei's wife had farther to travel before they finally came to rest. Counter-revolutionary 'white' forces overran the site of Ella's murder in Siberia, and assiduously collected the six bodies and considerable evidence. They had expected, no doubt, that when they overthrew the bolsheviks, certain retribution would follow for those who had executed them. That, of course, never happened. Her corpse, intended for a Moscow interment, was instead dispatched far to the east along the Trans-Siberian Railway. Through machinations too complicated to explain, it ended up two years later in Jerusalem, where it was buried in the crypt of a Russian convent dedicated to Mary Magdalene and located next to the Garden of Gethsemane.[17] The Holy Land can be a strange experience. Seeing this church, festooned with traditional multi-layered Orthodox onion domes, is a somewhat disorienting sight, but no less idiosyncratic than the great western door of Westminster Abbey in London, which has ten statues arrayed above it of twentieth-century religious (and, it must be said, political) martyrs. Ella is represented here; to her right is the Archbishop of Uganda, Janani Luwum, murdered in 1977 by Idi Amin (who is reputed to have done the deed himself), while to her left is Martin Luther King.

In Yekaterinburg, the House of Special Purpose was torn down by Boris Yeltsin, a local communist boss at the time. He believed, probably correctly, that at some point in a coming political thaw, the site might become a point of pilgrimage for right-wing monarchists. It is ironic that Yeltsin presided over Tsar Nicolas II's reinterment in St. Petersburg, in 1998, when the royal remains were transferred there, with considerable ceremony, from their gruesome burial pits twelve miles outside Yekaterinburg. These had been collected with assiduity by the government, after local sleuths had pointed the way. Three skulls, for example, had been discovered and taken home by amateur archaeologists in 1979. Feeling guilty, they reburied them in the same spot some time later, but not before having discovered a fourth in the process. They knew they had found the right place. All the Romanov corpses have been more or less discovered by now. People armed with metal detectors sometimes find fragments now and again around the site of the mine shaft (now a church), but whether these have anything to do with the Romanovs is usually disputed. As for the House of Special Purpose, it too has a religious building on its foundation, the Russian Orthodox Church of the Saviour on the Spilled Blood. Was there ever a more apt name?

Rasputin's eldest daughter Maria, who last saw her father getting into an automobile with Prince Yusupov, led a vicarious life. At one point she performed in a circus as a lion tamer, at another, during World War II, she was employed as a riveter at an American defence facility. Living off social security cheques, she died in Los Angeles on 27 September 1977.

Ireland

'The only way to deal with Ireland is for someone
to open a sluice and submerge her.'

David Lloyd George

Asquith's promise of Home Rule to the Redmondites, as they were called, came just about the time his own position in power grew wobbly. Five months later, in fact, he was forced to resign. In the interim, he had again assigned to Lloyd George the unpleasant task of trying to hammer out an agreement between Redmond and the Unionists, a task doomed to failure. Even the eloquent little Welshman, that 'slippery snake' as John Dillon called him, could not budge the intransigent men of Ulster, whereas Redmond, who was seen to give away the idea of a united Ireland in exchange … well, in exchange for nothing … was seen as increasingly irrelevant. In the aftermath of the executions, Redmond's power base began evaporating. An Irish nationalist in parliament explained the math to C. P. Scott, that before Maxwell's spree of killings, '99 percent of Nationalist Ireland was Redmondite; since the executions, 99 percent is Sinn Féin'. Redmond, politically twisting in the winds, was, additionally, no longer seen in London as a man who could 'deliver' anything. He was not even considered worth deceiving, as one historian put it, by unscrupulous politicians in London. The last months of his life were dreadful. His brother was killed on the western front; his son-in-law, whose appointment to a prison board in London he had arranged, oversaw the forced-feeding of a Republican prisoner who subsequently died; and he was even mugged on a Dublin street by a gang of Sinn Féin thugs. He died on 6 March 1918, and is buried in a shabby, generally locked cemetery in the middle of Wexford town. He is today a largely forgotten figure. John Dillon, accused of being 'the friend of England', followed him into the desert.

He lost his seat in parliament, as did nearly every other nationalist member, in the December 1918 general election. Éamon de Valera overwhelmed him in a landslide.

Lloyd George, in the meantime, had succeeded Asquith as prime minister, but in trying to form his own government he was forced to turn to the most unlikely partners of all (at least for him), the conservative/unionist crowd whom historically he had disdained. In order to win their support, Home Rule or any sort of solution to the Irish muddle became a dead letter for all intents and purposes. Sinn Féin was now the ascendant political entity in Ireland, and its members boycotted the parliament at Westminster, setting up a rump congress and shadow government of their own. The utter severance of communication and goodwill had the inevitable result of a slide towards open revolt, an interlude dominated by the ruthless Michael Collins, who initiated a campaign of violence towards (mostly) the Royal Irish Constabulary, largely made up of fellow Roman Catholics. It was not uncommon to read of some ordinary RIC policeman, walking home to lunch or dinner in a remote Irish village, being shot from behind or ambushed by gunmen, often on his doorstep in front of a horrified wife. Lloyd George grew fed up with that, especially as the Irish conscription issue heated up. Ireland would be dragooned. 'There were to be no judicial trials and punishments', he said in private to Scott. 'If men were to be shot, they were to be put up against a wall and shot on the spot'. When the fighting in Europe was over, he authorized the formation of ex-servicemen into flying squads called 'Black and Tans' or 'Auxiliaries', a frightening crew of renegades and madmen. These were, in many ways, the equivalent of the *Freikorps* in Berlin, and running pitched battles in the countryside with I.R.A. guerrillas became common occurrences, as did atrocities on both sides. In one rampage, Black and Tans burned down a goodly portion of the centre of Cork. The only thing Lloyd George did not do was formally declare war. He knew enough about public relations to stay away from doing that.

The prime minister had other things on his mind in 1919, mainly the Versailles Peace Conference. The Irish matter was an embarrassment, 'this skeleton in our closet' as Smuts put it. Here were the British, elucidating high-minded principles in Paris designed to allow small states to determine their own future, yet at the same time engaging in more or less open combat with a small, powerless opponent, attempting to coerce it into remaining a part of their imperialist empire. That was certainly the way a few Irishmen (many from America) tried to present the case in Paris, but their hands were tied by an unfortunate fact of life. The Irish rebels had fought on the side of Germany, or declared their intent to remain 'neutral' after their Easter 1916 defeat in Dublin, in either case hindering the war effort against a common foe. The conscription battle was really the last blow – shirking their duty – but the primary obstacle was actually President Woodrow Wilson, genetically a Presbyterian Orangeman. As far as Ireland was concerned, it 'was none of our business'. Lloyd George may have had his problems with Wilson, but in the Irish matter he was more than grateful.

Lloyd George eventually rammed a settlement down Irish throats (British liberal sentiment demanded a resolution, no matter what). A delegation including Michael Collins (formerly little more than a clerk), Arthur Griffith (journalist), and Erskine Childers (writer), locked horns for two months in London with the likes of the prime minister, Austen Chamberlain, Winston Churchill, Lord Birkenhead and others who must be considered the cream of Britain's political establishment. The result, predictably, was a British ultimatum: compromise or war – 'Resistance', as Lloyd George promised, 'would be brushed away as by the mere sweep of our arm'. Collins and the rest signed. The 26 southern counties of Ireland would be granted dominion status, six of the nine Ulster remaining a part of Britain. This treaty resulted in immediate civil war in Ireland. Collins, Childers and Griffith would all soon be dead, as well as perhaps 3,000 others.

The Rising had been bloody, but what followed outdid it in every way. Civil wars both past and present are often class wars, one stratum of a country (or tribe) versus another. In Russia, for example, the post-World War I conflict was generally depicted as tsarist and aristocratic circles fighting the bolsheviks. Those forces from which Easter Rising rebels were drawn, by contrast, proved remarkably homogeneous. Rural members were largely farmers or agricultural workers, with tradesmen interspersed, and very few people of a 'professional' caste; those from cities and towns were slightly more varied, but mainly working-class or lower middle-class individuals, with students mixed in. The Anglo-Irish ascendancy was barely represented, and Catholics were overwhelming in numbers. The resulting civil war was thus not fought between classes, but along political and ideological lines, some of stupefying pedantry (de Valera was a master of rhetorical contortion).[18] As such, the bitter strife cut deep to the bone among friends, neighbourhoods and even families, with no predictive characteristic as to how people might agree or differ. The results were horrific. If observers thought Maxwell was a brute, executing fifteen leaders of the Rising and overseeing the destruction of central Dublin, how were they to compare that to the Free State (or pro-Treaty) forces of 1922/23, who shot or hanged 101 of their former comrades and, with artillery borrowed from the British, demolished the Four Courts building along the Liffey in June 1922? By that point, as far as Lloyd George was concerned, this mess was all Ireland's problem, not his.

Von Richthoven's Many Graves

The corpse of Manfred von Richthofen has been laid to rest on four separate occasions. The first, behind British lines, occurred on the day after his death, and was allegedly vandalized by French farmers within a week. When the war ended, and the landscape tidied up, it was transferred to a nearby German military cemetery. In 1925, at the request of von Richthofen's mother (under pressure from nationalists and fellow flyers), he was reburied in Berlin's Invalidenfriedhof, a cemetery full of German military notables (Scharnhorst, von Schlieffen, Hoffmann and many more). In the 1930s, without consulting the family, Hitler ordered an ornate, heavy-handed and ostentatious monument erected at the gravesite, complete with sentry on special, wreath-laying occasions, which became a popular tourist attraction. It suffered more or less total devastation during the 1945 fall of the city and its aftermath, the Cold War, when the Berlin Wall was built right through the centre of the cemetery. East German guard troops, desperate for shelter, made crude huts from grave slabs pilfered *in situ*, and von Richthofen's memorial more or less disappeared (as did that of another famous internee, the notorious SS general, Reinhard Heydrich, assassinated in Prague during World War II). In 1975, before the demise of East Germany, the grave was moved yet again, to a family plot in Wiesbaden, full of artistic sculptures of nymphs playing harps and Grecians looking bereaved, as is so typical of German and Austrian cemeteries. Manfred is buried next to his younger brother Lothar, who died in 1922.

Actually, he is not. Lothar survived the war. In many ways, he was equally as proficient as his more famous brother. In two combat tours lasting just 90 days, he shot down thirty-three of his forty kills, and also was awarded the *Pour le Mérite*. He became a commercial pilot after 1918, flying mail routes between German cities; these flights often included passengers. On 5 July 1922, his engine failed and the plane he was piloting crashed, killing him and others. Among passengers who survived was Fern Andra, born in Illinois, but one of the most famous actresses during the war in German silent films. Lothar was buried in the family plot at Schweidnitz in Silesia, but after World War II the town cemetery, full of Germans, was destroyed and ploughed under by the Poles. Today it is covered by a football field; Lothar's corpse is in there somewhere, under the sod. His gravestone at Wiesbaden is a memorial, nothing more.

Part of the von Richthofen town house was converted after World War I into a museum by Manfred's mother, financially strapped during the postwar depression. All his hunting trophies, war souvenirs, medals and commemorative cups (sixty in all) were on display. During the dark days of April 1945, Frau von Richthofen, along with thousands of others, fled the oncoming Soviet armies. What happened to her collection of artefacts is somewhat unclear. An occasional cup is said to come up now and then on the auction block, but confirmation of such rumours has been impossible to confirm. The building is now a luxury hotel called (of course) The Red Baron, the inspiration of a Polish entrepreneur. The lobby and hotel rooms are covered with photographs of von Richthofen and his various planes. The receptionists and female employees are dressed in red stewardess costumes. The town is no longer known as Schweidnitz, but by its Polish nomenclature, Świdnica. Von Richthofen's genetic trait of relentless pursuit was amply carried on during World War II by a cousin, Wolfram von Richthofen, a thoroughly ruthless aviator who became one of the youngest field marshals in German history (he was a favourite of Hitler's). Wolfram's association with such despicable events as the bombing of Guernica during the Spanish civil war, and the pitiless battles over Stalingrad, give some indication that he stood most satisfied only within the maelstrom of battle.

The Afterlife of T. E. Lawrence

'It is said that in 1918 Marshal Foch was asked how Napoleon would have fought the Great War. "Superbly", said the Marshal; "but what the devil would we have done with him afterwards?" The Prince of Damascus solved the problem for Britannia. He simply walked away and became a nobody again under another name.'

George Bernard Shaw

Lawrence cut a romantic figure at the Versailles peace conference. Alongside the exotically dressed Faisal, he looked authoritative in his British officer's uniform, his head wrapped in a *keffiyeh* (the Arab headdress); but he made little headway for his and Faisal's cause. He left Paris deeply disillusioned, and still virtually unknown outside official circles. His great fame would not come until later.

For Lawrence, the closure of his Arabian adventure proved the end of his enjoyment of life, but not of his influence, which persisted somewhat longer. He did important work, as an aide to the new colonial secretary, Winston Churchill, for several months beginning in January 1921, and at the Cairo Conference later that year, all dealing with Middle Eastern matters. He more or less saw this period as a finale of sorts, an effort for him to tie up loose ends, particularly with regard to Faisal. By July 1922, he had pretty much had it, and resigned. 'The Arabs are like a page I have turned over', he explained to his sometime friend, Robert Graves. Churchill was disappointed, and posthumously chided Lawrence 'with hiding his talent in a napkin while the Empire needs its best'. 'I'm bored stiff', Lawrence wrote a friend instead. According to Philip Sassoon, Lawrence had that 'instinctive feeling that his life's work was done'.

Lawrence called the two plus years of his dramatic career in the desert a 'flash in the pan'. He had seventeen years more to think about it, reflect about it and write about it, but almost everything he did after the war was dramatically anti-climactic. T.E. in effect disappeared from life (though of course he did not entirely succeed. 'He was retiring and yet craved to be seen', the historian Lewis Namier wrote, 'sincerely shy [yet] naively exhibitionist').

If being at the centre of power bored Lawrence, it is difficult to say how satisfying his later life became as he submerged himself in roles of utter banality. He spent twelve years, under assumed names, as an enlisted man in both the RAF and the tank corps. 'I came here to eat dirt till its taste is normal to me'. His identity was well enough known in those services, but his desire for anonymity mostly respected. 'He said he had finished with the East', one of his friends later wrote. 'He made the army his monastery. He wanted to be "like a brown paper parcel" and have no decisions to make. [The sterility of the barracks] was his penance'. And sterility it certainly was, Lawrence 'of Arabia' (Lowell Thomas coined that descriptive) washing dishes, among other mundane duties. Sergeants, he observed, were 'messy feeders: plates were all butter and tomato sauce, and the washing water was cold'. Even then, Lawrence was distinctive. One of his army chums felt that 'it was obvious to me that legends would follow T.E. wherever he went, whether he turned brigand or evangelist. His whole life was a legend; and one had but to watch him scrubbing a barrack-room table to realize that no army table had been scrubbed in just that way before'.

Even though a common enlisted man, he often bristled when confronted with overbearing superiors. During one pointless inspection, his wing-commander noticed a few suspicious book titles in Lawrence's locker (one may well have been Joyce's *Ulysses*, which T. E. had in camp). 'Do you read that sort of thing?' he was asked. 'What were you in civil life?'

'Nothing special, sir'.

'Why did you join the Air Force?'

'I think I must have had a mental breakdown, sir.'

'Sergeant-Major, take this man's name; gross impertinence!'

He bought a derelict labourer's cottage in 1924 which he called Clouds Hill, in deep heather and mangy woods, located near the tank headquarters at Bovington Camp in Dorset, and renovated it over time to his own rather strange tastes. It had, for example, no kitchen (he usually ate and slept at camp); when guests came to Clouds Hill to listen to music or discuss books, they were supplied with can openers, Lawrence's offerings being confined to tinned meats and Heinz beans, but no alcohol. Visitors were many: E. M. Forster, Thomas Hardy and his wife, Siegfried Sassoon and other literary lights. George Bernard Shaw and his wife, Charlotte, became fast friends. Shaw even put a Lawrentian character, Private Meek, into one of his plays, *Too True To Be Good*.[19]

He spent his first years of 'retirement' writing enormously popular books, *Seven Pillars of Wisdom* (in painfully small editions), followed by a condensed version, *Revolt in the Desert* (a bestseller that sold 40,000 copies in just three weeks. T. E.'s publisher, Jonathan Cape, saw its revenue for that year jump from £2,000 to £28,000). What really put him in the spotlight was his willingness to become the subject of a travelling lecture tour by the well-known broadcaster Lowell Thomas, who allegedly grossed over $1,000,000 from the enterprise, in the process turning Lawrence, in the words of a critic, into 'a cheap and vulgar legend ... the whole war-time experience turned into farce'. Lawrence now spent considerable time and effort avoiding the fame he had, at first, assiduously craved, but thrashed back and forth mentally over the whole enterprise, condemning himself (and Thomas) on occasion, but also taking a secret enjoyment in all the hubbub ('The Arab war was not nearly as silly as Thomas makes out', he wrote in a 1921 letter; nonetheless, he went to Thomas's show several times, incognito, of course). Lawrence could, and often did, 'spread his peacock tail' according to a friend. Thomas said that Lawrence had an affinity for 'backing into the limelight'.

The spectacular success of the Thomas roadshow is not hard to understand. In the grim aftermath of the Somme, Passchendaele and the Dardanelles, people still looked for a hero. Industrialized battlefield mayhem and endless casualties still could not dim the allure of war as an item of popular interest. Lawrence's 'sideshow' in the desert 'was war as [many people] romantically dreamed it ought to be', wrote V. S. Pritchett: 'terrible, but at least apprehensible like an exotic work of art, small yet visionary and having the epic quality of individual combat, known then only to flying men.'

In his mind, Lawrence frequently teetered – 'I'm in a trough of the waves. Up and down it is, always'. He had a strong streak of self-disgust, as his letters attest. Often feeling worthless, he entertained suicidal thoughts many times. He was a man in anguish, with cross-currents of emotion torturing him continuously. 'There was in him a deep neurotic negation of life', wrote the historian Lewis Namier, a slight acquaintance. There was also the question of his sexuality, which again caused posthumous circumspection among his growing number of critics as to how truthful or wholesome a person he really was. Britain has rarely been kind to heroes who strayed from the straight and narrow path of respectability. Roger Casement learned that lesson.[20]

Lawrence was fully aware that he was being emotionally pulled into various directions, in keeping, as it were, with the contradictions inherent in his career and life, and how people might react in confusion. The only aspect of that which really interested him was portraiture. He enjoyed having artist friends sketch, draw and paint his likeness; he was eager to see how they saw him. Robert Graves wrote that T. E. 'knew a good deal about himself and wanted to know more. The various portrait treatments they made of him he found informative both about himself and about artists. Nobody painted the same man. One day in 1921, I was at Paddington Station with him waiting for the Oxford train. We met William Rothenstein: he had tea with us in a refreshment room. Rothenstein said that he had just been doing a portrait of Lawrence. "Oh", I said, "which Lawrence?"'[21]

Lawrence called *Seven Pillars of Wisdom*, the first draft of which he completed in 1919, 'my beastly thing' ('I wore my nerves into a mop' writing it, he later recalled). Notwithstanding his disdain, it is a unique and enormously complicated work and something of a metaphor as to the complexity of his character. The majority of war memoirs pale in comparison to this elaborately written, minutely observed, almost hyper-sensitive book. Whatever its faults, it is without doubt one-of-a-kind, a true epic.

The narrative seems straightforward in many respects, but in actuality it isn't. Lawrence was honest enough when he warned his friends to be careful. 'If people read [the book] as a history, then they mistake it', he wrote confidentially in a 1924 letter. But in fact he issued no such disclaimer for the general public, who mostly fell into lockstep, believing everything he wrote was an accurate portrayal of facts on the ground. In a generalized sense it was. But behind the broad-brush stroke there lay a long series of misrepresentations, inaccuracies and often serious lapses in candour, many of which initiated bitter controversy after Lawrence's death, when several historians disproved important details in the narration, which triggered several defensive responses. Lawrence's letters would not be collected and published until many of the disputants were dead, but, had they been widely known, more caution would probably have been called for by his admirers. 'On the whole I prefer lies to truth, particularly when they apply to me. I got discouraged trying to tell people the truth and finding they don't believe it, so I told them lies'. One fairly recent critic called the book 'Seven Pillars of Fiction', an overly harsh assessment.

If Lawrence had one predominant trait to his wartime exploits, it was recklessness. Among the Arabs, according to Robert Graves, he was nicknamed Prince Dynamite, 'for his explosive energy'. Plunging into long desert treks, attacking in situations where conventional tacticians would have hesitated, telling tall takes and/or lies if it furthered what he wanted, ignoring or evading what he clearly knew to be his superior's wishes (they were always 'butting into our show', as he complained) – these all revealed a headstrong and determined individual who would resist efforts to tame or control him. This lack of discretion characterized both *Seven Pillars* and the later years of his life.

That Lawrence was homosexually inclined is now a fairly given opinion among his most recent biographers, but, as was typical of the man, it is not an open and shut conclusion and defining its character too dogmatically is a dangerous path. Lawrence states in numerous letters that he hated being touched by anyone, had an aversion to sex and no interest in women. He stated bluntly to the author E. M. Forster that he was a virgin. It seems fair to conclude that this assertion might not be true.

The homoeroticism in *Seven Pillars* is hard to miss, beginning with his declaration of deep feeling for the Syrian youth, Dahoum.[22] This type of indiscretion is everywhere apparent, mostly from the idealized descriptions of noble and masculine Arab warriors whose affections often turned physical, 'quivering together in the yielding sand, with hot limbs in supreme embrace' (one is reminded of Achilles and his hyperbolic attachment to Patroclus in Homer's *Iliad*).[23] Lawrence adds the additional element of masochism to the mix, especially apparent in the long, often lugubriously described torment of his torture and implied rape on the ill-fated reconnaissance mission to Deraa, perhaps the most famous section of the book and previously alluded to in this narrative. After suffering assorted kicking and whipping – 'a gradual cracking apart of my whole being' – Lawrence confessed to 'a delicious warmth, probably sexual, swelling through me'. This startling revelation is stated without fanfare, without special emphasis, without any effort at subterfuge and certainly without a trace of shame. It is simply on the page in basic black and white. As such, the rumours that swirled around about his personal life at the various military installations where he was stationed after the war seem corroborative.

Rumours, of course, are just that, rumours, but one of Lawrence's biographers seems justified in his assertion that Lawrence 'was living dangerously close to scandal', so much so that several friends (and his brother) spent considerable efforts to douse and deny suspicions. It was certainly common knowledge that Lawrence had recruited several of his army comrades, in particular a John Bruce, known as Jock ('the roughest diamond of our tank corps hut', he called him), to administer beatings with a whip to his naked rear end, allegedly leading to orgasm (Freudians would probably point out the fact that Lawrence's mother, that zealous evangelical, was an avid believer in corporal punishment and frequently caned her son on his bare buttocks). These were not casual or languid play acts by Bruce and, apparently, others; some sessions occasioned seventy-five lashes.[24] His brother, while admitting to the beatings, said they were typical of early desert hermits, who flagellated themselves in order to suppress desire. Even Winston Churchill was 'in the know'. At Lawrence's funeral, he allegedly went up to John Bruce and said, 'Look to duty now, Jock', in other words, KEEP QUIET.[25]

Lawrence spent thirteen years in uniform, one in India where he began another literary project, a new English translation of Homer's *Odyssey*, an interesting choice to be sure. Ulysses, like Lawrence, had gone off to war and then returned, anonymously, to a different world and different circumstances: Ulysses to unravel whether his wife had remained faithful during the ten years of his absence, Lawrence coming home, exactly, to what? The postwar years were full of emptiness for many such men. Hemingway explored this theme in *The Sun Also Rises*, published in 1926. Two years later, Lawrence, the self-confessed 'extinct volcano', started his work on the *Odyssey*. He retired from the service in 1935. What he would have done with the rest of his life, and particularly during World War II, is an intriguing question. He was still, after all, a relatively youngish man.

He built a small thatched storage hut at Clouds Hill for his motorcycle; he owned seven, in succession, all Brough Superiors, and beautiful machines they were (Lawrence loved speed). On 13 May 1935, coming over a crest near Clouds Hill, he was startled to see two schoolboys on bikes in the middle of the road and, in swerving to avoid them, crashed into a grove of trees. A memorial stone marks the spot, though it is hard to find. Lawrence never said another word or regained consciousness, dying six days later. One result of his crash was a national campaign that motorcyclists should, in future, wear helmets.

Lawrence was buried nearby, Churchill one of the mourners, regretting the genuine talents of a man that he thought had gone wasted. Two years later a friend of Lawrence's, Eric Kennington, designed an effigy to be placed, as in mediaeval times, over a knight's sepulchre. Cathedrals all over Western Europe are full of such monuments, the warrior lying on his back in helmet, chain mail, full armour and shield, hands clasped in prayer, with his lady often by his side, their feet resting on a pillow or curled animal. Since Lawrence was a quintessential loner in many ways, Kennington featured his subject lying alone, but otherwise the reclining figure could be that of William the Conqueror, Prince Hal or the Black Prince, but with several notable exceptions. Instead of armour, shield and sword, Lawrence is depicted in full Arabian gear: a flowing *keffiyeh*, tribal robes, sandals, his right hand clutching the pommel, not of a sword but of the traditional curved belt dagger known as a *jambiya* that Lawrence may have commissioned in Mecca.[26] His head rests on a camel saddle, his feet on a stone carved with Hittite bulls. His legs are crossed, the ancient symbol of a crusader. By his head, Kennington had three books neatly stacked, Lawrence's favourite reading matter: *The Oxford Book of Verse*, Malory's *Morte d'Arthur* and *Anthologia Graeca*, better known as *The Greek Anthology*. The incongruity of this entire composition, medieval in tone but somewhat alien traditionally, so shocked the curate of the little parish church where Lawrence had been buried that he refused to countenance it. What in heaven's name did this Arab, gleaming white in Portland stone, have to do with his grey-drab village church of ancient lineage? A good question … but there will always be an England, and Kennington managed to find a more willing pastor in the nearby village of Wareham, and the effigy was placed there (but not before the dean of Salisbury Cathedral also rejected the project. He wanted Lawrence to be portrayed, upright, in an RAF uniform).

St. Martin's-on-the-Walls was locked tight when I visited it, but the key was available at a local shop down the street. When finished, I was to drop it off through a mail slot; things are casual out in the countryside. The interior, on this cold spring day, was dank, as usual. The Lawrence effigy, though shining bright as advertised, did seem inconsonant with the rest of the memorials here, but, then again, he was a unique personality and it seems right that he be out of place in this time-worn structure. Not many come here to see the tomb, I am told. Very few people know of its existence. It is one of the hidden wonders of World War I.

Legacies
The Middle East

> *And as for the unbelievers,*
> *Their words are a mirage in the desert.*
> *The thirsty man thinks it water*
> *Till, coming to it, he finds nothing.*

Koranic injunction

It is difficult to put into words the chaotic situations created in the Middle East after hostilities ended in 1918. The public utterances of Woodrow Wilson as regards 'the self-determination of peoples' did not help, nor the machinations at Versailles, which revealed once again that the voracious colonial appetites of the European contestants had not abated.

Borders never really meant much to Arabs. T. E. Lawrence's desire was larger and more grandiose, what historians call 'Pan-Arabism'. Neatly drawn maps, divisions of power established by treaties and documentation, did not conform with more inspired, and often otherworldly visions of Arab 'unity', which could be as amorphous as desert sands reaching beyond the horizon. Arabia, for want of another description, became a more or less defenceless cradle, there to be looted by imperialists from the West. Artificial nations were created, changed, altered, undermined, propped up, bribed, invaded, exploited and abused, the results of which continue to have their dire consequences as we proceed further into the twenty-first century.

Egypt, generally quiescent, erupted in revolt in the spring of 1919. The uprising was bloodily suppressed under Allenby's supervision, though he was not happy with the mindset of his troops, most of whom were fed up with war and wanted to go home. Allenby had Soviet revolutionaries in mind when he wondered if socialism wasn't at the core of their sullen attitudes. 'I can't shoot them all for mutiny', he glumly concluded, as though half-wishing that he could. The unrest was serious enough, however, that Britain finally granted Egypt independence in 1922, though its implementation was a sham. Britain maintained forces there until 1936, and even then would not relinquish military supervision of the Suez Canal.

British rule over Sudan lasted until 1954, and that of the vital Canal just another two years. Gamal Abdel Nasser, a charismatic Egyptian president, nationalized the waterway and moved to take over its operation in 1956. This led to the Franco-British intervention three months later, during the Second Arab-Israeli war, in an effort to re-establish control. Militarily, the operation, codenamed Musketeer, was successful, but the operation was roundly condemned by just about everyone in the international community. Lack of support from the Eisenhower administration proved fatal, and French and English forces withdrew in December. British Prime Minister Anthony Eden resigned after only two years in office. That old war horse Winston Churchill, though wary of the initial operation, could not fathom the pusillanimous finale. 'I cannot understand why our troops were halted. To go so far and not go on was madness.'

As for the Holy Land (or Palestine), the Balfour Declaration of 1917, which committed Britain to the creation of a Jewish homeland, has unsettled the region from then on to the present day. Britain exercised control of Palestine as a mandate after Versailles, and for nearly thirty years kept the peace, more or less, but often experienced long periods of violent upheavals, mostly occasioned by Arab discontent, the most serious of which took place between 1936 and 1939. These were brutally put down. After World War II, with Britain's economy in semi-ruins and its role in the world diminished, the government looked for just about any way out, and by 1948 all its troops had left. The formal creation of Israel that same year did nothing to settle matters; indeed, the new nation state fought for its life as it was attacked from all sides by its Arab neighbours, as it has, successfully, on several occasions since then. It remains the true power in the region. Geographically, the area is minuscule when compared with the rest of the world, but Palestine remains one of the great tinderboxes of the twenty-first century, certainly not the heritage that Britain hoped for or expected. How they could have thought otherwise is a mystery.

Lebanon became a French mandate after Versailles, and remained so until World War II. The war years were, to put it mildly, confused, given the rivalry between the Vichy, or pro-Axis government, and Free French forces opposed to them under the leadership of General de Gaulle. The French position after 1946 proved untenable; their troops were withdrawn that year, and Lebanese independence recognized. The country's history since then has been a seesaw. As of the publication date of this book, it can safely be said that Lebanon is at the lowest ebb since its creation, and on the verge of dissolution as a functioning state.

The French mandate of Syria was a perfect example of heavy-handed colonial rule. One of the moral dilemmas facing Britain was what to do with Faisal, and his appearance at Versailles, with Lawrence beside him, was but another inconvenience facing Lloyd George. How were they to reward him (to say nothing of his father, Sharif Hussein)? Both those men clung precariously to the McMahon correspondence, but even they recognized (the son more than the father) that the Sykes-Picot Agreement made every word of McMahon 'dead paper' (Lawrence's phrase). Lloyd George and Clemenceau had a brief and informal chat before the peace conference started (and before the annoying Woodrow Wilson had hit his stride), and between the two of them confirmed that they would implement Sykes-Picot to the hilt. Lloyd George essentially handed Faisal over to Clemenceau: he would be the token figurehead, ruling Syria as 'king' in name only. Faisal had little choice but to agree, but once settled in Damascus – 'settled' is not really the appropriate word – he found himself sucked under by Syrian nationalists, who gave him little choice other than to contest French rule. This masquerade of independence barely lasted four months. After a short battle outside the environs of Damascus, the city fell. The commanding French general celebrated his easy victory by visiting the grave of Saladin, the *bête noire* of Richard the Lionheart during the Third Crusade, at the Umayyad Mosque. 'Saladin, we're back', he said. Faisal was unceremoniously cast aside and expelled.

Unrest in the county erupted more seriously in the mid-1920s, and French forces suffered several embarrassing military defeats, though in the end they prevailed, however unsteadily. France finally agreed to Syrian independence in 1936, though the process was thrown into limbo both by internal French politics and then World War II, but resurrected in 1946 when French troops returned home. Despite the relative stability of the repressive regime of Hafez al-Assad from 1970 to 2000, the history of Syria has been one of turmoil and violence. Today, under the leadership of Assad's son, the country is currently in a state of suspended civil war, its economy in shambles.

In Mesopotamia (today's Iraq) the humiliating defeat of the Anglo-Indian army under General Charles Townshend in 1916 was revenged by a second invading force some eleven months later, again originating from Basra, which entered Baghdad on 11 March 1917. After the Ottoman collapse in 1918, Britain assumed administrative control of Iraq under mandate of the League of Nations. Correspondingly, Winston Churchill, now colonial secretary under Lloyd George, convened a working group of forty officials, military and administrative, in Cairo to finalize the details, T. E. Lawrence in attendance as a consultant. Only two Arabs were invited to attend (Churchill called his working party 'The Forty Thieves'). It was Lawrence, undoubtedly, who put forward the scheme to promote Faisal as the figurehead ruler of the new country, his way, as Churchill put it, to 'redeem in large measure the promises he had made to the Arab chiefs'. Faisal was a thorn in Lawrence's conscience, his 'king for a day' career in Syria, a farcical and ignoble denouement to the entire Arab Revolt of 1916. In Iraq, Lawrence saw redemption, and he seized it. 'Faisal owed me Damascus first of all', he wrote years later, 'and Baghdad second'.

Churchill, at Lloyd George's urging, was determined to clear the board, diplomatically speaking. He agreed to the notion of putting Faisal on yet another throne, though with the usual caveats that Faisal would do as he was told. The basis of post-World War I economics in the region that persisted for the next hundred years and continues as such today, was oil, and the potential of the Basra fields, in particular, was sturdily appreciated. Faisal, again, had little choice but to accept his new regal status, humiliating conditions notwithstanding. There can be little doubt that he owed much of this resurrection to Lawrence who, in effect, now considered all his debts to Faisal cleared. The two men never saw each other again, save for two instances when Faisal happened to be in England. These were not particularly successful encounters.[27]

In the course of these empire-building duties, Lawrence at least retained his sense of humour, as Robert Graves related in his biography. 'When a European monarch one day ... greeted him with the remark, "It is a bad day for us kings. Five new republics were proclaimed yesterday", Lawrence was able to answer, "Courage, sir! We just made three kingdoms in the East!"'

Iraq was granted its independence in 1932, though with the usual conditions (British military bases, rights of transit and so forth). Faisal died the next year (he was only fifty, but looked eighty). He was succeeded by his only son who ruled, shakily, for six years, to be followed by a grandson, also named Faisal, who took the throne at the tender age of three. Various regents and family members of varying capabilities ruled in his name until he came of age in 1953, but even then he relied primarily on others and was, essentially, out of touch with the realities of the ordinary Arab, and 'street' nationalism in general. His Hashemite cousin, Hussein of Jordon, requested Iraqi troops to assist during the Lebanon crisis of 1958, and Faisal agreed. Instead of marching into Jordon, however, these troops marched into Baghdad and staged an initially bloodless coup d'état on 14 July. Bloodless, that is, until 8 a.m. when Faisal and several members of his immediate family (as well as some servants) were machine-gunned to death at their palace as they were attempting to surrender. The king's unpopular prime minster, fleeing the city dressed as a woman, was discovered and lynched by a mob. So ended the Hashemite rule of Iraq. The present-day woes of this country are too familiar to relate here.

The only remnant of Hashemite rule left today is Jordan, another Churchill/Lawrence creation. Abdullah, Sharif Hussein's second son, a man whom Lawrence never truly cared for (but advised nonetheless), was selected to lead this new kingdom as emir after he had threatened to march on Damascus to support his brother there against the French (the process of his elevation is not easily or quickly described; in fact, it was inordinately complicated). He was essentially bought off with Transjordan (as it was called until 1946), probably the least blessed entity, in terms of natural resources or economic potential, of anywhere in the Middle East. Its biblical and symbolic importance, however, was potent, and Jewish settlers in Palestine were upset at its creation, and remained resentful for years to come. The antipathy was mutual. Abdullah dubbed himself a king in 1946 when Jordan was officially declared independent of any further British control.

Jordanian politics, like those of the other Arab states, constantly revolved around Israel. On 17 July 1951, the former prime minister of Lebanon was assassinated on his way home to Beirut. Extremists had been infuriated by rumours that he approved a peace treaty with Israel, among other complaints. Three days later, Abdullah was murdered during prayers at the Al-Aqsa Mosque in Jerusalem for the same reason. The killer was immediately shot in the resulting confusion, leaving conspiracy theorists to the conclusion that he, in his turn, had been killed to prevent any confession that might implicate those who had planned the assassination. The Hashemite dynastic succession prevailed, however, and that clan still rules in Jordon.

The final nagging piece of business to be decided by Churchill in Cairo was what to do with the Sharif of Mecca, Hussein bin Ali, and he handed that unpleasant task to Lawrence. As the originator of the Arab Revolt, Hussein certainly had cause for complaint. In his view, two of his sons, Faisal and Abdullah, had been coopted from their allegiance to him, bought off with the kingdoms of Syria (if briefly), but now with Iraq and Transjordan. All these and more had been claimed by the father as 'King of the Arabs', and here were his sons, betraying him with British assistance. The old man clung to the McMahon Agreement, now of course irrelevant. It was Lawrence's task to convince him of this reality.

Lawrence spent several weeks in Jeddah, on the Red Sea, meeting with Hussein, and sometimes with two others of the sharif's sons, Ali and Zaid. Whereas, in 1917, Hussein was courted by the British and lavishly attended to, the scales had now turned: he was no longer needed. Lawrence had never much liked Hussein, but he had certainly coddled him in the early days, when he needed to. His reports now were loaded with invective. In cables to the Foreign Office in London, he characterized the sharif as 'absurd', 'conceited', 'greedy', 'stupid' and so on. His patience running thin, Lawrence pretty much bullied Hussein into agreements that the sharif, after thinking things over, then repudiated. At one point, Hussein broke down and cried.

In October 1921, Lawrence left Jeddah without Hussein's agreement to the new arrangements settled upon by the colonial powers on the Middle East in general, and on Faisal and Abdullah specifically. As far as Lawrence was concerned, according to the literary critic Irving Howe, 'Arabia seemed far less admirable in peace than in war'. Hussein was no longer deemed a British 'client', as evinced by London's refusal to assist the sharif when Ibn Saud, his rival for control of the Arabian peninsula, and based in Riyadh, marched into Hejaz. Ironically, Ibn Saud's pretensions were supported to some degree with military supplies provided by officials in the Indian Office. All Lawrence had to say was, 'We sealed [his] doom'.

Ibn Saud was an adherent of the Wahhabi sect of Sunni Islam, a revivalist, puritanical and doctrinaire interpretation of the Koran popularized by a relatively unknown cleric two hundred years before, a short span indeed considering the religion's ancient pedigree (Lawrence called it 'a fanatical Moslem heresy'). Its harsh view of life seemed a reflection of the environment in which it thrived, the desert of central Arabia. Certainly the fanaticism of its warrior class, known as *Ikhwan* (The Brethren), was fearsome. In June 1924, Ibn Saud's force of some 3,000 *Ikhwan* invaded Hejaz. Hussein sent his son Ali to defend the city of Taif but, as he had done many times before during the Arab Revolt, Ali took fright and fled. The *Ikhwan* entered Taif and slaughtered almost everyone inside its walls, which sufficiently unnerved Sharif Hussein that he abdicated, succeeded by the hapless Ali early in October 1924. Ali quickly followed his father by abdicating two months later. Mecca fell on 5 December, and Ibn Saud absorbed Hejaz into his growing empire, which is known today as Saudi Arabia.[28]

Britain did Hussein a favour of sorts by eventually transporting him to Cyprus. His exile was softened to some degree by £800,000 of gold sovereigns that he reputedly took with him from Mecca. The embittered King of the Arabs died in 1930 at the age of seventy-nine.

It is difficult not to agree with the assessment by a modern scholar that 'the order of civilization' created in the Middle East by the victorious European powers was 'a mixture of the worst of several possible worlds'.

The 'Ex-Kaiser'

> *'In peace the kaiser was a war-lord, in war he*
> *evaded taking decisions, and in defeat he fled.'*

Former Chancellor von Bülow

The kaiser lived a long and boring retirement in Holland, two decades' worth. At first, his position was tenuous. Lloyd George called for elections in Britain almost immediately after the war's end, presumably to take advantage of people's relief that the whole ghastly mess was finally over. Britain was not in a euphoric mood by any means, and Lloyd George tried to generate some electoral heat by campaigning on a slogan that he called 'Hang the Kaiser'. Wilhelm should be extradited, he claimed, put on trial for war crimes and executed if found guilty (what other verdict was possible?). Whether or not the prime minister meant it was anyone's guess; he was, after all, the great 'foolometer', as Lord Esher put it, a man with the uncanny ability to read the public's mind at any given moment. A scurrilous rumour spread about London that George V had actually approached his opposite number in the Netherlands, Queen Wilhelmina, not to allow the kaiser's extradition, but instead to grant Wilhelm permanent asylum in her country. Too many kings had been overthrown, stripped of their property and dignities, even murdered, enough so to make any monarch with a healthy regard for self-preservation uneasy. Changing his dynastic name from the Germanic Saxe-Coburg-Gotha to House of Windsor could not disguise the truth that the British king was, after all, a German sympathizer.[29] How many Englishmen believed that we shall never know.

Wilhelm was certainly made nervous by such loose talk. 'An ocean of abuse, vilification, infamy, slanders and lies has rolled over me coming from London', he complained. He did not want details of the Schlieffen plan widely publicized in war documents released after the war; they would have revealed the embarrassing fact that Germany originally intended not only to invade Luxembourg and Belgium, but Holland as well. That would not have been good publicity given Wilhelm's current vulnerability. For the first two years of exile, he wondered at his eventual fate. The Dutch government found a nobleman of sufficient largesse, Count Godard Bentinck, to house the kaiser while it decided what to do with their uninvited guest. Bentinck had a beautiful estate and superb castle, Amerongen, surrounded by two moats (helpful to keep potential assassins away). The stay was supposed to last but a week or two; the kaiser stayed on for thirty months, members of his entourage coming and going at will. The count knew little of the kaiser's personal habits, much to his regret, especially Wilhelm's mania for woodcutting, his favourite exercise. It did not take long for the kaiser to cut down several thousand trees on Bentinck's property, which took years to reforest. He did not bother to ask permission from his host to do so. This poor gentleman was relieved indeed when Wilhelm was finally given permission to remain in Holland, whence the kaiser purchased a modest manor called Doorn, a few miles away.

Before leaving Amerongen, the kaiser decided a small gift was in order for his generous, and fortuitous, reception. He oversaw the construction of a small clinic for the nearby village, fully stocked with twelve beds and supervised by a German nun. The locals, however, would not frequent the place. 'They are frightened of it', a relation to the count later wrote, 'they think to go there means certain death'.

At Doorn, the kaiser (referred to in the press as the 'ex-kaiser', a term he detested), set up a miniature Hohenzollern court, regulated, as always, by reams of etiquette and protocol. Eventually the Republic allowed Wilhelm access to several of his bank accounts and personal possessions. A train with fifty-five boxcars eventually crossed the Dutch border, destined for Doorn, full of paintings, furniture, art treasures and, of course, uniforms. The kaiser dressed formally every day of his life, changing outfits several times as dinner schedules, guests or anniversaries required. At first, he was confined to the grounds of his estate, and no further. When his wife died, he was not allowed to accompany her body to Potsdam for burial. In time, however, he was granted limited freedom to tour the countryside in his automobile. The residents of Doorn, whom he allowed to walk through his estate as they wished, were respectful. They tipped their caps, or curtsied, whenever their paths might cross.

Sympathetic writers and journalists often received cordial welcomes to the manor house; they were treated to revisionist analyses of what had gone wrong. The kaiser never expressed any regret for anything, and his list of enemies was a long one (Hindenburg at the top, whom he considered on a par with Wallenstein, as well as British politicians, who 'engineered' (his words) an 'unjust war against me and my country'). For some years he entertained the hopes of a restoration, but these soon faded. His staff consisted not only of functionaries, but military attachés as well. These ex-officers were mostly chosen from among volunteers who came from Germany on set rotations. Wilhelm exasperated these men with his temper, always subject to extremes. 'How little the kaiser has changed', wrote one of these. 'Almost everything that occurred then still happens now, the only difference being that his actions, which then had grave significance and practical consequences, now do no damage'.

By the time his wife, Dona, died, at age sixty-three, her role in the kaiser's life had become formulaic. A 'thoroughly downtrodden' woman, the kaiser missed her only after she was gone. He now had no one to take care of him. Nineteen months into widowhood, he impetuously remarried, this time to Princess Hermine Reuss of Greiz, herself a widow with four children, and considerably younger than the kaiser. Socially ambitious, Hermine resented the string of snubs aimed her way. Many German monarchists refused to recognize her as 'Empress'. They also questioned her early enthusiasm for Hitler and the Nazis. She was foolish enough to think that if Hitler gained power as chancellor of Germany, the Hohenzollerns would be restored, Wilhelm again on the throne (with herself by his side). She evidently had not read *Mein Kampf* with sufficient attention. As was his wont, the kaiser soon tired of Hermine's company; he shut her out of his emotional life as thoroughly as he had her predecessor.

Wilhelm put little stock in Hitler or National Socialism. He delighted in the early twenties when various right-wing militarists attempted their various coups. The night he heard about the Kapp Putsch of 1920 (referred to by the diarist Count Harry Kessler as the 'Kapp farce'), he was overcome with delight. 'Tonight we will have champagne!' he told his staff. But he soon understood the Nazis for what they were, and saw little hope of returning to Germany as kaiser through any intercession from them. Despite the many anti-Semitic remarks that he routinely made, he deplored the *Kristallnacht* and other social excesses that he read about in the newspapers. Germany under Hitler was 'a mustard republic', in his opinion, 'brown and sharp'. On the eve of World War II, he entertained the British writer John Wheeler-Bennett at Doorn. Wheeler-Bennett was not altogether unsympathetic to the kaiser, though he disdained his miniature court with its ever-fawning retainers. The kaiser himself had no sense of finesse. When he was served, he ate like a pig; dinner was over when his plate was clean, before some guests had even begun. As for the company: 'Though the bluest of East Elbian blood flowed through their veins, they had the manners of wart-hogs and the political intelligence of low-class morons.'

Wheeler-Bennett was somewhat undone during his short stay. 'I was oppressed by a sense of nightmarish unreality. To discuss all morning the events and happenings of that old world which had crumbled in flames in 1914, and then go back to one's rooms in the afternoon and read in the daily papers of the increasingly inescapable probability of an imminent repetition, was an experience I will never forget.' Wilhelm asked him to 'come back and see me next summer, if you can. But you won't be able to, because the machine is running away from *him* [meaning Hitler] as it ran away with *me*'.

Kaiser Wilhelm II died on 4 June 1941. He had been offered asylum when World War II began by the British government, of all entities. The desire to hang him had abated over two decades, it seems. Hitler also made inquiries as to his safekeeping, wondering if he wished to reside in Berlin. Wilhelm politely refused, he would stay in Holland. The kaiser was, if anything, the proudest man on earth. Germany would have to get on its knees and beg him to return, and not as some pensioner of the state, but only as its leader. Hitler sent a troop of S.S. men to guard and patrol the compound. They bowed their heads whenever the kaiser walked by. Wilhelm specifically ordered that no swastika flags or Nazi symbols be displayed at his funeral; like so many of his pronouncements, this one too was ignored. Wilhelm now belonged, as Goebbels put it, where he deserved to be, in history's 'dustbin'.

Doorn today is a handsome museum. It does not take long to tour. Its most interesting exhibits involve the kaiser's wardrobe: uniforms, shakos, boots, medals and decorations beyond counting. A separate admission fee is required to see the mausoleum where Wilhelm is buried.

The crown prince also sought refuge in Holland in 1918, but he did not end up within the cosy environs of a magisterial country house. He was confined to the windswept island of Wieringen, one of a chain enclosing the Zuyderzee. The parson's house, without electricity or running water, was his home. The few inhabitants treated him warily at first. He had, after all, been caricatured as a blood-sucking monster all during the war years. His long-suffering wife spent her days in Berlin. She never reconciled herself to Friedrich Wilhelm's constant philandering, the temptations for which proved fortuitously non-existent on Wieringen.[30] Friedrich Wilhelm pottered about on the island; he wrote his memoirs, which were mendacious, superficial and largely devoid of insight. He spent a great deal of time, he related, just looking out of the window. In 1923, given permission to return to Germany, he became interested in politics, hoping for a Hohenzollern restoration. Since his father was universally regarded as literal poison, Friedrich Wilhelm was not shy about suggesting himself as a possible replacement. He very much courted Hitler and the Nazis, who in their turn viewed him briefly with marginal interest. Wilhelm regarded his son's manoeuvres with intense suspicion; the boy was dabbling in treason. There could be only one kaiser, as he said repeatedly.

Friedrich Wilhelm gradually withdrew from sight. He was a prop, carefully directed by Goebbels, on the occasion of Hitler's succession to the chancellorship in 1933, the highlight of which was a ceremony at the famous (or infamous) Potsdam Garrison Church attended by President von Hindenburg and a whole gallery of World War I generals, many in their antique spiked helmets. Hitler, dressed in a formal morning suit, resembled a butler, in the opinion of several observers (there would be few further occasions when a person could, in safety, mock the führer). The crown prince, in this particular spectacle, was dressed in the ferocious uniform of a death's head hussar. He was seated behind an empty throne-like chair, a tribute to the missing kaiser, who followed the proceedings on his radio from Doorn.

Hindenburg obsequiously saluted the 'symbolic' Wilhelm before descending into the crypt to commune with the spirit of Frederick the Great, who was buried there. Military symbols were about the only thing that could hold his attention anymore, senile as he was. After the whole affair was over, Hitler visited the crown prince at his Berlin address; when he left, his estranged wife had a servant open the windows 'to get the stench out'. Friedrich Wilhelm then vanished from public sight, to all intents and purposes, reappearing briefly in 1940. His own eldest son was killed in France during the *blitzkrieg*. The funeral in Berlin attracted 5,000 mourners, which shocked Hitler, who was accustomed to thinking of the Hohenzollerns as nonentities. He thereafter forbade any of the family from ever again serving in combat during the war. The last thing he wanted were Hohenzollern martyrs; the whole pack of them were 'slobbering pig dog aristocrats'. [31]

The end of the war found Friedrich Wilhelm in impoverished circumstances. He fled from Potsdam as the Red Army advanced from the east, a step quicker than his stepmother, Hermine, who was captured, imprisoned and maltreated by the Russians. She died in an internment camp, 1947. The crown prince ended up being arrested by the Free French in Austria, where he was recognized walking down the street. 'You have lost above all, monsieur, your sense of dignity', a French general said to him. 'After the collapse of your country, at the age of sixty-five years, the father of six children, you have no other interest than for your own comfort, the house of your idle hours, the woman of your pleasures. You are to be pitied, monsieur, and that is all I have to say to you'. Finally released, and after being forced to testify at the Nuremberg war crimes tribunal, he resided in the town of Hechingen in Swabia. The view from his window was of the immense castle Burg Hohenzollern, ancient seat of his dynasty, where he could not live since he had no funds to heat its eighty or so rooms. It is said his last female companion was a former chambermaid once in his employ, who also worked as a hairdresser in her many years of menial employment. He died in 1951 at age sixty-nine.

Miscellaneous Hardware

Twelve Big Berthas were manufactured by Krupp AG over the course of six years. While effective in Belgium, they proved less destructive when used during the Verdun campaign of 1916. The French forts, with the exception of

Vaux, had been modernized to some degree before the war; poured concrete with reinforced steel bars, strengthening their resistance. Some of the Big Berthas were more or less ruined by continuous use, requiring the replacement of their worn-out barrels over and over again (which may help account for Krupp AG's tremendous profit growth between 1916 and the following year, over 152 percent). Two Big Berthas survived the war; one disappeared within the bowels of allied military bureaucracy, one was shipped to the United States for detailed analysis, then stored at the Aberdeen Proving Ground in Maryland, whence it was sold for scrap metal in 1952.

In St. Petersburg, the original Finland Station is long gone, replaced by an ugly modern facility. The famous locomotive, # 293, that brought Lenin from Finland (twice) is preserved in a glass enclosure next to the rail yard. Several members of the proletariat, unemployed and/or intoxicated, lie around on benches alongside it. Solzhenitsyn called this engine 'the first chariot of socialism!'

The 25,000 rifles landed near Belfast in 1914 were never employed in France against Germans, though the thousands of rounds of smuggled ammunition were. The last-known use of these firearms was by tribesmen of Haile Selassie in their fight against invading Italians in 1940.

The French railway car where Foch insulted the German delegation in November 1918 – # 2419D – allegedly stands in the same clearing where the armistice terms were delivered, housed in a small museum adjacent to the site. After the war it became something of a shrine, a victory park assembled around it with statuary of various sorts (one of Foch), and derogatory inscriptions calling notice to the 'criminal pride of the German Reich'. Concrete slabs were poured to show the exact location of the railway cars where the two delegations were headquartered: one from which Foch dictated his terms, and one where the Germans collectively wept when they read them. Adolf Hitler returned the favour in 1939. After the French collapse, he ordered their representatives to surrender at the very same spot, which they did on a hot day in June. Hitler arrived first, took a quick look at the Word War I memorabilia, then entered # 2419D and took Foch's seat. The French arrived a few minutes later, and the surrender documents were read aloud. Hitler, a man on the go as it were (he had Britain to conquer next, then the Soviet Union) got up and walked out after only twelve minutes. After visiting Paris and his old trench works outside of Ypres, he returned to Berlin.

With customary Teutonic ruthlessness, the Clairière de l'Armistice as it was called (The Armistice Clearing) was then defaced. The statues were covered with swastikas and flags (or removed), the concrete footprint of the rail carriage stomped on and chipped away by souvenir hunters, and #

2419D jacked up on pilings and then carted off to a railway siding for a trip to Berlin. There it was ceremoniously placed in the *Lustgarten* as a victory totem, a huge open space in the very middle of the city where Hitler often harangued the mob, and was visited by thousands. Unfortunately, being as it was at the very epicentre, the *Lustgarten* was pulverized in the waning days of the second war, when a British air raid blew much of # 2419D into splinters. What was left, the S.S. hauled away and eventually burned. The museum at Compiègne today, in other words, does not house the real thing, symptomatic in a way as to how things are in our world today. If one wanders about the shadows of the current museum, one finally stumbles over the truth, exhibited in an obscure display case. There, the only remnant of # 2419D still left, an ordinary piece of metal, is exhibited with a small explanatory card. It states that the treasured railway car that one has just paid an admission fee to see is not # 2419D, but a compatriot car of similar provenance (actually, # 2439) but, as they say, it is not the real thing. For some reason, this visitor was extraordinarily disappointed at this revelation.

In 1983, off the Orkney coast, a group of Swedish salvage divers found the wreck of HMS *Hampshire*, sent to the bottom by a mine on 5 June 1916, and bringing Field Marshal Kitchener and 736 other souls down with her. One wonders what possessed them, but their employers proceeded to strip a considerable amount of scrap from the old hulk, including a propulsion shaft and its manganese screw propeller, weighting in at 35 tons. Since the *Hampshire* had been designated off limits (it was regarded as a war grave) much of this loot was eventually returned, albeit reluctantly.

When Scapa Flow in the Orkney chain served as the principal naval anchorage for the Grand Fleet in two wars, it presented a scene of considerably more bustle than it does today. A small ferry runs from the main island to Hoy, which is currently populated by more sheep than human beings (as a matter of fact, there are probably more graves in the small war cemetery on Hoy than the total resident population). Hoy was once the very nub of the Royal Navy's presence here, but most of its ramshackle buildings, never meant for permanency, have disappeared. A short walk from the ferry dock brings you to a museum, the former pumphouse that used to transfer precious fuel oil from a tank farm to the various battleships of the fleet. This unpresupposing building is probably visited by a couple of dozen people a year (an exaggeration, of course, but my point is made). In the forecourt are several rusting artillery pieces and, in its solitary glory, the *Hampshire*'s gigantic propeller. What seemed exciting to divers in 1983, sitting in a hundred feet of water and perhaps glistening as some sort of buried treasure, is anti-climactic here in this dingy environment. The best thing about Hoy is the ferry ride back and forth through its great expanse of gleaming, frigid water, with the windswept Orkneys all around you. War of any sort seems a long way off from here.

The end of the hostilities, and the transfer of so many borders, was embarrassing in many ways for the British Empire. Newly freed or independent states no longer felt the need to be reminded of their colonial bondage. Over the years, a steady stream of imperial monuments have made their way back to the mother country (as V. S. Pritchett remarked, 'To survive, a statue has to be on the winning side'). Ireland probably had the largest and most diverse collection, from Queen Victoria to any number of admirals and generals, some of Irish birth but many others not. Wellington's enormous monument in the city's Phoenix Park is too big to dismantle, but Admiral Nelson was more easily disposed of. There is a splendid photograph showing the courtyard of Kilmainham Hospital overflowing with statues neither needed nor desired ('Queen Victoria, For Sale'). Most were returned to Britain and resettled among a more genial audience of admirers. Lord Kitchener was likewise unloved in Khartoum, the capital city of present-day Sudan. His battlefield victory at Omdurman in 1898 was marked by special brutality, Kitchener spreading the word that wounded tribesmen, of whom there were several hundred, need not be given treatment or spared the sword. He then proceeded to desecrate the tomb of Muhammad Ahmad, the Mahdi (or Prophet) who had led the campaign which saw the death of General Charles Gordon thirteen years before, one of Britain's great nineteenth-century heroes (it is said that Kitchener intended to use the Mahdi's skull as an inkwell). Kitchener's splendid equestrian statue stood for years in the centre of Khartoum, agreeably so to English bureaucrats who lived and worked there, but offensive to just about everyone else. It now sits overlooking traffic in Chatham, a town several miles south-east of London.[32] To make matters even worse, a £2 coin issued by the Royal Mint to mark the centenary of the Great War's beginning immediately stirred controversy. It featured Kitchener's image, pointing at the viewer, and the now-famous exhortation 'Your Country Needs YOU'. It was immediately condemned by a Welsh politician as 'jingoistic'.

Animal Life (and Death)

The end of the war also coincided with the end of horse-drawn transport. 'Before' and 'After' photographs of Piccadilly Circus in London reveal this fact perfectly. In pre-war images, the confluence of six major city streets around the famous statue of Eros often showed almost a gridlock of vehicles – transport, haulage, private carriages, hackneys – mostly pulled by horses. In just four years, similar images show a radical change, the internal combustion engine sweeping everything aside. A few horses, but by now outnumbered.

One reason was simple attrition. Men died like flies all over the continent of Europe, but so did horses and mules in their thousands, and they were not easy to replace.[33] By the time Pershing's two million Americans had crossed over from the Atlantic, the situation had become dire, American agents combing neutral countries for mounts and beasts of burden of almost any size or description (they needed 32,000 fresh mounts a month). Even the rugged mountains of western and northern Portugal found themselves flooded with buyers, offering the sort of money that startled peasants had never seen before. Had the war lasted much longer, South America would not have been seen as so far away either.

Henry Ford had a great deal to do with all this. His revolutionary industrial schemes of mass production had served the war effort well. The 820,000 steel helmets that he manufactured for American doughboys was nothing in comparison to the over 39,000 vehicles of various sorts that he delivered to Europe, 25,000 of which were cars and ambulances, 8,000 trucks and, most critically, 6,000 tractors to Britain alone. Ford was many things (aside from rich and anti-Semitic): innovative, hard-working, a visionary and pacifist, but a deep thinker he was not. The tractor sales alone were a contributory factor to Britain's mounting casualty lists, freeing up manpower, mostly young and semi-literate boys from the farm, who could now be sent to the front. A man of conviction, he might have thought twice if he had realized that particular cause and effect.

By 1918, the age of the horse was over. World War I could never have been fought without them, but, as peace finally settled over Europe, they were largely replaced in the day-to-day life of millions of people.

In terms of dogs, German forces ran through almost 30,000 during the war, many of which were eaten as food supplies grew scarce in the latter days of the conflict. A German shepherd, since known as Rin Tin Tin, survived the final battles of 1918 and was rescued by an American serviceman, Lee Duncan, who brought him home, trained him and subsequently established a career in Hollywood for the dog in a series of silent films, twenty-seven in all. There have subsequently been countless Rin Tin Tins in both movies and television shows.

It seems impossible to verify, but apparently 16 million animals were harnessed in one way or another by the warring powers – everything from carrier pigeons to camels, oxen to mules and the aforementioned horses and canines. Public appeals were issued for people to donate their pet dogs for duty on the western front, especially if they were terriers. There were so many unburied cadavers in Flanders and France that the rat population multiplied exponentially. Nothing that a good Irish terrier couldn't handle.

Hitler

The most monumental postscript to World War I was Adolf Hitler. Enough has been written about this man's career that little need be added here. His wartime career was not much different than that of thousands of others. He displayed exemplary courage in the trenches around Ypres – the town was so close you could almost touch its famous tower, he said – was wounded, gassed and decorated for bravery. He wore his Iron Cross first class with great pride all his life. While a hyper-nationalist, he was not a crazed beserker during the war, a wild man like Ernst Jünger, whose book *Storm of Steel* galvanized German readers through multiple post-war editions. Jünger was the type of soldier Erich Maria Remarque did not portray in what has been called the finest book to come out of the 1914–18 war, *All Quiet on the Western Front*, a depiction of idealized youth deceived by misplaced wartime euphoria. Jünger was the man that Remarque's heroes were destined to become after four years of brutal combat, figures Otto Dix etched in his gruesome wartime renditions of front line, gas-masked soldiers charging forward into a No Man's Land devoid of life, tossing 'potato mashers' to and fro, looking for the opportunity (as one British veteran put it) of shoving their bayonets 'point, barrel, left and right and even the butt, right through his guts … your little bit of steel as far as you can stick it'. Hitler was hardened by the war, certainly, but his decorated feats mainly involved carrying dispatches back and forth through the maelstrom of combat. It was dangerous work, and it took guts to do it, but it is thought unlikely that Hitler ever killed anybody, however bloodthirsty his later rhetoric became.[34]

By the end of the war, German propaganda posters were depicting different-looking men from those of 1914. Gone were the images of enthusiastic boys surging forward in the attack. Now viewers looked at almost blank faces, submerged in grime and almost overwhelmed by their steel helmets, which had long since replaced the antique leather *pickelhaube*. The soldier was now an anonymous industrial cog, the 'new' man defined mostly by his hard anonymity. This was largely image, but who on the street had the perspicacity to notice?

Most veterans, no matter their nationality, fell into neither category portrayed by a Remarque or a Jünger. Many wanted simply hearth and home, however difficult the readjustment. Killing someone now was no longer an acceptable job description; it was murder. Looting a home in Belgium or molesting a peasant girl as a prize of war could not be brushed aside any longer, nor burning some innocent person's house to the ground in a fit of pique or battle-induced fury. In civil society, these anti-social acts would be called theft, rape and arson. Many surely missed the camaraderie of the trenches; exchanging chit-chat with your neighbour in a beer garden or pub just wasn't the same thing. And many suffered in silence, choosing to lose themselves in the banality of everyday civilian life, submerging into their subconsciousness, if they could, the incredible things they had seen and experienced. Who, after all, could understand what they had been through?

The interesting thing about Adolf Hitler's march from obscurity in the 1920s to international fame by the time of his appointment as chancellor in 1933, was his audience. His street fighting thugs in the early days, though amply sprinkled with disillusioned and race-baiting combat veterans, grew steadily augmented by men who had been too young to fight in World War I (and mostly regretted that fact). As they grew older, faced with a crumbling German economy with few jobs and fewer prospects, they grew attracted to Hitler's premise that it was no fault of theirs. Jews and traitors were the villains, not the youth of Germany. Many veterans shrugged when they heard Hitler's rants. His appeals for a return to glory were attractive, his refusal to accept a diminished standard for Germany struck the right chord. But they misunderstood Hitler's resolution, or the notion that he meant what he said. His threats of aggression and war seemed on the surface simple gamesmanship. They voted for him because they believed that no man who went through what they had would ever start the whole process over again. They did not understand that Hitler's years in the trenches were the happiest of his life. How could that be? Anyone who felt this way was surely insane.

Ypres

Mabel Clint, a nurse from Canada who served almost the entire war in Flanders, visited Ypres four months after the armistice, and a melancholy sight it was. She wondered if anything there could ever be put right again. Touring the Flanders battlefield today, almost a hundred years later, presents a very different dynamic. Ypres has been fully restored, the medieval cloth hall a stunning recreation. The Church of England on a side street is cluttered with brass memorials on its walls, many for Canadian units, and a Celtic cross adjoining the Catholic cathedral memorializes the Irish killed here. At the other side of town is the immense Menin Gate, one of the earliest British memorials commemorating the great war. Although conventionally designed, it is certainly a powerful and moving statement, perhaps the most popular such site for visitors from Britain even today, but illustrative nonetheless as to the enormity of loss that World War I represents, and the inability (both before and after) to conceptualize it. Originally conceived as a recognition for those thousands of men 'who have no known grave', the idea was to carve the name of every such individual on its walls. Over 54,000 are so memorialized on sixty huge panels, the problem being that the gate, big as it is, isn't big enough. Almost 90,000 dominion soldiers disappeared in the muck around Ypres, too many for the gate to physically accommodate. As is usual in such cases, the complete roster is contained in a Book of Remembrance, beautifully bound with superb calligraphy but, alas, effectively inaccessible. The additional names were engraved on another memorial wall at a military cemetery near Passchendaele. Today, tourists are moved by an evening ceremony featuring buglers, 'The Last Post', in keeping with the sentimentality that, with each passing year, tends to blur the bleak reality of what this place is all about. 'Daddy' Plumer gave a speech when the memorial was officially opened in 1927. About the men so honoured, the general said, 'He is not missing; he is here.' The war poet (and wounded veteran) Siegfried Sassoon remained unimpressed. He called the gate that 'sepulchre of shame'.[35]

Driving through it and continuing east, one can visit something a little more modest, a granite obelisk in the middle of a field set on a slightly rising headland, the Novie 85th Battalion monument to itself. One is reminded of the battalion's Gaelic motto, *Siol Na Fear Fearail*. This does not translate well into English, but its approximate meaning is 'Breed of Manly Men'. Perhaps the message that is meant to be conveyed, accompanied by bagpipes, is 'Here Comes Trouble'. The scenery, on the day I was there, was beautiful and green, with tractors tilling the soil far into the distance. This is not as serene a view as it appears, however. Every year farmers dredge up something. Bones are fairly common, not a surprise given that something like one million men who died here continue to fertilize the soil, their bodies having been just folded into the earth by artillery fire; brass buttons are a customary find, steel fragments from who knows what and, occasionally, live ordnance. Tractors have been known to blow up. World War I, it appears, might never end.[36]

Passchendaele village itself seems a pretty, if overly quiet, little farm community. It does not remind one of Sassoon's famous lines, 'I died in hell – (They called it Passchendaele)'. Aerial photographs taken after the hamlet's capture show that its industrious inhabitants, when they returned to the place after the war to rebuild, essentially started from scratch. The entire place had been blotted out.

Belgium has granted in perpetuity a good deal of land to Britain and the dominions, both for cemeteries and memorials. Some monuments, mostly British, are grandiose and unimpressive; the Canadians' tend to be restrained, aside, that is, from Vimy Ridge. The most often photographed is at a crossroads known as St. Julien. This minimalist sculpture is in the shape of a tapering plinth, surmounted by the gradually emerging head of a Canadian soldier, slightly bowed, leaning on his upturned rifle in, one can only infer, grief. There is no triumph to his countenance. As a matter of fact, I wondered if the sculptor had intended what I took to be the overall effect, the idea of a simple trooper buried up to his neck in mud. In Passchendaele centre there are outdoor Canadian interpretive plaques set in a circle to mark its capture. I do not know when these were written or erected, but they seem recent and appear to encapsulate the current thinking on what happened here. Acknowledging the incredible sacrifice made by Canadian soldiers, and the numbers who died on these slopes, it implies that the objectives set for these men by the British high command could be summarized in a single word: 'impossible'.

After sightseeing in Ypres and collecting souvenirs, Nurse Clint returned to Boulogne, the port she had disembarked from four years before. It presented a very different picture, as she related: 'Boulogne had gone to bed in peace, to make up some of its lost sleep. No cabs, no ambulances, no one about, trams stopped, and it was 1 a.m. With what energy we could muster, we started up the long, long hill to the hospital . . . one more long way to Tipperary . . . in the dark, carrying, for my part, three shell-cases, and a piece of the Cloth Hall. IT WAS RAINING!'

Able Seaman Pax G. Yates

The months following Armistice day, 1918, saw an amazing increase in baby names that somehow encapsulated the momentous reality of peace at last: in Britain, Victory, Poppy, Armistice and Peace were suddenly popular. For girls, the use of Irene, the Greek word for peace, jumped twenty percent over previous quarters. Perhaps the most poignant was the Latin word Pax. Pax G. Yates, resident of Chertsey, a London suburb, was born at exactly 11:00 a.m. on 18 November; his parents, forewarned as everyone else was, that the ceasefire would begin at 11 that day, named him Pax in honour of both the timing and the event. He was killed, twenty-one years later, serving in World War II.

Chapter 20

Mistakes: Who Must Shoulder the Blame?

'There died a myriad,
And of the best, among them,
For an old bitch gone in the teeth,
For a botched civilization.'

Ezra Pound

I

Retrospective judgments are handy things, though never capable of altering what actually happened. Their only real value, other than satisfying the natural tendency to assign blame, is whether future generations of politicians, generals, admirals, newspaper editors – whomever – actually 'change their ways' as a result of lessons learned. As is usually the case in exploring any facet of human behaviour, the proof is in the pudding … and oftentimes the resulting concoctions are not especially edifying.

Who among the major warring powers made the greater sum of mistakes? As a generalization, the answer to that must lie first in assessing which were the most poorly led, and in that sense all these nations were more or less equal in deficiency. Most historians belittle the kaiser, a man with severe psychological problems, whose varying emotional mood swings were disastrous towards the development of nuanced policies that Europe's most vibrant society and economy most certainly deserved. The high bar of accomplishment had been set by the incomparable Bismarck. Though that great chancellor departed the scene involuntarily, the baton could have successfully passed to Wilhelm had that impressionable young gentleman not been so eager to forge his own identity, the depths (if there were any) or complexities of which he had no understanding. Wilhelm's simple-minded vanity had a direct correlation to the launch of World War I, which is about as damning an admission as possible. Clemenceau, though injudicious in his language, was certainly within his rights to blame the war on 'the murderous incoherencies of an imperial degenerate'.

In Russia, Tsar Nicholas proved equally inept. One of the many clichés about World War I (in much the same category as the theory of French desire for revenge regarding the 'lost' provinces of Alsace-Lorraine) is the notion that Russia would do anything to protect its Slavic, Balkan clients from German and Austrian oppression. This has been exaggerated. During an earlier Balkan crisis, the tsar had written his mother that 'no *decent* person wants a war because of the Slavs. It's only those damned Jewish newspapers ... such as *New Times*, which wrote that public opinion in Russia is up in arms, which is a lie and a slander. There is a wholly understandable interest in war, but no agitation.' Nicholas could and should have sought a diplomatic resolution to the Sarajevo incident, no matter the provocations of a clearly demented Austria-Hungary that had momentarily lost its collective mind. It is a hallmark of wisdom to avoid the obvious. Nicholas took the easy way out by allowing his generals to box him into an emotive corner where war seemed the most direct solution. Unfortunately, this suited his essentially passive nature.

It is difficult to point an accusing finger at France. Her politics were confused, one government after another allowing for little or no continuity of policy, and a succession of inadequate leaders dragged through the mud by a vociferous press. When asked for his opinion in 1887 as to who the next president should be, Clemenceau, with his usual sympathy, said 'vote for the stupidest'. The shock waves of the Dreyfus affair should also never be underestimated. France was an aggrieved party in 1914, suffering the brunt of invasion. The nation did not want war, which is obscured to some degree by its reliance on the supremely aggressive strategy of *l'attaque à outrance*, a misplaced élan that would have done Napoleon proud, however inappropriate to the realities of modern war.

Britain lay in the grip of middle-class complacency. Herbert Henry Asquith was the wrong man in the wrong spot in 1914, his eye mostly trained on domestic and Irish politics while juggling his cabinet to appease as many political power groups as possible. Frances Stevenson recorded Lloyd George saying that the 'P.M. is absolutely devoid of all principles except one – that of retaining his position as Prime Minister. He will sacrifice everything except No. 10 Downing St. [David] says he is for all world like a Sultan with his harem of 23, using all his skills and wiles to prevent one of them from eloping.' Asquith allowed a drift towards war to accumulate momentum, instead of clearly stating his intentions, either yea or nay. This allowed the commotion and often downright hysteria generated by Belgian outrages to overcome rational thinking. Lord Esher, an astute observer, realized within a year of the war's beginning that British leadership (and that of the French, too) was unequal to the task. 'Twenty very able gentlemen in England, and about an equal number in France of similar age and habits, are trying to do something which long life, sedentary occupations, leisurely habits of mind render ludicrously impossible. I was educated, brought up and have lived all my life among these people. I know them. And I say that hardly one of them, except possibly in sobriety of temper and judgment, can be compared to what he was twenty years ago.' If nothing else, the war aged them even more.

An assessment of political leadership, therefore, presents a somewhat muddled parity. No nation was competently led, though the onus of greater ineptitude lies in Berlin, St. Petersburg and Vienna. In far-off, or so it seemed, America, President Wilson saw no specific entity to point a finger at; everyone was equally to blame, and the United States, in his opinion, had no real stake in the outcome. On the very eve of declaring war on Germany, Wilson still believed the greatest threat to his country was the 'yellow peril'. But he too was pulled into the conflict, despite all his own internal protestations to the contrary. Perhaps the only politician who took the bull by its horns was Lenin. He had a clarity of vision that all the others lacked. To survive, he had to drag Russia out of the war. He did so, despite the humiliations required, then turned his ruthless eye towards destroying all his rivals, one by one.

As regards military competence, there seems little question that Germany was by far the superior 'machine'. By that we by no means confine ourselves to equipment or mechanical inventiveness, in which she often lagged behind. Ludendorff failed to realize the potential of tanks, and British engineering skill produced better aircraft, which von Richthofen recognized early and often. But German staff work was superior, her fighting men determined, resolute and disciplined, her officer corps thoroughly dedicated. Even in the last months of the war, most German soldiers fought with near suicidal desperation. Demographics were her downfall, something Germany's generals should have recognized with more perception in 1914. Goading the United States into war was a misjudgment of colossal proportions. Just the threat of her millions of men was enough to collapse Germany's will in 1918.

On the sea, despite German ingenuity when it came to submarines, Britain had the finest navy in the world, ready to fight anywhere, anytime, come what may. She also had the most hidebound officers afloat. At Jutland she did what was necessary, fighting to a draw. A 'draw', in German terms, was the equivalent of a defeat.

II

Granting therefore a rough parity in both strengths and weaknesses, with some edge to Germany for military proficiency, we again pose the question: who made the most serious mistakes, mistakes whose consequences would dramatically affect the course of the war? The answer must be Imperial Germany.

Its prewar obsession with geography almost reached paranoia. As Schlieffen had said, Germany sat in the middle of the house; he assumed, as did the kaiser and many politicians, that this equalled a 'threat'. Germany, or so went the perception, was not surrounded by friends, but by enemies. Perhaps several centuries of racial conflict and military excursions back and forth across its territories presupposed such a cast of mind, but the fact remains that a more balanced appreciation of perceived dangers from east and/or west would certainly have served Germany better. Germany did not begin the war with ideas similar to Hitler's, which were a reversion to primitivism – simple conquest and spoliation, with the goal of a 'Greater Europe' somewhere on the horizon, dominated, of course, from Berlin. In 1914, even the deluded kaiser had no such objective in mind other than a generalized wish that Germany should 'have her place in the sun'. Germany sought security, first and foremost, having dark suspicions of all her neighbours, particularly France, and then Russia. Its militarists, for example, keenly noted the hundreds of miles of new Russian railway tracks all pointing in one direction – towards Germany. They also noted who largely financed these infrastructural improvements: the people of France.[1] That these men sought to gain this security through pre-emptive invasions, however, was no way to secure that goal.

The Schlieffen plan was a decided risk; even the great general himself knew that. He did not consider, nor did those who came after him, what the consequences would be if a quick, knock-out victory was not achieved on the battlefield. Where his strategy crushed German hopes, however, was not its military failure in the summer of 1914, but in what came after, now fashionably called 'the domino effect'. Bypassing the French frontier forts facing Germany meant violating Belgian neutrality; bypassing Belgian neutrality meant Britain's probable entry into the war. German war planners, with near criminal indifference, disregarded the immensity of this sequence. Britain's standing army was absurdly small and nothing to be afraid of; its prewar manoeuvres, observed by invited guests from all the European powers, were often laughingly inept. But Germany ignored the ripple effect. Britain is a small country indeed, its landmass not even equal to the state of Kansas, but her empire was then the largest in the world, her fleet the finest, her merchant marine the biggest and her young manhood considerable in numbers, relatively aggressive and eager for action – just waiting there to be pooled. Britain's entry further guaranteed a continental blockade of some sort; if effective, that guaranteed Germany's resort to U-boat warfare to break it (once they recognized the potential of that weapon), which in turn guaranteed some sort of significant response from another power, however unknown its potency, the United States. Demographically, economically, even militarily, Germany could not, over a protracted period of time, defeat such a coalition, as just a single statistic indicates: before the war, Germany generated 279 million tons of coal to France's 44 million. But production in the United States was an astounding 474 million. These were all ramifications that could have been avoided with more insight and less hubris.

German strategy should never have included the Belgian component. Britain had no treaty entanglement with France, only 'informal understandings', and might not have fought to save her, despite protestations to the contrary.[2] France, after all, had been the traditional enemy for centuries, and Francophobia was as pronounced in the Britain of 1914 as Anglophobia was in France. Instead of having two formidable opponents, Germany would face four.

If Germany considered war an inevitability, and managed to avoid the Belgian entanglement, what military strategy should have been followed? The consensus seems to be that Germany could have assumed a decidedly unromantic defensive posture in the west. France would not have been the first to violate the Belgian borders (in the first decade of the twentieth century, Brussels had been unsure, equally distrustful of both Paris and Berlin);[3] Germany had fortified much of its own frontier with France, and the French could have been relied upon to throw themselves wastefully against the prepared positions. Germany could have fought France to a draw in the west, concentrating her forces against an inferior Russian foe. In retrospect, Schlieffen was fundamentally wrong. He chose the wrong front by attacking to the west, not to the east.[4]

III

One of the most curious and damning aspects of World War I is that none of the eventual combatants had a certified, hard-and-fast political agenda. In most cases, countries reacted to circumstances that really did not concern them. The exceptions? Austria-Hungary and Russia. Vienna feared that its ragtag collection of member states, speaking ten different languages and encompassing some of the most difficult terrain, militarily speaking, imaginable, was on the verge of collapse. She was correct in that assumption. Playing the bully with a relatively weak Serbia was a way of cracking the whip and asserting authority, as a hoped-for object lesson to other subject peoples. One may certainly question the intelligence of such behaviour, and it seems safe to say that Austria-Hungary had no idea of what the consequences would be, effecting its disappearance as an empire in just four short years. One would think, given the centuries of Habsburg rule, that its leaders might have been experienced enough to avoid plunging over the cliff, but such was not to be the case. Austro-Hungarian belligerence was hinged by a sense of desperation, a knowledge that its foundation stones were crumbling. In attempting to shore itself up, it ironically took the most direct path to ruination.

Russia too had a legitimate stake in the Balkan arena. Slavic and religious imperatives were certainly within its appropriate purview, and there were strategic implications involving Turkey that could properly be considered worthy of a gambler's throw. But a strategy of reasoned restraint was certainly more in that nation's best interests, and a ruler more forceful and intelligent than Nicholas II might have had the maturity to resist his generals' pressure for war. As for the rest – Britain, Germany, France and especially Italy – there were not, broadly speaking, pressing imperatives on which to go to war. Blame here must rest at the top, among a fairly narrow spectrum of political leadership, perhaps not numbering more than a few dozen or so individuals sitting in offices and headquarters ranging from London, Berlin, Paris, Moscow and Rome (Prince von Bülow confined responsibility in Germany to a mere 'two or three'). These men (and they were all men) had wrapped themselves up too firmly in both 'theory' and 'paperwork': theory meaning too much time spent in assessing 'balances of power', and paperwork, as represented by the tangled web of treaties, position papers and yes, even train schedules, the details of which kept them up at night trying to fathom their multiple ramifications. One German diplomat was incredulous that Britain would launch itself into war over 'a scrap of paper', meaning its pledge to protect Belgium. Even allowing for antique notions of honour, to which all the upper crust of Europe's leaders seemed inordinately attached, this gentleman was correct. Was Belgium really worth nearly one million British dead?[5]

At the top of these national pyramids, excepting France, were several royal houses with respected and sometimes long pedigrees: the houses of Saxe-Coburg-Windsor in England, Habsburg in Vienna, Romanov in Russia and Hohenzollern in Germany. While the actual power that any of these crowned individuals actually wielded over affairs of state were varied, the fact remains that none of these gentlemen were at all competent given the complexity of issues facing them. George V of Britain rarely entertained an intelligent thought; he was obsessed with royal protocols and the pecking orders of aristocratic privileges, in keeping with the narrow-minded obsessions of his country's landed gentry. He had little or no sympathy with the ordinary working peoples of his country.[6] Franz Joseph was approaching senility and beset by family difficulties. He barely had a minute to spare for his successor, not that he would have remembered any fruitful advice that he might have passed along to smooth the path. Wilhelm delighted in overseeing uniforms and military decorations for his forces. It is said that he designed several dozen variations for the army alone. He was perhaps the greatest poseur of all the European monarchs, but in actual effect he was a hollow reed. Tsar Nicolas II was in a world all his own. Perhaps no other monarch involved in the Great War was so mediocre.

IV

Germany assumed the enmity and hostility of France and Russia. When such assumptions enter the realm of 'fact', the notion of 'preventive war' becomes acceptable. Generals such as von Moltke the Younger felt that significant hostilities, especially with France, were inevitable. He told the king of Belgium in 1913 that, because fate had decreed it, the grand battle should begin, the sooner the better. 'This time, the matter must be settled.'

The day-to-day atmospheric of army life is based on order, routine, obedience and a culture of certitude. Underlying the sameness of everyday tedium is a substratum of glamour. When war comes, occasions will develop that allow for displays of courage and initiative – bravery under fire, taking the battle to the enemy – which, with luck, will result in fame, promotion and professional security. Such elements, especially in peacetime, prove conducive to encouraging an aggressive attitude that can truly stand out only in offensive operations, as opposed to defensive. This mindset infected both the German and French officer corps, but was more malignant (in terms of actually starting a war) in the former cadre. It melded into the notion of 'preventive' war perfectly. Operations in that spirit protected the homeland and complemented the individual officer's dossier; it also added the welcome notion of 'control' to military operations. When standing on the defensive, soldiers had to react to what the enemy did; quite the contrary in offensive attacks, where the attacker chooses time, place and tactical opportunity.

Chapter 21

Residue: What Is 'Civilization'?

'We are face to face with the fact that pugnacity is still a part of human nature, and that civilization is in its infancy. Men will play at war when there are no battles to fight: their cinema films and magazine stories prove that war is a favourite food of their imagination. They volunteer for war without waiting to be compelled; and they go back to it after suffering its worst hardship.'

George Bernard Shaw, 1917

In his 1836 essay 'Civilization', John Stuart Mill wrote the following directive: 'Look at war', he wrote, 'the most serious business of a barbarous people.' Yet in 1914 which, if any of the many combatant nations, viewed itself as 'barbarous?' The answer, of course, is none. No war was ever fought more keenly for 'civilization' than the conflagration of 1914–18.

One can chalk up exaggeration as a commonplace of any war. During this conflict, entered into during an explosion of popular communication (most notably newspapers and the nascent world of motion pictures), and an increased awareness in the value of propaganda and mass indoctrination, perhaps no word was more embraced, enshrined, worshipped and abused than Civilization.[1] Only in Russia did it not become a *cause célèbre*, mostly due to the fact that its army was composed of illiterate peasants who, by and large, had absolutely no idea as to why they were fighting. For all the others, 'civilization' was the catchword: the allies were 'defending' it, the Germans were 'spreading' it (or something like it, *Kultur*). What they meant by that word was by and large as unfathomable to them as whatever was going through the minds of tsarist conscripts. Just what did it mean? (Shaw had the answer, 'mere wind and stink'.)

Woodrow Wilson received an honorary degree from the University of Louvain in 1919. He was awarded this piece of parchment standing amidst the ruins of its famous library, deliberately destroyed by 'the huns'. This was a defining moment for the revival of civilized values, what the war had been fought for. In fact, what Louvain represented was a medieval ethos that had no relation to the man in the street, its collection of ancient Celtic and Frankish manuscripts as far removed from modern concepts of relevance as the Dead Sea scrolls.

Other events of the war could be chalked up to noble sentiment, something worth dying for. Edith Cavell for one, 'plucky' Belgium another – those vile Germans; but then again, Roger Casement's tawdry execution, and the summary dispatch of Easter Rising survivors in Kilmainham jail, might justify a drift of recrimination in the opposite direction. Shaw was tempted to mention to his British army hosts, during his visit to the western front in 1917, that Arras didn't seem as badly damaged by war as he had been led to believe; the British had gutted central Dublin far worse than the Germans had Arras. But he decided on discretion, and remained silent.

'Civilization', in effect, was an afterthought. Since no one could readily justify going to war, an excuse was found in this single word. 'The great flourish of ideals', as one historian put it, does not disguise the fact that the war was not necessary. There was no reason that Hans Castorp, Thomas Mann's fictional hero of *The Magic Mountain*, had to succumb to the allure of military glory. After hundreds of pages of the most erudite conversation, undertaken in the glorious Alpine air of his sanatorium, what was the point of Castorp rushing forward in the tragic battle of Langemarck, 1914, to his death with 36,000 other university-aged young men, singing patriotic songs at the top of his lungs, a collective serenade that Hitler claimed in *Mein Kampf* to have heard from a distance (another of his lies, but never mind).[2]

In fact, the real meaning of civilization to most people, never verbalized and probably not understood, was what Clemenceau noted in his memoirs. 'The glory of our civilization is that it enables us – occasionally – to live an almost normal life', i.e., without war. Fair enough. Other than that, is there more? A. J. P. Taylor wondered if it meant central heating for all. He was, of course, not being serious.

'War and civilization were compatible', Taylor noted in the same essay. The entire preceding two centuries had witnessed the colonization of the entire globe, a succession of 'civilizing' white man's missions that were generally accomplished sword in hand, and with gruesome results for whatever native peoples stood in the way. The rationale was 'civilization', but as the controversial British politician Sir William Joynson-Hicks rightfully said, 'that is cant.... We did not conquer India for the benefit of Indians.' No truer words were ever spoken.[3]

The Japanese victory over Russia in 1905 was greeted with undeniable shock in all the European capitals. Somehow the cart had come before the horse. How was it possible for 'savages' to withstand the might of western culture (even if Russia was an unworthy champion of such values)? Talk of the 'decline of civilization' became more widespread than ever. The German historian Oswald Spengler called it *The Decline of the West*, his best-selling book published in 1918 which, perversely, gave his people some solace during the depressing years of the 1920s.

After the war many wondered, quite naturally, if it had all been worth it or, again using Mill, 'whether civilization is on the whole a good or an evil'. No one seemed to know the answer to that one, except perhaps those orators who spoke at the various consecrations of military cemeteries.

'Civilization' took a noisier turn after 1918, which added more unwanted confusion to the debate. The visible and audible tangibles of traditional culture – music, art and literature – largely turned sour and inconsonant. Stravinsky and jazz, Picasso and cubists, Joyce and Ezra Pound … who could make any sense out of them and their flamboyant rejection of 'mediocre kitsch-mongers' (Schoenberg's phrase)? Rupert Brooke's maudlin poetry seemed dated and wildly inappropriate; and after all, he hadn't died by a bullet, but from a mosquito bite.[4] Sassoon's poem, 'Suicide in the Trenches', seemed more the right note:

> You smug-faced crowds with kindling eye
> Who cheer when soldier lads march by,
> Sneak home and pray you'll never know
> The hell where youth and laughter go.

People settled down to more political strife, more injustice and the fruits of a world that had largely destroyed itself and could not, through the Versailles process, figure out how to repair the damage. The Soviet Union was effectively shunned from the community of nations. Austria, in the opinion of Repington, could no longer be regarded as a country, only as 'a sort of colony', its aristocracy formally banned, its economy ruined, its self-esteem destroyed (one member of the nobility entitled his memoirs *From Archduke to Grocer*, and he wasn't joking). France never recovered from the loss of its young manhood; defeat in World War II was preordained. Germany continued to subsist on turnip jelly, welcomed uncontrollable inflation and then Hitler. Paper money, printed in reams, lost all value. A man dragging a trunk down the streets of Berlin was asked what was in it. He replied, 'This is my purse'. Britain? She 'is finished', according to Clemenceau; 'she has seen the zenith of her glory.' Keynes agreed; according to him, the societal result of war in his country was dolorous, goals now guided by self-interest and nothing more: 'The rich to spend more and save less, the poor to spend more and work less.' C. P. Scott had argued that the end of the war 'ought to sound the death knell of all the autocracies – including that of our Foreign Office'. He was right. Diplomacy and, indeed, political advancement would no longer be the preserve of the landed aristocracy. The way to the top was now capitalistic, not genealogical. The middle class was ravaged by unrest. The divorce rate exploded threefold. 'Now Albert's coming back', Eliot wrote in *The Waste Land*, 'make yourself a bit smart....'

> He's been in the army four years, he wants a good time,
> And if you don't give it him, there's others will, I said.

Meanwhile the barkeep yells, 'HURRY UP PLEASE IT'S TIME'.

In his 1933 novel *Tender is the Night*, F. Scott Fitzgerald described a battlefield tour led by Dick Diver, his main character. The sight of the old trenches, the scattered and decaying equipment, the endless 'white caps of a great sea of graves', brought tears to the eyes of his more susceptible female companions – 'altogether it had been a watery day'. At the end of the afternoon, near the train station, they bought some sandwiches for the trip home, and a bottle of beaujolais. A band played *Yes, We Have No Bananas*. They clapped when the song was over. 'Then, leaving infinitesimal sections of Wurtemburgers, Prussian Guards, Chasseurs Alpins, Manchester mill hands and old Etonians to pursue their eternal dissolution under the warm rain, they took the train for Paris.' This particular war was over, but others would follow. It's called the human condition.

Notes

A note on expanded endnotes, with references and complete bibliography.
The length of this book and the economics of publishing today precluded the inclusion of complete endnotes and inclusive bibliography for this first edition. However, on the author's website, every reference for direct quotations and academic sourcing can be found, and conveniently arranged for each numbered page in the printed text. For example, if there is a statement or reference that requires sourcing on, let us say, page 235, a reader can go the website, scroll to page 235, and he or she will find it without difficulty. The site can be found at www.jamescharlesroy.com. Should a reader so wish, he may contact the author, via his website, and request a jpeg for complete endnotes and bibliography, free of charge. The author regrets any inconvenience.

Preface
1. In the space of just six weeks, Lawrence lost two brothers on the western front.

Chapter 1 – The European Landscape: Victoria's Webe
1. Victoria was the only legitimate offspring of her father, Edward, duke of Kent.
2. Gladstone returned the compliment, saying the queen 'is enough to kill any man'. Kenneth Rose, *King George V* (New York, 1984), p. 315.
3. Umberto had survived an earlier attempt on his life twenty-two years before. Because he was not killed, his assailant, an anarchist, could not be executed, but Umberto did ensure that the man's sentence of lifetime incarceration was as unpleasant as possible: he was shackled with forty pounds of iron chains, and imprisoned in a cell only four feet high.
4. Etiquette at such events was usually 'overpowering', according to one participant. At the Austro-Hungarian court, for instance, 'every step [is] regulated in a printed form'. When Wilhelm's father was still crown prince, he attended a formal reception hosted by King Edward VII. 'Uncle Bertie had given the King of Hawaii precedence over the crown prince because he was a king', Edward's niece later recounted, 'and when the crown prince objected, Bertie replied that the Hawaiian was either a king or he was an ordinary nigger, and if only a nigger he had no right to be present at all!' See Countess Alice of Athlone, *For My Grandchildren: Some Reminiscences of Her Royal Highness Princess Alice, Countess of Athlone* (London, 1967), pp. 96, 148–9; Edward Goschen, *The Diary of, 1900–1914*, ed. Christopher H. D. Howard (London, 1980), pp. 95–6. For examples of the stultifying court etiquette common to all the capital cities, see de Hegermann-Lindencrone, *The Sunny Side of Diplomatic Life, 1875–1912* (New York, 1914), pp. 279–84, and following.
5. George V of Britain, Albert I of Belgium, Alfonso XIII of Spain and Haakon VII of Norway all survived the turmoil and were effective rulers within the constraints of their countries' political traditions. Haakron, a Danish prince who had married Edward VII's youngest daughter, held his position for fifty-two years. Wilhelm of Germany, Manuel of Portugal and Ferdinand of Bulgaria were all deposed. George I of the Hellenes (Greece) was assassinated in 1913, and Frederick VIII of Denmark dropped dead during a walk through a park in Hamburg, 1912. The most famous heir apparent was Franz Ferdinand of Austria-Hungary, assassinated during a state visit to Sarajevo in 1914.

Chapter 2 – The Kaiser

1. Twenty-two were monarchies, three were former Hanseatic city states. J. C. G. Röhl, Nicolaus Sombart, eds., *Kaiser Wilhelm II, New Interpretations: The Corfu Papers* (Cambridge, 1982), p. 10.

2. 'Universal' to some degree, that is. The electoral process was clearly skewed to favour rural districts (largely conservative), instead of more heavily populated (and socialist) urban centres.

3. The Wittelsbachs were of a lineage far older and more distinguished than the Hohenzollerns, who were frequently regarded as parvenus. Napoleon, a commoner himself, was contemptuous of the Hohenzollerns, with the possible exception of Frederick the Great. He once said that the Prussian monarch Frederick William III 'looked like a tailor in the midst of kings'. Baron Beyens, *Germany Before the War* (London, 1916), pp. 56–7.

4. Cosima Wagner, the composer's second wife, noted that 'The kaiser is a very likeable man, but in order to clarify for him the basic principles of art I would have to spend three years alone with him on a deserted island.' Adolf Hitler, musically more knowledgeable than Wilhelm, was an enthusiastic patron of Wagner's music. Even William Shakespeare excited the emperor's wrath. After a performance of *Richard II*, the kaiser expressed his 'severe disapproval'; anything hinting (or reeking) of regicide was not worth seeing. Lamar Cecil, *Wilhelm II* (Chapel Hill, 1989, 1996), Vol. II, p. 46; Count Robert Zedlitz-Trützschler, *Twelve Years at the Imperial German Court*, trans. A. Kalish (New York, 1924), pp. 290–1.

5. Just a few days after his dismissal, Bismarck had this to say to visitors: 'I always said it would be a matter of three years. The first year the Emperor would be an infant. The second year he would be in leading strings. The third year he would be guided by me, and at the end of that year he would walk away by himself. I have been wrong by one year in my calculations.' Rose, *King George V*, op. cit., p. 166.

6. Bülow once wrote, 'Even a courageous spirit like my own takes fright at the sight of such abysmal ignorance of the true facts, such unworldly thoughts, emotions, judgments, such illusions.' J. C. G. Röhl, *Germany Without Bismarck : The Crisis of Government in the Second Reich, 1890–1900* (London, 1967), p. 268.

7. Much of Wilhelm's wrath regarding the 'yellow peril' of Chinese affairs had been prompted by the murder there of two German missionaries in 1897. Three years later the Boxer Rebellion also excited his anger. German troops joined those of eight other nations and Peking was eventually captured, the enemy scattered into the vast hinterland where they refused to give battle. With no glory to be won from a conventional, set-piece engagement, the entire subject, with its many annoying details, ceased to galvanize the kaiser's attention, and it was dropped from his daily monologues. Von Moltke the Younger felt the whole venture was based on 'greed', the desire to 'cut into the big Chinese cake'. Annika Mombauer, 'Wilhelm, Waldersee, and the Boxer Rebellion', in A. Mombauer, W. Deist, eds., *The Kaiser: New Research on Wilhelm II's Role in Imperial Germany* (Cambridge, 2003), pp. 91–118, 97 (ftn 22).

8. One particularly provocative (and unnecessary) remark sparked immediate irritation among the generals. During a public forum in 1908, Wilhelm said, 'I am well aware that efforts are being made to encircle Germany, but the German has never fought better than when he is attacked on all sides; let them all come.' As a Belgian diplomat observed of the kaiser, 'He is fond of the barracks, without having a taste for the battlefield ... is he really a soldier?' Zedlitz-Trützschler, *Twelve Years*, op. cit., p. 223; Beyens, *Germany Before the War*, op. cit., p. 25.

9. Wilhelm's theatrical posturing was especially annoying. When Edward Goschen, the new British ambassador to Germany in 1908, arrived to present his credentials in Berlin, he

described his reception: 'I was shown into a long room with the emperor standing at the far end – nearly. I bowed and bowed and bowed. But he had his Overlord face on – and never moved a muscle – not a smile, not a movement of any sort. He might as well have been cut out of stone.' Take Ionescu, later the prime minister of Romania, noted that the 'kaiser's stare is like nothing I have ever seen before, quite abnormal in its intensity, and distinctly suggestive of madness'. Goschen, *Diary*, op. cit., p. 182; Take Ionescu, *Some Personal Impressions* (New York, 1920), pp. 282, 285.

10. Einem was one of the few generals who supported the Hohenzollerns to the very last. A front-line commander for the entire war, he offered the crown prince his protection at Third Army headquarters during the final tumultuous days of November 1918, pledging to march troops into Berlin if necessary to guarantee his safe return to the royal palace. The crown prince instead followed his father's example, and fled to Holland. Isabel V. Hull, 'Military culture, Wilhelm II, and the end of the monarchy in the First World War', Mombauer, Deist, *The Kaiser: New Research*, op. cit., p. 247.

11. Eulenburg was embroiled in a notorious homosexual scandal beginning in 1907, largely initiated by muckracking journalists. Like Oscar Wilde, he too was forced to testify in public trials that deeply embarrassed the imperial court. Wilhelm, who seemed to have homoerotic impulses, was genuinely shocked by the revelations, saying that Eulenburg should be 'cleared or stoned', a typically overwrought reaction. Cecil, *Wilhelm II*, op. cit., Vol. II, p. 115.

Chapter 3 – Alfred von Schlieffen

1. William I bitterly resented Bismarck's insistence on restraint, calling it 'this sour apple', but the chancellor explained his intentions clearly in memoirs entitled *Reflections and Reminiscences*. 'We had to avoid wounding Austria too severely; we had to avoid leaving behind in her unnecessary bitterness of feeling or desire for revenge; we ought rather to preserve the possibility of becoming friends again with our adversary of the moment, and in any case to regard the Austrian state on the European chessboard and the renewal of friendly relations with her as a move open to us. If Austria were severely injured, she would become an ally of France and of every other opponent of ours; she would even sacrifice her anti-Russian interests for the sake of revenge on Prussia.' Otto von Bismarck, *Reflections and Reminiscences*, ed. T. S. Hamerow (New York, 1968), p. 147.

2. Carl von Clausewitz, a Prussian officer who served during the Napoleonic wars, had emerged as the theoretical genius of German military thinking, mostly on account of *Vom Kriege*, first published the year after his death (1832) by his wife. This and others of his works concentrated mostly on Napoleon's campaigns, to which Clausewitz gave a sense, form and cohesion, unlike the emperor himself. Napoleon's writings were, according to one historian, 'incoherent jumbles'; they 'tended to draw their author's intention to ascribe every military success to his own instinctive genius'. Dallas D. Irvine, 'The French Discovery of Clausewitz and Napoleon', *Journal of the American Military Institute*, Vol. 4, No. 3 (Autumn 1940), p. 144.

3. Adolf Hitler was equally contemptuous of the professional officer corps of the German army. In 1934 he famously remarked, 'None of you have read Clausewitz, or, if you have, you have not understood how to apply him to reality.' Jehuda L. Wallach, *The Dogma of the Battle of Annihilation: The Theories of Clausewitz and Schlieffen and Their Impact on the German Conduct of Two World Wars* (London, 1986), p. 301.

4. Although the officer corps were fervent believers in the monarchy, they often had no respect for individual monarchs, which was especially true with Wilhelm II, whom one (among many) generals considered a 'nitwit', and sought to circumvent or undermine whenever the kaiser intruded himself into military affairs, which was often. As Erich

von Manstein, who would achieve great fame during the Second World War, put it, 'One did not serve Wilhelm II, one served the King.' Eric Dorn Brose, *The Kaiser's Army: The Politics of Military Technology in Germany During the Machine Age, 1870–1918* (Oxford, 2001), p. 123; John Röhl, *Young Wilhelm* (Cambridge, 1998), p. 21.

5. These religious movements, rooted primarily in principles originating from the Reformation, were especially prevalent in German Lutheran circles. They stressed humility, piety and, in the workplace, proficiency.

6. The work of lyric poet Ludwig Hölty (d. 1776) was especially popular among those who trumpeted rural and straightforward Germanic virtues. 'The Old Farmer To His Son' contained his most famous lines:

   Use always fidelity and honesty
   Up to your cold grave,
   And stray not one inch
   From the ways of the Lord.

   Mozart put these to music, adapting an aria from *The Magic Flute*, and the bells of Potsdam's Garrison Church played a version of his theme daily.

7. The justly famous eleventh edition of the *Encyclopaedia Britannica*, an astounding compendium of knowledge and information, was published in 1910 and formed the basis for the following two editions (through 1926). It has no entry for von Schlieffen.

8. Ferdinand Foch had a similar opinion. Napoleon, he said, 'forgot that a man cannot be God'. B. H. Liddell Hart, *Reputations Ten Years After* (Boston, 1928), p. 178.

9. The British ambassador to Berlin disagreed. In February 1914 he reported his opinion that 'The bellicose desire for revenge ... is now outmoded. It only exists to a certain degree in theory. The wound of 1871 still burns in all French hearts, but nobody is inclined to risk his or his son's bones for the acquisition of Alsace-Lorraine.' Anthony Adamthwaite, *Grandeur and Misery: France's Bid for Power in Europe 1914–1940* (London, 1995), p. 18.

10. A key element in engineering efficiency regarding railways was to maintain constant speed as much as possible; frequent stops and variations in convoy speed had deleterious effects on both performance (especially fuel consumption) and the fluidity of the entire system (ideally in motion all at once).

11. In his memoirs, Ludendorff called Schlieffen 'one of the greatest soldiers who ever lived'. Erich Ludendorff, *Ludendorff's Own Story: August 1914–November 1918* (New York, 1919), Vol. I, p. 28.

12. Just three years before the outbreak of war, 58 per cent of Germany's population were urban dwellers, but only 7 per cent of new recruits were from inner city environments.

13. Meaning 'inferior imitators'.

14. Meaning that Germany's enemies will attack her.

Chapter 4 – Sarajevo: Where It All Began (And Why)

1. This was a violation of the minimum three requirements for royalty, according to King Umberto I of Italy, who allegedly wrote his son the following piece of advice: 'Remember: to be a king all you need to know is how to sign your name, read a newspaper, and mount a horse.' Frank Lorenz Müller, *Royal Heirs in Imperial Germany: The Future of Monarchy in Nineteenth-Century Bavaria, Saxony and Württemberg* (London, 2017), p. 82.

2. The marriage between Franz Joseph and Elisabeth was, typically for the times, between first cousins. It is ironical that, a year after the royal wedding, an Augustinian monk, Gregor Mendel, began his experiments on genetics at the monastery of Brünn, eighty miles from Vienna, the results of which, if known, might have discouraged such a union. Mendel originally began his studies with mice, but the then abbot at Brünn forced him to switch to peas, where the reproductive patterns required for research did not involve

sex. Mendel's findings did not long survive his death in 1884 (Darwin knew nothing of his work), largely due to the fact that many of his papers were destroyed by an overzealous monk cleaning up his chambers. At the turn of the twentieth century, however, his theories were rediscovered. The famous garden where Mendel grew thousands of peas still exists.

3. Losing his son in 1889 was one thing, as was the fate of his brother, Maximilian, executed by a firing squad full of peasants after an ill-advised attempt to become emperor of Mexico; but having his wife stabbed to death in 1898 by an anarchist was quite another. Though Empress Elisabeth had essentially deserted her husband, he nevertheless was deeply grieved at this loss. In an age rife with political assassinations, Franz Joseph was attacked but once, in 1853, as he walked about the old walls surrounding the capital. There is much to deride about the ostentatious uniforms that were the fashion of these times, but the emperor's rigid, heavily brocaded collar saved his life, blunting the knife thrust of his attacker who was busy yelling 'Long live Kossuth', a reference to the Hungarian patriot. As a token of appreciation, subscription monies were raised to build a church of thanksgiving near the site, the *Votivkirche*, a prominent though ugly addition to Vienna's skyline. The would-be assassin, a tailor, was promptly hanged.

4. The Mayerling tragedy might have received less attention had not court officials tried to obfuscate the entire affair in a series of maladroit and farcical attempts to suppress the truth. The corpse of Baroness Mary Vetsera, for example, Rudolph's mistress, was dressed in travelling attire, propped up in a carriage with two male attendants on either side of the body, and hustled from the murder scene as though she was still alive and nothing untoward had ever happened. She was secretly buried before her parents were even informed that she was dead. Other participants in the cover-up were equally clumsy. The pope, for instance, sanctioned a full funeral rite, despite its prohibition in cases of suicide. He was informed that the crown prince had suffered a derangement of mind sufficiently violent that it excused his mortal sin. Rebecca West wrote that Mary Vetsera, 'a very fat and plain little girl', could not possibly have inspired Rudolf to shoot himself on her account, adding yet another conspiratorial current that he was murdered because of his political views. Rebecca West, *Black Lamb and Grey Falcon: A Journey Through Yugoslavia* (London, 1994), pp. 6–7. For the episode in general, see Fritz Judtmann, *Mayerling: The Facts Behind the Legend*, trans. E. Osers (London, 1971).

5. In 1857, no longer feeling threatened, Franz Joseph authorized the demolition of Vienna's old walls. They and the glacis were replaced by the famous boulevard now called the Ringstrasse, full of public buildings and impressive town houses. Unlike Baron Haussman's reconstruction of central Paris, undertaken during Napoleon III's reign, Vienna's architecture from earlier epochs remained largely untouched during this project, though it later suffered from rampant real estate speculation and redevelopment. William M. Johnston, *The Austrian Mind: An Intellectual and Social History, 1848–1938* (Berkeley, 1972), pp. 147–9; Jasper Ridley, *Napoleon III and Eugénie* (New York, 1980), pp. 348–52.

6. Hungarians were famous for their racial sensitivities, touchy at best, impossible at worst in the opinion of many in Vienna. Within the Austro-Hungarian army, a polyglot assortment of troops, commands between officers and men below the rank of major were universally issued in German, and restricted to about seventy key phrases intended to cover most tactical situations. Magyar officers in charge of Magyar units were thus forbidden to address one another in their native tongue under battlefield conditions. The language issue was but one of many that roiled the atmosphere between these two peoples. It also confused their allies. It never occurred to Ludendorff, for example, that there were elements in the Austro-Hungarian army that did not understand conversational German. Out of 1,000 men in the Austro-Hungarian army, the proportional representation of

nationalities broke down as follows: 267 German-speaking Austrians, 223 Magyars, 125 Czechs, 85 Poles, 81 Ruthenians (Ukrainians, also called 'Little Russians'), 67 Croats/ Serbs, 64 Romanians, 38 Slovaks, 26 Slovenes and 14 Italians. Johnston, *The Austrian Mind*, op. cit., p. 51; Gordon A. Craig, 'The Military Cohesion of the Austro-German Alliance, 1914–1918', in *War, Politics, and Diplomacy*, op. cit., pp. 46–57; Gunther E. Rothenberg, 'The Habsburg Army in the First World War: 1914–1918', in eds. Robert Kann, et al., *The Habsburg Empire in World War I: Essays on the Intellectual, Military, Political and Economic Aspects of the Habsburg War Effort* (Boulder, CO, 1977), p. 74.

7. Franz Ferdinand's image was not helped by the fact that he was a superb shot and voracious hunter, having killed by his count over three thousand deer and untold numbers of birds. Writers interested in disparaging his character generally refer to him as 'a butcher', and Rebecca West, in her famous travelogue of the region, published in 1941, equated such ostentatious blood lust with 'his slow-working and clumsy mind'. A relation said he had the manners 'of a swine-herd', and that his political views were those of 'an outspoken ignoramus'. Ferdinand was not alone among European royalty in his love of killing animals. George V of Britain was a famous shot, and kept a tally for one year's hunting, 'Game Killed by Me During Season 1896–97', which recorded over 11,000 'kills'. These prodigious figures were the result of two developments: the double-barrelled 12-bore shotgun (increased rapidity of fire power), and artificially bred pheasants (more targets). Edmond Taylor, *The Fall of the Dynasties: The Collapse of the Old Order, 1905–1922* (New York, 1963), p. 12; West, *Black Lamb and Grey Falcon*, op. cit., p. 336; Leopold Wölfling, *My Life Story: From Archduke to Grocer* (New York, 1931), pp. 77, 80; Jane Ridley, *George V: Never a Dull Moment* (New York, 2021), p. 89; Geoffrey Wheatcroft, 'An Unexpectedly Modern Monarch', *New York Review of Books*, 7 April 2022, p. 40.

8. Franz Ferdinand deliberately did not travel as the heir apparent or member of the Habsburg family, but simply as an army officer, which allowed him by protocol to be accompanied by his wife, no matter what her station. This sort of evasion would anger the emperor, lessening his sense of outrage over the coming murders.

9. At the crypt of Artstetten Castle, now a museum, the two coffins are of equal height. When Archduke Karl came to the throne in 1916, one of his first actions was to dismiss Montenuovo. To his credit, Montenuovo was a great champion of Gustav Mahler.

10. The specific cause of their estrangement was the scandal involving Colonel Alfred Redl, a staff officer stationed in Prague, who was, in fact, a spy in the pay of St. Petersburg (a homosexual, he had been compromised by Russian agents and threatened with exposure). When uncovered, he was (with Conrad's approval) locked in a room, given a pistol and encouraged to use it. Franz Ferdinand, staunchly Catholic, was infuriated that an army code of honour could be used to force an individual to commit the mortal sin of suicide. Alan Palmer, *Twilight of the Habsburgs: The Life and Times of Emperor Francis Joseph* (New York, 1994), pp. 318–19.

11. Although Austrian society 'possessed military tastes', it had regressed to a lesser-power status when it came to investments for its armed forces. It spent less than a quarter of what Germany and Russia expended, and but a third of British or French budgets. Even Italy's budget exceeded that of the empire. One historian noted that subjects of the crown spent three times more for beer, wine and tobacco then they did on the armed forces. A. J. P. Taylor, *The Habsburg Monarchy 1809–1918: A History of the Austrian Empire and Austria-Hungary* (Chicago, 1976), p. 195; Rothenberg, 'The Habsburg Army in the First World War', op. cit., p. 73.

12. 'Undying loyalty to the German spirit'. Annika Mombauer, 'A Reluctant Military Leader? Helmuth von Moltke and the July Crisis of 1914', *War in History*, Vol. 6, No. 4 (November 1999), p. 444.

13. A recently published photograph from these times show troops milling around three crude gallows with dead bodies. On the back was written 'Priest, teacher and mayor'. Josef Rietveld, *1914–1918* (Vienna, 2013), p. 29.

Chapter 5 – Fort de Loncin

1. Alfred Krupp's emergence as one of Europe's most successful manufacturers was largely the result of his ingenious invention of *radreifen*, or railway wheels, in the early 1850s. His patents, which stood the test of many lawsuits, reduced the inherent instability of load-bearing wheels made from welded pieces of steel by introducing a single and seamless unit. The three rings, or wheels, symbolized Krupp's early fascination with railways and their equipment. There were times in his career, in fact, when he considered abandoning the development of weaponry in favour of more mundane items such as ships and land-based transport systems.
2. Fort Loncin alone had forced-air flow.
3. No one was satisfied with the defence of Antwerp, where Belgian garrison troops actually outnumbered the Germans. The city's defences, however, consisting of over forty forts or strong points, were hopelessly antiquated, and Churchill was unimpressed with the morale of the troops assigned to them. Contemporary reports are not in agreement regarding the city's military commander, General Victor Deguise. Some say he did what he could, handcuffed by the fact that many of his men simply deserted into Holland, and internment, when they realized that Big Bertha was on the way. Others indicate that he simply disappeared into one of the citadels and was finally ferreted out by the Germans, a thorough-going defeatist. It is said by some that General Hans von Beseler, the German commander, refused to shake Deguise's hand and ordered that his sword be stripped from him. Ian F. W. Beckett, *The Making of the First World War* (New Haven, 2012), pp. 21–30. See also John Keegan, *The First World War* (New York, 1999), p. 128; W. H-H. Waters, *Potsdam and Doorn* (London, 1935), pp. 134–5.
4. The statue was unveiled in 1920. The largest lettering is for the words, in four rows, of 'Brussels', 'Dawn', 'October 12th' and '1915'. As Ford Maddox Ford had one of his characters think in *Parade's End*, 'Why did they shoot them at dawn? To rub it in that they were never going to see another sunrise'. Ford Maddox Ford, *Parade's End* (New York, 1961) p. 338.

Chapter 7 – Gallipoli: The Sideshow

1. Another figure Churchill studied throughout his life was Napoleon. On his desk at Chartwell, the country estate he purchased in 1922, are two of his favourite possessions, statuettes of Napoleon and Admiral Nelson, a tribute to their shared character traits of megalomania. Many observers thought Churchill's admiration for Napoleon misplaced. John Morley, the distinguished liberal statesman, said to Prime Minister Asquith's wife that Winston 'would do better to study the drab heroes of life. Framing oneself upon Napoleon has proved a danger to many a man before him.' See Martin Gilbert, *Winston S. Churchill: 1914–1916* (London, 1971), pp. 781–2; Margo Asquith, *The Autobiography of*, ed. Mark Bonham Carter (Boston, 1963), p. 251.
2. Thirty thousand surplus men were organized into a land force called the Royal Naval Division, and incorporated into the army. They served on the western front and Gallipoli.
3. Asquith was an extremely intelligent, erudite, well-educated man. When the war started, he began re-reading all of Dickens to give his brain a rest. The 'zigzag' quotation was from P. J. Bailey's monumental poem *Festus*, and Asquith used the lightning allusion to two other figures of his era, Disraeli and Kaiser Wilhelm. M. Asquith, *Autobiography*, op. cit., p. 298.

4. George V excited Churchill's contempt on more than one occasion. 'The king talked more stupidly about the navy than I have ever heard him before", he once wrote; he was full of 'cheap and silly drivel'. Rose, *George V*, op. cit., pp. 160–1.

5. John Colville, Churchill's private secretary in the 1940s, perceptively remarked that 'what was magic in 1940' had, by 1955, been transformed into 'melodrama'. David Cannadine, *In Churchill's Shadow: Confronting the Past in Modern Britain* (Oxford, 2003), p. 109.

6. Asquith, who received his degree from Oxford, was generally quite fond of Churchill, though he lamented what he felt was his minister's superficial grasp of the classics, which he thought 'quite hopeless'. Roy Jenkins, *Churchill: A Biography* (New York, 2001), pp. 229–30.

7. Cyrus McCormick Jr., whose father made a fortune through his refinement and marketing of the mechanical reaper, estimated that sixty percent of Britain's annual import of cereals came from Russia. *The Papers of Woodrow Wilson*, ed. A. S. Link (Princeton, 1986), Vol. 53, p. 255.

8. The caliph was the spiritual head of Islam, a title claimed by the sultan of Ottoman Turkey, and generally recognized as such by most Sunni Muslims.

9. Mehmed V had succeeded his far more capable brother, Abdul Hamid II, in 1909, but never wielded true power. He had spent three decades of his life confined to the palace grounds, nearly a third of it in solitary confinement, where he became a passable poet. He died in 1918, and was succeeded by a half-brother, Mehmed VI, who ruled for fifty-two months.

10. Churchill could be forgiving about losses, real or projected, especially when it came to obsolete warships, 'the *surplus* fleet of Britain'. He said in January 1915 that 'to terrorize admirals for losing ships is to make sure of losing wars'. Gilbert, *Churchill*, op. cit., pp. 421, 185.

11. On the first occasion, in South Africa, his superiors thought him too young for such a distinguished award; in the second (again, versus the Boers, in 1899), the decoration was deemed unseemly because Hamilton, a major-general at the time, had personally ridden onto the battlefield to lead a redeeming charge. This was, apparently, behaviour too self-glorifying for a senior officer to engage in. George H. Cassar, "Sir Ian Hamilton", *The Oxford Dictionary of National Biography* (hereafter *DNB*), Vol. 24, pp. 819–20.

12. Some officers were issued maps from 1840, others with charts inaccurately annotated on the basis of sketchy aerial observation. Some had none at all. Ashley Ekins, 'A Ridge Too Far: The Obstacles to Allied Victory', A. Ekins, ed., *Gallipoli: A Ridge Too Far* (Wollombi, AU, 2013), pp. 95–7.

13. There was a chronic lack of sandbags at the front, in large measure because soldiers used the rough burlap of the bags to mend their shoddy uniforms.

14. *Mehmetçik* is a slang equivalent to 'Tommy', 'Yank', 'Ivan', and '*Poilu*'.

15. Achi Baba became an end in and of itself, though with cruel irony its capture would have meant nothing. Hamilton came to rationalize its value as that of an observation and artillery post that could have directed fire onto the forts guarding the Narrows. But after the war, in the company of his best staff officer, Lieutenant-Colonel Cecil Aspinall, and Keyes, he climbed Achi Baba, and was stunned to see that no direct view of the forts was afforded. The vile little hill was, as Keyes noted bitterly, a 'gigantic fraud'. Ekins, 'Ridge Too Far', op. cit., p. 83.

16. These were catalogued by one budding entomologist as blue- and green-bottle flies, scorpions, ticks, grasshoppers, beetles, horse flies, ants and ant-lions, mosquitoes, sand-flies, digger-wasps, praying mantises, 'ghastly' centipedes, and a vast profusion of spiders, the king of which was 'the brute', a species of tarantula. Compton Mackenzie, *Gallipoli Memories* (London, 1929), p. 98.

17. Churchill's desperation was a sorry sight for his friends to witness. He besieged Asquith with advice and pleas not to be forgotten. 'Amongst other things', one observer noted in his diary, 'Winston had said no one but I [i.e. himself] can bring the Dardanelles operations to a successful conclusion. When any man talks like that he is on his way to a lunatic asylum.' George Riddell recorded a conversation he had with Lloyd George at about this time: Riddell: 'Winston's mind is concentrated on the war'. LG: 'Yes, but it is more concentrated on Winston.' George Riddell, *Diaries, 1908–1923*, ed. J. M. McEwen (London, 1986), pp. 118, 162.

18. By contrast, Asquith did not write a single note to his son, a serving officer on the front. Rose, *George V*, op. cit., p. 194.

19. Churchill's fall was good news to many soldiers stuck on the Dardanelles. 'The men are very bitter against him' wrote one diarist. Percival Fenwick, *Gallipoli Diary* (Auckland, NZ, 2000), p. 60.

20. There were extenuating circumstances in Hammersley's case: he had suffered what can only be described as a mysterious nervous breakdown before the war began. He was still recovering from shattered nerves when called back into service for the Dardanelles operation, where at one point he was observed weeping. John Hargrave, *The Suvla Bay Landing* (London, 1964), p. 105.

21. The prime minister's wife, Margot Asquith, noted her opinion that this 'whole nation suffers from an excess of politeness'. Until Britons acted more like Germans, she felt, the war would last forever. M. Asquith, *Autobiography*, op. cit., pp. 363, 373.

22. Ellis Ashmead-Bartlett, correspondent for *The Daily Telegraph*, frustrated by the iron clamp of censorship at the front, wrote a long, deeply critical memorandum for the prime minister's private perusal, and entrusted it to an Australian colleague, Keith Murdoch, to hand-deliver in London. Murdoch was intercepted at Marseilles by military police who confiscated the highly damaging assessment. Murdoch continued to England, wrote up a summary of his own and Ashmead-Bartlett's conclusions, and managed to see that Asquith received it. When Hamilton heard about this affair, which he labelled 'camp gossip', he was unfazed. 'Tittle-tattle will effect no lodgement in the Asquithian brain', he noted. But when the gist of Murdoch's report made the rounds, it caused a sensation, and severely tarnished Hamilton's standing. (Murdoch was the father of Rupert Murdoch, the famous press baron of Australia, whose later career in Britain and the United States eclipsed in notoriety anything his father ever did.) Phillip Knightley, *The First Casualty: From the Crimea and Vietnam: The War Correspondent as Hero, Propagandist, and Myth Maker* (New York, 1975), pp. 100–103.

23. Many officers refused to look at the Dardanelles as anything but a waste of resources better reserved for the western front. Douglas Haig disparaged it as a needless distraction, comparing it to 'an American cinema show'. Sir Henry Wilson went so far as to confide in Foch that any good news from Gallipoli 'would be a disaster', since it would encourage the government in London to send even more supplies and men to what he considered a minor theatre of the war. Douglas Haig, *The Private Papers of Douglas Haig 1914–1919*, ed. Robert Blake (London, 1952), p. 90; Field-Marshal Sir Henry Wilson, *His Life and Diaries*, ed. C. E. Callwell (London, 1927), Vol. I, p. 240.

24. Pack animals and horses were not as fortunate. Most were slaughtered and left on the beaches. Liman von Sanders, *Five Years in Turkey* (Annapolis, 1927), p. 99.

25. Masefield wrote *Gallipoli* for immediate publication (1916). It was meant to take the sting off what was widely perceived as a huge collective blunder, and should be considered more or less a piece of propaganda. That having been said, it is the best written of the many eyewitness reports from the front, and there is much to be gleaned from reading between the lines. Masefield was supportive of Hamilton, and agreed with the general

that 'the Turks have been shaken to their hearts'. With more support, he suggests, the campaign would not have failed. *Gallipoli* was a best seller, going through seven editions; it was so successful that its author was asked to immortalize another fiasco, the Somme, one year later. See Jenny Macleod, 'The British Heroic-Romantic Myth of Gallipoli', in J. Macleod, ed., *Gallipoli: Making History* (London, 2004), pp. 73–85.

26. Despite the collective negativities associated with the Dardanelles, General Hunter-Weston's reputation as a 'thruster' gave him the opportunity to continue his military career. Invalided home from general exhaustion, abetted by sunstroke, he received command of XIII Corps in 1916, stationed in Flanders, where his men participated in the Somme bloodbath. Eighth Corps suffered 14,581 casualties in the by-now standard frontal attacks against prepared positions in broad daylight.

27. Australian losses at Gallipoli were 7,600 dead, New Zealand's, 2,400. France, the virtually unpublicized partner in this operation, lost considerably more than the ANZACs, many of these being colonial troops from North Africa. Britain's tally sheet came to over 25,000. Patricia Jalland, *Australian Ways of Death: A Social and Cultural History, 1840–1918* (Melbourne, AU, 2002), pp. 305, 322, 308.

28. Sir John French had felt the same way seven months previously. He solved his complaint by leaking embarrassing details about his 'shell shortage' to an accommodating news reporter, initiating a damaging scandal that severely damaged Asquith's government.

29. Diary entries by Dominion soldiers are generally more revealing than letters written home. Eighty percent of Australian troops were unmarried men under the age of twenty-five, who were predictably circumspect when they communicated unpleasant news to their understandably worried parents back on the home front. Letters to spouses are generally more candid.

Chapter 8 – Verdun

1. At the time of the Franco-Prussian War, about a third of all Saint-Cyr graduates were sons of *ancien régime* families. Douglas Porch, *The March to the Marne: The French Army 1871–1914* (Cambridge, 1981), p. 17.

2. Séré de Rivières lost his influence and position during one of the several political machinations that generally disturbed French politics after the Franco-Prussian War. Between the end of that war and World War I, for instance, there were forty-two different ministers of war. He died in 1895; his gravestone epitaph reads, in Latin, 'The Stones Will Testify'. Ibid., p. 255; personal observation, Père Lachaise Cemetery, Paris.

3. In all, French engineers built 459 fortifications, gun emplacements and secondary works along the north-eastern frontier, at a cost of some 660 million francs. Hew Strachan, 'From Cabinet War to Total War: The Perspective of Military Doctrine, 1861–1918', R. Chickering, S. Förster, eds., *Great War, Total War: Combat and Mobilization on the Western Front, 1914–1918* (Cambridge, 2000), p. 19.

4. At a pivotal moment during the Italian campaign of 1796, Napoleon's forces were stalled at a bridge in front of a village called Arcole. Gros depicted Napoleon in full martial glory, sword in one hand, tricolour in the other, leading his men forward to victory. Arcole was indeed a bloody affair, and Napoleon did not lack for courage there, but facts tell a different story. Napoleon's officers refused to allow him to expose himself so needlessly, and in the commotion and press of men, he was actually pushed into the swampy river below as the charge developed, emerging covered in mud and marshy debris. Alan Schom, *Napoleon Bonaparte* (New York, 1997), pp. 54–5.

5. The intellectual calibre of the officer corps was not considered high, perhaps another hold-over from the Napoleonic era. The military historian Jomini claimed that half of Napoleon's generals were illiterate and could not sign their names with anything but

an 'x' or a 'y'. Their achievements on the battlefield, however, would never be replicated. Porch, *Marne*, op. cit., pp. 37–41; Dallas D. Irvine, 'The French Discovery of Napoleon and Clausewitz', *Journal of the American Military Institute*, Vol. 4, No. 3 (Autumn 1940), p. 143.

6. There were few German general officers of any note not familiar with Clausewitz (at least vaguely), but the name was practically unknown in France until 1886, when *Vom Kriege* was finally translated by a French army officer and became something of a sensation within military circles. Though still smarting from their defeat in the Franco-Prussian war, it seemed reassuring to the French that only by studying Napoleon, via analyses by von Clausewitz, were the Germans able to defeat them in 1870. Ibid., pp. 144, 153–8.

7. Foch was not prescient when it came to aircraft, however; they were 'good sport' but, for the army, 'of no value'. He revised this opinion very quickly, especially coming to appreciate the value of aerial reconnaissance. Basil Liddell Hart, *Foch: The Man of Orleans* (London, 1931), p. 47.

8. Grandmaison's theories, particularly when taken out of context, must of necessity seem ridiculous to modern sensibilities. One well-respected commentator says that Grandmaison 'was not nearly as crazy as he was later made out to be'. John Mosier, *The Myth of the Great War: A New Military History of World War I* (New York, 2001), p. 196; Jonathan M. House, 'The Decisive Attack: A New Look at French Infantry Tactics on the Eve of World War I', *Military Affairs*, Vol. 40, No. 4 (December 1976), pp. 164–8.

9. The commander of Joffre's Fifth Army, Charles Lanrezac, had thought all along that Germany would violate Belgian neutrality and attack in force via that route. By 9 August he was convinced of it, and warned Joffre accordingly. The British military correspondent for *The Times*, Charles à Court Repington, was most proud of what he considered the greatest journalistic coup of his career, a 15 August column which outlined the entire German plan of attack (Haig was not impressed; he regarded Repington as 'a very conceited man'). Joffre did not admit any of this to himself for another week. Liddell Hart, *Foch*, op. cit., p. 81; C. à Court Repington, *The First World War, 1914–1918: Personal Experiences* (Boston, 1920), Vol. I, p. 24; A.J.A. Morris, ed., *The Letters of Lieutenant-Colonel Charles à Court Remington CMG Military Correspondent of "The Times" 1903–1918* (London, 1999), p. 289 (ftn. 127). Haig, *Private Papers*, op. cit., p. 219.

10. Relations between Lanrezac and Sir John French could not have been worse, due largely to language difficulties and the resultant lack of communication (to say nothing of respect). It is incredible how little effort was taken to provide translators between French and British commanders, who often spoke not a word of the other's language, nor had anyone on their staffs who did. Towards the end of August, Lanrezac and French barely spoke to each other, nor signalled what they intended to do with their respective forces. Of the two, Lanrezac was the more skilled and adroit commander. His contempt for Sir John began immediately, on their first meeting in Belgium. French asked Lanrezac a fairly simple question: would the Germans, if they reached a certain village on the Meuse, cross it or retrench? Lanrezac turned to an aide and replied, 'What does he think they will do when they get to the Meuse, piss in it?' Stephen Ryan, *Pétain the Soldier* (New York, 1969), p. 55 (ftn. 15).

11. After the guns finally went silent on the western front in 1918, the various participants, mostly now unemployed, resorted to memoirs to correct, alter and/or fudge the reality of their intentions and responsibilities. Von Kluck published his in 1920, and vehemently denied that his rashness was the cause of the Schlieffen Plan's failure. The role of the First Army was never anything other than 'a difficult and risky undertaking'; Von Moltke underestimated the French foe, not von Kluck; the command staff in faraway Luxembourg were pushing him to extremes, when in fact his assessment of the situation was far more

sober. Trying to have it both ways, however, Kluck succumbed to vanity. His unsanctioned pursuit of the French over the Marne he attributed to inspiration from a quote by Julius Caesar who, along with Napoleon, were the two generalissimos whom many of these officers most often linked to their own careers. 'In great and dangerous operations', von Kluck wrote, quoting the great Roman, 'one must act, not think'. One thing most of these recollections have in common was the claim that communications between the front and headquarters, as well as between the five army commanders themselves, were extremely poor and directly contributed to the invasion's ultimate failure. Von Moltke, who died in 1916, had no chance to comment or reply. He did write a short paper after his dismissal which contained 'nasty stuff', according to a fellow officer who read it, and von Moltke's wife was dissuaded from publishing it. It has since appeared in full. Alexander von Kluck, *The March on Paris and the Battle of the Marne 1914* (New York, 1920), pp. 94–5, 113, 121, 112, 114; Mombauer, *Von Moltke*, op. cit., p. 8. For Von Moltke's memo and its suppression, see T. H. Meyer, ed., *Light for the New Millennium – Rudolf Steiner's Association with Helmuth and Eliza von Moltke: Letters, Documents and After Death Communications* (London, 1997), pp. 93–129, 249–54.

12. Hentsch's role in his 52-hour tour of the front, and in the subsequent German withdrawal that he ordered, has been vigorously argued back and forth. The orders von Moltke gave him in Luxembourg were verbal. Did he misunderstand the scope of his authority, as some officers believed? Did he accurately reflect von Moltke's intentions? Had he become a defeatist by the sight of German troops retreating from the fields of battle in seeming confusion? He was certainly aware just leaving headquarters that whatever he did would be controversial. He discussed with a subordinate officer as they set out his worries that he might have been set up to be a scapegoat if things went wrong. Subsequent reactions proved so contentious that two years later he requested a hearing to adjudicate if he had acted properly, an inquiry that was chaired by Ludendorff himself. He was exonerated. Hentsch died in 1918 during the Romanian campaign. Holger H. Herwig, *The Marne, 1914: The Opening of World War I and the Battle That Changed the World* (New York, 2009), pp. 266–86; John E. Dahlquist, *A Study of the Mission of Lieutenant-Colonel von Hentsch, German General Staff, on 8th-10th September 1914, during the First Battle of the Marne* (Leavenworth, KS, 1931), pp. 5, 8; Meyer, *Light for the New Millennium*, op. cit., p. 90. See also J. E. Edmonds, 'The Scapegoat of the Battle of the Marne, 1914: Lieut.-Colonel Hentsch and the Order for the German Retreat', *The Army Quarterly*, Vol. 1 (January 1921), pp. 346–58; Wilhelm Muller-Loebnitz, 'The Mission of Lieutenant-Colonel Hentsch on September 8 to 10, 1914' (Typescript, 1933); Terence Zuber, *Inventing the Schlieffen Plan: German War Planning, 1871–1914* (Oxford, 2002), pp. 282–8; Annika Mombauer, *Helmuth von Moltke and the Origins of the First World War* (Cambridge, 2001), pp. 256–60; Robert B. Asprey, *The First Battle of the Marne* (Philadelphia, 1962), pp. 138–58, 172–3; Keegan, *First World War*, op. cit., pp. 120–22. For Ludendorff's decision at the court of inquiry, see Ralph H. Lutz, ed., *Fall of the German Empire, 1914–1918*, trans. D. G. Rempel, G. Rendtorff (Stanford, 1932), pp. 605–606.

13. The eastern front was often something of a playground for Ludendorff. 'We always merely set an intermediate objective, and then discovered where to go next.' Zuber, *Inventing the Schlieffen Plan*, op. cit., pp. 300–301; David T. Zabecki, *The German 1918 Offensives: A Case Study in the Operational Level of War* (London, 2006), p. 109.

14. This basic lesson of World War I, for example, fully grasped by von Falkenhayn, took Foch many more months to learn. For Foch, 'any improvements in firearms is bound to strengthen the offensive', an opinion that von Falkenhayn would have found ridiculous. Cyril Falls, *Marshal Foch* (London, 1939), p. 4.

15. Author's emphasis.

16. The Iron Cross second-class was freely distributed; in such numbers, according to the Austrian liaison officer at general headquarters, that a soldier had to commit suicide to avoid being given one. Awarding decorations could be tiring work. It has been estimated, for example, that George V of Britain pinned over 50,000 decorations on individual soldier's tunics. Barbara Tuchman, *The Guns of August* (New York, 1962), p. 244; H. C. G. Matthew, 'George V', *DNB*, Vol. 21, pp. 869–71.

17. To his credit, von Falkenhayn anticipated the Somme campaign as an allied response to Verdun. Robert T. Foley, *German Strategy and the Path to Verdun: Erich von Falkenhayn and the Development of Attrition, 1870–1916* (Cambridge, 2005), pp. 191–3.

18. Liddell Hart suggested that this might indicate a perpetual confusion in Foch's mind. His rhetorical aggressiveness helped 'him to triumphs of defence that had been conceived by him as offence'. Liddell Hart, *Foch*, op. cit., p. 24.

19. *Chasseurs* were light infantrymen, generally regarded as elite troops who specialized in rapid deployments.

20. German pioneers usually accompanied the infantry in frontal attacks. They carried special cutters to clear the way through barbed wire, were trained in explosives to undermine bunkers and machine gun nests, and generally carried as many hand grenades (the famous 'potato mashers') as they could drape around their necks, and belts or jam in their haversacks. Their mortality rate was very high.

21. *Poilu* was an affectionate nickname for the French foot soldier, the equivalent of 'Tommy' and 'Doughboy'. It translates loosely as 'hairy one', in reference to their beards and unkempt appearance. *Poilus* had another nickname, *les grognards* or 'the grumblers', said to have originated with Napoleon's Old Guards, who were notorious for speaking their minds.

22. During the Parisian Commune, anti-clerical revolutionaries had raided the college and taken away several monks and lay workers as hostages. During the capture of Paris by the army in May 1871, these men were hastily executed against a wall on Avenue d'Italie by the insurrectionists.

23. There is some difference of opinion as to who coined the phrase *Voie Sacrée*. It was, according to most historians, the right-wing nationalist writer Maurice Barrès, a vociferous champion of the war. He at one point noted that 'the individual is nothing', which may account for his tolerance of high casualties. The track 'is the sacred road', he wrote. 'A river was flowing towards the troops. It is France, they thought, coming to our aid.' A satirical newspaper of the times called Barrès a 'brainwasher'. A decided minority of commentators suggest credit belongs to the French novelist Georges Bernanos, himself a veteran of the Verdun battle who was wounded there several times. He is best remembered today for *Diary of a Country Priest*. The road was mainly called *La Route* by soldiers and those who worked on it. Ian Ousby, *The Road to Verdun: France, Nationalism and the First World War* (London, 2002), p. 7; Maurice Barrès, 'Les Déraciné', *Romans et Voyages* (Paris, 1994), p. 615; 'Biographie: Maurice Barrès – Homme politique' (Internet resource: Académie Française website).

24. Earlier in the war Pétain was presented with the problem of soldiers who shot themselves in the foot, hand or arm in order to escape the trenches for care behind the lines. After initially deciding to execute them, he changed his mind. Some twenty-five men were bound, then thrown into No Man's Land, there to suffer their fate. Pétain was not a soft-hearted individual. Jean-Raymond Tournoux, *Sons of France: Pétain and De Gaulle*, trans. O. Coburn (New York, 1966), p. 30. The veracity of this widely disseminated incident is disputed in Stephen Ryan, *Pétain the Soldier* (New York, 1969), pp. 130–1.

25. Eventually this single line would employ 75 steam engines, pulling over 800 railway cars and, for artillery pieces, flatbeds.

26. The most common photographs of the Verdun campaign are usually pre- and post-battle images of Fort Douaumont. Nineteen-fifteen aerial photographs show the structure's polygonal design very clearly, its moats and walls perfectly delineated, with surrounding slopes smooth and grassy. Images just a year later present an entirely different perspective. The outline of the structure is faintly evident, but other features have simply disappeared. The countryside is a vast pockmarked wasteland. Like Côte 304, constant shelling had simply evaporated much of the fort's multi-foot layer of protective earth and sand.

27. Stellenbosch is a city on the south-western edge of South Africa. During the Boer War it was an assembly point for British forces. Officers deemed incompetent were generally removed from the field to Stellenbosch for eventual return to Britain and 'retirement'. It was thus the British equivalent of Limoges.

28. For German officers, shooting oneself in the side of the head was usually a foolproof way to confront insoluble problems. In von Stülpnagel's case, personal disgrace, a sham trial, torture and a horrible execution was all that awaited him in Germany, and he knew it. Unfortunately for him, the bullet did not enter his brain and produce instant death; it merely managed to put out both his eyes. On or about 30 August 1944, he was strangled by the Gestapo.

29. The Scottish novelist Allan Massie, in his 1989 novel *A Question of Loyalties*, has Pétain squarely acknowledging the psychological importance of Verdun, no matter its military irrelevance, in an imaginary 1936 interview. 'The corporal,' he has the marshal saying, 'always believes that the General Staff are idiots, he believes that he could correct their blunders or avoid repeating them. He does not realise that blunders are an inescapable feature of war, because choice in military affairs lies generally between the bad and the worse. The defence of Verdun was appalling; failure to defend it would have been intolerable.' Allan Massie, *A Question of Loyalties* (Edinburgh, 2002), p. 152.

30. Six hundred thousand North Africans, mostly Moroccans and Tunisians, served in the French army during this war.

31. In 1936, an attempt at reconciliation had taken place on the battlefield in a peace celebration called *Veillée de Verdun*. Five hundred German veterans arrived to participate, but in the actual ceremonies they marched with battle flags adorned with swastikas, somewhat spoiling the intended pacifistic atmosphere. As for the Mitterrand and Kohl demonstration of unity, some European leaders mocked it. Margaret Thatcher professed herself untouched. '"Wasn't it moving", she was privately asked afterwards? "No, it was *not*", she answered. "Two grown men holding hands!" ' Mitterrand was captured by German forces near Verdun during World War II, and Kohl's father fought there in World War I. See 'Mitterand and Kohl Honor Dead of Verdun', *The New York Times*, 22 September 1984; Charles Moore, *Margaret Thatcher, The Authorized Biography – At Her Zenith: In London, Washington and Moscow* (New York, 2016), pp. 388–9.

Chapter 9 – Field Marshal Sir Douglas Haig

1. Asquith's inability to cope with the turmoil of war was illustrative of the departments of state over which he presided, most of which were understaffed, bureaucratically misled and antique in approach. Very few officials of the times were equipped to handle the exigencies of multiple crises. The Foreign Office in 1914, for example, numbered 176 individuals, of whom a full quarter were messengers, doormen, porters and office cleaners. David Cannadine, *The Rise and Fall of the British Aristocracy* (New York, 1990), p. 281.

2. Kitchener didn't value what the king thought either. King George's son, the Prince of Wales, presented an early problem. The young man's desire to see action was commendable and, given Kitchener's insouciance about casualties, he didn't care if the prince was killed or injured. Being captured, however, was a different matter; it would not do to have a

member of the royal family paraded about in Germany as some sort of prize, and Edward was never formally allowed to go near any fighting, a prohibition he occasionally evaded. Harold Nicolson, *King George the Fifth: His Life and Reign* (London, 1970), p. 253.

3. In the early days of Mons, there were only about 36,000 British troops on the continent, not many more than Wellington had commanded at nearby Waterloo a century before. Martin Gilbert, *The First World War: A Complete History* (New York, 1994), pp. 57–8.

4. Journalists found Kitchener impossible to deal with as well; both his reticence and refusal to let others act independently or with some knowledge of his intent, made the job of fact-checking or gaining insight nearly impossible. Repington of *The Times*, the foremost military reporter in Britain, gained little access. Kitchener told him to talk to subordinates, but since the field marshal 'did everything himself, it was useless to talk to anyone else'. Repington, *Letters*, op. cit., p. 29.

5. A newspaper correspondent noted that 'every man with a cabbage patch is now claiming an exemption on agricultural grounds'. John Terraine, *Ordeal of Victory* (Philadelphia, 1963), p. 323.

6. Jan Smuts, South African soldier and politician, arrived in England in March 1917 after successfully campaigning against German forces in his homeland. He was immediately asked to join the war cabinet.

7. Another first: in all previous wars, most deaths were from disease, not battle. In World War I, it was quite the reverse. The exception was the Ottoman army, where twice as many soldiers died from their wounds than were killed in combat, an indictment of the primitive medical services provided, as well as the indifference of Turkish officers to the fate of their men, most of whom were easily replaceable Anatolian peasants.

8. Lloyd George privately told the editor of the *Manchester Guardian* in September 1915 that Germany was producing 320,000 shells a week versus Britain's 30,000.

9. It is not clear if Wilson ever intended his diary to be published, or if he planned to purge it of many indiscreet remarks and judgments in case he did. He was assassinated on the front stoop of his townhouse on London's Eaton Square by two Irish gunmen in 1922, and the diary was left to an associate to edit and put into shape. Nonetheless, it caused an uproar, and many personalities skewered by the sharp-tongued, opinionated and egotistical Wilson, reacted in anger and denials. It is, however, a delight to read, for the author was, unlike so many of his colleagues, an intelligent and literate individual. An acquaintance, in his own journal, jotted down a typically quick riposte on Wilson's part at a dinner party attended by Asquith and Sir John French. 'Mr. Asquith, with a singular want of tact seeing who was his host, remarked to Sir John, "It is a curious thing, Field-Marshal, that this war has produced no great generals". The rest of us at table naturally cocked our ears at this. But Henry Wilson chimed in, "No, Prime Minister, nor has it produced a statesman."' Wilson, *Diaries*, op. cit., Vol. I, p. 230.

10. Andrew Bonar Law was a native of New Brunswick, Canada, but grew up in Scotland. A successful businessman, he won a seat in parliament in 1895, and rose to become a prominent figure in the Conservative Party. He was a key 'provocateur' in the campaign to unseat Asquith. George Curzon, whose ancestors could be traced to the Norman invasion, was a rather typical product of the English aristocracy, much concerned with the 'honour' of his ancient family. Educated at Eton and Oxford, profoundly traditional in his views and opinions, he entered parliament at only twenty-six years of age, initiating a rapid rise in politics and government (he was viceroy of India between 1899 and 1905). Lloyd George appointed him to the war cabinet, but Robertson considered him 'a gas bag'. Alfred Milner, a fierce critic of Asquith, was also brought into the cabinet by Lloyd George, where his political and administrative skills were dedicated to pursuing the war. Partially disillusioned by the enormous devastation of the conflict, however, he was in

favour of negotiating an early peace with Germany. By 1918 he was an exhausted man. Haig, *Private Papers*, op., cit., p. 251.

11. People of appropriate bloodlines returned the insults. Richard Haldane considered Lloyd George 'really an illiterate with an unbalanced mind', and the king was described by Haldane as going 'into a most violent diatribe against Ll. George', something he did with some frequency. H. C. G. Matthew, 'Richard Haldane', *DNB*, Vol. 24, p. 521; Stephen Roskill, *Hankey: Man of Secrets, Vol. I, 1877–1918* (London, 1970), p. 283. See also Frances Stevenson, *Lloyd George: A Diary by Frances Stevenson*, ed. A. J. P. Taylor (New York, 1971), pp. 147–8.

12. Haig & Haig is Scotland's oldest whiskey distillery, its three-sided bottle famous the world over for its 'dimples'. *Don't be vague, ask for Haig*, was one of the best-known advertising slogans ever devised in the United Kingdom. Haig's sister married into the Jameson family, famous for its Irish whiskey.

13. This precaution was perhaps the result of a mishap by the king during one of his visits to the front. On a mount provided by Haig himself, George V took a fall while reviewing the troops. Considering the emphasis so often placed on horsemanship and just about everything else regarding matters equine, this was embarrassing. Haig devoted a lengthy and obsequious passage in his diary to the accident, fearing perhaps the royal wrath (though privately he wrote 'Few bruises have received so much attention'). His pelvis fractured, physicians kept the king in bed for several days, and George himself later wrote that he held the horse and, by extension, Haig, blameless. Haig's solicitousness for the king's well-being contrasts sharply to the coldness he often displayed for the casualty figures piling up on his desk. His French counterpart, Ferdinand Foch, though an artilleryman by profession, had attended the famous cavalry school at Saumer and was a fine rider. 'Not once during four years, save for ceremonial parades, did I have occasion to show my horsemanship. In fact, I ceased to handle a horse from the day I began to handle troops in war. What a joke!' Haig, *Private Papers*, op. cit., p. 110; Rose, *George V*, op. cit., pp. 181–2; Liddell Hart, *Foch*, op. cit., pp. 14–15.

14. H. G. Wells was of the opinion that career soldiers, especially cavalrymen, disdained the tank because 'it gave an unprofessional protection to the common soldiers within it'. Wells, an early critic on the conduct of this war, was disdainful of the military profession. 'No man of high intellectual property would willingly imprison his gifts in such a calling', he wrote. H. G. Wells, *The Outline of History: Being a Plain History of Life and Mankind* (New York, 1926), Vol. II, p. 670.

15. C. S. Forester, the creator of Horatio Hornblower, viciously satirized Haig in his short novel, *The General*, published in 1936, in which the protagonist, Sir Herbert Curzon, had the restraint to wait at least a week before seeking the hand in marriage of the plain, though unmistakably well-born, Lady Emily Winter-Willoughby. 'For a fleeting moment Curzon, as his eyes wandered over her face, was conscious of a likeness between her features and those of Bingo, the best polo pony he ever had'. C. S. Forester, *The General* (Harmondsworth, 1965), p. 59.

16. *The Bing Boys* revues were a series of popular musical productions that ran for over a thousand performances beginning in April 1916, overshadowed only by *The Maid of the Mountains* (1,352 shows) and *Chu Chin Chow* (2,235). A young naval officer wrote in his memoirs that 'no one who was in London during the First World War will ever forget [*The Bing Boys*] … Thousands and thousands of men, who now sleep in a field which is forever England, looked into a pair of shining eyes as the great audience sang the chorus of

If you were the only girl in the world
And I were the only boy …

17. Alfred Harmsworth, ennobled at only forty years of age as Baron (later Viscount) Northcliffe, was the most powerful newspaper baron in Britain (according to Aitken, he controlled half the London market), a man who wielded incredible influence through both the printed word and private counsels to the rich and famous. In his memoirs, Lloyd George called him the 'kettledrum of Sir Douglas Haig'. *The Times*, Northcliffe's most influential paper, was 'among the most inebriated of all our journals with the Haigean triumphs'. Though a master of popular journalism, many of his publications were ridiculed by more discriminating readers. One prime minister called the *Daily Mail* 'a newspaper run by office boys for office boys'. Whatever their disdain, Northcliffe took politics seriously, the war very seriously and himself most seriously of all, the diarist George Riddell writing that 'his opinion of himself is colossal'. His coverage of the alleged shell scandal of 1915 brought Asquith's government to its knees. He is reported to have said that 'a newspaper proprietor should have no friends'. The generals despised the press, albeit realizing their importance. To Haig, newspapers belonged in the 'gutter', and he loathed the time he had to waste giving interviews. 'I think I understand what you gentlemen want', Robertson once said to a group of journalists. 'You want to get hold of little stories on heroism, and so forth, and to write them up in a bright way to make good reading for Mary Anne in the kitchen.' Lord Beaverbrook, *Men and Power, 1917– 1918* (London, 1956), pp. 59, xxi; David Lloyd George, *War Memoirs* (Boston, 1933), Vol. IV, pp. 416, 441; D. George Boyce, 'Alfred Harmsworth', *DNB*, Vol. 25, p. 342; Riddell, *Diaries*, op. cit., p. 108; Haig, *Private Papers*, op. cit., p. 351; Duff Cooper, *Haig* (London, 1935–1936), Vol. I, p. 342; Stephen Badsey, *The British Army in Battle and Its Image 1914–1918* (London, 2009), p. 21.

18. These press wars between the generals and Lloyd George did no one any credit, according to Hankey, who called them 'a case of the 'pot calling the kettle black'. Roskill, *Hankey*, op. cit., p. 451.

19. Masefield never wrote a poetical 'chronicle' but he did compose two short prose works about the battle, *The Old Front Line* and *The Battle of the Somme*. Neither did well, either critically or financially.

20. Henry Wilson at this point in the war was in command of a corps. Though no shrinking violet, he recoiled from some of the senseless, precipitate attacks that he was ordered to undertake. In one instance, as he records in his diary, he refused point-blank to consider an advance for which his men were not ready. 'I said I could not do it with even a moderate chance of success. Of course, I could lose 5,000–6,000 men any day Haig liked, but I could not take and keep the Vimy trenches before September 1'. Wilson, *Diaries*, op. cit., Vol. I, p. 290.

21. Haig's outburst, ill-considered and fusty, was outdone by one of his generals, Sir Edmund Allenby. Outraged by the slovenly attire of an infantryman he saw in the trenches, Allenby launched into a tirade that did not cease until he was informed that the man was dead. Terraine, *Ordeal of Victory*, op. cit., p. 106.

22. Although dismissed by many of his colleagues as hopelessly outdated in his views, Field Marshal French correctly assessed the larger picture that had prompted Ludendorff's retrenchment. 'He thought the enemy was awaiting the result of the U-boat war', reported Repington after a meeting with French. 'If it failed, he considered that they would either resume peace negotiations or try a great blow at England as a mighty gamble.' French was correct on all counts. Repington, *Personal Experiences*, op. cit., Vol. II, p. 490.

23. The late Lord Kitchener had been furious about the plethora of loose lips in London. 'My colleagues', said Kitchener, 'tell military secrets to their wives, all except —, who tells them to other people's wives.' Maurice Hankey, secretary to the war cabinet, agreed, complaining vociferously about 'mischievous gossiping women'. As far as he was

concerned, 'The real danger of secrets leaking out lies in these high society gatherings'. Lord Beaverbrook, *Politicians and the War 1914–1916* (London, 1928), p. 69; Roskill, *Hankey*, op. cit., 422.

24. John of Bohemia, not wishing to miss the upcoming battle of 26 August 1346, ordered his fellow knights to lead him onto the field. Because of his blindness, several tied together their horses' bridles and they charged *en masse*. All were killed. Crécy has long been termed the last chivalric battle, given the fact that English and Welsh archers killed over a third of France's nobility in a single afternoon with the weapons of a common man, the longbows

25. He added in the same entry that 'I am sorry to say that the Australians are not nearly so'. Haig, *Private Papers*, op. cit., p. 290.

Chapter 10 – Ireland 'That sad, beautiful, bitch of a country'

1. Sally Phipps, the daughter of the Irish novelist Molly Keane, had this to say about the Anglo-Irish caste: 'They lived in a half-mythical place and they deluded themselves about the nature of Ireland. Their empathy with the landscape made them feel part of it, and because they mostly got on well with the people around them, and with those who worked for them, they thought they were loved .... They did not think of themselves as English. They were rooted in the land of Ireland. They called themselves Irish and very few of them reflected on the uneasy nature of this Irishness. It was only by sticking to their blinkers that they could keep going. Molly said of her poet mother: "She would have dismissed Yeats as just another Irish patriot. She couldn't think that the English had ever done anything wrong".' Sally Phipps, *Molly Keane: A Life* (London, 2017), p. 34.

2. Asquith's behaviour infuriated all parties, but especially those of conservative/unionist bent. 'He has behaved like a cardsharper', wrote one, 'and should never be received into a gentleman's house again.' R. F. Foster, *Modern Ireland 1600–1972* (London, 1988), p. 471.

3. A reference to the infamous Treaty of Limerick 1691, which ended the Jacobite resistance in Ireland to William of Orange.

4. In June 1890 he met Joseph Conrad in the Congo (*Heart of Darkness*), who was impressed. 'Thinks, speaks well, most intelligent and very sympathetic.' Conrad admired Casement's courage as he waded into the interior on his various missions. 'He could tell you things!' R. Curle, ed., 'Conrad's Diary', *Yale Review*, Vol. XV, 1926, p. 259; C. T. Watts, ed., *The Letters of Joseph Conrad to R. B. Cunningham Graham* (Cambridge, 1969), p. 149.

5. Called O'Connell Street since 1924.

6. Michael Collins, whom C. P. Scott styled a 'quite agreeable savage', disliked Pearse and his 'poeticism'. A pragmatic and ruthless man of action, Collins wanted nothing to do with 'Greek tragedy'. Dorothy Macardle, *The Irish Republic* (London, 1968), pp. 155–6; C. P. Scott, *The Political Diaries of C. P. Scott 1911–1918*, ed. T. Wilson (Ithaca, 1970), p. 404; Rex Taylor, *Michael Collins* (London, 1958), p. 33; Declan Kiberd, 'The Easter Rebellion: Poetry or Drama?' in *The 1916 Rising: Then and Now* (Conference paper, The Ireland Institute and Dublin University History Society, 21–22 April 2006).

7. Nelson's Pillar, 134 feet high, was built in 1809 as a memorial to Admiral Horatio Nelson. Ascendancy Ireland also built a huge monument to the Duke of Wellington, born an Irishman but contemptuous of the fact, in Dublin's Phoenix Park. The Pillar was blown up by the outlawed I.R.A. on the fiftieth anniversary of the Rising in 1966.

8. To be fair, the archbishop, Randall Davidson, privately pressed for a reprieve, having met Casement during the furore over results of his reports on the Congo and Amazon. He would not sign any public petitions, however. Brian Inglis, *Roger Casement* (New York, 1973), pp. 253–4.

9. Casement had not wanted to be buried in Pentonville, 'this dreadful place', but in his native County Antrim. The British prime minister in 1965, Harold Wilson, forbade

that wish, given the horrendous sectarian upheavals then transpiring in Ulster. An elaborate funeral procession for Casement would have certainly provoked rioting. The 'body' returned to Dublin was probably not Casement's, according to a former prisoner at Pentonville, who was a member of the work party that dug up the general site of the first burial, which was full of assorted bones. The outline of a skeleton was put together by this group from the general pile, and put in the casket for its return to Ireland. Brendan Ó Cathaoir, 'Casement Found Peace in Pentonville Prison Before Execution, Said Priest', *The Irish Times*, 15 April 2001.

Chapter 11 – The Great War at Sea

1. Wilhelm's enthusiasm for light cruisers helped contribute to the construction of five *Hertha* class warships. Officers from the British navy dubbed these 'ten-minute cruisers', about the time required for their destruction. Patrick J. Kelly, *Tirpitz and the Imperial German Navy* (Bloomington, IN, 2011), p. 484 (ftn. 59).

2. Heligoland ('Germany's Gibraltar', as a correspondent labelled it in 1913) is less than a single square mile in area and presents a bold, red-cliffed frontage to the west, with several freestanding rock stacks 150 feet in height, but then slopes down dramatically to sea level on its eastern shores where the predominant view encompasses sandy beaches and dunes. A popular (and exclusive) summer resort in the early nineteenth century, the waterfront was fully developed with hotels, cottages and boarding houses. The island was militarized during Wilhelm's reign, and its population evacuated when the Great War began. During World War II it was heavily bombed by the RAF, the village destroyed; and between 1945 and 1947, as a target range, subjected to some of the largest non-nuclear explosions ever recorded. Heligoland has now reverted to its status as a holiday resort, but only after extensive clean-ups to remove explosives and other hazardous materials. Stanley Shaw, *William of Germany* (London, 1913), p. 144.

3. These included several episodes involving South Africa, culminating in the Boer War 1899–1902; the Morocco crisis of 1905; and the incident involving an obscure German gunboat, the *Panther*, when it behaved provocatively in the harbour of Agadir, Morocco, 1911.

4. Mahan's most influential book, *The Influence of Sea Power Upon History*, published in 1890, was read by every imperialist in every capital of the world, from Teddy Roosevelt to von Tirpitz to Fisher to the entire staff of the Japanese navy. Its theses had an often baleful effect on strategists and dreamers contemplating colonial empires or militaristic expansion, and remained in vogue through World War II.

5. The projected completion of the improved Kiel Canal.

6. Three years later Churchill admitted to a colleague 'that he had been "a bit above himself" at the Admiralty'. Roskill, *Hankey*, op. cit., p. 415.

7. The whole ponderous exercise, in fact, required two high tides to complete. Jellicoe's most important subordinate, David Beatty, whose battlecruisers, intended in any set battle to be the screen for Jellicoe's dreadnoughts, was the exact temperamental opposite of his commander. The very personification of 'dash' and ostentation, wearing specially designed uniforms and always wearing his hat at a rakish, piratical angle, he and his flamboyant wife cut a wide and 'jolly' swath through both London society and the Big House set. An instinctive eagerness for battle, being the huntsman he was, coloured his judgment in ways that undercut the fleet's effectiveness as a cohesive fighting unit. His impulsive nature is reflected in a vignette from 1931. A houseguest of the admiral's recorded that Beatty, then sixty years old, 'was convalescing from a fearful accident which had smashed his jaw, and a nurse was in attendance as we sat at lunch. Suddenly a pack of hounds appeared and could be seen in full cry streaming across the park. David Beatty rushed out of the room and, brushing aside all protests, mounted a pony and disappeared in pursuit'.

Beatty's many defenders would scoff at the implications of such behaviour, stating that the admiral 'had an adequate amount of caution in his nature'. Kelly, *Tirpitz*, op. cit., pp. 262, 376; Stephen King-Hall, *My Naval Life 1906–1929* (London, 1952), p. 141; Rear-Admiral W. S. Chalmers, *The Life and Letters of David, Earl Beatty* (London, 1951), p. 266.

8. 'Calibre' refers to the diameter of the gun barrel through which a shell will pass when fired.

9. Displacement tonnage is a naval ship standard, and means the weight of water taken up by the vessel in question. When submerged, the class of U-boat described above displaced 864 tons.

10. Fisher considered such hysterics as sanctimonious humbug. When von Tirpitz resigned in March 1916, Fisher composed a parody letter of condolence to his opposite number which somehow appeared in the press. 'I don't blame you for the submarine business', he wrote; 'I'd have done the same myself.' Lord Fisher of Kilverstone, *Fear God and Dread Nought: The Correspondence of Admiral of the Fleet Lord Fisher of Kilverstone*, ed. Arthur J. Marder (Cambridge, MA, 1952–1959), Vol. III, pp. 112–13.

11. The term 'Middle East' was coined by Mahan.

12. Hypocrisy was not confined to one or another power, but was shared. Germans considered the arming of merchantmen as an affront to decent military behaviour. A Captain Fryatt of the small packet ship *Brussels*, obeying Admiralty procedures, charged *U-33* when it surfaced to shell him, forcing the submarine to dive. For his actions, the Admiralty rewarded Fryatt with an engraved gold watch. Sixteen months later, however, the *Brussels* was captured by German destroyers and Fryatt, the incriminating watch in his pocket, was arrested. During brief court martial proceedings, he was charged with being an 'irregular' combatant fighting out of uniform, was found guilty and shot two hours after sentencing, a punishment the kaiser personally approved. The German chaplain who counselled Fryatt before his death then sent a letter to his widow saying, in effect, that he deserved to die. Liza Verity, 'Charles Fryatt', *DNB*, Vol. 21, pp. 112–13.

13. The mysterious Room 40 at Admiralty headquarters in London, with the aid of several captured code books, was often able to reconstruct various commands and sailing instructions as they were transmitted from German fleet headquarters. The Germans assisted this process by a stubborn refusal to admit the very possibility of interception, and by their persistent verbosity on the airwaves.

14. One thing very wrong with Beatty's battlecruisers was insufficient armour plating, sacrificed by Fisher to achieve better speed. Watertight bulkhead containments were also inferior to the Germans, as well as vitally important magazine protection. When gun turrets on British ships suffered a direct hit, protective devices to prevent an explosive chain reaction below decks where shells and munitions were stored, proved poorly designed or deactivated. Beatty's two cruisers that went down essentially blew to pieces. King-Hall, *My Naval Life*, op. cit., p. 132.

15. The previously referenced *Southampton* was engaged in several of these actions and suffered serious damage and loss of life, as reported in Sub-Lieutenant Stephen King-Hall's memoir. After taking a direct hit, King-Hall said to himself, 'What is it going to feel like to blow up? Let me see, how had the *Queen Mary* looked?' King-Hall somehow came into possession of the *Southampton*'s battle flag from Jutland, which he gave to the captain of its replacement, a light cruiser that fought in World War II. He asked that the tattered remnant always be flown during combat, and when the second *Southampton* went down off Malta in January 1941, crippled after attacks by Stuka dive bombers, she did so with this flag flying from its main. *The Fighting at Jutland: The Personal Experiences of Forty-five Officers and Men of the British Fleet*, eds. H. W. Fawcett, G. W. W. Hooper (London, 1921), p. 164.

16. An estrangement grew between Jellicoe and Beatty, the latter in particular being conscious that his performance might be criticized. Reports and dispatches were carefully crafted and monitored by both men to shed the best available light on their tactics and decisions, which were subjected to intense scrutiny for any and all discrepancies. It did not help matters when Jellicoe admitted that 'the whole thing was most confusing'. One defender of Jellicoe went so far as to write later that when it came to discussing Jutland, 'those two neglected goddesses JUSTICE AND TRUTH [are] now worshipped in [but] an obscure corner of the British Pantheon'. Beatty's wife wrote her husband a typically intemperate assessment. 'Now that it is all over there seems to be very little to say except to "curse" Jellicoe for not going at them as the Battlecruisers did & never stopped until we had annihilated them. I hear he was frightened to death in case he "might" lose a Battleship.... He failed hopelessly.' Jellicoe did not recommend Beatty as his successor to the grand fleet, as he 'had made many mistakes'. Fisher was also unhappy after the battle, though unrepentant, at the criticism he expected to receive. You will see, he wrote a colleague, 'there'll be an outcry for ships as heavily armoured as a Spithead fort! *That* will be the *red* herring! And why didn't Lord Fisher put on more armour? *Hang Lord Fisher!*' George V was another member of the Beatty 'club'. A. Temple Patterson, ed., *The Jellicoe Papers: Selections from the Private and Official Correspondence of Admiral of the Fleet Earl Jellicoe of Scapa, Vol. I, 1893–1916* (London, 1966), p. 271; Admiral Sir Reginald Bacon, *The Jutland Scandal* (London, 1925), frontpiece; B. McL. Ranft, ed., *The Beatty Papers: Selections from the Private and Official Correspondence of Admiral of the Fleet Earl Beatty* (Aldershot, 1989), p. 369; Fisher, *Correspondence*, op. cit., Vol. III, pp. 395–8, 353; Ridley, *George V*, op. cit., p. 397.

17. During World War II, Churchill personally vetoed the notion of naming a new battleship HMS *Jellicoe*, opting for the *Anson*. Paul G. Halpern, *A Naval History of World War I* (Annapolis, 1994), p. 326.

18. Some bodies were eventually found even farther afield. The German writer Johann Kinau, famous for his sea novel *Seefahrt ist Not!* (under the pseudonym Gorch Fock), died at Jutland. His corpse drifted all the way to Sweden. A three-masted naval training barque was named in his honour in the 1930s. Scuttled in the waning days of World War II when it was bombarded by Russian tanks, it sailed under a variety of Soviet-bloc flags thereafter. It is currently a rather decrepit tourist attraction in the former GDR port of Stralsund, on the Baltic.

19. Fisher was also upset. 'A fleet, magnificent, five times bigger than the enemy, and takes no risks! A man I heard of – his wife, separated from him, died in Florence. He was on the stock exchange. They telegraphed "Shall we cremate, embalm, or bury?" "Do all three," he replied; "take no risks."' Fisher, *Correspondence*, op. cit., Vol. III, p. 566 (ftn. 1).

20. British manufactures of explosive materials were shoddy all through the war. Some estimates are that over thirty per cent of artillery shells failed to explode, and Fisher fulminated against the quality of torpedoes, which often did not detonate upon impact. They 'seem to be filled with sawdust!!!' Fisher, *Fear God and Dread Nought*, op. cit., Vol. 3, p. 197.

21. Eighteen superior long-range U-boats were under construction in 1918 but never finished. Capable of 12,000-mile-range with bigger guns, and much faster speeds, they were designed to engage unescorted convoys in mid-ocean from farther distances during surface attacks. Halpern, *Naval History*, op. cit., pp. 421–2.

22. Prince George, duke of Cambridge, then the retrograde commander in chief of the British army, reacted to the tragedy with these remarks to a group of cadets at the military academy at Woolwich: 'A good deal has been said of late as to freedom being given to inferiors to question and disobey the orders of a superior officer. Discipline must be the law, and must prevail. It is better to go wrong according to orders than to go wrong in

opposition to orders.' Fisher's reaction to that kind of attitude was typical of him: 'In war the first principle is to disobey orders. *Any fool can obey orders!*' Richard Hough, *Admirals in Collision* (New York, 1959), p. 163; Fisher, *Correspondence*, op. cit., Vol. III, p. 151. See also Edward M. Spiers, 'Prince George, second duke of Cambridge', *DNB*, Vol. 21, pp. 799–803.

23. Fisher looked at it the other way around: how one man could make a colossal blunder and affect the lives of many thousands: 'The generals may be asses, but the men, being lions, may pull the battle through on shore; but in a sea fight, if the admiral is an ass, millions of lions are useless! ... We must rely on Providence and a good Admiral!' Fisher, *Correspondence*, op. cit., Vol. I, p. 311.

24. As if to confirm the disdain Lloyd George and Churchill had for the intellectual calibre of officers wandering about amid the 'antique walls' of the Admiralty, Jellicoe was replaced by a 'society' figure, Sir Rosslyn Wemyss. Much admired by the king as 'an absolute gentleman', he was suave and polished, his manners honed by the command of several royal yachts, with their constant retinue of aristocratic and titled guests. Like Jellicoe, he was not an early champion of convoys. Fisher wrote a friend in exasperation that 'it will be soon found out that he has no brains!' Viscount Reginald Esher, *Journals and Letters*, ed. Viscount Oliver Esher (London, 1938), Vol. IV, pp. 115, 102; Fisher, *Correspondence*, op. cit., Vol. III, p. 481. See also James Goldrick, 'Rosslyn Wemyss', *DNB*, Vol. 58, pp. 102–105.

25. Convoys at first protected only loaded ships sailing to Britain. Ships returning in ballast generally proceeded without an escort, and these vessels remained vulnerable to attack. By August 1917, outbound ships began steaming in convoys as well, and their losses dropped dramatically. Whether incoming or outgoing, the first convoys generally assembled at a predetermined location on the open seas to join together in formation. They travelled to and from Liverpool, Bristol, Southampton or whatever their destination happened to be, independently. U-boats therefore began attacking them at those stages of their voyage. By the end of the war, such individual sailings were avoided where possible, most ships steaming from start to finish in convoys.

26. Well over 100 degrees Fahrenheit.

27. Bergen continued painting marine subjects after the war, both civilian and military. A committed Nazi, he received several commissions from the *Kriegsmarine* after 1939, several dealing with the ill-fated *Bismarck*. He died in 1964. His work became more internationally known in 1964 when *Life* magazine did a series on World War I that featured several paintings. Bergen's name also resurfaced in 2007 when officials from Germany's naval academy near Flensburg formally requested the return of his huge canvas, *Wreath in the North Sea in Memory of the Battle of Jutland*, from the National Maritime Museum in Greenwich, England. It had been looted in 1945 from the academy's mess hall. It depicts a large commemorative wreath floating in North Sea waters on the site of the great naval battle, its ribbons emblazoned with swastikas. For Bergen portfolio, see *Life*, 17 April 1964, pp. 58–80. For an image of *Wreath in the North Sea*, see www.rmg. co.uk/file/1978.

28. Some behaviour by the Royal Navy also raised eyebrows. In August 1915 the Q-ship *Baralong*, flying a neutral flag, came to assist the steamer *Nicosian* when attacked by *U-27*, and succeeded in fooling the sub's commander up until the last minute, when it opened a devastating fusillade, landing 34 hits. Several of the U-boat survivors, instead of swimming to the *Baralong*, made for the *Nicosian* instead, which prompted the naval officer in charge, Godfrey Herbert, to machine-gun German sailors in the water. The few who made it to the *Nicosian* were hunted down and killed by a naval boarding party. German propagandists said they were not given the chance to surrender, but were summarily executed; the U-boat commander, it was also alleged, was shot by the *Baralong*'s

captain as he swam towards that ship hoping to be rescued. Herbert reportedly yelled at him 'What about the *Lusitania*, you bastard?' British naval authorities tried to quell any reports on the incident, but unfortunately for them several passengers on the *Nicosian* were Americans who related what happened once they reached shore. German reaction was predictable, a promise of retribution; any sailor aboard the *Baralong* who might be captured later on during the war would be summarily shot. The *Baralong* was immediately transferred to the Mediterranean theatre, and her name changed, a transfer for obvious reasons not noted in Lloyd's Marine Register. Dwight R. Messimer, *Verscholler: World War I U-boat Losses* (Annapolis, 2002), pp. 46–7, 61–2; Halpern, *Naval History*, op. cit., p. 301; E. Keble Chatterton, *Q-Ships and Their Story* (Boston, 1923), pp. 20–31.

Chapter 12 – 'Halifax Wrecked'

1. Hoover had arranged for the evacuation of Americans and neutrals from Europe when hostilities broke out in Belgium during August 1914. An organizational genius, he headed the Relief Commission until America joined the war in 1917, its purpose being to feed that country's civilian population, its farmlands now engulfed in static trench warfare and its coastline entirely blocked off from merchant shipping. With a monthly budget of $11 million, Hoover arranged for over two and a half million tons of food supplies to be shipped overseas to Belgium. Negotiations with German authorities were especially ticklish. Hoover crossed the North Sea forty times for meetings and conferences. One of his major concerns, aside from the practicalities of delivering relief through battle zones, was to prevent Germans from diverting foodstuffs to their own troops.

Chapter 13 – Manfred von Richthofen

1. Volunteering to be an observer was the equivalent of a death wish. A younger brother of T. E. Lawrence 'of Arabia' was dead within a week of his arrival at the front, shot down over enemy lines in October 1915. The whereabouts of his grave, if he ever had one, is unknown.

2. Captain Albert Ball of the Royal Flying Corps epitomized the dash of English flyers, having no hesitation at all in attacking German formations where he could be outnumbered 7–1. An exceptional fighter with fast reflexes and superb vision (incredibly so because he eschewed goggles and helmets), his seemingly placid disposition disguised exceptional competitiveness. Early in his career, he 'buzzed' a German airfield, challenging any and all to a fight. Two pilots responded, and both were shot down. Ball, like Richthofen, was not a gregarious personality. He lived apart from his squad mates in a hut he made himself (with a small garden plot which he tended). According to a fellow officer, 'we called him "The Lonely Testicle".' Ball disappeared into a cloud on 7 May 1917. His plane apparently suffered an engine failure, and he crashed behind enemy lines. As was typical of the great aces, he was emotionally done in a very quick span of time. 'Am feeling very old', he wrote in a letter to his parents. 'I do get tired of always living to kill, and am really beginning to feel like a murderer.' Ball shot down forty-four German planes. Leon Bennett, *Fall of the Red Baron: World War I Aerial Tactics and the Death of von Richthofen* (Solihull, UK, 2011), p. 172; David Gunby, 'Albert Ball', *DNB*, Vol. 3, pp. 553–5.

3. Eddie Rickenbacker, the formidable ace of the American flying corps (22 kills and four balloons in just three months) was initially deemed to be too old for combat. He was twenty-seven. Bennett, *Fall of the Red Baron*, op. cit., p. 185.

4. Von Richthofen witnessed several bombing raids from the ground, and was generally contemptuous of what he considered 'very pretty fireworks'. Anyone who 'filled their pants' experiencing one of these raids was nothing but 'a coward'. Peter Kilduff, *Richthofen: Beyond the Legend of the Red Baron* (London, 1993), p. 90; Rittmeister Manfred Freiherr von Richthofen, *The Red Air Fighter* (London, 1918), p. 105.

5. The war had made Fokker a wealthy man. In 1914 he had sold 32 airplanes to Imperial Germany; four years later, his annual output had climbed to 1,500. His challenge after the armistice was to extricate his holdings, both financial and material, out of Germany. As the principal parties were haggling at Versailles, Fokker, bribing freely, managed to smuggle some 220 unfinished airplanes and 400 engines into Holland (mostly his newest fighter, the Fokker D VII), where he re-established his aviation company. The D VII would have been quite the beast had it been introduced earlier in the war. With more manoeuvrability, speeds of 125 mph and a ceiling of 20,000 feet, many felt it would have swept the sky clean. Always considered a somewhat shady businessman, Fokker eventually emigrated to the United States, where he became a citizen. His American subsidiary was purchased by General Motors in 1930. A. R. Weyl, *Fokker: The Creative Years* (London, 1965), pp. 352, 355–6; Henri Hegener, *Fokker – The Man and the Aircraft* (Letchworth, UK, 1961), pp. 37–8; William E. Burrows, *Richthofen: A True History of the Red Baron* (New York, 1969), p. 211 (ftn.).
6. 'You have to be lucky.'
7. Göring also was awarded the *Pour le Mérite*, on the basis of twenty-two kills. His record was often criticized as inflated (deliberately so), but current scholarship credits him with seventeen confirmed victories.

Chapter 14 – St. Petersburg ... then Petrograd ... then Leninburg

1. Tsar Nicholas, in his heart, felt the same way. He considered Peter the Great, the most illustrious of his ancestors, nothing more than 'an adventurer'. A. Mossolov, *At the Court of the Last Tsar*, trans. E. W. Dickes (London, 1935), p. 16.
2. This attempt on his life occurred the day after Archduke Franz Ferdinand's murder.
3. Of perhaps less prestige, he was briefly alluded to in F. Scott Fitzgerald's *The Great Gatsby*, where Gatsby produced a medal honouring his valour given him by Nicola. Like so much of Gatsby's talk, one had to wonder how truthful any of it really was. F. Scott Fitzgerald, *The Great Gatsby* (New York, 1953), pp. 66–7.
4. The French ambassador, a man much in sympathy with the Russian character, gave his impression of a typical salon. 'I called on Madame S —— for tea rather late this evening. Her company numbered about a dozen. Conversation was general and very lively. The subjects of discussion were spiritualism, ghosts, palmistry, divination, telepathy, the transmigration of souls and sorcery. Nearly every man and woman present told some personal anecdote or incident received from direct tradition. These agitating problems had been warmly debated for two hours already, so after smoking a cigarette I retired, as once a conversation of this kind is in full swing it may last until the morning.' Maurice Paléologue, *An Ambassador's Memoirs*, trans. F. A. Holt (New York, 1972), Vol. II, p. 118.
5. Grand Duke Alexander said of the tsar's boyhood tutors, 'They taught him all they knew, which proved to be little'. As far as his military career went, 'it appealed to his passive nature. One executed orders and did not have to worry over the vast problems handled by one's superiors'. Grand Duke Alexander of Russia, *Once a Grand Duke* (New York, 1932), p. 165–6.
6. Maria Pavlovna was the daughter of Grand Duke Pavel, Sergei's younger brother and another uncle to the tsar. In 1902, eleven years after the death of his first wife, Duke Pavel married his mistress, completing a trifecta of mistakes when it came to royal protocol: the woman had lived in sin with the duke and given birth to a son out of wedlock, was a commoner and, worst of all, divorced from her first husband. Nicholas, a prude of the first order, forced his uncle into exile and consigned the guardianship of his two children to Sergei and Ella. These were the sorts of things that consumed the tsar's attentions. In time for the war, Nicholas rehabilitated Pavel, allowed him to return to Russia, and gave him a nominal command in the Russian army. As things turned out, this was an

unfortunate turn of grace for the grand duke, who was caught up in the revolutionary tumult of 1917 and beyond. Arrested by the bolsheviks, he was executed in 1919 in the great fortress of Saints Peter and Paul in Petrograd. His remains, at first discarded in an open pit, were rediscovered in 2011, and a representational portion (they were difficult to identify definitively) reinterred with those of the tsar's family in the garrison church. 'Les Russes pensent avoir retrouvé les restes de princes Romanov', *Tribune de Genève*, 6 August 2011.

7. Anna Vyrubova, whom Prince Felix Yusupov described as 'of limited and undeveloped intelligence', was the tsarina's closest confidant, living in a house on the edge of Tsarskoe Selo's grounds. She shared most of Alexandra's enthusiasms (especially when it came to Rasputin), was deeply religious and utterly attached to the imperial family. Her social graces were few, and she was exceedingly plain, both physically and in her mode of dress. The elegant Maurice Paléologue stated that 'no royal favourite ever looked more unpretentious'. Vyrubova and other intimates in the royal circle were too sympathetic and emotionally tied to the empress for their (and her) own good. They were indiscriminate in their affection and unsophisticated when it came to life beyond the palace walls. 'Although they were devoted to her', said one observer, 'none of them had the ability to interpret the trend of events'. Of Vyrubova in particular, Paléologue wrote in 1915, 'I am horrified to think that anyone so thoroughly mediocre, so lacking … in refinement, can have any influence in times like these on the destinies of Russia!' Prince Youssoupoff, *Rasputin: His Malignant Influence and His Assassination*, trans. O. Rayner (London, 1927), p. 21; Paléologue, *Memoirs*, op. cit., Vol. II, pp. 50, 51; Count Kokovtsov, *Out of My Past: Memoirs*, ed. H. H. Fisher, trans. L. Matveev (Stanford, 1935), p. 454.

8. In order to conform to other events described in this book, all dates in Chapter 14 are Gregorian, or 'new style', even though until 1918 Russians adhered to the Julian Calendar, commonly referred to as 'old style', a thirteen-day difference. This can be undeniably confusing, the famous 'October Days', for example, having taken place, by 'new style' standards, in November. One of Leon Trotsky's 'reforms' was to bring Russian dates into general European usage.

9. This manoeuvre came close to sparking a war with Britain when Russian ships opened fire on several fishing trawlers in the English Channel during a night action, mistaking them for Japanese torpedo boats, and killing several civilians. The officer who initiated this action was allegedly drunk on the national drink, vodka.

10. Tsushima is an island chain midway between the southern Japanese mainland and the tip of Korea. The battle was fought in the Strait of Tsushima, which separates the islands from Japan.

11. The war was a learning experience for many European officers who had been sent as observers. Most of these were of junior ranks and their recommendations were largely ignored by traditionalists ensconced in their respective high commands. Warnings about the efficacy of machine guns, frontal attacks on prepared positions and the high casualty counts that modern weaponry could inflict were lost in the welter of paperwork and formal reports that were produced. Part of this neglect was due to the generalized contempt for orientals and their perceived incapacity to fight a modern war. Among those present who were important figures in the Great War were Sir Ian Hamilton (Dardanelles) and Max Hoffmann (Tannenberg and the eastern front). Then Captain John J. Pershing of the United States army was also an official observer. See David Walder, *The Short, Victorious War: The Russo-Japanese Conflict of 1904–1905* (London, 1973), p. 67; Keith Nelson, '"That Dangerous and Difficult Enterprise": British Military Thinking and the Russo-Japanese War', *War and Society*, Vol. 9 (1991), pp. 17–37.

12. An indication that Japan should no longer be conceptually marginalized was realized by some, who noted the chief Japanese negotiator was a graduate of Harvard University. As

for Witte, Trotsky characterized him as 'a plebeian *parvenu* among the noble ranks of the upper bureaucracy'. Leon Trotsky, *1905*, trans. A. Bostock (New York, 1971), p. 118.

13. These naval disturbances were ruthlessly suppressed; some estimates are that 2,000 sailors were executed. The battleship *Potemkin* incident was immortalized by one of the most famous propaganda films ever made, directed by Sergei Eisenstein and released in 1925.

14. Stolypin, who effectively juggled his loyalty to the tsar's person with the realization that change must be achieved, was writing at his desk when the bomb went off. People thought he was a dead man when they first saw him, since his inkwell had exploded in his face, covering him in a gory-looking mess. His luck ran out in Kiev on the night of 18 September 1911, the denouement of yet another of Rasputin's predictions. The *starets* had seen Stolypin's carriage pass, and had said prophetically, 'Death is after him. Death is driving behind him.' That night, at the opera, he was shot by an assassin. Looking up at the royal box he saluted Nicholas, there with two of his daughters, and then collapsed, dying four days later (his assassin following, hanged five days after that). Colin Wilson, *Rasputin and The Fall of the Romanovs* (New York, 1964), p. 135.

15. While the smears that Rasputin had slept with the tsar's daughters appear patently false, he did bed the resident nurse of the imperial children. The empress seems to have considered that the girl was at fault, and dismissed her.

16. Freud took great interest in the dichotomy of Rasputin's moral character, calling his lifestyle 'the happy union of sinful satisfaction of instincts and pious suppression of them – the very ideal of pleasure with payment'. René Fülöp-Miller, *Rasputin: The Holy Devil* (New York, 1962), endnote. Presumably Freud meant 'consequences' by his use of the word 'payment'.

17. Paul I was son and heir to Catherine the Great, between whom relations were frigid. She would have preferred, for instance, that Paul's son, the future Alexander I, succeed her to the throne, just one sign of her disdain. Paul ruled for only five years after Catherine's death. His army reforms, erratic foreign policy initiatives and measures concerning the condition of serfs and peasants, made him deeply unpopular among the nobility. In 1801, a group of inebriated officers, led by a German mercenary, Count von Bennigsen (who would later command several battles against Napoleon) barged into Paul's apartments at the palace in St. Petersburg. They discovered the tsar behind the curtain drapes, hauled him to a table and demanded his abdication. The tsar demurred, upon which he was slapped, punched and generally abused. Carried away by drink, the officers lost control of themselves. Paul was thrown to the floor, kicked repeatedly and then strangled. Tsarevich Alexander was in the palace when all these events took place. He was awakened by his father's murderers and told he was now the tsar. 'Time to grow up!' he was allegedly told, 'Go and rule!' It is a moot point how much Alexander knew about the conspiracy beforehand. *Eras of Elegance: The House of Romanovs* (Internet resource).

18. Vladimir Purishkevich escaped arrest, fleeing to sympathetic army friends at the Romanian front. He became deeply involved in 'White Russian' intrigues following the fall of the dynasty. He died of typhus in 1920.

19. Kerensky noted that 'too much paper was wasted during the Revolution'. Alexander F. Kerensky, *Catastrophe: Kerensky's Own Story of the Russian Revolution* (New York, 1927), p. 33.

20. There is some confusion as to whether locomotive # 293 is the actual engine that brought Lenin to the Finland Station. See Catherine Merridale, *Lenin on the Train* (New York, 2017), figure 34 (no citation for this claim).

21. *Pravda*'s circulation in the city itself was a mere 45,000, with another allotment of that number for the country at large, a ridiculous circulation considering Russia's population. That should not be used to underestimate its influence, which grew with every train that departed Petrograd, bundles of *Pravda*s on board, bound for Moscow and beyond.

22. Lenin even wrote a paper on the subject, entitled 'On Compromises'.

23. 'You Red men of Kronstadt!' he called this rabble of malcontents. Kronstadt was the major naval base for the Baltic fleet, downriver from Petrograd. Like their compatriots in Kiel, Germany, the Russian navy was a hotbed of sedition as the war dragged on, a situation that never occurred in the British Royal Navy. Four years later, the Kronstadt garrison mutinied against the bolsheviks. Lenin condemned them as 'petit-bourgeois counter-revolutionaries', and Trotsky ordered their ruthless suppression. Isaac Deutscher, *Trotsky: 1879–1940* (Oxford, 1970), Vol. I, p. 272; Robert Service, *Trotsky: A Biography* (Cambridge, 2009), p. 283. For Kronstadt mutiny, see pp. 282–7.

24. John Reed, born in Portland, Oregon and educated at Harvard, was probably the most famous radical journalist the United States ever produced, and perhaps the most controversial. He was lampooned as 'Jack the Liar' (Lenin's wife wrote that his most famous book, *Ten Days that Shook the World*, was full of 'legends and inaccuracies') and repeatedly scorned by the mainstream press. It did not help that many of his articles (some little better than rants) were often to be found in obscure and generally ridiculed leftist newssheets and journals. His life of adventure, intrigue and socialist commitment is the stuff of legend, however; the numbers of historical and literary figures with whom he mixed, beyond the telling; the saga of his final days, full of disillusionment and pathos, a true tragedy. George Kennan was one of the few establishment figures to give Reed his due. Though he called him a 'foolish and rebellious child', he also wrote that he should 'be neither forgotten nor ridiculed'. John Dos Passos called him 'the best American writer of his time …the last of the great race of war correspondents who ducked under censorship and risked their skins for a story'. Reed, who died on 17 October 1920, is buried in Moscow's Kremlin wall. John Reed, *Ten Days that Shook the World* (New York, 1960), p. xlvi; George F. Kennan, *Russia Leaves the War* (Princeton, 1956), p. 69; John Dos Passos, *1919* (Boston, 1991), p. 10.

25. Reed was honest enough to report that many members of any given audience were often confused and dumbfounded by the continuous rhetoric, noting in one case a soldier 'grimacing with the pain of his intellectual processes'. Reed, *Ten Days*, op. cit., p. 244.

26. Nicholas seemed to have put away his several prejudices against Britain. During the war with Japan, the tsar had called the English 'mangy enemies' for their alliance with Japan, to say nothing of the fact that the battleships that crushed the Baltic fleet at Tsushima had been built in Newcastle upon Tyne. He also had expressed the opinion that 'an Englishman is a *zhid* (Jew)'. Roderick R. McLean, 'Dreams of a German Europe: World War II and the Treaty of Björkö of 1905', Mombauer, Deist, eds., *The Kaiser*, op. cit., p. 127; Count Witte, *Memoirs*, ed. and trans. A. Yarmolinsky (New York, 1921), p. 189.

27. Marie Antoinette was a favourite of monarchists. Prince Yusupov's wife, Irina, wore a veil on her wedding day which once belonged to Louis XVI's unfortunate wife. It was held in place by 'a tiara of rock-crystal and diamonds', he noted proudly. Prince Felix Youssoupoff (Yusupov), *Lost Splendor*, trans. A. Green, N. Katkoff (New York, 1954), p. 174.

28. Lenin was congenitally unable to feel sympathy for any monarchist, however innocent their behaviour or progressive their views. Nikolai Mikhailovich had consistently warned the tsar to change his ways or face the very worst. The empress was so furious with him after one of his lectures to Nicholas that she suggested he be sent to Siberia since his views 'become next to high treason'. In the same letter she added, 'He is the incarnation of all that's evil'. Andrei Maylunas, Sergei Mironenko, eds., *A Lifelong Passion: Nicholas and Alexandra, Their Own Story* (New York, 1997), p. 479.

29. Marat, associated with the radical Jacobins, and Théroigne de Méricourt with the Girondists, were two notorious firebrands of the French Revolution.

30. Countess Cantacuzène, the granddaughter of Ulysses S. Grant, was born in the White House, 1876. Her father, Grant's eldest son, was a professional soldier who served in all

manner of campaigns, including Custer's Indian wars. Julia Dent Grant married Prince Cantacuzène in 1899 after a whirlwind, two-week courtship that began in Cannes, France and ended in Newport, Rhode Island with a lavish society wedding. The prince, who owned immense estates in the Ukraine, served Tsar Nicholas as a general of cossacks and, briefly, as his chief of staff. He and his wife escaped to Finland in 1917, she allegedly with family jewels sewed into her clothing. After the tsar's death, they refrained from any further political activity, and retired to Sarasota, Florida. She died in 1975 at ninety-nine years of age.

31. Aside from liquor and valuables, the most prized pieces of loot commandeered from private town houses and palaces were automobiles. Kokovtsov's doorman, unbeknownst to him 'a regular bolshevik', had led the mob to the count's private garage and made off with his three cars. Two days later Kokovtsov went to his safety deposit box at a local bank and removed 20,000 rubles worth of stock certificates. He was denounced in the lobby and arrested by a group of half-drunken soldiers, who then loaded him into a car to take him to prison. An officer climbed onto the running board and yelled to passersby, 'Here goes the former tsarist minister, the thief, Count Kokovtsov, caught red-handed dragging from the bank a million rubles with which to rescue the tsar'. Kokovtsov, *Memoirs*, op. cit., p. 482.

32. Sukhomlinov, unlike many other tsarist officials, actually survived. Tried by the provisional government for his incompetence at the beginning of the war, he was convicted and sentenced to penal punishment. Kokovtsov considered him 'one of the most guilty for the catastrophe that befell Russia', but 'I do not believe he was a traitor'. Surprisingly released on humanitarian grounds (old age) in May 1918, he managed to flee to Berlin via Finland, where he died in 1926. Ibid., pp. 487–8.

33. Romanovs and aristocrats were not the only émigrés to flee Petrograd, whose population was culled by two-thirds in just the three years between 1917 and 1920. Master craftsman and jeweller extraordinaire Peter Carl Fabergé managed to escape in the autumn of 1918. He died, close to penury and largely in stunned amazement, two years later in Switzerland. George Balanchine, dancer and choreographer, fled at twenty years of age, in 1924, leaving behind pretty much everything and everybody. He remembered dancing in *The Sleeping Beauty* at the old imperial theatre, its stalls crowded with the proletariat, the tsar long gone. Even in winter, the heat was never on. The internationally famous philosopher Isaiah Berlin, who spent his career mostly at Oxford, remembered seeing a tsarist policeman hauled off by a Petrograd mob, to what fate he could only guess. His parents, prosperous Jews, fled the city in 1920. Alissa Zinovyevna Rosenbaum was born just weeks after the infamous 1905 massacre. Her family was also Jewish, the despised underclass, but her father was a successful pharmacist until a chaotic day in 1917 when armed bolshevik guards stormed through his shop and threw him out, confiscating every bit of inventory there was. 'Looting the looters' was how Lenin phrased this particular wave of violence. Nine years later Rosenbaum emigrated to New York City, changing her name to Ayn Rand. 'No one helped me', she wrote in her most famous novel, *Atlas Shrugged*. Elizabeth Kendall, *Balanchine and the Lost Muse: Revolution and the Making of a Choreographer* (New York, 2013), pp. 104–53; A. Ryan, 'Sir Isaiah Berlin', *DNB*, Vol. 5, pp. 402–3; Anne C. Heller, *Ayn Rand and the World She Made* (New York, 2009), p. 31; Ayn Rand, *Atlas Shrugged* (New York, 2005), author's note, n/p. See also Lesley Chamberlain, *Lenin's Private War: The Voyage of the Philosophy Steamer and the Exile of the Intelligentsia* (New York, 2006).

34. *The Times* would not print Lord Lansdowne's letter outlining his proposals. They were defeatist.

35. These negotiations were handled by Trotsky himself. On the other side of the table sat Max Hoffmann, now a general and in charge of the entire eastern theatre. Trotsky enjoyed jousting with his stiff-necked Prussian counterpart, infuriating him with provocations and revolutionary dogma (he called their sessions 'a Marxist propagandist class for beginners'). But in the end a German diplomat put it best: 'The bolsheviks got their power through advocating peace. They can retain it only on condition they make peace.' Russia ceded over thirty percent of its territory. Leon Trotsky, *My Life: An Attempt at an Autobiography* (New York, 1970), pp. 372, 371. See also George Kennan, *Russia and the West Under Lenin and Stalin* (Boston, 1961), p. 39.

36. Ironside was certainly a colourful personality. It has been said that Richard Hannay, the central character of John Buchan's enormously popular adventure tales, *The Thirty-Nine Steps* being the best known, was modelled on him.

37. Anti-Semitism in all ranks of Russian society was pronounced, but within two elements it was supreme: the peasantry and the officer corps, both united in the army (i.e., those who led and those who were led). In the ghastly war theatre of Galicia, in particular, atrocities against the Jewish population were everyday occurrences, and no accurate number of those killed has ever been compiled, owing in large measure to the matter-of-factness of such events. Generally regarded as spies, Jews were routinely rounded up as hostages, to be executed upon any suspicious activity that a paranoid general might perceive in the surrounding countryside. Countess Kleinmichel recorded the experiences of a young officer, seated at the mess table, who was ordered by his commander to execute two Jews. 'You can come back and finish your dinner afterwards.' As he left his meal, a third Jew was hauled in. 'God loves a trinity. Take him and hang him with the others.' M. Kleinmichel, *Memories of a Shipwrecked World, Being the Memoirs of Countess Kleinmichel* (New York, 1923), pp. 190–93.

Chapter 15 – T. E. Lawrence, 'of Arabia'

1. To say nothing of Arabia in general, 'terra incognita until well after World War I'. Muhammad Munayyir, *The Hejaz Railway and the Muslim Pilgrimage: A Case of Ottoman Political Propaganda*, ed. J. Landau (Detroit, 1971), p. 25.

2. In gathering materials for his Oxford thesis, Lawrence cycled 2,500 miles through France, visiting more than fifty medieval sites during the summer holidays of 1908, all in less than two months. The next year, and much farther afield, he trekked some thousand miles alone through Palestine, visiting remote crusader castles there, many unknown in England, taking three months and at times walking thirty miles a day in heat of over 100 degrees. G. B. Shaw once wrote that vegetarians have more stamina than people who eat steaks every day. G. B. Shaw, 'Preface on the Prospects of Christianity', *Androcles and the Lion: An Old Fable Renovated* (Harmondsworth, 1983), p. 22.

3. As coincidence would have it, Lawrence's mother was also illegitimate, which he did not learn until 1919. His father died in 1919; his grave, in Oxford, is 'unmarked and untended'.

4. Since 1918, this important site has been marked on the Turkish side of the Syrian-Turkish border.

5. It has been claimed that a Bedouin could sustain himself for thirty days on camel milk alone. A unique characteristic of the animal's internal digestive system (to conserve water) is that its excrement is discharged in a dry state, and thus is available almost immediately for use as fuel in a campfire.

6. The army was 78 percent Indian, with an additional 3,800 camp followers, who served as porters, water carriers, cooks and so on. Indian soldiers were fed considerably less than their British counterparts, and other aspects of army life, such as medical services, were likewise inferior.

7. After surrendering, Townshend, along with all his officers, were given the choice of remaining with their men in captivity or being separated from them. All but one, a Gurkha, chose the latter. Townshend was sent to spent the remainder of the war in the environs of Constantinople, accompanied by his Portuguese cook, an Indian servant and two British orderlies. He requested that his dog, Spot, be repatriated to England. Along the way, at one small town, 'I shot 6 couple of sand grouse before breakfast'. His last imprisonment was on an island near Constantinople, in a villa, it seems, where he was treated as an honoured guest. A launch was put at his disposal, and he made frequent trips to the capital city, often to receptions at the sultan's palace or for lunch at the American embassy, where he caught up on the latest newspapers from London. Things were pleasant enough that he urged his wife to join him, who refused. The image, she explained to him, was all wrong, which was certainly true, especially after the war when reports surfaced of the abominable treatment his men had endured at the hands of Turkish guards. Muslim Indian prisoners had been encouraged to enlist in the Ottoman army after the surrender of Kut, to fight the infidels. Most accepted. The others were subjected to a death march along the likes of Bataan twenty-six years later, then were largely worked and starved on construction projects. Estimates vary, but it appears close to half did not survive. Townshend barely mentioned any of this in his memoirs, which even a sympathetic biographer called 'vainglorious'. Rudyard Kipling, as usual, had something to say on the subject:

   > They shall not return to us, the resolute, the young,
   > The eager and whole-hearted whom we gave:
   > But the men who left them thriftily to die in their own dung,
   > Shall they come with years and honour to the grave?

   The answer to that was yes. Despite the king's opinion that Townshend should have remained with his troops, he was awarded the Knight Commander of the Bath the year following his surrender, and later was elected to parliament. Haig considered him 'a semi-lunatic'. Charles Townshend, *My Campaign in Mesopotamia* (London, 1920), pp. 359, 364; Russell Braddon, *The Siege* (New York, 1970), pp. 258, 290; T. R. Moreman, 'Sir Charles Vere Ferrers Townshend (1861–1924)', *DNB*, Vol. 55, p. 151; Rudyard Kipling, 'Mesopotamia', *Complete Verse* (New York, 1989), p. 298; Lawrence James, *The Golden Warrior: The Life and Legend of Lawrence of Arabia* (New York, 1993), p. 126; Scott Anderson, *Lawrence in Arabia* (New York: Doubleday, 2013), p. 523 (ftn. 178); A. J. Barker, *Townshend of Kut: A Biography of Major-General Sir Charles Townshend, K.C.B., D.S.O.* (London, 1967), p. 218. See also Norman Dixon, *On the Psychology of Military Incompetence* (New York, 1976), pp. 95–109.

8. Caliphate means the Islamic state, or regions under Muslim control, no matter the artificiality of political boundaries. The caliph, from the Arabic word *khalifah*, meaning 'successor', is the honorific ruler.

9. Many of Lawrence's descriptions of service with Faisal, and notes he made for officers either following in his footsteps or dealing separately with Arab leaders, are strongly reminiscent of Count Baldesar Castiglione's *The Book of the Courtier* (1528), a hugely influential compendium of advice for would-be advisers to Machiavellian kings. A copy was found in Lawrence's library after his death. A. W. Lawrence, ed., *T. E. Lawrence by His Friends* (London, 1937), p. 481.

10. War had interrupted construction of the intended final link to Mecca, some 230 miles farther south from Medina.

11. At one point, Lawrence was in charge of 30,000 gold sovereigns, 1,000 coins to a bag. One camel carried two bags, along with other gear. Arabs generally disdained being paid with paper currency; it was gold sovereigns that mattered to them. These coins came to be

nicknamed 'the cavalry of St. George', given the depiction on its obverse side of England's patron saint, mounted on a horse, nude aside from shin armour, slaying a dragon, a design by Benedetto Pistrucci, a native of Rome. It is said that Pistrucci, eating dinner at a restaurant near his hotel in London, employed the services of an Italian waiter as his model for St. George. For Pistrucci, see his 'Autobiography', trans. A. Billing, *The Science of Gems, Jewels, Coins and Medals, Ancient and Modern* (London, 1867), pp. 135–91; and Roderick Farey, 'Benedetto Pistrucci (1782–1855), Part 1', *Coin News* (September 2014), pp. 51–3.

12. The Ageyl and Hadheyl were Arabic clans.

13. Chaim Weizmann, president of the Zionist Federation and a prime mover in the creation of a Jewish homeland, met Lawrence several times in 1917. 'Lawrence never regarded the policy of the Jewish National Home as in any way incompatible with assurances given the Arabs. He did not think the aims and aspirations of the Jewish people in Palestine contrary to the interests of the Arabs'. It is difficult to see in this exchange anything other than a conscious daydream on both men's part. A. W. Lawrence, *Lawrence by His Friends*, op. cit., p. 221.

14. Nejdi (or Najd), the centre of the Arabian peninsula, associated with the Al Saud clan.

15. It has been estimated that Lawrence attacked and destroyed seventy-nine trains in two years. Bertram Wyatt-Brown, 'Lawrence of Arabia: Image and Reality', *Journal of the Historical Society*, Vol. 9, No. 4 (December 2009), p. 528.

Chapter 16 – Berlin: Black Hours in a Red Tide

1. While Lloyd George was delighted to be rid of Robertson, preferring the Irishman's outgoing personality, he remained disappointed in Wilson's unrepentant 'western' views when it came to war strategy; 'Wully redivivus', as the prime minister referred to him. 'It is Irish instead of Scotch, but it is still whisky'. Roskill, *Hankey*, op. cit., pp. 584, 586.

2. Charteris blamed most difficulties regarding the army's performance on politicians sitting at their ease in London. 'We have been starved of men' was one of his common complaints. Brigadier-General John Charteris, *At G. H. Q.* (London, 1931), p. 294.

3. Another exchange was a little less optimistic. Clemenceau said to Foch, 'Well, you've got the job you so much wanted.' 'A fine gift', the marshal replied; 'you give me a lost battle and tell me to win it.' Foch was determined that the English and French not be split apart by the attacking Germans. He did not want a situation where the two powers would have to decide whether to fall back to the channel ports or retire towards Paris. '*Ni l'un, ni l'autre* ... It will not come to that – *jamais, jamais, jamais*.' Terraine, *Ordeal of Victory*, op. cit., p. 424; Roskill, *Hankey*, op. cit., p. 536. Foch's 'stout' remark translates as 'Neither one nor the other ... It will not come to that – never, never, never.'

4. The bolshevik 'ambassador' to London (he was never formally accredited) was expelled after only nine months for revolutionary behaviour. He was not a gentleman, but an individual of 'utter crudity'. Scott, *Political Diaries*, op. cit., pp. 329, 331.

5. Von Müller called German communiques an 'entirely incorrect if not to say downright dishonest picture of events'. *The Kaiser and His Court: The Diaries, Note Books and Letters of Admiral Georg Alexander von Müller, Chief of the Naval Cabinet, 1914–1918*, ed. W. Görlitz, trans. M. Savill (New York, 1961), p. 373.

6. Even the officer corps might have baulked at that. A brigadier was quoted in May 1918 as saying that 'this is my ninth offensive ... I've had a belly full'. Ibid, p. 359.

7. Marx himself would have been slightly more tactful; he simply called organizations such as SPD an example of 'bourgeois' socialism. Jonathan Sperber, *Karl Marx: A Nineteenth-Century Life* (New York, 2013), p. 211.

8. Ludendorff wrote scathing attacks on Hindenburg after the war. German reviewers called some of these articles 'poisonous gas'. 'Erich Ludendorff' (Wikipedia: Internet resource), ftn. 18.

9. Actually the empress was in very poor health, having suffered the first of several recurring heart attacks earlier in the year.

10. The soon-to-be former king of Württemberg jotted in his diary that Hindenburg on this occasion had failed in his duty, Gröner, after all, being a Swabian. 'Gröner was right to do what he did', he wrote, 'but he should have said to [Hindenburg]: "Find a Prussian to say these things"'. John Wheeler-Bennett, *The Nemesis of Power: The German Army in Politics, 1918–1945* (New York, 2005), p. 22 (ftn. 1).

11. The kaiser's bother, Prince Henry, was the titular commander in chief of the navy. When the fleet mutinied in Kiel, beginning on 3 November, he had no such scruples about flying the red flag, which he ordered placed on his car. With difficulty, he managed to escape the city dressed as a civilian. He would never wear a uniform again except at émigré dinner parties.

12. The vast estate of Krieblowitz, where the famous Marshal Blücher died and was buried, reverted to Poland after the war, and was thus lost to the family. In 1945, during the advance of Red Army troops, the Blücher mausoleum was vandalized, the old marshal's casket dug up, opened and desecrated. It is said that Russian soldiers used his skull as a football. All that was left of his remains were buried at a local church in 1989. The mausoleum today still stands, a relic of German history that is understandably, like others, not respected in modern-day Poland.

Chapter 17 – Versailles: Where It All Ended (or Should Have)

1. Wilson returned the conceit, once remarking that House's mind 'is not first class'. David M. Esposito, 'Imagined Power: The Secret Life of Colonel House', *The Historian*, Vol. 60, No. 4 (June 1998), p. 741.

2. Theodore Roosevelt, the former president, was certainly the loudest of Wilson's detractors. He was not nicknamed T. 'Vesuvius' Roosevelt for nothing. During these latter stages of his public career, Roosevelt's rhetoric reached such extremes that many wondered if he had lost not only his sense of perspective, but some of his sanity as well. Edmund Morris, *Colonel Roosevelt* (New York, 2011), p. 403.

3. German obtuseness was not restricted to the Atlantic Ocean. Revelations that Germany was involved in conspiracies to involve Mexico in any future state of belligerency with the United States (Mexico would be awarded Arizona, New Mexico and Texas) raised yet another needless uproar that made Wilson's decision for war easier. The unreality of the scheme matched the quixotic adventure of 'Emperor' Maximilian of Mexico half a century before.

4. The title 'general' seemed extraordinarily generous to some, considering that Villa was little more than a freebooting guerrilla.

5. Feelings were rarely neutral when it came to the Dreyfus affair. The American-born wife of the Danish ambassador to France recorded this scene as she walked through Place de la Concorde. 'People rush about the streets pushing, howling, and screaming at the top of their lungs, "Conspuez Zola!" which I cannot translate in other words than "Spit on Zola!"' Lillie de Hegermann-Lindencrone, *The Sunny Side of Diplomatic Life, 1875–1912* (New York, 1914), p. 264.

6. The cabinet of Aristide Briand was particularly feeble. At seventy-five, Clemenceau refused to accept a position, saying 'No, I am too young.' Stevenson, *Diary*, op. cit., p. 81.

7. E. E. Cummings, like Hemingway an ambulance driver, described his return to Paris in the autumn of 1917. 'The streets. *Les rues de Paris.* I walked past Notre Dame. I bought tobacco. Jews are peddling things with American trade-marks on them, because in a day or two it's Christmas I suppose. Jesus it is cold. Dirty snow. Huddling people. *La guerre.* Always *La guerre.* And chill.' E. E. Cummings, *The Enormous Room* (New York, 1934), p. 330.

8. The desire for replacement troops, at least for the British, did not include men of colour. One of the divisions offered by Pershing was the 92nd, a segregated African-American unit. Haig declined their use. Lord Milner, in putting together the official response, noted the 'administrative difficulties' that accepting Pershing's offer would entail. John J. Pershing, *My Experiences in the World War* (New York, 1931), Vol. II, pp. 45–6.

9. Bitterly disappointed at having been left on the home front (training recruits in Pennsylvania) was another later-to-be-famous general, Dwight Eisenhower.

10. As far as President Wilson was concerned, 'We won the war at Château-Thierry'. Arthur S. Link, et al., eds., *The Papers of Woodrow Wilson* (Princeton, 1983), Vol. 53, p. 314.

11. Named after the Russian general Aleksei Brusilov, one of the better tsarist officers, but who, like so many of that cadre, seemed often oblivious of casualties.

12. On the freedom of the seas issue, Shaw wrote that 'a claim on the part of any one Power to dominate the naval armaments of all other nations and treat the oceans and the Mediterranean as its own peculiar territory, needs only to be stated to appear utterly outrageous to everyone except the claimants'. Bernard Shaw, *What I Really Wrote About the War* (New York, 1932), p. 5.

13. For some reason, Douglas Haig invited Shaw to visit the front in 1917, an offer the famous playwright accepted. Shaw called it 'a joy ride' (even though the things he saw were grim – he was told 'go flat on your face if anything comes over'). Haig did not know quite what to make of Shaw who, in his turn, observed that the field marshal had 'a well closed mind'. Shaw wrote frequently about the war, during the war, but his strange persona coloured people's reactions to what he had to say. The Dubliner James Stephens said the usual thing: 'On Saturday I got *The Irish Times*, and found in it a long article by Bernard Shaw. One reads things written by Shaw. Why one does read them I do not know exactly, except that it is a habit we got into years ago, and we read an article by Shaw just as we put our boots on in the morning – that is, without thinking about it, and without any idea of rewards.' Shaw, *What I Really Wrote*, op. cit., pp. 289, 223, 216; James Stephens, *The Insurrection in Dublin* (New York, 1999). See also Haig, *Private Papers*, op. cit., pp. 194–5.

14. It is interesting to note that *The Times*, in reporting the election results, grossly misunderstood the possible effect of the president's defeat, editorializing that 'their importance is psychological rather than concrete'. Lodge would foretell his bitter opposition to Wilson's ideas in a speech he delivered in Boston on 13 November, just two days after the armistice, the headline of a local paper reporting 'Lodge warns Against Pacifist Sentimentality in Making Peace Terms'. *Papers of Woodrow Wilson*, op. cit., pp. 44, 83.

15. Lloyd George said of Lansing, 'He just did what he was told, and was never told to do very much.' Wilson unceremoniously called for his resignation in 1920, prompting a quip from Clemenceau that 'I got my bullet during the conference; Lansing got his after.' Lansing was the uncle of a future secretary of state, John Foster Dulles. David Lloyd George, *Memoirs of the Peace Conference* (New Haven, 1939), Vol. I, p. 156; John Dos Passos, *Mr. Wilson's War* (Garden City, NY, 1962), p. 489.

16. The influenza pandemic first raised its alarming head at the beginning of 1918, 'an enemy almost as barbarous and relentless as the Germans', according to a British journalist. It lasted for approximately two years and ravaged the entire world. Press censorship in Europe minimized its importance, mostly to dampen panic. It came to be called the Spanish Flu, largely because King Alfonso XIII nearly died of it and Spain, having not been a party to the war, placed no restrictions on reporting the disease, giving the impression that it had originated there. Scott, *Political Diaries*, op. cit., pp. 232–3; John N. Barry, *The Great Influenza: The Epic Story of the Deadliest Plague in History* (New York, 2004), p. 171.

17. On Armistice Day, British forces held 75 miles of line, American forces nearly 90. The French army, by contrast, held 230. In manpower, roughly the same per centages applied: of the total, Britain contributed 28 percent, America 31 per cent, and France 41 percent. Spears also seemed to forget that the war was fought largely on French soil, with all the inherent destruction which that implied. Donald Smyth, *Pershing: General of the Armies* (Bloomington, IN, 1986), pp. 233–4.

18. The blockade was not lifted until March, a delay C. P. Scott considered 'a crime'. The German industrialist Walther Rathenau told a journalist that the needless suffering thereby caused was counterproductive in every way. 'When you clean up a city, you don't isolate the unhealthy quarters. You give them light, water, and the necessities of life'. Scott, *Political Diaries*, op. cit., p. 373; Maurice Berger, *Germany After The Armistice: A Report, Based on the Personal Testimony of Representative Germans, Concerning the Conditions Existing in 1919* (New York, 1920), p. 96.

19. By the autumn of 1916, Britain was spending almost $200 million a month with American purveyors of war materials, foodstuffs and assorted necessities both on its own behalf and also those of France and Italy. Three months later, its gold reserves were being drawn down by the astounding amount of £5 million a day, nearly half of it earmarked for American purchases, a figure that so alarmed the economist John Maynard Keynes that he saw a future for his country as nothing less than that of a serf on a medieval manor, subservient to his wealthy master. He later estimated that the total amount of money spent or borrowed by Britain amounted to ten trillion dollars, certainly an exaggeration. Alec Cairncross, 'John Maynard Keynes', *DNB*, Vol. 31, p. 486; John Maynard Keynes, *The Economic Consequences of the Peace* (New York, 1920), p. 274; Patrick Devlin, *Too Proud to Fight: Woodrow Wilson's Neutrality* (London, 1975), p. 548.

20. Clemenceau was also mildly contemptuous of the United States. It was 'the only country that had passed from barbarism to decadence without the intervening stage of civilization'. Wilson, *Rasputin*, op. cit., p. 72.

21. Henry Cabot Lodge led the attack from the Senate floor, rejecting the most important parts of the Covenant which interfered, as he saw it, with America's freedom of action. As the *Congressional Record* stated, Lodge felt the American public especially should question Article X and its 'very perilous promise to guarantee, by force if necessary, the political independence and territorial integrity of all members of the League. The American people would do well to consider carefully whether they were willing to have the United States forced into a war by decision of the League and against their own will'. In general, he saw no reason to abandon the foreign policy principles established by President Washington in his farewell address, and the anti-European posture of the Monroe Doctrine. *Papers of Woodrow Wilson*, op. cit., Vol. 55, p. 312.

22. He also caught the flu and missed several meetings. 'Clemenceau was very pleased at Wilson's absence', Lloyd George's mistress noted in her diary, '& could not conceal his joy. "He is *worse* today," he said to David, & doubled up with laughter.' Stevenson, *Diary*, op. cit., p. 178.

23. Nicolson, who spent a good deal of his time at Versailles arranging new borders (often without any expertise to do so), would have sided with Colonel House. His diary entry for 5 March is typical: 'Work hard all morning. Maps, plans, partitions, watersheds, canalization – all these intricate processes of thought which have become a jog-trot in my brain. The strain moral and mental is great: even the puddles in the pavements assume for me the shapes of frontiers, salients, corridors, neutralized channels, demilitarized zones, islands, duck beaks.' Harold Nicolson, *Peacemaking 1919: Being Reminiscences of the Paris Peace Conference* (Boston, 1933), p. 277.

24. A Zionist at the conference was wary of the Arab entourage. He thought Faisal 'a splendid specimen of a man surrounded by the scum of the earth'. Scott, *Political Diaries*, op. cit., p. 360.

25. The same writer was also upset watching German prisoners of war working on clearing rubble, side by side with French coloured troops. Walter Simons, 'Personal Letters of Dr. Walter Simons to His Wife, Written at Versailles (April 30–June 12, 1919)', in Adam Lackau, ed., *The German Delegation at the Paris Peace Conference* (New York, 1941).

26. Walther Rathenau, an immensely wealthy German industrialist, had held pivotal offices in the Imperial government during the war. Though a Jew, the kaiser was aware of his importance to the war effort and graced him with his company on several occasions. Wilhelm even suggested that Rathenau convert to Christianity so that a grateful kaiser could elevate him to the aristocracy or give him an honorary commission in some elite regiment. No socialist, Rathenau felt it his duty to serve in the Weimar Republic as its foreign minister. Controversy over Versailles, and later treaties with the Soviet Union, led extremists to assassinate him in 1922. No longer grateful, Wilhelm II remarked that Rathenau's fate was exactly what he deserved. See Hartmut Pogge von Strandmann, 'Rathenau, Wilhelm II, and the Perception of *Wilhelminismus*', in Mombauer, Deist, eds., *The Kaiser: New Research*, op. cit., pp. 273, 277.

27. Keynes abruptly left Paris on 19 May. Although the co-author of the treaty's article 231, known as the 'war guilt clause' and the source of such angst among the German delegation (and of Brockdorff-Rantzau in particular, who resigned largely on its account), Keynes was for a magnanimous peace based on principles that later could be seen as the inspiration for the Marshall Plan of post-World War II. What he experienced in Paris, he later wrote, was 'a nightmare'. Upon returning to England, he authored a blistering account of the goings-on in Paris, the results of which he condemned as vicious and certain to produce considerable turmoil in the future. *The Economic Consequences of the Peace* was a bestseller all over the world (he wrote it in only three months and made a small fortune from its proceeds). Its rabid tone and exaggerations, as well as its treatment of Woodrow Wilson, caused considerable controversy. Charles Seymour, future president of Yale University and a member of the American delegation, denounced the book as propaganda, 'bilious and contentious …an imaginative travesty', in a review he wrote of it in 1919, and defended Wilson. 'The essence of statesmanship', he wrote, was the art of compromise, a virtue he said Keynes should recognize, as its greatest practitioner was William Gladstone, with whom Keynes was surely familiar. Keynes, *Economic Consequences*, op. cit., pp. 5–6; Charles Seymour, 'A Great Opportunity Missed', *Yale Review*, Vol. IX, October 1919, pp. 857–61.

28. Mark Twain agreed, writing that Roosevelt was 'clearly insane'. Stephen Kinzer, *The True Flag: Theodore Roosevelt, Mark Twain, and the Birth of American Empire* (New York, 2017), p. 13.

29. Roosevelt saw in Wilson's rhetorical inconsistencies a 'really nauseous hypocrisy'. Devlin, *Too Proud to Fight*, op. cit., p. 684.

Chapter 18 – Known & Unknown Soldier(s)

1. Spencer, who served as a medical orderly during some of his wartime service, was fascinated by surgery. He at least spared his viewers, and the Behrends, from one proposed subject, a patient opened up on the operating table. 'I should love to do a fresco of an operation', he wrote a friend, 'and have the incision in the belly in the middle of the picture, and all the forceps radiating from it'. During World War II, Spencer was an official war artist, spending much of his time in Glasgow where he created a series of brilliant paintings depicting the shipyards in their full activity. Spencer did much of his sketching

on rolls of toilet paper, which he prized for strength and portability. During the same time frame, the Behrends continued their patronage of difficult artists, commissioning Benjamin Britten, a conscientious objector and habitué of homosexual circles, to compose his String Quartet No. 2, first performed in 1945. Duncan Robinson, *Stanley Spencer at Burghclere: The Oratory of All Souls Sandham Memorial Chapel, Hampshire* (London, 2012), p. 7; Robert Upstone, 'Sir Stanley Spencer: Portrait of Louis Behrend' (The Tate: Internet resource).

2. The British had some difficulty settling on a name. 'Unknown Comrade' was first considered, but rejected due to the general opprobrium felt for bolshevism. 'Unknown Warrior' was finally selected.

3. Fussiness over medals and decorations have always been a special feature of British society. Lifers who had survived the entire four years of World War I were a self-conscious fraternity, generally awarded with three special medals: The Mons Star, the British War Medal and the Victory Medal. These were generally known as Pip, Squeak and Wilfred. British humour ... who would understand it other than the British themselves?

4. The original Cenotaph memorial hastily designed by Lutyens, past which allied troops had marched in the Victory parade of 1919, was meant to be temporary. It was made of wood, plaster and canvas. It proved so moving to the general public, however, that Lutyens reworked the design slightly, and its permanent replacement was unveiled by the king in time for Armistice Day 1920. Not everyone was thrilled with the design, however. The archbishop of Canterbury regarded it as altogether too 'pagan' for his liking.

5. Kipling, at the start of the war, was an enthusiastic jingoist. His son John, who had dreadful eyesight, was failed trying to join the Royal Navy, and failed again when he turned to the army. Kipling pulled strings, and John was finally taken on by the Irish Guards. On his second day of combat, at Loos in 1915, he was killed, at eighteen years of age. His name is on the village memorial outside the little parish church of Burwash in east Sussex, where the Kiplings lived in baronial splendour.

6. King George V visited the war cemeteries in France and Belgium during the spring of 1922. Kipling's first verse in his commemorative poem marking the event reads:
   Our King went forth on pilgrimage
   His prayers and vows to pay
   To them that saved our heritage
   And cast their own away.
   The same year, T. S. Eliot wrote 'The Waste Land'. Sassoon began the war years writing the type of sentimental verse that he would later excoriate. Once he had seen combat, his friend and fellow poet Robert Graves 'told him, in my old-soldier manner, that he would soon change his style'. As for Kipling, King George, over time, came to appreciate his talents. The king evolved into a prolific reader later in his life, though his tastes were middlebrow and hardly refined. At first he considered Kipling's work as 'coarse,' as he did D. H. Lawrence's, whose *Lady Chatterley's Lover* he threw into the fire one evening when his son caught him reading it. But when George needed a catchy phrase for a speech, or, indeed, an entire delivery, Kipling came to the rescue, and became more duly regarded at Buckingham Palace. There was never any doubt, as Kingsley Amis was to say, that Kipling was anything but a 'writer of obvious talent.' Rudyard Kipling, *1922* (The Kipling Society: Internet resource, 2010); Graves, *Good-bye to All That* (New York, 1998), p. 175; Ridley, *George V*, op. cit., pp. 201, 396.

7. The Messines memorial features an Irish round tower, among other things, and several slabs with engraved remarks (as well as a plaque urging reconciliation in Ireland, a conflict as remorseless as anything on the western front). A snippet of poetry by Patrick MacGill, London Irish Rifles, runs as follows:

'I wish I were back again
In the glens of Donegal,
They'll call me coward if I return
But a hero if I fall!'
Patrick MacGill, 'A Lament', *Soldier Songs* (New York, 1917), p. 31.

8. Despite the prevalence of 'shell shock' cases induced by the ferocity of combat in World War I, it remained a 'syndrome' usually out of favour among the ranks of professional officers, most infamously by General George Patton in Sicily during World War II. Infuriated by malingerers who professed they 'had had enough', Patton said, to no one in particular, 'There's no such thing as shell shock. It's an invention of the Jews'. Patton was presumably referring to psychoanalysts, a large proportion of whom were Jewish. Antony Beevor, *The Second World War* (New York, 2012), p. 498.

9. St. John the Divine in New York City is technically somewhat larger but also, technically, not yet completed.

10. The Legion has raised millions of pounds over the years through the annual sale of commemorative poppies, inspired by the poem 'In Flanders Fields' by the Canadian soldier John McCrae.

Chapter 19 – Postscripts

1. In 1922, Britain requested military participation from Canada for a projected expedition against Turkey, a plea that was rejected.

2. The Habsburgs, having opposed the *Anschluss* with Germany in 1938, were not especially favoured by the Nazis. During the invasion of Belgium, Empress Zita's residence was attacked by German bombers, which scored a direct hit that came close to killing her. She and her family followed the miserable example of countless other refugees, fleeing south, over the Pyrenees, through Spain and finally into Portugal. After some anxious weeks there, they managed to secure passage to the United States.

3. Then Lieutenant-Colonel George Patton, who wrote a staff study of the campaign, was of the opinion that at Suvla Bay allied foot soldiers did not so much lose to their Turkish counterparts as did their officers. 'Had the two sets of commanders changed sides it is believed that the landing would have been as great a success as it was a dismal failure'. He also noted that 'the valor and persistence of the Turkish infantry has never been justly evaluated'. Lieutenant-Colonel G. S. Patton Jr., *The Defense of Gallipoli: A General Staff Study* (Fort Shafter, HI, 1936), p. 62.

4. Von Sanders eventually ended up in Malta, where he was arrested by British authorities and held for six months. There was some agitation to try him for alleged war crimes, but these subsided. He used the time to write his memoirs.

5. The subsequent experiences by many of these men give some indication of the precarious environment of Turkish politics: Enver Pasha (killed in battle); Talaat Pasha (murdered in Berlin by an Armenian); Mehmed Cavid (executed for treason); Ahmed Djemal (assassinated, also by Armenians), among others. The grand vizier (or prime minister) Mehmed Said Halim, also died violently, killed in Rome by Romanian assassins.

6. His friend and confidant, Lord Riddell, recorded Lloyd George's gradual embitterment as the long years of 'retirement' (though often very busy) stretched ahead. The former PM 'is like a pretty woman', he wrote, 'who has been absolutely the rage and who now is being somewhat neglected. Even the smallest attentions are gratifying, whereas in other times they would have been disregarded.' Only eighteen months after Lloyd George's resignation, Riddell noted that 'iron has entered into his soul. He is resentful of the way in which he had fallen into the background'. Riddell, *Diaries*, op. cit., pp. 384, 386.

7. In 1924, Kemal formally ended the caliphate as well, a deed foretold by one of the sultan's ministers. 'I can see in that man's eyes', he said referring to Kemal, 'that he means to abolish all religion'. Patrick Kinross, *Atatürk: The Rebirth of a Nation* (London, 1993), p. 152.

8. The king's somewhat simplistic view of the army undoubtedly reflected his opinion of the larger civilian population as well: everyone is 'happy'. His popularity as king was certainly genuine, if sometimes lukewarm, George Orwell noting during the monarch's silver jubilee in 1935 signs which read, 'Poor but Loyal'. George Orwell, *The English People* (New York, 1974), p. 26.

9. Maxime Weygand, commander in chief from 1931 to 1935, and then again in 1940, disapproved of too many tanks on the grounds that the 'army of mechanics [required to service them] would be a regular hotbed of Communism'. Weygand was Foch's most important staff officer during World War I. De Gaulle called him 'by nature a brilliant second man'. Janet Flanner, *Pétain: The Old Man of France* (New York, 1944), p. 34; Jean Lacouture, *De Gaulle: The Rebel, 1890–1944* (New York, 1990), p. 130. See also Michael S. Neiberg, *Foch: Supreme Allied Commander in the Great War* (Washington, 2003), pp. 22–3.

10. Changing governments was a political sport in France, as parties splintered, reformed and fell apart with bewildering frequency. One pre-World War I premier said of his ideological colleagues, both truthfully and humorously, 'I am their leader, and must follow them.' Adamthwaite, *Grandeur and Misery*, op. cit., p. 11.

11. As Roy Jenkins, an able biographer of Churchill, glowingly put it, 'The flower of the BEF was back behind the white cliffs of Dover'. The prime minister did confess before the House of Commons, however, that 'Wars are not won by evacuations'. Jenkins, *Churchill*, op. cit., p. 597.

12. Leopold III decided to remain in Belgium, a decision that enormously complicated his life, and that of the country, until the final denouement in 1951, when he finally abdicated the throne.

13. Pétain's government returned the favour, condemning de Gaulle to death, *in absentia*, for treason.

14. The villa where Trotsky was housed in Turkey, on an island in the Sea of Marmara, was the same where General Charles Townshend was sent after his surrender of Kut in 1916. Karl E. Meyer, Shareen Blair Brysac, *Kingmakers: The Invention of the Modern Middle East* (New York, 2008), p. 137.

15. Maria Feodorovna, despite the change in her circumstances, remained politically unenlightened for the remainder of her long life (she died in 1928 at the age of eighty). 'The Revolution of Trotsky and Kerensky was not Russian', she told a visitor in Denmark, 'but Jewish, and for that reason the Soviet will not endure'. She was right about the eventual fate of the communist state, but it took nearly a century for her prediction to come true. H. R. H. the Infanta Eulalia, *Memoirs of a Spanish Princess*, trans. P. Mégroz (New York, 1937), p. 236.

16. Queen's Mary's addiction to expensive jewellry was widely noted by contemporaries in and around the court, as well her stinginess when it came to paying market value. Her reputation as a 'kleptomaniac' is, however, evidently untrue, according to George V's most recent biographer. Ridley, *George V*, op. cit., pp. 371, 501 (ftn. 22).

17. Also buried within this monastery is Princess Alice of Greece, a niece of Grand Duchess Elizabeth, and the daughter of Prince Louis of Battenberg, once first lord of the Admiralty and mentioned previously in this narrative. She was the mother of the late Prince Philip of England, consort of the late queen. Her life, while not quite as tragic as Ella's, was nonetheless peripatetic and adventure filled, replete with incidents of genuine tragedy. She asked to be buried next to her aunt in Jerusalem, a request not realized for almost twenty years.

18. Many politicians in Britain could not then, and cannot now, fathom the complexities of difference that separated many of the Irish from one another, nor the violence of their opinions. They 'don't know what they want', a British lawyer said, 'and are prepared to fight to the death to get it.' Smuts, who participated in many of the negotiations, was appalled at the Irish participants. 'Not impressed by any of them', C. P. Scott recorded in his diary after a chat with him. 'No big man among them'. Sidney Underwood, President of Law Society, speech of 13 April 1961. See *Encarta: Book of Quotations*, ed. B. Swainson, et al., (New York, 2000), p. 570; Scott, *Political Diaries*, op. cit., p. 201.

19. In his stage directions, Shaw noted that Meek, despite being militarily proper, had 'something exasperatingly and inexplicably wrong about him'. Lawrence's library at Clouds Hill was exceptionally interesting. At one time he had said that an individual should own no more than 150 books; when you bought a title that meant something to you, you had to discard one to make room. As was common with Lawrence, he flouted this maxim. When inventoried after his death, the collection exceeded 1,200 eclectic volumes, many signed first editions, such as James Joyce's *Ulysses*, number 36 of 100 copies (Shakespeare and Company, 1922). Unsurprisingly, poetry, both classical and modern, was well represented, everything from Aeschylus to Ezra Pound. Travel books detailing the Middle East found shelf space. Novelists that he liked included both the famous and the obscure: in the latter camp, James Hanley, whose violent and graphic novel *Boy* would have had an obvious appeal to Lawrence; and Francis Yeats-Brown, who wrote an inscription in his *Dogs of War* to T. E., 'that sabre-rattling militarist' (Lawrence did not own Yeats-Brown's war memoir, *Caught by the Turks*, but probably had read it). Among the better known were Conrad (14 titles), Hart Crane (10), Faulkner (7), Hardy (13), and so on, with the most titles belonging to D. H. Lawrence (26), jarring perhaps, given that D. H. penned a dim view of T. E. in *Lady Chatterley's Lover* ('too much advertisement behind all the humility'). Lawrence voraciously read books about World War I, especially those relating to his career, but he saved very few. 'I have read too many war books. They are like drams, and I cannot leave them alone, though I think I really hate them'. Lawrence's music collection, much valued by him, was more conventional: Mozart (his favourite), Bach, Beethoven, Elgar, Schubert and Handel were well represented. George Bernard Shaw, 'Too True To Be Good, A Political Extravaganza', *Three Plays* (London, 1934), pp. 49–50; A. W. Lawrence, *T. E. Lawrence by His Friends*, op. cit., pp. 333, 476–510, 523–9; T. E. to Frederic Manning, *The Selected Letters of T. E. Lawrence*, ed. M. Brown (New York, 1989), p. 438. See also pp. 409–410 (to Herbert Read re. *All Quiet on the Western Front*), and p. 439 (to Charlotte Shaw); Robert Graves, *Lawrence and the Arabs* (London, 1927), p. 437.

20. Casement, of course, was considered a traitor by most Englishmen, having actively consorted with the enemy. Such would not have been the opinion of many Irishmen. Throughout its history, Irish revolutionaries routinely collaborated with anyone if it helped the cause (see the Great O'Neill with Spaniards, Wolfe Tone and the French, among many others). Regardless of circumstance, the stigma of homosexuality was inflammatory material in the early twentieth century, which is why British authorities used it to tarnish Casement, and why T. E.'s brother, among others, tried suppressing damaging rumours of same.

21. Rothenstein was a well-known and well-connected artist, who, on the recommendation of *The Times*'s correspondent, Charles à Court Repington, travelled to the Western Front in 1917 to paint war scenes. His German-sounding name resulted in difficulties; he once was detained by the French, who found drawings of fortifications on his person, which caused several anxious moments. 'One hears tales of suspected spies being summarily executed'. Mary Lago, 'Sir William Rothenstein (1872–1945)', *DNB*, Vol. 47, pp. 896–8;

William Rothenstein, *Men and Memories: Recollections, 1872–1938* (Columbia, MO., 1978), pp. 175–8.

22. Lawrence's brother described the dedication in *Seven Pillars* as a 'a literary exercise in memory of his own youth'. During the final drive to Damascus in the autumn of 1918, Lawrence learned that Dahoum had died at Carchemish of typhoid fever several months before, the news of which devastated him. A. H. Lawrence, *Lawrence by His Friends*, op. cit., p. 592.

23. In what has become known as the Oxford Text, completed in 1922 with just eight copies privately printed (330,000 words), Lawrence wrote that the Deraa experience, whatever it may have entailed, 'resulted in a longing for a repetition of the experience [akin to] the striving moth towards its flame'. Lawrence trimmed this version by half for what is called the Subscriber Edition (202 copies), and cut even more in a still shorter abridgement published in 1927 as *Revolt in the Desert*. The 'striving moth' descriptive did not survive in either. In 1927, Lawrence also finished *The Mint*, a description of day-to-day barracks life in the RAF, which he had joined under his service pseudonym, 352087 A/c Ross. It too contained homoerotic passages, as well as scatological details and smutty language. These so scandalized Air Marshal Hugh Trenchard, who had assisted Lawrence in his quixotic enlistments into the air force (there were two of them), that the book remained unpublished until 1955. The exact number of the Subscriber Edition is uncertain, but between 200 and 206 copies is generally accepted. Wilson, *Authorized Biography*, op. cit., discusses the evolution of the various editions in detail, particularly pp. 671, 706, 726–30, 780, 782–6, 1136 (# 29); see also his 'Seven Pillars of Wisdom – Triumph and Tragedy', *T. E. Lawrence Studies* (Internet resource, May 2008).

24. T. E. also paid Bruce to be his bodyguard in the barracks, the membership of which consisted of 'animals'. That T. E. required protection was proven by the fact that four of his drunken comrades severely beat him on one occasion (after Bruce had been transferred to a different camp). Lawrence suffered a cracked rib and facial bruising. Harold Orlans, *T. E. Lawrence: Biography of a Broken Hero* (Jefferson, NC, 2002), pp. 62, 67.

25. In a letter Robert Graves wrote in 1954 to Basil Liddell Hart, he stated in no uncertain terms that 'the suggestion that [T. E.] was homosexual is absurd and indecent'. He might have changed his mind, at least privately, fourteen years later when *The Sunday Times* began running a five-part series on Lawrence, largely based on the explicit reminiscences of Jock Bruce, then in his sixties and financially strapped (how much the newspaper paid Bruce is obscure). Up until then, Lawrence's reputation had reached its zenith, based in large measure on David Lean's spectacular four-hour film, *Lawrence of Arabia*, released in 1962, becoming a worldwide hit that grossed $80 million, an astonishing sum at the time (shades of Lowell Thomas). Graves also benefited from the film. His friendship with T. E., once very close, had dimmed since the publication of Graves's biography in 1928, *Lawrence and the Arabs*, a work its subject intensely disliked. Nevertheless, Graves wrote in 1959 that 'since his death there's always been something coming from him to help me whenever things got rough: sale of his MSS letters in 1936 for £2000; money from *Lawrence of Arabia* film rights, twice since then: £1000 and £3000'. Robert Graves, *Between Moon and Moon, Selected Letters of, 1946–1972*, ed. P. O'Prey (London, 1984), pp. 123, 186. Revelations by Bruce formed the background of the 1969 book, *The Secret Lives of Lawrence of Arabia*, by two journalists at *The Times* (Philip Knightly and Colin Simpson). Wilson, in his *Authorized Biography*, op. cit., dismisses Bruce pretty much out of hand, pp. 750–51, 873, and particularly 1134 (# 7).

26. Lawrence was uneven when it came to money. He sold his dagger, an artefact full of meaning to him, to help finance his various renovation projects at Clouds Hill; but he often casually gave away the royalties he received from book sales. 'He is not bothered

about his bank balance', wrote Robert Graves; 'at the moment, he has no bank balance'. Kennington had been an official army artist during the war. One of his commissions was to depict Canadian units on the front, which he did. His best-known, of kilted soldiers from the 16th Battalion (Canadian Scottish) marching through a wasted battleground, he entitled *The Victims*, which infuriated their commanding officer. Kennington then changed it to *The Conquerors*. Graves, *Lawrence*, op. cit., p. 45.

27. Gertrude Bell was also an extremely important figure during this period in Iraqi history. 'You may rely on one thing', however, as she wrote a friend, 'I'll never engage in creating a king again'. Bell died on 12 July 1926, from an overdose of sleeping pills, in Baghdad. She was buried more or less immediately. Whether her death was accidental or not will never be known. Amal Vinogradov, 'The 1920 Revolt in Iraq Reconsidered: The Role of Tribes in National Politics', *International Journal of Middle East Studies*, Vol. 3, No. 2 (April 1972), p. 139.

28. Lawrence called Ibn Saud 'the last protest of the desert against Europe', but that was not exactly true. Elements of the *Ikhwan* rebelled in 1929, sensing in Ibn Saud a growing inclination towards temporizing with the West. Not believing in anything 'modern', whether it be religion or weaponry, the camel-riding *Ikhwan* were destroyed in battle by Ibn Saud loyalists with machine guns, motorized amoured cars and, helpfully assisted by British pilots, four aeroplanes. A. H. Lawrence, *Lawrence by His Friends*, op. cit., p. 231.

29. The kaiser thought this ploy was amusing, saying he looked forward to seeing Shakespeare's revised play, *The Merry Wives of Saxe-Coburg-Gotha*. Miranda Carter, *George, Nicholas and Wilhelm: Three Royal Cousins and the Road to World War I* (New York, 2009), p. xxiii.

30. Princess Catherine Radziwill, a Russian émigré with a vivid sense of imagination, wrote a series of gossipy biographies in the 1920s profiling important European celebrities, often using a pseudonym. She claimed that among his many other abusive tendencies, Friedrich Wilhelm beat his wife, Cecilie of Mecklenburg, with his riding whip. The marriage for Cecilie was a personal disaster. After the war, the couple were rarely together. Count Paul Vassili (Princess Catherine Radziwell), *The Disillusions of a Crown Princess, Being the Story of the Courtship and Married Life of Cecile, Ex-Crown Princess of Germany* (London, 1920), pp. 157–8.

31. The crown prince had five other children. Many of the conspirators who plotted to assassinate Hitler on 20 July 1944, were thorough-going monarchists. They carefully sifted through the Hohenzollern family tree in search of suitable candidates. Friedrich Wilhelm was dismissed out of hand, his reputation as a libertine had irrevocably soiled his public image. One of his remaining sons was also scratched off, because he was an ardent Nazi. Louis Ferdinand, the crown prince's now eldest, proved the most promising possibility. He was a man of considerable common sense; in the brutal round-up after 20 July he was interrogated by the Gestapo, but released. After World War II he worked in Detroit for the Ford Motor Company, on the assembly line, to broaden his experience with the proletariat.

32. General Gordon's Sudanese statue suffered a similar fate. Cast in 1902, it experienced a torturous trip to Khartoum, its ship sinking in the Thames after a collision, then undergoing three tide changes before retrieval from the mud and slime. Its second conveyance, a barge on the Nile, also sank en route. It was shipped back to London in 1959, and now graces the grounds of a state boarding school.

33. Robert Graves was more disturbed by seeing carcasses of horses and mules than he was of human beings. 'It seemed wrong for animals to be dragged into the war like this.' Graves, *Good-bye to All That*, op. cit., p. 209.

34. Hitler did participate in the First Battle of Ypres in October 1914 as a front-line combatant, which was certainly a horrific experience. His description of his role in that battle in *Mein Kamph* has been judged by some historians as exaggerated, despite the fact

that his unit suffered near catastrophic losses. In it, he never mentioned that he had ever killed an enemy soldier.

35. Siegfried is not to be confused with his cousin Philip, who served Haig as an aide-de-camp.

36. In the immediate aftermath of hostilities, the use of labour battalions was generally employed to clear the battlefields around Ypres of debris and unexploded shells. There are several headstones in adjoining military cemeteries which attest to the dangerousness of such work, often undertaken by immigrant workers from India and China whose epitaphs, in their native languages, are also joined with an English phrase, 'A Noble Duty Bravely Done'. It has been estimated that almost one-third of the artillery shells fired on the western front failed to explode, for a variety of reasons (war profiteering, short cuts in the manufacturing process and incompetent production techniques are all blamed in various measure). This leaves a varied and profuse collection of unexploded ordnance that often lies just below the surface of Belgian and French farmland. Caches of up to 1,000 shells are not uncommon finds, the most dangerous of which are gas canisters. In April 2001, over 15,000 residents in and around Vimy Ridge had to be evacuated when rainy weather conditions destabilized an outdoor collection depot of stored World War I shells that was leaking gas (16,000 projectiles, weighing 173 tons). Belgium alone employs 150 bomb disposal specialists. In 2001 they received 3,000 telephone calls from farmers who had unearthed explosives. *The Guardian*, 14 April 2001; *The Globe and Mail*, 20 April 2001; D. Webster, *Aftermath: The Remnants of War* (New York, 1999).

Chapter 20 – Mistakes: Who Must Shoulder the Blame?

1. After Britain, France had the largest colonial empire, but a mere 9 per cent of its overseas investments were spread about these largely Third-World appendages, as opposed to 25 per cent in the Soviet Union. Railway construction bonds issued by the tsarist government proved worthless after the revolution. Adamthwaite, *Grandeur and Misery*, op. cit., p. 23.

2. In an irony that few observers noted, G. B. Shaw felt that Belgium, in fact, had saved Great Britain. 'What have we done for Belgium?' he wrote in 1914. 'Have we saved her from invasion? Were we at her side with half a million men when the avalanche fell on her? Or were we safe in our own country praising her heroism.... We have not protected Belgium: Belgium has protected us at the cost of being conquered by Germany.' Shaw, *What I Really Wrote*, op. cit., p. 49.

3. Von Schlieffen would have disagreed; in several of his war games, he assumed that French forces would automatically enter Belgium. Jack Snyder, *The Ideology of the Offensive: Military Decision Making and the Disasters of 1914* (Ithaca, 1984), p. 145.

4. This, at least, was Haig's opinion. Two years after the war, he wrote a memo that said, 'There could be no serious doubt of the enemy's ability to roll back the Russians if he were left free to concentrate against them'. Haig, *Private Papers*, op. cit., p. 366.

5. C. P. Scott, the influential editor of *The Manchester Guardian*, noted in his diary that only two members of Asquith's cabinet were in favour of war at the beginning of Germany's invasion. 'The violation of Belgian neutrality altered the situation [completely]'. Scott, *Political Diaries*, op. cit., p. 96.

6. The king was disturbed by the many outbreaks of Germanophobia in Britain as the Great War progressed. Politicians demanded that the kaiser and his son be stripped of their honorary commands in various regiments of the British army, but George demurred. The gentlemanly procedure would be for the two royals to 'remain on the army list until they themselves resigned', presumably via the mails of neutral countries. Nicolson, *King George V*, op. cit., p. 249.

Chapter 21 – Residue: What is 'Civilization'?

1. In the United States, the Associated Press reportedly serviced over 90 million readers. Emmet Crozier, *American Reporters on the Western Front, 1914–1918* (New York, 1959), p. 186.

2. As an extenuating circumstance for his hero's obliviousness of the oncoming 'thunderbolt' of war, Mann described his hero as 'a man who, despite many warnings, had neglected to read the papers … with their wild, chaotic contents'. Thomas Mann, *The Magic Mountain*, trans. H. T. Lowe-Porter (New York, 1969), pp. 706–16; John Keegan, *A History of Warfare* (New York, 1993), pp. 358–9. See also Bernd Hüppauf, 'Langemarck, Verdun and the Myth of a *New Man* in Germany after the First World War', *War and Society*, Vol. 6, No. 2 (September 1988), pp. 82–4.

3. The only non-European country in the early part of the century that pursued the 'colony' trade was Japan. Rana Mitter, 'The Smooth Path to Pearl Harbor', *The New York Review of Books*, 22 May 2014, p. 21.

4. Brooke, the 'Young Apollo', whose sexual confusions defy easy analysis, was buried on the Greek island of Skyros. By coincidence, Skyros was the island where Achilles's mother sent her son to hide, so that he would not be drawn into the Trojan War, where she feared his death. He spent his time there dressed as a woman.

Credits for illustrations, maps and copyrighted materials

Section I

Maps

Schlieffen Plan: © Dana Blennerhassett Roy

Verdun: Everett Collection/Alamy Stock Photos

Gallipoli: © Dana Blennerhassett Roy

Arabia: Estate of Heather Perry (also known as Herry Perry), drawn for Robert Graves's 1927 book, *Lawrence and the Arabs* (London, Jonathan Cape).

Copyrighted material

Small portions of Chapter 6 appeared previously in *The Vanished Kingdom* by James Charles Roy, copyright © 1999. Reprinted by permission of Basic Books, an imprint of Hachette Book Group, Inc.

Extracts from *The Waste Land* by T. S. Eliot, by permission Faber & Faber.

Extracts from the poetry of Siegfried Sassoon, © Siegfried Sassoon by kind permission of the Estate of George Sassoon.

Acknowledgments

As a long-time reader of histories and non-fiction in general, I often peruse the acknowledgments page(s) as a matter of curiosity. At times, I am astounded at their length and the numbers of people for whom thanks are felt to be in order. One recent example listed over four hundred names, probably more people than I have ever met in my entire life span of seventy-six years. The author even included her dog walker.

My acknowledgments will be brief. This book has been, even more so than my other works, a genuine solo adventure. I have consulted very few authorities on the subject (other than through their printed works), laboured in a bare number of libraries (though heavily) and done all the spadework and research trips on my own. As such, any error of fact or mistaken interpretation found in this book is my responsibility and no one else's.

I list my own thanks here to the usual suspects: the fine production crew at Pen & Sword, headed by Harriet Fielding, and my editor there, Lester Crook. Readers who have read all or parts of the manuscript, and helped me with their comments: Beth Welch, Laura Henderson and particularly my agent, Jonathan Williams, who has assisted me in more ways than I can count. For their work regarding illustrations and maps, Dana Blennerhassett Roy (especially), and Steve Morello (especially); also Ralph Brown, Frank Rockland, Andrew Hewitt, Dominic Lee, Kevin Austin, John Ansley (Marist College), Andrew Derrick and Lloyd Leichentritt (www.fokkerdr1.com).

For comradeship and support, as well as the recipients of any number of odd requests: Alix and Dan Hackett, Jill Baker and Jeffrey Bishop, Sana Morrow, Julie Roy Jeffrey, James Pethica and, last of all my wife, Jan Victoria, to whom this book is dedicated.

James Charles Roy
April 11, 2022
Pine Island
Newbury, Massachusetts

Index